B
A
S
I
Computing

BASIC Computing

Don Mittleman
Oberlin College

HBJ HARCOURT BRACE JOVANOVICH, INC.
New York San Diego Chicago San Francisco Atlanta
London Sydney Toronto

PHOTO CREDITS

Page 4 top left: Bell System's Hospital Communications Management System; bottom left: Radio Shack; top right: Anderson-Jacobson Co.; middle right: Digital Engineering; bottom right: See 'n Say® Talking-Learning System is a registered trademark of Mattel, Inc.

Page 5 top left: Techtran Industries, Inc.; bottom: Honeywell; top right: Formation, Inc.; middle right: Dysan Corporation

Printed in the United States of America
Library of Congress Catalog Card Number: 81-83082
ISBN: 0-15-504910-0

With love to Guy, Meg, and Jef,
and especially to Dee

PREFACE

In the nearly 40 years since the computer was first used, we have come to depend more and more on quantitative methods of data handling and problem solving. Today the computer is employed by an astonishing variety of disciplines: economics, psychology, medicine, and even the performances of dancers and athletes have been improved by the use of quantitative methods and the computer. Unfortunately, the computer has also acquired a "big brother" image, feared and distrusted by many people. Eliminating this negative image means acquiring the ability to use the computer and applying that knowledge to our advantage both personally and professionally.

BASIC Computing is dedicated to the idea that using a computer can be both easy *and* fun. The book introduces students to programming and the problem-solving capabilities of the computer using the simple structure of the BASIC language.

Programming is covered in a step-by-step way in the early chapters. In Chapters 1 and 2, every effort is made to make the beginner comfortable while approaching the terminal for the first time. Where they exist, parallels with such commonly understood tools as the typewriter and the hand-held digital calculator are stressed. The differences, when they exist, are also pointed out.

The most difficult task for most people is translating ideas expressed in words into operations expressed in symbols. No one has yet devised an algorithm (recipe) to do this. We can, however, illustrate this translation in a variety of situations with the expectation that the reader will gain sufficient insight from the examples to extend and apply them to more complex situations. Tricks that focus attention on how to effect the translation from words into symbols and make the translation easier should be used freely. One such device is the flow chart, which is illustrated extensively in Chapter 3 of the book.

Because interactive computing is highly motivating for students, Chapter 4 introduces students to computing using interactive examples. INPUT is preferred to READ, which is postponed to Chapter 7. Only the minimal number of BASIC statements is presented—just enough to illustrate how a program is written and how the computer executes it. This is done with the BASIC instructions INPUT, LET, PRINT, and END and the BASIC commands LIST and RUN.

Since one of the most powerful features of any computer program is its ability to make decisions and modify its future action based on prior information, the conditional transfer instruction is covered late in Chapter 4. Internal documentation is stressed and the REMARK instruction is explained. Attention is also directed to the intrinsic functions, such as INT(X). Finally, the RENUMBER, SAVE, and LOAD commands are explained.

By this time, students have had much to learn: how to translate word problems into BASIC statements using a flow chart as a guide and how to direct the computer to carry out their intentions. During the course of learning all this, frustrating situations invariably arise, and an explanation is needed to minimize, if not eliminate, these frustrations. Thus, in Chapter 5, the interrelationship between computer hardware and some of the system commands of immediate relevance is discussed.

Chapter 6 discusses LOOPS, the technique that helps to solve problems by repeating the same or similar computations more times than is humanly possible. The machine's great speed and indifference to tedium are the features stressed here, but sometimes speed alone is not enough. Hints in the text point to problems whose solutions need more than such brute force methods. Some of these problems are made explicit later in the book.

The uses of READ, DATA, and RESTORE are illustrated in Chapter 7. The use of the conditional transfer is extended from situations with only two possible outcomes to situations with several possible outcomes.

In Chapter 8 random numbers are introduced and their use in simulating games and processes is illustrated. This is followed by a chapter on lists and arrays, which are applied to sorting (alphabetizing) and testing magic squares. The string capabilities of BASIC are kept in the background until Chapter 11, in which several applications are presented.

Topics covered after Chapter 11 will depend on the instructor and the amount of time remaining in the course. A one-semester hour course could conclude with the presentation of the material covered in Chapter 12, "Functions and Subroutines" and possibly BASIC's MAT statements (Chapter 15).

If the material is offered in a two-semester hour course, this is a proper place to leave BASIC temporarily and introduce students to the data-handling capabilities of the computer (Chapter 13). This background is needed to understand the CHANGE instruction (Chapter 14) and how, for example, a computer alphabetizes.

If matrices have not already been discussed, they can be naturally introduced at this point as an extension of the earlier discussion on lists and arrays. Several examples in Chapter 16 illustrate the use of matrices.

During the presentation of the previous material, the ability to format output was limited because only commas, semicolons, and TAB were available. The greater flexibility that PRINTUSING provides is presented and illustrated in Chapter 16.

Chapter 17 introduces files—what they are and how to construct and use them. This could be the concluding topic for a two-semester hour course.

If more time is available, Chapters 18 through 21 delve into the structure of keyed files and sequential files. Binary coded decimal files and binary files are fully discussed. By the time students finish Chapter 21, they will be able to read hexadecimal dumps.

Chapter 22 is a collection of odds and ends that are useful to students who want a little more information. Finally, a glossary of terms appears at the back of the book. Since different computer systems use different terminology, the glossary serves as a cross-reference to the concepts presented in this book. For students familiar with one system, the glossary should provide the bridge to ease their way into another system.

Don Mittleman

CONTENTS

1 Getting Started

When the computer was introduced some 30 years ago, its most imaginative and enthusiastic proponents saw only a limited horizon for its applicability. Born out of necessity, the computer fulfilled the military's need for artillery firing tables. Its successful adaption to the reduction of census data led to its acceptance by commerce, industry, art, and science. Today, computers routinely solve problems in art and architecture, in medicine and music, in physics and philology. It is difficult to imagine any area in which the computer has not made a contribution. Although, we have not yet reached the stage at which the computer is as commonplace as television or the automobile, it seems but a small step away.

Most people agree that computer technology has brought about tremendous changes in our social structure; some even feel that these changes have been too many and too fast. The more conservative seers predict continued change and continued growth; the more radical envision an explosive growth occurring when the first generation of children growing up feeling as comfortable with the computer as with the telephone reach maturity and add their contributions to our intellectual heritage.

The growth of computer acceptance rests on two cornerstones. The first is the identification of activities that in fact require little or no human intelligence. For example, the actual process of reducing massive census data to a manageable and meaningful form requires little ability. To have recognized that the process can be described by a sequence of simple operations and to have brought together the resources to achieve the end result took intelligence and insight. Someone was smart enough to get the computer to do the simple and tedious work.

The second cornerstone is the capability of the computer to understand us rather than demand that we understand it. By analogy, driving an automobile does not require advanced training in engineering (nor should it, although at times this would seem helpful). Similarly, to communicate with a computer should not be beyond the capabilities of an intelligent person. From that earlier time when only a small handful of experts knew and understood the computer's language and did "speak" it, billions of dollars have been spent to educate the computer to make it smart enough to understand our daily parlance. Although complete success still eludes us (remember, we have difficulties communicating with one another), partial success has been achieved. Many computer languages exist; generally, each has been tailored for a specific class of problems and a specific audience. For example, FORTRAN was developed for the scientist and engineer,

COBOL for the business community. For those interested in list processing, LISP was created; for the mathematician, APL.

One feature common to all these computer languages is their highly structured and, consequently, seemingly artificial format. To learn one is like learning a new algebra, with more rules and conventions than the algebra learned in high school. For the beginner, this raises psychological difficulties that interfere with the acceptance of the computer as something that can be fun. How nice it would be if there were a computer language like simple English. We wouldn't have to spend too much time and effort learning the language; instead, we could put our time and effort into getting the computer to solve our problems. Furthermore, if the language were sufficiently general so that it could be used by people whose interests covered a wide spectrum, it would have more universal appeal. Finally, if after learning such a language, other more specialized languages could readily be assimilated, a bridge, for those who want it, would have been built. The language that comes closest to these goals is BASIC.[1]

When learning to drive a car, we must learn a few technical words and their definitions. We should know the ignition, the brake, the accelerator, and so on. Similarly, when learning about computers, we need to learn a few technical words. First, the **terminal** is the device through which information is entered into the computer and through which the computer responds. Second, the **main memory** is the storage area in the computer where the data and the instructions needed for the solution of a problem are initially entered and temporarily stored. The main memory of a computer may be likened to the array of mailboxes in a large post office. Each mailbox is identified by an address—a number, a letter, or a combination of both; the contents of each box depends on the mail received and when it is removed. In the computer, in addition to the initial data and instructions, intermediate results and the final answer are stored in the main memory. Ultimately, the final answer is transmitted electrically to the terminal, where it appears in a discernible form.

The third component of a computer is the **CPU,** or **the central processing unit,** to which data stored in the main memory are transmitted along with instructions for manipulating them. The actual computations—additions, subtractions, comparisons, and so on—are carried out in the CPU, and the results are returned to the main memory. The number of back and forth transmissions between the CPU and the main memory generally

Functionally, data and instructions are entered initially from the terminal into the main memory. The required computations are carried out in the CPU and the results returned to main memory. At this point, the results can be presented at the terminal, permanently stored, or both. If you wish, the instructions used to carry out the computation may be permanently stored and, if ever needed again, retrieved.

In the preceding paragraphs, we presented an overview of what is to follow. More important, we have attempted to provide the rationale for studying in detail the functioning of the terminal and how it communicates with the main memory. The terminal is the point at which the human and the computer interact. Think of the computer as a person with neither sight nor hearing; you must have some way of communicating with this person. Anne Sullivan tapped out messages to Helen Keller on her hand; you type out messages to the computer on the terminal.

Many installations require that when you begin to use the computer, you identify yourself. The ensuing dialogue is known by various names, for example, LOGON, LOGIN, and SIGNON. In this chapter, we shall illustrate a typical procedure for identifying yourself to the computer.

Because many computers are multi-lingual, you will need to indicate the you wish to communicate in BASIC. How this is done will also be illustrated.

---

[1]BASIC is an acronym for *B*eginner's *A*ll-purpose *S*ymbolic *I*nstruction *C*ode, initially developed in 1963 by John G. Kemeny and Thomas E. Kurtz of Dartmouth College.

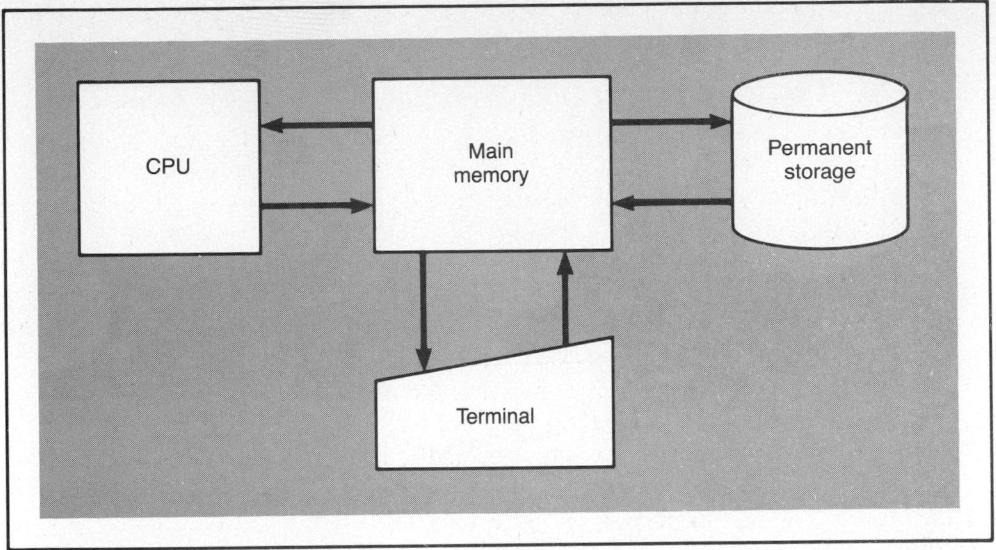

FIGURE 1-1

runs into the billions, depending on the specific problem being solved. When the final answer is obtained, it is transmitted from the CPU, by way of the main memory, to the terminal.

The fourth major component of a computing system is its **permanent storage.** Most problems solved with computers are repetitive in nature. When you go to the bank to make a deposit or withdrawal, the same set of instructions is used to update your balance as is used for all other customers. It would be a waste of time and effort if these instructions had to be repeatedly entered into the computer for each transaction. The instructions are entered once into the computer and stored there in permanent form. As needed, a copy of this permanently stored set of instructions (called a **computer program**) is brought into the main memory, where it is used to process your transaction. The more common devices used to provide permanent storage are disks, drums, tapes, and cassettes.

Schematically, these four components[2] relate to each other as depicted in Figure 1-1.

Several games and demonstrations, programs that have been previously stored in the computer, are frequently available for your use. To make you feel welcome and comfortable using the terminal, we shall show you how to call these forth, play the games, and work the demonstrations.

We shall assume that a keyboard, similar to that of a typewriter, is available for you to "speak" to the computer. Because typing errors are common and the computer is not yet smart enough to interpret what you "mean" but only what you "say," we shall show you how to correct typing errors.

Finally, saying "good-bye" to the computer is also formalized. The procedure, known as signing off or logging off, will be illustrated.

Communicating with the Computer: The Terminal

Although terminals that understand spoken language do exist, their level of comprehension is currently so limited that we shall not consider them here. Terminals that speak are also available and, for what follows, could be considered a viable option. Their

[2]The four major components of a computer—known as "hardware"—will be discussed in detail in Chapter 5.

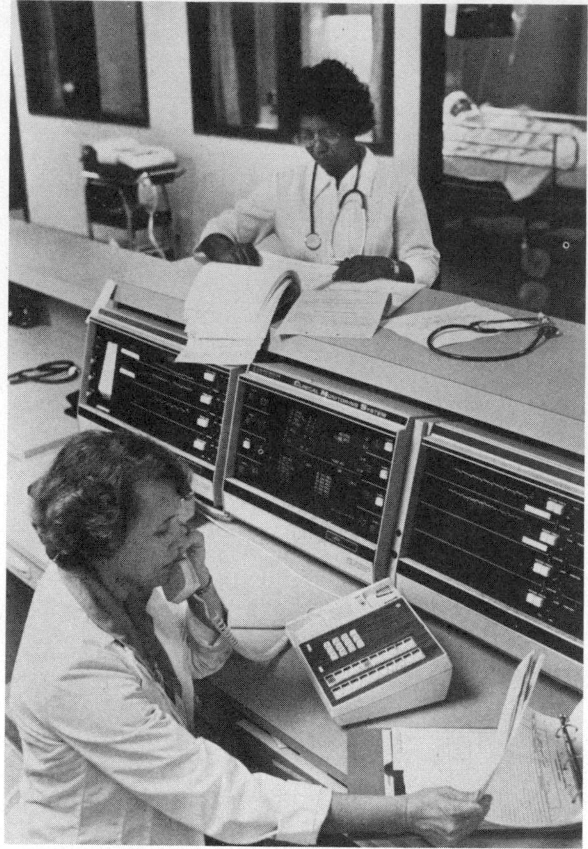

AUDIO-INPUT DEVICE.
DATA CAN BE ENTERED INTO A COMPUTER VIA A TELEPHONE.

HARD COPY PRINTER WITH KEYBOARD

GRAPHIC CATHODE RAY TUBE (CRT) TERMINAL

ALPHANUMERIC CATHODE RAY TUBE (CRT) TERMINAL

AUDIO-OUTPUT DEVICE.
COMPUTER TOY CAN MAKE AN AUDIO RESPONSE TO DATA ENTERED BY CHILD.

EXAMPLES OF PERMANENT STORAGE DEVICES

TAPE DRIVE

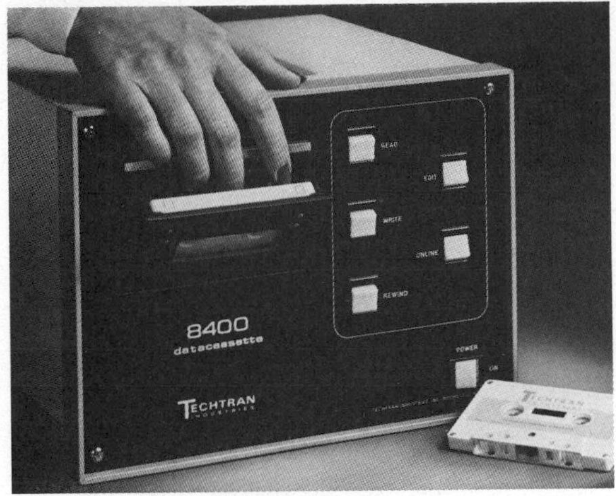

CASSETTE

CROSS SECTION OF A DISC PACK

FLOPPY DISC

usefulness for our purposes, however, is questionable. We shall limit our discussion, therefore, to the more readily available computer types. Of these, the terminal that resembles the electric typewriter, in that it has a keyboard and a hard-copy printing mechanism, is the most widely used. An alternative to the printer is the alphanumeric CRT (cathode ray tube)—a television screen on which the computer can display both alphabetic and numeric characters. Information is entered into the computer by way of a keyboard; information from the computer is either printed or displayed on a CRT.

Both types of terminals are widely used; more than 200 different models are currently available. Either type may be used to test the programs and solve the problems in this book. In the beginning, however, you will benefit from using the typewriter terminal because it will document your work on paper for future reference. Work displayed on the CRT will be lost unless a special printer, an expensive device that attaches to the CRT, is available.

The Half-Duplex and Full-Duplex Modes

On a typewriter, the printer is activated each time a key is struck; that is, the two operations—striking a key and seeing the result—are physically and logically linked. This is not necessarily so on a computer terminal.

If the computer and terminal communicate in the **half-duplex** mode, when a key is struck at the terminal keyboard, the corresponding character is printed and the appropriate electric signal is simultaneously transmitted to the computer. Both events are initiated from the terminal, and the parallel with the operation of the typewriter is apparent.

If the computer and terminal communicate in the **full-duplex** mode, when a key is struck at the terminal keyboard, the appropriate signal is also sent to the computer. The computer, however, after receiving and interpreting the signal, returns its own signal to the terminal. The return signal activates the printer or CRT, and the character corresponding to that signal is then made visible. Because the computer is in control of the situation after receiving the incoming signal, it can return a modified signal. In fact, it can decide to return no signal. In the next section, we shall see how suppressing the return signal can ensure the security of your computer account.

In both the half-duplex and the full-duplex modes of operation, the computer, when it has information to convey to you, will, on its own initiative, send the message to your printer or CRT.

The Terminal

Turning on the terminal may involve nothing more than being sure that the electric plug is secured in the proper outlet and that the power switch on the terminal is turned to the ON position.[3] For the simplest computer configuration, nothing more is required, because it is composed of only one terminal and one computer, which understands only BASIC. If you are using a personal computer that can converse in another language in addition to BASIC, a labeled key on the keyboard is usually provided so that you may select BASIC as the language you wish to use. If no key is evident, it may be necessary to refer to the manual supplied by the manufacturer to learn how to prepare the computer to converse in BASIC.

Before we explore the intervening steps required to use one of the larger computers, we shall examine the keyboard in greater detail. A typical terminal keyboard is shown in Figure 1-2. In spite of the many similarities between a terminal keyboard and a typewriter keyboard, there are differences. One major difference is that many terminals have only upper-case (capital) letters.

---

[3]Locating the power on-off switch may pose a problem. If the switch is not on or near the keyboard, you will have to look for it on the back of or underneath the terminal. Sometimes it is on the side.

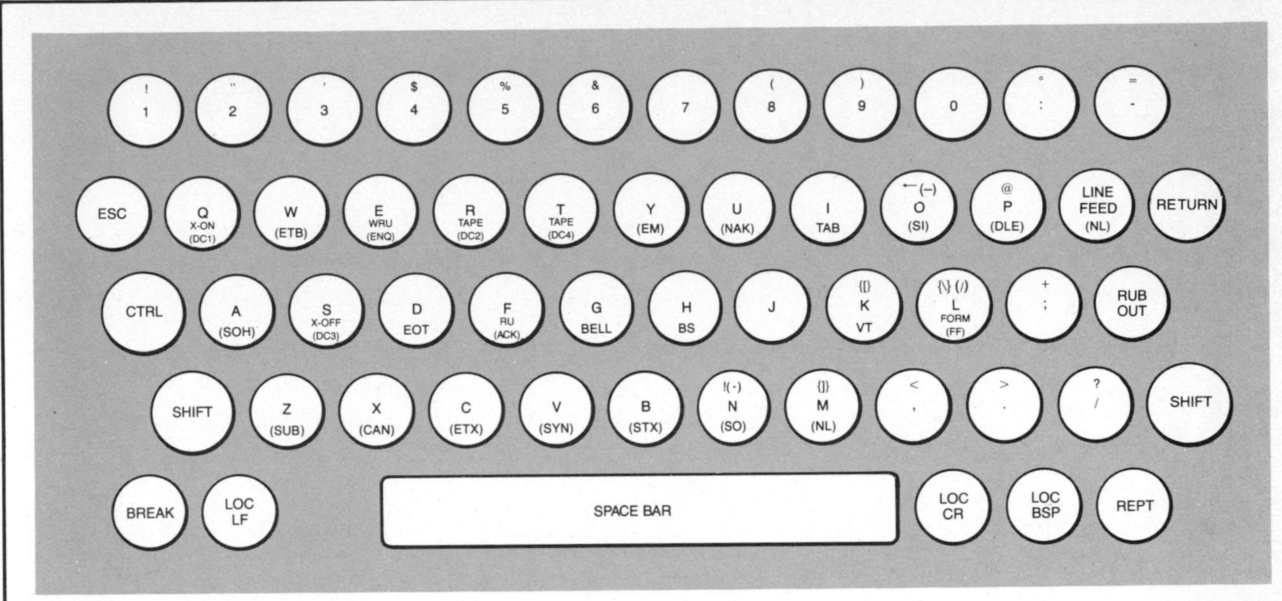

FIGURE 1-2

Suppose you want to type a short sentence on an electric typewriter. As you strike each key, the corresponding character is printed on a sheet of paper. When you finish the sentence, you strike the RETURN key, causing the carriage to move to its leftmost position and the paper to advance one line. If you were typing an instruction to a computer, you would perform the identical operations. As you strike each key, a distinct electric signal corresponding to that key is sent to the computer, which temporarily stores this information and prints an image corresponding to the key you struck. Until you press the RETURN key, the line of typed characters hangs in limbo. The computer has neither accepted nor rejected it. Only after you press the RETURN key does the computer begin to process the information you typed on the line. At that time, the printer advances to the next line and the computer is ready to receive the next instruction you type. We shall use the symbol <CR> (for carriage return) to indicate that the RETURN key should be pressed.

On some typewriters, the lower-case l is also used as the symbol for the number 1. Because the terminal keyboard may not contain any lower-case letters, a separate key is needed for the number 1. Even if lower-case letters are available, to avoid confusing the computer, we must distinguish between the lower-case letter l and the number 1. Two separate keys are also provided to distinguish between the letter O and the number 0. Some terminals print Ø for the number and O for the letter; others print Ø for the letter and 0 for the number. Some terminals distinguish between the two characters by a slight difference in shape: the letter O is more rounded and the number 0 is more elongated.

Logging On

Rather than a simple or personal computer, you may be working at a terminal with shared access to a larger computer. Access to the larger computer may be achieved in two ways. The terminal may be connected directly to the computer, in which case it is only necessary to turn on the power switch to activate the system. When the number of available terminals exceeds the number of "ports" (entry points into the computer to which communication lines may be connected) or when the distance between the terminal and the computer precludes a direct connection, ordinary telephone lines are used.

In this case, the terminal is connected to the telephone line via an acoustic coupler.[4] The coupler is wired to the terminal (or it may be an integral part of the terminal) and activated when the terminal's power is turned on. The telephone is used to call the computer. If you have dailed the correct number, which you obtain from the computer center, the computer will answer your ring—it generally says "hello" with a high-pitched whiny sound. When you hear this, place the phone in the cradle of the coupler. The telephone handset must be carefully placed in the cradle; the positions for the mouthpiece and the earpiece are distinct, and a tight fit is required to exclude extraneous noise. When the handset is in place, wait for the computer's first message to be printed on the terminal.[5] This is the beginning of the LOGON (logging on) or SIGNON (signing on) procedure.

The computer may be capable of serving a number of different terminals simultaneously and may have to know in advance the type of terminal you are using. You should therefore be prepared for the computer's first message to be a request to identify the terminal. The computer center will give you the precise format for your response. Be sure to ask before attempting the LOGON procedure.

After you have indicated the terminal you are using (if required), press <CR>. The computer will ask you to identify yourself. The more obvious reasons for this request are to verify that you are an authorized user, to maintain accounting records, and to allocate resources within the computer for your needs. The precise procedure for identifying yourself will vary among different installations. The following sequence illustrates the initial dialogue that may take place between you and the computer. Remember, however, that your computer center will give you the precise format to follow for your particular installation.

Assuming you have made contact with the computer, the first message you may see is

```
TERMINAL:
```

For our example, we shall assume that you are using a TELETYPE® MODEL 33, for which the proper response is TTY33. In the dialogue that follows, your responses are underlined. (The underline, of course, would not appear on your printout.)

```
TERMINAL:TTY33    <CR>
```

Remember, the symbol <CR> does not appear on your printout. You press <CR> simply to signal that all the intended information has been entered and you want the computer to act. At this point, the computer asks you to identify yourself by typing:

```
OTS AT YOUR SERVICE
LOGON PLEASE:
```

You would respond by typing your ID number (ST123456), your ID code word (HUMBLE), your intended use of the computer—in this example, for your introductory sociology course 101 (SOC101), and your password (FANCY). You now see:

```
OTS AT YOUR SERVICE
LOGON PLEASE: ST 123456,HUMBLE,(SOC101),            <CR>
```

You should remember several things about this response. First, expect minor differences at your installation. For example, the order in which the information is to be entered

---

[4]There may be several switches on the acoustic coupler. The DUPLEX switch should be set to HALF or FULL, depending on the computer. If the coupler has a BAUD RATE switch, set it at 110, unless you know that a higher rate is either acceptable or expected.

[5]Some computers may require that you press <CR> or the BREAK key before the message will appear.

may be different, or the commas and parentheses may be replaced by other symbols. Second, note that underlined blank spaces follow (SOC101),. To enhance the security of your account on the computer, the password FANCY that you typed was not echoed back to the terminal.[6] The computer "knew" that you typed FANCY, but it has been instructed not to exhibit it. Thus, if an unauthorized person happens to see your printout, the LOGON information needed to access your account would be incomplete and the data stored there would be secure. Again, not all systems work this way. Some print the password; others suppress the printing of the entire sequence (the ID number, code word, intended use, and password). In general, systems that print the password also provide a means to suppress it.

Occasionally, the computer may be slow to signal LOGON. In such cases, you may try several different keys to catch the computer's attention. Some of the more commonly used keys are the BREAK key, the ESC (ESCAPE) key, the ATTEN (ATTENTION) key, and <CR>. If the computer does not respond within a minute or two after these keys are struck, something is probably wrong with the terminal, the coupler, the telephone line, or the computer itself. If this happens, you should request help from the computer center.

Calling the BASIC Processor

If you are using a computer that can converse only in BASIC or that can call the BASIC interpreter with an external switch, you are now ready to familiarize yourself with the computer and the language. If you are using a large computer that uses additional languages, you will have to indicate to it that you will be working in BASIC. The sequence of steps you should take are approximated in the following discussion.

You will recognize that you are successfully logged on when the computer responds with some general type of information, welcoming you to the system or notifying you of special conditions, such as hours of operation or maintenance. The computer will also display a special symbol to prompt you to respond. The particular character representing the prompt symbol varies with the particular computer installation. One system may employ @; another, #; a third, *. In this book, we shall use ! as the system prompt symbol. When you see the first !, type BASIC and <CR>.

The computer may respond with some nonessential information, (such as the currently available form of BASIC) and will then exhibit another prompt symbol. In this book, we shall use > as the BASIC language prompt symbol. Remember, the prompt symbol ! (indicating that you have successfully logged on) and the prompt symbol > (indicating that the computer is ready to converse in BASIC) are not standard. You will have to familiarize yourself with the corresponding symbols on your computer system.

Your printout now looks like this:

```
OTS AT YOUR SERVICE
LOGON PLEASE: ST 123456,HUMBLE,(SOC101),______          <CR>
ON AT 12:34 SEPT 27, '81
!BASIC                                                  <CR>
```

Computer Games and Demonstrations

Playing a few computer games or working through some demonstration programs, if these are available on your system, will help you relate to the terminal and the computer. The computer, naturally, may not realize you are a novice and will probably ask you if you want to write a new program or examine one you have previously written and stored.

[6] Assume that this computer operates in the full-duplex mode.

One common method is for the computer to ask

```
NEW OR OLD?    <CR>
>
```

Some systems do not print the request explicitly but simply respond with the appropriate prompt symbol (in our case, >). Your response would depend on the circumstances. At this point, you are ready to run one of the demonstration programs, but first you must know what programs are available and how to call them up. Again, there is no universal way to do this. One technique is to type

```
>OLD          <CR>
>ACC GAMES    <CR>
```

What you have done is to inform the computer that you want to direct it to an account called GAMES. (Remember, your account has been named HUMBLE.) The computer responds with the prompt symbol >, and you type CAT for CATALOGUE. In effect, you are asking the computer to list the names of all the programs contained in the account GAMES. The computer responds by printing the list. At this point, the printout will look approximately like this (again, your responses are underlined here):

```
TERMINAL:TTY33                                              <CR>

OTS AT YOUR SERVICE
LOGON PLEASE: ST 123456,HUMBLE,(SOC101),                    <CR>

ON AT 12:34 SEPT 27, '81

!BASIC                                                      <CR>

NEW OR OLD?
>OLD                                                        <CR>
>ACC GAMES                                                  <CR>
>CAT                                                        <CR>

**ACCOUNT**
GAMES

BASEBALL
CRAPS
GOLF
MARKET
POLLUTE
QUBIC
TICTAC

>
```

Notice that after the computer has listed the names of the available games, it responds with the prompt symbol >. It is waiting for your next instruction. Suppose you play a fair game of tic-tac-toe and you want to try your skill against the computer. Because the program TICTAC resides in the GAMES account, you must direct the computer to that account again and then ask for TICTAC. Continuing our sample printout, the paper in front of you would show

```
QUBIC
TICTAC

>OLD          <CR>
>ACC GAMES    <CR>
>TICTAC       <CR>
>
```

Again, the prompt symbol indicates that the computer is waiting for a further command. Since you intend to play tic-tac-toe, you type RUN <CR> and wait for the game to start. The last four lines of print are now

```
>OLD             <CR>
>ACC GAMES       <CR>
>TICTAC          <CR>
>RUN             <CR>
```

The BASIC command RUN orders the computer to start the program. The computer will tell you how to play the game.

After several games of tic-tac-toe, you decide to try another game. The TICTAC program itself should contain instructions for terminating play; if it does, follow them. If it does not, locate and press the BREAK key. This stops whatever the computer is doing and should cause the prompt symbol > to appear. (Some computers may print the system prompt symbol ! instead. This means that you are no longer in BASIC and will have to call it up again by typing BASIC and <CR>.)

Suppose that now you would like to try your luck at CRAPS. The calling sequence is the same as the sequence you used to call up TICTAC.

```
>OLD             <CR>
>ACC GAMES       <CR>
>CRAPS           <CR>
>RUN             <CR>
```

Continue to play the games and work through the demonstrations until you feel comfortable with the terminal and the computer. Feel free to experiment with your responses, since there is little you can inadvertently do that will damage either the terminal or the computer.

Correcting Typing Errors

Before we conclude this introduction, there is one more elementary operation you should master. How do you correct typing errors? Suppose that your ID number is JM765432, your code word is WORLD, your password is JUNGLE, and you intend to use the computer to solve a problem assigned in your physics course, PHYS227. While logging on, you inadvertently type your ID number as JN765 and then discover your error. Examine the keyboard until you locate the key labeled RUBOUT or DELETE. Striking this key once will erase the character 5 in your ID number; striking the key a second time will rub out the 6; a third time, the 7; and a fourth time, the letter N. You may now resume typing with the correct letter M, followed by the digits 765432.

Most computer print mechanisms do not backspace but move forward each time a key is struck. Therefore, your printout would probably contain four marks indicating that the RUBOUT key was pressed four times. In this book, we shall use the backslash \ to indicate that the RUBOUT key has been struck. Assuming that you do not make any other typing errors, the corrected line of type in this example would be

```
LOGON PLEASE:JN765\\\\M765432,WORLD,(PHYS227),        <CR>
```

Multiple corrections per line may be made simply by repeating the above rubout procedure each time an error occurs.

If you are working with a sophisticated CRT unit, striking the RUBOUT key may actually erase the character from the screen and backspace the print mechanism. If this happens, what you see on the screen is identical to what the computer sees. This process, called *editing,* will be discussed later in the book.

If you fail to detect an error, the computer will detect it and respond with an error message after you press <CR>. What you type must be identical to your ID number, code word, and password before the computer recognizes you as an authorized user. For example, if you had not detected the N error in your ID number, the computer would have rejected your attempt to log on, indicated that the ID number was wrong, and asked you to try again.

At times, you can depend on the computer's capability to detect errors to reduce the amount of retyping and rubouts. For example, if you type a long line and then discover an error near the beginning, you may simply stop typing and press <CR>. The computer will print its error message and reject the line. You may then retype the line from the beginning. As you gain experience working with the keyboard, you will learn to choose the correction procedure best suited to the particular situation at hand.

Signing Off

When you have finished working with the computer, you must sign off. To do this, you type BYE or OFF and <CR> the next time the computer prints either prompt symbol ! or >. This will indicate to the computer that the sessions is finished.

The computer can now record the charges you incurred and reallocate its internal resources to other users. Many computers will notify you of the charges you incurred, and you may regard this as a signal that you have been signed off. Before leaving, remember to turn off the electricity. If you are using a telephone connection, remove the handset from the cradle and return it to the telephone base.

Summary

Familiarity with a typewriter can help you understand a computer terminal. You have been given instructions that enable you to log on and to call the BASIC interpreter. You have learned how to call up games and demonstration programs (if available) to help you become familiar with the terminal keyboard. And you have been shown how to correct typing errors and, when you are finished, how to sign off.

Expect the details to vary from one computer system to the next. The fundamental operations, however—logging on, calling the BASIC interpreter, calling up and running stored programs, correcting typing errors, and signing off—are general procedures that must be followed by all computer users. The details of carrying out these operations on a specific terminal at a specific installation can be quickly mastered, forgotten, and relearned as you are exposed to different terminals and computers.

Exercises

1.1 Name the four main components of a computing system and describe the function of each.

1.2 Can you imagine a means (not described in the text) whereby you and a computer could communicate?

1.3 What operations would you expect the CPU to perform? Why?

1.4 List some areas in which the computer has been used to solve problems. Can you list areas in which it has not been used? Can you list areas in which you believe it cannot be used?

1.5 Write instructions to log on your computer in sufficient detail so that a person who knows nothing about computers can follow them.

Computer Arithmetic

2

Now that you have learned how to log on, log off, and play games with a computer, you are ready to learn how to use a computer to solve problems. First, however, you will need to know some of the fundamental concepts of computer arithmetic.

There are five basic arithmetic operations that a computer performs immediately and directly: addition, subtraction, multiplication, division, and exponentiation. Initially, we shall describe these five operations as they apply to integers[1] because this is the easiest way to follow each step of the computation and to verify the answer. Remember, however, that all numbers are not integers. In a computer, a noninteger is represented in two different ways. We shall refer to one representation as the "computer decimal notation" and the other as the "floating point" or "scientific notation." Both will be described and illustrated in this chapter. The arithmetic rules demonstrated for integers extend to this larger class of numbers.

In algebra, letters (known as *literals*) are used to stand for numbers. We may think of performing specified arithmetic operations on numbers by combining in the appropriate way the literal symbols that stand for them. Thus, in algebra, we think of adding two literal symbols when we want to add the numbers they represent. We can do the same with the computer. We shall use letters to stand for numbers and combine these literals according to the rules of algebra. In fact, the five basic arithmetic operations apply to literals in a computer in the same way that they apply to literals in algebra.

The Arithmetic Operations

Many computers may be used as desk or hand calculators. For example, if you want to add 3 and 5, the familiar way to write this is 3 + 5. If you used a hand calculator, you would press the 3 button, then the plus sign button, the 5 button, and finally the equal sign button, and the answer 8 would be displayed. To have the computer do the same task, the sequence is as follows. After calling the BASIC interpreter, when you see the > prompt symbol, type PRINT 3+5 <CR>, and the computer will respond with the answer, 8. At your terminal, you would see:

[1]The integers are: . . . , −4, −3, −2, −1, 0, 1, 2, 3, ...

```
>PRINT 3+5
 8
```

You use the BASIC instruction PRINT so that the computer will present the answer to you so that you can see it.

To subtract two integers, say 12 minus 7, you would type: PRINT 12 − 7 <CR> and the computer would respond with the answer, 5

```
>PRINT 12 - 7
 5
```

The symbols for addition and subtraction are the familiar ones, + and −. Multiplication and division are handled similarly, except that a new symbol, *, is used for multiplication. The symbol for division is the familiar slash, /. Thus, 3*5 = 15 and 24/6 = 4. At the terminal, if you typed PRINT 3*5 <CR> and then PRINT 24/6 <CR>, you would see:

```
>PRINT 3*5
 15
>PRINT 24/6
 4
```

Addition, subtraction, multiplication, and division may be combined on one line. For example,

```
>PRINT 12-7+3*5-8/2+3
 19
```

The computer performs the computation as follows. First, it scans the line from left to right and finds six arithmetic operations. By convention, multiplication and division have a higher priority than addition and subtraction and must be performed first. Multiplication and division, having the same priority, are performed as they occur from left to right. Thus, the first step in reducing the expression to a single number is to multiply 3 by 5 and substitute 15; this yields: 12 − 7 + 15 − 8/2 + 3. The second step is to divide 8 by 2 and substitute the result, 4; the expression then looks like: 12 − 7 + 15 − 4 + 3. At this time, the computer has made one full sweep of the line from left to right and performed all multiplications and divisions, reducing the complexity of the problem to one involving only additions and subtractions.

Addition and subtraction, having the same priority, also are performed as they occur from left to right. On the second sweep through the line, they are performed in the following sequence:

```
12-7+15-4+3
    5+15-4+3
       20-4+3
          16+3
             19
```

The answer, therefore, is 19.

The fifth arithmetic operation is exponentiation, or raising a number to a power. In arithmetic and algebra, this relationship is normally expressed by writing the two numbers on different lines. For example, four cubed, 4 times 4 times 4, or, in computer notation, 4*4*4, would be written 4^3. Generally, the digit 3 is smaller in size than the 4, and its position is a half-line above that of the 4. On the terminal printer or the CRT, however, this flexibility for modifying the size of the characters and specifying their positions relative to one another is not available, and we must use another scheme. To indicate exponentiation, the preferred symbol is ^ (circumflex); unfortunately, it is not available on all terminals. Alternatives are ↑ and **. Thus, 4*4*4 may be written 4^3 or 4↑3 or 4**3. Examine your keyboard to discover which symbol is used.

On the computer, exponentiation has a higher priority than multiplication and division. Thus, as the expression is scanned from left to right, exponentiation is performed first. For example, suppose we want to evaluate:

12 − 7 + 3*5 − 4^2 − 8/2 + 3 + 2^3

On the first sweep through, the computer detects two exponentiations and carries out the leftmost one first. At the end of this sweep, the expression is

12 − 7 + 3*5 − 16 − 8/2 + 3 + 8

On the second sweep through, the multiplications and divisions are performed, and the line looks like

12 − 7 + 15 − 16 − 4 + 3 + 8

At the end of the third sweep, after the additions and subtractions have been performed, the answer is obtained, 11. As an exercise, at your terminal, type: PRINT 12 − 7 + 3*5 − 4^2 − 8/2 + 3 + 2^3 <CR> and verify that the answer is 11:

On Parentheses

Some special comments should be made about division. If you were to see $\frac{48}{6*2}$ in an arithmetic or algebra text, its meaning would be clear. You would first evaluate the denominator to get 12 and then divide 48 by 12 to get 4. The computer will give the same answer if you exercise care in writing the instructions.

There are two ways to write $\frac{48}{6*2}$. The first is $\frac{48}{6*2}$; The second is 48/6/2. In the first expression, using the parentheses, you are instructing the computer to do the computation within the parentheses first, so that you would get 48/12 and, then, by following the preceding rules, get 4. The second method instructs the computer first to divide 48 by 6, obtaining 8, and then to divide this result by 2, which results in 4.

The most common error is to type $\frac{48}{6*2}$. By omitting the parentheses, you are directing the computer first to divide 48 by 6 to get 8, and then to multiply the 8 by 2 to get 16. Wrong! Note that the same rules apply in algebra.

Similar observations apply to the calculation $\frac{48}{6+2}$. The computer will give the correct answer if the formula is entered correctly: 48/(6+2). The parentheses require the computer to calculate 6+2 first and then to divide 48 by 8 to yield 6, the correct answer. Omitting the parentheses leads to a wrong answer because the formula 48/6+2 means first to divide 48 by 6 to get 8, and then to add 2 to this to get 10.

Parentheses, as the examples illustrate, can be used to modify, and in particular, to specify the order in which a computation is to be carried out. If an expression contains only one set of parentheses, then the part contained within the parentheses is evaluated first and reduced to a single number. The parentheses then become superfluous and may be removed, yielding an expression that you know how to evaluate. For example, evaluate:

2 − 3*(1 + 3^2)/2

The quantity within the parentheses is evaluated first.

1 + 3^2 = 1 + 3*3 = 1 + 9 = 10

The original expression may now be rewritten

2 − 3*(10)/2

The parentheses may be removed and the expression evaluated.

2 − 3*10/2
2 − 30/2
2 − 15
− 13

If an expression contains parentheses nested within parentheses, the computer will evaluate the most deeply nested ones first, remove them, and continue working outwards. For example, evaluate:

13 + 3*(1 + 21/(16 − 3^2) + 5*(12 − 2*(3 + 8/4)))

The innermost nested parentheses, nested three deep, contain the expression

(3 + 8/4)

which when evaluated equals 5.

The original expression may now be written:

13 + 3*(1 + 21/(16 − 3^2) + 5*(12 − 2*5))

Two expressions are contained within parentheses nested two deep; the leftmost one is evaluated first: (16 − 3^2) = (16 − 9) = 7, and then the right one: (12 − 2*5) = (12 − 10) = 2. The original expression may now be rewritten:

13 + 3*(1 + 21/7 + 5*2)

The expression within the parentheses is evaluated:

(1 + 21/7 + 5*2) = (1 + 3 + 10) = (14)

and the original expression rewritten:

13 + 3*(14)

which is calculated to be 55.

Looking at the last formula, note that the familiar algebraic notation 3(14), indicating that the numbers 3 and 14 are to be multiplied, does not carry over unchanged to computer notation. The multiplication symbol, which is implicit in algebra, must be made explicit for the computer. Thus, we must write, 3*(14).

As a consequence of these conventions, certain circumstances arise in which the result obtained is different from the result you might expect if you blithely transformed an algebraic formula into a BASIC formula. For example, consider the algebraic expression

$$\lim_{x \to 0^+} x^x = 1$$

It would be nice if 0^0 were evaluated as 1. Not all computers give 1 as the answer. To try it on your computer, type: PRINT 0^0 <CR> and see what answer is given.

The arithmetic expression 4^{3^2} means first calculate 3^2, which is 9, and then determine 4^9 which is 262,144. If you unthinkingly write 4^3^2, the computer will evaluate this according to the rules given above. Because there are two operations of the same priority, the leftmost one is performed first, 4^3 = 64, and then 64^2 = 4096. To properly evaluate 4^{3^2}, we must use parentheses: 4^(3^2) = 4^(9) = 262,144. At your terminal type PRINT 4^3^2 <CR> and PRINT 4^(3^2) <CR> and see the difference.[2]

[2]Computer systems exist for which, for the special case of repeated exponentiation, the computation is performed from "right to left" rather than "left to right." In these systems, parentheses are not needed; 4^{3^2} would be evaluated properly if you typed PRINT 4^3^2 <CR>.

Summary of Arithmetic Rules

The preceding are the basic rules that the computer follows to evaluate arithmetic and algebraic expressions in BASIC. In review, they are:

1. Evaluate expressions within parentheses first, starting with the most deeply nested ones and work outward.
2. The priorities for execution of arithmetic operations are:
   a. exponentiation
   b. multiplication and division
   c. addition and subtraction
3. Given an expression containing operations of the same priority, the order in which the operations are performed is from left to right.

Representation of Nonintegers

So far, we have introduced the basic operations of arithmetic—addition, subtraction, multiplication, division, and exponentiation—and illustrated how the computer evaluates arithmetic expressions built from the integers and these operations. The illustrations were chosen so that all intermediate steps and the final answers were also integers. While addition, subtraction, and multiplication of two integers always produce an integer, division and exponentiation do not. For example, 3/5 is not an integer; nor is 2^(−3).

Decimal Representation

When nonintegers are printed at your terminal, they appear in one of two forms. The computer decimal format reserves eight print positions.[3] The first position contains a minus sign if the number is negative; it is blank if the decimal is not negative. Of the remaining seven positions, six are for digits and one is for the decimal point. The various combinations are illustrated as follows:

1.	1/2 = .500000	−1/2 = −.500000
2.	5/4 = 1.25000	−5/4 = −1.25000
3.	91/8 = 11.3750	−91/8 = −11.3750
4.	3011/8 = 376.375	−3011/8 = −376.375
5.	30864/25 = 1234.56	−30864/25 = −1234.56
6.	24691/2 = 12345.5	−24691/2 = −12345.5
7.	1000000/3 = 333333.	−1000000/3 = −333333.

In the first six of the above lines, the answers are exact. For the seventh line, it is impossible to construct an example that is exact and has six digits preceding the decimal point because such a number is an integer and would be printed as such. The answer printed on the seventh line was rounded.[4] The computer actually determined the seventh digit, the one that should appear in the next position, found it was less than 5, and dropped it. If the seventh digit had been five or greater, then the answer printed would have been rounded up. For example,

```
 1000001/3 =  333334.
-1000001/3 = -333334.
```

[3]This may vary from one system to the next; some may reserve only 7 while others may use 9.

[4]Rounding will be discussed in detail in Chapter 4 (page 51) when we write a computer program to round numbers.

Other examples of rounding are:

```
6/7 = .857143                (rounded up)
65/7 = 9.28571               (rounded down)
7197532/11 = 654321.         (rounded down)
7197537/11 = 654322.         (rounded up)
```

All the arithmetic rules previously described for integers apply to the broader class of integers and decimals. For example:

```
27.3+37.45*16.276-84.48/7.23=625.152
- 18.46 + 2.1^3.6/4/78 = -18.4137
(-12.457)*(-.0621)+103.32^(-2.4)=.773594
```

The rules will fail, as should be expected, when the operations called for are not defined. Thus, while (−2)^(3) = −8, 2^(1/3)=1.25992, and (−2)^(−3)= −.125000 are all calculable and correct, (−2)^(1/3) may not be calculable by your computer. Generally, a negative number raised to a noninteger power is not a decimal. Unless your computer handles algebraically complex (imaginary) numbers, it will not respond with the correct numerical answer; it should produce an error message telling you what has gone wrong.

In certain cases, you can circumvent this shortcoming by rewriting the expression to be evaluated. For example, (−2)^(1/3) would be rejected by the computer, but the answer could be obtained by rewriting it as −(2)^(1/3)= −1.25992. However, (−2)^(1/2) would also be rejected by the computer, and there is no way to rewrite it to make it acceptable to a computer that does not handle complex numbers.

In summary, the rules for evaluating arithmetic expressions, previously given for integers, apply equally to computer decimals. The one exception occurs when a negative number, either integer or decimal, is raised to a noninteger power. Although mathematically it is possible to provide an answer in this case, most BASIC interpreters are not equipped to do so and indicate their shortcoming with an error message.

Floating-Point Representation

The second way to express nonintegers is the scientific, or floating-point, format. For this notation, 12 print positions are used.[5] The first position is reserved for the sign; the minus sign is printed, the plus sign generally is omitted. The second position is for one of the digits 1 through 9; 0 is not acceptable. The third position is for the decimal point; the next five positions are for digits. The ninth position contains the letter E, which is the clue that floating-point, or scientific, notation is being used. The tenth position is again reserved for the sign, either plus or minus. The last two positions are reserved for two digits. For example, consider the expressions

```
-4.56789E+08
 3.12127E-12
```

In the more familiar scientific notation, the number −4.56789E+08 is expressed -4.56789×10^{8}; the number 3.12127E−12 is 3.12127×10^{-12}.

What may we expect from different computers? First, the number of digits following the decimal point may not be five. Second, if the exponent is positive, the plus sign that follows the E may be omitted; obviously, the minus sign cannot be. Third, the number of

[5]Some systems use fewer than 12, some more.

digits available for the exponent, while generally two rarely may be only one; on extremely large computers it may be three. We shall, in this book, assume that two digits are available for the exponent.

The rules for evaluating arithmetic expressions, given previously for integers and computer decimals, apply equally to numbers expressed in floating-point notation. Again, the computer may balk if asked to raise a negative number to a nonintegral power.

Algebraic Expressions

In each of the above illustrations, we applied the rules for evaluating arithmetic expressions to numerical quantities only. In elementary algebra, however, you learned that the rules of arithmetic also apply to literals. Thus, in algebra, you can evaluate such literal expressions as A+B, B−C, C*D, D/A, and A^B, provided you know beforehand the numerical values of A, B, C, and D.

The computer, still operating as a desk calculator, also can perform the standard arithmetic operations on literals, provided that the values of the literals are known beforehand. In the following example, we first assign arbitrary values to the literals A, B, C, and D and then let the computer evaluate the prescribed algebraic expressions.

```
>LET A=3
>LET B=5
>LET C=7
>LET D=11
>PRINT A+B
 8
>PRINT C-D
-4
>PRINT A*D
 33
>PRINT D/A
 3.66667
 PRINT B^C
 78125
>PRINT C^D
 1.97733E+09
>PRINT A*(B+C)
 36
>PRINT (A-B)/(C-D)
 .500000
>PRINT 3*C+4/2^A-(C-6/B)*2^A
-24.9000
```

Summary

In this chapter, we introduced representations of three kinds of computer numbers: integers, computer decimals, and floating-point numbers. The rules of ordinary arithmetic were shown to apply to all three types. To ensure that the correct answer is obtained, you must exercise care in specifying the order in which the various arithmetic operations are carried out. The extension of these rules to literals, to algebra, is valid also.

All of this is prelude to what is to follow. Obviously, you must know how a computer goes about evaluating arithmetic and algebraic expressions if you expect to get meaningful results from the programs you soon will be writing.

When the computer is used as it was in the examples in this chapter—that is, as a desk calculator—we shall refer to it being used in the "immediate mode."

Exercises

2.1 Using the rules that a computer would follow, compute with a pencil and paper:

a. 3+5−2+4−6
b. 5+8−12−10+1
c. 3*2+2*5−12/2
d. 2+26/2−5*3−2^5
e. 2*3*4
f. 4*3^2

2.2 At your terminal, verify that your answers are correct

2.3 Evaluate each of the following:

a. 3*5*7+5*7*9−7*11*13−11*13*17
b. 2/3+6/7−10/9
c. 5*7/2−4/3*8
d. 12/5/7+2*7−3
e. 12/5*3+2*(7−3)
f. 8+3^4
g. (1−4)^5
h. 3^4*5^2−29*41^2
i. 9^3*5^6−(3*5)^6

2.4 Evaluate the following algebraic expression for each set of indicated values:

A+2*B*(C/3−4/(D−A/B)+C^D)

a. A=1, B=2, C=3, D=4
b. A=B=C=D=2
c. A=1.2, B=2.3, C=3.4, D=4.5
d. A=5.4, B=4.3, C=3.2, D=2.1
e. A=6, B=7, C=8, D=9

In Exercises 5-7, the formulas are written as the computer would expect you to enter them. Rewrite each formula in standard algebraic notation. Test each expression for the values of the variables specified.

F=9*C/5+32
C=0, 50, 100

2.6 A=P*(1+I/100/K)^(Y*K)

P	I	K	Y
1000	10	1	1
1000	10	1	2
1000	10	12	1
1000	10	4	5
1000	10	4	10

2.7 S=D*((1+I/100/K)^(Y*K)−1)/(I/100/K)

D	I	K	Y
1000	10	1	1
1000	10	2	1
500	10	2	5
100	10	2	10

In Exercises 8–10, the formulas are written in standard algebraic notation. Rewrite each formula in a computer-acceptable form. Test each for the values of the variables specified.

2.8 $C = \frac{5}{9}(F - 32)$

$F = 32, 122, 212$

2.9 $P = \dfrac{A}{\left(1 + \dfrac{I}{100K}\right)^{YK}} = A\left(1 + \dfrac{I}{100K}\right)^{-YK}$

A	I	K	Y
1500	10	1	1
1500	10	2	1
1500	10	1	2
1500	10	2	2

2.10 $D = S\dfrac{\dfrac{I}{100K}}{\left(1 + \dfrac{I}{100K}\right)^{YK} - 1}$

S	I	K	Y
2500	10	2	1
8000	10	2	2
20000	10	2	5
40000	10	2	10

3 Flow Charts

A Perspective

In solving problems, there is no substitute for insight. Experience gained by observing how similar problems are solved helps to sharpen one's perception. Beyond this, however, certain techniques may be used to organize and give structure to the steps to be taken in thinking about a solution. These techniques give a deeper understanding of the solution process. One such technique is called **flow-charting.** In this chapter, we shall dissect a variety of problems and expose their parts and interrelationships in order to show with examples how the pieces may be reassembled using flow charts.

Flow charts, also called flow diagrams, serve several purposes. For one, they present the solution to a problem in a form that another person, familiar with the symbolism of flow-charting and the language used, can understand. For another, a flow chart may represent an intermediate stage in the preparation of instructions to a computer. A flow chart forces one to describe in clear detail the various steps to be taken in arriving at a solution; it can pinpoint errors in logic for problems incorrectly solved.

We shall apply flow-charting to a variety of problems. In each example, after the problem has been posed, a verbal description of the steps needed to obtain the solution is given. This description is then translated into a flow chart. As you examine how this translation is effected, you will acquire background and experience in flow-charting. The knowledge gained may then be brought to bear on flow-charting new problems.

Our first illustration is not a computer problem; it simply consists of directions for going to and from a supermarket. We shall introduce four flow-charting symbols in this example; the remaining two that will be used are introduced in the second and third examples. Of the other examples and exercises, most are for problems that may be solved on a computer. The broader intent, however, is to provide material that illustrates how flow-charting helps solve problems.

In solving most real problems, it is necessary to cut through the verbiage to get to and symbolize the essence. Do not be concerned if some words or ideas are unfamiliar to you; no one is knowledgeable in all areas. It is only by studying a variety of problems that the experience underlying insight is acquired.

A Trip to the Supermarket

Assume you are visiting a friend in a totally unfamiliar town. Dinner is to be a cook-out, and you offer to go to the supermarket to buy the necessary groceries. Your friend gives you the following directions: "As you leave the driveway, turn right and go to the third traffic light. Make a right turn onto the cross street, Congress Avenue. Go to the second cross street, Perry Boulevard, and turn left. Continue on Perry for about a half mile and you'll see the supermarket, the Penny Pincher, on your right.

"Unfortunately, Perry Boulevard is under construction and you may not be able to get through between Congress and the Penny Pincher. In that case, turn around, go back to Congress, turn right, and continue to the second street on the right-hand side past the second traffic light. This is Alpine. Go right onto Alpine, and about three miles down the street on your left is the Mighty Miser.

"Try the Penny Pincher first, though, because it's cheaper and closer. If they don't have something, you will have to go to Mighty Miser anyway."

As he is giving you these directions, your friend draws the map in Figure 3-1.

The instructions are sufficiently explicit, and you have no difficulty finding your way.

A Flow Chart

After dinner, while catching up on old times and discussing your friend's main interest, which is the history of Byzantine dancing, you decide to show him how you would flow-chart his directions to the supermarket.

FIGURE 3-1

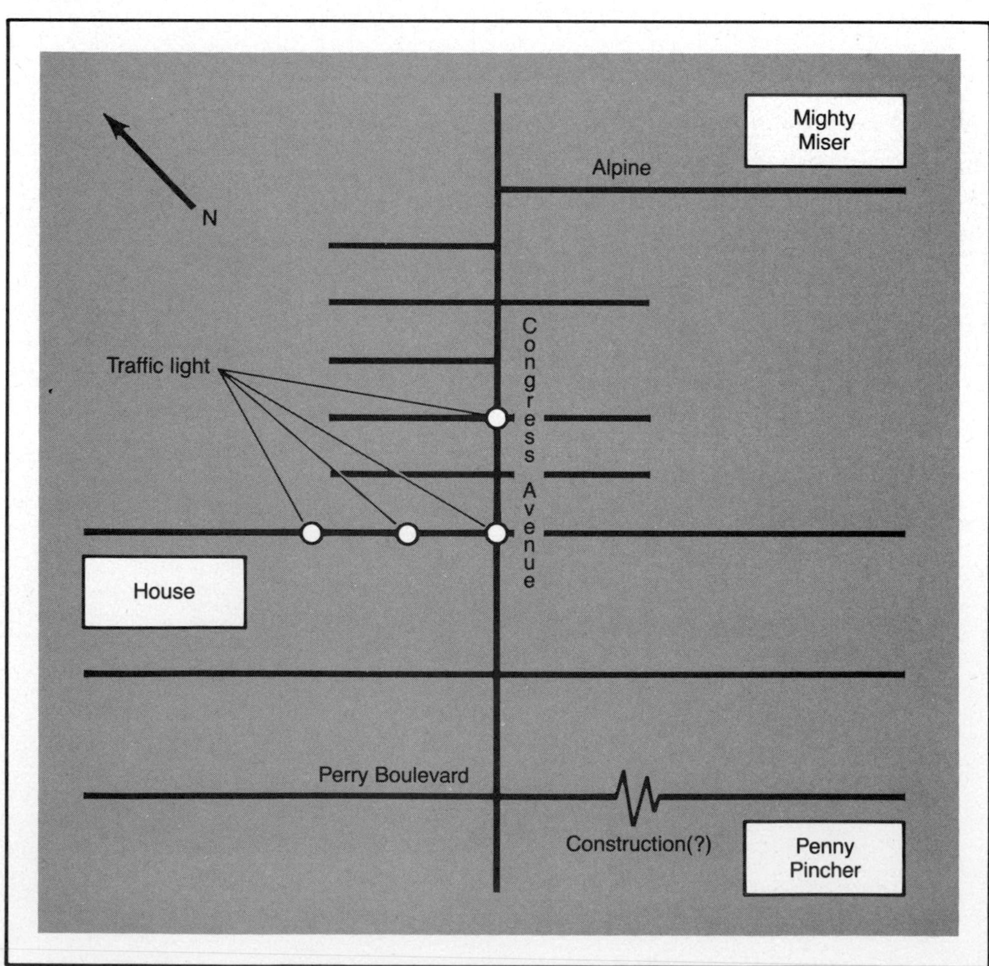

As you and your friend examine your flow chart, illustrated in Figure 3-2, you point out the feasibility of preparing directions for almost any process using this technique and, in particular, the salient features of this one. The symbol ( ) is always reserved for the beginning and ending of the entire process. The rectangle [ ]

FIGURE 3-2

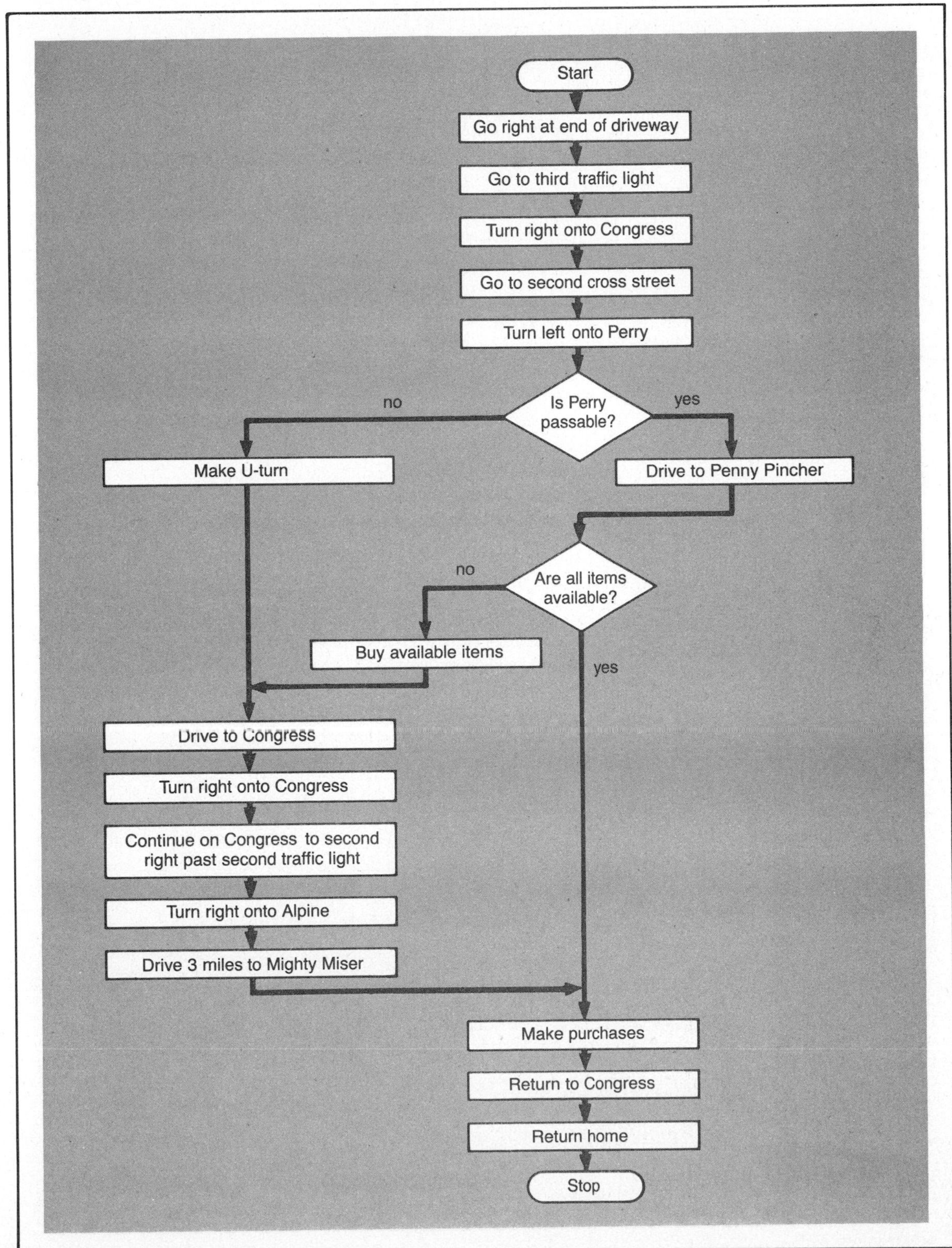

is reserved for performing a specified task; the diamond shape ◇ is used to indicate where decisions are to be made. Arrows → indicate the flow of action from start to finish.

You remain reticent about the variety of symbols reserved for other operations, feeling these might be best explained in the context of specific problems in which they arise naturally. You both agree it may be too difficult to describe, using a flow chart, the body movements of the ancient forms of Byzantine dance.

Two lessons are to be learned from this illustration. First, a flow chart may be used to describe a process. The degree of complexity of the process depends on the problem posed; the degree of detail of the flow chart is dictated by the clarity desired. The other more obvious lesson is the introduction and use of four flow-charting symbols.

Tossing Pennies

As you will see in Chapter 8, computers may be programed to simulate random processes and, thus, may be used to imitate games that depend on such processes. One such problem and a corresponding flow chart are described in the following example. We shall also introduce the flow-chart symbol for input and output—for entering data into the computer and getting answers from it.

Two young people, Art and Bill, each with some pennies in his pocket, have some time to kill waiting for friends. They decide to while away the time tossing pennies at a line. The game is played as follows: Two parallel lines, about 15 feet apart, are marked off. Standing behind one line, each player tosses a penny toward the other line. The player whose penny is closer to the second line wins the other's penny. Art tosses first; after the first game, the winner tosses first. If either player goes broke before their friends arrive, the game is over; otherwise, the game ends when their friends arrive.

A Flow Chart

The flow chart in Figure 3-3 parallels the description of the game. In this flowchart, an additional symbol, the parallelogram, ▱, is used. Because the number of pennies that Art and Bill have varies from one day to the next, and we want the flowchart to apply to the general rather than the specific case, it is desirable to have as input to the process the amount each has on that particular day. In a similar vein, if either has won all his opponent's pennies, or if the game ended with the arrival of their friends, we want to be told this. The parallelogram signals that input or output is expected. Examine the flow chart carefully to see how it describes the game. Notice that each step of the process is described.

A Road Map from Here to There

Of the other symbols that may be used, you need to know only one more. When the flow diagram for a problem becomes so large an unwieldy that it cannot fit on a single sheet of paper or when the only way it can be drawn is with intersecting lines, the symbol ○, a circle, is used. We shall illustrate its use in the following examples.

Figure 3-4 is a schematic road map depicting the routes available to a motorist going from Appleton to Georgetown. Of the three roads leaving Appleton, the first goes to Beaver, the second to Charleston and the third to Downers. From each of these three towns, two roads lead to Elmyra and Falmouth, and finally, one road leads from Elmyra and one from Falmouth to Georgetown.

When the weather is pleasant, the route from Appleton to Beaver is the prettiest and quickest; the other two roads out of Appleton are under construction at such times and, consequently, are not passable. In case of rain, however, only the road from Appleton to Charleston may be used; in case of snow, only the road from Appleton to Downers is open.

Beaver is famous for its art museum, and if you pass through town, you must spend at least a day viewing the collection. Charleston is known for its wineries and the siren

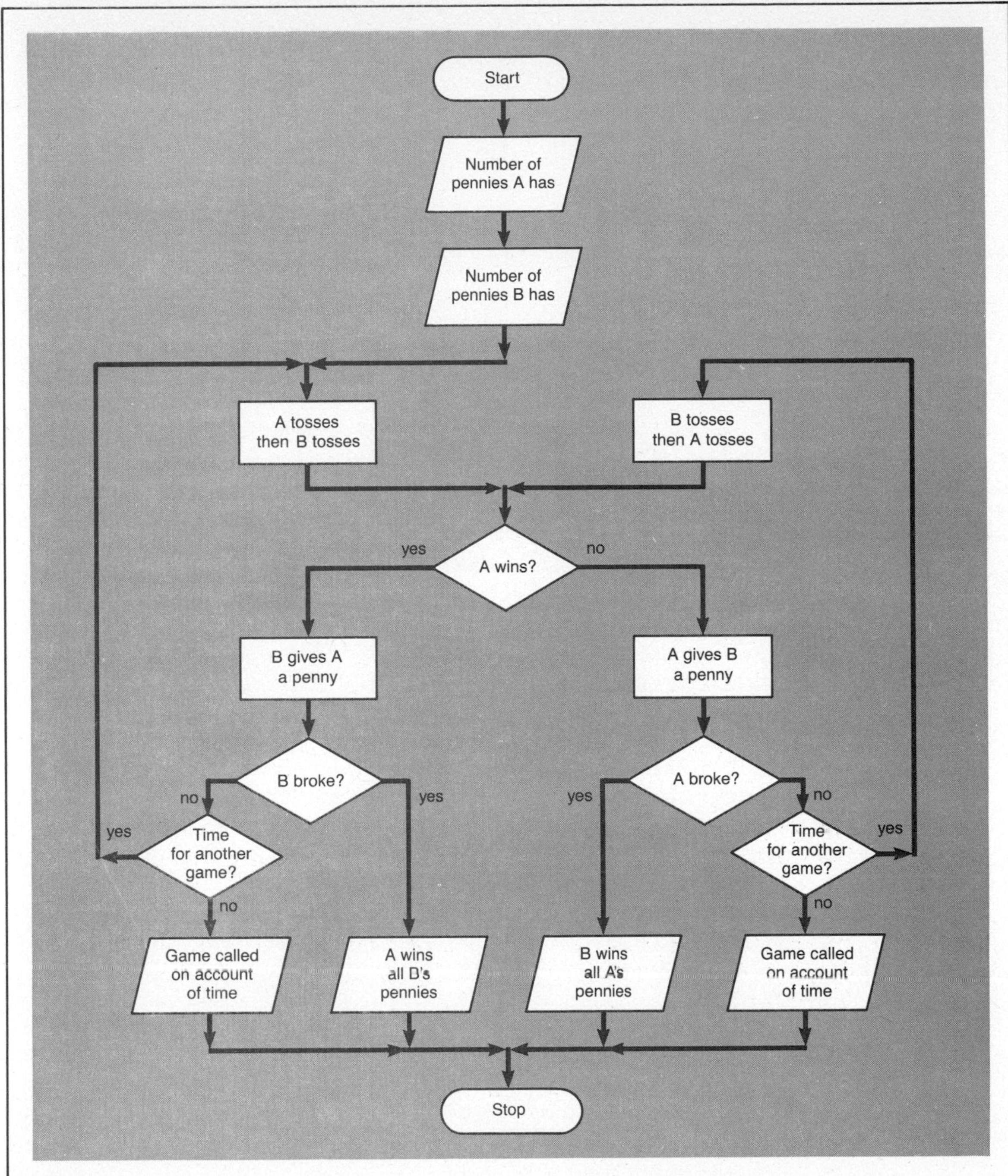

FIGURE 3-3

song of free samples has kept many a visitor overnight. Downers is located in horse country, and its restored Shaker village is renowned for its quaint lodging houses and fine dining facilities. No one has ever driven through without stopping.

If you get to Beaver, the road to Elmyra is open in good weather only; the road to Falmouth, which is under construction when the weather is fair, may be used only when there is no crew working, that is, when the weather is bad. The social life in Charleston is such that many people find themselves with limited funds when they are ready to leave. If your money supply is running short, head for Elmyra with its many friendly loan offices; if your funds are ample, head for Falmouth. If you are in Downers and have lots of time, go to Falmouth; if time is running short and you are in a hurry, go directly to Elmyra.

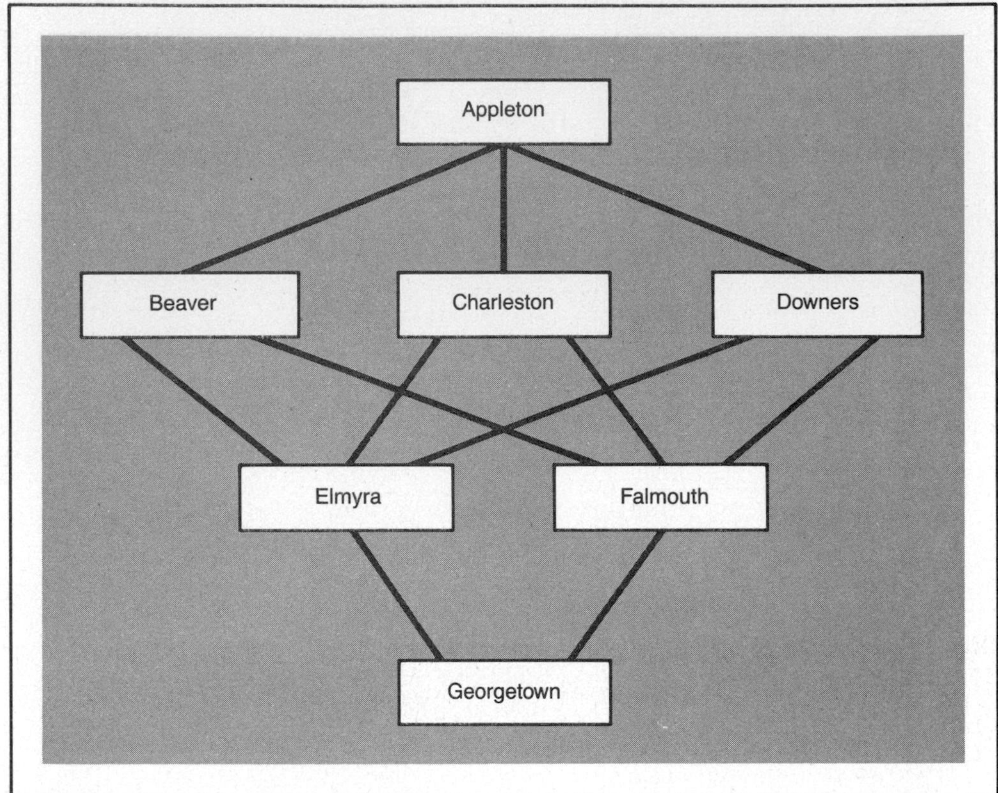

FIGURE 3-4

The roads between Elmyra and Georgetown and between Falmouth and Georgetown are excellent in all kinds of weather, toll free, and suitable for high speeds.

How can we make sense of all this and decide which way to go? The flow chart in Figure 3-5 parallels the above description.

A Graph

The complexity of a flow chart is inherent in the nature of the particular problem, as the following discussion will show. Consider a seemingly different problem, one that may be more familiar. Three houses, H1, H2, and H3, are to be served by three utilities, gas, water, and electricity. Is it possible to join each house to each of the three utilities so that no two service lines cross? The answer is no.[1]

It is easy to see from Figure 3-6 (although difficult to prove) that eight pipelines may be placed with no two crossing but that the ninth always cuts one of the eight. How does this relate to the road map problem?

First, delete the roads from Elmyra and Falmouth to Georgetown, and relabel Appleton as the electric station, Elmyra as the gasworks, and Falmouth as the waterworks. Then, relabel the three cities Beaver, Charlestown, and Downers as the three houses. The two diagrams are now equivalent, as shown in Figure 3-7.

It is therefore impossible to arrange the network of roads so that there is no intersection, and the corresponding flow chart must exhibit this same complexity. In fact, the correspondence between the road map and the flow diagram is as follows: Appleton corresponds to the upper diamond containing "weather?," Beaver to the lower diamond containing "weather?," Charleston to the diamond containing "money?," and Downers to the diamond containing "time?." Again, the lines from Elmyra and Falmouth to George-

[1]Claude Berge, *The Theory of Graphs and Its Applications* (N.Y.: John Wiley & Sons, 1962), pp. 207–213.

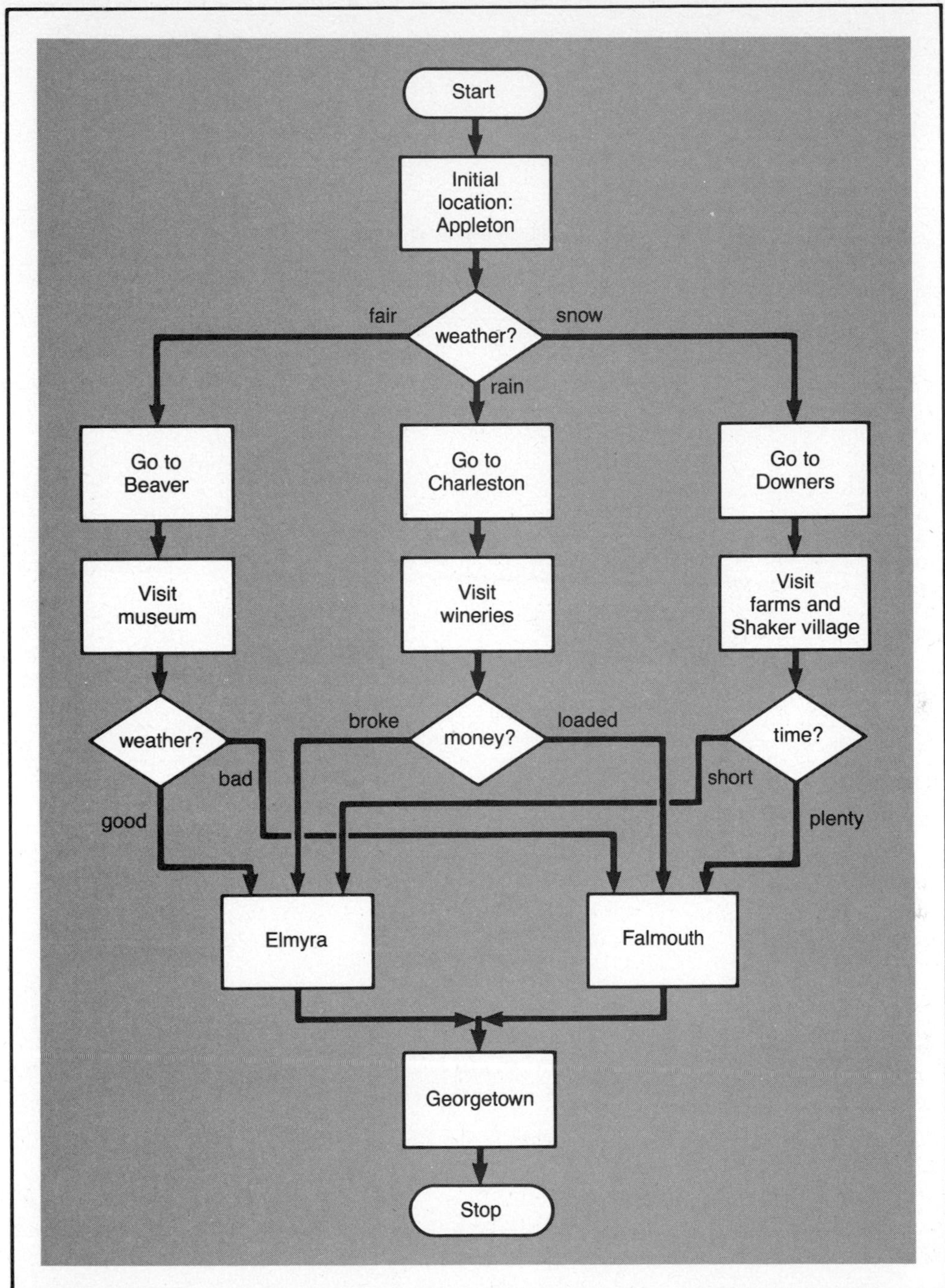

FIGURE 3-5

town may be disregarded. Having established this correspondence between the abbreviated road map and the abbreviated flow chart, you must conclude it is impossible to draw the flow chart without intersecting lines.

You should now be aware of the complexity that may result when you try to flowchart even a relatively simple problem. Generally, the logic of the flow chart is easier to specify and understand when there are no intersecting lines. To achieve this clarification, the connector symbol, ○ , is used at the appropriate places, as shown in Figure 3-8. While only one connector is really needed, we have used two in order to further simplify both the drawing and the logic.

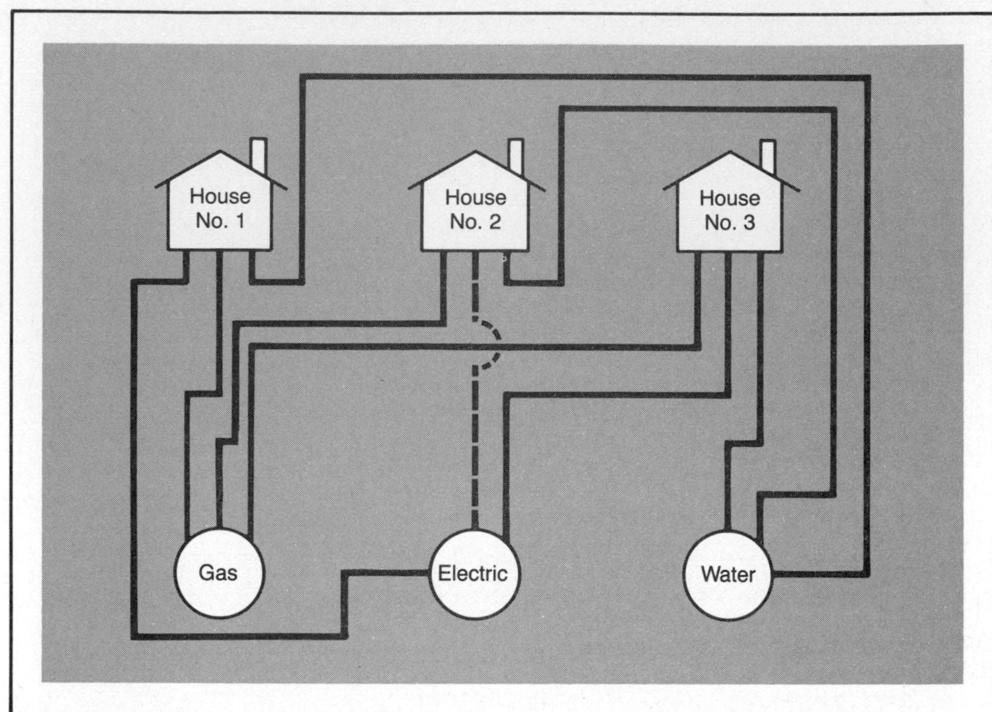

FIGURE 3-6

FIGURE 3-7

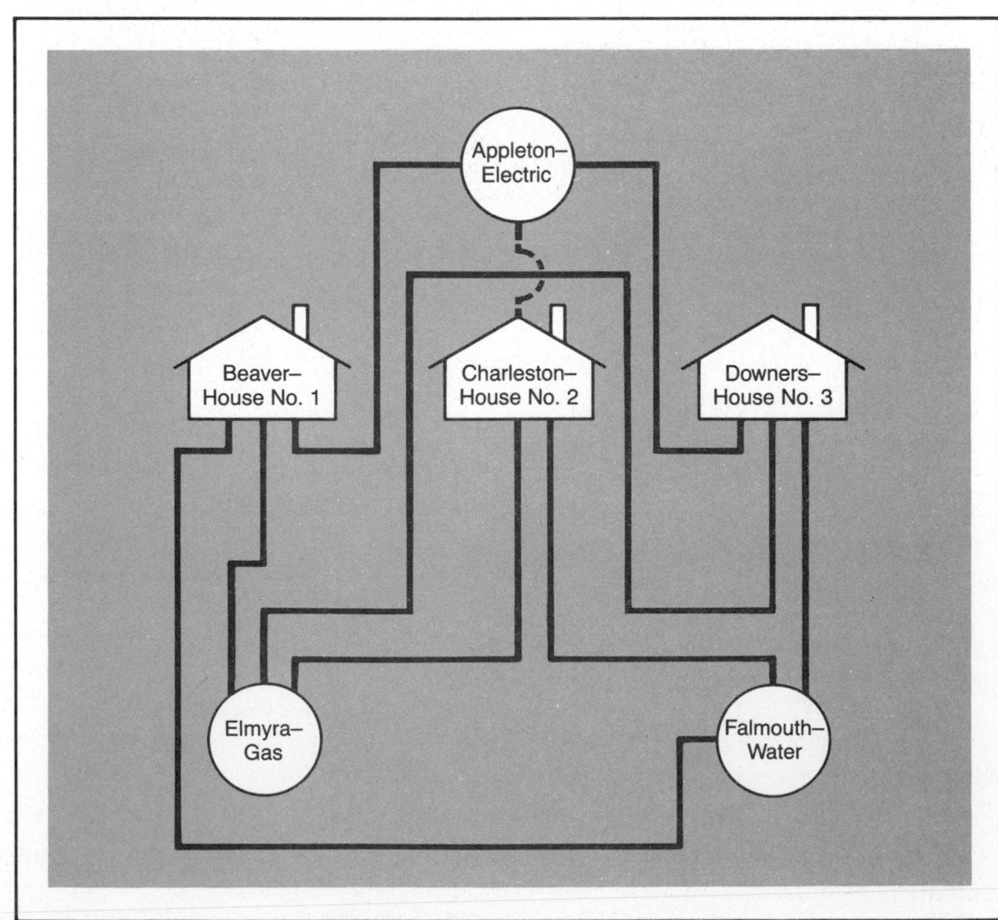

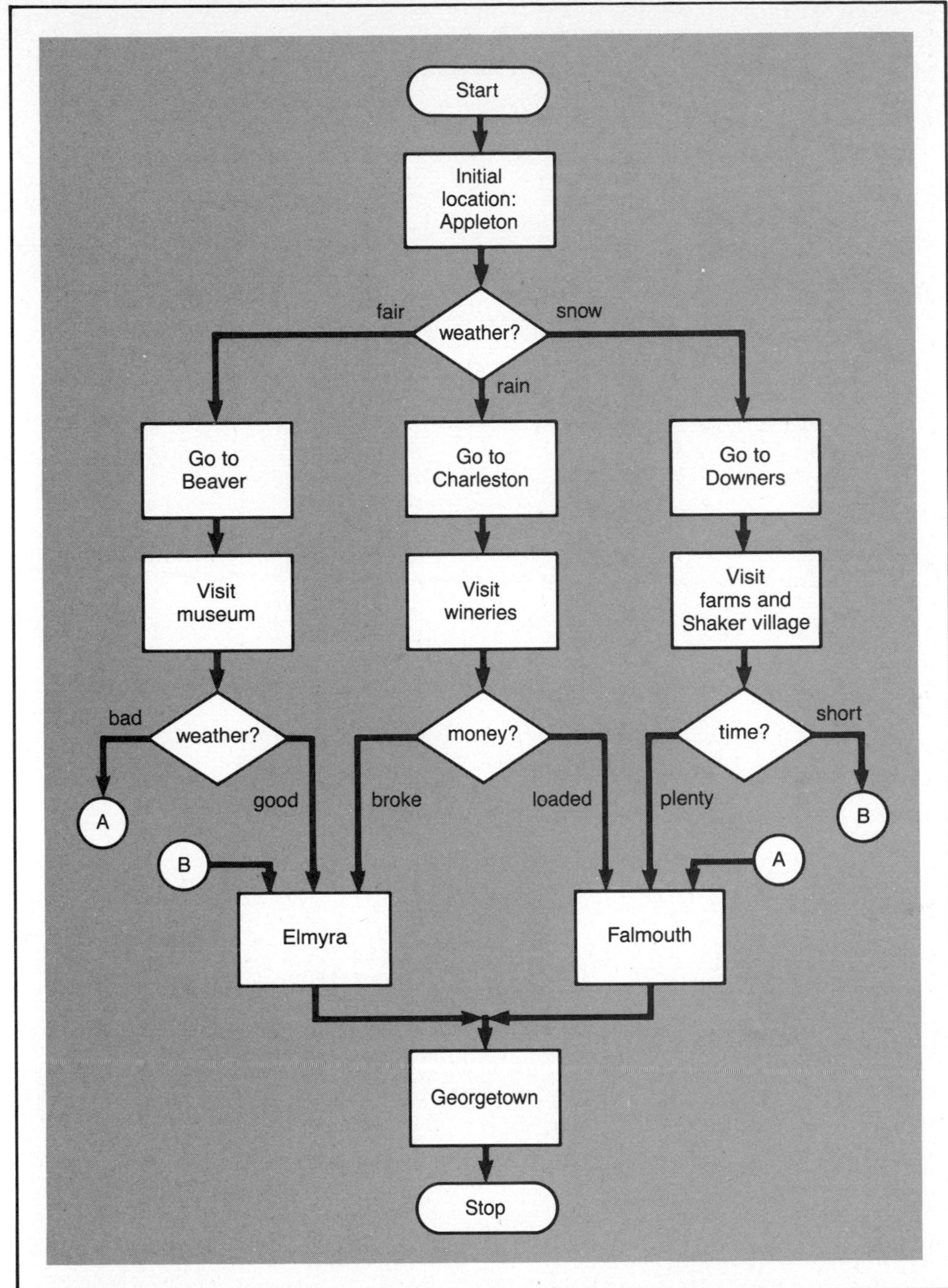

FIGURE 3-8

You are now acquainted with the six most fundamental flow chart symbols—the only ones to be used in this book. You should know the function of each and its use as illustrated in the specific examples. We shall use flow charting as a problem solving aid in the rest of this book. To increase your familiarity with the use of flow charts, we offer another illustration, followed by some exercises designed to test your understanding.

Scissors, Rock, and Paper

While there is generally only one answer to a problem, there may be different ways to arrive at it. In the following example—a two-person game popular with children—two different analyses are given, as are two different flow charts.

Charles chooses at random one of three objects: scissors, rock, or paper. Simultaneously, Dorothy also picks one of the three. Charles's selection is unknown to Dorothy as is hers to him. The two choices are then compared. If they are the same, there is no payoff; when different, the winner is decided according to the following rules:

1. paper covers rock; paper wins;
2. rock breaks scissors; rock wins;
3. scissors cuts paper; scissors wins.

FIGURE 3-9

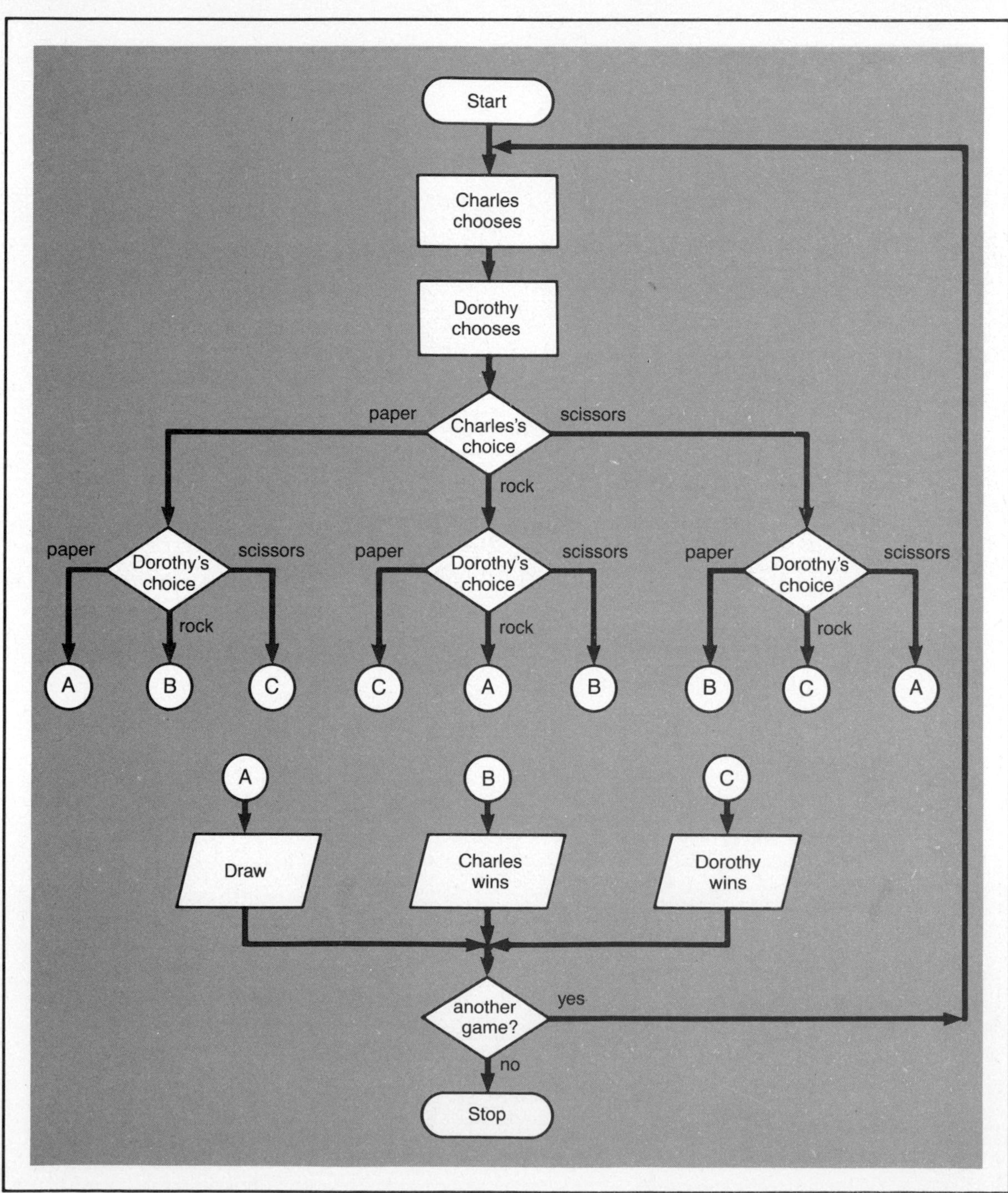

A flow chart describing the game appears in Figure 3-9. Clearly, the use of the connector symbol reduces the complexity of the flow chart by eliminating intersecting flow lines. In other, more complex situations, it serves also to clarify the logic.

A Second Solution

The complexity of the flow chart, and correspondingly that of the solution, may sometimes be reduced by reformulating the problem. We can do this with the above example in the following way. There are nine possible outcomes, namely:

1. Charles–rock
   Dorothy–rock
2. Charles–paper
   Dorothy–paper
3. Charles–scissors
   Dorothy–scissors
4. Charles–rock
   Dorothy–paper
5. Charles–paper
   Dorothy–scissors
6. Charles–scissors
   Dorothy–rock
7. Charles–rock
   Dorothy–scissors
8. Charles–paper
   Dorothy–rock
9. Charles–scissors
   Dorothy–paper

The first three outcomes lead to a draw, the second three to a win for Dorothy, and the last three to a win for Charles. Thus, the outcome of the game is equivalent to picking one of the three numbers, 1, 2, or 3, at random and saying that if the number 1 is picked, the game is a draw, if 2 is picked, Dorothy wins, and if 3 is picked, Charles wins. Figure 3-10 is a flow chart for this procedure.

FIGURE 3–10

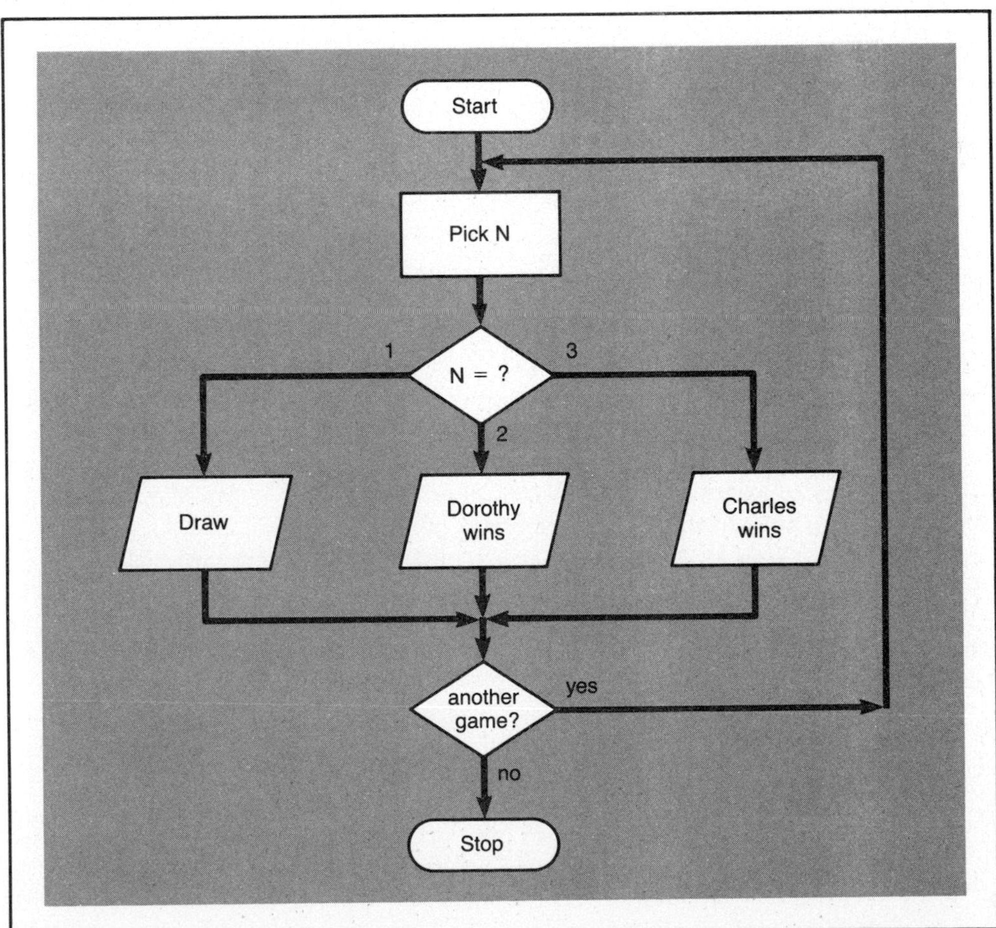

Exercises

3.1 Describe the first two hours of your routine after awakening in the morning. Draw a flow chart that parallels this description.

3.2 Describe the mental process you go through during the involuntary blinking of your eyelid. Draw a flow chart that parallels this description.

3.3 Craps The game of craps is played as follows: In its simplest form, it is the player against the house. The player places his bet and the house covers it with an equal amount of money; this becomes the pot. The player then throws two dice for the first time. If, on the first throw, a total of either 7 or 11 points comes up, the player wins the pot. The game is over and he has the option of continuing to play or passing the dice to another player.

If on the first throw, however, a total of either 2, 3, or 12 points comes up, the player loses and the house takes the pot. Again, the game is over, but the player still has the option of continuing to play or passing the dice.

Suppose, on the first throw, one of the totals 4, 5, 6, 8, 9, or 10 comes up. Under these circumstances, the player retrieves the dice and continues to throw them until one of two events occurs. If, for example, on the first throw, the number 6 comes up, he continues to throw the dice until either a 6 or a 7 occurs. If the 6 comes up, the player wins and again has the option of continuing or passing the dice. If a 7 occurs, however, he loses; the house takes the pot and the dice pass to the next player. In the illustration, the number 6 could have been any of the numbers, 4, 5, 6, 8, 9 or 10.

Draw a flow chart for the game of craps.

3.4 When Is Easter Sunday? When Constantine convened the Council of Nicaea in A.D. 325, great disputes had arisen among the Christians regarding the proper day for celebrating Easter, which in turn governs all other movable feasts. In order to terminate the dissensions, the Council decreed that: "1st, Easter must be celebrated on a Sunday; 2nd, this Sunday must follow the 14th day of the paschal moon, so that if the 14th day of the paschal moon falls on a Sunday then Easter must be celebrated on the Sunday following; 3rd, the paschal moon is that of which the 14th day falls on or next follows the day of the vernal equinox; 4th, the equinox is fixed invariably in the calendar on the 21st of March."[2]

As stated by the Encyclopaedia Britannica, "The observance of this rule renders it necessary to reconcile three periods which have no common measure, namely, the week, the lunar month, and the solar year; and as this can only be done approximately, and within certain limits, the determination of Easter is an affair of considerable nicety and complication."[3]

With the reform of the Julian calendar under Pope Gregory X in 1582, it became possible to devise an arithmetic scheme to calculate the date for Easter Sunday in subsequent years. The architects of the Gregorian calendar and the method for calculating Easter were Aloysius Lilius, an astronomer and physician from Naples, who unfortunately died before the introduction of the new calendar, and the German Jesuit mathematician Christopher Calvius, who published an 800 page folio on the subject in 1603. The following form of their algorithm is taken from D. E. Knuth's *The Art of Computer Programming.*[4]

1. Denote the year by N.
2. Divide N by 19; add 1 to the remainder and call this A.
3. Divide N by 100; add 1 to the integer part and call this B.
4. Let C equal the integer part of (3*B/4) − 12.

---

[2] *Encyclopaedia Britannica,* Vol. 4, p. 997, The Encyclopaedia Britannica Co., New York, 1910 (eleventh edition).
[3] *Ibid.* p. 992.
[4] D. E. Knuth, *The Art of Computer Programming, Vol. 1, Fundamental Algorithms,* (Reading, Mass.: 1968. Addison-Wesley Publishing Co.,) pp. 155–156.

5. Let D equal the integer part of ((8*B+5)/25) − 5.
6. Let E equal the integer part of (5*N/4) − C − 10.
7. Calculate the remainder of (11*A+20+D−C)/30 and call this F.
8. If F=25 and A>11 then increase F by 1.
9. If F=24, increase F by 1.
10. Let G=44−F.
11. If G is less than 21 then increase G by 30.
12. Let H equal the remainder of (E+G)/7.
13. Let J=G+7−H.
14. If J does not exceed 31, Easter Sunday is on MARCH J, N.
    If J exceeds 31, then Easter Sunday is on APRIL (J-31), N.

The following table, derived from this algorithm, gives the dates for Easter Sunday for the years 1954 through 2009.

```
APRIL 18    1954
APRIL 10    1955
APRIL  1    1956
APRIL 21    1957
APRIL  6    1958
MARCH 29    1959
APRIL 17    1960
APRIL  2    1961
APRIL 22    1962
APRIL 14    1963
MARCH 29    1964
APRIL 18    1965
APRIL 10    1966
MARCH 26    1967
APRIL 14    1968
APRIL  6    1969
MARCH 29    1970
APRIL 11    1971
APRIL  2    1972
APRIL 22    1973
APRIL 14    1974
MARCH 30    1975
APRIL 18    1976
APRIL 10    1977
MARCH 26    1978
APRIL 15    1979
APRIL  6    1980
APRIL 19    1981
APRIL 11    1982
APRIL  3    1983
APRIL 22    1984
APRIL  7    1985
MARCH 30    1986
APRIL 19    1987
APRIL  3    1988
MARCH 26    1989
APRIL 15    1990
MARCH 31    1991
APRIL 19    1992
APRIL 11    1993
APRIL  3    1994
APRIL 16    1995
APRIL  7    1996
MARCH 30    1997
APRIL 12    1998
APRIL  4    1999
APRIL 23    2000
APRIL 15    2001
MARCH 31    2002
APRIL 20    2003
APRIL 11    2004
MARCH 27    2005
APRIL 16    2006
APRIL  8    2007
MARCH 23    2008
APRIL 12    2009
```

Draw a flow chart that illustrates how the date for Easter Sunday is calculated.

The Gauss Algorithm for Easter Sunday As you have already seen, the solution to a problem may be obtained using different lines of reasoning. Conceivably, different algorithms could yield the same result. The Prince of Mathematicians, Johann Carl Friedrick Gauss, apparently had devised an alternative algorithm for determining the date of Easter Sunday.[5]

> This formula for determining the date upon which Easter will fall was derived by Karl Gauss, German mathematician and is recorded in one of the essays of an English author, Christopher Morley.
> a. Divide the number of the year by 19; let the remainder equal A.
> b. Divide the number of the year by 4; let the remainder equal B.
> c. Divide the number of the year by 7; let the remainder equal C.
> d. Divide 19A plus 24 by 30; let the remainder equal D.
> e. Divide 2B plus 4C plus 6D plus 5 by 7; let the remainder equal E.
> f. Easter will be 22 plus D plus E and, if the number exceeds 31, the month will be April instead of March.

Figure 3-11 illustrates a flow chart for Gauss's method for determining Easter Sunday.

Unfortunately, the dates produced by the two algorithms do not agree. For the years 1600–1699, all the dates predicted by Gauss's method fall on a Wednesday; for the years 1700–1799, all fall on a Tuesday; for 1800–1899, all fall on Monday. For the 200-year period 1900–2099, however, all the dates Guass's method yields do fall on Sunday.

There is another difference between the dates obtained by the two methods. For the years 1700–1799, most of the Tuesdays calculated by Guass's algorithm follow Easter Sunday; for 17 of these years, however, the Tuesday precedes Easter. For the years 1800–1899, all of the Mondays predicted by Gauss's method follow Easter Sunday. For the 200 years, 1900–2099, Guass's method does determine the correct Sunday except for the years 1954, 1981, 2049, and 2076, when it yields the Sunday after Easter.

For the years 2100–2199, similar differences arise. The dates predicted by Gauss's method all fall on Saturday, generally the Saturday preceding Easter.

Occasionally, for 16 of the 100 years, the method predicts the Saturday following Easter. Looking still further ahead, for example to the years 2200–2210, Gauss's algorithm picks the Friday before Easter Sunday, except in 2201, when it yields the Friday following. As a final observation, in the year 2209, Easter falls on March 26 whereas Gauss's method calculates the date to be April 20, a Friday 26 days later.

3.5 Which Coins Are Gold? One of the more intriguing problems that fill our lore is that of the crown of Hieron. The king of Syracuse had ordered a crown of gold from a silversmith of dubious integrity. After the crown was delivered and paid for, Hieron, suspecting that the gold may have been adulterated with silver, asked Archimedes to put his mind to the problem. As the story goes, Archimedes was in his bath when he discovered by observing his own body, that an object immersed in a fluid loses in weight an amount equal to that of the displaced fluid. So excited was he by this discovery that he ran through the streets of the city stark naked, shouting "Eureka, eureka!" ("I have found it, I have found it!") or, at least, legend has it so. There is no record indicating the guilt of the goldsmith; the story would seem to be enhanced if we believe he was.

Assume you are given twelve seemingly identical coins, purportedly gold, and you are told that one of them has been debased. You do not know if the counterfeit coin is heavier or lighter than the true ones; you are asked to decide this and to discover the false coin. The only instrument available to you is a beam balance.

A solution may be obtained as follows:

---

[5]Alan J. Perlis, *Introduction to Computer Science* (N.Y.: Harper and Row, 1975), pp. 262–263.

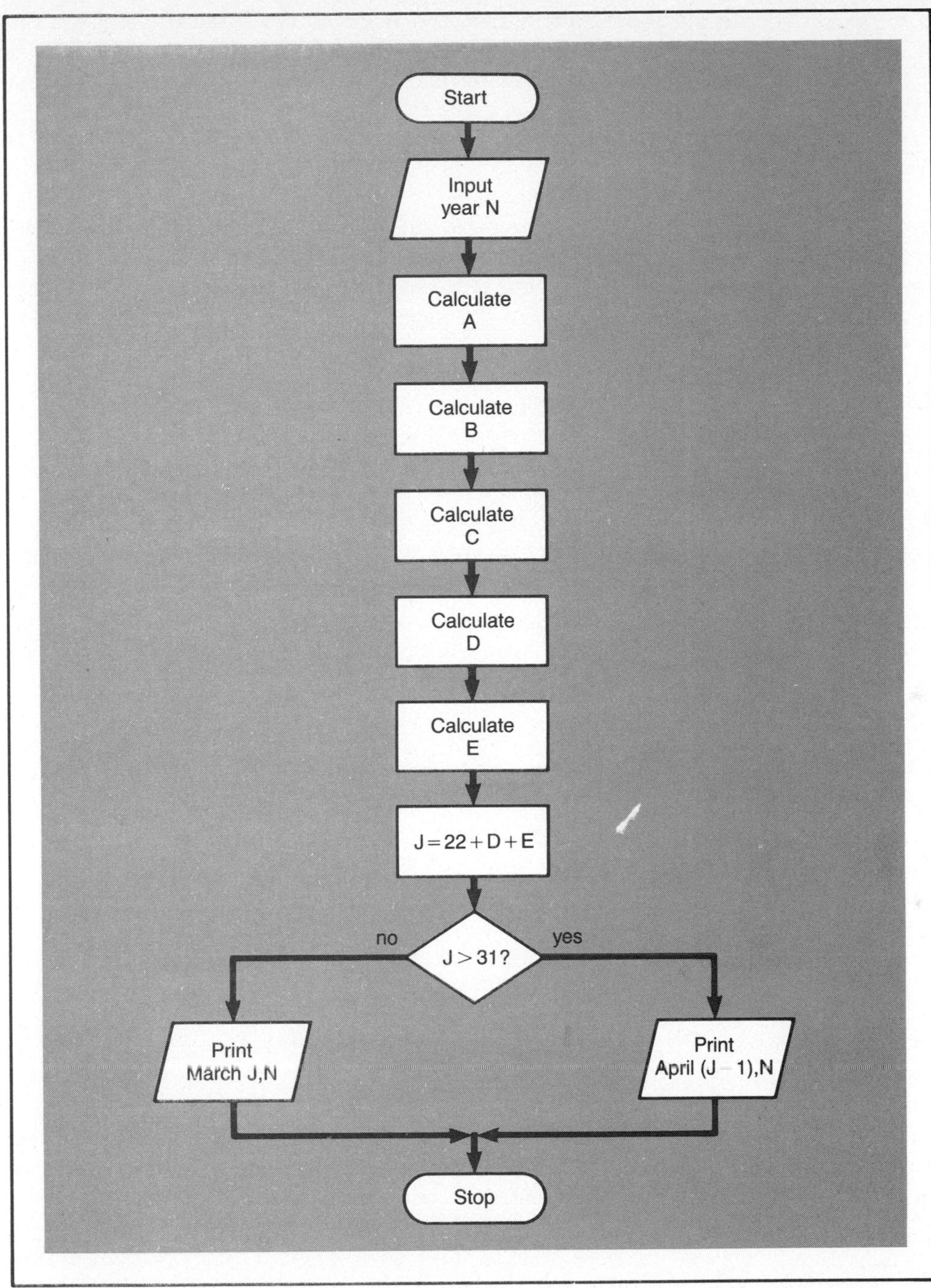

FIGURE 3-11

1. Place one coin on each side of the balance; the balance will indicate if the two are equal or unequal in weight.
2. If the two are equal, you know both are true; if the two are unequal, one must be degraded.
3. If the two are equal, remove one from the balance and replace it with a third coin. If these two are equal, repeat the process until you find two that are unequal. You have found the false coin and the way that the balance tips will indicate if it is lighter or heavier than a true one.
4. If, in Step 2, the weights are unequal, remove the heavier coin and replace it with a true coin. If the balance tips as before (note that it cannot tip in the opposite

direction), the false coin is the one that has been left on the balance and is lighter than the rest; if the balance arms are equal the false coin is the one that has been removed, and it is heavier than the rest.

Draw a flow chart indicating how, using this method, the counterfeit coin may be detected.

3.6 Another Solution The solution as given requires a minimum of two comparisons (if you are lucky) and a maximum of eleven. A not-too-difficult variant needs no more than three weighings to detect the debased coin and determine if it is heavier or lighter. (If you don't know the solution, you might try to discover it for yourself before reading further.) The procedure is as follows:

1. Label the coins A1, A2, A3, A4, B1, B2, B3, B4, C1, C2, C3, C4.
2. Compare the A and B groups. There are three possibilities: case (a): the A group is heavier than the B group; case (b): the A group is lighter than the B group; case (c): the groups are equal in weight.
3. If case (b) arises, interchange the labels on the two groups.
4. Case (a): We know that the C group contains only true coins. Compare (A1, A2, A3, B1) and (A4, C1, C2, C3). Three possibilities exist: case (a1): The two sets are equal in weight, which implies that the bad coin is among B2, B3, B4 and is lighter; case (a2): (A1, A2, A3, B1) is heavier than (A4, C1, C2, C3), which implies that the base coin is among A1, A2, A3 and is heavier; case (a3): (A1, A2, A3, B1) is lighter than (A4, C1, C2, C3), which imples that either A4 is the base coin and is heavier or B1 is the base coin and is lighter.
5. Case (a1): We know that the bad coin is among B2, B3, B4 and is lighter. Compare B2 and B3. If they are equal in weight, B4 is the false coin; if B2 is heavier than B3, B3 is the false coin; if B2 is lighter than B3, B2 is the false coin.
6. Case (a2): Compare A1 and A2. If they are equal in weight, A3 is the debased coin and is heavier; if A1 is heavier than A2, A1 is the adulterated coin and is heavier; if A1 is lighter than A2, A2 is the counterfeit and is heavier.
7. Case (a3): Compare B1 with a true coin. If they are equal, A4 is the altered coin and is heavier; if B1 is lighter than the true coin, B1 is the adulterated coin and is lighter; it is impossible that B1 be heavier than a true coin.
8. Case (c): You know that the false coin is among those labeled C. Compare (A1, A2, A3) and (C1, C2, C3). Again, three possibilities arise: case (c1): the two sets are equal in weight; case (c2): the C set is heavier; case (c3): the C set is lighter.
9. Cases (c1): If the two sets are equal in weight, then C4 is the false coin. Compare C4 with any true coin and record whether it is lighter or heavier.
10. Case (c2): One of the three coins C1, C2, C3 is heavier. Compare C1 and C2. If these are equal, C3 is the base coin and is heavier; if C1 is heavier than C2, C1 is the base coin; if C1 is lighter than C2, C2 is the base coin.
11. Case (c3): One of the three coins C1, C2, C3 is false and is lighter than a true coin. Compare C1 and C2. If these are equal, C3 is the bad coin, if C1 is heavier than C2, C2 is the false one; if C1 is lighter than C2, C1 is the counterfeit coin.

Draw a flow chart that describes this procedure.

4 Writing Your First Program

Before you can write a program in BASIC, you must know the formal vocabulary and sentence structure of the language. As a first requirement, you must know how the language provides a means for you to enter data into the computer. Two BASIC instructions—INPUT and LET—are provided for this purpose. After the data are entered, they may be manipulated according to the arithmetic rules discussed in Chapter 2. After the answers have been determined, you must be able to instruct the computer to display them for you; the BASIC instruction PRINT does this.

While many problems may be solved on the computer just by the judicious application of arithmetic rules, there will be times when you will want the computer to make a decision based on prior information. The BASIC instruction, IF—THEN—, can do this.

As you write a program, you will want to *document* it—in other words, provide in clear language your understanding of the intent of the overall program (the problem it is supposed to solve) as well as the intent of the several subsections of the program (the steps you are taking to arrive at the solution). Documentation serves two purposes. After you have put an undocumented program aside for several weeks, it will be difficult for you to read it, to recall the problem it was to solve, and your method for arriving at the solution. Also, if your program is to be used by someone else, that person will have no idea of what you intended the program to accomplish nor how you achieved that goal unless you tell him or her. The BASIC instruction REMARK provides the means for you to express your intent at appropriate places in the program.

The statement END serves the purposes of letting the computer know when a program is at its end. You will want the computer to interact with your program while you are writing it and after it is written. There are numerous BASIC system commands that do this. **BASIC system commands** are words that you do not use within a program but that instruct the computer to do something to your program. Of these, RUN, LIST, RENUMBER, SAVE, and LOAD will be explained as the occasion for their use arises.

To enhance the arithmetic capabilities of the language beyond addition, subtraction, multiplication, division, and exponentiation, BASIC is endowed with several intrinsic functions. INT(X) is one of these intrinsic functions. We shall illustrate its use in a program that rounds numbers.

In this chapter, we shall discuss and illustrate each of these BASIC instructions and commands.

Writing a Program

Up to this point, you have learned how to log on and log off a computer, to interact with computer programs written by others, and some of the basics of computer arithmetic. Now, the time has come for you to write your first program.

Line Numbers

Certain conventions have been adopted for writing computer programs. Because the computer will perform the operations in the order you indicate, you must specify this order by assigning a line number to each instruction. When you write your program, assign line numbers to the instructions sequentially—the lowest number to the first statement to be executed and successively higher numbers to succeeding statements.

It is good practice not to assign such consecutive numbers as 1, 2, 3, but instead to use a sequence such as 10, 20, 30. The reason for this is that after you have entered several statements, you may want to go back and insert additional lines that are to be executed between previously written instructions. When this occurs, and it will in almost every program you write, you will have unused line numbers available between any two line numbers previously chosen.

An Addition Program

For your first program, you are to take two arbitrary numbers and have the computer add them and print their sum. Let the symbols X and Y represent the two numbers to be added and let Z represent their sum. The program must do three things: (1) tell you to enter numerical values for X and Y, (2) have the computer calculate their sum and assign this to the variable Z, and (3) print the result for you to see.

A flow diagram that parallels these operations is shown in Figure 4-1.

The INPUT Statement

Assume that you have logged on, called the BASIC interpreter, and the computer is waiting for your first instruction. Because there is no special statement that tells the computer you are starting a program, there is no instruction corresponding to START in the flow diagram. The next symbol in the flow chart contains the words "Input X." After you see the prompt character >, type

```
10 INPUT X     <CR>
```

The computer will accept this and indicate its acceptance by issuing another prompt character >. Now, type the instruction that corresponds to the next symbol in the flow diagram, "Input Y":

```
20 INPUT Y     <CR>
```

You have now programmed two INPUT statements.

The LET Statement

The instruction corresponding to the addition formula in the flow diagram is typed after the next prompt symbol.

```
30 LET Z=X+Y     <CR>
```

The statement LET Z=X+Y is not an algebraic equation; rather, it is the assignment of the sum of the numerical values associated with the variables X and Y to the variable Z. In general, the assignment instruction takes an algebraic expression, which appears to the right of the equal symbol, evaluates it, and assigns that numerical value to the single variable name that appears to the left of the equal sign.

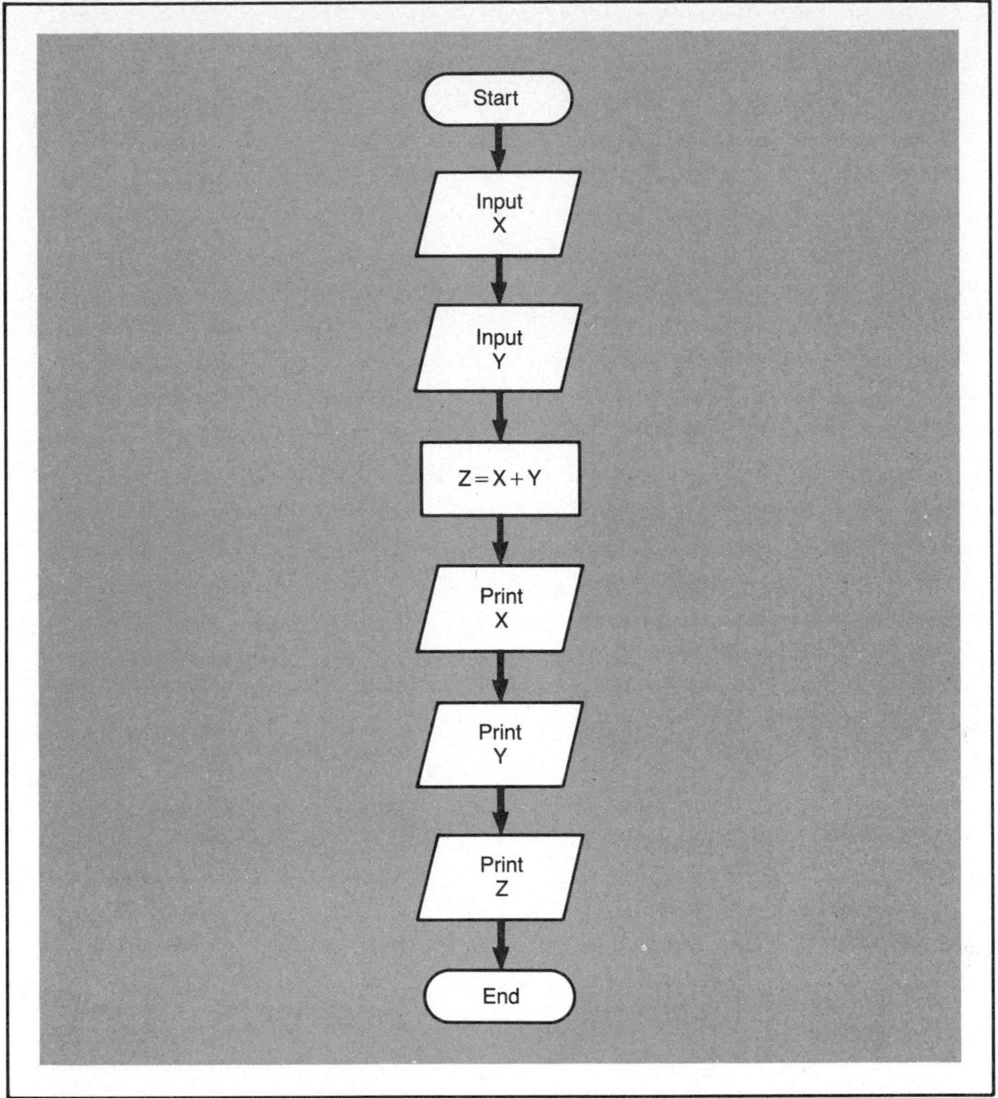

FIGURE 4-1

The assign statement may at times appear idiosyncratic. For example:

```
100 LET W=W+1
```

is a perfectly good statement in BASIC, although as an algebraic statement it makes no sense. Line 100 is interpreted by the computer as follows: Add 1 to whatever numerical value had been assigned to the variable W before the execution of line 100, and assign this new number to the variable W. For example, if the numerical value assigned to the variable W immediately before the execution of line 100 was 72.45, then the numerical value assigned to W after line 100 is executed is 73.45.

The PRINT Statement

When the program is executed, you will want to assure yourself that the computer has accepted the values you intended to assign to X and Y. Therefore, you will want the computer to repeat these values back to you rather than just give the result. This is accomplished by entering:

```
40 PRINT "X="X     <CR>
```

and, after the next >, entering:

```
50 PRINT "Y="Y     <CR>
```

Similarly, you may instruct the computer to print the value assigned to the variable Z in line 30. After the >, type

```
60 PRINT "Z="Z     <CR>
```

When, in a PRINT statement, literal information is enclosed within quotation marks, the computer prints that information exactly as it appears. Thus, the symbols Z=, Y=, and Z=, because they appear within quotation marks in lines 40, 50, and 60, respectively, will be printed when the program is executed. For X, Y, and Z, however, the computer will print the appropriate numerical values.

The END Statement

At this point in the program, because the computer will have completed its assigned task, you want to indicate that the program is ended. After the next prompt symbol, type

```
70 END     <CR>
```

At your terminal you should now see, either printed or displayed on the cathode ray tube, the following:

```
>10 INPUT X
>20 INPUT Y
>30 LET Z=X+Y
>40 PRINT "X="X
>50 PRINT "-Y="Y
>60 PRINT "Z="Z
>70 END
```

Executing Your Program: The RUN Command

Although your program has been entered into the computer, it resides there in a dormant mode. In order to use it to add two specific numbers, you must get the computer to execute the program. You do this by typing RUN and <CR> after the next prompt. The computer will respond with a ?, which is its way of asking for the number you want to assign to the variable X. For example, suppose you type 5 and press <CR>. The computer will then come back with a second ?. This time the computer is asking you to specify the value to be assigned to the variable Y. Suppose you choose 13. After typing 13 and hitting <CR>, the computer will print X=5, then go to the next line and print Y=13, and then go to the next line and print Z=18.

After printing these three lines, the computer will print 70 HALT. This indicates that it has come to the END of the program and, as far as it is concerned, its assigned task is completed. The number 70 refers to the last line that was executed.[1]

Your complete printout now looks like this:

```
>10 INPUT X
>20 INPUT Y
>30 LET Z=X+Y
```

[1]The indication that the program has run to completion is different on different computers.

```
>40 PRINT "X="X
>50 PRINT "Y="Y
>60 PRINT "Z="Z
>70 END
>RUN
?5
?13
X= 5
Y= 13
Z= 18
    70 HALT
```

Modifying the Program

As you review the output and the method by which the numbers 5 and 13 were entered into the computer, certain questions might occur to you. For instance, is there a way to specify that the first ? refers to the symbol X and the second ? refers to Y? The answer is yes. In your program, before the INPUT statement on line 10, insert the following: 5 PRINT "X=" <CR>, and between the input statements on lines 10 and 20, insert: 15 PRINT "Y="<CR>. Make these insertions after you see 70 HALT.

Your complete printout now looks like this:

```
>10 INPUT X
>20 INPUT Y
>30 LET Z=X+Y
>40 PRINT "X="X
>50 PRINT "Y="Y
>60 PRINT "Z="Z
>70 END
>RUN
 ?5
 ?13
 X =  5
 Y = 13
 Z = 18

     70 HALT
>5 PRINT "X="     <CR>
>15 PRINT "Y="     <CR>
```

The LIST Command

The program now consists of nine lines. We did not, however, enter these lines into the computer in the order of their assigned line numbers. Suppose you want to see what the program looks like with the statements appearing in order—that is, with their line numbers in increasing order. To do this, when the prompt symbol next appears, type LIST and <CR>. The computer will produce a listing, in sequential order, of all the statements you have entered. The output will look like this:

```
5 PRINT "X="
10 INPUT X
15 PRINT "Y ="
20 INPUT Y
30 LET Z=X+Y
40 PRINT "X="X
50 PRINT "Y="Y
60 PRINT "Z="Z
70 END
```

To see the effect of introducing lines 5 and 15 into your program, type RUN and <CR>.

The completed run will look like this:

```
X=
?5
Y=
?13
X =  5
     13
Y = 18
Z = 70 HALT
```

This illustrates the effect of statements inserted between previously written ones.

Observe that during program execution, X= appears on one line and ? on the next. We may have these appear on the same line by placing a semicolon after the last character on line 5. To have Y = and ? appear on the same line, place a semicolon[2] after the last character on line 15. At present, the only way we can do this is to completely retype these two lines. We have a line numbered 5, but we want to replace it with a new line numbered 5. After the prompt symbol >, type:

```
5 PRINT "X=";     <CR>
```

This replaces the old line 5. Similarly, to replace line 15 by the new line 15, type:

```
15 PRINT "Y=";     <CR>
```

To see the program as it is currently stored in the computer, type LIST and <CR>. The computer will respond as follows:

```
5 PRINT "X=";
10 INPUT X
15 PRINT "Y=";
20 INPUT Y
30 LET Z=X+Y
40 PRINT "X="X
50 PRINT "Y="Y
60 PRINT "Z="Z
70 END
```

To show the effect of the change, type RUN and <CR>. The completed run will look like this:

```
X =  5
Y = 13
Z = 18
Y= 13
Z= 18
   70 HALT
```

Variable Names

In the above example, the three variables were named X, Y, and Z. The convention for naming variables is that any of the 26 letters A through Z may be used, as well as any letter *followed* by one of the digits 0, 1, 2, 3, 4, 5, 6, 7, 8, 9. Thus, 286 different variables may be named.

Typical variable names are E6, Q9, F, R, and Z2; unacceptable variable names are AB, C12, and 9G.

---

[2]Some systems use a comma.

Illustration: The Future Value of an Investment

The concepts, statements, and commands introduced thus far may be applied to a variety of problems. One class of business problem encompassing interest, depreciation, and annuities may be solved using one fundamental formula and variants of it.

Suppose John deposits \$1000 in a savings account in a local bank that pays 6 percent interest, computed annually. At the end of one year, he will have on deposit his original \$1000 plus the interest—(.06) × \$1000 = \$60—or a total of 1000 × (1 + .06) dollars = \$1060.

If the bank compounds interest semiannually, then at the end of the first six months, the amount on deposit will be \$1000 × (1 + .06/2) = \$1030 and at the end of the year, \$1030.00 × (1 + .06/2) = \$1,060.90. You should convince yourself that the same answer is obtained if the formula $1000 \times (1 + .06/2)^2$ is used. If interest is compounded quarterly (every three months), the amount of money on deposit at the end of the year will be $\$1000(1 + .06/4)^4 = \$1061.36$.

If K represents the number of times per year that interest is compounded, then at the end of the year, the amount on deposit will be

$$1000 \times \left(1 + \frac{.06}{K}\right)^{K}$$

If the period of investment is two years, then at the end of that time, the amount on deposit will be:

$$1000 \times \left(1 + \frac{.06}{K}\right)^{2K} \text{ dollars;}$$

and in general, if the money is left for Y years, then, at the end of the investment period, the amount on deposit will be:

$$1000 \times \left(1 + \frac{.06}{K}\right)^{YK} \text{ dollars.}$$

Since the interest paid by banks varies, the formula may be further generalized to accommodate other interest rates. Thus, if the nominal annual interest rate is I percent, the modified form of the formula is

$$1000 \times \left(1 + \frac{I}{100K}\right)^{YK}$$

For example, if the interst rate is $5\frac{3}{4}$ percent, the formula is:

$$1000 \times \left(1 + \frac{5.75}{100K}\right)^{YK}$$

Finally, if instead of an initial deposit of \$1000, an arbitrary principal P is deposited, the formula becomes:

$$A = P\left(1 + \frac{I}{100K}\right)^{YK}$$

where the symbol A is used to denote the final amount (see Chapter 2, Exercise 2.6).

Now that we have a general formula, the next task is to write a computer program that, with the initial principal, the nominal annual rate of interest, the frequency with which the interest is compounded, and the number of years the money is left on deposit as input, computes the final amount on deposit. An appropriate flow diagram is shown in Figure 4-2.

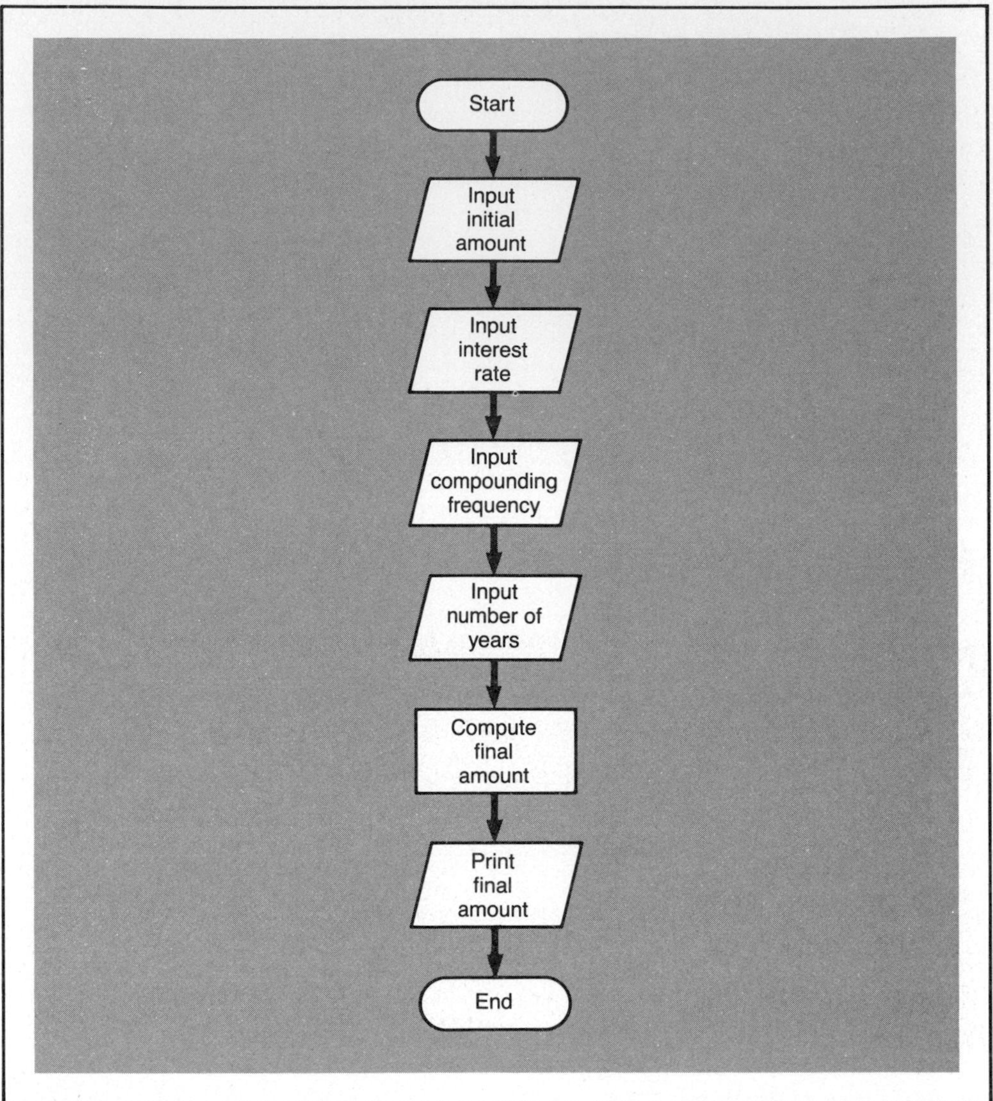

FIGURE 4-2

The program derived from this flow chart is as follows:

```
 LIST

10 PRINT "THIS PROGRAM CALCULATES THE FUTURE VALUE OF AN INVESTMENT."
20 PRINT "AS THE COMPUTER REQUESTS THE DATA, INPUT THE AMOUNT OF THE"
30 PRINT "ORIGINAL DEPOSIT, THE NOMINAL ANNUAL INTEREST RATE, THE"
40 PRINT "NUMBER OF TIMES PER YEAR THAT INTEREST IS COMPOUNDED AND"
50 PRINT "THE NUMBER OF YEARS.  THE COMPUTER WILL THEN PRINT FOR YOU"
60 PRINT "THE FUTURE VALUE OF YOUR INVESTMENT."
70 PRINT
80 *****************************
90 REMARK: THIS SECTION REQUESTS THE INPUT DATA.
100 *****************************
110 PRINT "WHAT IS YOUR ORIGINAL INVESTMENT";
120 INPUT P
130 PRINT "WHAT IS THE NOMINAL ANNUAL INTEREST RATE";
140 INPUT I
150 PRINT "HOW MANY TIMES PER YEAR IS INTEREST COMPOUNDED";
160 INPUT K
170 PRINT "FOR HOW MANY YEARS WILL THIS INVESTMENT BE MADE";
180 INPUT Y
190 *****************************
```

```
200 REM: THIS SECTION CALCULATES THE FUTURE VALUE OF THE INVESTMENT.
210 ******************************
220 LET A=P*(1+I/100/K)^(Y*K)
230 ******************************
240 REM: THE INFORMATION IS PRINTED.
250 ******************************
260 PRINT
270 PRINT "THE FUTURE VALUE OF THE DEPOSIT  =$" A
280 ******************************
290 END
```

Recall from the previous program that whenever you want the computer to print literal information, you must use the statement PRINT followed by an opening quotation mark, then the text to be printed, and finally a closing quotation mark. In this program, we have used this format to instruct the user of the program, that is, the person for whom the computer is to perform the calculation.

Notice on line 70 that nothing follows the word PRINT. Actually, the <CR> was struck immediately after the letter T in PRINT. The effect is to have the computer print nothing, which is equivalent to asking the computer to skip a line. This may be observed in the following printout, which appears after the program is run:

```
 RUN

THIS PROGRAM CALCULATES THE FUTURE VALUE OF AN INVESTMENT.
AS THE COMPUTER REQUESTS THE DATA, INPUT THE AMOUNT OF THE
ORIGINAL DEPOSIT, THE NOMINAL ANNUAL INTEREST RATE, THE
NUMBER OF TIMES PER YEAR THAT INTEREST IS COMPOUNDED AND
THE NUMBER OF YEARS.  THE COMPUTER WILL THEN PRINT FOR YOU
THE FUTURE VALUE OF YOUR INVESTMENT.

WHAT IS YOUR ORIGINAL INVESTMENT  ?1000
WHAT IS THE NOMINAL ANNUAL INTEREST RATE  ?6
HOW MANY TIMES PER YEAR IS INTEREST COMPOUNDED  ?2
FOR HOW MANY YEARS WILL THIS INVESTMENT BE MADE   ?1

THE FUTURE VALUE OF THE DEPOSIT  =$ 1060.90

     290 HALT
```

The Remark Statement

Lines 90, 200, and 240 introduce a new instruction, REMARK. During the course of writing a program, it is good practice not only to segment the various parts—the input section, the section in which the computation is made, and the output section—but also to insert comments at appropriate places. To accomplish this, immediately after a line number, enter REM (or REMARK) and follow this with your comments. When the program is run, the computer will ignore this line.[3]

The IF—THEN— Statement

Until now, each time we wanted to make a calculation, we had to issue the RUN command. If, however, the program is to be used repeatedly (for example, if you want to compare the effect of different interest rates or varying periods of investment), you may want the program to restart itself after each computation. To accomplish this, a new instruction, called "conditional transfer," is used. The form of the instruction is:

(line number) IF (expression) THEN (line number)

---

[3]On the computer on which this program was written, if the first character is an asterisk, the line is also ignored during execution of the program. Thus, lines 80, 100, 190, 210, 230, 250, and 280 are not executed. This was done to segment the program and make it easier to read.

The word "expression" simply means any valid BASIC expression. We shall illustrate the use of conditional transfer by amending the above program to permit the user to decide if another calculation is to be made. First, we should modify the flow diagram, as shown in Figure 4-3, to reflect this change. To modify the program, after line 270, insert

```
275 PRINT
```

and, after line 280, insert

```
281 REM: THIS SECTION ASKS IF YOU WANT TO REPEAT THE CALCULATION
282 ********************************
283 PRINT "ANOTHER CALCULATION? RESPOND '1' FOR 'YES', '2' FOR 'NO'.";
```

FIGURE 4-3

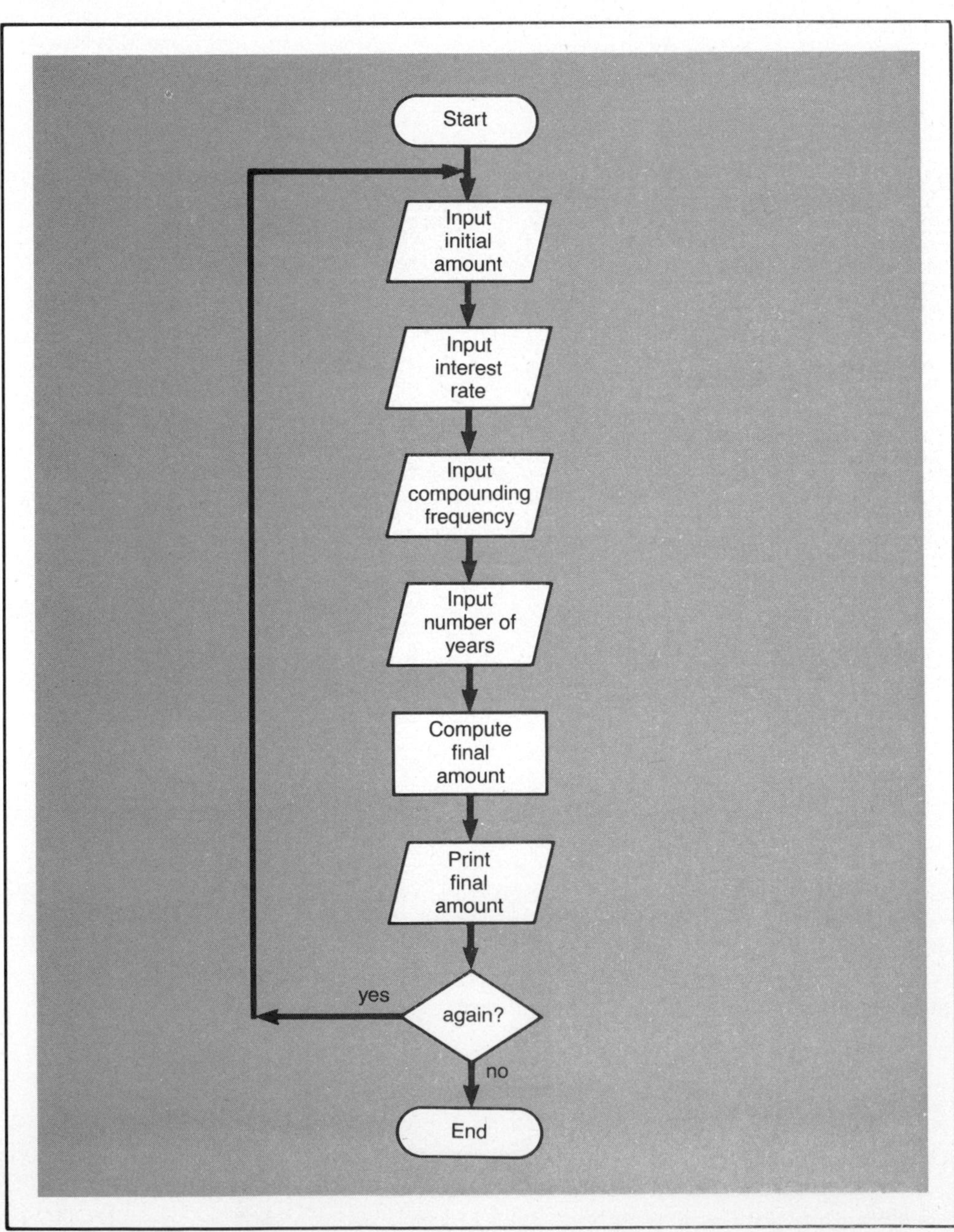

```
284 INPUT X
285 IF X=1 THEN 70
286 ******************************
```

After making the insertions, we may obtain a copy of the new program by typing LIST. The first part of the program is the same as on pages 46–47; the end of the program looks like this:

```
240 REM: THE INFORMATION IS PRINTED.
250 ******************************
260 PRINT
270 PRINT "THE FUTURE VALUE OF THE DEPOSIT  =$" A
275 PRINT
280 ******************************
281 REM: THIS SECTION ASKS IF YOU WANT TO REPEAT THE CALCULATION.
282 ******************************
283 PRINT "ANOTHER CALCULATION? RESPOND '1' FOR 'YES', '2' FOR 'NO'.";
284 INPUT X
285 IF X=1 THEN 70
286 ******************************
290 END
```

The modified program may now be run, as follows:

```
RUN


THIS PROGRAM CALCULATES THE FUTURE VALUE OF AN INVESTMENT.
AS THE COMPUTER REQUESTS THE DATA, INPUT THE AMOUNT OF THE
ORIGINAL DEPOSIT, THE NOMINAL ANNUAL INTEREST RATE, THE
NUMBER OF TIMES PER YEAR THAT INTEREST IS COMPOUNDED AND
THE NUMBER OF YEARS.  THE COMPUTER WILL THEN PRINT FOR YOU
THE FUTURE VALUE OF YOUR INVESTMENT.

WHAT IS YOUR ORIGINAL INVESTMENT  ?1000
WHAT IS THE NOMINAL ANNUAL INTEREST RATE  ?6
HOW MANY TIMES PER YEAR IS INTEREST COMPOUNDED  ?2
FOR HOW MANY YEARS WILL THIS INVESTMENT BE MADE   ?1

THE FUTURE VALUE OF THE DEPOSIT  =$ 1060.90

ANOTHER CALCULATION? RESPOND '1' FOR 'YES', '2' FOR 'NO'.   ?1

WHAT IS YOUR ORIGINAL INVESTMENT  ?1000
WHAT IS THE NOMINAL ANNUAL INTEREST RATE  ?6
HOW MANY TIMES PER YEAR IS INTEREST COMPOUNDED  ?4
FOR HOW MANY YEARS WILL THIS INVESTMENT BE MADE   ?1

THE FUTURE VALUE OF THE DEPOSIT  =$ 1061.36

ANOTHER CALCULATION? RESPOND '1' FOR 'YES', '2' FOR 'NO'.   ?1

WHAT IS YOUR ORIGINAL INVESTMENT  ?1000
WHAT IS THE NOMINAL ANNUAL INTEREST RATE  ?6
HOW MANY TIMES PER YEAR IS INTEREST COMPOUNDED  ?12
FOR HOW MANY YEARS WILL THIS INVESTMENT BE MADE   ?2

THE FUTURE VALUE OF THE DEPOSIT  =$ 1127.16

ANOTHER CALCULATION? RESPOND '1' FOR 'YES', '2' FOR 'NO'.   ?2

   290 HALT
```

Examine in detail the effect of these new lines of code. Line 275 separates the answer to the computation and the inquiry as to whether another calculation is wanted. It has only the cosmetic effect of making the printout of the run more readable. Lines 283 and 284 are similar to statements used previously. Line 285 provides for the conditional transfer. The value of X has been previously determined. If X equals 1, then control of the program is transferred to line 70 and the program continues from that point forward. If X does not equal 1, that is, if X is any other character, even though the user was instructed to use 2, then line 285 is totally ignored and the program proceeds to line 290 END.

Control could just as easily have been transferred to line 110 and the program would have run as well. Again, the only difference would be cosmetic: The blank line between the statement:

```
ANOTHER CALCULATION? RESPOND '1' FOR 'YES', '2' FOR 'NO'.
```

and

```
WHAT IS YOUR ORIGINAL INVESTMENT?
```

would not have been there. To improve the graphic quality of the output, control was transferred to line 70.

The BASIC expression "X = 1" in line 285 is simple; for more sophisticated situations, more complicated expressions may be used. These will be illustrated as the need for them arises.

Review

You have seen that when you write a computer program, you must precede each instruction to the computer by a line number. Although the order in which you type the instructions may be arbitrary, the computer will execute each instruction in the order of assigned line numbers.

Data may be entered into the computer by means of the INPUT instruction, manipulated according to the arithmetic rules discussed in Chapter 2, and the results presented by the computer by the PRINT statement. We have used the PRINT statement in two different ways: first, to tell the computer to print literal information (by enclosing the literal string[4] between quotation marks) and, second, to tell the computer to print the numerical result of a computation (by using the symbol associated with that numerical value).

We also introduced the concept of assignment. In the first of the two examples, when you typed

```
30 LET Z=X+Y
```

you assigned the sum of the numerical values associated with the variables X and Y to the variable Z. Similarly, in the second program, when you typed

```
220 LET A = P*(1 +I/100/K)^(Y*K)
```

you assigned the numerical value that resulted from performing the computation specified by the formula to the right of the equal sign to the variable A. In both cases, the assignment used the BASIC language instruction LET.

The conditional transfer instruction was introduced. Whenever, during the course of writing a program, a decision is required, the BASIC statement:

```
IF (expression)THEN (line number)
```

may be used.

[4] A *string* is a sequence of characters: letters of the alphabet, digits, and punctuation.

Finally, a word about documentation. While you are writing a program, all the steps may be perfectly clear in your mind. If, however, another person is to be able to read your program (not run it, but read it for an understanding of your logic as well as what you intend the program to accomplish), clues as to what you have in mind at the various stages of the writing are quite helpful. You will find these clues helpful also after you have put the program aside for some time and return to it at a later date for revision. We used the REM instruction to insert nonexecutable statements into the program.

If you have carried out the preceding directions carefully, then you have successfully written two computer programs. The repertoire of BASIC instructions (the statements you used to build the programs) and the BASIC commands (the statements to the computer that cause it to do something to your program) was quite limited. As you learn more instructions and more commands, a greater variety of problems will become tractable to computer solutions, and the ease with which you will write these programs will increase. We shall take some first steps in that direction in the remainder of this chapter.

Rounding

In calculating federal income tax, the law allows the figures to be rounded to the nearest dollar. Consider the following circumstances. Kevin has approximately $9000 to invest. He has found a bank that pays 12 percent interest, compounded daily, if he agrees to leave his money on deposit for a minimum of one year. He quickly agrees and eagerly sets out to modify our computer program to calculate his taxable income from this venture. The modified program is as follows.

```
    LIST

1Ø PRINT "THIS PROGRAM CALCULATES THE FUTURE VALUE OF AN INVESTMENT."
2Ø PRINT "AS THE COMPUTER REQUESTS THE DATA, INPUT THE AMOUNT OF THE"
3Ø PRINT "ORIGINAL DEPOSIT, THE NOMINAL ANNUAL INTEREST RATE, THE"
4Ø PRINT "NUMBER OF TIMES PER YEAR THAT INTEREST IS COMPOUNDED AND"
5Ø PRINT "THE NUMBER OF YEARS.  THE COMPUTER WILL THEN PRINT FOR YOU"
6Ø PRINT "THE FUTURE VALUE OF YOUR INVESTMENT."
61 PRINT
62 PRINT "THE PROGRAM WAS MODIFIED TO DELETE THE PRINTING OF THE "
63 PRINT "FUTURE VALUE OF THE INVESTMENT.  INSTEAD, THE TAXABLE"
64 PRINT "INCOME IS REPORTED, BOTH UNROUNDED AND ROUNDED"
65 PRINT "TO THE NEAREST DOLLAR."
7Ø PRINT
8Ø *******************************
9Ø REMARK: THIS SECTION REQUESTS THE INPUT DATA.
1ØØ *******************************
11Ø PRINT "WHAT IS YOUR ORIGINAL INVESTMENT";
12Ø INPUT P
13Ø PRINT "WHAT IS THE NOMINAL ANNUAL INTEREST RATE";
14Ø INPUT I
15Ø PRINT "HOW MANY TIMES PER YEAR IS INTEREST COMPOUNDED";
16Ø INPUT K
17Ø PRINT "FOR HOW MANY YEARS WILL THIS INVESTMENT BE MADE";
18Ø INPUT Y
19Ø *******************************
2ØØ REM: THIS SECTION CALCULATES THE FUTURE VALUE OF THE INVESTMENT.
2Ø5 REM: THE TAXABLE INCOME IS ALSO CALCULATED, BOTH ROUNDED AND UNROUNDED"
21Ø *******************************
22Ø LET A=P*(1+I/1ØØ/K)^(Y*K)
221 LET T=A-P
222 LET R=INT(T+.5)
23Ø *******************************
24Ø REM: THE INFORMATION IS PRINTED.
25Ø *******************************
26Ø PRINT
261 PRINT "THE UNROUNDED TAXABLE INCOME = $" T
262 PRINT "THE ROUNDED TAXABLE INCOME = $" R
275 PRINT
28Ø *******************************
```

```
281 REM: THIS SECTION ASKS IF YOU WANT TO REPEAT THE CALCULATION.
282 ******************************
283 PRINT "ANOTHER CALCULATION? RESPOND '1' FOR 'YES', '2' FOR 'NO'.";
284 INPUT X
285 IF X=1 THEN 70
286 ******************************
290 END
```

First, in lines 61–65 Kevin added the information that reflects the new intent of the program. He inserted an additional REM at line 205. In line 221, the difference between the future value of the investment and the amount initially invested, the taxable income, is determined and labeled T.

The INT(X) Function

Line 222 requires special attention. Imbedded within the BASIC language are several mathematical functions. Of these, one is the "integer value" function. For any argument X, the value of INT(X) is the largest integer less than or equal to X. The following examples are illustrative: $INT(5.4)=5$, $INT(3)=3$, $INT(.67)=0$, $INT(0)=0$, $INT(-.5)=-1$, $INT(-4.56)=-5$, $INT(-6)=-6$.

Another way to think of INT(X) is as follows. Consider the number line extending from minus infinity to plus infinity ($-\infty$ to $+\infty$), and partition it into intervals of unit length. The leftmost end point of each interval is to be an integer and is to be included in the interval; the rightmost end point of the interval is to extend to the next integer but is *not* to include it. A typical interval consists of all numbers X such that $N \leq X < N + 1$ where N is an arbitrary integer. The function INT(X) assigns to each number X that integer value N that is the leftmost end point of the interval in which X lies.

We may adapt the integer value function to enable us to round numbers. First, however, recall the meaning of rounding a number. Again, start with the number line, and for each integer N, construct the unit interval extending from $N - ½$ to $N + ½$; the interval is to include its leftmost end point but not its rightmost end point. A typical interval is represented by $[N - ½, N + ½)$, where the bracket indicates that $N - ½$ is included in the interval and the parenthesis indicates that $N + ½$ is excluded from the interval. An alternative representation is $N - ½ \leq X < N + ½$. No two intervals have a number in common, and every number on the number line lies in an interval. In particular, note that each interval contains one integer, N. Rounding a number T to the nearest integer means replacing T by the integer found in the interval in which T lies.

This definition is equivalent to the more familiar rule, which states: Any number whose decimal part is .5 or greater is rounded up to the next higher integer and any number whose decimal part is less than .5 is rounded down.

The definition of INT(X) and the concept of rounding a number T to its nearest integer may be joined: $INT(T + .5)$ rounds T to the nearest integer. In other words, for any T such that $N - ½ \leq T < N + ½$, $N \leq (T + .5) < N + 1$ and $INT(T + .5) = N$.

Returning to the new program, two new PRINT statements were added at lines 261 and 262, and line 270, no longer germane, was deleted. The remainder of the program is as before. A sample run might appear as follows.

```
RUN

THIS PROGRAM CALCULATES THE FUTURE VALUE OF AN INVESTMENT.
AS THE COMPUTER REQUESTS THE DATA, INPUT THE AMOUNT OF THE
ORIGINAL DEPOSIT, THE NOMINAL ANNUAL INTEREST RATE, THE
NUMBER OF TIMES PER YEAR THAT INTEREST IS COMPOUNDED AND
THE NUMBER OF YEARS.  THE COMPUTER WILL THEN PRINT FOR YOU
THE FUTURE VALUE OF YOUR INVESTMENT.
```

```
THE PROGRAM WAS MODIFIED TO DELETE THE PRINTING OF THE
FUTURE VALUE OF THE INVESTMENT.  INSTEAD, THE TAXABLE
INCOME IS REPORTED, BOTH UNROUNDED AND ROUNDED
TO THE NEAREST DOLLAR.

WHAT IS YOUR ORIGINAL INVESTMENT  ?9000
WHAT IS THE NOMINAL ANNUAL INTEREST RATE  ?12
HOW MANY TIMES PER YEAR IS INTEREST COMPOUNDED  ?365
FOR HOW MANY YEARS WILL THIS INVESTMENT BE MADE   ?1

THE UNROUNDED TAXABLE INCOME = $ 1147.27
THE ROUNDED TAXABLE INCOME = $ 1147

ANOTHER CALCULATION? RESPOND '1' FOR 'YES', '2' FOR 'NO'.    ?1

WHAT IS YOUR ORIGINAL INVESTMENT  ?8900
WHAT IS THE NOMINAL ANNUAL INTEREST RATE  ?12
HOW MANY TIMES PER YEAR IS INTEREST COMPOUNDED  ?365
FOR HOW MANY YEARS WILL THIS INVESTMENT BE MADE   ?1

THE UNROUNDED TAXABLE INCOME = $ 1134.52
THE ROUNDED TAXABLE INCOME = $ 1135

ANOTHER CALCULATION? RESPOND '1' FOR 'YES', '2' FOR 'NO'.    ?2

     290 HALT
```

When the program was run for an initial investment of $9,000, the taxable income was rounded down from $1147.27 to $1147; when it was run for an initial investment of $8900, the taxable income of $1134.52 was rounded up to $1135.

In this illustration, the decimal point was properly placed to effect the rounding to the nearest integer, that is, the nearest dollar. Because in other applications, we may not want to round to the nearest integer, a minor modification of the above formula permits us to round to any number of decimal places. For example, X = 34.5271 when rounded to two decimal places is 34.53. The computer performs this operation in the following way. First move the decimal point two places to the right; this is done by multiplying X by 100 or X*10^2 = 3452.71. The decimal point is now properly positioned, and INT(X*10^2+.5) effects the rounding to the nearest integer, 3453. The decimal point can now be returned to its original position, two places to the left. This is done by dividing 3453 by 100, or 3453/10^2 to get 34.53, the answer.

Reexamining the steps taken, it can be seen these may be subsumed in a single BASIC expression:

```
INT(X*10^P + .5)/(10^P)
```

The number X will be rounded to P decimal places; in the above illustration, P was equal to 2. Any other positive integer value of P would do as well; X would be rounded to P decimal places.

When dealing with such large numbers as 347,926,871 that you want to round to, let us say, the nearest thousand, choose P = −3; the result will be 3.47927E+08. (Recall from Chapter 2 how the computer expresses numbers in scientific notation.) Thus, to round numbers to decimal positions left of the decimal point, use negative integer values for P. The following program illustrates this process.

```
LIST

10 REM: THIS PROGRAM ILLUSTRATES HOW NUMBERS MAY BE ROUNDED
20 PRINT
30 PRINT "INPUT THE NUMBER TO BE ROUNDED";
40 INPUT X
50 PRINT "TO HOW MANY DECIMAL PLACES";
60 INPUT P
70 LET Y=INT(X*10^P+.5)/(10^P)
```

```
80 PRINT
90 PRINT "THE NUMBER" X " ROUNDED TO " P " PLACES =" Y
100 PRINT
110 PRINT "AGAIN? RESPOND '1' FOR 'YES', '2' FOR 'NO'.";
120 INPUT A
130 IF A=1 THEN 20
140 END
```

```
 RUN

INPUT THE NUMBER TO BE ROUNDED  ?3.67281
TO HOW MANY DECIMAL PLACES  ?2

THE NUMBER 3.67281 ROUNDED TO  2 PLACES = 3.67000

AGAIN? RESPOND '1' FOR 'YES', '2' FOR 'NO'.   ?1

INPUT THE NUMBER TO BE ROUNDED  ?3.67281
TO HOW MANY DECIMAL PLACES  ?3

THE NUMBER 3.67281 ROUNDED TO  3 PLACES = 3.67300

AGAIN? RESPOND '1' FOR 'YES', '2' FOR 'NO'.   ?1

INPUT THE NUMBER TO BE ROUNDED  ?3.67281
TO HOW MANY DECIMAL PLACES  ?4

THE NUMBER 3.67281 ROUNDED TO  4 PLACES = 3.67280

AGAIN? RESPOND '1' FOR 'YES', '2' FOR 'NO'.   ?1

INPUT THE NUMBER TO BE ROUNDED  ?3.67281
TO HOW MANY DECIMAL PLACES  ?0

THE NUMBER 3.67281 ROUNDED TO  0 PLACES = 4

AGAIN? RESPOND '1' FOR 'YES', '2' FOR 'NO'.   ?1

INPUT THE NUMBER TO BE ROUNDED  ?347926871
TO HOW MANY DECIMAL PLACES  ?-3

THE NUMBER 347926871 ROUNDED TO -3 PLACES = 3.47927E+08

AGAIN? RESPOND '1' FOR 'YES', '2' FOR 'NO'.   ?1

INPUT THE NUMBER TO BE ROUNDED  ?347926871
TO HOW MANY DECIMAL PLACES  ?-5

THE NUMBER 347926871 ROUNDED TO -5 PLACES = 3.47900E+08

AGAIN? RESPOND '1' FOR 'YES', '2' FOR 'NO'.   ?1

INPUT THE NUMBER TO BE ROUNDED  ?347926871
TO HOW MANY DECIMAL PLACES  ?-7

THE NUMBER 347926871 ROUNDED TO -7 PLACES = 3.50000E+08

AGAIN? RESPOND '1' FOR 'YES', '2' FOR 'NO'.   ?2

     140 HALT
```

In line 90, the PRINT statement is used in yet another way; both numeric and alphabetic strings are mixed on one line to achieve the desired format for the output. The numeric values are printed by referring to their symbolic names, X, Y, and P; the alphabetic strings are enclosed within quotation marks.

Some BASIC System Commands

The RENUMBER Command

Let us return to Kevin's program (pages 51–52). The line numbers are getting too closely packed together. If further modification is needed, line numbers may not be available to permit insertions at the appropriate places. To improve the appearance of the program listing (and enhance its readability) and to provide additional line numbers for possible future modifications, the system command REN (the abbreviation for RENUMBER) is used. Assuming the program is in main storage, type REN <CR> after you see the prompt >. The computer will scan each line of the program and renumber it, starting with 100 (on this computer, although another computer may start with 10) and then increase each succeeding line by 10 (which is fairly universal). When applied to Kevin's program, the result is as follows:

```
REN

LIST

100 PRINT "THIS PROGRAM CALCULATES THE FUTURE VALUE OF AN INVESTMENT."
110 PRINT "AS THE COMPUTER REQUESTS THE DATA, INPUT THE AMOUNT OF THE"
120 PRINT "ORIGINAL DEPOSIT, THE NOMINAL ANNUAL INTEREST RATE, THE"
130 PRINT "NUMBER OF TIMES PER YEAR THAT INTEREST IS COMPOUNDED AND"
140 PRINT "THE NUMBER OF YEARS.  THE COMPUTER WILL THEN PRINT FOR YOU"
150 PRINT "THE FUTURE VALUE OF YOUR INVESTMENT."
160 PRINT
170 PRINT "THE PROGRAM WAS MODIFIED TO DELETE THE PRINTING OF THE "
180 PRINT "FUTURE VALUE OF THE INVESTMENT.  INSTEAD, THE TAXABLE"
190 PRINT "INCOME IS REPORTED, BOTH UNROUNDED AND ROUNDED"
200 PRINT "TO THE NEAREST DOLLAR."
210 PRINT
220 ******************************
230 REMARK: THIS SECTION REQUESTS THE INPUT DATA.
240 ******************************
250 PRINT "WHAT IS YOUR ORIGINAL INVESTMENT";
260 INPUT P
270 PRINT "WHAT IS THE NOMINAL ANNUAL INTEREST RATE";
280 INPUT I
290 PRINT "HOW MANY TIMES PER YEAR IS INTEREST COMPOUNDED";
300 INPUT K
310 PRINT "FOR HOW MANY YEARS WILL THIS INVESTMENT BE MADE";
320 INPUT Y
330 ******************************
340 REM: THIS SECTION CALCULATES THE FUTURE VALUE OF THE INVESTMENT.
350 REM: THE TAXABLE INCOME IS ALSO CALCULATED, BOTH ROUNDED AND UNROUNDED"
360 ******************************
370 LET A=P*(1+I/100/K)^(Y*K)
380 LET T=A-P
390 LET R=INT(T+.5)
400 ******************************
410 REM: THE INFORMATION IS PRINTED.
420 ******************************
430 PRINT
440 PRINT "THE UNROUNDED TAXABLE INCOME = $" T
450 PRINT "THE ROUNDED TAXABLE INCOME = $" R
460 PRINT
470 ******************************
480 REM: THIS SECTION ASKS IF YOU WANT TO REPEAT THE CALCULATION.
490 ******************************
500 PRINT "ANOTHER CALCULATION? RESPOND '1' FOR 'YES', '2' FOR 'NO'.";
510 INPUT X
520 IF X=1 THEN 210
530 ******************************
540 END
```

It is not remarkable that the REN command sequentially assigns increasing line numbers to successive lines of code. It is remarkable, however, that it goes into each line of code and properly modifies the line numbers used within BASIC statements. For example, in

Kevin's program in its original form, line 285 refers to line 70. What had been line number 70 in the original numbering system is now line 210. The computer makes the necessary change in old line 285 for you. The only exception is that while the line numbers of REM statements are renumbered, nothing within a REM statement is altered. Because of this, within a REM statement it is good practice not to refer to sections of code by line numbers; the reference may not be appropriate after renumbering.

The SAVE and LOAD Commands

Kevin's fortunes are not limited to the single investment for which he designed his program. He has others and wants to retain his program for future use. Of course, he could always retype it into the computer, but this is a waste of time and effort. Instead, he wants to save it in the computer and call it forth at some future time when he needs it again.

On some computers, when you log on, the computer asks if the program you intend to work with is a new one or an old one. Since, presumably this is your first program, it is a new one, and in this case the computer expects you to type NEW, followed by a name of your choosing. Normally, you would choose a name that reminds you of the intent of the program. For example, John may have chosen INT for "interest calculation" and Kevin may have chosen TAX for "tax calculation." Because John was not interested in saving his program, he would have done nothing but log off when he was finished. Kevin, wanting to save his program, would have typed:

```
SAVE TAX
```

and then logged off. When Kevin logs on again and the computer asks OLD OR NEW, he can respond OLD TAX, and this will recall his program.

Some computers do not ask OLD OR NEW. On the computer on which most programs used in this book were produced, the OLD OR NEW query is not asked when logging on. Rather, just before logging off, Kevin would type

```
SAVE ON TAX
```

and this computer would store the program for future use. At that future time when he logged on, Kevin would type

```
LOAD TAX
```

and the computer would recall his program.

Suppose that Kevin had originally saved his TAX program before renumbering the lines. Because he has decided that the renumbered version is easier to read, he would rather save it. On some computers, if he were now to type SAVE TAX, the computer would respond with a message indicating that he had already saved a program under that name. Appropriately, he would type RESAVE TAX, and the computer would erase the old version of his program and replace it with the new one. On the computer on which these programs were written, the corresponding command is SAVE OVER TAX.[5]

Review

In addition to the BASIC language instructions reviewed above, one intrinsic BASIC function was introduced; the INT(X) function was used to round a number to any desired number of decimal places.

---

[5]See also Chapter 22.

System commands were also extended. These now include: LIST, to exhibit the program as it exists currently within the computer; RUN, used when you played games and used now to activate and run your own program; REN, to renumber your program lines and to provide space between line numbers that have become too closely packed; the SAVE commands to store programs for future use; and OLD or LOAD to recall an old program.

Illustration: Conversion from the English to the Metric System of Measurements

Having successfully flow-charted and written your first computer programs, you are now ready for a second task.

The United States is slowly but inexorably converting from the English to the metric system of measurements. Thus, measurements of length will be made in kilometers, meters, and centimeters instead of the more familiar miles, yards, feet, and inches. To facilitate the transition, it is desirable to prepare a program to do this conversion. Knowing one conversion factor, 39.37 inches = 1 meter, such a program is within your reach.

Before writing the program—in fact, before even trying to draw an appropriate flow chart—try the conversion on special cases, just to trace the logic involved. Suppose you start with 1 mile and convert this to the metric system. Because the conversion relationship is expressed in terms of inches, you must first convert the mile to inches: 1 mile = 1760 yards = 5280 feet = 63,360 inches. From 39.37 inches = 1 meter, note that 1 inch = 1/39.37 meters. Thus, 1 mile = 63,360/39.37 meters = 1609.3472 meters = 1 kilometer + 609 meters + 34.72 centimeters.

From this exercise, you can see that if the input is in miles, yards, feet, and inches, it is necessary first to convert everything to inches. Once the total number of inches is known, dividing this number by 39.37 yields the number of meters. Next, you will want to determine the number of kilometers, meters, and centimeters, where the numbers of kilometers and meters are to be nonnegative integers and you intend to round the number of centimeters to two decimal places.

To convert from miles, yards, and feet to inches requires only multiplying by the appropriate factors. Given the number of meters, however, such as 2745.33124, you must first determine the number of kilometers. This is done by dividing 2745.33124 by 1000 and using INT(X)

```
INT(2745.33124/1000) = INT(2.74533124) = 2
```

But do not lose track of the remainder, .74533124. The computer gets this by subtraction:

```
2.74533124 - INT(2.74533124)
```

If now, .74533124 is multiplied by 1000, you get 745.33124. The number of meters is found by taking INT(745.33124) = 745; there are 745 meters. But again, you must not lose track of the remainder, which the computer finds by subtraction:

```
745.33124 - INT(745.33124) = .33124
```

This remainder, multiplied by 100, yields the number of centimeters, 33.124. Since the number of centimeters is given to more than 2 decimal places, you round to two decimal places before printing the answer.

The flow chart, which may now be drawn, is shown in Figure 4-4. A program based on this flow chart follows.

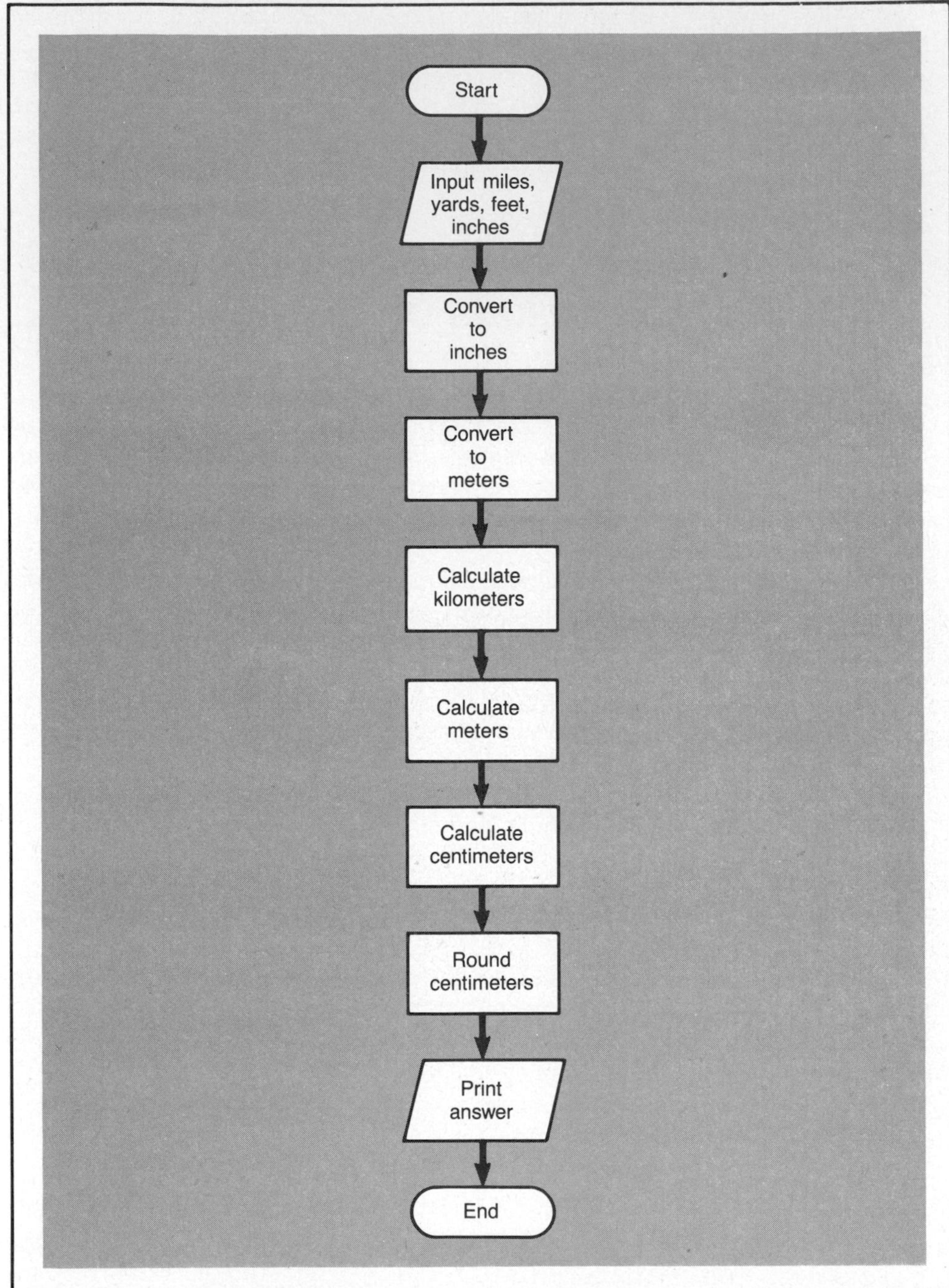

FIGURE 4-4

```
LIST

10 REM: THIS PROGRAMS CONVERTS MILES, YARDS, FEET AND INCHES TO
20 REM: KILOMETERS, METERS, AND CENTIMETERS.  THE CENTIMETERS
30 REM: ARE ROUNDED TO TWO DECIMAL PLACES.
40 ******************************
50 REM: IN THIS SECTION THE INPUT DATA ARE COLLECTED.
60 ******************************
70 PRINT "INPUT THE NUMBER OF MILES";
80 INPUT A
```

```
90 PRINT "THE NUMBER OF YARDS";
100 INPUT B
110 PRINT "THE NUMBER OF FEET";
120 INPUT C
130 PRINT "THE NUMBER OF INCHES";
140 INPUT D
150 ******************************
160 REM: EVERYTHING IS CONVERTED TO INCHES.
170 ******************************
180 LET E=D+12*C+36*B+63360*A
190 ******************************
200 REM: THE INCHES ARE CONVERTED TO METERS.
210 ******************************
220 LET F=E/39.37
230 ******************************
240 REM: WE NOW CALCULATE THE NUMBER OF KILOMETERS.
250 ******************************
260 LET G=INT(F/1000)
270 ******************************
280 REM: WE CALCULATE THE REMAINING NUMBER OF METERS.
290 ******************************
300 LET H=F-1000*G
310 ******************************
320 REM: WE CALCULATE THE INTEGRAL NUMBER OF METERS.
330 ******************************
340 LET J=INT(H)
350 ******************************
360 REM: WE CALCULATE THE REMAINDER.
370 ******************************
380 LET K=H-J
390 ******************************
400 REM: CONVERT THE REMAINDER, WHICH IS IN METERS AND IS < 1, TO CENTIMETERS.
410 ******************************
420 LET L=100*K
430 ******************************
440 REM: ROUND TO TWO DECIMAL PLACES.
450 ******************************
460 LET M=INT(L*100+.5)/100
470 ******************************
480 REM: WE NOW PRINT THE ANSWER.
490 ******************************
500 PRINT
510 PRINT A " MILES";
520 PRINT B " YARDS";
530 PRINT C " FEET";
540 PRINT D " INCHES"
550 PRINT
560 PRINT "ARE EQUAL TO"
570 PRINT
580 PRINT G " KILOMETERS";
590 PRINT J " METERS";
600 PRINT M " CENTIMETERS."
610 END
```

Several trial runs show that the program produces correct results:

```
 RUN

INPUT THE NUMBER OF MILES    ?1
THE NUMBER OF YARDS    ?0
THE NUMBER OF FEET  ?0
THE NUMBER OF INCHES  ?0

 1 MILES    0 YARDS    0 FEET    0 INCHES

ARE EQUAL TO

 1 KILOMETERS    609 METERS    34.7200 CENTIMETERS.

     610 HALT
```

```
 RUN

INPUT THE NUMBER OF MILES    ?0
THE NUMBER OF YARDS    ?1
THE NUMBER OF FEET  ?0
THE NUMBER OF INCHES   ?3.37

 0 MILES   1 YARDS   0 FEET    3.37000 INCHES

ARE EQUAL TO

 0 KILOMETERS    0 METERS    100 CENTIMETERS.

     610 HALT

 RUN

INPUT THE NUMBER OF MILES    ?0
THE NUMBER OF YARDS    ?0
THE NUMBER OF FEET  ?3
THE NUMBER OF INCHES   ?3.37

 0 MILES   0 YARDS   3 FEET    3.37000 INCHES

ARE EQUAL TO

 0 KILOMETERS    0 METERS    100 CENTIMETERS.

     610 HALT

 RUN

INPUT THE NUMBER OF MILES    ?0
THE NUMBER OF YARDS    ?0
THE NUMBER OF FEET  ?0
THE NUMBER OF INCHES   ?39.37

 0 MILES   0 YARDS   0 FEET    39.3700 INCHES

ARE EQUAL TO

 0 KILOMETERS    1 METERS    0 CENTIMETERS.

     610 HALT
```

The repetition of the zero-valued inputs and outputs reveals a lack of professionalism. It is within your grasp to correct this. From the program listing, note that each PRINT statement in lines 510–530, 580, and 590 terminates in a semicolon—the signal to the computer not to advance the print mechanism on the terminal to the next line but to hold it on the line currently being printed. If, between lines 500 and 510, you interpose a conditional transfer that jumps line 510 if A=0, then, under these circumstances, you will avoid the unnecessary printout. Similarly, line 520 may be skipped if B=0 and line 530 if C=0. For the moment, you will not want to suppress the printing of line 540 under any circumstances.

Similar comments apply to line 580 if G=0 and line 590 if J=0. Again, the printing of line 600 is not to be suppressed.

The section of the flow chart that refers to the output must now be modified. The block, Print Answer in Figure 4-4, should be replaced by the flow chart in Figure 4-5.

The program coding that accompanies this modification to the flow chart is the insertion of conditional transfers between lines 500 and 510, between lines 510 and 520, and between lines 520 and 530. Also, conditional transfers are inserted between lines 570 and 580 and between lines 580 and 590. The modified section of the code follows:

```
480 REM: WE NOW PRINT THE ANSWER.
490 ******************************
500 PRINT
505 IF A=0 THEN 515
```

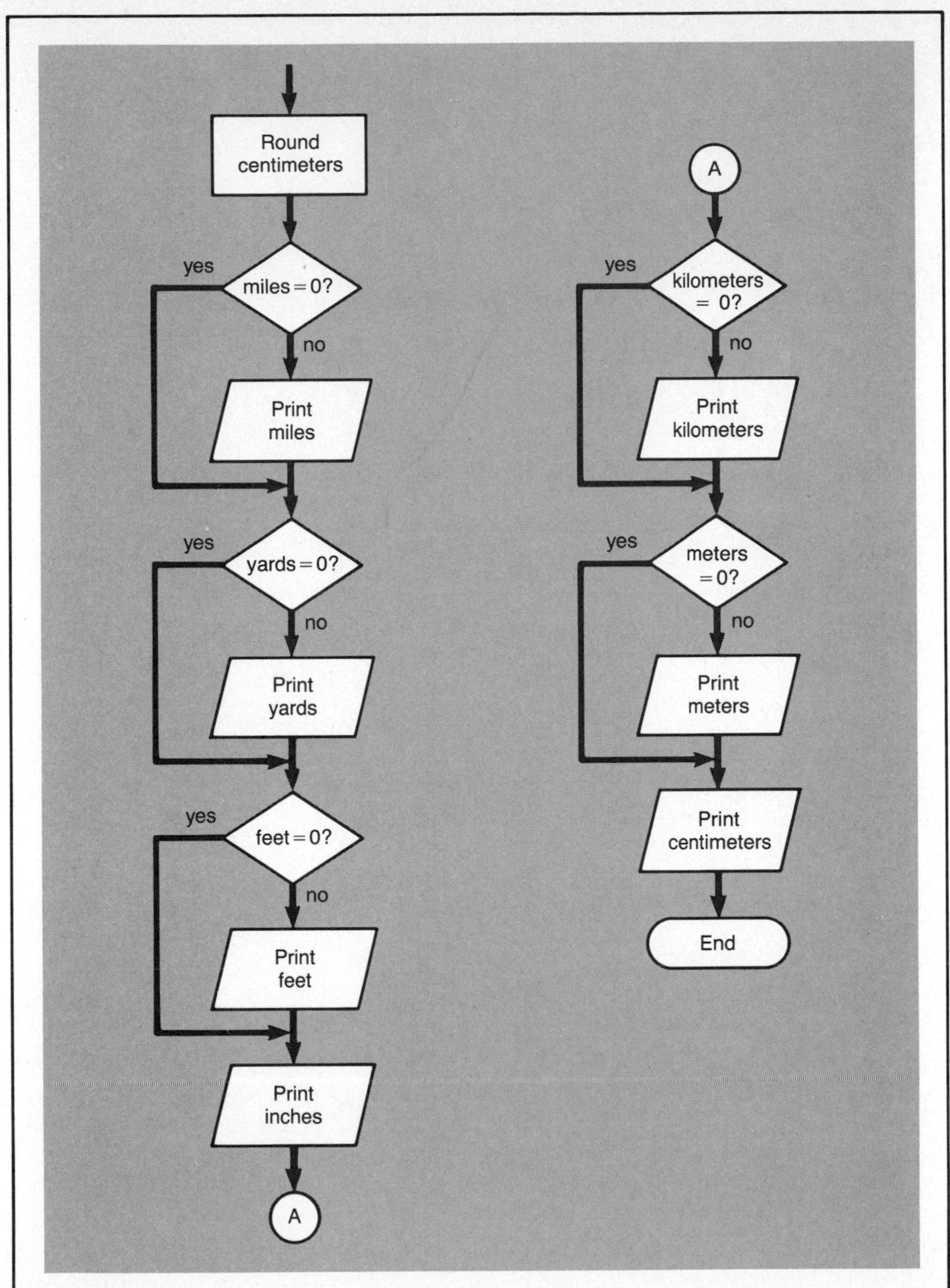

FIGURE 4-5

```
510 PRINT A " MILES";
515 IF B=0 THEN 525
520 PRINT B " YARDS";
525 IF C=0 THEN 540
530 PRINT C " FEET";
540 PRINT D " INCHES"
550 PRINT
560 PRINT "ARE EQUAL TO"
570 PRINT
575 IF G=O THEN 585
580 PRINT G " KILOMETERS";
585 IF J=0 THEN 600
590 PRINT J " METERS";
600 PRINT M " CENTIMETERS."
610 END
```

As the following run shows, the output from this modified program suppresses the unnecessary printing.

```
RUN

INPUT THE NUMBER OF MILES    ?1
THE NUMBER OF YARDS   ?0
THE NUMBER OF FEET  ?0
THE NUMBER OF INCHES   ?0

 1 MILES    0 INCHES

ARE EQUAL TO

 1 KILOMETERS    609 METERS     34.7200 CENTIMETERS.


 RUN

INPUT THE NUMBER OF MILES    ?0
THE NUMBER OF YARDS   ?1
THE NUMBER OF FEET  ?0
THE NUMBER OF INCHES   ?3.37

 1 YARDS   3.37000 INCHES

ARE EQUAL TO

 100 CENTIMETERS.


 RUN

INPUT THE NUMBER OF MILES    ?0
THE NUMBER OF YARDS   ?0
THE NUMBER OF FEET  ?3
THE NUMBER OF INCHES   ?3.37

 3 FEET    3.37000 INCHES

ARE EQUAL TO

 100 CENTIMETERS.


 RUN

INPUT THE NUMBER OF MILES    ?0
THE NUMBER OF YARDS   ?0
THE NUMBER OF FEET  ?0
THE NUMBER OF INCHES   ?39.37

 39.3700 INCHES

ARE EQUAL TO

 1 METERS    0 CENTIMETERS.
```

While the output is now more graphically pleasing, it would be further enhanced if you suppressed the printing of "0 inches," provided, of course, that the number of miles, yards, and feet are all not zero simultaneously. In that case, you will want the printout to read "0 inches." We may translate this logic into a sequence of conditional transfer statements. Observe first that each of the three numbers A, B, and C is greater than or equal to zero, so that their sum is also greater than or equal to zero. In fact, their sum equals zero only if A=B=C=0. Thus, you will want to insert one conditional statement of the form:

IF A+B+C=0 THEN (print D)

Second, note that if A+B+C ≠ 0, then you need to know if D=0. Thus, the form of the second conditional statement may be:

```
IF D > 0 THEN (print D)
```

Injecting this logic into the appropriate section of the flow chart modifies it as shown in Figure 4-6.

A similar situation arises when the metric output is to be printed; the logic for handling it parallels that given above. The modified flow chart is shown in Figure 4-7.

The code needs to be modified to accommodate these changes. Before doing this, however, the program is renumbered so that it is easier to follow, and the significant portion, from old line 290 to the end, now looks like this:

```
480 REM: WE NOW PRINT THE ANSWER.
490 ******************************
500 PRINT
510 IF A=0 THEN 530
520 PRINT A " MILES";
530 IF B=0 THEN 550
540 PRINT B " YARDS";
550 IF C=0 THEN 570
560 PRINT C " FEET";
570 PRINT D " INCHES"
580 PRINT
590 PRINT "ARE EQUAL TO"
600 PRINT
610 IF G=O THEN 630
620 PRINT G " KILOMETERS";
630 IF J=0 THEN 650
640 PRINT J " METERS";
650 PRINT M " CENTIMETERS."
660 END
```

From the flow chart, you see that between lines 500 and 510 you want to insert the statement

```
505 IF A+B+C=0 THEN 570
```

and between lines 560 and 570,

```
565 IF D=0 THEN 580
```

These insertions require that line 550 be changed from:

```
550 IF C = 0 THEN 570
```

to:

```
550 IF C=0 THEN 565
```

that a semicolon be added at the end of line 570, which in turn requires an additional PRINT statement at line 585. Similarly, between lines 600 and 610, you insert:

```
605 if G+J=0 THEN 650
```

and between 640 and 650:

```
645 IF M=0 THEN 660
```

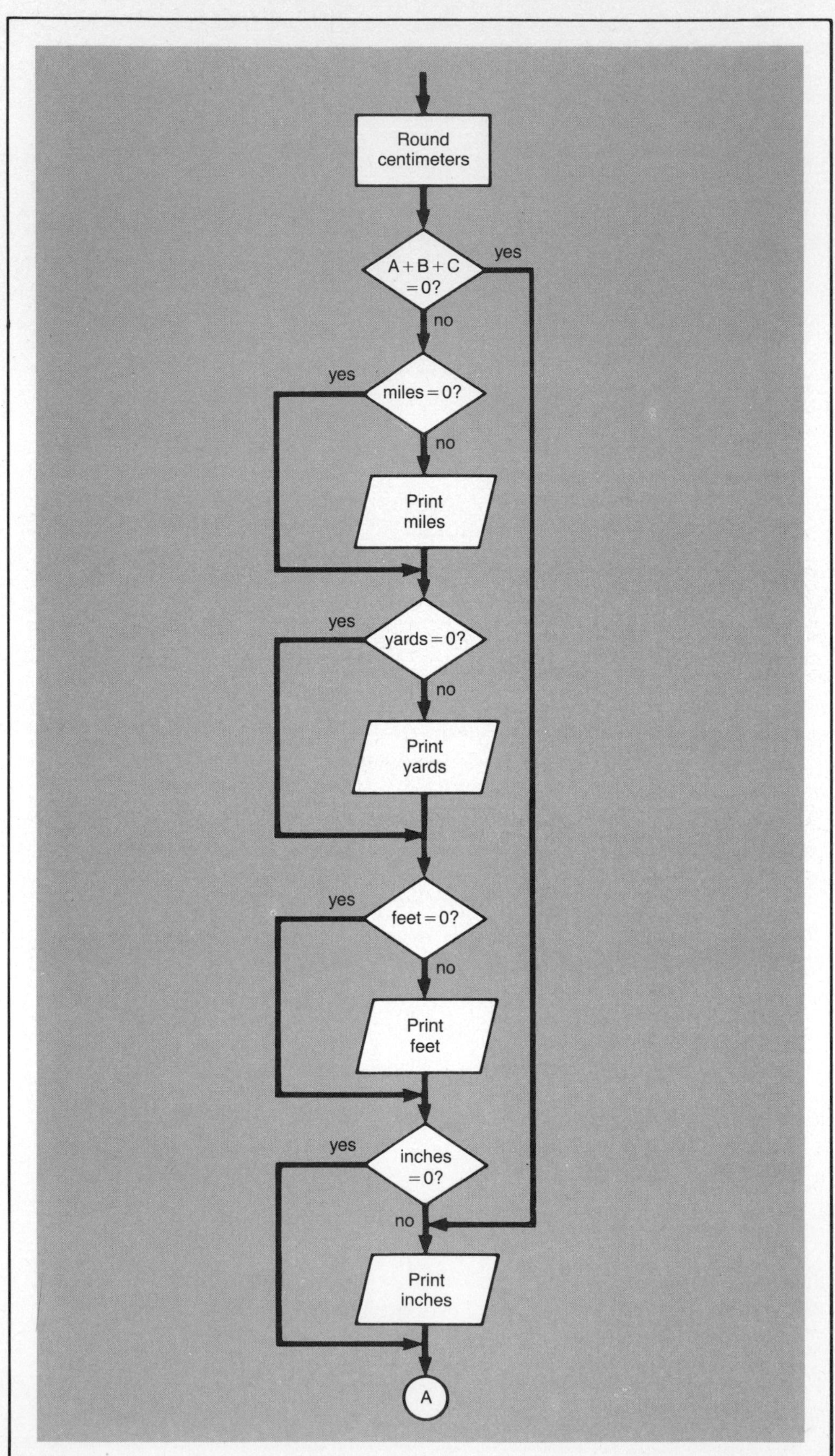
Round centimeters
A + B + C = 0?
yes
no
miles = 0?
yes
no
Print miles
yards = 0?
yes
no
Print yards
feet = 0?
yes
no
Print feet
inches = 0?
yes
no
Print inches
A

FIGURE 4-6

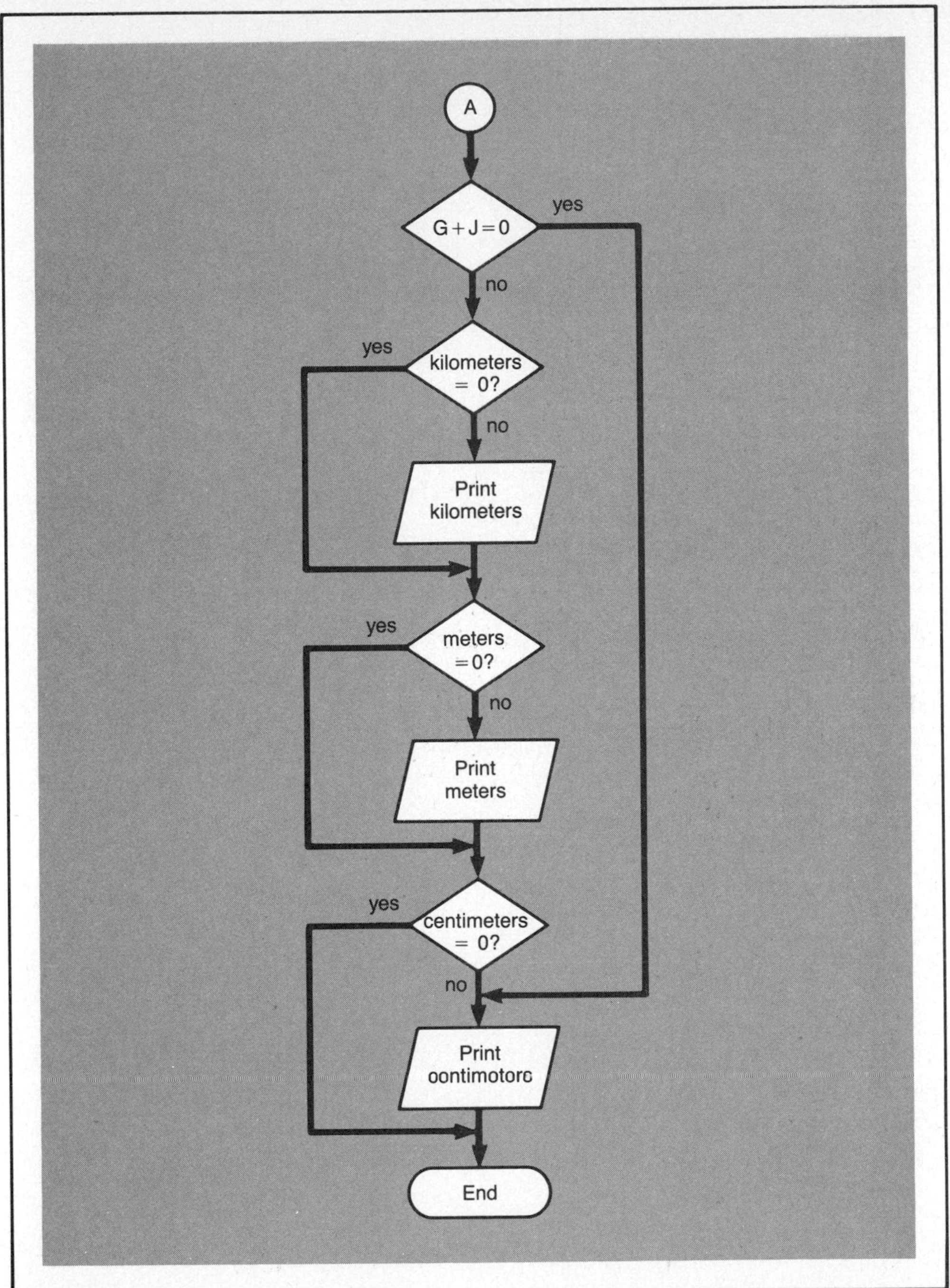

FIGURE 4-7

With these changes, the program is:

```
LIST

10 REM: THIS PROGRAMS CONVERTS MILES, YARDS, FEET AND INCHES TO
20 REM: KILOMETERS, METERS, AND CENTIMETERS.  THE CENTIMETERS
30 REM: ARE ROUNDED TO TWO DECIMAL PLACES.
40 ******************************
50 REM: IN THIS SECTION THE INPUT DATA ARE COLLECTED.
60 ******************************
70 PRINT "INPUT THE NUMBER OF MILES";
80 INPUT A
```

```
90 PRINT "THE NUMBER OF YARDS";
100 INPUT B
110 PRINT "THE NUMBER OF FEET";
120 INPUT C
130 PRINT "THE NUMBER OF INCHES";
140 INPUT D
150 ******************************
160 REM: EVERYTHING IS CONVERTED TO INCHES.
170 ******************************
180 LET E=D+12*C+36*B+63360*A
190 ******************************
200 REM: THE INCHES ARE CONVERTED TO METERS.
210 ******************************
220 LET F=E/39.37
230 ******************************
240 REM: WE NOW CALCULATE THE NUMBER OF KILOMETERS.
250 ******************************
260 LET G=INT(F/1000)
270 ******************************
280 REM: WE CALCULATE THE REMAINING NUMBER OF METERS.
290 ******************************
300 LET H=F-1000*G
310 ******************************
320 REM: WE CALCULATE THE INTEGRAL NUMBER OF METERS.
330 ******************************
340 LET J=INT(H)
350 ******************************
360 REM: WE CALCULATE THE REMAINDER.
370 ******************************
380 LET K=H-J
390 ******************************
400 REM: CONVERT THE REMAINDER, WHICH IS IN METERS AND IS < 1, TO CENTIMETERS.
410 ******************************
420 LET L=100*K
430 ******************************
440 REM: ROUND TO TWO DECIMAL PLACES.
450 ******************************
460 LET M=INT(L*100+.5)/100
470 ******************************
480 REM: WE NOW PRINT THE ANSWER.
490 ******************************
500 PRINT
505 IF A+B+C=0 THEN 570
510 IF A=0 THEN 530
520 PRINT A " MILES";
530 IF B=0 THEN 550
540 PRINT B " YARDS";
550 IF C=0 THEN 565
560 PRINT C " FEET";
565 IF D=0 THEN 580
570 PRINT D " INCHES";
580 PRINT
585 PRINT
590 PRINT "ARE EQUAL TO"
600 PRINT
605 IF G+J=0 THEN 650
610 IF G=O THEN 630
620 PRINT G " KILOMETERS";
630 IF J=0 THEN 650
640 PRINT J " METERS";
645 IF M=0 THEN 660
650 PRINT M " CENTIMETERS."
660 END
```

```
 RUN

INPUT THE NUMBER OF MILES   ?1
THE NUMBER OF YARDS   ?0
THE NUMBER OF FEET  ?0
THE NUMBER OF INCHES  ?0

 1 MILES

ARE EQUAL TO

 1 KILOMETERS    609 METERS    34.7200 CENTIMETERS.


 RUN

INPUT THE NUMBER OF MILES   ?0
THE NUMBER OF YARDS   ?1
THE NUMBER OF FEET  ?0
THE NUMBER OF INCHES  ?3.37

 1 YARDS   3.37000 INCHES

ARE EQUAL TO

 100 CENTIMETERS.


 RUN

INPUT THE NUMBER OF MILES   ?0
THE NUMBER OF YARDS   ?0
THE NUMBER OF FEET  ?0
THE NUMBER OF INCHES  ?39.37

 39.3700 INCHES

ARE EQUAL TO

 1 METERS

 RUN

INPUT THE NUMBER OF MILES   ?0
THE NUMBER OF YARDS   ?0
THE NUMBER OF FEET  ?0
THE NUMBER OF INCHES  ?0

 0 INCHES

ARE EQUAL TO

 0 CENTIMETERS.
```

Exercises

4.1 Your local Savings and Loan Association pays interest at an annual rate of 7.5 percent, compounded daily. How much should you deposit today so that at the end of 5 years you will have $4000 on deposit?

The general formula for solving this problem is:

$$P = \frac{A}{\left(1 + \frac{I}{100K}\right)^{YK}}$$

In this problem, A = 4000, K = 365, Y = 5, and I = 7.5. Draw a flow diagram that indicates the input data needed, the calculation to be performed, and the printout. Using your flow chart as a model, write the computer program. Include documentation at the appropriate places. (See Chapter 2, Exercise 2.9.)

4.2 At regular intervals during the year, say K times a year, a dollar amount, D, is deducted from your salary and placed in a retirement fund. The fund pays interest at an annual rate of 1 percent. If the number of years until your retirement is Y, the lump sum, S, available to you upon retirement is given by the formula:

$$S = D\left(\frac{(1 + I/100K)^{ky} - 1}{I/100K}\right)$$

Prepare a flow chart that indicates the input data needed, the calculation to be performed, and the printout. Using the flow chart as a guide, write the corresponding computer program. Include documentation where appropriate. (See Chapter 2, Exercise 2.7.)

4.3 If, in Exercise 2, your goal is to accumulate a lump sum of S dollars upon retirement and you want to know how much should be deducted each period, the formula to use is:

$$D = S\left(\frac{I/100K}{(1 + I/100K)^{ky} - 1}\right)$$

Modify the flow diagram and the computer program of Exercise 4.2 in order to calculate the required deduction. The documentation must be changed also. (See Chapter 2, Exercise 2.10.)

4.4 (a) Assume you are given linear measurements in kilometers, meters, and centimeters. Draw the flow diagram, and from it, write the computer program that will convert the distances to miles, yards, feet, and inches. The number of miles, yards, and feet should be integral, and the number of inches should be rounded to two decimal places.

(b) If a zero occurs in either the input or the output, suppress the printing of the associated unit of length except when all inputs are zero. In that case, have the computer print: "0 centimeters equal 0 inches."

4.5 The conversion of liquid measure from the English to the metric system is based on the following definition: 1 quart = .9464 liters. Also, in the English system, 1 pint = 16 fluid ounces, 1 quart = 2 pints, and 1 gallon = 4 quarts. In the metric system, 1 centiliter = 10 milliliters, 1 deciliter = 10 centiliters, and 1 liter = 10 deciliters.
(a) Draw a flow diagram and write a program that asks for input in the English system and prints out the equivalent measure in the metric system.
(b) Draw a flow diagram and write a program that requests input in the metric system and prints the equivalent measure in the English system.

5 On the Hardware and Some System Commands

Your ability to solve problems on a computer, as well as the ease with which you can do so, will increase as you become more familiar with computer hardware (the physical components of the system) and computer software (those programs, generally manufacturer supplied, that ensure that the instructions you write and the commands you issue are faithfully executed). Thus far, your exposure to the hardware, to the system commands, and to the BASIC language instructions and commands has been minimal—just enough to show you how a computer solves a problem. The purpose of this chapter is not so much to provide additional tools to enable you to solve more complex problems, but rather to make it easier for you to manage the computer. This will be done by providing an understanding of some of its inner workings. With that as the intent, three general concepts are discussed. The first of these is the hardware. As you already know, there are four major components: the input-output (abbreviated I/O and consisting of the terminal), the main storage, the central processing unit (CPU), and the permanent storage (generally a disk). For the moment, enough has been said about the terminal; we shall talk more about the other three. Second, the flow of information within and between these components is controlled by the executive system; we shall paint a picture showing how this program oversees all operations within the computer. Finally, we shall expand somewhat on some of the commands available to you, both within BASIC and under the operating system. After you finish this chapter, you will have a better understanding of how the computer goes about solving your problems, and you will be able, using your terminal, to manipulate the computer with greater ease.

The narrative is presented in the order in which you are apt to encounter difficulties as you attempt to increase your facility with the equipment. The several sections attempt to anticipate your needs and respond to them.

The Main Memory

As you sit at your terminal and type instructions to the computer, the information is stored in the computer's **main memory.** As discussed in Chapter 1, one way to visualize the main memory is as a collection of mail boxes like those in a large post office. Although each box has a number (an address) permanently affixed to it, the contents of each box depend on whatever happens to have been sent and whatever happens to have been taken out. Thus, in the computer's main memory there will be a section of 286 boxes, the addresses of which are the 286 possible variable names discussed in Chapter 4. What happens to be in each box depends on what you put there. Recall the addition problem in Chapter 4. When the number 5 was assigned to the variable X, conceptually, you were sending a slip of paper with the number 5 written on it and having that piece of paper placed in the box whose address is X. This imagery is valid in general: Whenever a numerical value is assigned to a variable, think of that number as being written on a slip of paper and the paper placed in the box whose address is the variable name.

Other boxes contain the instructions you have written. One box will contain the instruction for addition, another for subtraction, another for multiplication, and so on. There will be a box that contains the instruction INPUT and another containing PRINT. In fact, there will be a box containing each of the various instructions you will write in your program, at least one for each instruction. After your program is written and entered into the main memory of the computer, it resides there like so many letters in the mail boxes until someone comes along and starts to deliver them.

The Executive Program

Imagine a town with one central hub and an exceptionally smart traffic director standing at this intersection. Many roads come into and leave the hub, and each motorist stops and asks directions while passing through. The computer's traffic director is called the executive program. Not only must it keep the traffic moving, but it must be sure that each motorist goes to the correct destination. You previously met this director when you logged on and off. When you logged on, you were effectively showing that you had a valid driver's license; when logging off, you were indicating you intended to leave town. When you call the BASIC language processor, you are asking to be directed to a specific section of the computer, as if asking to be directed to a specific suburb. (You may make other requests of the executive program, and you will learn of these in due course.) After you ask to be directed to BASIC and get there, you find a second traffic director in that suburb. This one knows how to direct the computer to carry out the BASIC system commands: LIST, RUN, SAVE, LOAD, and so on.

The BASIC Processor and the CPU

After you log on and call the BASIC interpreter, all information from your terminal is managed by the director handling traffic in BASIC. As you enter your program into the computer, he directs the several elements of each instruction to the proper address in the local post office. When you run your program, however, he has more to do. There is an entirely separate county, called the CPU (Central Processing Unit), where all arithmetic operations are performed and all logical decisions are made. Thus, when your addition program is run, the director must first send a message back to you at your terminal and ask you to indicate the numerical value you want placed in the letter box marked X. When you have done this, the value is marked on a piece of paper that is placed in the letter box marked X. The director then sends a second message to you inquiring what numerical value you want placed in the letter box marked Y. Again, that value is written on a piece of paper and the paper put into the letter box marked Y. Since your next instruction was to add the two numerical values, the director sends a messenger to the box labeled X, where the messenger makes a copy of the contents of the box and delivers this copy to the addition component of the CPU. A copy of the contents of the box labeled Y is then made and also delivered to the CPU. The addition section of the CPU, recognizing that it has two numbers, adds them and calls for a messenger to take the result back to BASICland. The BASIC director orders the messenger to go to the letter box marked Z, to remove and destroy whatever happens to be in the box at that time, and place the result of the addition into the box.

The next set of directions issued by the director are: (1) copy the contents of the box marked X, carry this to your terminal, and display (PRINT) it there, (2) copy the contents of the box marked Y, carry this to your terminal, and print it, and (3) copy the contents of the box marked Z, carry it to your terminal, and print it. You are informed that the assigned task is completed when the message HALT appears at your terminal.

The preceding, personified description of how a computer executes a program in BASIC will prove helpful when extended to other programs you will encounter and when writing your own.

Basic System Commands

Once you are in BASIC, in addition to the language statements, such as LET, PRINT, and IF—THEN—, there is the set of BASIC system commands, for example, LIST and RUN. The difference between a BASIC statement, or instruction, and a BASIC command is as follows. **Statements** (or instructions) are words you use within your program; they tell the computer what to do with the data in your program. A BASIC **command** is an order to the computer to do something to your program; commands are not used within a program. We shall illustrate how these apply by reexamining the operations previously discussed.

SAVE and LOAD When writing and running a program, only the terminal (the I/O, input/output), the main memory, and the CPU are used. Imagine you have finished writing a program and want to save it for future use, as Kevin wanted to save his TAX program. It need not be a complete program; partial programs, or whatever has been completed, may be saved. To know what you are saving, you can look into the main memory before saving what is there. Type the BASIC system command LIST and the contents will be displayed. To save what you see before you, use the appropriate SAVE command. With this done, a copy of the program, as it exists in the main memory, is recorded in permanent storage, generally on a disk. If now you log off, the program in the main memory is wiped out, but the copy on disk remains. Thus, at some future time, when you log on, you can retrieve the program from the disk. At this time, the program is not actually removed from the disk, but a copy is made and placed into main memory when the BASIC system command LOAD is issued. If the program has been stored on disk under the name PROBE, you bring it into main memory by typing

```
>LOAD PROBE          <CR>
```
[1]

LIST With the copy now in main memory, you are free to operate on it as you wish, either run, list, or modify it. If you intend to modify the program, you may not remember its details. If you type

```
>LIST          <CR>
```

the entire program will be displayed. If it is too long or if only a portion is needed, you may type

```
>LIST 150          <CR>
```

to see the statement at line 150, or

```
>LIST 90-120          <CR>
```

---

[1] A common alternative is: >OLD PROBE <CR>.

to see all statements having line numbers between 90 and 120 inclusive. You may see any combination of lines simply by specifying the lines you want to see. For example,

```
>LIST 90-120, 300, 425-450          <CR>
```

Having isolated the section of interest, you decide to make changes. These changes, however, apply only to the copy in main memory. You now have the option of storing this new version on disk under another name and also retaining the original version of PROBE or, by erasing the earlier one, storing the modified version under the old name.

DELETE At some point, you will want to delete something you have written, a situation that arises for different reasons. Suppose you complete a section of code and, on reviewing what you typed, decide to delete a specific line. For example, you have typed

```
70 PRINT "TO EACH ONE BE TRUE"
```

and wish to delete it, After the > prompt, type

```
70          <CR>
```

Line 70 is now gone. An alternative procedure is to use the BASIC system command DELETE. In this case, type

```
DEL 70          <CR>
```

The DELETE command is used also to remove sets of lines. For example,

```
>DEL 80-110,175,225-300          <CR>
```

Suppose you complete one program and your interest turns to another. Before beginning the second program, it is important to wipe clean the main memory. Otherwise, remnants of the old program may be interspersed in the new one, producing unexpected and spurious results. You may delete the first program by using the DEL command with the first and last line numbers of the program, or your computer may have a CLEAR command that does the same. In this case, you would type

```
CLEAR          <CR>
```

The first program may not be the only thing cluttering up the main memory. Values assigned to some of the variables used in the earlier program may be lurking there. To erase them, it is good practice to "initialize" all variables at the beginning of each program—in other words, to set all variables equal to zero. On some systems, the BASIC system command NUL does this for you. You would type

```
NUL          <CR>
```

CLEAR and NUL affect programs and variables only in main memory; they have no effect on programs or data stored on disk. Using CLEAR and NUL puts the main memory into a pristine state ready for your first instruction.

The time will come when you will want to delete a program that has been saved on disk. For example, it may be that your allotted disk storage space is getting crowded and you want to remove programs no longer current. Because each program in the disk storage area is identified by a name, you use that name with the DELETE command to remove the program from the disk. For a program stored under the name SIMPLE, for example, the specific command is

```
DELETE SIMPLE        <CR>
```

This use of DELETE affects nothing in main memory; it affects only the named program on disk.[2]

With the DELETE command available, the SAVE OVER or RESAVE command is superfluous although handy. With the corrected version of your program in main memory, delete the old version from disk and then save the new one. This requires two steps; RESAVE or SAVE OVER requires only one.

CATALOG What if you want to know the programs you have on disk or, at least, to recall their names? The BASIC system command CAT, the abbreviation for CATALOG, instructs the computer to display the names of all programs in your account. Recall that we used the CAT command in Chapter 1 to have the computer display the list of games available under the account GAMES (see page 10).

Errors

You have seen that while typing a program you may make typing errors that you may not detect before striking <CR>. The computer is not deterred. When the rules of BASIC are violated, it detects the error and responds with an error message, a typical one being BAD STME (statement). When that happens, simply retype the line correctly and continue.

It may be that during the course of writing the program, you typed each statement correctly but the totality of statements is logically inconsistent or incomplete. Errors of this kind are detected only after you have issued the RUN command and before the first statement is executed. When detected, an error message is printed. One such error message might be ARRAY CLASS CONFLICT.

Finally, errors may occur during the execution of the program. For example, if during the course of running the program and perhaps after some partial results have been obtained, division by zero occurs, the program will halt and an error message DIV BY ZERO will appear. To correct this, it is necessary to examine the logic behind the program and correct the program accordingly. Alternatively, you may devise a means to check for a zero divisor and circumvent that section of the program when division by zero is to occur.

These three types of errors are referred to, respectively, as (1) syntax errors, (2) logical errors, and (3) pragmatic errors.

Executive System Commands

In our description thus far of the executive system, we have emphasized how it manages the flow of BASIC commands, instructions, and data within the computer. We mentioned, however, that each motorist—you—can interact with it. This is done by explicit executive operating system commands. Of the commands that are available, you have consciously used two: one to call the BASIC interpreter and the other—OFF or BYE—to log off. Additional system commands are described below.

Correcting a Line

You have seen how typing errors may be corrected using the RUBOUT key; this is an implicit system command that deletes one character at a time. In one sense, all commands to the computer must be made explicitly; if you do nothing, nothing happens. Thus, you

[2]On some systems the command is KILL SIMPLE <CR>; others use UNSAVE SIMPLE <CR>.

can say there is no implicit system command. There are certain system commands, however, that are used so naturally and routinely that the terminal manufacturer provides a single key for them, for example, <CR> and RUBOUT. We refer to these commands as "implicit." On the other hand, to call the BASIC interpreter and to log off requires that you consciously type BASIC<CR> and OFF<CR> or BYE<CR>. This type of command we refer to as an explicit system command.

In addition, you know that if you discover an error while typing a line, you may stop and hit <CR> (an implicit operating system command) and the computer will respond with an error message. You may then retype the line, starting with the same line number. If this seems too slow, press and hold the CTRL (control) key and strike X. The computer will ignore everything you typed since the last <CR>; the print head will reposition itself at the beginning of the line and you may begin retyping. Effectively, CTRL X erases a partially entered line without producing an error message and permits you to start again. The symbol X^C is frequently used to represent CTRL X.

Viewing

Sometimes a line is cluttered with several changes and it is difficult to recognize what the computer has accepted. (Obviously, this will not occur on those CRT systems that erase errors when RUBOUT is used; there, what you see is what the computer sees.) There is an executive system command that shows that portion of the line accepted to this point. On one computer it is ESC R; striking ESC R will have the computer print back the current contents of a partial line. You may then continue and finish the line.

Interrupting a Run

Assume your program is running and partial results are being printed. On seeing these, you decide to stop the run. Press the BREAK key (another implicit operating system command); program execution will stop, but the program will remain in the execution mode. Generally, if you next strike <CR>, the program will continue running. Pressing the BREAK key twice halts further execution; the computer will still be in BASIC and your program will still be in main memory. You may proceed as you wish.

If for some reason you panic and want to hit the panic button, press and hold the CTRL key while you strike Y. This will bring the computer to an immediate halt; the disadvantage is that you will be at the executive system level. You will have to reenter BASIC; the program in main memory may be lost, and you may have to reload it from disk or retype it completely.

While the operations attributed to CTRL X, ESC R, BREAK, and CTRL Y are fairly universal, their exact names are different on different computers. You will have to learn them as they apply to your machine.

Conclusion

The purpose of this chapter was to make it easier for you to manage the computer and to interact with it. The organization of the hardware is universal in that all computers have a main memory, a CPU, and I/O capabilities. It is only the very smallest that do not provide permanent storage such as disk, drum, tape, or cassette. Since you are working in BASIC, a BASIC interpreter must exist as well as a set of BASIC system commands. The existence of a general operating system and the ability to use some of its commands directly from your terminal is a function of the level of complexity and versatility of the computer. Only the smallest ones, those dedicated solely to BASIC, may not have an executive operating system; more complex ones certainly will.

Exercises

5.1 Assume you are writing a program to multiply three numbers. Two statements in your program are:

```
120 PRINT "X=";
130 INPUT X
```

a. Describe what happens in the computer as you enter each of these two lines.
b. Describe what happens in the computer when these two lines are executed during a run.

5.2 Assume that you have successfully written a program and want to save it for future use. Describe the various steps you take at your terminal to accomplish this. What does the computer do in response to what you do?

5.3 You intend to modify a program you have saved in permanent storage. What commands will you issue to accomplish this? What does the computer do in response to these commands?

5.4 Illustrate by an example you have tried on the computer: (a) a syntax error, (b) a logical error, and (c) a pragmatic error.

5.5 Correct an error in a line you are typing by each of the three methods described in the chapter.

5.6 If you were to run the following program:

```
10 LET X=1
20 PRINT X,
30 LET X=X+1
40 IF X<>0 THEN 20
50 END
```

the integers 1, 2, 3, . . . will be printed across and down the page. (The symbol <> means "not equal to.") The program never gets to line 50 and never halts. Describe what happens in each case as you use the several options discussed in the chapter to stop the program.

5.7 If your computer responds to ESC R, describe what it does. Otherwise, find the equivalent of ESC R on your computer, test its functioning, and describe what it does.

6 Loops

A powerful technique for solving many problems on a computer uses the concept of iteration, or looping. To "iterate," which is synonymous with "reiterate," means to repeat. For example, a formula is evaluated for one set of values of the variables and then evaluated again and again for different sets of values of the variables. In this chapter, we shall present two general methods for writing "loops"; one uses the IF—THEN—statement, which we have previously discussed, and the other uses the FOR—NEXT—instruction.

We shall also introduce some other useful techniques. First, we shall discuss a method for formatting output to enhance its appearance. This method may be applied, for example, to the preparation of a table of numbers. Second, a need for the BASIC instructions STOP and the unconditional GOTO (line number) arises when a program (or section of a program) logically terminates for different reasons. We shall illustrate the use of these instructions. Third, it is sometimes convenient to know when two quantities are unequal; the symbol not equal to, <>, is introduced and its use illustrated. Fourth, in all the illustrations offered thus far, each statement was written on a separate line. At times we might want to write several BASIC statements on the same line. We shall illustrate a technique for doing this.

Illustrative material intended to provide background for using loops to solve problems is drawn from numerical cryptograms, the elementary theory of numbers, and geometry.

Lucy's One-upmanship

In his enthusiasm to exhibit his newly gained programming skills, John showed the program he had written to calculate the future value of an investment to his sister, Lucy. Being adept at one-upmanship, she quickly pointed out that the program, while logical and consistent, did not reflect the real world. Banks do not calculate future values according to the formula John used. Instead, at the end of each interest period, the interest is calculated, truncated to the penny, and added to the old balance to produce a new balance. Over many periods, the effect of the truncation, which is always in the bank's favor, while not large, becomes noticeable. Lucy suggested to John that he rethink the problem, redraw his flow chart, and rewrite the program. Then, he could determine also the difference between the two methods of computation.

FIGURE 6-1

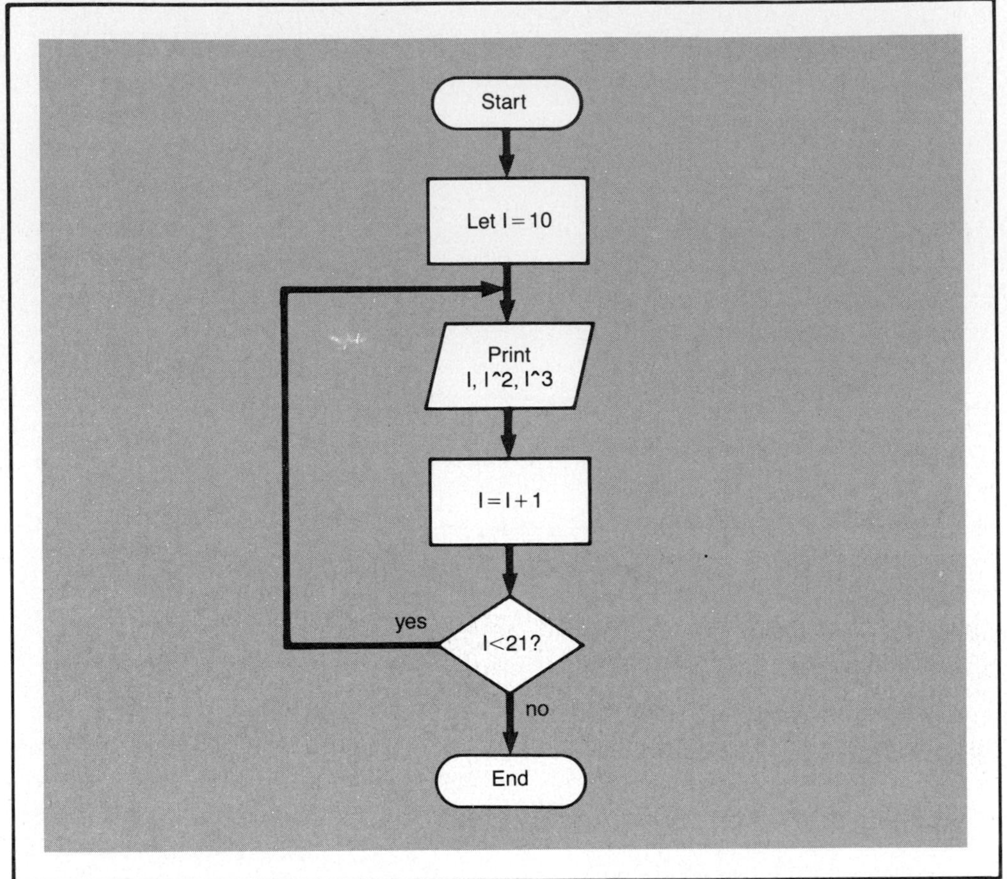

Muttering to himself, John opens his *BASIC Computing* and leafs through it, hoping to find enough information to help him meet Lucy's challenge.

The IF—THEN—Statement

To some extent, a BASIC instruction needed to generate a loop is already available. As the following program illustrates, the IF—THEN— statement suffices. Suppose you want to prepare a table of numbers from 10 to 20 with their squares and cubes. The operations would be first to print 10, then print its square, and then its cube. Next, increase 10 by 1 to get 11. Now, print 11, then its square, and then its cube. Next, increase 11 by 1 to 12 and continue. If this process is repeated until you reach 20, the table will be generated. It is necessary to stop when 21 is reached.

A flow diagram that reflects these instructions appears in Figure 6-1. A program, carrying out the intent of the flow chart, is not difficult:

```
10 LET I=10
20 PRINT
30 PRINT I,I^2,I^3
40 LET I=I+1
50 IF I<21 THEN 30
60 END
```

```
10           100          1000
11           121          1331
12           144          1728
```

```
13            169            2197
14            196            2744
15            225            3375
16            256            4096
17            289            4913
18            324            5832
19            361            6859
20            400            8000
```

Formatting Output Using the Comma

As you examine the program, you should find nothing unfamiliar, except line 30. In our earlier programs, literal strings and numerical values were interspersed on a single line without punctuation, and the output seemed reasonably natural. Now, however, the output appears in the form of a table. Most terminals have a line width of 72 characters, which we may think of as divided into six fields: The first five fields have a width of fourteen characters each, and the sixth field has a width of two characters.[1] Because no comma precedes the first I in line 30, the value if I is printed in the first field; the comma that separates I from I^2 tells the computer that the value of I^2 is to be printed in the field after the one in which I is printed (in this case, field 2), and the comma that separates I^2 from I^3 instructs the computer to print the value of I^3 in the field after the one in which the value of I^2 is printed (in this case, field 3).

If we were to rewrite line 30 as:

```
30 PRINT I,,I^2,,I^3
```

then the value of I would appear in the first field, the second field would be blank, and the value of I^2 would appear in the third field. The fourth field would be blank, and the value of I^3 would be in the fifth field.[2]

```
10 LET I=10
20 PRINT
30 PRINT I,,I^2,,I^3
40 LET I=I+1
50 IF I<21 THEN 30
60 END
```

```
10                            100                           1000
11                            121                           1331
12                            144                           1728
13                            169                           2197
14                            196                           2744
15                            225                           3375
16                            256                           4096
17                            289                           4913
18                            324                           5832
19                            361                           6859
20                            400                           8000
```

If line 30 were written:

```
30 PRINT ,I,,I^2,,I^3
```

then the first, third, and fifth fields would be blank. The value of I would appear in the second field, that of I^2 in the fourth, and that of I^3 in the sixth. However, since the

---

[1]Some computers divide the 72 characters into four fields of 15 characters each and one of 12.

[2]On some computers, line 30 would be written:
30 PRINT I,"",I^2,"",I^3
The "" are needed to produce the blank field.

sixth field can contain at most two characters and four are required to print the value of I^3, it is printed in the next available field, in this case, the first field of the next line. The run in this case would appear as follows:

```
10 LET I=10
20 PRINT
30 PRINT ,I,,I^2,,I^3
40 LET I=I+1
50 IF I<21 THEN 30
60 END

              10                          100
1000
              11                          121
1331
              12                          144
1728
              13                          169
2197
              14                          196
2744
              15                          225
3375
              16                          256
4096
              17                          289
4913
              18                          324
5832
              19                          361
6859
              20                          400
8000
```

In a PRINT statement, the comma positions the print mechanism so that printing begins in the next available field.

The FOR—NEXT— Statement

The concept of iteration so thoroughly permeates computing that a special instruction has been devised to make writing loops even easier. This instruction is referred to as the FOR—NEXT— loop. The following program consists of only three lines.

```
10 FOR I=10 TO 20
20 PRINT I,,I^2,,I^3
30 NEXT I
```

The computer executes these instructions as follows. At line 10, one counter is reserved for I and initially set at 10; a second counter is set at 20, the final value of I. Control goes to line 20, which is then executed. Control passes to line 30 and the counter reserved for I is increased by 1. At this point, I = 11. With I = 11, the computer compares the contents of the register I, namely 11, with the contents of the second register, namely 20, and since 11 < 20, proceeds to execute line 20. It continues on to line 30, where I is set equal to 12. Control returns to line 10, and this time 12 is compared with the contents of the second register, that is, 20. Because 12 < 20, the computer executes line 20, and so on. Eventually, I = 20 and line 20 is executed. Line 30 then sets the counter I to the next number, to 21. 21 is now compared with 20. Because 21 is greater than 20, the value of the I counter is reduced by 1 (it is now back to 20), and control is transferred to the instruction following line 30. Since there is none in this example, execution is halted. The run appears as follows.

```
10                   100                  1000
11                   121                  1331
12                   144                  1728
13                   169                  2197
14                   196                  2744
15                   225                  3375
16                   256                  4096
17                   289                  4913
18                   324                  5832
19                   361                  6859
20                   400                  8000
```

Omitting the END Statement

In previously written programs, the last statement has been END. In this one, the END statement was omitted. In both cases, the computer halted after executing the last statement of the program.

Some computers require an END statement, others do not; some will print the line number of the last line executed, others will not. You should be able to discover quite easily for yourself the option your computer provides.

Increment Control

In the preceding example, the increment for the variable I was +1. The illustration is easily modified for increments other than 1. For example, for a step size of .5, the only change is to modify line 10 as follows:

```
10 FOR I=10 TO 20 STEP .5
```

The program and run appear as follows.

```
10 FOR I=10 TO 20 STEP .5
20 PRINT I,,I^2,,I^3
30 NEXT I

10                   100                  1000
10.5000              110.250              1157.63
11                   121                  1331
11.5000              132.250              1520.88
12                   144                  1728
12.5000              156.250              1953.13
13                   169                  2197
13.5000              182.250              2460.38
14                   196                  2744
14.5000              210.250              3048.63
15                   225                  3375
15.5000              240.250              3723.88
16                   256                  4096
16.5000              272.250              4492.13
17                   289                  4913
17.5000              306.250              5359.38
18                   324                  5832
18.5000              342.250              6331.63
19                   361                  6859
19.5000              380.250              7414.88
20                   400                  8000
```

Another variant is to use a decrement rather than an increment for the step size. For example, we could begin with 20 and decrease by steps of .5 to 10. Line 10 would then be written

```
FOR I=20 TO 10 STEP -.5
```

The listing and output would be as follows.

```
10 FOR I=20 TO 10 STEP -.5
20 PRINT I,,I^2,,I^3
30 NEXT I
```

```
20                        400                       8000
19.5000                   380.250                   7414.88
19                        361                       6859
18.5000                   342.250                   6331.63
18                        324                       5832
17.5000                   306.250                   5359.38
17                        289                       4913
16.5000                   272.250                   4492.13
16                        256                       4096
15.5000                   240.250                   3723.88
15                        225                       3375
14.5000                   210.250                   3048.63
14                        196                       2744
13.5000                   182.250                   2460.38
13                        169                       2197
12.5000                   156.250                   1953.13
12                        144                       1728
11.5000                   132.250                   1520.88
11                        121                       1331
10.5000                   110.250                   1157.63
10                        100                       1000
```

John's Future Value of an Investment

Fortified with his newly gained knowledge, John examines his old flow chart and draws a new one (Figure 6-2) incorporating Lucy's suggested logic. The several components of the flow chart are translated into code, producing the following program.

```
10 REM: THIS PROGRAM CALCULATES INTEREST ON A DEPOSIT AS A
20 REM: BANK MIGHT DO IT. AT THE END OF EACH PERIOD, THE INTEREST IS
30 REM: CALCULATED, TRUNCATED TO THE PENNY AND CREDITED TO THE
40 REM: ACCOUNT.  THE EFFECT OF THE TRUNCATION IS CUMULATIVE AND
50 REM: THE FUTURE VALUE WILL BE SLIGHTLY DIFFERENT FROM THAT
60 REM: CALCULATED WITHOUT TRUNCATION.
70 REM: THIS SECTION ASKS FOR THE INPUT DATA
80 PRINT "INITIAL DEPOSIT"; & INPUT P
90 PRINT "INTEREST RATE"; & INPUT I
100 PRINT "FREQUENCY INTEREST COMPOUNDED"; & INPUT K
110 PRINT "HOW MANY YEARS"; & INPUT Y
120 REM: THIS SECTION CALCULATES AND PRINTS THE AMOUNT ON DEPOSIT
130 REM: AT THE END OF EACH INTEREST PERIOD.
140 Q=P
150 FOR J=1 TO Y*K
160 X=Q*(I/100/K)
170 X=INT(X*100)/100
180 Q=Q+X
190 PRINT "THE BALANCE AT THE END OF PERIOD"J" ="Q
200 NEXT J
210 REM: WE CALCULATE THE FUTURE VALUE EXACTLY.
220 PRINT & PRINT "EXACT VALUE =";
230 PRINT P*(1+I/100/K)^(Y*K)
240 END
```

John's first run appears as follows.

```
INITIAL DEPOSIT   ?1000
INTEREST RATE   ?7
FREQUENCY INTEREST COMPOUNDED   ?4
HOW MANY YEARS  ?1
THE BALANCE AT THE END OF PERIOD 1 = 1017.49
THE BALANCE AT THE END OF PERIOD 2 = 1035.29
THE BALANCE AT THE END OF PERIOD 3 = 1053.40
THE BALANCE AT THE END OF PERIOD 4 = 1071.83

EXACT VALUE =     1071.86
```

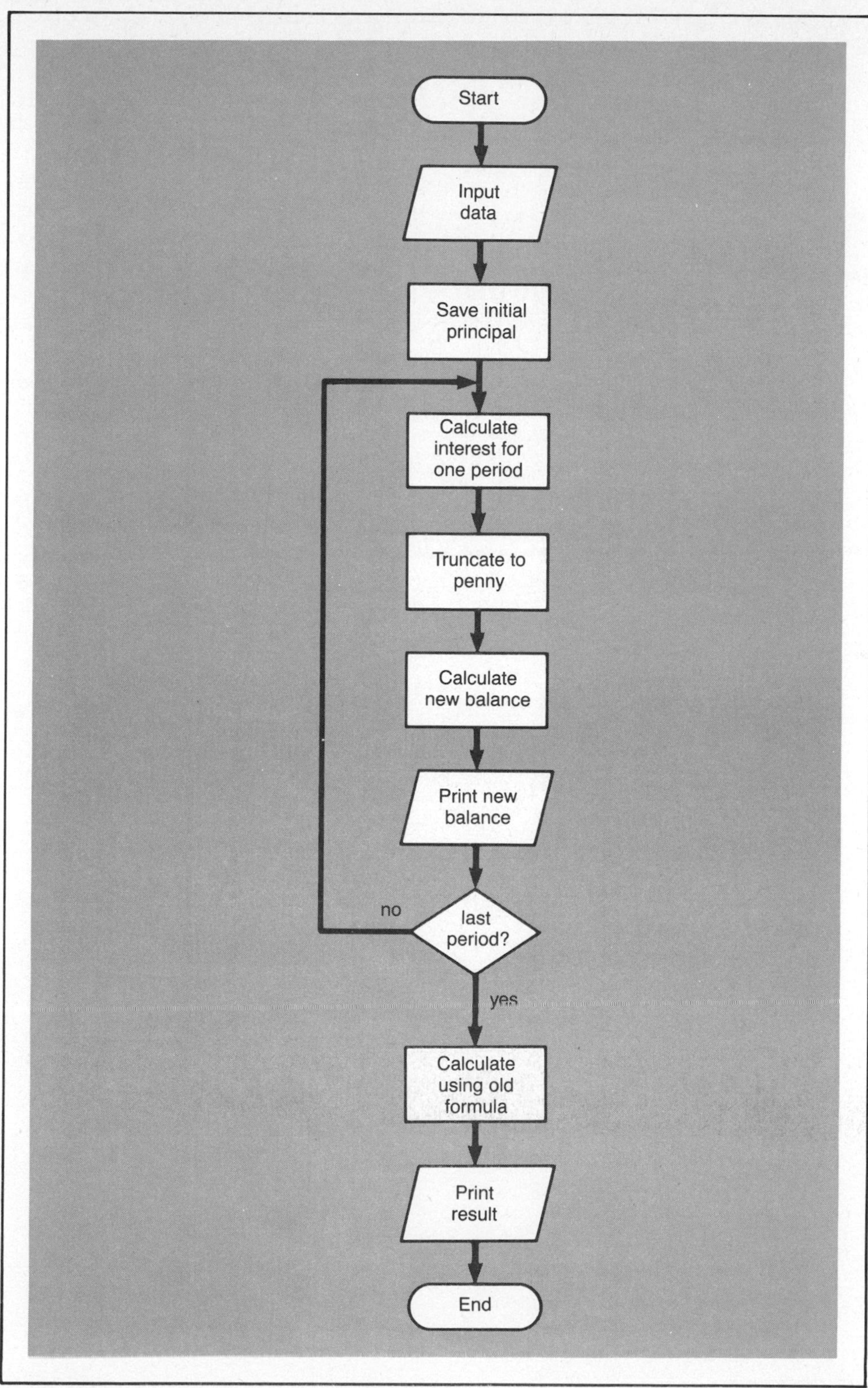

FIGURE 6-2

Multiple Statements Per Line In John's new program, note that the data are requested and input in lines 80–110. Each line contains two BASIC statements, the first a PRINT statement, the second an INPUT. Multiple BASIC statements may be typed on one line; the computer recognizes the second and subsequent ones when it encounters the ampersand, &.[3] Typing multiple statements on one line is a matter of personal preference; it was done in this program because of the intimate link between each PRINT statement and the following INPUT. The primary disadvantage is that it is impossible to refer directly to the second statement; because references within a program are to line numbers only, the computer must always first execute the leading statement.

Omitting LET Look again at John's new program. Because the principal changes at the end of each interest period and it is necessary to remember the original amount, a copy is made of it (line 140). It is this copy that is updated after each interest period. Note that lines 140 and 160–180 are assignment instructions but that the word LET has been omitted. On most computers, it is not necessary to include LET in the assignment statement. Therefore, we shall not use it in the future except for emphasis.

The Main Loop The loop in this program is contained between lines 150 and 200. In line 150, the variable J is a dummy variable in that it has no role in the subsequent computation; it is used only to keep track of the number of interest periods as the program progresses through them. Also, note that the last value of J is specified by the BASIC expression Y*K rather than by an explicit number. The same option exists for the first value. When STEP is omitted, the computer assumes that you want the value 1 (referred to as the default value); any other step size must be given explicitly. In line 160, the interest for the period is calculated; in line 170, it is truncated to the penny; in line 180, the new balance is determined. Line 190 parallels the posting as it might appear in John's passbook.

Multiple FOR—NEXT— Statements

Assume you want to print a multiplication table for two variables, A and B. The variable A is to assume values 1 through 4; B is to assume values 1 through 3. A program and run that does this follows:

```
10 FOR A=1 TO 4
20 FOR B=1 TO 3
30 LET C=A*B
40 PRINT "A="A,"B="B,"C="C
50 NEXT B
60 NEXT A
70 PRINT "DONE"
80 END
```

```
A= 1          B= 1          C= 1
A= 1          B= 2          C= 2
A= 1          B= 3          C= 3
A= 2          B= 1          C= 2
A= 2          B= 2          C= 4
A= 2          B= 3          C= 6
A= 3          B= 1          C= 3
A= 3          B= 2          C= 6
A= 3          B= 3          C= 9
A= 4          B= 1          C= 4
A= 4          B= 2          C= 8
A= 4          B= 3          C= 12
DONE
```

The significant feature of this program is the nesting of the two FOR—NEXT— statements. Observe that both the FOR— and the NEXT— statements for the variable B lie between the FOR—and the NEXT—statements for the variable A. Furthermore, the

[3] Some computers use the backslash, others accept both.

output is instructive in that it shows that when a double loop is executed, first, the outer loop takes its initial value, A = 1, then the inner loop runs through all its assigned values, B = 1, 2 and 3. When the inner loop is finished, control is returned to the outer loop and its index is incremented, in this case, A = 2. The inner loop again runs through all its assigned values. Control returns to the outer loop and the index is incremented again, A = 3, and the inner loop runs through all its assigned values. Again back to the outer loop, and A = 4; to the inner loop, and B = 1, 2, and 3. At this point, control is returned to the outer loop, and the computer, recognizing that the final value of A has been used, proceeds to execute the next instruction, in this case, line 70.

When more than two loops are nested, the same principles apply. First, both the FOR— statement and the NEXT— statement for an inner loop must lie between the FOR— and the NEXT— statements for an outer loop. Second, all outer loops are initialized to their first values, and then the innermost loop runs through all its values. The index of the second-to-the-innermost loop is incremented, and the innermost loop runs through all its values. This continues until the index of the second-to-the-innermost loop has run through all its values, at which point the index of the third-to-the-innermost loop is incremented; the whole procedure involving the two innermost loops repeats. This method for incrementing each index continues until the outermost loop has run through all its values; control is then transferred to the statement following the NEXT statement of the outermost loop.

If multiple loops are improperly nested, an error message is printed. For example:

```
10 FOR A=1 TO 4
20 FOR B =1 TO 3
30 LET C=A*B
40 PRINT,"A="A,"B="B,"C="C
50 NEXT A
60 NEXT B
70 PRINT, "DONE"
80 END
```

```
50 FOR-NEXT ERR
60 FOR-NEXT ERR
```

The error message occurred because the B loop is not nested within the A loop.

An Application of Nested Loops to Numerical Cryptograms

Numerical cryptograms are regarded by some people as challenging recreational puzzles. A numerical cryptogram is a formula containing several letters for which digits must be found that, when substituted for the letters, yield a correct arithmetic result. For example, find four digits A, B, C, and D so that the four-digit number ABCD = $(A + BC + D)^2$. Using mathematical theory and deductive reasoning to solve this is difficult; the computer provides another method: brute force.

The computer is to test all 10,000 possible combinations of the digits 0 to 9 that can occur in a four-digit number and discover which, if any, work. First, we shall review decimal notation. The letters A, B, C, and D represent digits; the notation ABCD means the integer $A*10^3 + B*10^2 + C*10 + D$. Similarly, the notation BC means the integer $B*10 + C$.

Let each of the symbols A, B, C, and D be replaced, in some orderly way, by one of the digits 0, 1, . . . , 9 and have the computer test

$$A*10^3 + B*10^2 + C*10 + D = (A + B*10 + C + D)^2$$

If it works, the program is to print the values of A, B, C, and D and continue to the next case; if not, the program continues to the next case. A flag is inserted to indicate that all possibilities have been tested. The flow chart in Figure 6-3 graphically illustrates these conditions. A program and run reflecting the intent of the logic and the flow chart follow.

```
10 REM: THIS PROGRAM USES BRUTE FORCE TO DETERMINE THE VALUES OF A,B,C,D
20 REM: FOR WHICH ABCD=(A+BC+D)^2
30 FOR A=0 TO 9
40 FOR B=0 TO 9
50 FOR C=0 TO 9
60 FOR D=0 TO 9
70 IF (A+B*10+C+D)^2=A*10^3+B*10^2+C*10+D THEN 250
80 NEXT D
90 NEXT C
100 NEXT B
110 NEXT A
120 PRINT
130 PRINT "DONE"
140 GOTO 280
250 PRINT
260 PRINT "A="A,"B="B,"C="C,"D="D
270 GOTO 80
280 END
```

FIGURE 6-3

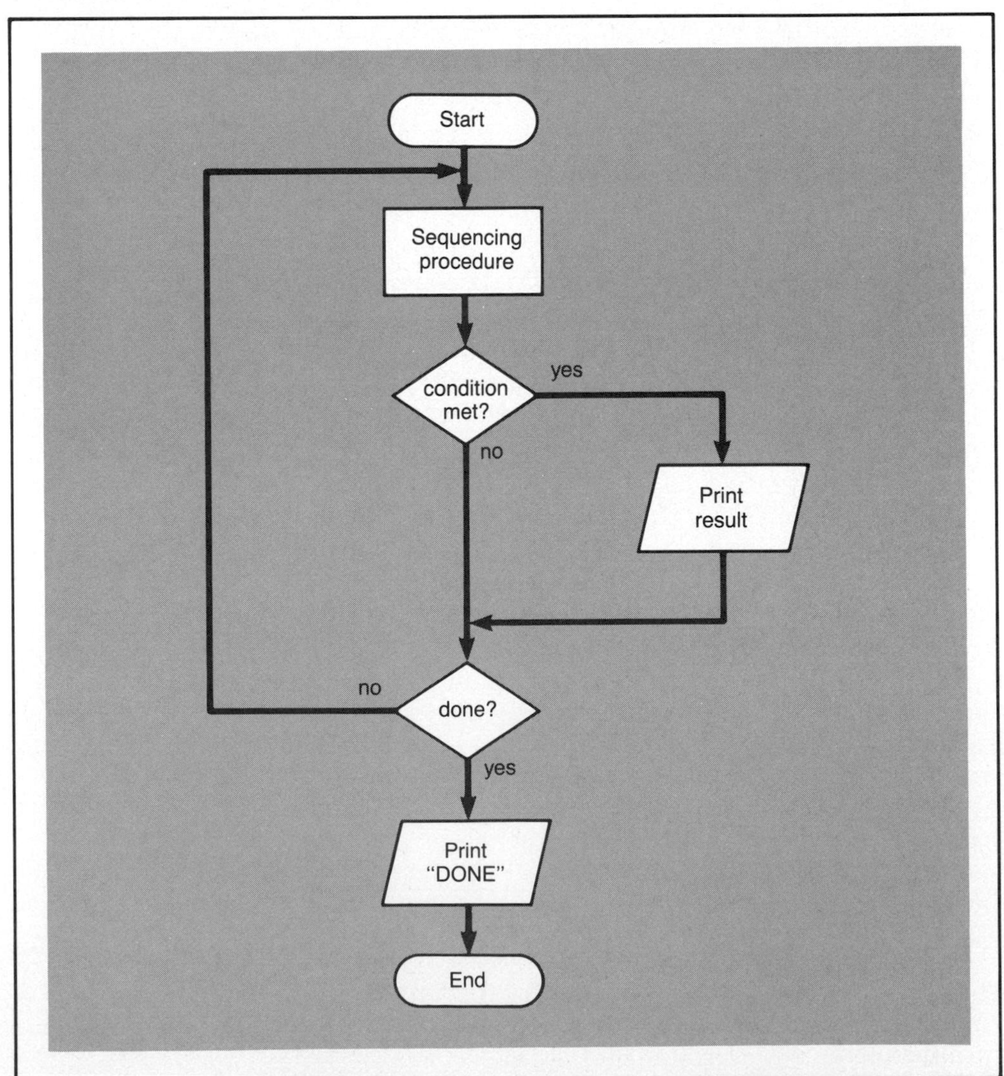

```
A= 0            B= 0            C= 0            D= 0

A= 0            B= 0            C= 0            D= 1

A= 0            B= 0            C= 8            D= 1

A= 0            B= 1            C= 0            D= 0

A= 1            B= 2            C= 9            D= 6

A= 6            B= 7            C= 2            D= 4

DONE
```

Of the six correct answers to this problem, the largest four-digit number is 6724. Check for yourself that $6724 = (6 + 72 + 4)^2$.

GOTO and STOP

The points of interest in the program are the multiple FOR—NEXT— loops and the introduction of another BASIC language statement, the unconditional GOTO (line number). When GOTO (line number) is encountered, the computer executes it without reservation; control is transferred to the specified line number and the program continues from that point.

The GOTO statement was used twice in this program. An alternative program would substitute the BASIC language instruction STOP in line 140. With this change made, the program is listed and run in the following illustration.

```
10 REM: THIS PROGRAM USES BRUTE FORCE TO DETERMINE THE VALUES OF A,B,C,D
20 REM: FOR WHICH ABCD=(A+BC+D)^2
30 FOR A=0 TO 9
40 FOR B=0 TO 9
50 FOR C=0 TO 9
60 FOR D=0 TO 9
70 IF (A+B*10+C+D)^2=A*10^3+B*10^2+C*10+D THEN 250
80 NEXT D
90 NEXT C
100 NEXT B
110 NEXT A
120 PRINT
130 PRINT "DONE"
140 STOP
250 PRINT
260 PRINT "A="A,"B="B,"C="C,"D="D
270 GOTO 80
280 END
```

```
A= 0            B= 0            C= 0            D= 0

A= 0            B= 0            C= 0            D= 1

A= 0            B= 0            C= 8            D= 1

A= 0            B= 1            C= 0            D= 0

A= 1            B= 2            C= 9            D= 6

A= 6            B= 7            C= 2            D= 4

DONE
```

When STOP is encountered, the execution of the program terminates. The STOP statement generally is used when there are alternative ways a program can terminate. Because logically parallel paths through a program can only be entered sequentially, there must be some way to stop the program when it has logically terminated but executable statements occur further along. This situation occurs here; the two lines of code

120 and 130 and the two lines of code 250 and 260 cannot physically occupy the same position in the program, one must precede the other. And yet, conceivably, the program could terminate after either set is executed. Thus, when the program is logically finished, at line 140, lines 250–270 are not executed by using either GOTO or STOP.

Illustration: A Diophantine Equation

A "Diophantine" equation is a polynomial equation for which the unknowns are to be rational numbers. An illustration that requires only minor modification to the preceding sequence of instructions asks that you find four digits A, B, C, and D such that (A^B)*(C^D) = ABCD. A problem, previously raised, may arise. How does your computer handle 0^0? Some interpret it as zero, others as one. It may happen that if you simply change line 70 in the program given in our previous example (page 87) to reflect the new algebraic condition, you may get a pragmatic error message that stems from the characteristics of your computer. Should this happen, run the A and C loops from 1 to 9 instead of from 0 to 9. This will obviate the difficulty.

```
10 REM: THIS PROGRAM USES BRUTE FORCE TO DETERMINE THE VALUES OF A,B,C,D
20 REM: FOR WHICH (A^B)*(C^D)=ABCD
30 FOR A=1 TO 9
40 FOR B=0 TO 9
50 FOR C=1 TO 9
60 FOR D=0 TO 9
70 IF (A^B)*(C^D)=A*10^3+B*10^2+C*10+D THEN 250
80 NEXT D
90 NEXT C
100 NEXT B
110 NEXT A
120 PRINT
130 PRINT "DONE"
140 STOP
250 PRINT
260 PRINT "A="A,"B="B,"C="C,"D="D
270 GOTO 80
280 END
```

```
A= 2            B= 5            C= 9            D= 2

DONE
```

Illustrations

The following examples illustrate computer solutions for a variety of problems. They are intended to help you gain insight into solutions to similar ones. You may, however, skim or omit this section without loss of continuity with the material still to be presented.

SEND + MORE = MONEY

While the number of numerical cryptograms is legion, perhaps the one seen most often is the following:

```
 SEND
 MORE
-----
MONEY
```

The problem is to replace each letter by a digit, different letters by different digits, and create an example in addition.

The complete analysis of this cryptogram without using a computer is not difficult; however, the purpose is to write a program that, although obvious and naive, solves it.

First, observe that eight different letters are used. Thus, a computer program that attempts to find all possible answers for this cryptogram would contain eight nested loops. The equation

SEND + MORE = MONEY

may be rewritten

MONEY − SEND − MORE = 0

and, when translated into an arithmetic form understandable to the computer, becomes

M*10^4+(O−S−M)*10^3+(N−E−O)*10^2+(E−N−R)*10+(Y−D−E)=0

The flow diagram in Figure 6-3 (page 86) suffices; the program follows.

```
10 REM: THE PURPOSE OF THIS PROGRAM IS TO SOLVE THE CRYPTOGRAM
20 REM:          SEND
30 REM:          MORE
40 REM:         -----
50 REM:         MONEY
60 FOR M=0 TO 9
70 FOR O=0 TO 9
80 FOR Y=0 TO 9
90 FOR E=0 TO 9
100 FOR N=0 TO 9
110 FOR D=0 TO 9
120 FOR R=0 TO9
130 FOR S=0 TO 9
140 IF M*10^4+(O-S-M)*10^3+(N-E-O)*10^2+(E-N-R)*10+(Y-D-E)=0 THEN 260
150 NEXT S
160 NEXT R
170 NEXT D
180 NEXT N
190 NEXT E
200 NEXT Y
210 NEXT O
220 NEXT M
230 PRINT
240 PRINT "DONE"
250 STOP
260 PRINT
270 PRINT "              "S*10^3+E*10^2+N*10+D
280 PRINT "              "M*10^3+O*10^2+R*10+E
290 PRINT "             -----"
300 PRINT "             "M*10^4+O*10^3+N*10^2+E*10+Y
310 PRINT
320 PRINT
330 GOTO 150
340 END
```

Number of Cases Trouble arises when this program is to be run. If all eight variables assume all 10 possible values, then the number of cases the computer is to examine is 10^8, or 100 million. While a computer is thought of as working in the microsecond range, that is, capable of performing certain operations in one microsecond or less, so that a hundred million operations require only one hundred seconds, or less than two minutes, the operations performed at this speed are the most fundamental ones. Each operation in this particular program, however, is a combination of many such elementary ones and thus, we should not expect the computer to make the 100 million different comparisons in less than two minutes.

We may reduce the time required to solve the cryptogram with a little human reasonableness. First, the loops for M and S need not go from 0 to 9 but only from 1 to 9, because if either M or S is equal to zero, the flavor of the problem is lost. Second, M must be equal to one. Whenever any two digits are added, their sum is between 0 and 18. When the sum is less than 10, the carry to the next higher place is zero; when the sum is 10 or greater, the carry to the next place is 1. Since M=0 is excluded, it must be that M=1. (Although this type of reasoning, properly continued, will solve the cryptogram, we shall take a different tack. We shall let the computer enumerate and test the remaining cases.) Thus far, the number of cases to be tested has been reduced from 10^8 to $9*10^6$—quite a saving.

On examining the program, we can see that most of the time will be spent executing line 140. Can some of this time be saved? Because the only solutions of interest are those for which different digits correspond to different letters, there is no point in evaluating line 140 when this condition fails. Thus, we want the program to skip line 140 if two letters have the same numerical value. To accomplish this, it is better to redraw the flow chart in Figure 6-3, although it is only the box "Sequencing procedure" that requires change. A new flow chart appears in Figure 6-4.

How shall we modify the program to reflect these changes? First, we change line 60 to read LET M=1, and delete line 220. Second, in line 130, we set the S loop to run from 2 to 9; we know that S ≠ 0, 1. The major changes, however, are to be the additional instructions that cause the program to skip unnecessary comparisons; these new instructions will be tests to determine if two of the variables are assigned the same value. The

FIGURE 6-4

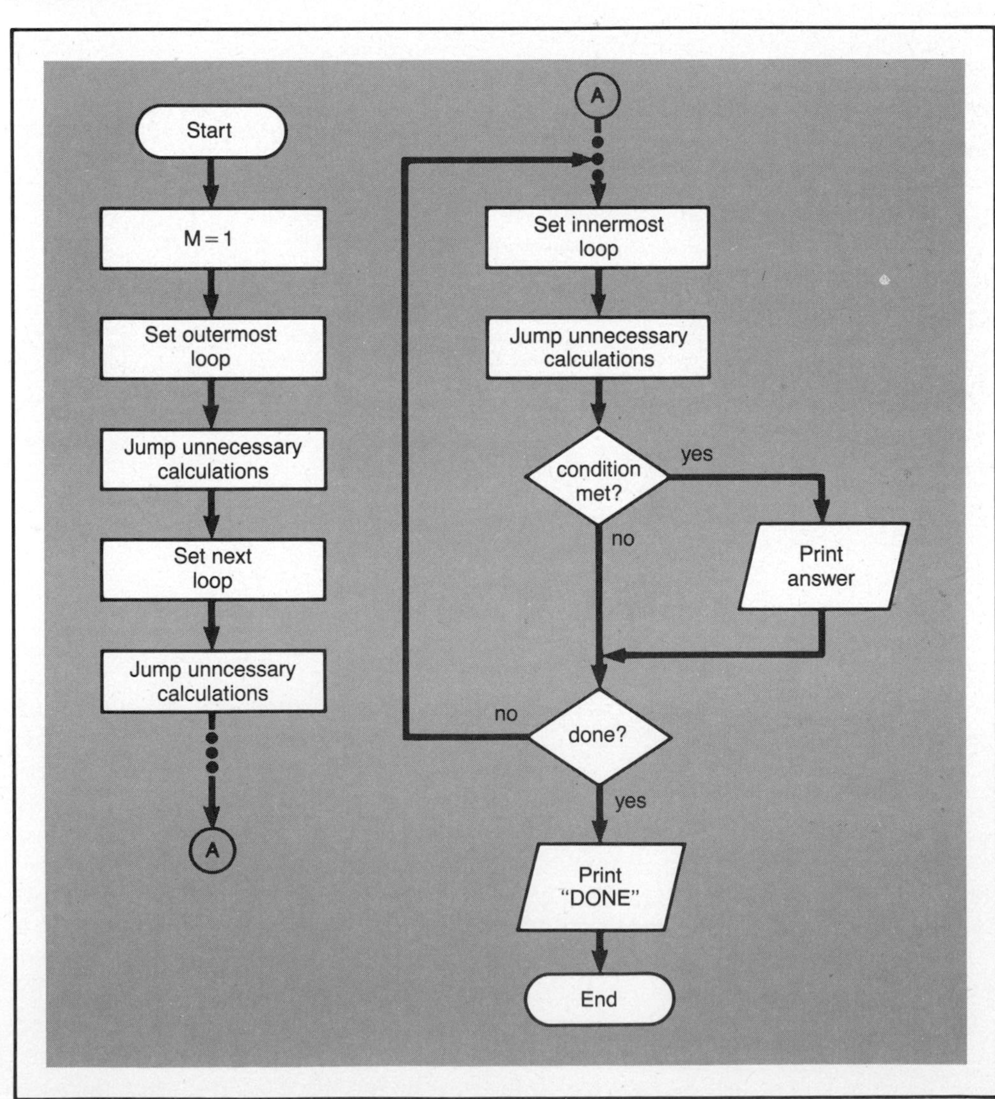

specific test used can best be understood from a typical example. Suppose there are four variables, A, B, C, and D, and the program is to decide if, at any time during execution, B=A or C=A or D=A. We could use the conditional construction

```
IF B=A THEN —
IF C=A THEN —
IF D=A THEN —
```

This, however, requires three program steps and three comparisons. Is there a shorter way? The expression (A−B)*(A−C)*(A−D) is equal to zero if and only if at least one of the three factors is zero or, equivalently, if B or C or D equals A. It is this construction that is used.

Between lines 70 and 80, insert

```
75 IF (O−1)=0 THEN 210
```

This says that if the variable O=1 (the value of M), there is no point in looking at this case; go to the next value for O (line 210).

Between lines 80 and 90, insert:

```
85 IF (Y−1)*(Y−O)=0 THEN 200
```

This says that if Y = M = 1 or if Y = O, there is no point in looking at this case; go to the next value of Y (line 200).

The appropriate insertions for the other variables are made at lines 95, 105, 115, 125, and 135.

After the insertions are made, the program is renumbered to look like this:

```
10 REM: THE PURPOSE OF THIS PROGRAM IS TO SOLVE THE CRYPTOGRAM
20 REM:          SEND
30 REM:          MORE
40 REM:         -----
50 REM:         MONEY
60 LET M=1
70 FOR O=0 TO 9
80 IF (O-1)=0 THEN 280
90 FOR Y=0 TO 9
100 IF (Y-1)*(Y-O)=0 THEN 270
110 FOR E=0 TO 9
120 IF (E-1)*(E-O)*(E-Y)=0 THEN 260
130 FOR N=0 TO 9
140 IF (N-1)*(N-O)*(N-Y)*(N-E)=0 THEN 250
150 FOR D=0 TO 9
160 IF (D-1)*(D-O)*(D-Y)*(D-E)*(D-N)=0 THEN 240
170 FOR R=0 TO9
180 IF (R-1)*(R-O)*(R-Y)*(R-E)*(R-N)*(R-D)=0 THEN 230
190 FOR S=2 TO 9
200 IF (S-O)*(S-Y)*(S-E)*(S-N)*(S-D)*(S-R)=0 THEN 220
210 IF M*10^4+(O-S-M)*10^3+(N-E-O)*10^2+(E-N-R)*10+(Y-D-E)=0 THEN 320
220 NEXT S
230 NEXT R
240 NEXT D
250 NEXT N
260 NEXT E
270 NEXT Y
280 NEXT O
290 PRINT
300 PRINT "DONE"
310 STOP
320 PRINT
330 PRINT "                    "S*10^3+E*10^2+N*10+D
340 PRINT "                    "M*10^3+O*10^2+R*10+E
350 PRINT "                    -----"
360 PRINT "                   "M*10^4+O*10^3+N*10^2+E*10+Y
```

```
370 PRINT
380 PRINT
390 GOTO 220
400 END
```

```
                 9567
                 1085
                -----
                10652


DONE
```

Observe that at line 60, M = 1. The FOR part for the FOR—NEXT— loops are set for each of the remaining variables in lines 70, 90, 110, 130, 150, 170, and 190. To skip the unnecessary comparisons, the appropriate conditional transfers appear in lines 80, 100, 120, 140, 160, 180, and 200.

When the number of cases was reduced in this way, the run time on a medium-sized computer was approximately 5 minutes. This time will vary, depending on the computer on which the program is run, as well as, if it is a time-sharing computer, the number of other users being served simultaneously. When run on a second, larger computer, the corresponding run time was approximately 1.5 minutes.

Counting the Number of Cases Although the number of times line 210 was tested was reduced considerably from 100 million, the exact number of times it was executed is not known. Although we could trace the logic of the program and try to determine this, which would be quite a formidable task, an easier way is to have the program keep track. We can introduce a counter into the program so that each time line 210 is executed, the counter is increased by 1. Just before the program stops, the counter is displayed. Thus, the number of times line 210 was executed is determined.

```
10 REM: THE PURPOSE OF THIS PROGRAM IS TO SOLVE THE CRYPTOGRAM
20 REM:          SEND
30 REM:          MORE
40 REM:         -----
50 REM:         MONEY
55 I=0
60 LET M=1
70 FOR O=0 TO 9
80 IF (O-1)=0 THEN 280
90 FOR Y=0 TO 9
100 IF (Y-1)*(Y-O)=0 THEN 270
110 FOR E=0 TO 9
120 IF (E-1)*(E-O)*(E-Y)=0 THEN 260
130 FOR N=0 TO 9
140 IF (N-1)*(N-O)*(N-Y)*(N-E)=0 THEN 250
150 FOR D=0 TO 9
160 IF (D-1)*(D-O)*(D-Y)*(D-E)*(D-N)=0 THEN 240
170 FOR R=0 TO 9
180 IF (R-1)*(R-O)*(R-Y)*(R-E)*(R-N)*(R-D)=0 THEN 230
190 FOR S=2 TO 9
200 IF (S-O)*(S-Y)*(S-E)*(S-N)*(S-D)*(S-R)=0 THEN 220
205 I=I+1
210 IF M*10^4+(O-S-M)*10^3+(N-E-O)*10^2+(E-N-R)*10+(Y-D-E)=0 THEN 320
220 NEXT S
230 NEXT R
240 NEXT D
250 NEXT N
260 NEXT E
270 NEXT Y
280 NEXT O
290 PRINT
300 PRINT "DONE"
```

```
305 PRINT "NUMBER OF LOOPS=" I
310 STOP
320 PRINT
330 PRINT "                    "S*10^3+E*10^2+N*10+D
340 PRINT "                    "M*10^3+O*10^2+R*10+E
350 PRINT "                    -----"
360 PRINT "                   "M*10^4+O*10^3+N*10^2+E*10+Y
370 PRINT
380 PRINT
390 GOTO 220
400 END
```

```
 9567
 1085
-----
10652


DONE
NUMBER OF LOOPS= 161280
```

The counter is given the variable name I and is initialized (set equal to zero) at line 55. Just before line 210 is executed, I is increased by 1, line 205. The number of times that line 210 is executed is accumulated in the counter I and is printed at line 305 immediately preceding STOP. As we can see from the run, line 210 was executed 161,280 times. Since the program ran in about 1.5 minutes, roughly 100,000 comparisons were made in 1 minute. The time needed to have made the 100 million tests, therefore, would have been about 16 hours.

Two More Cryptograms

A variant of the preceding problem is the cryptogram

```
 SAVE
 MORE
-----
MONEY
```

In this example, nine digits are used, and you should expect that if the preceding program is modified and executed, the run time should be approximately 10 times greater, perhaps about 15 minutes.

For those who take the time and make the effort to solve it, there are four answers. To verify that you have found these, examine that solution for which SAVE is smallest and MORE is largest. Then look at page YAR; the four answers are given in a footnote.

For the cryptogram

```
 SEND
 MORE
 GOLD
-----
MONEY
```

all 10 digits are needed. If the number of nested loops can be reduced to no more than seven or eight, it would not be unreasonable to solve it by enumerating the remaining possibilities. While the computer is fast, it is not a jinni; human thought and analysis are still needed to reduce intractable problems to a level at which the computer may help solve them.

An Alternative Procedure for Solving Numerical Cryptograms

There is an alternative method, more arithmetic, for solving cryptograms. We shall describe it as it applies to SEND + MORE = MONEY. The various steps relate to the corresponding line numbers in the program that follows (page 95). Although it is by no means significant, we shall use the knowledge that M = 1 (line 10) and S ≠ 0,1 (line 240); it shortens the execution time.

The units' column in the addition translates into the equation (line 60)

```
Y=D+E
```

If D successively assumes values from 0 to 9 excluding 1 (which is the value of M) (lines 20 and 30), and E assumes values from 0 to 9 excluding 1 and the previously selected value for D (lines 40 and 50), then the values assigned to Y include only those of possible interest. The values of Y are between 0 and 18. Examine the digit in the units' place and the digit in the tens' place separately. The digit in the tens' place,

```
Y1=INT(Y/10)    (line 70)
```

will be either 0 or 1 and tells you what to carry from the units' to the tens' place.

```
Y2=Y-Y1*10    (line 80)
```

is the digit in the units' place. If Y2 = 1 or Y2 = D or Y2 = E—one of the previously assigned values—this case is to be excluded and you are to proceed immediately to the next value of E (line 90).

The tens' column of the original problem translates into

```
E1=N+R+carry from the ones' column.
```

The symbol E1 is used here because E has been used previously; you must determine if the digit in the units' place of E1 is E. If it is, the program continues; if not, the program jumps to the next possibility. Before this is done, however, the appropriate loops for N and R are set.

The loop for N is set in line 100; in line 110, those values of N that have been assigned to prior variables are excluded. Similarly, line 120 sets the loop for R and line 130 excludes those values of R that have been assigned to prior variables.

Now, to line 140 and the equation

```
E1=N+R+Y1
```

where Y1 is the carry from the ones' column. Since E1 may be greater than 9, it is necessary to determine both its units' digit and its tens' digit. This is done in lines 150 and 160; E2 is the digit in the tens' place, and E3 is the digit in the ones' place. The value of E3 must be the same as the value of E previously stored; if not, the previously picked values of the variables cannot lead to a solution and the program should proceed to the next possibility. This condition is tested in line 170.

The possibilities for addition in the hundreds' place are examined next.

```
N1=E+O+carry from the tens' column
```

Since N has been used, the new variable N1 is introduced; you must find out if the digit in the units' place of N1 is equal to N. Since the variable name O has not been used before, it is set into a loop, lines 180 and 360; those values that have been used up to this point are excluded in line 190.

For N1, the digit in the tens' place (call it N2) and the digit in the units' place (call it N3) are found. N3 is tested to see if it equals the previously assigned value of N (line 230). If not, it cannot be used and the program jumps to the next case, line 360.

Examine now the possibilities for addition in the thousands' place, remembering that M = 1 and that the carry from the hundreds' place is N2. Since O has been used, the symbol O1 is introduced:

O1 = S + 1 + N2 (line 260)

After setting the loop for S (line 240) (remember S ≠ 0, 1), exclude those values used by the other variables (line 250). In lines 270 and 280 the digit in the tens' place and the digit in the ones' place of O1 are determined. The digit in the tens' place, O2, must be M, that is, 1 (lines 290) and the digit in the ones' place must be the value previously assigned to O (line 300). If either of these conditions fails, the program jumps to the next possibility.

If there are digits that may be assigned to all the variables with all the exclusions satisfied, these digits, with their appropriate assignment, solve the cryptogram. The printout, if there is any, is given in lines 310–340.

The program and run follow.

```
10 M=1
20 FOR D=Ø TO 9
30 IF (D-1)=Ø THEN 4ØØ
40 FOR E=Ø TO 9
50 IF (E-1)*(E-D)=Ø THEN 39Ø
60 Y=D+E
70 Y1=INT(Y/1Ø)
80 Y2=Y-Y1*1Ø
90 IF (Y2-E)*(Y2-D)*(Y2-1)=Ø THEN 39Ø
1ØØ FOR N=Ø TO 9
11Ø IF (N-1)*(N-D)*(N-E)*(N-Y2)=Ø THEN 38Ø
12Ø FOR R=Ø TO 9
13Ø IF (R-1)*(R-N)*(R-D)*(R-E)*(R-Y2)=Ø THEN 37Ø
14Ø E1=N+R+Y1
15Ø E2=INT(E1/1Ø)
16Ø E3=E1-E2*1Ø
17Ø IF E3<>E THEN 37Ø
18Ø FOR O=Ø TO 9
19Ø IF (O-1)*(O-R)*(O-N)*(O-D)*(O-E)*(O-Y2)=Ø THEN 36Ø
2ØØ N1=E+O+E2
21Ø N2=INT(N1/1Ø)
22Ø N3=N1-N2*1Ø
23Ø IF N3<>N THEN 36Ø
24Ø FOR S=2 TO 9
25Ø IF (S-O)*(S-R)*(S-N)*(S-D)*(S-E)*(S-Y2)=Ø THEN 35Ø
26Ø O1=S+1+N2
27Ø O2=INT(O1/1Ø)
28Ø O3=O1-O2*1Ø
29Ø IF O2-1<>Ø THEN 35Ø
3ØØ IF O3-O<>O THEN 35Ø
31Ø PRINT "          " S*1Ø^3+E*1Ø^2+N*1Ø+D
32Ø PRINT "          " M*1Ø^3+O*1Ø^2+R*1Ø+E
33Ø PRINT "          -----"
34Ø PRINT "         " M*1Ø^4+O*1Ø^3+N*1Ø^2+E*1Ø+Y2
35Ø NEXT S
36Ø NEXT O
37Ø NEXT R
38Ø NEXT N
39Ø NEXT E
4ØØ NEXT D
```

```
  9567
  1Ø85
 -----
 1Ø652
```

When this program was run, the execution time dropped from the previous program's 1.5 minutes to a few seconds.

Diophantine Equations: Hardy's Taxicab

C. P. Snow, in his foreword to G. H. Hardy's *A Mathematician's Apology,*[4] tells of Hardy's visit to his colleague and collaborator, Ramanujan in a hospital at Putney. "It was on one of those visits that there happened the incident of the taxicab number. Hardy had gone out to Putney by taxi, as usual his chosen method of conveyance. He went into the room where Ramanujan was lying. Hardy, always inept about introducing a conversation, said, probably without a greeting, and certainly as his first remark: 'I thought the number of my taxicab was ____. It seemed to me rather a dull number.' To which Ramanujan replied: 'No, Hardy! No, Hardy! It is a very interesting number. It is the smallest number expressible as the sum of two cubes in two different ways.' "

The license number of Hardy's taxicab can be found in the following way. Let the four numbers be X_1, X_2 and Y_1, Y_2, with $X_1^3 + X_2^3 = Y_1^3 + Y_2^3$. A search for possible values is to be made with the understanding that X_1 is to be the largest number. The number X_2 cannot be as large as X_1, for if it is, the left-hand side of the equation would be $2X_1^3$, and this implies that at least one of the two numbers Y_1 or Y_2, if these are unequal, would have to be greater than X_1, a contradiction. Thus, the largest that X_2 can be is $X_1 - 1$.

Similarly, Y_1 cannot be as large as X_1 for if $Y_1 = X_1$, then $Y_2 = X_2$, and clearly this is not a solution. Thus, the largest that Y_1 can be is $X_1 - 1$. Also, we can assume that $Y_2 \leqslant Y_1$. Furthermore, none of the numbers is zero, for if one were, say $X_2 = 0$, then the equation reduces to

$$X_1^3 = Y_1^3 + Y_2^3$$

which is known to have no integer solutions.

A program to find the taxicab's license number follows:

```
10 FOR X1=1 TO 100
20 FOR X2=1 TO X1-1
30 FOR Y1=1 TO X1-1
40 FOR Y2=1 TO Y1
50 IF X1^3+X2^3=Y1^3+Y2^3 THEN 500
60 NEXT Y2
70 NEXT Y1
80 NEXT X2
90 NEXT X1
500 PRINT X1;X2;X1^3+X2^3,,Y1;Y2;Y1^3+Y2^3


12    1    1729                              10    9    1729
```

Thus, the license number is found to be 1729, which can be represented two different ways as the sum of two cubes:

$$12^3 + 1^3 = 1729 = 10^3 + 9^3$$

Exercises

6.1 Serious consideration should be given to writing programs with a minimum of GOTO statements in order to simplify the logic and minimize the possibility of error. Refer to the program on page 86. Verify, by writing and running the program, that the modification of line 270 from

```
270 GOTO 80
```

[4]G. H. Hardy, *A Mathematician's Apology* (Cambridge: Cambridge University Press, 1967) p. 37.

to

```
270 IF (A−9)^2 + (B−9)^2 + (C−9)^2 + (D−9)^2 <> 0 then 80
```

leaves the answers unaltered. Remember that <> means "not equal to."

6.2 One of the fringe benefits offered employees of the Underseas Excavation Corporation is a retirement bonus based on length of service. Retirement is mandatory on June 30 following the 70th birthday; a check is presented to the employee on that date. Monies are deposited in a trust fund that pays 7.5 percent interest, compounded monthly; payments to the fund are $25, also made monthly. To explain the plan, the company provides a table (Table 6-1) showing each prospective employee the amount to be expected upon retirement provided he begins working for UEC at the age shown. Draw a flow diagram and write a computer program that produces this table. Allow for

TABLE 6-1
Underseas Excavation Corporation
Retirement Bonus

AGE	VALUE OF ANNUITY
20	$164,111.00
21	152,000.00
22	140,762.00
23	130,333.00
24	120,656.00
25	111,676.00
26	103,342.00
27	95,609.50
28	88,433.70
29	81.774.80
30	75,595.60
31	69,861.50
32	64,540.50
33	59,602.90
34	55,020.90
35	50,769.10
36	46,823.50
37	43,162.20
38	39,764.60
39	36,611.80
40	33,686.10
41	30,971.20
42	28,451.90
43	26,114.10
44	23,944.70
45	21,931.50
46	20,063.40
47	18,329.90
48	16,721.20
49	15,228.50
50	13,843.30
51	12,557.80
52	11,365.00
53	10,258.10
54	9230.96
55	8277.81
56	7393.31
57	6572.54
58	5810.90
59	5104.12
60	4448.26

different starting ages, different ages at which the table ends, different ages at which retirement takes place, different interest rates, and different amounts to be deposited each period. Although the frequency of compounding is the same as the frequency with which deposits are made, this number may change; it may be as high as 52 if the company has a weekly payroll, 26 if the payroll is biweekly, 24 if the payroll is semimonthly, and 12 if the payroll is monthly.

The following hints and notation may prove helpful. Let A equal the employee's starting age, also the age at which the table starts; let B equal the age at which the last entry is made into the table; let Z equal the retirement age. Then, Y=Z−A is the maximum number of years that an employee may be with the company, Y=Z−B will be the last entry in the table. Let R equal amount deposited each period, K equal the number of periods per year, I equal the nominal yearly interest rate, and S equal the final value of the annuity. The formula that relates these various quantities is:

```
S = R* ((1 + I/100/K)^(Y* K) - 1)/(I/100/K)
```

6.3 The Underseas Excavation Corporation is only one of several corporations that offer this type of retirement plan in their recruiting literature. The Seven Seas Exploration Corporation offers a similar plan; it differs only in that the interest rate is 7.25 percent. Underseas Search, Inc. offers a plan identical in all respects except that the interest rate is 7 percent.

The trade-off is as follows: UEC offers two weeks' vacation for the first three years of employment, three weeks after three years, and one month after seven full years of employment. SSEC offers one month of vacation to start, six weeks after eight years, and two months after fifteen years of service. USI offers three weeks the first year, then one additional day after each additional six months of service.

The Worldwide Employment Agency recruits for all three firms. In an effort to explain the different fringe benefits offered by the three companies, WEA prepared Table 6-2.

WEA ran the program of Exercise 6.2 three times, obtained the three lists, and then had a secretary prepare the table. Clearly, it is possible to modify the original program and have the table printed by the new version. Modify your flow diagram and your program from Exercise 6.2 to accomplish this.

6.4 Using the procedure illustrated on pages 93–95, solve the cryptogram:

```
 SEND
 MORE
 GOLD
-----
MONEY
```

6.5 Three integers (X, Y, Z) that solve the equation

$$Z^2 = X^2 + Y^2$$

are called a Pythagorean triple. Draw a flow chart and write a program that calculates all Pythagorean triples for Z=5 to Z=N and for which Y≤X≤Z. Your program should request as input a value for N, an integer greater than 5.

6.6 While there are no integer solutions to the equation

$$Z^3 = X1^3 + X2^3$$

there are integer solutions to the equation

$$Z^3 = X1^3 + X2^2 + X3^3$$

TABLE 6-2
Value of Annuity

AGE	UEC	SSEC	USI
20	$164,111.00	$149,452.00	$136,202.00
21	152,000.00	138,742.00	126,731.00
22	140,762.00	128,779.00	117,898.00
23	130,333.00	119,511.00	109,661.00
24	120,656.00	110,888.00	101,979.00
25	111,676.00	102,868.00	94,814.90
26	103,342.00	95,405.90	88,133.80
27	95,609.50	88,464.60	81,903.20
28	88,433.70	82,007.30	76,092.70
29	81,774.80	76,000.03	70,673.80
30	75,595.60	70,412.10	65,620.30
31	69,861.50	65,213.60	60,907.50
32	64,540.50	60,377.70	56,512.40
33	59,602.90	55,878.90	52,413.60
34	55,020.90	51,693.80	48,591.10
35	50,769.10	47,800.60	45,026.40
36	46,823.50	44,178.90	41,701.90
37	43,162.20	40,809.70	38,601.60
38	39,764.60	37,675.40	35,710.30
39	36,611.80	34,759.70	33,013.90
40	33,686.10	32,047.30	30,499.30
41	30,971.20	29,524.10	28,154.20
42	28,451.90	27,176.80	25,967.20
43	26,114.10	24,993.20	23,927.70
44	23,944.70	22,961.80	22,025.60
45	21,931.50	21,072.10	20,251.80
46	20,063.40	19,314.20	18,597.60
47	18,329.90	17,678.80	17,054.80
48	16,721.20	16,157.50	15,616.10
49	15,228.50	14,742.30	14,274.40
50	13,843.30	13,425.80	13,023.20
51	12,557.80	12,201.00	11,856.30
52	11,365.00	11,061.70	10,768.00
53	10,258.10	10,001.80	9,753.15
54	9,230.96	9,015.80	8,806.70
55	8,277.81	8,098.58	7,924.06
56	7,393.31	7,245.31	7,100.92
57	6,572.54	6,451.54	6,333.27
58	5,810.90	5,713.12	5,617.37
59	5,104.12	5,026.19	4,949.74
60	4,448.26	4,387.17	4,327.12

Draw a flow chart and write a program that exhibits all such quadruples for which $Z \leq 100$.

6.7 Most curves studied in mathematics—the straight line, the circle, the conics—are smooth and pleasing to the eye. Every once in a while, a pathological curve appears to excite our interest and suggest how much more there is to know. One such is the snowflake curve.

A triangle is a simple polygon of three sides, a quadrilateral is one of four sides. There are simple polygons of N sides where N is any positive integer. For each of these, both the perimeter and the area are finite. Also, the area and perimeter of a circle are both finite, as are the area and perimeter of an ellipse. The snowflake curve is pathological in that while the area within it is finite, its perimeter is infinite.

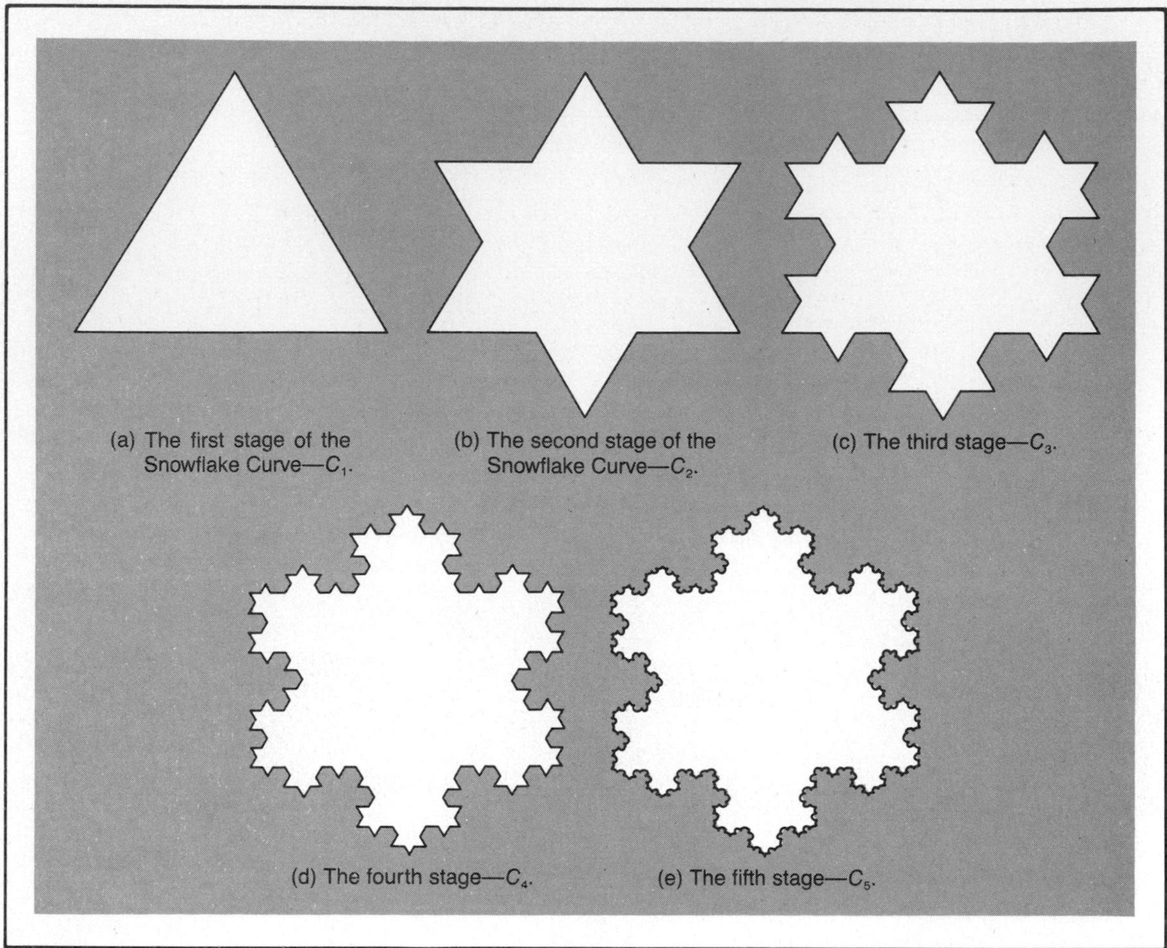

FIGURE 6-5

A snowflake curve is constructed as follows. Start with an equilateral triangle and let the length of each side be 1; call this curve C_1. Its perimeter is 3. Trisect each of the three sides, and on each of the middle thirds erect an equilateral triangle, pointing outward. Erase the three line segments common to the new and old triangles; call the resulting curve C_2. Its perimeter is $3+1$.

To construct C_3, on the middle third of each side of C_2 erect an equilateral triangle, pointing outward. Again, erase the 12 line segments common to the new and old figures; call the final curve C_3. Its perimeter is $3 + 1 + 4/3$. Repeat the process, erecting equilateral triangles pointing outward on each middle third of each side of C_3 and erase the parts common to the old and new figures; call the curve C_4. Its perimeter is $3 + 1 + 4/3 + (4/3)^2$. If the process is repeated until the curve C_n is constructed, its perimeter will be

$$3+1+\left(\frac{4}{3}\right)+\left(\frac{4}{3}\right)^2+\left(\frac{4}{3}\right)^3+\ldots+\left(\frac{4}{3}\right)^{n-2}$$

At successive stages, the perimeter of C_2 is obtained by adding to the perimeter of C_{n-1} a positive integral power of 4/3, a number that grows rapidly as the number of stages increases. The snowflake is defined as the limiting curve obtained from this construction as the number of stages approaches infinity; its perimeter is greater than any finite number, that is, it is infinite. See Figure 6-5.

From the construction, it is easily seen that the area within the snowflake curve is finite. In fact, since the original equilateral triangle had sides of length 1, the triangle can be inscribed in a circle of radius $\sqrt{3}/3$. Also, each C_n lies within this circle, and thus, its area is less than that of the circle, $\pi/3$. The snowflake curve also lies within the circle. Just as the perimeter of each C_n can be calculated, so can its area.

If the area of the original triangle is denoted by A_1, ($A_1 = (\sqrt{3}/4)L^2$, where L is the length of a side of the triangle), the area of C_2 is $A_1(1 + 3(1/3^2))$ and that of C_3 is $A_1(1 + 3(1/3)^2 + 4{\cdot}3(1/3)^4)$. The area of C_4 is equal to the area of $C_3 + C_3 + A_1(4^2 3(1/3)^6)$. The area of C_n is calculated recursively, that is, each C_n is computed from the one preceding it (from C_{n-1}). The area of C_n equals area of $C_{n-1} + A_1(4^{n-2}3(1/9^{n-1})$. As the number of sides increases, the area of C_n approaches $(8/5)A_1$, that is, $(8/5)(\sqrt{3}/4)L^2 = 2(\sqrt{3}/5)L^2$.

Draw a flow chart and write a computer program that does the following. For any positive number K, find the smallest integer N such that the perimeter of C_N is greater than K. Find the area within this C_N.

On READ/DATA, RESTORE, and ON— GOTO— Statements 7

In this chapter, we shall review and extend the properties of the BASIC statements LET and INPUT, which we used earlier to enter data into a program, and we shall introduce a third method for assigning a numerical value to a variable, which uses the pair of BASIC instructions READ and DATA. Examples, illustrating the use of READ and DATA, will be given. At times, you may want to modify the order in which the data are read; the supplementary instruction RESTORE will enable you to do so. We shall further enlarge your repertoire of BASIC instructions by introducing ON—GOTO—, a useful instruction when you are confronted by a decision process with multiple (more than two) possible outcomes. Finally, two more intrinsic BASIC functions, "the absolute value of X," ABS(X), and "the sign of X," SGN(X), will be described.

Thus far, we have used only the INPUT and LET statements to enter data into a program. Another mode for assigning numerical values to variables uses the pair of BASIC statements READ and DATA. When the amount of data is relatively small and static, LET may suffice; if the interactive characteristic of the system is to be stressed or the data to be entered are not known beforehand, INPUT may be the preferred mode. When the data are voluminous and the interactive capabilities are not needed, however, the READ/DATA instructions may be preferable. When the READ/DATA instructions are used, the data are supplied within the program, so that an entire program may be run without pause to request data from the user. Before examining the READ/DATA format, however, we shall complete our description of LET and INPUT.

More on LET

In Chapter 4, we assigned values to variables using the LET instruction. For example,

```
10 LET A= 7.53
```

One statement was used for each assignment. Later, we saw that the word LET may not be necessary. For computer systems that accept multiple statements on one line, we were able to write

```
10 A= 7.53 & B= −4.376
```

As previously noted, some systems use the ampersand, &, as the connector, some the backslash, /, some both. For assignment statements and for some computers, however, the use of either connector may not be mandatory; you may type

```
10 A= 7.53, B= -4.376
```

using the comma to separate the two assignments. In fact, you may go further. Again, with the limitation on connectors noted above, the three assignments

```
10 X=1
20 Y=3
30 Z=X+7-2*Y
```

may be written on one line:

```
10 X=1, Y=3 Z=X+7-2*Y
```

When multiple assignments are made on one line, the sequence in which the assignments are made must correspond to the order in which the variables are to be used. For example, if the above statement were written

```
10 X=1, Z=X+7-2*Y, Y=3
```

then, while 1 is assigned to X and 3 to Y, the value assigned to Z is uncertain since it depends on the value that was assigned to Y before 3 was assigned to Y.

More on INPUT

In earlier illustraions that called for the use of INPUT, only one variable per line was used. Multiple inputs per line are possible. Consider the following program that, when the height, length, and width are given, calculates the volume of a three-dimensional rectangular box.

```
10 PRINT
20 PRINT "ENTER HEIGHT, LENGTH AND WIDTH"
30 INPUT H,L,W
40 PRINT
50 PRINT "VOLUME="H*L*W
60 PRINT
70 PRINT "IF YOU WISH TO REPEAT, TYPE 1, OTHERWISE 0."
80 INPUT Q
90 IF Q=1 THEN 10
100 END
```

```
ENTER HEIGHT, LENGTH AND WIDTH
?2,3,4

VOLUME= 24

IF YOU WISH TO REPEAT, TYPE 1, OTHERWISE 0
?1

ENTER HEIGHT, LENGTH AND WIDTH
?1
ILLEGAL INPUT. RETYPE?1,2
ILLEGAL INPUT. RETYPE?1,2,3

VOLUME= 6
```

```
IF YOU WISH TO REPEAT, TYPE 1, OTHERWISE Ø
?1

ENTER HEIGHT, LENGTH AND WIDTH
?1 2 3
ILLEGAL INPUT. RETYPE?1,2,3

VOLUME= 6

IF YOU WISH TO REPEAT, TYPE 1, OTHERWISE Ø
?Ø
```

As you can see, line 30 asks for input values for the three variables H, L, and W. When the program was run, three values, separated by commas, were entered. Note that on this particular computer, when we tried to separate the three values any other way, by entering one at a time, or with spaces between them, the computer balked. On another computer, however, the data could be entered one at a time, or separated by spaces, or as before, separated by commas.

If a manual that goes into this level of detail is available for your computer, you will find the prescribed format there. Alternatively, simply repeating this exercise as an experiment will reveal how your computer functions.

The READ/DATA Statements

In addition to LET and INPUT, a third method for assigning numerical values to variables uses the READ/DATA instructions. Suppose you want to know the average of three numbers. If this is all that you want to know, then INPUT will suffice. If you wish to calculate the average many times, however, for many sets of three numbers, then the READ/DATA assignment mode may be preferred. In this way, you will not have to sit at the terminal while the program is run and wait for the computer to ask for your input. Examine the following program:

```
1Ø FOR I=1 TO 5
2Ø READ A,B,C
3Ø X=(A+B+C)/3
4Ø PRINT "A="A,"B="B,"C="C
5Ø PRINT "AVERAGE="X
6Ø PRINT
7Ø NEXT I
8Ø DATA 56,75,48
9Ø DATA 69,89,71,82,93,24
1ØØ DATA 75,66
11Ø DATA 57,48,39,47
12Ø END

A= 56          B= 75          C= 48
AVERAGE= 59.6667

A= 69          B= 89          C= 71
AVERAGE= 76.3333

A= 82          B= 93          C= 24
AVERAGE= 66.3333

A= 75          B= 66          C= 57
AVERAGE= 66

A= 48          B= 39          C= 47
AVERAGE= 44.6667
```

Lines 10 and 70 indicate that the calculation is to be repeated five times. Line 20 instructs the computer to read three numbers and assign them to the variables A, B, and C. Line 80 is the starting point at which the data are stored. During the execution of the program, the number initially assigned to the variable A is 56, to the variable B, 75, and to C, 48. After the assignments are made, the average, X, is calculated (line 30). Lines 40 and 50 are PRINT statements showing the values used and their average. Line 60 skips a line, and line 70 returns control to line 20. At this point, the computer, *remembering* it has read the first three data elements, reads the next three, those given in line 90, the data elements 69, 89, and 71. After reading this second set of three, the average is computed and the output printed by lines 40 and 50. Again, line 70 transfers control to line 20 and the next three data elements, 82, 93, and 24, are read, their average calculated, and the result printed. Control returns to line 20. Now, the program is to read three values, but line 100 has only two. This causes no trouble at all, because the computer picks up the 75 and 66 from line 100 and assigns these to the variables A and B, respectively. It then looks for the next DATA statement and, finding one at line 110, takes the first element from line 110—57—and assigns it to C. The average is computed and printed. Line 70 transfers control to line 20, and the last three data elements 48, 39 and 47 are read, the average calculated, and the result printed.

The location of DATA statements within a program is not significant. They need not be at the end and may be scattered anywhere throughout the program, including before line 10.

Too Many or Too Few Data Elements

We may now modify the program in anticipation of two questions. First, what happens when there are too many data elements? Second, what if there are too few?

By changing the loop to run from 1 to 3, that is, by changing

```
10 FOR I=1 TO 5
```

to

```
10 FOR I=1 TO 3
```

and rerunning the program, nothing surprising happens. The READ statement will be executed three times, nine of the data elements will be used, and six will remain unused.

If the loop is changed to run from 1 to 6, the READ statement should be executed six times. This requires eighteen data elements, however, and there are only fifteen in the program. In this case, when there are too few data elements, an error message, OUT OF DATA, is usually printed and execution stops.

```
10 FOR I=1 TO 6
20 READ A,B,C
30 X=(A+B+C)/3
40 PRINT "A="A,"B="B,"C="C
50 PRINT "AVERAGE="X
60 PRINT
70 NEXT I
80 DATA 56,75,48
90 DATA 69,89,71,82,93,94
100 DATA 75,66
110 DATA 57,48,39,47
120 END
```

```
A= 56           B= 75           C= 48
AVERAGE= 59.6667

A= 69           B= 89           C= 71
AVERAGE= 76.3333

A= 82           B= 93           C= 94
AVERAGE= 89.6667
```

```
A= 75           B= 66           C= 57
AVERAGE= 66

A= 48           B= 39           C= 47
AVERAGE= 44.6667


      20 OUT OF DATA
```

The RESTORE Instruction

You have seen that with the READ/DATA instructions, the computer reads sequentially through the data, "remembering" after each READ the last element used and selecting the next one for the next READ. Situations arise, however, in which it is desirable to *reuse* data. The RESTORE instruction permits this. As the following program illustrates, the RESTORE instruction restarts READ at the *first* DATA element.

```
10 FOR I=1 TO 3
20 READ A,B,C
30 X=(A+B+C)/3
40 PRINT "A="A,"B="B,"C="C
50 PRINT "AVERAGE="X
60 PRINT
70 RESTORE
80 NEXT I
90 DATA 56,75,48
100 DATA 69,89,71
110 DATA 82,93,84
120 END
```

```
A= 56           B= 75           C= 48
AVERAGE= 59.6667

A= 56           B= 75           C= 48
AVERAGE= 59.6667

A= 56           B= 75           C= 48
AVERAGE= 59.6667
```

After line 20 is executed the first time and the data elements from line 90 are read, the computer is *poised* to read the next data elements from line 100. Before READ is executed again, however, the RESTORE at line 70 occurs and the program is directed to read the data elements from the first DATA line. After line 20 is executed a second time, the program is again poised to read the next DATA elements from line 100, but again line 70 occurs before the next READ and line 90 is READ a third time.

RESTORE (Line Number)

Some computer systems have extended the RESTORE command to permit it to be used with a line number. When RESTORE with no line number is used, the next data element read is the first one in the program; when RESTORE (line number) is used, the net data element read is the first one at the specified line. The following program is illustrative.

```
10 FOR I=1 TO 3
20 READ A,B,C
30 X=(A+B+C)/3
40 PRINT "A="A,"B="B,"C="C
50 PRINT "AVERAGE="X
60 PRINT
70 IF I=1 THEN 160
80 IF I=2 THEN 180
90 NEXT I
100 STOP
```

```
110 DATA 56,75,48
120 DATA 69,89,71
130 DATA 82,93,94
140 DATA 75,66,57
150 DATA 48,39,47
160 RESTORE 150
170 GOTO 90
180 RESTORE
190 GOTO 90
200 END
```

```
A= 56          B= 75          C= 48
AVERAGE= 59.6667

A= 48          B= 39          C= 47
AVERAGE= 44.6667

A= 56          B= 75          C= 48
AVERAGE= 59.6667
```

The first time through the loop, A, B and C are read from line 110, where the first DATA elements are found, and the output is then printed. Since at this point I = 1, control goes to line 160. At line 160, RESTORE 150 directs that the next data elements are to be read from line 150. Control returns to line 20, and A, B, and C are read from line 150. After the output is printed, the counter I = 2 and the program jumps to line 180. At 180, RESTORE with no line number is executed. Control returns to line 20, and when A, B, and C are read, the values assigned are the first from the sets of data elements, that is, A, B, and C are read.

A flow chart for this program appears in Figure 7-1.

The ON—GOTO— Concept: An Example

We are frequently confronted with situations that offer alternative paths of action, and we must decide which one to follow. If there are only two possibilities, then our procedure for choosing parallels the BASIC instruction IF—THEN—. When we have multiple choices, however, analyzing them as a sequence of two alternatives, while possible, is neither natural nor expeditious. We think differently, and BASIC provides a different instruction: ON—GOTO—. The following admittedly contrived illustration shows how you might spend a week of your life.

If on Monday, Wednesday, and Friday, you go to school at 9:00 A.M., on Tuesday and Thursday at 1:30 P.M., on Saturday to work at 8:00 A.M. and on Sunday, stay at home, then, depending on the day of the week, you follow one of four different routines. If the days are numbered sequentially 1 through 7, beginning with Sunday, the following sequence of pseudoinstructions parallels your weekly routine.

```
10 INPUT I (the number of the day of the week)
20 IF (I-2)*(I-4)*(I-6)=0 THEN 200
30 IF (I-3)*(I-5)= 0 THEN 300
40 IF (I-7)=0 THEN 400
100 FOLLOW SUNDAY ROUTINE
      ...
190 STOP
200 FOLLOW MONDAY, WEDNESDAY, FRIDAY ROUTINE
      ...
290 STOP
300 FOLLOW TUESDAY, THURSDAY ROUTINE
      ...
390 STOP
400 FOLLOW SATURDAY ROUTINE
      ...
490 STOP
500 END
```

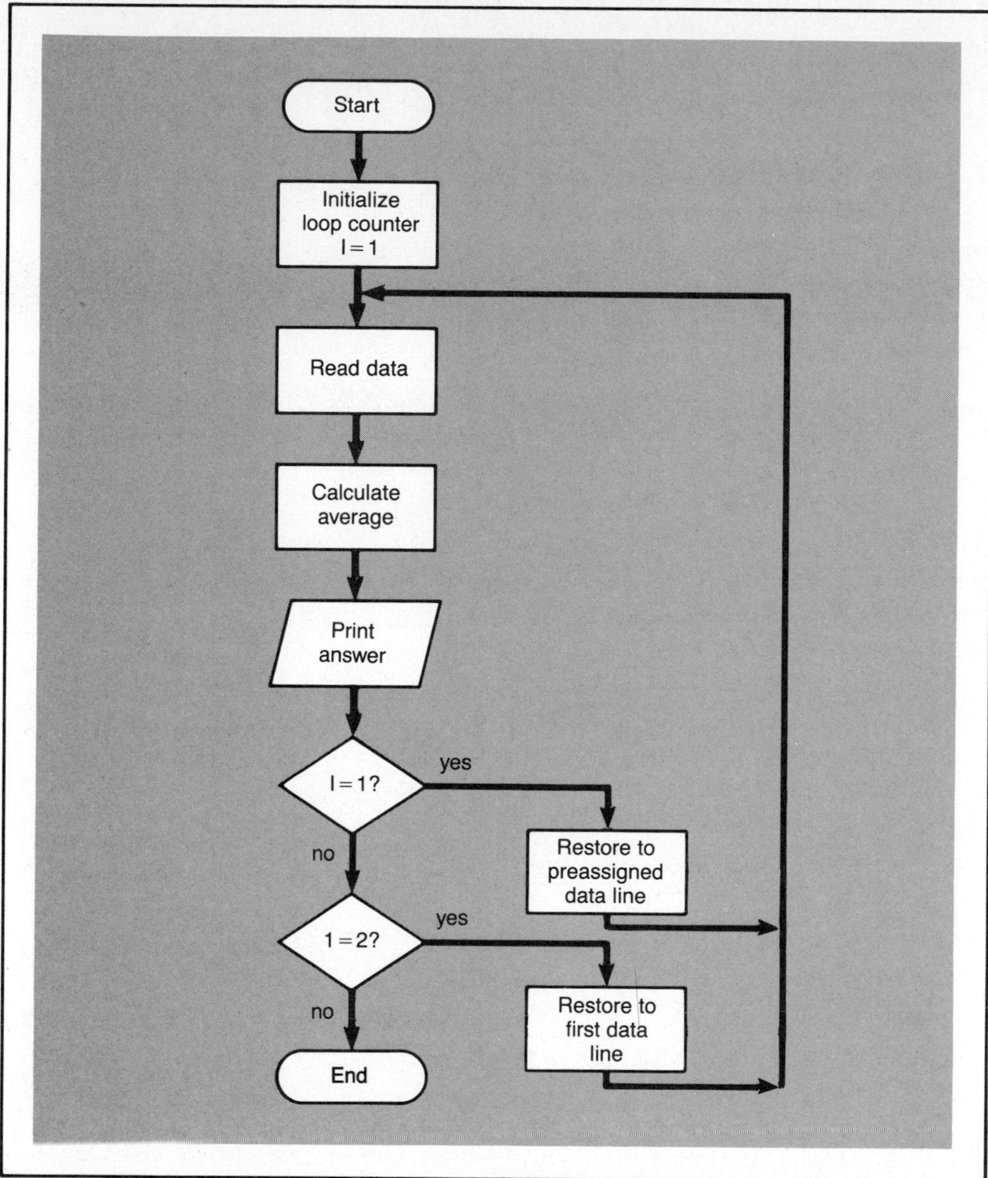

FIGURE 7-1

A flow chart for this program is shown in Figure 7-2.

The flow chart uses only the familiar, elementary symbols. The decision process depends on the answers to three questions. First, is it Monday, Wednesday, or Friday? The answer is either yes or no. If yes, you follow the Monday, Wednesday, Friday path; if no, the second question is asked. Is it Tuesday or Thursday? Again, the answer is either yes or no. If yes, you follow the Tuesday, Thursday routine; if no, the response to the third question decides whether you follow the Saturday or Sunday routine.

The ON—GOTO— Statement

Most choices are not simply either/or, and the decision-making process may be more complicated than deciding your daily routine. Even when it is possible to resolve the problem with a sequence of questions, each with only two answers, the flow-charting and the coding may become unwieldly. Any technique that reduces the effort is useful.

There is a BASIC statement that can replace the three lines 20, 30, and 40 in the above pseudoprogram. The form of the statement is:

ON (expression) GOTO (ln_1,ln_2, . . . ln_k)

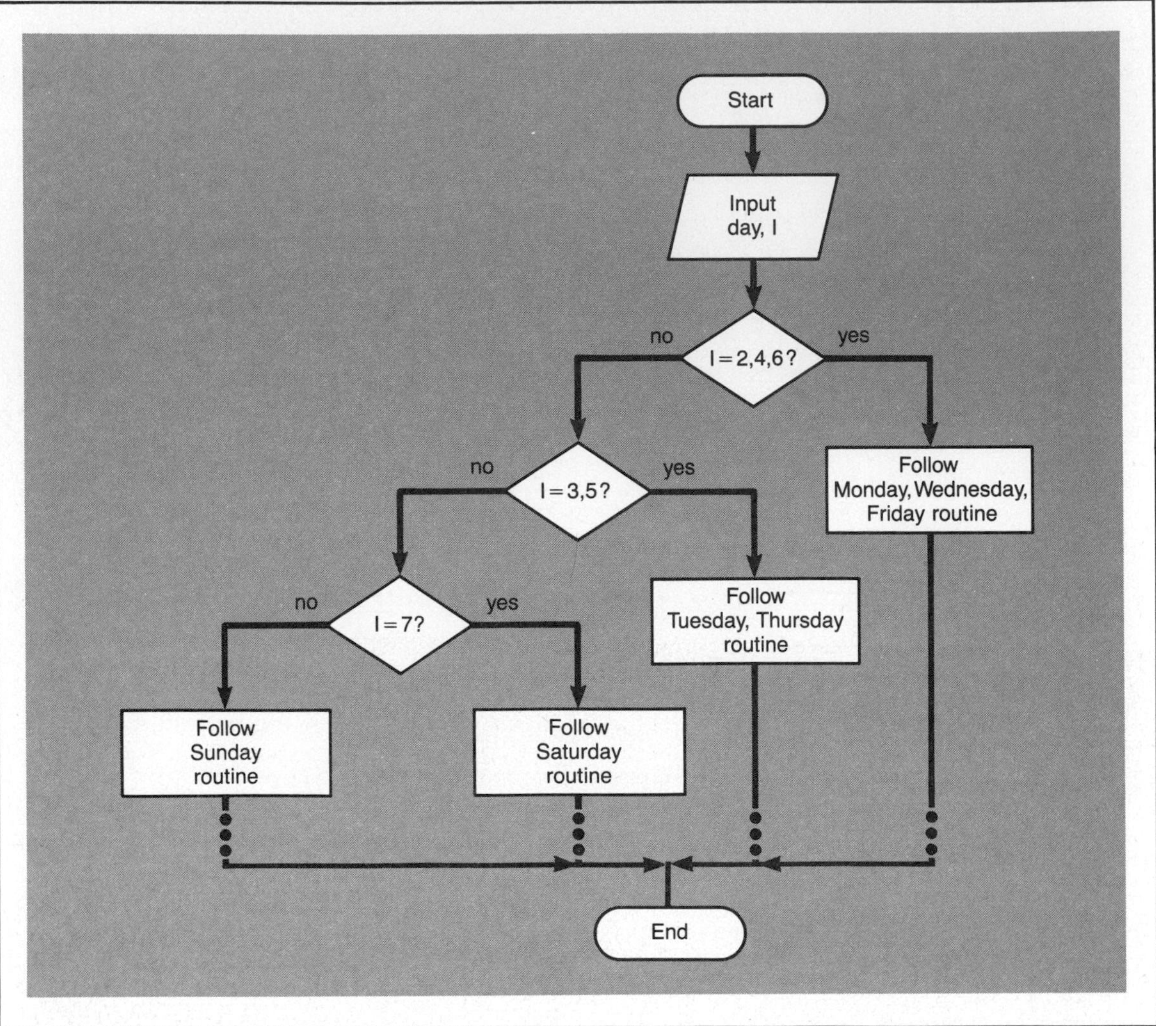

FIGURE 7-2

where ln_1,ln_2, . . . ,ln_k are line numbers. When used in the above pseudoprogram, lines 30 and 40 are deleted and line 20 is replaced by:

```
20 ON I GOTO 100,200,300,200,300,200,400
```

where I denotes the day of the week. If I = 1, control is transferred to the line number that appears first in the sequence after GOTO, line 100; if I = 2, control goes to the line number that appears second, line 200; and so on, until if I = 7, control is transferred to line 400.

In the example, the expression after ON in the ON—GOTO— statement is the variable I; under other circumstances, any valid BASIC expression would do. In fact, if a more general expression is used, it would, for whatever values of the variables, be evaluated first. If not an integer, the value would be truncated and control would be transferred to the appropriate line.

Exceptional Cases

What happens if, after the expression is evaluated and truncated, its value is less than one or greater than the number of line numbers that follow GOTO? It depends on the computer. Some halt and print an error message; others ignore the line completely and proceed to the next executable statement. You will have to experiment to find out what your computer does. The following programs illustrate the weekly pattern and the exceptions described above. The modified flow chart appears in Figure 7-3. A program that accompanies the flow chart and simultaneously illustrates what happens when an error condition occurs follows.

```
10 FOR I=1 TO 8
20 PRINT "I="I
30 ON I GOTO 100,200,300,200,300,200,400
40 STOP
100 PRINT "FOLLOW SUNDAY ROUTINE"
110 GOTO 500
200 PRINT "FOLLOW MONDAY, WEDNESDAY, FRIDAY ROUTINE"
210 GOTO 500
300 PRINT "FOLLOW TUESDAY, THURSDAY ROUTINE"
310 GOTO 500
400 PRINT "TODAY IS SATURDAY"
410 GOTO 500
500 NEXT I
510 END
```

```
I= 1
FOLLOW SUNDAY ROUTINE
I= 2
FOLLOW MONDAY, WEDNESDAY, FRIDAY ROUTINE
I= 3
FOLLOW TUESDAY, THURSDAY ROUTINE
I= 4
FOLLOW MONDAY, WEDNESDAY, FRIDAY ROUTINE
```

FIGURE 7-3

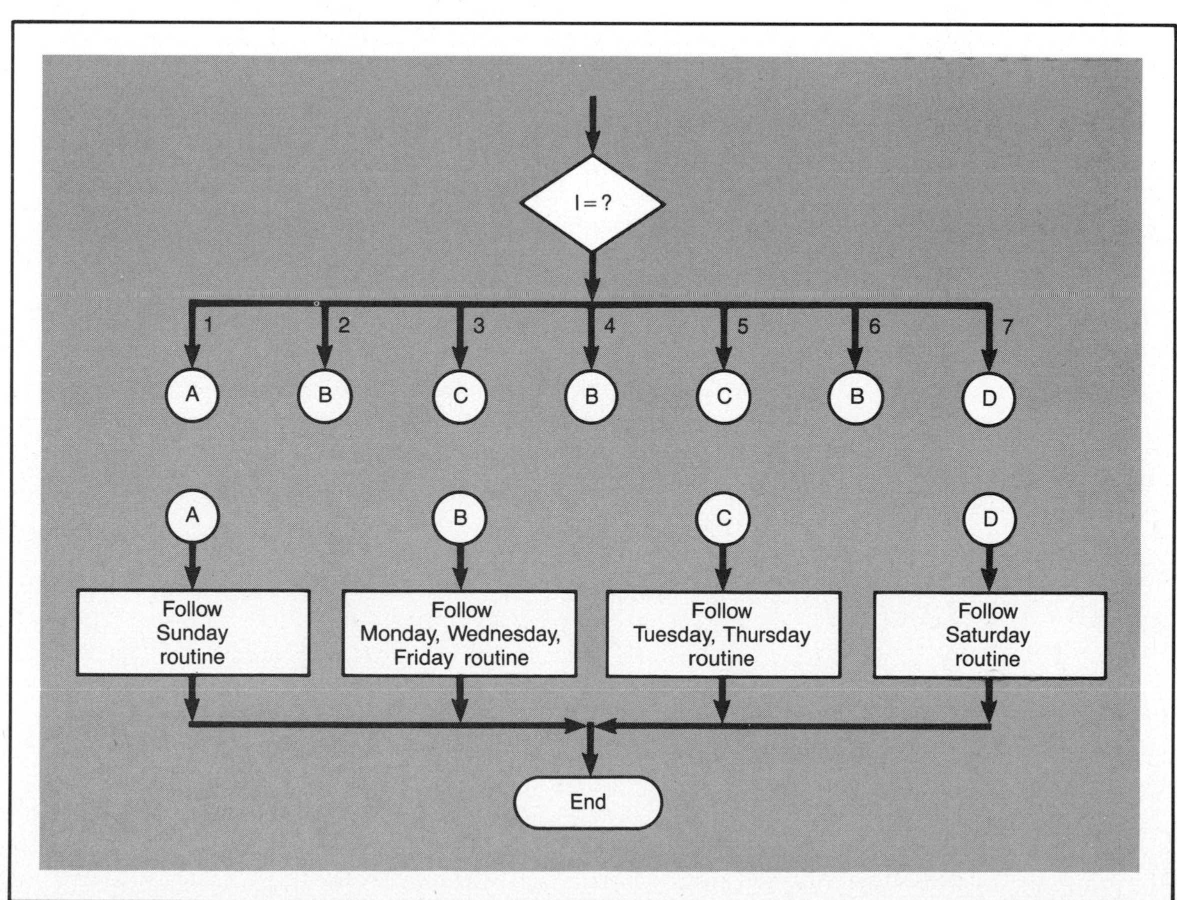

```
I= 5
FOLLOW TUESDAY, THURSDAY ROUTINE
I= 6
FOLLOW MONDAY, WEDNESDAY, FRIDAY ROUTINE
I=7
TODAY IS SATURDAY
I=8

INVALID COMPUTED GOTO IN 30
```

The program was run on a computer that, when a value of I less than 1 or greater than the number of line numbers that follow the GOTO occurs, halts and prints an error message. As the variable I went from 1 through 7, the ON—GOTO— instruction functioned as described; when I was equal to 8, an error message was printed and execution stopped.

As a further illustration of an error condition, a second program was written by changing the variable I to I − 1, at line 30, in the last program. Thus, the expression to be evaluated is to take on the values 0, 1, 2, ... 7. When this modified version was run, the first value encountered at line 30 was 0, an error message was printed and the computer halted.

```
10 FOR I=1 TO 8
20 PRINT "I="I
30 ON I-1 GOTO 100,200,300,200,300,200,400
40 STOP
100 PRINT "FOLLOW SUNDAY ROUTINE"
110 GOTO 500
200 PRINT "FOLLOW MONDAY, WEDNESDAY, FRIDAY ROUTINE"
210 GOTO 500
300 PRINT "FOLLOW TUESDAY, THURSDAY ROUTINE"
310 GOTO 500
400 PRINT "TODAY IS SATURDAY"
410 GOTO 500
500 NEXT I
510 END
```

```
I= 1

INVALID COMPUTED GOTO IN 30
```

These two programs also were run on a computer that ignores the ON—GOTO— instruction if the truncated value of the expression following ON does not specify one of the line numbers following GOTO. The printout that follows shows that when this occurred, line 30 was ignored and the computer executed the STOP at line 40. Any other valid BASIC instruction at line 40 would do, and the program would continue from that line forward.

```
10 FOR I=1 TO 8
20 PRINT "I="I
30 ON I GOTO 100,200,300,200,300,200,400
40 PRINT "THE PROGRAM HAS REACHED LINE 40 AND WILL STOP" & STOP
100 PRINT "FOLLOW SUNDAY ROUTINE"
110 GOTO 500
200 PRINT "FOLLOW MONDAY, WEDNESDAY, FRIDAY ROUTINE"
210 GOTO 500
300 PRINT "FOLLOW TUESDAY, THURSDAY ROUTINE"
310 GOTO 500
400 PRINT "TODAY IS SATURDAY"
410 GOTO 500
500 NEXT I
510 END
```

```
I= 1
FOLLOW SUNDAY ROUTINE
I= 2
FOLLOW MONDAY, WEDNESDAY, FRIDAY ROUTINE
I= 3
FOLLOW TUESDAY, THURSDAY ROUTINE
I= 4
FOLLOW MONDAY, WEDNESDAY, FRIDAY ROUTINE
I= 5
FOLLOW TUESDAY, THURSDAY ROUTINE
I= 6
FOLLOW MONDAY, WEDNESDAY, FRIDAY ROUTINE
I= 7
TODAY IS SATURDAY
I= 8
THE PROGRAM HAS REACHED LINE 40 AND WILL STOP
```

```
10 FOR I=1 TO 8
20 PRINT "I="I
30 ON I-1 GOTO 100,200,300,200,300,200,400
40 PRINT "THE PROGRAM HAS REACHED LINE 40 AND WILL STOP" & STOP
100 PRINT "FOLLOW SUNDAY ROUTINE"
110 GOTO 500
200 PRINT "FOLLOW MONDAY, WEDNESDAY, FRIDAY ROUTINE"
210 GOTO 500
300 PRINT "FOLLOW TUESDAY, THURSDAY ROUTINE"
310 GOTO 500
400 PRINT "TODAY IS SATURDAY"
410 GOTO 500
500 NEXT I
510 END
```

```
I= 1
THE PROGRAM HAS REACHED LINE 40 AND WILL STOP
```

A Tax Problem

The solutions to many problems depend on finding an interval within which a variable lies. Consider a graduated real estate tax whereby for property values \$9,999.99 or less, the tax is 1 percent of the appraised value; for values between \$10,000.00 and \$49,999.99, the tax is \$100.00 plus 2 percent of the value in excess of \$10,000.00; for properties valued between \$50,000.00 and \$99,999.99, the tax is \$900.00 plus 3 percent of the value in excess of \$50,000; for properties valued between \$100,000.00 and \$199,999.99, the tax is \$2400.00 plus 4 percent of the value in excess of \$100,000.00; and for properties with values \$200,000.00 or greater, the tax is \$6400 plus 5 percent of the value in excess of \$200,000.00 Given the value of any property, you are to devise a sequence of questions that enables you to locate the tax group in which the property belongs. If property is valued at \$65,000, one sequence might be: Is 65000 < 10000?; no; is 65000 < 50000?; no; is 65000 < 100000; yes; put it into tax class 3.

You have seen how the programing for a sequence of questions may be simplified by using the ON—GOTO— construction. In the illustration of your daily routine, however, the expression was easily discovered; it was the variable I, representing the day of the week. What might be the appropriate expression for the tax structure described? First, notice that there are five classes and, therefore, the expression sought is to have five outcomes, 1, 2, 3, 4, and 5. Before the needed expression can be constructed, however, another intrinsic BASIC function is needed.

Two Intrinsic Functions: ABS(X) and SGN(X)

Before a magician can pull a rabbit out of a hat, he has to anticipate using that trick in his act and prepare for it before going on stage. In a similar vein, the developers of BASIC anticipated that there would be a need for mathematical functions to solve problems like the tax problem, and therefore, several such functions were built into the BASIC interpreter. One, INT(X), we used before. Two more that will prove invaluable are ABS(X) and SGN(X). The function ABS(X), called "absolute value of X," is equal to X if X is greater than or equal to zero and is equal to −X if X is negative. For example, ABS(5)=5, ABS(−3)=3, ABS(0)=0. The function SGN(X), referred to as "sign of X," is equal to 1 if X is positive, −1 if X is negative, and 0 if X is 0.

The two functions are intimately related; the value of one may be found from the other. If X is positive or negative:

```
SGN(X)=ABS(X)/X;
```

if X=O,

```
SGN(X)=ABS(X)
```

And, ABS(X) = X*SGN(X) for all X.

The SGN(X) function will be used to construct the expression for the tax problem. How would you go about associating a $65,000 property with tax class 3? As a first step, you might notice that the product (X−50000)*(100000−X) is positive for all values of X between 50,000 and 100,000 and negative for all other values of X. (For the moment, we shall exclude the two cases for which X=50,000 and X=100,000.) Then, SGN((X−50000)*(100000−X)) is +1 for all properties belonging in tax class 3 and −1 for all others. This suggests that we define five functions as follows:

$$
\begin{aligned}
F_1 &= \mathrm{SGN}(X^*(10000-X)\\
F_2 &= \mathrm{SGN}((X-10000)^*(50000-X))\\
F_3 &= \mathrm{SGN}((X-50000)^*(100000-X))\\
F_4 &= \mathrm{SGN}((X-100000)^*(200000-X))\\
F_5 &= \mathrm{SGN}(X-200000)
\end{aligned}
$$

For those properties that belong in tax class 1, $F_1 = +1$ and all the other F's, F_2, F_3, F_4, and F_5, are equal to −1; for those properties in class 2, $F_2 = +1$ and the other F's, F_1, F_3, F_4, and F_5, are equal to −1. For those properties the values of which exceed $200,000, $F_5 = +1$ and the other F's are −1. (Later, we shall worry about those properties valued exactly at the end points of the intervals.) Now, we construct the expression

$$F = \frac{1}{2}\left(1^*F_1 + 2^*F_2 + 3^*F_3 + 4^*F_4 + 5^*F_5 + \frac{(5)^*(6)}{2}\right)$$

If the value of the property places it in the first class, F=1; if the value places it in the second class, F=2; and so on, until if the value places it in the 5th class, F=5. Thus, the needed expression has been constructed.

To generalize this expression so that it may be used for other problems, for which the number of classes is not 5 but k, you would construct such k functions as F_k and define F as

$$F = \frac{1}{2}\left(1F_1 + 2F_2 + 3F_3 + \ldots + kF_k + \frac{k(k+1)}{2}\right)$$

One troublesome point remains: What happens if the value of a property is exactly at one of the end points of an interval? Because all property values are at most to the penny, the possibility of a value being exactly $10,000 or $50,000 or $100,000 or $200,000 may be circumvented by adding 1 mil to all property values and then evaluating the expression F. Nor will this cause a problem if the value happens to be $9,999.99 or $49,999.99 or $99,999.99 or $199,999.99, because the addition of 1 mil (adding 1 in the third decimal place) will not put the property into the next higher tax class. This adjustment eliminates the possibility of the value of any property coinciding with an end-point of an interval.

The flow chart in Figure 7-4 illustrates these ideas. A program for assigning properties to tax classes follows.

```
10 REM: THIS PROGRAM ILLUSTRATES THE USE OF THE ON--GOTO--
20 REM: STATEMENT AS IT IS APPLIED TO A TAX PROGRAM.
30 PRINT
40 PRINT "WHAT IS THE VALUE OF THE PROPERTY"; & INPUT V
50 REM: TO ELMINATE TROUBLESOME CASES, ADD 1 MIL TO V
60 X=V+.001
70 REM: SET UP THE FUNCTIONS FK.
80 F1=SGN(10000-X)
90 F2=SGN((50000-X)*(X-10000))
```

FIGURE 7-4

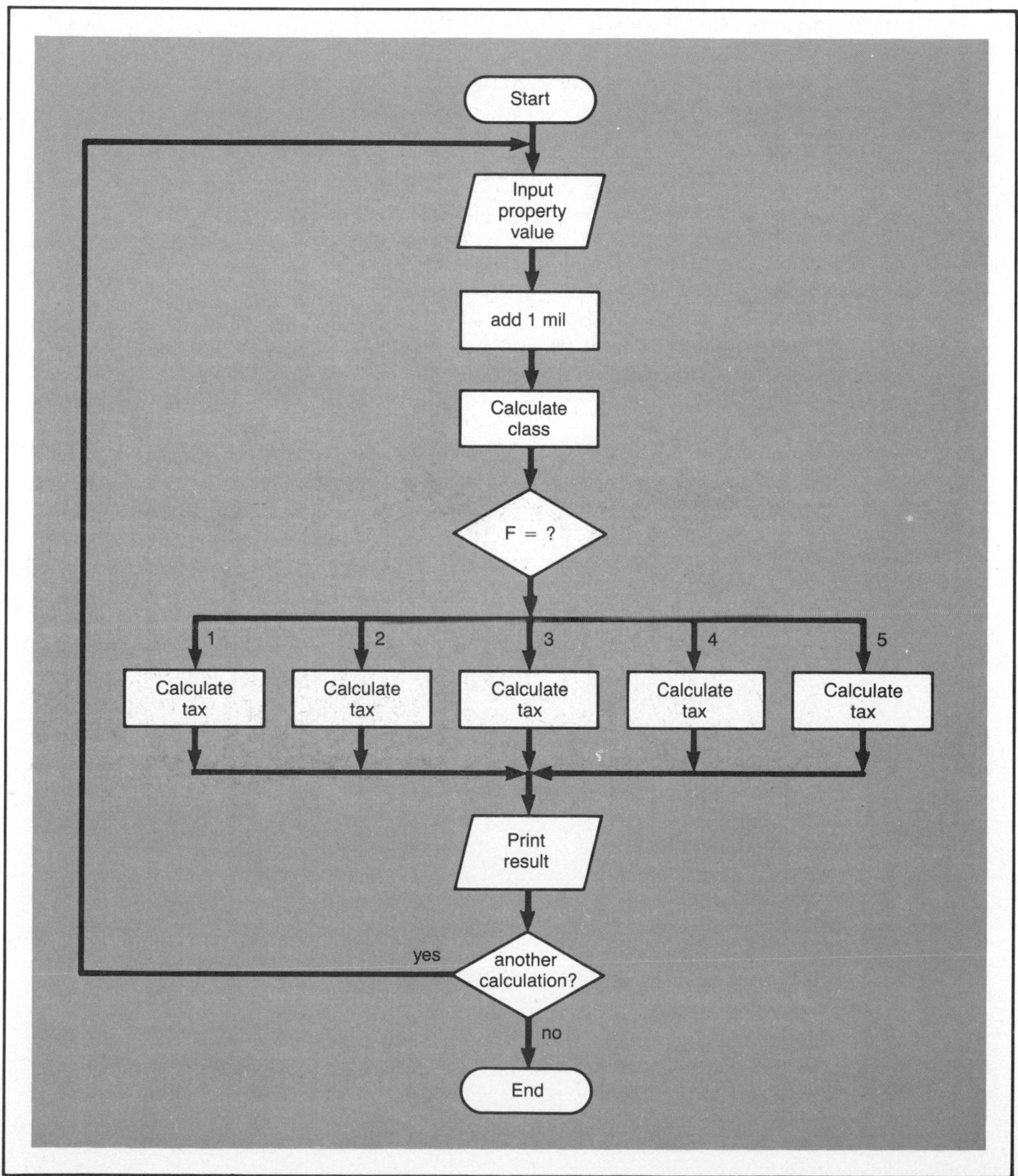

```
100 F3=SGN((100000-X)*(X-50000))
110 F4=SGN((200000-X)*(X-100000))
120 F5=SGN(X-200000)
130 F=(1*F1+2*F2+3*F3+4*F4+5*F5+15)/2
140 ON F GOTO 160,200,240,280,320
150 REM: TAX PROGRAM FOR PROPERTY IN CLASS 1
160 PRINT "THIS PROPERTY IS IN TAX CLASS 1"
170 T=.01*V
180 GOTO 360
190 REM: TAX PROGRAM FOR PROPERTY IN TAX CLASS 2
200 PRINT "THIS PROPERTY IS IN TAX CLASS 2"
210 T=100+.02*(V-10000)
220 GOTO 360
230 REM: TAX PROGRAM FOR PROPERTY IN CLASS 3
240 PRINT "THIS PROPERTY IS IN TAX CLASS 3"
250 T=900+.03*(V-50000)
260 GOTO 360
270 REM: TAX PROGRAM FOR PROPERTY IN CLASS 4.
280 PRINT "THIS PROPERTY IS IN TAX CLASS 4"
290 T=2400+.04*(V-100000)
300 GOTO 360
310 REM: TAX PROGRAM FOR PROPERTY IN CLASS 5
320 PRINT "THIS PROPERTY IS IN CLASS 5"
330 T=6400+.05*(V-200000)
340 GOTO 360
350 REM: ALL CALCULATIONS HAVE BEEN MADE; PRINT TAX.
360 PRINT "THE TAX IS $" T
370 REM: TO RERUN PROGRAM FOR DIFFERENT INPUT
380 PRINT
390 PRINT "RERUN PROGRAM? TYPE 1 FOR 'YES', 0 FOR 'NO'"; & INPUT Q
400 IF Q=1 THEN 30
410 END
```

```
WHAT IS THE VALUE OF THE PROPERTY   ?10000
THIS PROPERTY IS IN TAX CLASS 2
THE TAX IS $ 100

RERUN PROGRAM? TYPE 1 FOR 'YES', 0 FOR 'NO'   ?1

WHAT IS THE VALUE OF THE PROPERTY   ?5000
THIS PROPERTY IS IN TAX CLASS 1
THE TAX IS $ 50

RERUN PROGRAM? TYPE 1 FOR 'YES', 0 FOR 'NO'   ?1

WHAT IS THE VALUE OF THE PROPERTY   ?30000
THIS PROPERTY IS IN TAX CLASS 2
THE TAX IS $ 500

RERUN PROGRAM? TYPE 1 FOR 'YES', 0 FOR 'NO'   ?1

WHAT IS THE VALUE OF THE PROPERTY   ?75000
THIS PROPERTY IS IN TAX CLASS 3
THE TAX IS $ 1650.00

RERUN PROGRAM? TYPE 1 FOR 'YES', 0 FOR 'NO'   ?1

WHAT IS THE VALUE OF THE PROPERTY   ?150000
THIS PROPERTY IS IN TAX CLASS 4
THE TAX IS $ 4400.00

RERUN PROGRAM? TYPE 1 FOR 'YES', 0 FOR 'NO'   ?1

WHAT IS THE VALUE OF THE PROPERTY   ?300000
THIS PROPERTY IS IN CLASS 5
THE TAX IS $ 11400

RERUN PROGRAM? TYPE 1 FOR 'YES', 0 FOR 'NO'   ?0
```

Exercises

7.1 Professor Newcomb teaches three classes. The grading systems from one class to the next are similar but not identical because the classes are at different levels. In each class, the final grade is determined by multiplying each of five examination scores by a weighting factor, adding the results, and reducing the answer to the familiar range from 0 to 100. Thus, the first score G_1 is multiplied by a weight A_1, the second score G_2 by a weight A_2, and so on. The final grade is then calculated from the formula

$$G = \frac{(A_1G_1 + A_2G_2 + A_3G_3 + A_4G_4 + A_5G_5)}{(A_1 + A_2 + A_3 + A_4 + A_5)}$$

In the first class, each weight equals 20; in the second, $A_1 = A_2 = A_3 = A_4 = 15$, $A_5 = 40$; in the third, $A_1 = 5$, $A_2 = A_3 = 10$, $A_4 = 20$, $A_5 = 55$.

In the first class, the letter grade A is given to those students whose numerical grade is 90 or above, B to those whose numerical grade is at least 80 but less than 90, C to those whose grade is at least 70 but less than 80, D to those whose grade is at least 60 but less than 70, and F to those whose final grade is less than 60.

In the second class, A is given to those who score 80 or more, B to those who score at least 60 but less than 80, C to those who score at least 40 but less than 60 and F to those who fail to score at least 40.

In the third class, those who score 70 or more get A, those who score at least 40 but less than 70, get B and those who score below 40 get F.

Professor Newcomb wants you to write a computer program that has as input the class number 1, 2, or 3 and the five examination scores: the output is to be the final letter grade.

In an effort to be helpful, Newcomb makes the following observations. Knowing the class number, you know the weights to be assigned to each examination score. You can get the computer to read the correct weights by directing the READ instruction to the proper DATA line using the RESTORE (line number) instruction. When the weights appropriate for the class have been read, and the five examination scores are known, the final grade score can be computed. Since, for each class, the cut-off points between letter grades are different, it is necessary to know which class is being graded. Thus, although there are at most five final letter grades, A, B, C, D, and F, the final letter grade is determined by different scores in the different classes.

Prepare a flow chart and BASIC computer program for Professor Newcomb.

7.2 Professor Oswald's circumstances are identical to those of Professor Newcomb except that Oswald's computer does not have the RESTORE (line number) statement. Using Newcomb's flow chart as a starting point, Oswald finds that it can serve his purpose as well. Although the flow chart is the same, the program must be modified. How is he to accomplish the same results using only RESTORE? The solution Oswald devised is based on the fact that the variables $A_1, A_2, \ldots, A_5$ remember only the last set of values read. Thus, if he uses READ once, he gets the proper weights for the first class; if he uses READ twice, he gets the proper weights for the second class; if he uses it three times, he gets the proper weights for the third class. This can be done in a loop. After each time the loop is used, however, the READ pointer must be repositioned to its initial place. This is exactly what the RESTORE command does.

Rewrite Newcomb's program so that it will run on Oswald's computer.

7.3 In a certain state, license plates for automobiles are of the form XRT-456— any three alphabetic letters followed by a three digit number. To spread the workload associated with reissuing plates, the expiration dates of the old plates are staggered. All plates in which the middle digit is 0 expire January 31, new plates may be bought between January 1 and January 31; plates for which the middle digit is 1 expire February 28

(February 29 on leap years); new plates are available beginning February 1. Continuing this way, all plates for which the middle digit is 9 expire October 31 and new ones may be purchased beginning October 1. New plates for trucks and buses are issued during November and December.

Draw a flow chart and write a program that, given any three-digit number greater than or equal to 100, will return the name of the month during which replacement license plates are issued.

7.4 In Yoknapatawpha County, the income tax is graduated. For incomes less than $10,000, the tax is 1 percent; for incomes of $10,000–19,999, the tax is $100 plus 3 percent of the income in excess of $10,000; for incomes of $20,000–29,999, the tax is $400 plus 5 percent of the amount in excess of $20,000; for incomes of $30,000–39,999, the tax is $900 plus 7 percent of the amount in excess of $30,000; for incomes of $40,000–49,999, the tax is $1600 plus 9 percent of the amount in excess of $40,000; for incomes of $50,000–59,999, the tax is $2500 plus 11 percent of the amount in excess of $60,000; for incomes in excess of $60,000, the tax is $3600 plus 15 percent of the amount in excess of $60,000.

Each taxpayer submits a form containing a statement of his or her income and the tax previously paid that year including the amount currently submitted. If the total tax paid is more than the tax due, a request may be made for a refund of the overpayment. If the difference between the tax paid and the tax calculated by the formula is less than $1, no tax is due and no refund will be made. If the difference is greater than $1, it is rounded to the nearest dollar. This is the tax still owed or the amount to be refunded.

Polly Quinter, the local tax collector, is responsible for obtaining a program that reads each person's reported income, computes the tax owed, and compares that figure with the amount tendered by the individual. She wants to see the data presented in the following tabular form:

TAXABLE INCOME	TAX PAID	TAX DUE	REFUND DUE
12,500	175		140
38,000	1,600		
22,000	450	50	

The problem of preparing the table was given to Polly's programing staff with the following list of test data (the first figure in each couple is the income, the second is the tax paid):

10000,100; 20000,400; 30000,900; 40000,1600; 50000,2500; 60000,3600; 9000,100; 9000,0; 11000,100; 11000,200; 45000,2050; 45000,2000; 45000,2200; 55000,3050; 55000,3200; 55000,2900; 65000,4350; 65000,4500; 65000,4000; 90000,8100; 90000,8000; 9000,8500.

Polly asked her staff to prepare a flow chart and program and test it on these data. Meanwhile, using a desk calculator, she prepared her own table. When she is satisfied that the program operates according to specifications, she will test it on other data. Eventually she wants to run the program for all persons in the county; this is generally a number between 3500 and 4000. The exact number will be known only when all the forms for the year are in.

As a member of the programing staff, you are assigned the task of preparing the flow chart, writing, and checking out the program.

8 Random Numbers

Random processes surface in many places. They occur in tossing coins and in playing dice. Poker and bridge hands from a well-shuffled deck of cards are other examples. Less obvious, probability has been spectacularly successful in solving problems in physics. Business decisions involve an element of uncertainty; the discipline of operations research has provided useful results. Although many questions involving random events have been answered using the classical methods of mathematical probability and statistics, there are many more still that have not succumbed to these techniques. A different approach is needed.

The French mathematician and philosopher Jean le Rond d'Alembert confessed in his article on probabilities in the famous *Encyclopédie* that he did not fully understand some of the elementary theorems on multiplying independent probabilities. He nevertheless foresaw and suggested that approximations to a desired probability might be obtained experimentally. For example, you may know that when you toss a fair coin, the probability of heads coming up is 1⁄2 but you may not know how to calculate the probability of getting two heads simultaneously when you toss two coins. The correct answer is 1⁄4; d'Alembert thought it was 1⁄3. He might have realized his mistake if he had followed his own advice and experimented. You could take two coins, toss them, and count the experiment successful if you get two heads, a failure otherwise. If you perform this experiment 100 times and divide the number of successes by the total number of trials, you will get an estimate of the probability of getting two heads when you toss two coins.

Tossing the coins 100 times is time consuming and dull. Of course, if there were no other way to go, that is what you would have to do. If you could use a computer to *simulate* this experiment, however, the tedium of the experiment and the possibility of recording a result erroneously, would be reduced. Moreover, it might be possible to replicate the experiment many times or, equivalently, extend the number of trials to 1000, 10,000, or more. If the computer is to be able to simulate this experiment, it must be able to decide, on a random basis, if the coin has landed head or tail.

The answer to the Buffon Needle Problem is not so easily obtained. For this problem, rule a surface with a series of parallel lines one unit apart. Now, toss a needle, also of length 1, so that it falls "at random" on the surface. What is the probability that the needle will cross a line?

If you attempted to model this process, you would use the distance from the center of the needle to any one line as one random variable, call it x, and the angle that the needle makes with the perpendicular to the lines as a second random variable, call it ϕ.

This is illustrated in Figure 8-1. As you may readily see from the figure, the needle crosses the line if $x \leq 1/2 \cos \phi$ and $-\pi/2 < \phi < \pi/2$. These inequalities are graphically depicted in Figure 8-2, where the ratio of the shaded area to the area of the rectangle equals the probability that the needle crosses the line.

The simulation consists of taking two random numbers, the first, x, between 0 and 1/2, and the second, ϕ, between $-\pi/2$ and $\pi/2$ and checking to see if $x \leq 1/2 \cos \phi$. If it is, the experiment is a success; if not, it is a failure. Repeat the experiment many times and calculate the ratio of the number of successes to the total number of trials. This ratio is an estimate of the probability that, on any one trial, the needle will cross a line.

Solved analytically, the probability turns out to be $2/\pi$. Georges Louis Leclerc, Count de Buffon, the eighteenth-century naturalist who formulated and solved this problem, observed that the experiment offered a way to estimate π. In 1901, the Italian mathematician M. Lazzarini made 3408 tosses and calculated a value of π equal to 3.1415929, an error of only .0000003.[1] With so few tosses, so small an error can only be fortuitous. Later in this chapter, we shall simulate a simpler experiment to estimate π.

Surprisingly enough, the application of such techniques to business situations has become widespread. We shall offer an illustration in this chapter.

The ability to solve problems in such diverse areas rests on two cornerstones: (1) the programmer's ability to properly model the problem and (2) the computer's ability to generate random numbers. In BASIC, random numbers are generated by the intrinsic function RND(X). We shall introduce RND(X) and demonstrate its use.

Revisiting an Old Problem

Remember Art and Bill pitching pennies while they waited for their friends? A flow chart paralleling the situation was given in Figure 3-3 (page 27), although at that time for another purpose. We now want to write a computer program that parallels the flow chart.

[1]M. Lazzarini, Un Applicazione Del Calcolo Della Probabilita, Periodico Di Matematica, series 2, vol. 4, 1901, pp. 140–43.

FIGURE 8-1

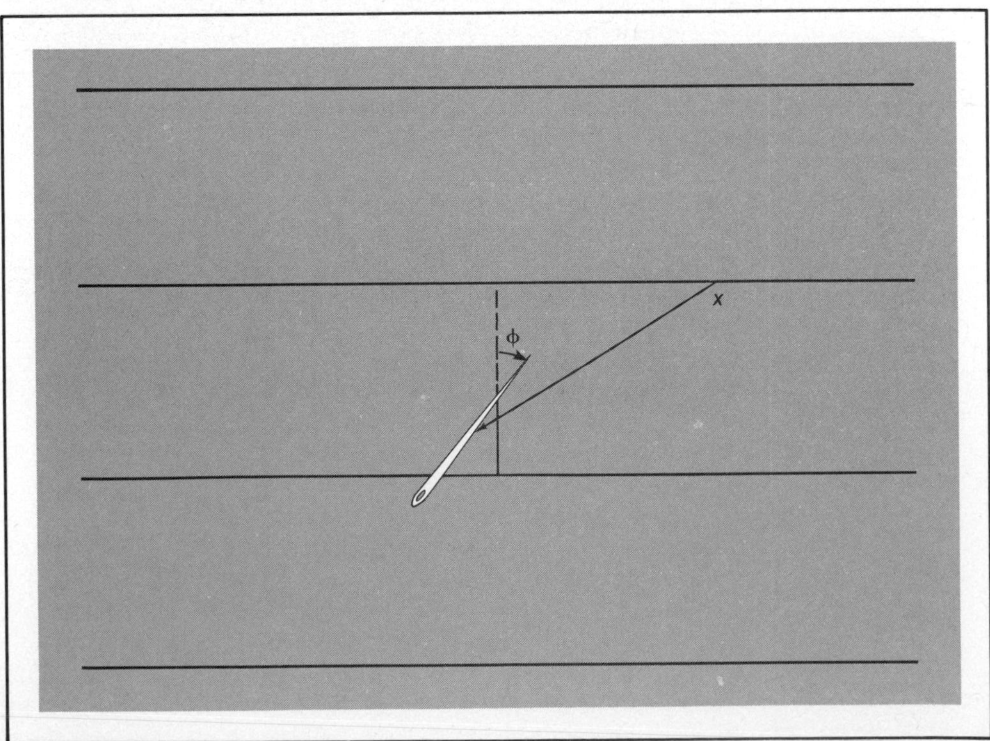

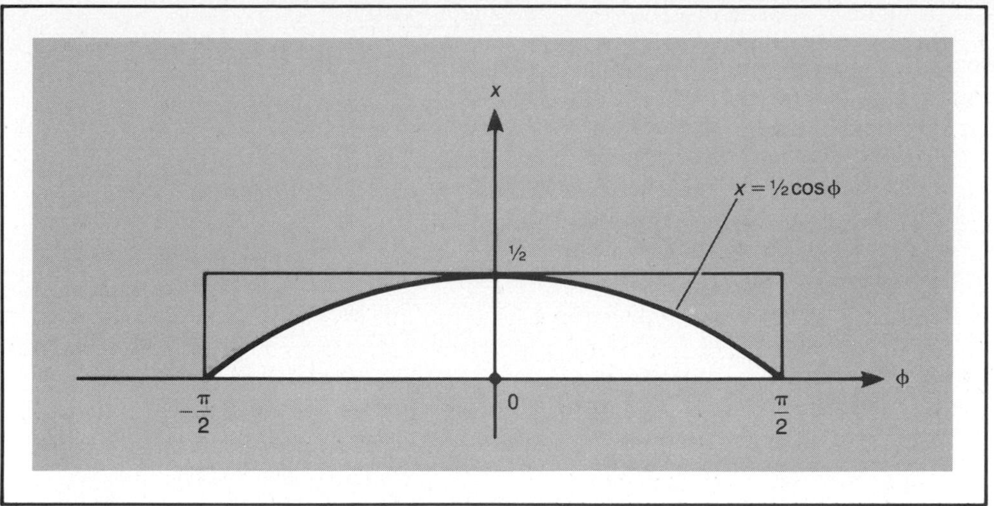

FIGURE 8-2

The flow chart, however, calls for an ingredient that is missing. First, there must be a way to decide the winner of each game, and second, there must be a way to decide if Art's and Bill's friends have arrived.

Assume that Art and Bill are evenly matched and that the outcome of each game is a random event; in effect, each has a 50 percent chance of winning. Also, although their friends are not expected immediately when Art and Bill start playing, as the number of games played increases, so does the probability of the friends' arrival. Thus, the arrival time of the friends is also a random event, with low probability in the beginning and increasing probability as time goes on.

In the next section, we shall introduce the random number generator RND(X) and illustrate a way of incorporating random numbers into a program.

An Intrinsic BASIC Function: RND(X)

We have presented three intrinsic BASIC functions: INT(X), ABS(X), and SGN(X). A fourth one is RND(X). Suppose we use RND(X) in a statement such as:

```
10 LET Y = RND(X)
```

The effect of this statement is to assign a decimal number between 0 and 1 to the variable Y. The significant feature is that when the statement is used repeatedly, *different* decimal numbers are assigned. Thus, when we run the program

```
10 FOR I = 1 TO 5
20 LET Y = RND(X)
30 PRINT Y
40 NEXT I
```

the output *might* be:

```
.496821
.872234
.172957
.362712
.611593
```

If we run the program again, however, the output *might* be:

```
.297193
.913928
.727516
.207315
.582617
```

The numbers are generated in a seemingly random sequence; knowing any of them in the sequence does not enable us to predict the next one. There is, however, one unifying feature: the numbers generated are uniformly distributed between 0 and 1. In other words, for any long sequence, approximately half lie between 0 and .5 and half between .5 and 1; for 10,000 numbers and the 10 intervals 0 to .1, .1 to .2, . . . , .9 to 1, approximately 1000 lie in each interval. If $l < 1$ is the length of an interval I lying within the interval 0 to 1, then the probability that the decimal Y = RND(X) lies in the interval I is l.

Using RND(X)

The RND(X) function may be used to simulate the outcome of each game played by Art and Bill. If we associate a randomly generated number greater than .5 with Art winning and one less than .5 with Bill winning, assuming the two are evenly matched, the outcome of each game may be decided. If Art is the better player, we could divide the interval 0 to 1 into the two subintervals 0 to .4 and .4 to 1. This is equivalent to saying that 60 percent of the time we expect Art to win and 40 percent of the time we expect Bill to win. Other subdivisions could reflect other evaluations of their abilities.

Now, concerning the arrival time of the friends, the situation to be simulated is that if the number of games played is small, the probability of the friends' having arrived is small; as the number of games played increases, so does the probability of the friends' arrival. Again, divide the unit interval into two parts, one from 0 to P and the other from P to 1. Associate the arrival probability with that of a random number falling in the interval O to P, and for the sake of illustration, choose P = N/(N + 1000), where N is the number of games played.[2]

The computer generates a random number. If it is less than P, we use this to indicate that the friends have arrived and play has stopped; if it is greater than P, their friends have not yet arrived and there is time for another game.

The following program reflects this analysis. Several runs follow the program.

```
10 PRINT
20 PRINT " THE NUMBER OF PENNIES THAT ART STARTS WITH";\INPUT A
30 IF A>0 THEN 60
40 PRINT " ART MUST START WITH SOME PENNIES. TRY AGAIN."
50 GOTO 20
60 PRINT " THE NUMBER OF PENNIES THAT BILL STARTS WITH=";\INPUT B
70 IF B>0 THEN 100
80 PRINT " BILL MUST START WITH SOME PENNIES. TRY AGAIN."
90 GOTO 60
100 A1=A & B1=B
110 REM: ART TOSSES FIRST, THEN BILL.
120 REM: N COUNTS THE NUMBER OF GAMES PLAYED
130 N=0
140 X=RND(1)
150 REM: IF X<.5, ART LOSES; IF X>.5, ART WINS
160 IF X<.5 THEN 240
170 A=A+1,B=B-1,N=N+1
180 REM: IS BILL BROKE; IS THERE TIME FOR ANOTHER TOSS?
190 IF B>0 THEN 320
```

[2] The formula we have chosen is direct and intuitive and illustrates the use of RND(X). A procedure based on waiting line theory would require an excursion into aspects of probability theory inappropriate at this level.

```
200 PRINT
210 PRINT, " BILL IS BROKE. ART HAS WON"B1" PENNIES."
220 PRINT, N" GAMES WERE PLAYED."
230 STOP
240 A=A-1,B=B+1,N=N+1
250 REM: IS ART BROKE; IS THERE TIME FOR ANOTHER TOSS?
260 IF A>0 THEN 320
270 PRINT
280 PRINT," ART IS BROKE. BILL HAS WON"A1" PENNIES."
290 PRINT, N" GAMES WERE PLAYED."
300 STOP
310 REM: DID FRIENDS ARRIVE?
320 P=N/(N+1000)
330 X=RND(1)
340 IF X>P THEN 140
350 PRINT
360 PRINT, " FRIENDS ARRIVED."
370 REM: PAY OFF SITUATION WHEN FRIENDS ARRIVE AND INTERRUPT PLAY.
380 IF A<=A1 THEN 420
390 PRINT, " ART HAS WON"A-A1" PENNIES FROM BILL."
400 PRINT, N " GAMES WERE PLAYED."
410 STOP
420 IF A=A1 THEN 460
430 PRINT," BILL HAS WON"B-B1" PENNIES FROM ART."
440 PRINT, N " GAMES WERE PLAYED."
450 STOP
460 PRINT, " THEY BROKE EVEN."
470 PRINT, N " GAMES WERE PLAYED."
480 STOP


THE NUMBER OF PENNIES THAT ART STARTS WITH=  ?3
THE NUMBER OF PENNIES THAT BILL STARTS WITH=  ?3

              ART IS BROKE. BILL HAS WON 3 PENNIES.
              23 GAMES WERE PLAYED.



THE NUMBER OF PENNIES THAT ART STARTS WITH=  ?3
THE NUMBER OF PENNIES THAT BILL STARTS WITH=  ?3

              BILL IS BROKE. ART HAS WON 3 PENNIES.
              15 GAMES WERE PLAYED.



THE NUMBER OF PENNIES THAT ART STARTS WITH=  ?5
THE NUMBER OF PENNIES THAT BILL STARTS WITH=  ?5

              FRIENDS ARRIVED.
              ART HAS WON 1 PENNIES FROM BILL
              23 GAMES WERE PLAYED.



THE NUMBER OF PENNIES THAT ART STARTS WITH=  ?20
THE NUMBER OF PENNIES THAT BILL STARTS WITH=  ?20

              FRIENDS ARRIVED.
              BILL HAS WON 9 PENNIES FROM ART.
              27 GAMES WERE PLAYED.



THE NUMBER OF PENNIES THAT ART STARTS WITH=  ?20
THE NUMBER OF PENNIES THAT BILL STARTS WITH=  ?20

              FRIENDS ARRIVED.
              THEY BROKE EVEN.
              10 GAMES WERE PLAYED.
*
```

The function RND(1), for which the argument was set equal to 1, is used in lines 140 and 330. Each time the program executes one of these lines, another random number is obtained. We show several runs to illustrate the output and, in particular, to emphasize that the same input can lead to different output.

In line 160, the winner is decided. If Art wins, he collects the penny (line 170) and the program asks if Bill is broke, line 190. If he is, lines 200–220 are printed and the program stops. If Bill is not broke, the program goes to line 320 to decide if their friends have arrived. The variable P is defined in line 320 and a new random number selected in line 330. When N is small, P is small and the probability that the random variable X > P is large. Thus, another game can be played and the program goes back to line 140. If N is large, however, P is close to 1 and the probability that X > P is small. In turn, this implies that the friends probably have arrived since the last game and play would now be over.

To print how much has been won and lost, the computer remembers the original amounts (line 100) and, knowing the current status, terminates via one of the sequences (200–230), (270–300), (350–360, 390–410), (350–360, 430–450), (350–360, 460–480).

Reproducible Random Sequences

The two significant properties of RND(X) are first, the unpredictability of successive numbers, and second, the uniform distribution of the numbers in the sequence. If a program prints a list of 100 randomly generated numbers, there is no discernable pattern except the uniform distribution. If the program is run again, will the same list of 100 numbers be generated? The answer could be yes or no.

Each computer can generate a sequence of random numbers that can be replicated and thus, once seen, is predictable. For the computer on which the program on pages 122–23 was run, a reproducible sequence is obtained by setting the argument X equal to 0. For any other value of X, the sequence is unpredictable.

The following programs illustrate this for lists of 25 numbers.

```
 10 FOR I=1 TO 5
 20 PRINT RND(0),RND(0),RND(0),RND(0),RND(0)
 30 NEXT I
>

 .445282        .353333        .112460        .494758        .956412
 .285648        .106182        6.62574E-02    .441906        5.51176E-02
 .353555        .625270        .569627        .790333        .615352
 .579120        .936548        .407208        1.43185E-02    .421038
 .397360        .594821        .992685        .602720        .682154

      30 HALT
>

 .445282        .353333        .112460        .494758        .956412
 .285648        .106182        6.62574E-02    .441906        5.51176E-02
 .353555        .625270        .569627        .790333        .615352
 .579120        .936548        .407208        1.43185E-02    .421038
 .397360        .594821        .992685        .602720        .682154

      30 HALT
>

 10 FOR I=1 TO 5
 20 PRINT RND(1),RND(1),RND(1),RND(1),RND(1)
 30 NEXT I
>

 .332124        5.84135E-02    .361367        .642482        .602585
 .833177        .575794        .956172        .554887        .723773
```

```
 .348656        .577982        .329983        .778066        .698549
 .188694        .845228        .373116        .631646        .431833
 .906186        .550621        .148048        .932701        .263769

       30 HALT
>

 .354389        .274073        .454939        .262981        .483430
 .533756        .851666        .306187        .172131        .277104
 .113447        .186745        9.94510E-02    .915998        .600930
 .361598        .761216        .312913        2.65391E-02    .343014
 .819235        .828279        .596563        .124863        .380112

       30 HALT
>
```

For other computers, the argument chosen to generate reproducible sequences is different. For some, the random sequence Y generated from

```
10 Y = RND(X)
```

for negative values of X is *not* reproducible; for each nonnegative X, a reproducible sequence, depending on the specific value of X picked, is generated. For a third group of computers, this convention is reversed.

A fourth class of computers uses

```
10 Y = RND
```

omitting the argument, or

```
10 Y = RND(X)
```

for any X, to generate a reproducible sequence. To get a nonreproducible sequence, the additional statement

```
5 RANDOMIZE
```

is required.

Why would we need to generate the same sequence of random numbers? The answer becomes apparent during the writing and testing of a program. As changes and corrections are made and the modified program run and rerun, it is comforting not to have to take into account an unpredictable sequence of random numbers. After the program has been thoroughly tested and is known to be correct, the change from a reproducible to a nonreproducible sequence may be made.[3]

Tossing Dice

The probability distribution for the outcomes of tossing two dice, although far different from the uniform distribution, may be obtained from the uniform distribution. Since RND(X) is a random number between 0 and 1, 6*RND(X) is a random number between 0 and 6. The value of INT(6*RND(X)) is one of the digits 0, 1, 2, 3, 4, and 5, and the probability of any one occurring is 1/6. For the expression: INT(6*RND(X)) + 1, the value is one of the digits 1, 2, 3, 4, 5, 6, again each with probability 1/6.

[3]For an explanation of the theory behind RND(X), see R. W. Hamming, *Introduction to Applied Numerical Analysis*, (N.Y.: McGraw-Hill, 1971), pp. 313–19.

To simulate the tossing of two dice, therefore, we may write:

```
Y1 = INT(6*RND(X)) + 1
Y2 = INT(6*RND(X)) + 1
Y  = Y1 + Y2
```

The possible outcomes for Y are the integers 2 through 12, and their distribution is identical with the distribution of points obtained by tossing two dice.

The following program simulates 10 tosses of 2 dice.

```
10 PRINT
20 PRINT ,"FIRST DIE","SECOND DIE","SUM"
30 PRINT
40 FOR I=1 TO 10
50 Y1=INT(6*RND(1))+1
60 Y2=INT(6*RND(1))+1
70 Y=Y1+Y2
80 PRINT ,Y1,Y2,Y
90 NEXT I
>

              FIRST DIE      SECOND DIE     SUM

               4              1              5
               2              3              5
               1              2              3
               5              4              9
               3              4              7
               1              6              7
               2              6              8
               4              5              9
               3              3              6
               1              6              7

       90 HALT
>
```

The Monte Carlo Method

The phrase "Monte Carlo" applies to a procedure whereby a random process is used to obtain a nonrandom result. The following method for approximating π affords a simple illustration. The unshaded area in Figure 8-3 is a quarter circle of radius 1. From elementary geometry, we know that its area is $\pi/4$. Let X and Y be independent random variables, each uniformly distributed on the interval 0 to 1. Randomly select an X and a Y. If $X^2 + Y^2 \leq 1$, consider the choice successful; otherwise, unsuccessful. We can repeat this many times and tally both the number of trials and the number of successes. Then, π is approximated by

$$4\left(\frac{\text{Number of successes}}{\text{Number of trials}}\right)$$

The following program simulates this experiment:

```
10 PRINT "HOW MANY TRIALS"; & INPUT N
20 S=0
30 FOR I=1 TO N
40 X=RND(1) & Y=RND(1)
50 IF X^2+Y^2>1 THEN 70
60 S=S+1
70 NEXT I
80 PRINT "AN APPROXIMATION TO PI IS" 4*(S/N)
>
```

When run three times for N = 100,000, the answers were: 3.13156, 3.14640, and 3.14128. To 5 decimal places, π = 3.14159; the error in each case is less than .5 percent.

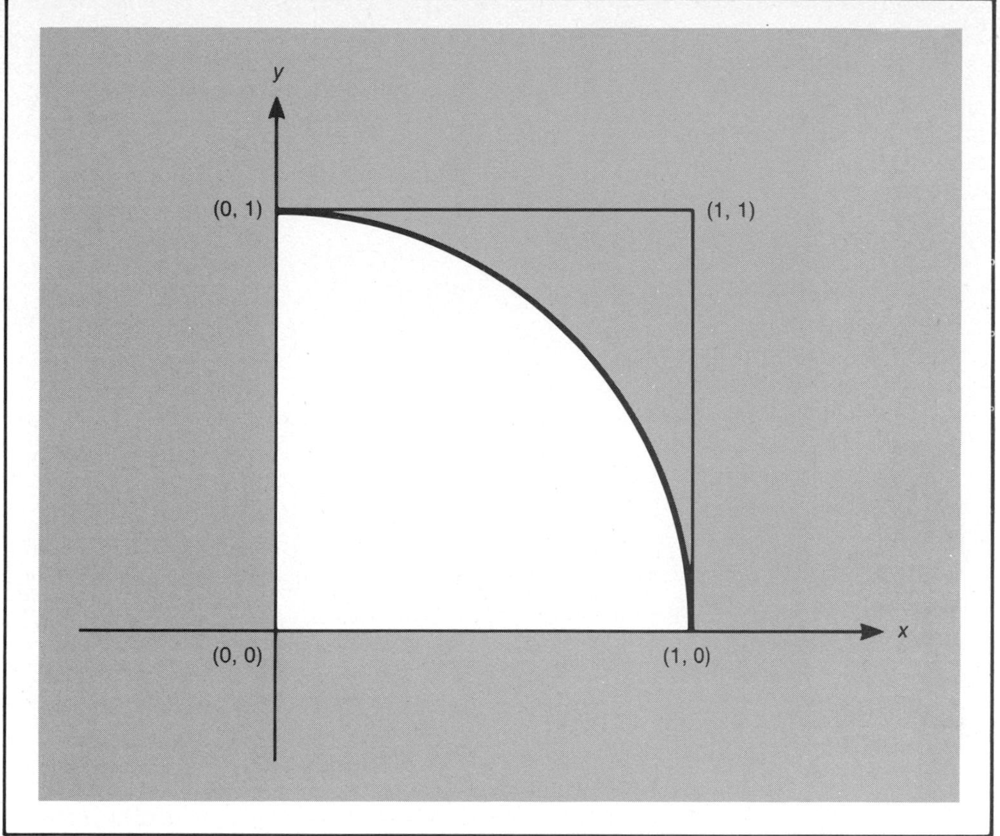

FIGURE 8-3

Illustration of the Monte Carlo Method

The Shur-Grip Company manufactures zippers, rivets, and clips. Based on the company's past sales and manufacturing experiences, the managers know that the price–quantity curve per 1000 zippers is:

$$Y_z = -.5X_1 + 80$$

where X_1 is the number of zippers produced in units of 1000, and Y_z is the unit selling price. The cost of manufacturing and marketing one unit is \$5. The profit on the sale of X_1 units is:

$$P_z = X_1Y_z - 5X_1 = -.5X_1^2 + 75X_1 \qquad (1)$$

For 10,000 rivets, the price-quantity curve is:

$$Y_r = -.25X_2 + 100$$

and the marketing and manufacturing cost is \$10. Here, X_2 is the number of rivets produced in units of 10,000, and Y_r is the unit selling price. The profit is:

$$P_r = X_2Y_r - 10X_2 = -.25X_2^2 + 90X_2 \qquad (2)$$

Finally, the clips are manufactured and sold in lots of 500, and the price-quantity curve is:

$$Y_c = .3X_3 + 105$$

where X_3 represents the number of lots and Y_c is the unit selling price. The marketing and manufacturing cost per lot is \$15. The profit is:

$$P_c = X_3Y_c - 15X_3 = .3X_3^2 + 90X_3 \qquad (3)$$

Upon examining the equation for P_z, we can see that if $0 \leq X_1 \leq 150$, then $P_z \leq 0$, whereas if $X_1 > 150$, then $P_z < 0$. These inequalities indicate that the company makes money if $1 < X_1 < 149$ but that it will lose money if it produces more than 150 units of zippers. It breaks even if it produces 0 or 150 lots. Similarly, $P_r \geq 0$ only if $0 \leq X_2 \leq 360$, that is, the company stands to make a profit if the number of units of rivets produced is between 1 and 359 (neither profit nor loss occurs if 0 or 360 units are produced) but will lose money if more than 360 units are produced. Finally, $P_c \geq 0$ if $X_3 \geq 0$, that is, the company makes a profit on every unit of clips produced. The more units produced, the greater the profit.

The total profit picture is given by the equation:

$$P = P_z + P_r + P_c = -.5X_1^2 + 75X_1 - .25X_2^2 + 90X_2 + .3X_3^2 + 90X_3 \tag{4}$$

The company's objective is to maximize its total profit, P. There are certain limitations, however. Twelve people are employed in the manufacturing operation, which consists of three divisions: molding, machining, and finishing, known as Divisions A, B, and C, respectively. Each division employs four people, and the plant is on a 40-hour week. Thus, there are 160 worker-hours per week available in each division. In Division A, it takes 1 hour to process 1 unit of zippers, 1 hour to process 1 unit of rivets, and 1 hour to process 1 unit of clips. Thus, the total number of units of the three products that can be processed in the molding division is:

$$X_1 + X_2 + X_3 \leq 160 \tag{5}$$

In the machining division, B, it takes 3 hours to handle 1 unit of zippers, 2 hours for the 10,000 rivets, and 1 hour for the unit of clips. The total number of units that can be processed in Division B therefore, is:

$$3X_1 + 2X_2 + X_3 \leq 160 \tag{6}$$

In the finishing division, C, 1 hour is required for 1 unit of zippers, 1 hour for 1 unit of rivets, but 5 hours for 1 unit of clips. Thus, the total number of units that can be handled in Division C is:

$$X_1 + X_2 + 5X_3 \leq 160 \tag{7}$$

From the inequality (6), we can see that $X_1 \leq 160/3$, or, since X_1 must be an integer, that $X_1 \leq 53$. Thus, there are two constraints on X_1, $X_1 \leq 53$ and $X_1 \leq 150$, and consequently, X_1 cannot be greater than the smaller of these two numbers. Similarly, again from inequality (6), $X_2 \leq 80$ and X_2 cannot be greater than the smaller of the two numbers 80 and 360, namely 80. Finally, from inequality (7), X_3 cannot exceed 160/5, or 32.

The problem then becomes to maximize the total profit subject to these additional constraints. The simplest and most straightforward method for solving this is to evaluate P for all triplets (X_1, X_2, X_3) for $X_1 = 0, \ldots, 53$, $X_2 = 0, \ldots, 80$, and $X_3 = 0, \ldots, 32$ and where the triplets also satisfy the inequalities (5), (6), and (7). We would then select that triplet for which P is maximum. In all, 144,342 combinations would be selected, those that do not satisfy the inequalities (5), (6), and (7) discarded, and P evaluated for the remainder. From the totality of P's evaluated, we would select the maximum. Also, out of curiosity and interest, we would like to know how many times P is actually evaluated. Clearly, this is not a job to be done with paper and pencil; it is ideal for a computer.

The flow chart in Figure 8-4 reflects this logic, and the program that follows carries out the intent of the flow chart.

```
10 P1=-1
20 I=0
30 FOR X1=0 TO 53
40 FOR X2=0 TO 80
50 FOR X3=0 TO 32
60 IF X1+X2+X3>160 THEN 130
70 IF 3*X1+2*X2+X3>160 THEN 130
80 IF X1+X2+5*X3>160 THEN 130
```

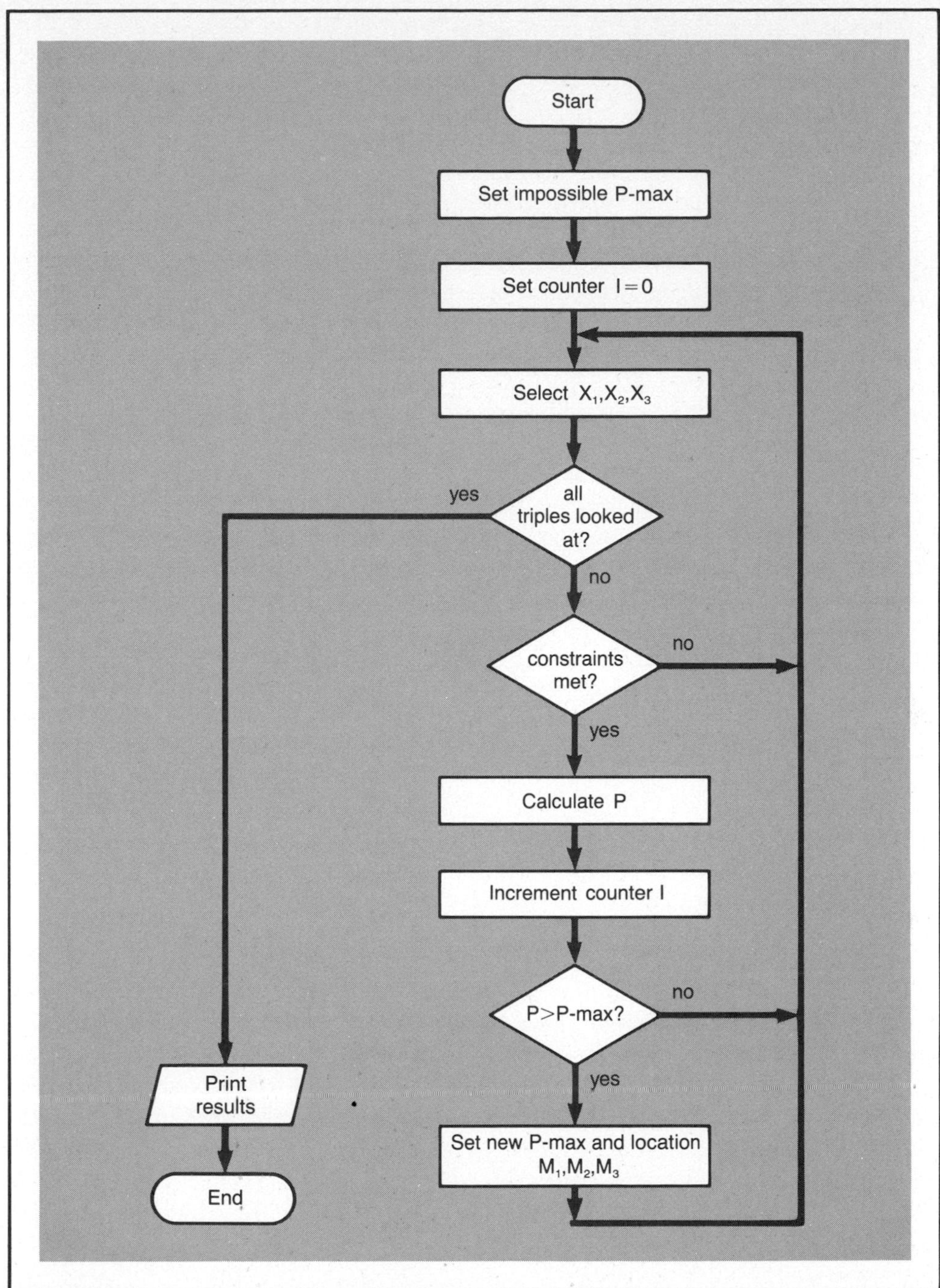

FIGURE 8-4

```
 90 P=-.5*X1^2+75*X1-.25*X2^2+90*X2+.3*X3^2+90*X3
 100 I=I+1
 110 IF P>P1 THEN 160
 120 NEXT X3
 130 NEXT X2
 140 NEXT X1
 150 GOTO 180
 160 P1=P,M1=X1,M2=X2,M3=X3
 170 GOTO 120
 180 PRINT "P-MAX="P1" FOR X1="M1",X2="M2" AND X3="M3
 190 PRINT "THE NUMBER OF CASES EXAMINED="I
 200 END
>
```

```
P-MAX= 6829.20 FOR X1= 2,X2= 68 AND X3= 18
THE NUMBER OF CASES EXAMINED= 47573

        200 HALT
>
```

In line 10, P1, which represents P-max, is set equal to −1, an impossible situation.[4]

In line 20, the counter I that will eventually specify how many times P is evaluated, is set equal to zero. Lines 30, 40, 50 and 120, 130, 140 set-up the triple loop. The time constraints are given in lines 60, 70, and 80. Note that, from the way the nested loops are written, if a constraint is violated, it is probably because X_3 is too large. For that reason, control is transferred to line 130 rather than to line 120. If the constraints are satisfied, P is calculated in line 90 and the counter, I, increased by 1 at line 100. If P is greater than the currently stored value of P1, then control goes to line 160, where the new P1 is stored and the triple of values (X1, X2, X3), which produced this new P-max, is recorded. Control returns to line 120 and a new triad is tested.

After all cases have been tested, the program reaches line 150, control is transferred to line 180, and the results are printed. The P-max has been found and that combination (X_1, X_2, X_3) that produces it is given. Also, the total number of cases examined is known.

The computer time to solve this problem is relatively short—just a few minutes on a medium-sized machine. The problem was formulated, however, so that the answer could be obtained in such a short time. If you have a problem for which there are 10 products and the range of possible values for each X_i is from 0 to 100, then the number of possible situations you might have to examine is on the order of 10^{20}, and there is no computer fast enough to examine this number of cases in a reasonable amount of time. Even if you could do one billion (10^9) calculations per second (unheard of at this time) it would still take more than thirty centuries to examine all cases. A different approach is necessary.

Imagine that all 10^{20} feasible combinations have been obtained and, for the sake of illustration, suppose the profits range from 0 to 100. Draw the line graph for which, at each of the 101 values, the height is the percentage of answers that have that value. A typical graph is given in Figure 8-5.

What we are looking for is that solution for which the profit is 100. Suppose we were to pick at random 500 sets of $(X_1, X_2, \ldots, X_{10})$ that satisfy the constraints. Calculate P for each of these 500 sets and record P-max and that set $(X_1, \ldots, X_{10})$ that produced it. What is the probability that the P-max thus calculated is within 5 percent of the true maximum?

This question cannot be answered without detailed knowledge of the actual shape of the graph. What can be stated, however, is that the probability that the P-max thus determined lies within the shaded region (which constitutes 5 percent of the area under the curve) is

$$1 - (.95)^{500} = .9999999999927255$$

If we want to know the probability that P-max lies within the double-hatched region (1 percent of the area under the curve), this is

$$1 - (.99)^{500} = .9934$$

More realistically, if 1,000,000 trials are made, then the probability that P-max lies within the right-hand end region (1 percent of the total area), is $1 - (.99)^{1{,}000{,}000} = .99\ldots99$;

[4]This device is universally used when we search for the maximum of a function. First, to get started, we pick a value for the maximum that we know is too small and then let the computer pick the higher values. Normally, we will find that the value initially picked is −99999; in this example, −1 will do since we know there are triplets for which the profit is positive.

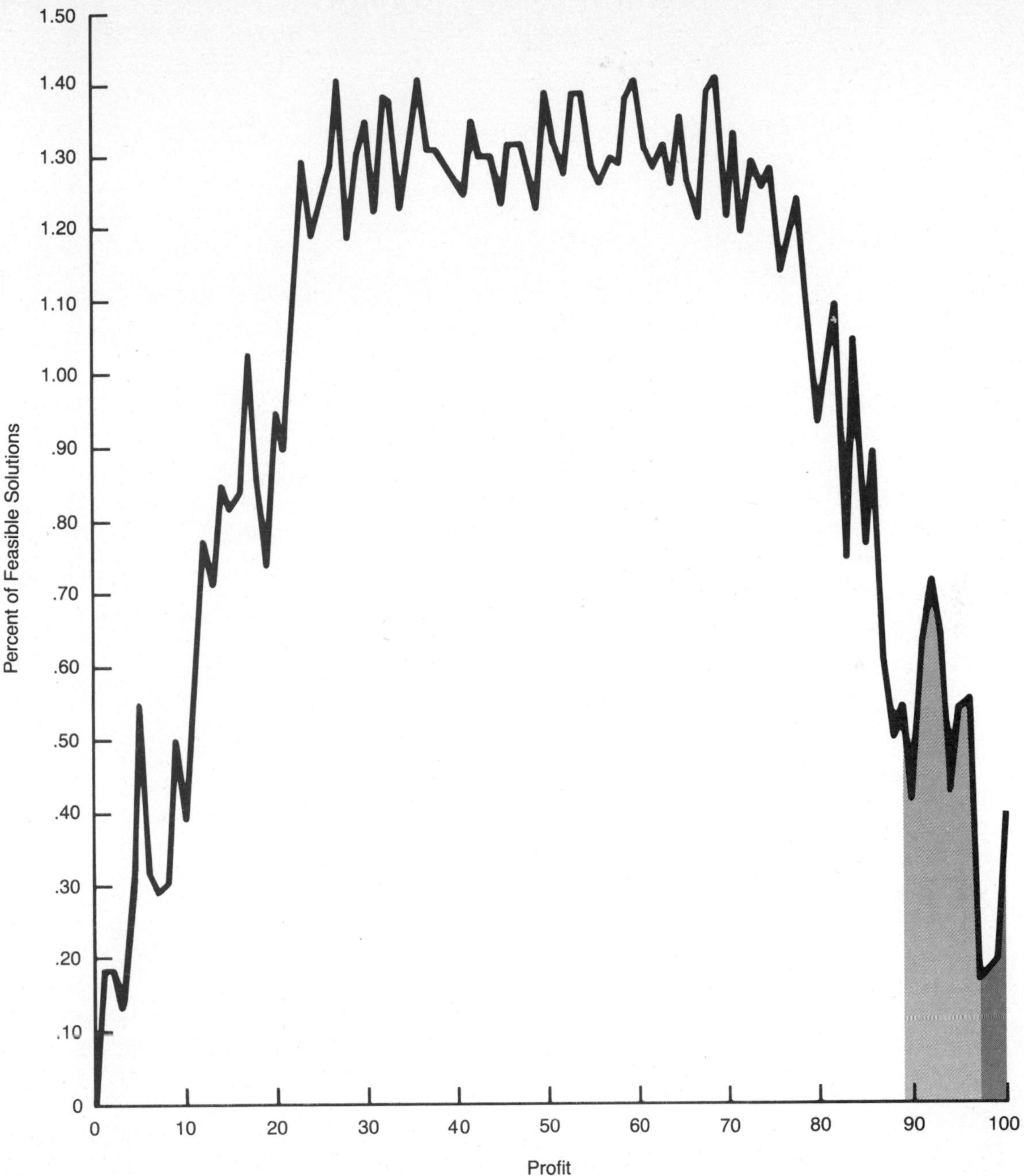

FIGURE 8-5

where 9's appear in more than 100 decimal places. Again, for 1,000,000 trials, that probability that P-max lies within the end region making up .01 percent of the total area is

$$1 - (.9999)^{1,000,000} = .999 \ldots 9 \ldots$$

when 9 occurs in the first 43 decimal places. The probability that P-max lies within the end region making up only .00001 percent of the total area is

$$1 - (.99999)^{1,000,000} = .999954602301925$$

For illustrative purposes, we shall rework the previous problem using this probabilistic approach for a sample size of 500. First, however, we need a new flow chart (Figure 8-6).

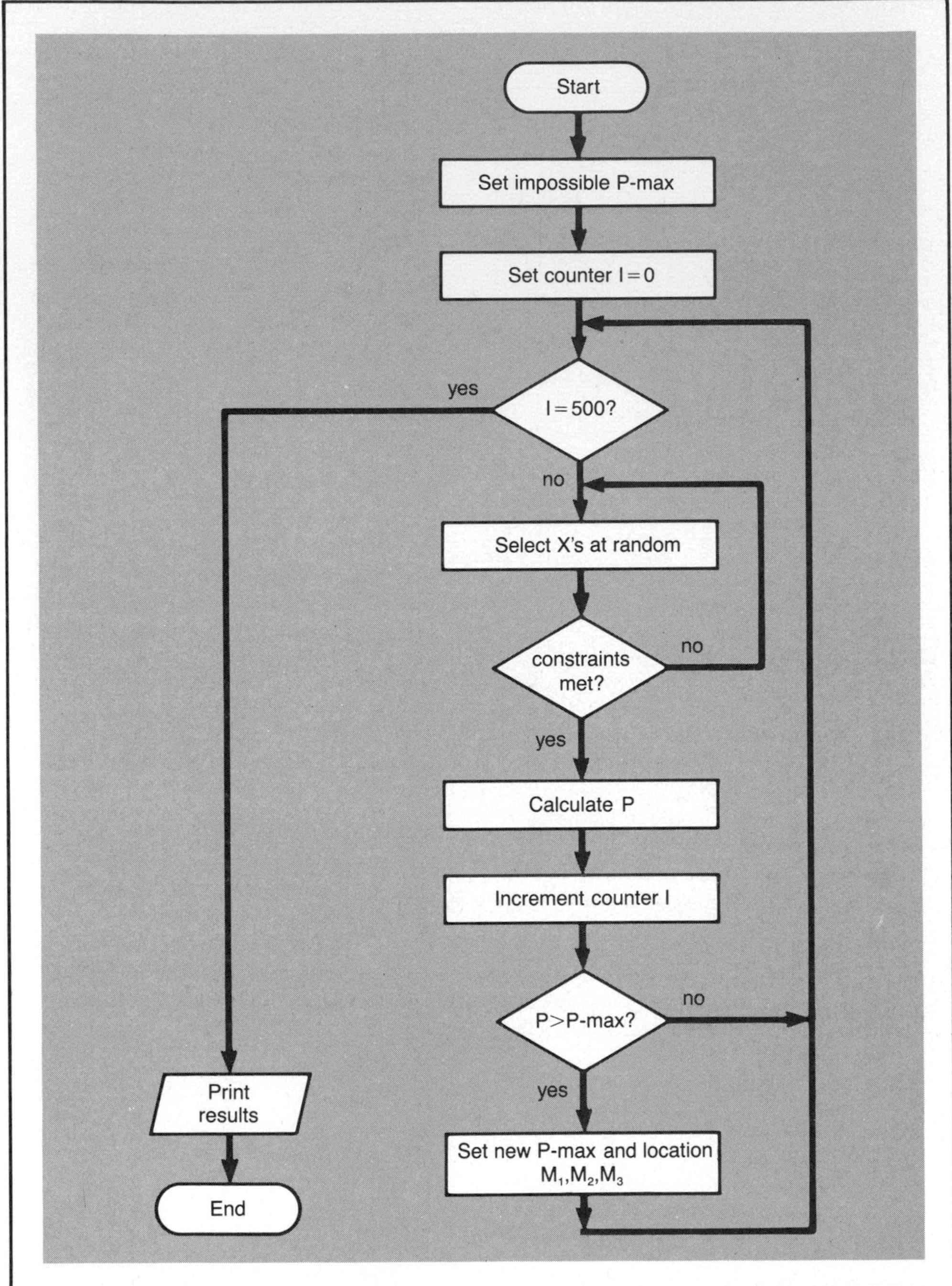

FIGURE 8-6

The computer program accompanying this chart follows:

```
10 P1=-1
20 I=0
30 IF I=500 THEN 160
40 X1=INT(54*RND(1))
50 X2=INT(81*RND(1))
60 X3=INT(33*RND(1))
70 IF X1+X2+X3>160 THEN 40
80 IF 3*X1+2*X2+X3>160 THEN 40
90 IF X1+X2+5*X3>160 THEN 40
100 P=-.5*X1^2+75*X1-.25*X2^2+90*X2+.3*X3^2+90*X3
```

```
 110 I=I+1
 120 IF P>P1 THEN 140
 130 GOTO 30
 140 P1=P,M1=X1,M2=X2,M3=X3
 150 GOTO 30
 160 PRINT "P-MAX="P1" FOR X1="M1",X2="M2" AND X3="M3
 170 PRINT "THE NUMBER OF CASES EXAMINED="I
 180 END
>
```

Three random integers, the first in the range 0 to 53, the second in the range 0 to 80, and the third in the range 0 to 32 are selected (Lines 40, 50, 60). The constraint equations, lines 70, 80, 90, are as in the previous program. From this point on, the program is as before, except that now the counter I is used to terminate the run, lines 30 and 160–180. The results of five runs follow.

```
P-MAX= 6639.45 FOR X1= 5,X2= 61 AND X3= 18
THE NUMBER OF CASES EXAMINED= 500

     180 HALT
>


P-MAX= 6772.95 FOR X1= 2,X2= 67 AND X3= 18
THE NUMBER OF CASES EXAMINED= 500

     180 HALT
>


P-MAX= 6579.70 FOR X1= 5,X2= 60 AND X3= 18
THE NUMBER OF CASES EXAMINED= 500

     180 HALT
>


P-MAX= 6527.70 FOR X1= 1,X2= 64 AND X3= 18
THE NUMBER OF CASES EXAMINED= 500

     180 HALT
>


P-MAX= 6608.45 FOR X1= 6,X2= 61 AND X3= 17
THE NUMBER OF CASES EXAMINED= 500

     180 HALT
>
```

From these runs, we can see that P-max varied from a low of 6579.70 to a high of 6772.95. The percentage error varied from

$$\left(\frac{6829.20 - 6579.70}{6829.20}\right) \times 100 = 3.65\%$$

to

$$\frac{6829.20 - 6772.95}{6829.20} \times 100 = .82\%$$

If we did not know the true P-max, we would suspect that it is close to 6772.95 and the values of (X_1, X_2, X_3) for the true P-max are close to (2, 67, 18). If this is indeed the case, we can go back to the previous program (pages 128–29) and limit the search to values of (X1, X2, X3) close to (2, 67, 18). This was done by taking 0 ≤ X1 ≤ 5, 64 ≤ X2 ≤ 70 and 15 ≤ X3 ≤ 21. The true P-max and the corresponding values of X_1, X_2, and X_3 were then obtained.

```
10 P1=-1
20 I=0
30 FOR X1=0 TO 5
40 FOR X2=64 TO 70
50 FOR X3=15 TO 21
60 IF X1+X2+X3>160 THEN 130
70 IF 3*X1+2*X2+X3>160 THEN 130
80 IF X1+X2+5*X3>160 THEN 130
90 P=-.5*X1^2+75*X1-.25*X2^2+90*X2+.3*X3^2+90*X3
100 I=I+1
110 IF P>P1 THEN 160
120 NEXT X3
130 NEXT X2
140 NEXT X1
150 GOTO 180
160 P1=P,M1=X1,M2=X2,M3=X3
170 GOTO 120
180 PRINT "P-MAX="P1" FOR X1="M1",X2="M2" AND X3="M3
190 PRINT "THE NUMBER OF CASES EXAMINED="I
200 END
>


P-MAX= 6829.20 FOR X1= 2,X2= 68 AND X3= 18
THE NUMBER OF CASES EXAMINED= 110

    200 HALT
>
```

Once computer programs are written and running, it is relatively easy to change the values of the variables.

The management of Shur-Grip noted that for this optimum solution, 160 worker-hours are needed in both Divisions B and C, keeping the employees there hopping, whereas only 88 worker-hours are needed in Division A, allowing excessive free time for coffee breaks. The managers wanted to see if they could improve the profit picture as well as distribute the workload more evenly if they were to have only three employees in Department A and assign the fourth half time to Department B and half time to Department C. As far as the program above is concerned, this means modifying the constraints so that inequalities (5), (6), and (7) become

$$x_1 + x_2 + x_3 \leq 120 \quad (5.1)$$
$$3x_1 + 2x_2 + x_3 \leq 180 \quad (6.1)$$
$$x_1 + x_2 + 5x_3 \leq 180 \quad (7.1)$$

In the loop, lines 30, 40, 50, the upper limits for (X1, X2, X3) change from (53, 80, 32) to (60, 90, 36). With these changes in the program, it was run.

```
10 P1=-1
20 I=0
30 FOR X1=0 TO 60
40 FOR X2=0 TO 90
50 FOR X3=0 TO 36
60 IF X1+X2+X3>120 THEN 130
70 IF 3*X1+2*X2+X3>180 THEN 130
80 IF X1+X2+5*X3>180 THEN 130
90 P=-.5*X1^2+75*X1-.25*X2^2+90*X2+.3*X3^2+90*X3
100 I=I+1
110 IF P>P1 THEN 160
120 NEXT X3
130 NEXT X2
```

```
 140 NEXT X1
 150 GOTO 180
 160 P1=P,M1=X1,M2=X2,M3=X3
 170 GOTO 120
 180 PRINT "P-MAX="P1" FOR X1="M1",X2="M2" AND X3="M3
 190 PRINT "THE NUMBER OF CASES EXAMINED="I
 200 END
>


P-MAX= 7520 FOR X1= 0,X2= 80 AND X3= 20
THE NUMBER OF CASES EXAMINED= 67228

     200 HALT
>
```

Management's hunch was confirmed. It might be noted that the excessive free time still available to the employees in Division A could be used to provide coffee breaks for the employees in Divisions B and C by temporarily shifting the Division A people to the other two divisions.

The Monte Carlo procedure previously described was then tried. The modified program and five runs follow.

```
 10 P1=-1
 20 I=0
 30 IF I=500 THEN 160
 40 X1=INT(61*RND(1))
 50 X2=INT(91*RND(1))
 60 X3=INT(37*RND(1))
 70 IF X1+X2+X3>120 THEN 40
 80 IF 3*X1+2*X2+X3>180 THEN 40
 90 IF X1+X2+5*X3>180 THEN 40
 100 P=-.5*X1^2+75*X1-.25*X2^2+90*X2+.3*X3^2+90*X3
 110 I=I+1
 120 IF P>P1 THEN 140
 130 GOTO 30
 140 P1=P,M1=X1,M2=X2,M3=X3
 150 GOTO 30
 160 PRINT "P-MAX="P1" FOR X1="M1",X2="M2" AND X3="M3
 170 PRINT "THE NUMBER OF CASES EXAMINED="I
 180 END
>


P-MAX= 7239 FOR X1= 10,X2= 62 AND X3= 20
THE NUMBER OF CASES EXAMINED= 500

     180 HALT
>


P-MAX= 7230.30 FOR X1= 14,X2= 56 AND X3= 21
THE NUMBER OF CASES EXAMINED= 500

     180 HALT
>


P-MAX= 7400.05 FOR X1= 10,X2= 63 AND X3= 21
THE NUMBER OF CASES EXAMINED= 500

     180 HALT
>
```

```
P-MAX= 7250.25 FOR X1= 15,X2= 57 AND X3= 20
THE NUMBER OF CASES EXAMINED= 500

     180 HALT
>
```

```
P-MAX= 7418.30 FOR X1= 6,X2= 68 AND X3= 21
THE NUMBER OF CASES EXAMINED= 500

     180 HALT
>
```

Again, P-max and the values of X1, X2, X3 that produced it are readily seen. The percentage error is (7520 − 7418.30)/7520 × 100 = 1.35 percent. Again, the neighborhood of X1 = 6, X2 = 68, and X3 = 21 was searched to see if the P-max could be improved. The range of X's are: $3 \leq X1 \leq 9$, $65 \leq X2 \leq 71$, and $18 \leq X3 \leq 24$. The above program was modified and run with the following results.

```
 10 P1=-1
 20 I=0
 30 FOR X1=3 TO 9
 40 FOR X2=65 TO 71
 50 FOR X3=18 TO 24
 60 IF X1+X2+X3>120 THEN 130
 70 IF 3*X1+2*X2+X3>180 THEN 130
 80 IF X1+X2+5*X3>180 THEN 130
 90 P=-.5*X1^2+75*X1-.25*X2^2+90*X2+.3*X3^2+90*X3
 100 I=I+1
 110 IF P>P1 THEN 160
 120 NEXT X3
 130 NEXT X2
 140 NEXT X1
 150 GOTO 180
 160 P1=P,M1=X1,M2=X2,M3=X3
 170 GOTO 120
 180 PRINT "P-MAX="P1" FOR X1="M1",X2="M2" AND X3="M3
 190 PRINT "THE NUMBER OF CASES EXAMINED="I
 200 END
>
```

```
P-MAX= 7507.80 FOR X1= 9,X2= 66 AND X3= 21
THE NUMBER OF CASES EXAMINED= 162

     200 HALT
>
```

An improvement was obtained. This new P-max occurred at one of the end-points of the search interval, however, and with the possibility in mind there may be further improvement, the process was repeated using X1 = 9, X2 = 66, and X3 = 21 as the center of a new search interval. When run, the same result, P-max = 7507.80, and the same values for the X's (9, 66, 21) were obtained. The percentage error between this new value and the true value is

$$\frac{7520 - 7507.80}{7520} \times 100 = .16\%$$

Note, however, the radical change in the quantities of zippers, rivets, and clips produced. For the true P-max, the numbers are 0, 80, and 20; for the Monte-Carlo-located P-max, they are 9, 66, and 21.

To understand why we did not find the true P-max, we redrew the graph (Figure 8-5) in exaggerated form as shown in Figure 8-7.

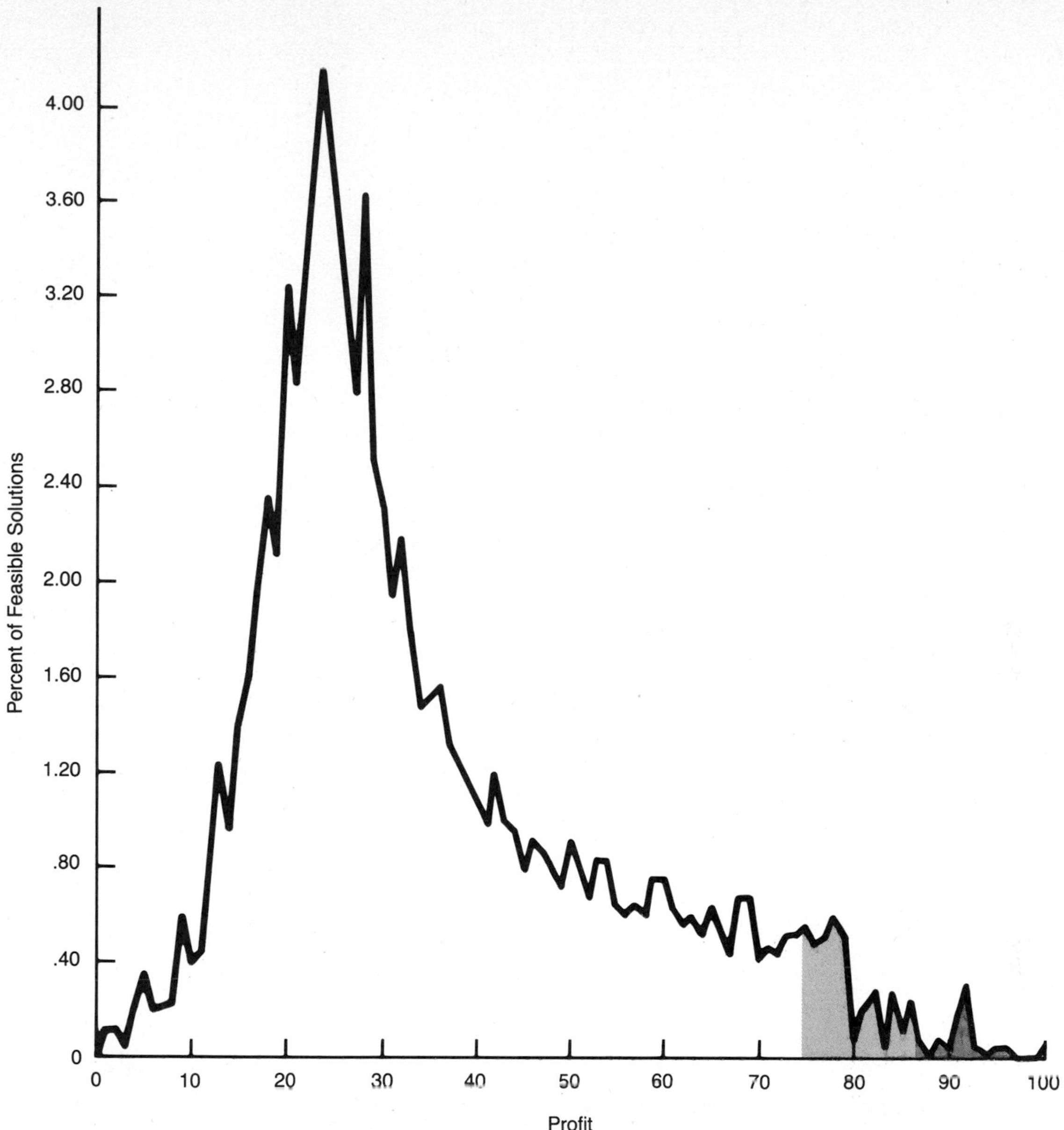

FIGURE 8-7

From the graph, it should be clear that when the distribution of values has a long tail or in the extreme case, when P-max is an isolated point far to the right, the Monte Carlo technique does not guarantee that we will get within some fixed percentage of the true P-max. All it does say is that the probability of landing within the shaded area is high. But the lower end of the hatched area can be far away from P-max and, consequently, the percentage error of P-max determined this way may be relatively high.

Exercises

8.1 The game of craps was described in Exercise 3.3 in Chapter 3. Using the description given on page 34, write a program that simulates craps.

8.2 The two-person game "Scissors, Rock, and Paper" was described in Chapter 3. We discussed two methods for analyzing it and drew the corresponding flow charts.

Write a program that simulates the game using the first method. Play it several hundred times, and observe the frequencies with which Charles wins, Dorothy wins, and the game is a draw.

8.3 An urn contains 99 white balls and 1 red one. You reach into it and pick a ball. If it is red, you win $99; if not, the ball is replaced and you get a second chance. If you pick the red ball on the second try, you win $98; if not, it is replaced and you get a third chance. This process is repeated until you pick the red ball. If you get the red ball before the hundredth try, there is a positive payoff to you; on pick number 100, there is no payoff and the game ends.

Draw a flow chart and write a computer program that simulates this game. Play it 100 times and compute your average winnings. This is an estimate of the "fair price" for you to pay to play the game.

8.4 Quentin, a not-too-clever, slightly myopic mouse, finds himself at one corner of a rectangular box consisting of twelve straight wire edges and eight corners. A piece of cheese is lodged at the diametrically opposite corner. The dimensions of the box are 24 inches × 30 inches × 36 inches.

Quentin's olfactory sense is just keen enough so that he is aware that food is nearby but not keen enough to lead him unerringly to it. He picks at random one of the three edges labeled *a, b,* and *c,* and runs along it until he reaches the next vertex. Here he again makes a random choice as to which edge to traverse next. He proceeds in this way until he either reaches the cheese or dies of hunger or exhaustion. Quentin runs at an average rate of 1 foot per second. Draw a flow chart and write a program that simulates Quentin's behavior. Have the program calculate the average length of time it takes Quentin to reach the cheese if he were to carry out this task 100 times. (*Hint:* Label the sides as shown; all the *a* sides are parallel and equal in length, as are all the *b* sides and all the *c* sides. One *a,* one *b,* and one *c* side emanates from each vertex. Therefore, at each corner Quentin must choose either an *a* or a *b* or a *c* side. Set up three counters: A, B, and C. Each time Quentin traverses an *a* side, increase the A counter by one; each time he chooses a *b* side, increase the B counter by one; each time he chooses a *c* side, increase the C counter by one. The *first* time that all three counters are simultaneously

FIGURE 8-8

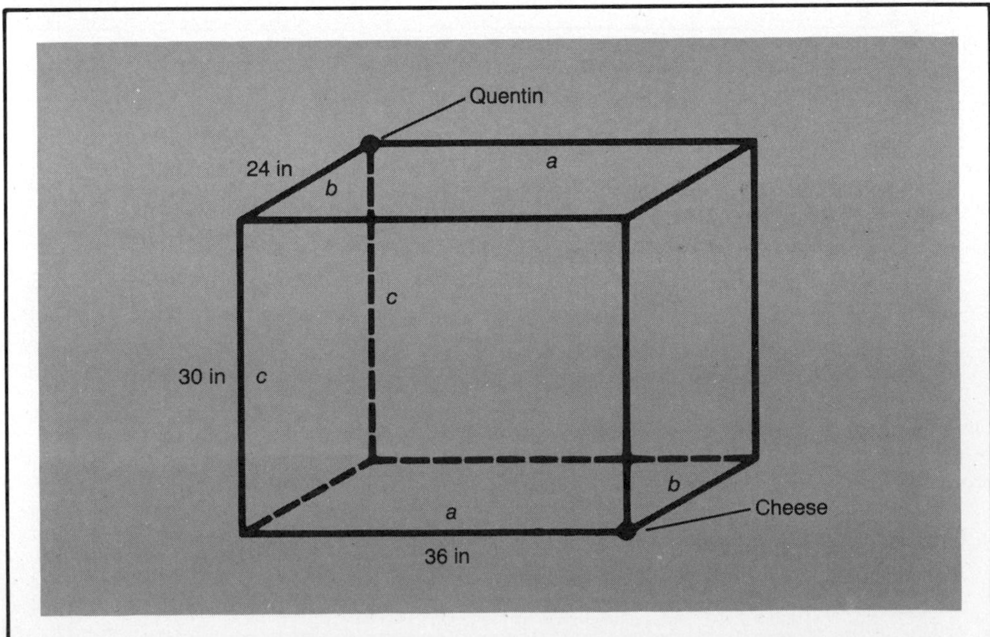

odd numbers corresponds to Quentin reaching the cheese. Why? Knowing how many times he traverses each side and being told the length of each side, you can calculate the length of his path. From here on, you are on your own.)

8.5 Rosamunda, a not-too-distant cousin of Quentin, one day found herself in similar circumstances. Rosamunda, however, was smart enough never to retrace an edge she had just traversed. Although as she leaves the first vertex the first time, she has three possible edges to choose from, she has only to choose between two alternatives at each corner therafter. Draw a flow chart and write a computer program that simulates Rosamunda's behavior. Have the program calculate the average length of time it would take her to reach the cheese if she were to perform the task 100 times.

8.6 Shortly after the Shur-Grip Company shut down its zipper production and reassigned its personnel so that there were only three people in Division A and four and one-half in each of Divisions B and C, the giant of the industry, Reliable Fasteners, Inc., began to eye Shur-Grip for a possible takeover. From Reliable's point of view, the Shur-Grip profit picture was just marginal; if it could be improved slightly, say 5 percent, it would become a desirable acquisition. Reliable began to explore Shur-Grip's operation, noting, in particular, the 20 hours of slack time in Division A. Reliable's managers speculated as to what would happen if those 20 hours were distributed between Divisions B and C. They knew that if such a change were to be made, the union would require that the 20 hours be divided into blocks no smaller than 4 hours each; that is, they could assign a person 4 hours to Division A, 8 hours to B, and 8 hours to C but not 2, 9, and 9. Obviously, there are other possibilities: 0 hours to A, 12 hours to B, 8 hours to C; or 0 to A, 8 to B, and 12 to C. Guess at the one possibility you feel most likely to increase profits. Either modify the program given in the text or write your own and determine if your guess is correct. Also, test the Monte Carlo technique and see how close the answer obtained using it agrees with the absolute maximum you have found. If you were a consultant to Reliable, would you recommend the takeover?

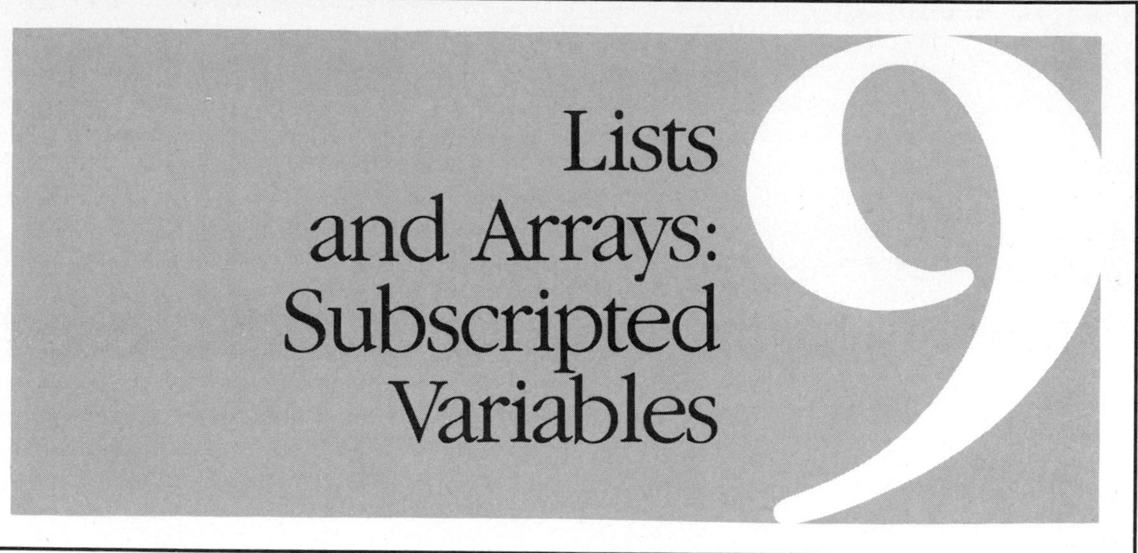

9 Lists and Arrays: Subscripted Variables

In this chapter, we shall extend the idea of a single variable name, first to a list of variables and then to an array of variables. As you know, a single variable is represented by a letter or a letter followed by a digit. Thus, B and Q7 are names for single variables. A *list* of variables is represented by a letter with a single *subscript* attached to it. Thus, a list of twenty-seven variables may be represented by:

$$T_1, T_2, T_3, \ldots, T_{27}$$

An *array* of variables is represented by a letter with two subscripts attached to it. Thus, an array of variables may be represented by and at the same time thought of as arranged as in the following display:

$$\begin{array}{cccccc}
S_{1,1} & S_{1,2} & S_{1,3} & S_{1,4} & \ldots & S_{1,23} \\
S_{2,1} & S_{2,2} & S_{2,3} & S_{2,4} & \ldots & S_{2,23} \\
 & & & \ldots & & \\
S_{47,1} & S_{47,2} & S_{47,3} & S_{47,4} & \ldots & S_{47,23}
\end{array}$$

In all, there are 47 × 23, or 1081 variables in the array $S_{m,n}$, where m = 1,2,3, . . . ,47 and n = 1,2,3, . . . ,23. There are 47 rows and 23 columns.[1]

Before a list or array may be used in BASIC, its size must be specified. This is done with a *dimension* statement.

We shall illustrate the use of lists with several examples, including (1) finding the smallest (or largest) number in a set of numbers, (2) sorting a sequence of numbers, and (3) tallying. We shall use lists to solve, in two different ways, a birthday problem.

Using an industrial example, we shall illustrate the use of arrays to record the utilization of equipment in a machine shop and to keep records of employees' time.

A Birthday Party

At a large party recently, I offered to take bets that there were at least two people present who celebrate their birthdays on the same day. Of the thirty to forty guests, several reached for their wallets; others backed away, knowing I rarely make anything but sure

[1]Lists and arrays play a central role in scores of problems; we shall explore them fully in Chapter 15, "Matrices."

bets. My host, who had recently acquired a microcomputer, retreated quickly to his study to consider my offer. He later told me that he formulated the problem in the following terms. If he could have 365 variables, one for each day of the year, then he could initially assign zero to each of these. He would then get his computer to give him a sequence of forty random numbers between 1 and 365. This would be tantamount to ordering his guests in some arbitrary fashion and sequentially recording their birthdays. As a random number came off the computer (equivalent to a guest announcing his or her birthday), the value in the corresponding variable would be changed from zero to one. At some point, it will happen that when my host goes to change the value assigned to one of the variables from zero to one, he will find it has already been changed. At that moment, he will have found two people with the same birthday. He reasoned this could happen when there were only two people (very unlikely) and that it must happen when there are more than 365 people. But at what point in between might it happen?

Having only recently acquired his computer and having read only a few pages in the manual, he knew he could assign at most 286 variables. Was there a way around this limitation?

Lists

Thus far, we have focused attention on problems for which a few variables were sufficient. In addition, the meanings attached to these variables were specific and distinct. For example, in one problem, the symbol Y stood for year and I for interest. We may want to solve problems, however, that require large numbers of variables. More important, the meaning attached to these variables may be more readily grasped by considering all of them as belonging to a class.

Consider a 300-seat auditorium that has been reserved for an examination. Three hundred students, each identified by an ID number, are to be assigned seats for the exam. The most natural association is to create a list of three hundred subscripted variables X_1, $X_2, \ldots, X_{300}$ to represent the seats and to assign each student, by means of his or her ID number, to a specific seat, that is, to one of the variables. The ID of the first student would be assigned to X_1, the ID of the second to X_2, and so on, until the ID of the 300th student is assigned to X_{300}.

Because problems of this type frequently occur, BASIC has been given the capability of handling subscripted variables. The physical limitations of the terminals, however, dictate that instead of writing X_1, we must write X(1); instead of X_{15}, we must write X(15). Thus, for the 300 seats in the auditorium we would use the 300 variables X(I), where I takes the integer values 1, 2, 3, . . . , 300.

The Dimension Statement

Before subscripted variables may be used, the computer must know that we intend to use them. This is signaled by a dimension statement, DIM, generally written at the beginning of the program. Thus, for example, we would write:

```
>10 DIM X(350)
```

to indicate we are setting up a subscripted variable X(I) for which the subscript may take the values from 1 through 350.[2] While only 300 people are to be assigned, and we intend to use no more than 300 of the subscripted values, there is little harm in using a number in the DIM statement that exceeds by some reasonable amount the number needed in the problem. It is unreasonable, however, to use a number in the DIM statement that far exceeds the number of subscripted variables actually needed.

The following program reads and prints ID numbers for 10 students.[3] Observe that

[2]For some computers, the maximum number of variables in a list is as few as 255; for others, as many as 32,767.
[3]For some computers, for a list of ten or fewer variables, the DIM statement may be omitted.

the name of the variable used to represent the identification number is I and that at lines 80, 90, and 100 the symbol K represents the subscript. Since no particular significance is attached to the subscript, at lines 140, 150, and 160 the symbol J is used. When used this way, the subscript is often referred to as a dummy variable.

```
10 REM: THIS PROGRAM ILLUSTRATES THE USE OF SUBSCRIPTED VARIABLES,
20 REM: WHICH CONCEPT IS OFTEN REFERRED TO AS A LIST.
30 REM: WE SHALL CREATE A LIST OF ID NUMBERS FOR 10 STUDENTS.
40 REM: N REFERS TO THE LENGTH OF THE LIST
50 READ N
60 DATA 10
70 DIM I(25)
80 FOR K=1 TO N
90 READ I(K)
100 NEXT K
110 DATA 1231234,2342345,3453456,4564567,5675678,6786789
120 DATA 1122334,2233445,3344556,4455667
130 PRINT
140 FOR J=1 TO N
150 PRINT I(J),
160 NEXT J
170 PRINT
```

```
1231234        2342345        3453456        4564567        5675678
6786789        1122334        2233445        3344556        4455667
```

If a program requires more than one list, we must use a dimension statement for each list. Thus, if A(I) and B(J) are two lists of 20 and 30 elements, respectively, we write:

```
10 DIM A(20), B(30)
```

The maximum number of named lists in a program is 26: A(I), B(J), . . . , Z(K). BASIC does not recognize a letter followed by a digit as a legal name for a subscripted variable; if attempted, an error message is printed.

Illustration: The Smallest Number in a List

How may we go about finding the smallest (or largest) number in a list of numbers? First, 15 randomly generated integers between −100 and 100 are assigned to the variables X(1), . . . , X(15). To discover the numbers generated, the program includes an instruction to print them. To emphasize that the symbol used to represent the subscript is not significant, we have used I in lines 20–40 and J in lines 50–70.

```
10 DIM X(20)
20 FOR I=1 TO 15
30 X(I)=INT(201*RND(1))-100
40 NEXT I
50 FOR J=1 TO 15
60 PRINT X(J);
70 NEXT J
```

```
-17   -87    31   -36   -99   -66    93   -51    64    40    67    38
 29    30   -81
```

The following algorithm, or procedure, finds the smallest number and its position in the list. Let the variable A be the smallest number found thus far and K its position in the list. Initially, A = X(1) and K = 1. Next, compare X(2) and A; if X(2) < A, replace the current value of A by the value of X(2), let K = 2, and go to X(3). Otherwise, ignore X(2) and proceed to X(3). If X(3) < A, replace the current value of A by X(3), let K = 3 and go to X(4); otherwise, ignore X(3) and proceed to X(4). Repeat this process until the list is exhausted. The final value of A is the smallest number in the list, and its position is given by the value of K. A flow chart illustrating this process appears in Figure 9-1.

A code implementing this procedure is appended after line 70 of the above program. The new program and the result of executing it is:

```
10 DIM X(20)
20 FOR I=1 TO 15
30 X(I)=INT(201*RND(1))-100
40 NEXT I
50 FOR J=1 TO 15
60 PRINT X(J);
70 NEXT J
80 PRINT
90 A=X(1) \ K=1
100 FOR I=2 TO 15
110 IF X(I)>=A THEN 130
120 A=X(I) \ K=I
130 NEXT I
140 PRINT
150 PRINT "MINIMUM = "A
160 PRINT "POSITION IN LIST IS"K
```

FIGURE 9-1

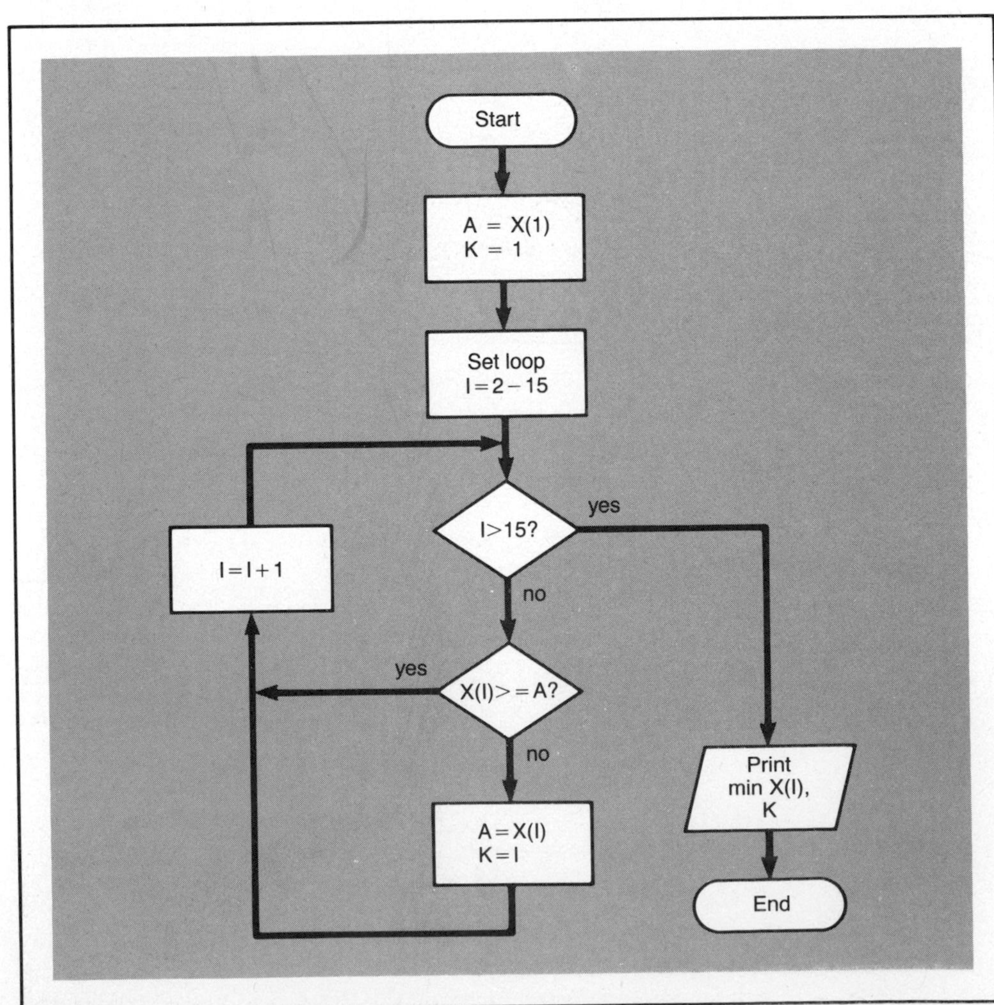

```
-24    -26    55    -33    -92    -58    84    16    -56    -77    42    -60
 65    -69     2

MINIMUM = -92
POSITION IN LIST IS 5
```

If we want to find the maximum and its position in the list, we change line 110 to read:

```
110 KF X(I) < = A THEN 130
```

Line 150 should be changed so that MAXIMUM replaces MINIMUM.

Sorting

Sorting is one of the more important applications of lists. When you pay bills by check, they are received at your bank in random order. Generally, in order to help you reconcile your checkbook with the bank statement, the bank will list the amounts written, sorted by check number. Also, major credit agencies receive charge slips from a variety of sources and for a variety of customers. These charges are entered into the computer as they are received. Monthly, this accumulated list is sorted by account number and the invoices prepared. The objective is, given a list of arbitrarily arranged numbers, to rearrange the entries either in increasing or decreasing order.[4] From the viewpoint of simplicity of logic, the "bubble" method is straightforward.

The Bubble Sort

Starting with an unordered sequence of numbers, we wish to arrange them in increasing order. The underlying process is to compare two adjacent numbers, starting with the first and second, and if these are in the correct order, leave them alone; if not, interchange them. Next, compare the second and third numbers. If these are in the order wanted, leave them alone; if not, interchange them.

Proceed this way through the entire list. At the end of the first pass through the list, the largest number in the list has been moved to the last place and assigned to the variable with the largest subscript.

Return to the beginning of the modified list and start again. Compare the first two numbers, ordering them as required; then compare the second and third numbers, again ordering them, then the third and fourth numbers, and so on. After the second run through, the second largest number in the original list is assigned to the variable with the second largest subscript. Return to the beginning of the list and repeat the process, continuing until it is totally sorted.

If there are N elements in the original list, then during the first pass through, $N-1$ comparisons are made; during the second pass through only $N-2$ comparisons are needed, since the method assures that the largest number has already been assigned to the variable with the largest index. As the looping through the list continues, the number of comparisons needed is reduced by 1 each time. To totally sort the list, the number of comparisons needed is

$$(N-1) + (N-2) + \ldots + (1) = \frac{N(N-1)}{2}$$

The flow chart in Figure 9-2 describes the bubble sort. Since there are N elements in the list, there must be $N-1$ passes through it. This is indicated by an outer loop that runs from 1 to $N-1$. On any one pass, say the Ith time through the list, only $N - I$

[4]Later, we shall use these same ideas to alphabetize a list of names. See Chapter 11.

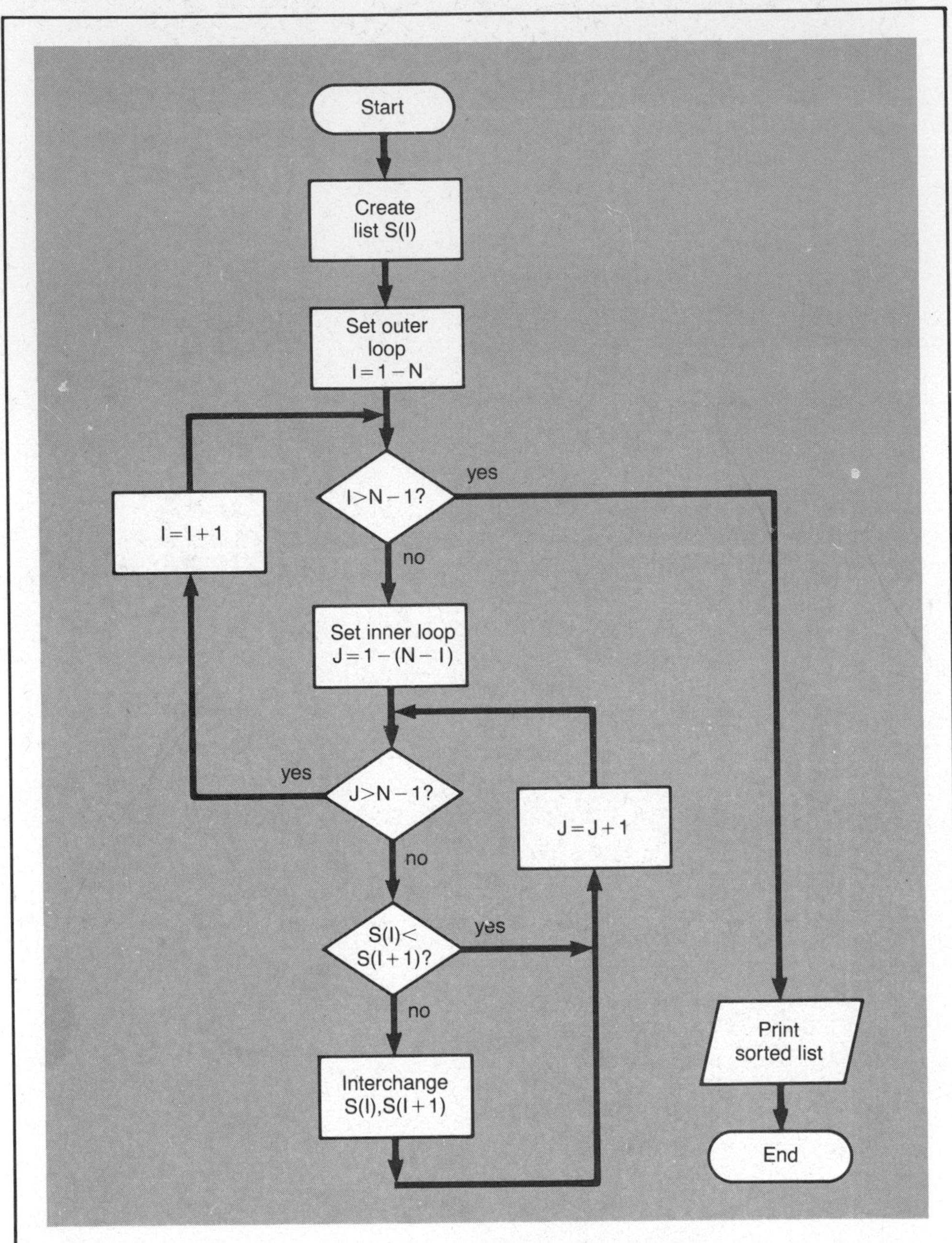

FIGURE 9-2

comparisons are made. This is done in an inner loop; the index J goes from 1 to N − I. The comparisons between successive pairs of elements in the list are made within this inner loop. After the list is totally sorted, it is printed. The program for the bubble sort follows:

```
10 DIM S(25)
20 N=24
30 REM: A RANDOM LIST IS GENERATED AND PRINTED.
40 FOR I=1 TO N
50 S(I)=INT(201*RND(1))-100
60 NEXT I
70 FOR J=1 TO N
80 PRINT S(J);
90 NEXT J
100 PRINT \ PRINT
```

```
110 REM: WE ENTER THE BUBBLE SORT ROUTINE
120 FOR I=1 TO N-1
130    FOR J=1 TO N-I
140 REM: WE COMPARE S(J) AND S(J+1)
150       IF S(J)<=S(J+1) THEN 200
160 REM: WE SWITCH S(J) AND S(J+1)
170       X=S(J+1)
180       S(J+1)=S(J)
190       S(J)=X
200    NEXT J
210 NEXT I
220 FOR I=1 TO N
230 PRINT S(I);
240 NEXT I
```

```
-49    65    24   -41   -54    44   -59    54    52    28   -96   -27
100    44   -34   -77   -87   -29    66   -10   -53   -22   -61    38

-96   -87   -77   -61   -59   -54   -53   -49   -41   -34   -29   -27
-22   -10    24    28    38    44    44    52    54    65    66   100
```

The first part of the program, lines 10–90, creates and exhibits the list to be sorted. Suppose α is the number initially assigned to the variable S(J) and β to the variable S(J+1). At line 150, α and β are compared. If α is less than β, the program continues to the next comparison by jumping to line 200. If, however, α is greater than β, then we want to end up with β assigned to S(J) and α to S(J+1). The precise technique used to interchange the two numbers is given in lines 170–190.

Imagine three memory locations whose addresses are S(J), S(J+1), and X. Immediately prior to the execution of line 170, the status of these three locations may be depicted by:

Memory location	S(J)	S(J+1)	X
Contents	α	β	anything

After line 170 is executed, β is assigned to the variable X and the status of the three memory locations is:

Memory location	S(J)	S(J+1)	X
Contents	α	β	β

After line 180, α is assigned to S(J+1) and the three memory locations look like:

Memory location	S(J)	S(J+1)	X
Contents	α	α	β

If we had not previously saved β by assigning it to X, it would be lost forever; having assigned β to X, we still have it. It can now be used to replace α in S(J). This is done in line 190, and the status of the three locations becomes:

Memory location	S(J)	S(J+1)	X
Contents	β	α	β

The contents of memory locations S(J) and S(J+1) have been interchanged.

Tallying

Another important application of lists is tallying. Back in Yoknapatawpha County, Polly Quinter has another task for her computer staff. The state government prepares an annual report listing the number of homes that fall into specific classes of appraised property value. The classes are arranged in intervals of $10,000.

In class 1 are the properties whose value is less than $10,000, in class 2 those whose value is at least $10,000 but less than $20,000, and so on. All properties of at least $200,000 are lumped together into one class. In all, there are 21 such classes.

Having the data of appraised property values for her county available to her, Polly wants an analogous table to compare property values in Yoknapatawpha County with those in the rest of the state.

The procedure she visualizes begins with 21 empty boxes labeled 0–10K, 10K–20K, . . . , 190K–200K, over 200K, and a big bag of beans. As each property value is read, a bean is placed in the appropriate box. After all the properties are accounted for, the number of beans in each box is counted and the results tabulated. A graph such as the one in Fig. 9-3 may then be prepared.

Polly's prior experience with her computer staff encourages her to take a more modern approach. Showing the table produced by the state to her staff (Table 9-1), she

TABLE 9-1

CLASS NUMBER	NUMBER OF HOMES
1	90,215
2	78,567
3	70,111
4	62,345
5	76,327
6	72,107
7	69,820
8	59,272
9	53,897
10	46,227
11	41,648
12	39,787
13	36,274
14	28,132
15	24,812
16	20,010
17	18,567
18	17,456
19	9,864
29	6,196
21	13,456

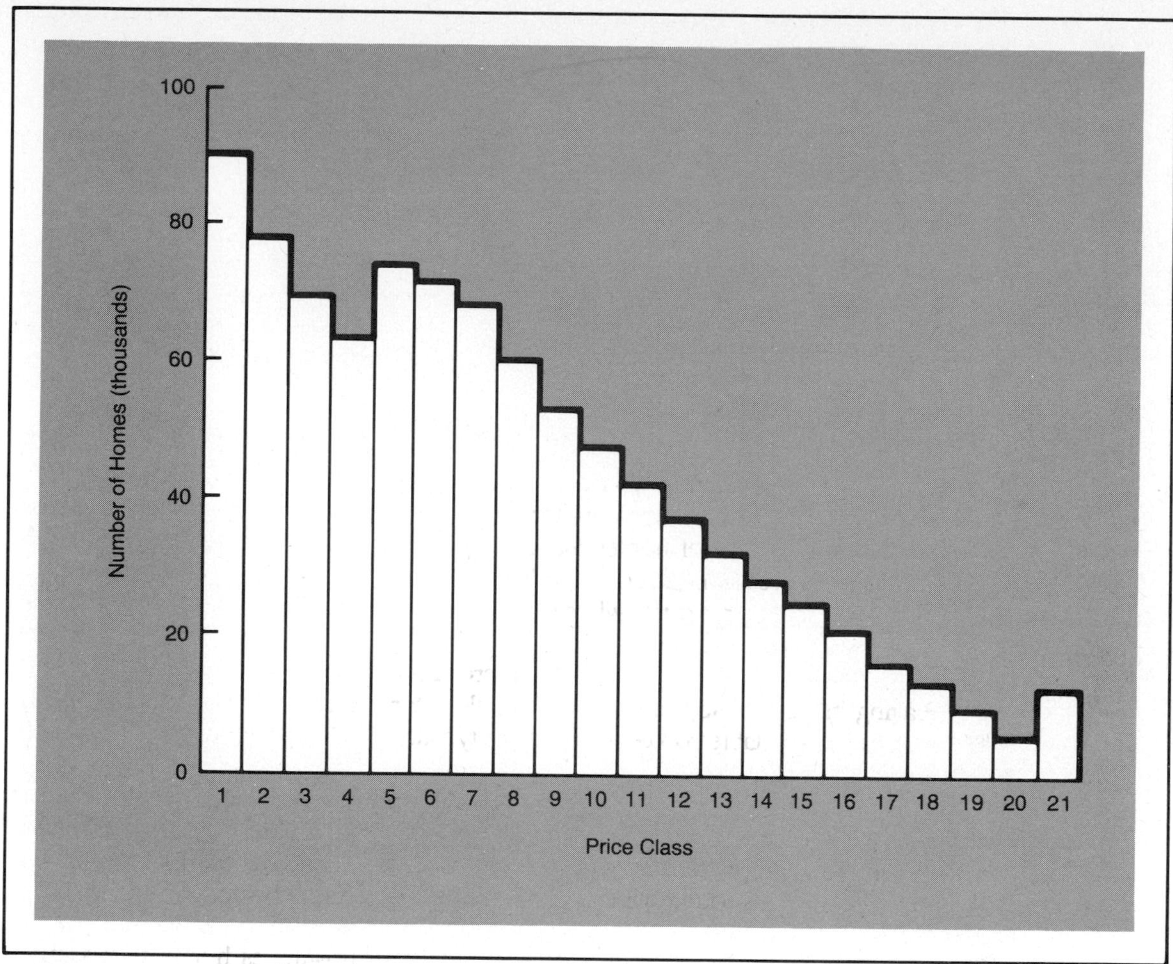

FIGURE 9-3

asks for a computer program that, given the data for Yoknapatawpha County, would produce an analogous report. She asks for a flow chart as well as assurance that the program works. The assurance is to take the form of a test run on selected data. The flow chart is shown in Figure 9-4.

Polly's staff writes and tests the following program:

```
10 DIM P(100),N(25)
20 PRINT"HOW MANY PROPERTIES ARE THERE"; \ INPUT H
30 REM: AT PRESENT THERE ARE 21 CLASSES; LATER THERE MAY A DIFFERENT NUMBER
40 REM: LET K REPRESENT THE NUMBER OF CLASSES.
50 K=21
60 REM: THE CLASSES ARE DENOTED BY N(C).
70 REM: INITIALLY, THE NUMBER OF PROPERTIES IN EACH CLASS IS ZERO.
80 FOR I=1 TO K
90 N(I)=0
100 NEXT I
110 REM: EACH PROPERTY VALUE IS READ AND THE CLASS IN WHICH IT BELONGS
120 REM: IS DETERMINED.
130 FOR I=1 TO H
140 READ P(I)
150 C=INT(P(I)/10000)+1
160 IF C<K+1 THEN 180
170 C=K
180 N(C)=N(C)+1
190 NEXT I
200 REM: THE TALLYING IS DONE. PRINT THE RESULTS.
210 PRINT & PRINT
```

```
220 PRINT,"     PROPERTY VALUES"
230 PRINT
240 PRINT ,"AT LEAST"," BUT LESS THAN","NUMBER"
250 PRINT
260 FOR I=1 TO K-1
270 PRINT ,(I-1)*10^4,I*10^4,,N(I)
280 NEXT I
290 PRINT ,"IN EXCESS OF $200,000",,N(K)
300 DATA 4000,4500,5500,5600,5700,12100,13400,85000,250000,300000
310 DATA 25600,29900,45900,78650,98760,45630,89070,35555,56600
320 DATA 100500,115000,125000,139000,147000,152000,168900,175123,186000,199999
330 DATA 34500
```

```
HOW MANY PROPERTIES ARE THERE   ?30

                      PROPERTY VALUES

                 AT LEAST        BUT LESS THAN                NUMBER

                  0              10000                          5
                  10000          20000                          2
                  20000          30000                          2
                  30000          40000                          2
                  40000          50000                          2
                  50000          60000                          1
                  60000          70000                          0
                  70000          80000                          1
                  80000          90000                          2
                  90000          100000                         1
                  100000         110000                         1
                  110000         120000                         1
                  120000         130000                         1
                  130000         140000                         1
                  140000         150000                         1
                  150000         160000                         1
                  160000         170000                         1
                  170000         180000                         1
                  180000         190000                         1
                  190000         200000                         1
                 IN EXCESS OF $200,000                          2
```

The only parts of this program that may be unfamiliar to you are lines 130 through 190. Lines 130 and 190 are instructions for a loop; these offer no difficulty. Line 140 assigns a value to P(I), the value of the Ith property. The class number C to which the property value P(I) is to be assigned is determined in line 150. Because all properties of value $200,000 or greater are to be lumped into one class, the class number, C, is tested to see if it is less than 22. If C is less than 22, the program jumps line 170; if C is greater than 21, it is set equal to 21 (line 170). In line 180, the actual tallying is done. For any given class, say C = 3, N(3) is increased by 1 each time a property belonging in class 3 occurs.

The remainder of the program is concerned only with the format of the printout.

More on Birthdays

The next time I saw my host from the birthday party (see pages 141-42), he had read about subscripted variables and lists and had written a program to determine how many people there should be in a group so that at least two have the same birthday. He had modified his original thinking only slightly and presented his solution in the following form. He constructed a list of 365 variables, D(1), . . . , D(365), one for each day of the year, and initially set each variable equal to zero. He then turned to his random number generator

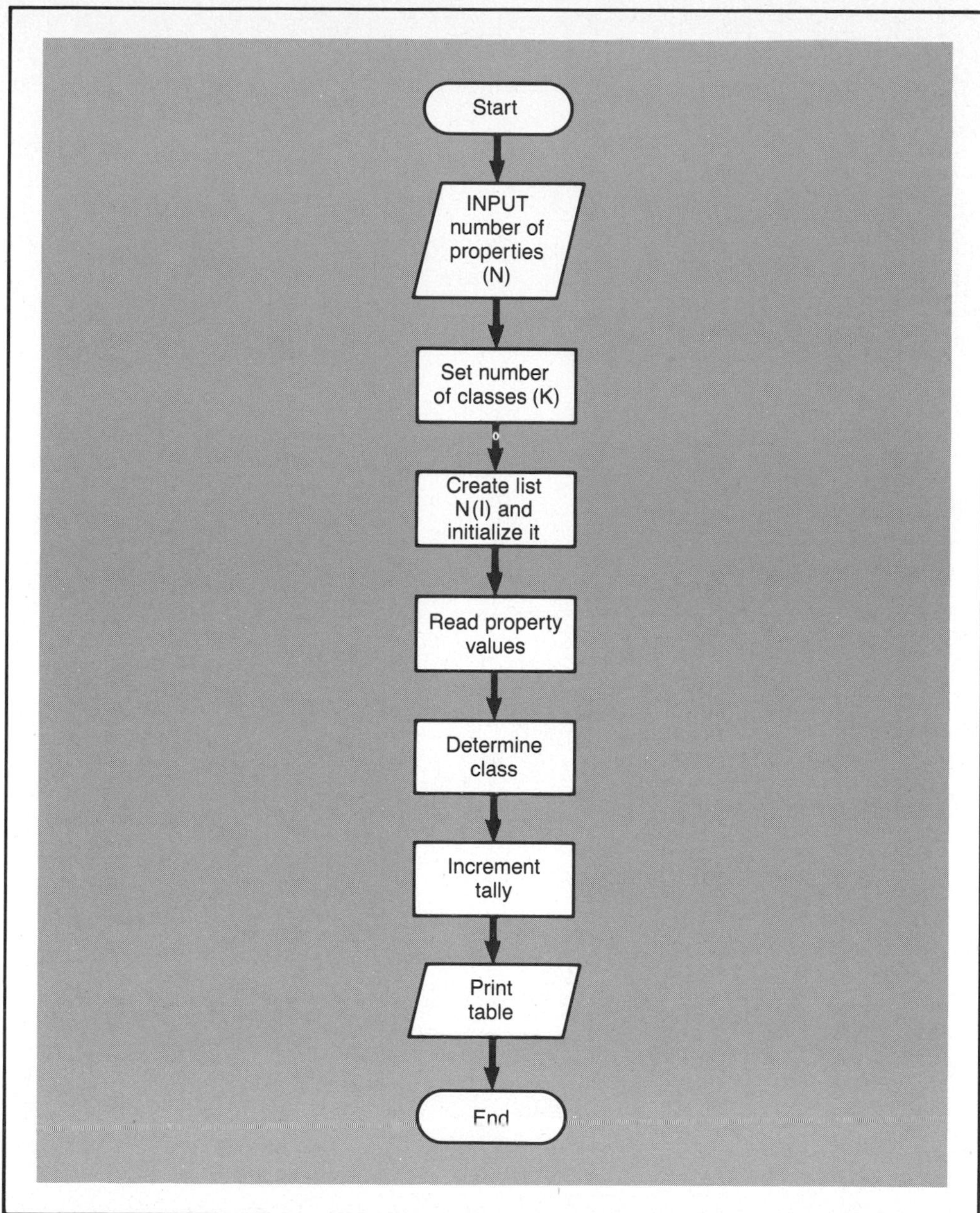

FIGURE 9-4

and sequentially selected randomly generated integers between 1 and 365. As each random integer, say J, was selected, he did three things: (1) he increased the entry in D(J) by one, (2) he recorded the number of random integers that had been selected to that point, and (3) he examined the entry in D(J) to see if it was one or two. If it was one, he knew he had not yet found two people with the same birthday, whereas if the entry was two, then he had found two people whose birthdays coincided. The number of randomly selected integers corresponded to the number of people he had to ask before finding the pair.

My friend recognized that doing the experiment only once would be misleading. If he repeated it many times, say 10,000, he could record how often he found two people with the same birthday when the number of random selections was 2, 3, 4, . . . , 366. Accordingly, he set up a second list of 366 variables, N(1), N(2), . . . , N(366), and tallied in N(J) the number of times success was achieved on the Jth selection. (He noted that N(1) = 0.) He let S represent the total number of trials (S = 10,000), so that N(2)/S became an estimate of the relative frequency that, in a group consisting of only two people, they would have the same birthday, [N(2) + N(3)]/S an estimate of the relative frequency that, in a group of three people, at least two would have the same birthday, . . . , [N(2) + N(3) + . . . + N(K)]/S an estimate of the relative frequency that in a group of K people there would be at least two having the same birthday. He believed he did not need to know the value of the expression [N(2) + N(3) + . . . + N(K)]/S for all values of K from 2 to 366. Accordingly, he devised two traps to limit the number of computations that should be made. First, he conjectured that, even for S = 10,000 trials, the possibility that N(K) $\neq$ 0 for *all* K = 2 to 366 was extremely unlikely. Therefore, if he summed N(K) for K = 2 to some value A, possibly less than 366, so that the sum $\sum_{K=2}^{A} N(K) = S$, he would know that for all K > A, N(K) = 0. Thus, any future computation could be limited to values of K $\leqq$ A. (See lines 220–290, below.) Second, he felt that knowing the relative frequency of success from 0 to perhaps as much as 75 percent would give him the insight he needed. (See lines 300–370.)

He had dutifully drawn the flow chart in Figure 9-5. He then showed me his program and the output from 10,000 trials.

```
10 REM: SET UP THE TWO LISTS
20 DIM D(365),N(366)
30 PRINT "HOW MANY TRIALS"; & INPUT S & PRINT
40 REM: INITIALIZE THE N(I) LIST
50 FOR I=1 TO 366 & N(I)=0 & NEXT I
60 FOR J=1 TO S
70 REM: INITIALIZE THE D(I) LIST
80 FOR I=1 TO 365 & D(I)=0 & NEXT I
90 REM: THIS NEXT SECTION CALCULATES THE NUMBER
100 REM: OF RANDOMLY GENERATED INTEGERS UNTIL THE FIRST
110 REM: REPETITION OCCURS AND TALLIES THESE
120 K=0
130 Y=INT(365*RND(0))+1
140 K=K+1
150 D(Y)=D(Y)+1
160 IF D(Y)=2 THEN 180
170 GOTO 130
180 N(K)=N(K)+1
190 NEXT J
200 REM: THE RESULTS ARE PRINTED
210 PRINT "K","N(K)","SUM"
220 REM: THERE IS NO POINT IN PRINTING K AND N(K) IF
230 REM: ALL S CASES ARE ACCOUNTED FOR.  THUS, THE LAST
240 REM: VALUE THAT IS OF INTEREST IS DETERMINED.
250 M=0
260 FOR A=2 TO 366
270 M=M+N(A)
280 IF M=S THEN 320
290 NEXT A
300 REM: ONLY THOSE VALUES OF K, N(K) AND THE RELATIVE FREQUENCY
310 REM: FOR WHICH M/S<.75 ARE PRINTED.
320 M=0
330 FOR K=2 TO A
340 M=M+N(K)
350 IF M/S>.75 THEN 370
360 PRINT K,N(K),M/S
370 NEXT K
380 END
```

```
HOW MANY TRIALS    ?10000

K               N(K)            SUM
 2               29              2.90000E-03
 3               63              9.20000E-03
 4               99              1.91000E-02
 5               110             3.01000E-02
```

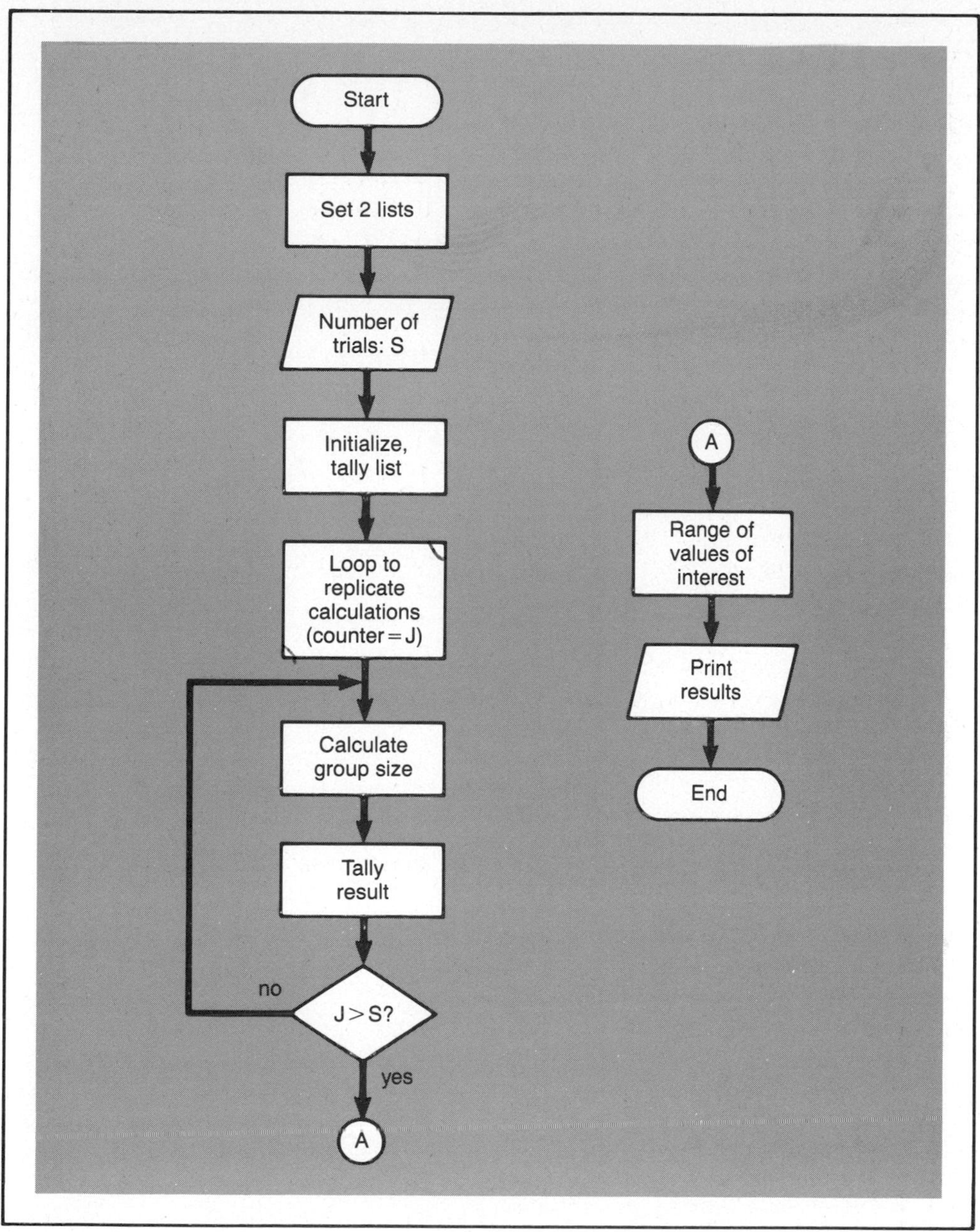

FIGURE 9-5

```
6              160          4.61000E-02
7              165          6.26000E-02
8              170          7.96000E-02
9              190          9.86000E-02
10             208          .119400
11             238          .143200
12             250          .168200
13             270          .195200
14             314          .226600
15             324          .259000
16             310          .290000
17             348          .324800
18             292          .354000
19             307          .384700
20             318          .416500
21             317          .448200
22             345          .482700
23             279          .510600
```

```
24          305          .541100
25          327          .573800
26          290          .602800
27          291          .631900
28          251          .657000
29          267          .683700
30          244          .708100
31          247          .732800
```

My friend concluded with the observation that, apparently, in a group of size 22, the probability of finding two people with the same birthday is slightly less than 1/2, whereas in a group of size 23, this probability is slightly greater than 1/2.

Another Solution

As we have seen, there may be more than one way to analyze and solve a problem. The following procedure offers another solution to the birthday problem.

Start with an arbitrary group of size N, say N = 20, and ask if it contains two people with the same birthday. If the answer is yes, record this as a successful experiment; otherwise record it as unsuccessful. Repeat the experiment for a second group of 20 and again record the result as successful or unsuccessful. Repeat the experiment many times, say 10,000, each time recording the outcome as either successful or unsuccessful. The number of successes divided by the number of trials (10,000) is an estimate of the relative frequency of finding two people in a group of size N, 20, who share the same birthday.

Increase N by 1 and repeat the process. Stop when you feel N is sufficiently large, say N = 35. It is this solution, for N ranging from 2 to 35, that is now flow charted and programed. The flow chart appears in Figure 9-6. The program follows.

```
10 DIM Y(40)
20 REM: LET N BE THE NUMBER OF PEOPLE IN THE GROUP
30 PRINT
40 PRINT "N","PROBABILITY"
50 PRINT
60 FOR N=2 TO 35
70 Z=0
80 REM: FOR EACH N, THE EXPERIMENT IS TO BE RUN 10000 TIMES.
90 FOR K=1 TO 10000
100 REM: THERE ARE N PEOPLE, GET THEIR BIRTHDAYS.
110 FOR L=1 TO N
120 Y(L)=INT(365*RND(0))+1
130 NEXT L
140 REM: ARE THERE TWO PEOPLE WITH THE SAME BIRTHDAY?
150 FOR I=1 TO N-1
160 FOR J=I+1 TO N
170 IF Y(I)=Y(J) THEN 240
180 NEXT J
190 NEXT I
200 GOTO 250
210 REM: Z COUNTS THE NUMBER OF TIMES THE EXPERIMENT IS
220 REM: SUCCESSFUL, I.E., HOW MANY TIMES, IN A GROUP OF SIZE
230 REM: N, THERE ARE TWO PEOPLE WITH THE SAME BIRTHDAY.
240 Z=Z+1
250 NEXT K
260 PRINT N,Z/10000
270 NEXT N
```

The program was run with the following result:

```
N              PROBABILITY

 2              3.20000E-03
 3              8.30000E-03
 4              1.61000E-02
 5              3.04000E-02
 6              4.05000E-02
```

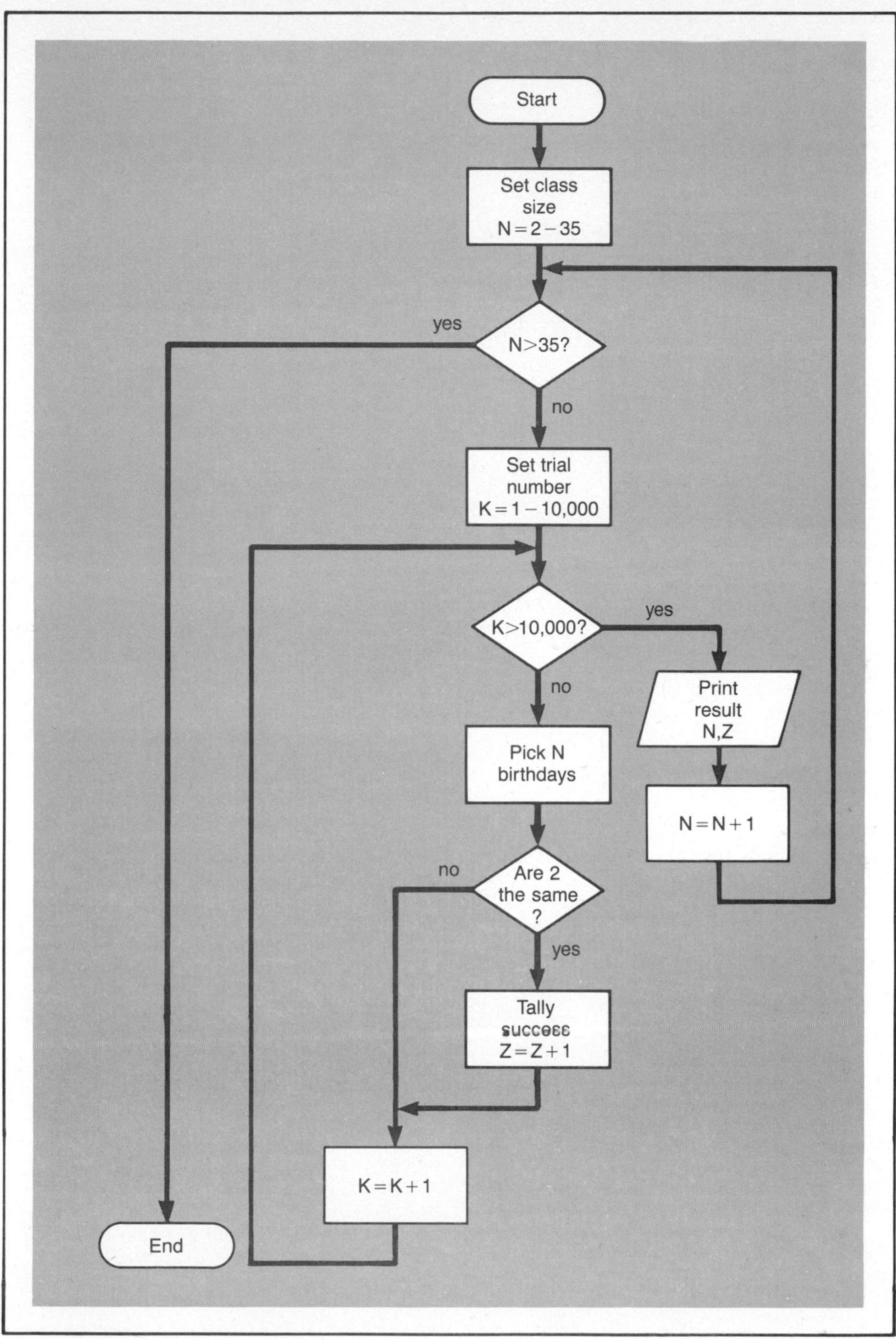

FIGURE 9-6

```
7              5.84000E-02
8              7.20000E-02
9              9.19000E-02
10             .113900
11             .142700
12             .162500
13             .200000
14             .225500
```

```
15          .252500
16          .281400
17          .316300
18          .344000
19          .381000
20          .413800
21          .448200
22          .476200
23          .508500
24          .542000
25          .563000
26          .607000
27          .627900
28          .656800
29          .689700
30          .701800
31          .731000
32          .760200
33          .770800
34          .795300
35          .807000
```

These two simulations may be replaced by an exact formula for calculating the probability P, that in a group of size N, there are at least two persons with the same birthday.[5] The formula is:

$$P = 1 - \left(1 - \frac{1}{365}\right)\left(1 - \frac{2}{365}\right)\cdots\left(1 - \frac{N-1}{365}\right)$$

The formula is tabulated in Table 9-2.

TABLE 9-2
The Probability That at Least Two People in a Group Share the Same Birthday

GROUP SIZE	PROBABILITY	GROUP SIZE	PROBABILITY	GROUP SIZE	PROBABILITY
		21	.443688	41	.903152
2	2.73973E-03	22	.475695	42	.914030
3	8.20417E-03	23	.507297	43	.923923
4	1.63559E-02	24	.538344	44	.932885
5	2.71356E-02	25	.568700	45	.940976
6	4.04625E-02	26	.598241	46	.948253
7	5.62357E-02	27	.626859	47	.954774
8	7.43353E-02	28	.654461	48	.960598
9	9.46238E-02	29	.680969	49	.965780
10	.116948	30	.706316	50	.970374
11	.141141	31	.730455	51	.974432
12	.167025	32	.753348	52	.978005
13	.194410	33	.774972	53	.981138
14	.223103	34	.795317	54	.983877
15	.252901	35	.814383	55	.986262
16	.283604	36	.832182	56	.988332
17	.315008	37	.848734	57	.990122
18	.346911	38	.864068	58	.991665
19	.379119	39	.878220	59	.992989
20	.411438	40	.891232	60	.994123

[5] William Feller, *An Introduction to Probability Theory and Its Applications,* Vol. 1 (New York: John Wiley & Sons, 1958) 2nd Edition, pp. 31–32, 45–47.

Arrays

In addition to handling lists (single subscripted variables), BASIC handles arrays (double subscripted variables). Arrays are needed, for example, when we want to study populations based on two-way classifications. Suppose we want to examine the average annual income, I, as a function of age, A, and education, E. We would create a table in which a row, A, would represent an age group: A = 1 means 15–25 years old, A = 2 means 25–35 years, . . . , A = 12 means 125–135 years, and a column, E, would represent an educational level. Thus, E = 1 would mean less than one year of elementary school completed, E = 2 would mean one year of elementary school completed, . . . , E = 13 would mean high school completed. E = 17 would indicate four years of college completed, E = 18 a Master's degree and E = 19 a Doctor's degree. The average annual income, I, would then be an entry in the table. (For those entries for which there are insufficient data, the number −1 is used. A dot indicates some numerical entry not germane to the discussion.) From Table 9-3, we would read, for example: $I_{5,13}$ = $15,000.

In mathematical notation, an array is represented by A_{ij}, *where the subscripts i* and j are integers with $i = 1, 2, \ldots, N$ and $j = 1, 2, \ldots, M$. In BASIC, the corresponding symbol is A(I,J). As with single subscripted variables, a DIM statement is required.[6] Thus, if the array A(I,J) has 12 rows and 19 columns, we write:

```
>10 DIM A(12,19)
```

It is permissible, of course, to use

```
>10 DIM A(15,20)
```

and still, in the program, limit I to 12 values and J to 19. The first index always refers to the row number, the second to the column.

TABLE 9-3
Average Annual Income (I)
as a Function of Age (A) and Education (E)

A↓ E→	1	2	3	···	13		···		19
1	−1	50	300	·	8,000	·	·	·	−1
2	2,000	3,000	3,500	·	9,000	·	·	·	20,000
3	·	·	·	·	·	·	·	·	·
4	·	·	·	·	·	·	·	·	·
5	4,000	·	·	·	15,000	·	·	·	32,000
	·	·	·	·	·	·	·	·	·
⋮	·	·	·	·	·	·	·	·	·
	·	·	·	·	·	·	·	·	·
12	−1	·	·	·	1,200	·	·	·	−1

[6] As with lists, if both indexes I and J of an array are ten or less, the DIM statement may not be needed.

The following examples illustrate how arrays are read and printed. The array we want the computer to read is:

```
20 30 40 50 60 70 80 90
21 31 41 51 61 71 81 91
25 35 45 55 65 75 85 95
```

The eight numbers in the first row are to be assigned to the eight variables A(1,1), A(1,2), A(1,3), . . . , A(1,8), respectively; the eight numbers in the second row to the variables A(2,1), A(2,2), . . . ,A(2,8), respectively; and the eight numbers in the third row to the variables A(3,1), A(3,2), . . . ,A(3,8), respectively. In the following program, this is done in lines 10 through 50. Lines 60 through 90 print the 24 values of the subscripted variables A(I,J).

```
10 FOR I=1 TO 3
20 FOR J=1 TO 8
30 READ A(I,J)
40 NEXT J
50 NEXT I
60 FOR I=1 TO 3
70 FOR J=1 TO 8
80 PRINT "A("I","J")=" A(I,J)
90 NEXT J
100 NEXT I
110 DATA 20,30,40,50,60,70,80,90
120 DATA 21,31,41,51,61,71,81,91
130 DATA 25,35,45,55,65,75,85,95
```

```
A( 1, 1)= 20
A( 1, 2)= 30
A( 1, 3)= 40
A( 1, 4)= 50
A( 1, 5)= 60
A( 1, 6)= 70
A( 1, 7)= 80
A( 1, 8)= 90
A( 2, 1)= 21
A( 2, 2)= 31
A( 2, 3)= 41
A( 2, 4)= 51
A( 2, 5)= 61
A( 2, 6)= 71
A( 2, 7)= 81
A( 2, 8)= 91
A( 3, 1)= 25
A( 3, 2)= 35
A( 3, 3)= 45
A( 3, 4)= 55
A( 3, 5)= 65
A( 3, 6)= 75
A( 3, 7)= 85
A( 3, 8)= 95
```

We may modify the program to print the output in tabular form. In line 80, the identification is dropped and a comma is inserted after A(I,J). Line 80 becomes

```
80 PRINT A(I,J),
```

With this modification, the program output looks like this:

```
20            30            40            50            60
70            80            90            21            31
41            51            61            71            81
91            25            35            45            55
65            75            85            95
```

We attempt to print three lines with eight entries each by modifying this last program. We insert: 95 PRINT. The new program is listed and run as follows.

```
10 FOR I=1 TO 3
20 FOR J=1 TO 8
30 READ A(I,J)
40 NEXT J
50 NEXT I
60 FOR I=1 TO 3
70 FOR J=1 TO 8
80 PRINT A(I,J),
90 NEXT J
100 NEXT I
110 DATA 20,30,40,50,60,70,80,90
120 DATA 21,31,41,51,61,71,81,91
130 DATA 25,35,45,55,65,75,85,95
```

```
 20              30              40              50              60
 70              80              90
 21              31              41              51              61
 71              81              91
 25              35              45              55              65
 75              85              95
```

Because there are only five fields on a line and eight fields are needed, 80 PRINT A(I, J), lists eight values before going to the next line.

If, in line 80, we replace the comma after A(I,J) with a semicolon, the printing is more closely packed and the result is as follows:

```
20    30    40    50    60    70    80    90
21    31    41    51    61    71    81    91
25    35    45    55    65    75    85    95
```

You may have noticed that we omitted the dimension statement. For the computer on which these programs were run, DIM A(3,8) may be omitted because the range for the indexes does not exceed ten.

As with lists, if more than one array is needed, the DIM statement must explicitly indicate this. For example, if three arrays, A, B, and C, are needed, the DIM statement would be:

```
10 DIM A(12,15), B(18,22), C(11,31)
```

Lists and arrays may be dimensioned in one or more statements. The same name, however, cannot be used for both a list and an array. Thus,

```
10 DIM S(25,30), S(15)
```

is illegal; if attempted, an error message will be printed.

Illustration: Machine Utilization and Overtime

To illustrate the use of arrays, we shall consider the following problem. The machine shop of the ABC Hardware Company contains 12 different kinds of machine tools: lathes, drills, milling machines, and so on. The cost of operating each of these is determined from prior experience. At the end of the day, each of 15 employees enters on a time card the number of hours worked on each machine. Thus, at the end of a typical day, an array like the one illustrated in Table 9-4 is produced. Blank entries represent zeros.

TABLE 9-4

Employee Number	Machine Number 1	2	3	4	5	6	7	8	9	10	11	12
1	2		3		1	1				1		
2		1			2					3		2
3									7		1	
4		1		1	1			1		1	1	2
5	1	4					3					
6			1	2		1	1		1	1		1
7	1			1	1	1		1			1	2
8	1		1	1	1	1	1	2				
9		1	2		1	2			2			
10	1	1		3							3	2
11	2		1	1		2		1		1		
12		2	1		2		2	1				
13				1	1		2	2		2	1	2
14			1	1		1	1	1	1		1	1
15	2	1			1			1		1	2	

Management's first concerns are to determine the total number of hours each machine is used and the number of hours of overtime, if any, each employee worked. To determine the utilization of each machine, each column of the array is summed. To find out if any employee worked overtime that day, each row of the array is summed and compared with 8. If an employee worked more than 8 hours on a particular day, the amount of overtime is noted. A flow chart of the task is shown in Figure 9-7. From this flow chart, the following program was written and run.

```
1Ø DIM H(15,12)
2Ø **********
3Ø REM: THIS SECTION READS THE DATA AND CONSTRUCTS THE ARRAY.
4Ø **********
5Ø FOR I=1 TO 15
6Ø FOR J=1 TO 12
7Ø READ H(I,J)
8Ø NEXT J
9Ø NEXT I
1ØØ DATA 2,Ø,3,Ø,1,1,Ø,Ø,Ø,1,Ø,Ø
11Ø DATA Ø,1,Ø,Ø,2,Ø,Ø,Ø,Ø,3,Ø,2
12Ø DATA Ø,Ø,Ø,Ø,Ø,Ø,Ø,Ø,7,Ø,1,Ø
13Ø DATA Ø,1,Ø,1,Ø,1,Ø,1,Ø,1,1,2
```

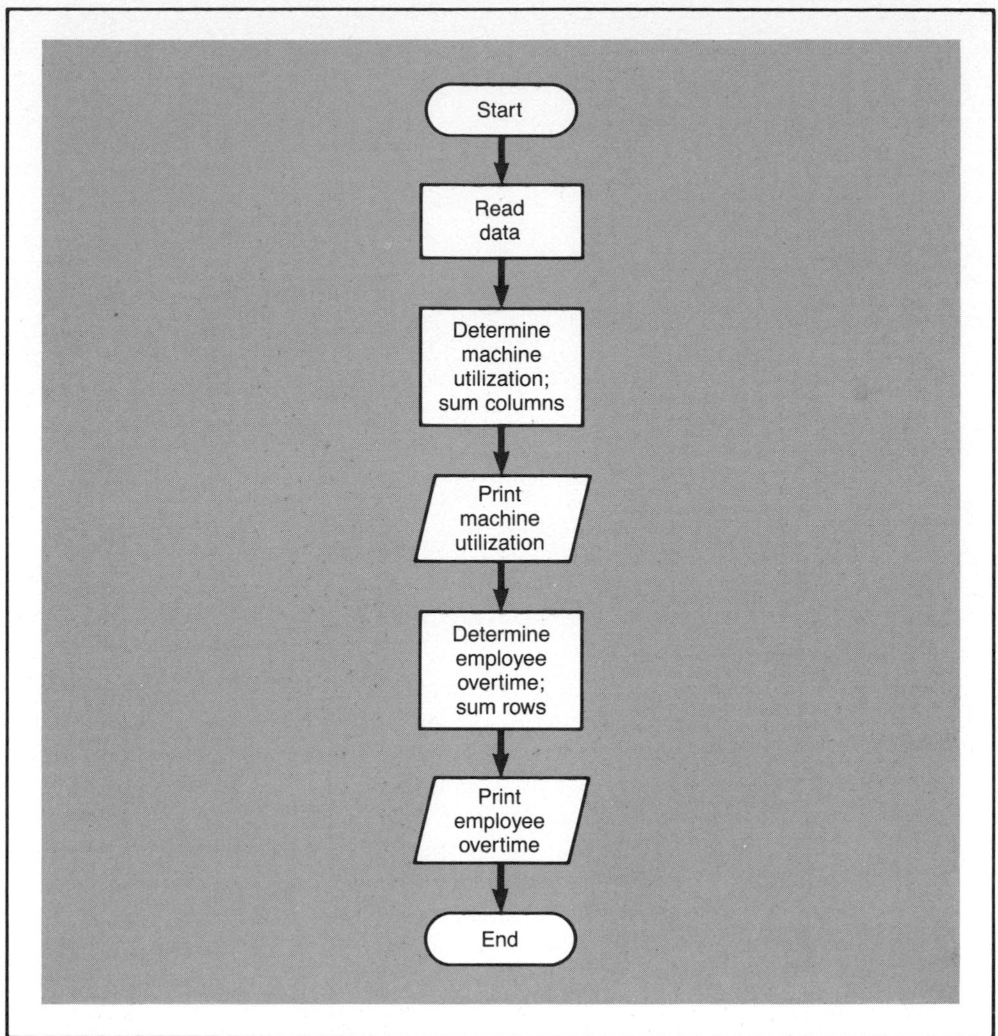

FIGURE 9-7

```
140 DATA 1,4,0,0,0,0,3,0,0,0,0,0
150 DATA 0,0,1,2,0,1,1,0,1,1,0,1
160 DATA 1,0,0,1,1,1,0,1,0,0,1,2
170 DATA 1,0,1,1,1,1,1,2,0,0,0,0
180 DATA 0,1,2,0,1,2,0,0,2,0,0,0
190 DATA 1,1,0,3,0,0,0,0,0,0,3,2
200 DATA 2,0,1,1,0,2,0,1,0,1,0,0
210 DATA 0,2,1,0,2,0,2,1,0,0,0,0
220 DATA 0,0,0,1,1,0,2,2,0,2,1,2
230 DATA 0,0,1,1,0,1,1,1,1,0,1,1
240 DATA 2,1,0,0,1,0,0,1,0,1,2,0
250 **********
260 REM: THIS SECTION DETERMINES THE MACHINE UTILIZATION.
270 **********
280 ;&;
290 FOR J=1 TO 12
300 A=0
310 FOR I=1 TO 15
320 A=A+H(I,J)
330 NEXT I
340 PRINT"MACHINE NUMBER"J" WAS UTILIZED"A" HOURS."
350 NEXT J
360 **********
370 REM: THIS SECTION DETERMINES WHICH EMPLOYEES WORKED OVERTIME.
380 **********
390 ;&;
```

```
400 FOR I=1 TO 15
410 B=0
420 FOR J=1 TO 12
430 B=B+H(I,J)
440 NEXT J
450 IF B<=8 THEN 470
460 PRINT "EMPLOYEE NUMBER"I" WORKED"B-8" HOURS OVERTIME."
470 NEXT I
```

```
MACHINE NUMBER 1 WAS UTILIZED 10 HOURS.
MACHINE NUMBER 2 WAS UTILIZED 11 HOURS.
MACHINE NUMBER 3 WAS UTILIZED 10 HOURS.
MACHINE NUMBER 4 WAS UTILIZED 11 HOURS.
MACHINE NUMBER 5 WAS UTILIZED 10 HOURS.
MACHINE NUMBER 6 WAS UTILIZED 10 HOURS.
MACHINE NUMBER 7 WAS UTILIZED 10 HOURS.
MACHINE NUMBER 8 WAS UTILIZED 10 HOURS.
MACHINE NUMBER 9 WAS UTILIZED 11 HOURS.
MACHINE NUMBER 10 WAS UTILIZED 10 HOURS.
MACHINE NUMBER 11 WAS UTILIZED 10 HOURS.
MACHINE NUMBER 12 WAS UTILIZED 12 HOURS.


EMPLOYEE NUMBER 10 WORKED 2 HOURS OVERTIME.
EMPLOYEE NUMBER 13 WORKED 3 HOURS OVERTIME.
```

To sum the numbers in a column, hold the J for that column constant and sum down the rows, I. This is done in lines 290–350. To sum the numbers in a row, hold the I for that row constant and sum across the columns, J. This is done in lines 400–440.

The only other symbol that may be unfamiliar to you appears in lines 280 and 390. Many computer systems recognize that the word PRINT occurs frequently. In an effort to reduce the tedium of writing PRINT each time, a special character is assigned to represent the word. For the computer for which this program was written and run, if the first symbol following the line number is a semicolon, it is interpreted to mean PRINT. Thus, "280 ; & ;" means "280 PRINT & PRINT." The use of the semicolon in this context may not be the convention adopted for your computer. On some it is "?". Refer to your manual to discover if and how this has been implemented on your system.

Exercises

9.1 Randomly select 15 numbers between −100 and +100 and print them in the order selected. Draw a flow chart and write a program that simultaneously finds both the maximum and the minimum values and their positions in the list.

Hint: Let A be the smallest number found thus far and K its position; let B be the largest found thus far and L its position. Initially, A = B = X(1) and K = L = 1. Next, compare X(2) and A; if X(2) < A, replace the current value of A with X(2), let K = 2, and go to X(3). If X(2) ≥ A, compare X(2) and B. If X(2) > B, replace the current value of B with X(2), let L = 2 and go to X(3). If X(2) ≤ B, go to X(3). Repeat this process until the list is exhausted. The final value of A is the smallest number in the list, and its position is given by K; B is the largest number and its position is L.

9.2 In a class of 25 students, the names are first alphabetized manually and then a number from 1 to 25 is assigned sequentially to each name. The students' grades on the first examination are stored in the computer in a list L_1, those on the second exam in a list L_2, and the scores on the final exam in a list L_3. The semester score for each student is determined by taking 25 percent of the first score plus 20 percent of the second and 55 percent of the third.

Draw a flow chart and write a program that prepares L_4, a fourth list consisting of the final scores.

You may use INPUT, READ/DATA, or generate the scores for each exam randomly.

In any case, the scores for each of the three exams are to be integers between 0 and 100. The final scores, the entires of the list L_4, are to be rounded to the nearest integer.

Print the four lists L_1, L_2, L_3, L_4

Sort and print L_4.

9.3 Modify the bubble sort program on pages 146–47 so that the output is a list arranged in decreasing order. Test your program.

9.4 (a) The mean $\overline{X}$ of a sequence of numbers $X_1, X_2, \ldots, X_N$ is given by the formula

$$\overline{X} = \frac{\left[\sum_{i=1}^{N} X_i\right]}{N}$$

where $\sum_{i=1}^{N} X_i = X_1 + X_2 + \ldots + X_N$.

Start with a sequence of numbers given in a list, X(I), and compute the mean. Your program should ask for, as input, the number of elements in the list X(I). You may generate the list X(I) using the random number generator.

(b) During August, the Dow-Jones average fluctuated between 820.47 and 875.29. For the 23 days that the stock market was open, the closing values of the Dow-Jones average were:

DAY	DOW-JONES AVERAGE	DAY	DOW-JONES AVERAGE	DAY	DOW-JONES AVERAGE
1	843.96	9	827.82	17	861.19
2	842.14	10	833.91	18	862.21
3	830.73	11	837.17	19	860.27
4	835.16	12	846.22	20	872.51
5	829.55	13	852.74	21	875.29
6	820.47	14	857.81	22	868.44
7	822.59	15	863.37	23	865.32
8	821.18	16	858.12		

Draw a flow chart and write a computer program that calculates the average of the Dow-Jones daily averages for the month of August. Because, in any one month, the number of days that the stock market is open varies, your program should be general enough to apply to any month.

9.5 (a) Assume there are N points on a line, located at distances $X_1, \ldots, X_N$ from a fixed point, 0. If X_i is positive, it lies to the right of 0; if X_i is negative, it lies to the left of 0. At each point, there is a positive mass M_i.

X_3 X_9 X_1 X_N X_7

M_3 M_9 ↑ M_1 M_N M_7

0

The center of mass $\overline{X}$ of this system is defined by the equation

$$\overline{X} = \frac{\left[\sum_{i=1}^{N} M_i X_i\right]}{\left[\sum_{i=1}^{N} M_i\right]} = \frac{M_1X_1 + M_2X_2 + \ldots + M_NX_N}{M_1 + M_2 \quad + \ldots + M_N}$$

Assume that N is an arbitrary positive integer and that the M_i and X_i are stored in two lists, each of length N. After drawing the flow chart, write a program that computes $\overline{X}$. Test it on data of your choosing.

(b) A large automobile agency sold 450 cars last month. In an effort to reduce inventory, no reasonable offer was refused. When the books were closed for the month, it was found that $100 was lost on each of 25 cars and $40 was lost on each of 50 cars. On the profit side, $85 was earned on each of 125 cars, $125 on each of 75 cars, $165 on each of 90 cars, $210 on each of 45 cars and $235 on each of the remaining cars. The formula given in part (a) can be used to calculate the average profit (or loss) on each car. Draw the flow chart, write the program, and calculate the average profit.

9.6 Let M_i and X_i be defined as in Exercise 9.5(a). The moment of inertia I of the mass system about the point 0 is given by the formula

$$I = \sum_{i=1}^{N} M_i X_i^2 = M_1 X_1^2 + M_2 X_2^2 + \ldots + M_N X_N^2$$

Draw a flow chart and write a program that computes the moment of inertia. Test it on data of your choosing.

9.7 The moment of inertia about the center of mass is given by the formula

$$I_c = \sum_{i=1}^{N} M_i (X_i - \overline{X})^2$$

which also can be written as

$$I_c = \sum_{i=1}^{N} M_i X_i^2 - (\overline{X})^2 \cdot \left[\sum_{i=1}^{N} M_i\right]$$

Draw a flow chart and write a program that calculates the moment of inertia about the center of mass. Test it on data of your choosing.

9.8 If the sum of the masses, $\sum_{i=1}^{N} M_i$, equals 1, the formulas in Exercise 9.7 have statistical interpretations. The center of mass is referred to as the mean of the distribution, the moment of inertia about 0 as the second moment about 0, and the moment of inertia about the center of mass as the variance. If the masses M_i are equal, so that each M_i = 1/N, then the formula for the mean of the distribution becomes

$$\overline{X} = \frac{\sum_{i=1}^{N} X_i}{N}$$

and the formula[7] for the variance, σ^2, becomes

$$\sigma^2 = \frac{\sum_{i=1}^{N} X_i^2 - N\overline{X}^2}{N}$$

The standard variation is the square root of the variance.

The sales force of the ABC Hardware Company consists of 43 persons, each having a territory of approximately a thousand retail outlets. At the end of the fiscal year, the sales record for each agent is reviewed. The average and standard deviation of the 43 records are calculated. Those agents whose sales exceed the mean by one standard deviation receive a $2000 bonus; those whose sales exceed the mean by two standard

[7]The denominator of this formula should be N − 1 rather than N when analyzing sample data rather than data from the entire population. With this change, σ^2 is an unbiased estimate of the population variance. For large N, the modification is obviously trivial.

deviations receive an additional bonus of $3000 (a total of $5000). An agent whose sales fall below the mean by two standard deviations is terminated.

Draw a flow chart and write a program that will identify each agent who is to get a bonus and the amount and those agents who are to be terminated. Test the program on data of your choice.

Hint: Think of each agent as identified by an integer between 1 and 43, and assign to each subscripted variable X_i, the dollar amount agent i sold.

9.9 The median of a distribution may be loosely defined as that point on the X-axis for which half the total mass, $\sum_{i=1}^{N} M_i$, lies to its left and half to its right. In some cases, the point is uniquely determined; in others, any point in an interval may serve. In this latter situation, the midpoint of the interval is customarily defined as the median. See Figure 9-8.

Write a program that calculates the median of a distribution. Test the program on data of your choice.

9.10 The local supermarket offers detergent for sale in a variety of packages. Brand X sells for $3.47 for 46 ounces, $2.15 for 28 ounces, $1.16 for 15 ounces, and $0.60 for 8 ounces. Brand Y sells for $3.68 for 51 ounces, $1.99 for 26 ounces, $1.24 for 16 ounces, and $0.75 for 10 ounces.

Write a program that enables you to determine the best buy, namely, the lowest price per ounce.

9.11 Two supermarkets, the Mighty Midget and the Klassy Kupboard, advertise in the local newspaper. Current prices for selected items are as follows:

	KLASSY KUPBOARD	MIGHTY MIDGET		KLASSY KUPBOARD	MIGHTY MIDGET
Bread (per pound)			**Coffee (per pound)**		
White	$ .90	$ .95	Brand A	$2.60	$2.75
Rye	1.10	.80	B	2.75	2.30
Milk			C	2.50	2.10
$\frac{1}{2}$ gal.	1.05	1.25	**Butter**		
			Brand A	1.95	1.25
1 gal.	2.05	2.00	B	1.25	1.80

Prepare a shopping list of the things you need. Assume that the two supermarkets are at opposite ends of town and it is too expensive and time-consuming to make some of your purchases at one and the remainder at the other.

Write a program that determines at which supermarket your total cost is lower. Test your program against different shopping lists.

9.12 Add the following consideration to Exercise 9.11: The cost of transportation to the Mighty Midget is $1.50 per round trip and to the Klassy Kupboard $2.25 per round trip; it is $3.25 if you decide to shop at both. Modify your program so that the transportation costs are included. You are sufficiently wealthy so that a difference of $.25 or less may be ignored.

9.13 The same problem as the property value tally on pages 148–51 appears in many guises. For example, suppose an examination is given to a class of 75 students and there is a grade distribution from the lowest of 10 to the highest of 100. You want to know

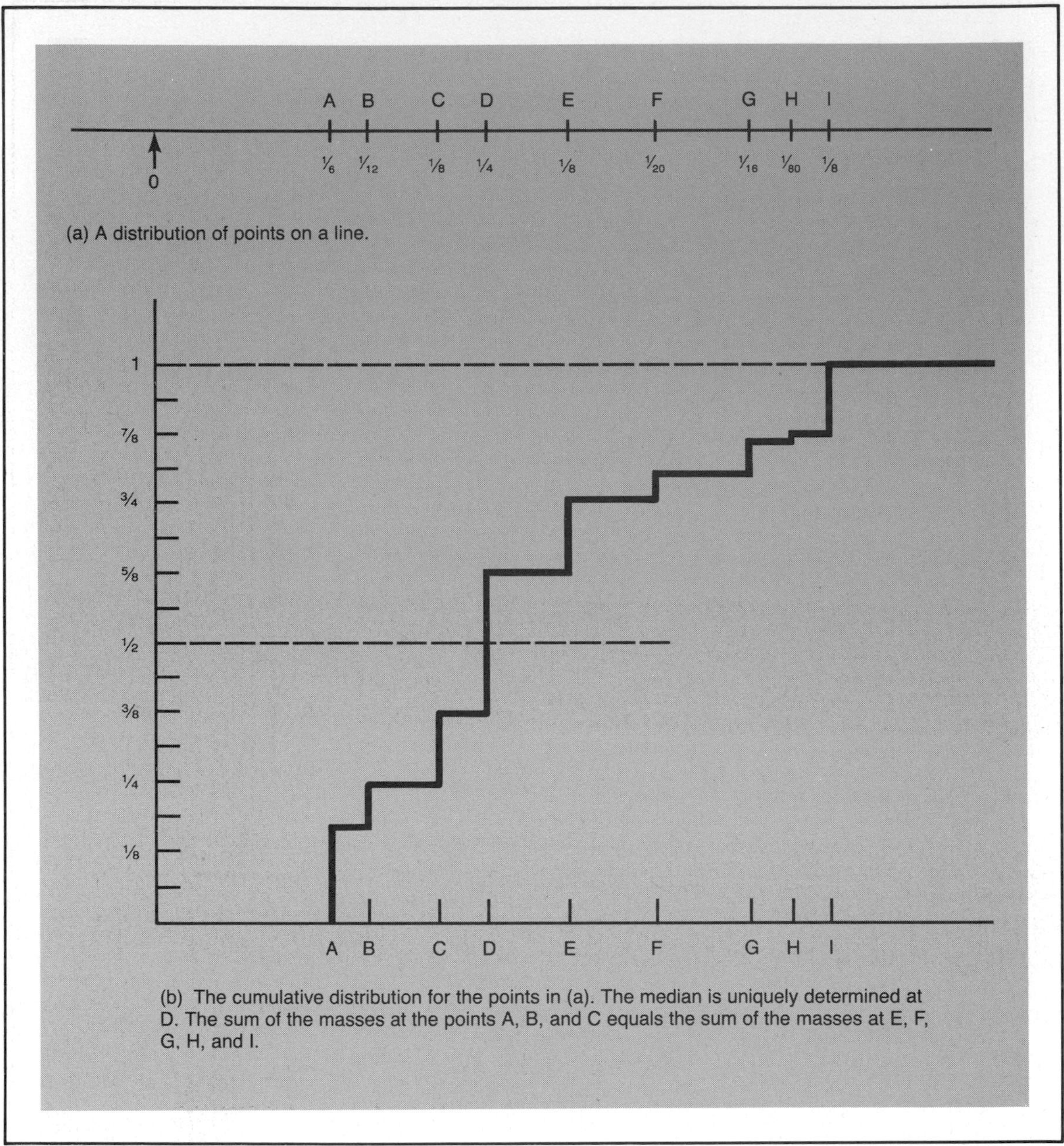
A B C D E F G H I
1/6 1/12 1/8 1/4 1/8 1/20 1/16 1/80 1/8
0
(a) A distribution of points on a line.
1
7/8
3/4
5/8
1/2
3/8
1/4
1/8
A B C D E F G H I
(b) The cumulative distribution for the points in (a). The median is uniquely determined at D. The sum of the masses at the points A, B, and C equals the sum of the masses at E, F, G, H, and I.

FIGURE 9-8(a) and (b)

how many grades are between 10 and 19, between 20 and 29, . . . , 80 and 89, and 90 and 100. Modify the program on pages 148-50 to accommodate this situation.

9.14 A magic square is a square array of numbers, no two of which are equal and such that the sums of each row, of each column, and the two main diagonals are the same. The order is defined as the number of rows. Magic squares of order 3, 5, and 7 are shown on the next page.

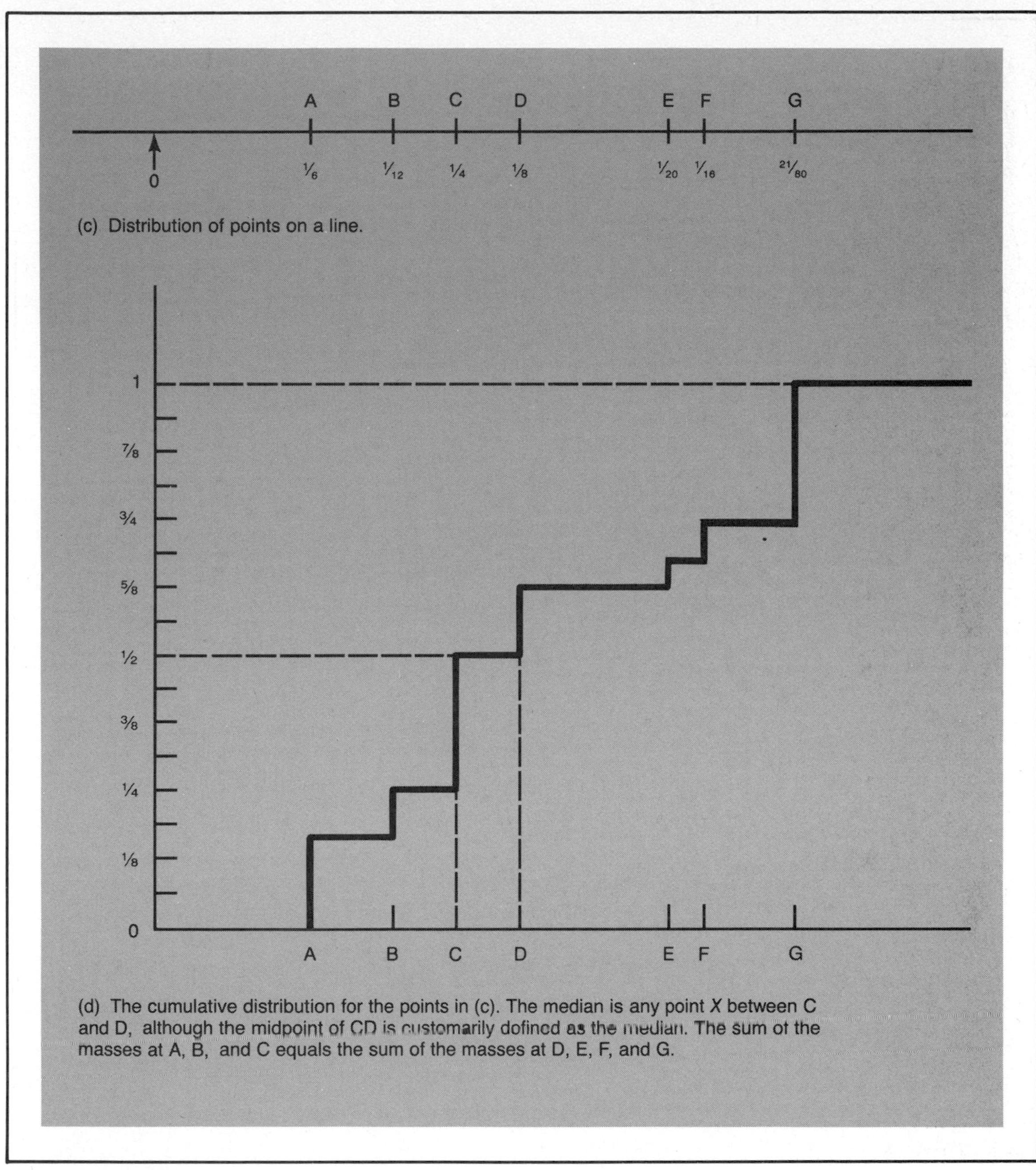

(c) Distribution of points on a line.

(d) The cumulative distribution for the points in (c). The median is any point X between C and D, although the midpoint of CD is customarily defined as the median. The sum of the masses at A, B, and C equals the sum of the masses at D, E, F, and G.

FIGURE 9-8(c) and (d)

2	7	6
9	5	1
4	3	8

3	16	9	22	15
20	8	21	14	2
7	25	13	1	19
24	12	5	18	6
11	4	17	10	23

4	29	12	37	20	45	28
35	11	36	19	44	27	3
10	42	18	43	26	2	34
41	17	49	25	1	33	9
16	48	24	7	32	8	40
47	23	6	31	14	39	15
22	5	30	13	38	21	46

The following algorithm generates a magic square of odd order N.

Lay out a checkered board of N^2 places and label each square with its row number and column number. The illustration is for N = 7.

1,1	1,2	1,3	1,4	1,5	1,6	1,7
2,1	2,2	2,3	2,4	2,5	2,6	2,7
3,1	3,2	3,3	3,4	3,5	3,6	3,7
4,1	4,2	4,3	4,4	4,5	4,6	4,7
5,1	5,2	5,3	5,4	5,5	5,6	5,7
6,1	6,2	6,3	6,4	6,5	6,6	6,7
7,1	7,2	7,3	7,4	7,5	7,6	7,7

Adjoin N squares to the upper edge; similarly, adjoin N squares to the right edge and label as indicated.

7,1	7,2	7,3	7,4	7,5	7,6	7,7	
1,1	1,2	1,3	1,4	1,5	1,6	1,7	1,1
2,1	2,2	2,3	2,4	2,5	2,6	2,7	2,1
3,1	3,2	3,3	3,4	3,5	3,6	3,7	3,1
4,1	4,2	4,3	4,4	4,5	4,6	4,7	4,1
5,1	5,2	5,3	5,4	5,5	5,6	5,7	5,1
6,1	6,2	6,3	6,4	6,5	6,6	6,7	6,1
7,1	7,2	7,3	7,4	7,5	7,6	7,7	7,1

Place the number 1 in the first square to the right of the center. (In the illustration, in the square marked 4, 5.) Go to the right one square and up one, and insert the number 2; continue to the right one unit and up one unit, entering successive integers in each square. When you reach a right-hand or upper edge (first encountered when you try to enter 4, next when you try to enter 5), place the number on the square with the same coordinates and continue. At some places you will reach an impasse (first encountered at 7); the next square will have had a number already assigned to it. Jump two places to the right, enter 8, and continue the diagonal motion. The following illustrates this for the first 16 numbers.

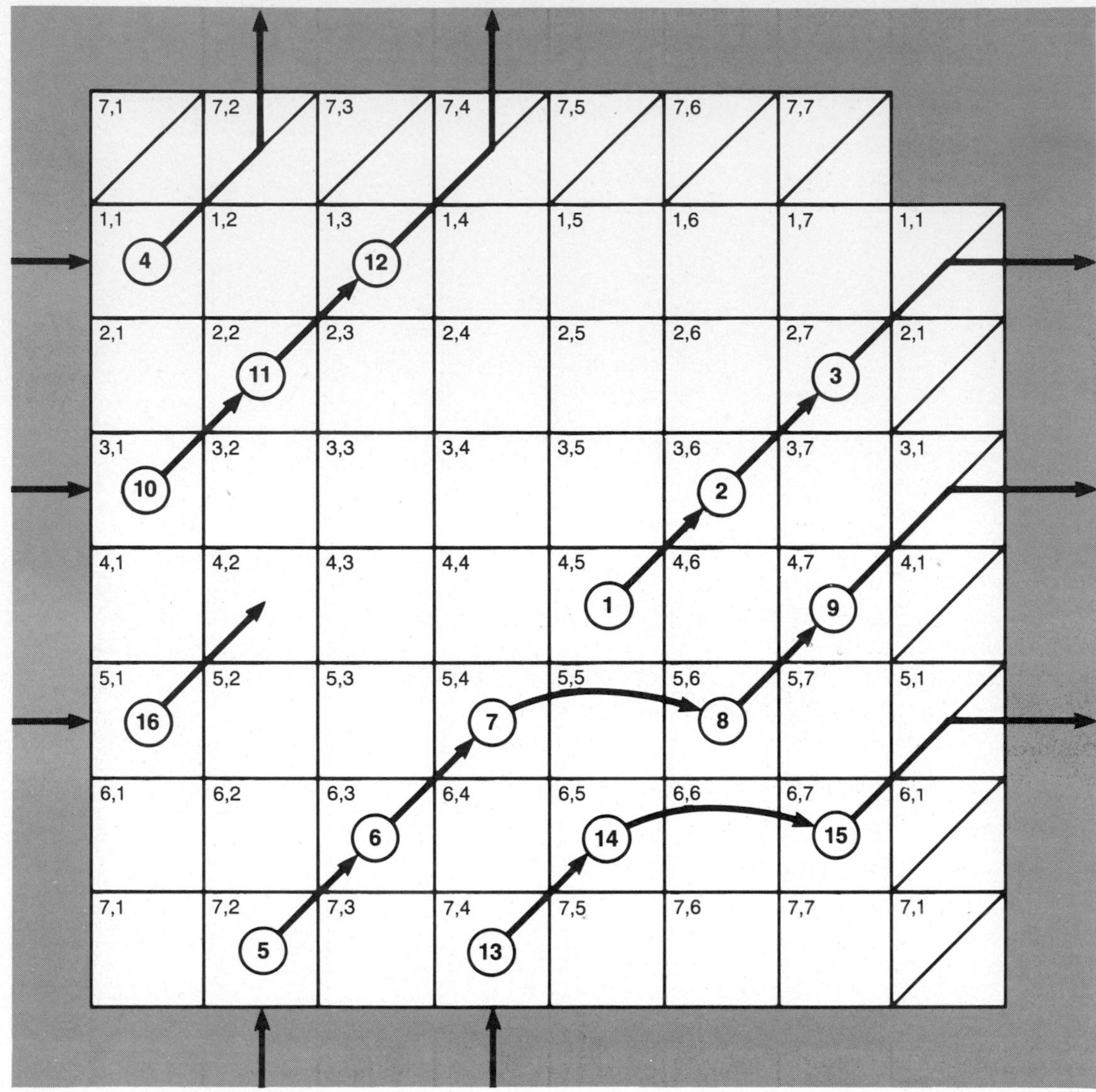

Continue entering successive numbers until all squares are numbered; you will have constructed a magic square of order N.

Use the above algorithm (or any other you know) to generate a magic square of order greater than 7.

Prepare a flow diagram and write a program that tests any square array of numbers to determine if it is a magic square. (Remember: All elements must be different positive integers; if the sum of the numbers in the first row is K, then the sum in every other row, in each column, and along the two main diagonals must also equal K. For magic squares of the type described and for N = 3, the sum is K = 15; for N = 5, it is K = 65. For a magic square of the type described and of order N, $K = (N^3 + N)/2$.)

9.15 In the example for the ABC Hardware Company, the current hourly cost for operating each machine is:

MACHINE	COST	MACHINE	COST	MACHINE	COST
1	$4.50	5	7.00	9	7.50
2	6.25	6	8.25	10	4.75
3	3.75	7	9.50	11	8.00
4	2.50	8	9.25	12	2.75

The costs are adjusted on a monthly basis.

Write a program that combines the daily utilization report with these costs and calculates the cost, on a daily basis, of operating the machine room.

9.16 The Dyke Distributing Company employs three salespersons—A. Jones, B. Knight, and C. Loomis—to sell five products—pliers, screwdrivers, hammers, saws, and planes. Each salesperson calls on only one customer each day and at the end of the day phones in the daily order. For example, Jones may have sold 25 gross of pliers, 50 gross of screwdrivers, 10 gross of hammers, 80 gross of saws, and 60 gross of planes on a given day.

The pliers cost $8.33 per dozen, and sell for $34.75; the screwdrivers cost $14.47 per dozen and sell for $55.98; the hammers cost $11.13 and sell for $43.27; the saws cost $16.95 and sell for $74.75; and the planes cost $9.90 and sell for $40.50. Of the difference between the selling price and the cost, 10 percent goes to the salesperson as a commission.

For each salesperson, enter the daily order, calculate the cost of all items that person sold, compute the total bill to the customer, the gross profit, and the salesperson's commission.

For the home office, compute the total number of each item sold, the total cost by item to produce those quantities, the total cost for all five items, the total income per item, the total income for all five items, the gross profit, and the net profit after the commissions are paid.

Draw a flow chart and write a computer program that automates these calculations.

10 The TAB Function

Printed material is our foremost means of effective communication. Although the content of the page carries the message, the form in which it is printed enhances our ability to capture the ideas. We have used the comma, the semicolon, and quotation marks to organize printed material on a page of computer printout. BASIC provides two additional instructions that we can use to format output. On a typewriter, if we want our typescript to be in a tabular format, we use the TAB key. Similarly, on the computer, the purpose of TAB is to produce output arranged in a particular format. Whereas on the typewriter TAB is set externally, on the computer TAB is an intrinsic BASIC function and is used internally in a program. Because it is under program control, TAB is more versatile than its typewriter counterpart; you will see it used to prepare mathematical tables, to print poetry, to graph mathematical functions, and to produce bar graphs. The remaining BASIC instruction concerned with output format, PRINTUSING, will be discussed in Chapter 16.

TAB

As you know, we have used the comma and the semicolon to control the positions of characters in a PRINT statement. Because the print mechanism on a terminal behaves much like that on a typewriter, it is not surprising that the equivalent of the TAB key exists in BASIC. In its simplest form, TAB is used with the PRINT statement in the following way:

```
10 PRINT "123456789012345678901234567890"
20 PRINT TAB(20) "75"
30 PRINT TAB(20) "STRING"
40 PRINT TAB(20) "***"
```

```
123456789012345678901234567890
                    75
                    STRING
                    ***
```

In each of the program's four lines, the information to be printed is placed between quotation marks, and the computer prints it exactly as written. The purpose of line 10 is to locate for you each print column on the paper; for illustration, only the first thirty are given. When lines 20, 30, and 40 are executed, the print head moves to print position 20, as indicated by TAB(20), and prints the information within the quotation marks.

Assume that a numerical variable X having the value 67 is to be printed beginning in column 30. The BASIC instruction is

```
>10 PRINT TAB(30)""X
```

The double quotation marks are necessary. An alternative would be to use a semicolon, as follows:

```
10 PRINT "1234567890123456789012345678901234567890"
20 PRINT TAB(30) "" X
30 PRINT TAB(30) ; X
```

```
1234567890123456789012345678901234567890
                              67
                              67
```

If we omit the double quotation marks and the semicolon and simply type:

```
10 PRINT TAB(30) X
```

an error message is printed:

```
10 PRINT TAB(30) X
10 BAD FORMULA
```

Note that the number 67 is printed beginning in position 31 rather than position 30. Position 30 is reserved for a possible minus (−) sign.

Not all computers implement the TAB function exactly this way; it depends on the numbering scheme chosen by the people responsible for the BASIC interpreter. Some number the print positions 1, 2, 3, . . . , 72; others start with 0 and use 0, 1, 2, 3, . . . 71. Thus, when you execute PRINT TAB(30)"" X on one machine, the print mechanism moves to print position 30 (which coincides with print column 30) and prints the numerical value of X, starting with a blank space if the number is positive.

```
10 PRINT "PRINT COLUMN"
20 PRINT "12345678901234567890123456789012345678901234567890"
30 PRINT "PRINT POSITION"
40 PRINT "12345678901234567890123456789012345678901234567890"
50 X=1234567
60 Y=-X
70 PRINT TAB(30)""X
80 PRINT TAB(30)""Y
```

```
PRINT COLUMN
12345678901234567890123456789012345678901234567890
PRINT POSITION
12345678901234567890123456789012345678901234567890
                               1234567
                              -1234567
```

On another machine, however, the same instruction again moves the print mechanism to print position 30 (but now this coincides with print column 31) and prints the numerical value of X, including the blank space if the number is positive.

```
10 PRINT "PRINT COLUMN"
20 PRINT "12345678901234567890123456789012345678901234567890"
30 PRINT "PRINT POSITION"
40 PRINT "01234567890123456789012345678901234567890123456789"
50 X=1234567
60 Y=-X
70 PRINT TAB(30)""X
80 PRINT TAB(30)""Y
```

```
PRINT COLUMN
12345678901234567890123456789012345678901234567890
PRINT POSITION
01234567890123456789012345678901234567890123456789
                               1234567
                              -1234567
```

To discover which of these two possibilities is implemented on your computer, try the two programs given above. One of your outputs will coincide with one of the above, which will identify the scheme used on your computer.

Variable Argument

Another feature of TAB control is that the argument may be a variable rather than a preassigned numerical value. In the following example, the value is the number assigned to the variable K.

```
10 PRINT "PRINT COLUMN"
20 PRINT "12345678901234567890123456789012345678901234567890"
30 X=1234567
40 Y=-X
50 FOR K=10 TO 15
60 PRINT TAB(K)""X
70 PRINT TAB(K)""Y
80 PRINT TAB(K) "*"
90 NEXT K
```

```
PRINT COLUMN
12345678901234567890123456789012345678901234567890
          1234567
         -1234567
         *
           1234567
          -1234567
          *
            1234567
           -1234567
           *
             1234567
            -1234567
            *
              1234567
             -1234567
             *
               1234567
              -1234567
              *
```

In the next example, the argument of the TAB function is 10 + I/10.

```
10 PRINT"123456789012345678901234567890"
20 FOR I=10 TO 33 STEP 2
30 PRINT I""TAB(10+I/10)"A"
40 NEXT I
```

```
123456789012345678901234567890
 10       A
 12       A
 14       A
 16       A
 18       A
 20        A
 22        A
 24        A
 26        A
 28        A
 30         A
 32         A
```

When I = 10, the value of the argument is 11 and the letter A appears in the 11th print position. For I = 12, 14, 16, and 18, the value is 11.2, 11.4, 11.6, and 11.8, respectively. In each case, the number is truncated and the letter A appears in the 11th print position. When the variable I takes the value 20, 22, 24, 26, and 28, the argument takes the values 12, 12.2, 12.4, 12.6, and 12.8, respectively, is truncated where needed to 12, and the letter A appears in the 12th print position. Similarly, when I takes the values 30 and 32, the argument takes the values 13 and 13.2 (truncated to 13), and A appears in the 13th position.

In line 30, the double quotation marks ("") are used to separate the variable I from the expression TAB(10 + I/10). Alternatively, a semicolon could be used to produce the identical output. When a numerical variable immediately precedes or follows a TAB instruction, the two must be separated by either a semicolon or double quotation marks. If you forget to do this, an error message will appear.

Multiple TABs Per Line

One PRINT statement may contain several TABs. The following program prints a table of squares and cubes of a sequence of numbers:

```
10 ;\;
20 PRINT TAB(15) "NUMBER" TAB(35) "SQUARE" TAB(55) "CUBE"
30 PRINT
40 FOR I=1 TO 10
50 ; TAB(15) ; I ; TAB(35) "" I^2 ; TAB(55) ; I^3
60 NEXT I
```

```
              NUMBER              SQUARE              CUBE

               1                   1                   1
               2                   4                   8
               3                   9                   27
               4                   16                  64
               5                   25                  125
               6                   36                  216
               7                   49                  343
               8                   64                  512
               9                   81                  729
               10                  100                 1000
```

Remember, line 10 is equivalent to

```
10 PRINT & PRINT
```

In line 20, three strings, NUMBER, SQUARE, and CUBE are used, each enclosed within quotation marks. Each quotation mark serves a double purpose: first, it alerts the computer that strings are being used; second, because it is generally illegal to have two expressions in juxtaposition, it serves as a separator.

The first semicolon in line 50 is again a PRINT statement; the other semicolons are used to separate the several expressions appearing in the line.

TAB Ignored

If, as a line is being printed, the print head has already passed the position called for in a TAB statement, that TAB is ignored and printing continues as if the TAB did not exist. The following one-line program illustrates this.

```
10 PRINT TAB(10) "THIS IS THE" TAB(15) " FOREST PRIMEVAL"
```

```
          THIS IS THE FOREST PRIMEVAL
```

Note that the phrase "THIS IS THE", which begins in position number 10, extends past position number 15. The computer ignores the expression TAB(15) and continues printing the remaining two words "FOREST PRIMEVAL". The space in the printout between the words THE and FOREST is achieved by introducing a space after the quotation mark and before the letter F in the word FOREST.

TAB(0)

There is another useful feature of the TAB command. If a PRINT statement terminates with a TAB to a print position that is to the left of the current print position, for example, TAB(0), the next PRINT statement is taken as a continuation of the previous line, provided that when the second string is linked to the first, there are enough print positions on the one line to print the concatenated string. "Concatenate" is a term meaning to join together two or more character strings into a single string. If there are not enough print positions on the line, the TAB(0) is ignored and the second string is printed on the next line. Examine the following program and run.

```
10 PRINT "THIS IS THE" TAB(0)
20 PRINT " FOREST PRIMEVAL"
30 PRINT "MARY HAD A LITTLE LAMB, ITS FLEECE WAS WHITE AS SNOW" TAB(0)
40 PRINT " AND EVERYWHERE ..."
50 PRINT "MARY, MARY, QUITE CONTRARY, HOW DOES YOUR GARDEN GROW?" TAB(0)
60 PRINT " WITH SILVER BELLS, AND ..."
```

```
THIS IS THE FOREST PRIMEVAL
MARY HAD A LITTLE LAMB, ITS FLEECE WAS WHITE AS SNOW AND EVERYWHERE ...
MARY, MARY, QUITE CONTRARY, HOW DOES YOUR GARDEN GROW?
 WITH SILVER BELLS, AND ...
```

In lines 10 and 20, the two strings, when concatenated, could be printed on one line and this was done. Similarly, the output of lines 30 and 40 are printed on one line. The number of characters in the two strings in lines 50 and 60, however, is greater than 72 (the number of print positions available on this particular terminal), and consequently, the TAB(0) is ignored and each string is printed on a separate line.

The following is an extreme example of the use of TAB(0) to keep the terminal printing on one line.

```
10 PRINT "1234567890123456789012345678901234567890" TAB(0)
20 PRINT "12345678901234567890123456789012"
30 ; "MARY " TAB(0)
40 ; "HAD " TAB(0)
50 ; "A LITTLE LAMB " TAB(0)
60 ; "ITS FLEECE WAS WHITE " TAB(0)
70 ; "AS SNOW AND " TAB(0)
80 ; "EVERYWHERE " TAB(0)
90 ; "THAT " TAB(0)
100 ; "MARY " TAB(0)
110 ; "WENT " TAB(0)
120 ; "THE LAMB " TAB(0)
130 ; "WAS SURE " TAB(0)
140 ; "TO GO"
```

```
123456789012345678901234567890123456789012345678901234567890123456789012
MARY HAD A LITTLE LAMB ITS FLEECE WAS WHITE AS SNOW AND EVERYWHERE THAT
MARY WENT THE LAMB WAS SURE TO GO
```

```
REM: NOTE THAT THE LINE CONTAINS EXACTLY 72 CHARACTERS; THE 'BLANK'
REM: AFTER 'THAT' IN LINE 90 COUNTS AS A CHARACTER.  IF 'EVERYWHERE'
REM: IS CHANGED TO 'EVERY WHERE' THEN 'THAT ', WHICH REQUIRES FIVE
REN: CHARACTERS, GOES TO THE NEXT LINE.
```

```
80 ; "EVERY WHERE " TAB(0)
```

```
123456789012345678901234567890123456789012345678901234567890123456789012
MARY HAD A LITTLE LAMB ITS FLEESE WAS WHITE AS SNOW AND EVERY WHERE
THAT MARY WENT THE LAMB WAS SURE TO GO
```

As we have seen, if the expression in TAB(expression) is not an integer, it is truncated to an integer. If it is less than zero, it is set equal to zero. Thus, for K=3, TAB((K − 10)/4) would be equivalent to TAB(0).

Not all computer systems adhere to the convention described. When multiple TABs occur on one line and there is a call for a position already passed, the print mechanism proceeds to the next line and moves to the specified position. Thus, the output of the program:

```
10 PRINT "1234567890123456789012345678901234567890"
20 PRINT TAB(10) "THIS IS THE" TAB(15) " FOREST PRIMEVAL"
```

is:

```
1234567890123456789012345678901234567890
         THIS IS THE
               FOREST PRIMEVAL
```

Three Applications of the TAB Function

Formatting Poetry

We have already demonstrated one application of the TAB function, that is, to prepare tabular data. As you may know, typesetting on modern equipment is under computer control. The "office of the future," which is already here, processes endless amounts of textual material. Our second application of the TAB function is using the computer to format lines of poetry. (When you become familiar with string manipulation, in Chapter 11, we shall use the computer to prepare personalized form letters.)

```
10 REM: THIS IS AN ILLUSTRATION OF AN APPLICATION OF THE
20 REM: TAB(X) FUNCTION TO FORMATING LINES OF POETRY.
30 REM: THE POEM 'YOU SAY YOU LOVE' BY JOHN KEATS CONSISTS
40 REM: OF FIVE STANZAS; ONLY THE FIFTH IS REPRODUCED.
50 A=20,X=5,Y=7,Z=9
60 ; & ;
70 ; TAB(A) "V"
80 ; & ;
90 ; TAB(X) "O BREATHE A WORD OR TWO OF FIRE!"
100 ; TAB(Y) "SMILE, AS IF THOSE WORDS SHOULD BURN ME,"
110 ; TAB(X) "SQUEEZE AS LOVERS SHOULD-O KISS"
120 ; TAB(Y) "AND IN THY HEART INURN ME!"
130 ; TAB(Z) "O LOVE ME TRULY!"
140 ;
```

```
                    V


  O BREATHE A WORD OR TWO OF FIRE!
    SMILE, AS IF THOSE WORDS SHOULD BURN ME,
  SQUEEZE AS LOVERS SHOULD-O KISS
    AND IN THY HEART INURN ME!
      O LOVE ME TRULY!
```

The graphic quality of the printout reflects the limitations of the terminal, which prints only upper case letters. If your terminal has lower case letters and if your BASIC interpreter accepts them as characters within strings, then lines 90–130 may be rewritten as follows.

```
90 ; TAB(X) "O breathe a word or two of fire!"
100 ; TAB(Y) "Smile, as if those words should burn me,"
110 ; TAB(X) "Squeeze as lovers should-O kiss"
120 ; TAB(Y) "And in thy heart inurn me!"
130 ; TAB(Z) "O love me truly!"
```

The printout from this modified version of the program is:

```
              V


O breathe a word or two of fire!
  Smile, as if those words should burn me,
Squeeze as lovers should-O kiss
  And in thy heart inurn me!
    O love me truly!
```

For comparison, the printed version is as follows:

V

O breathe a word or two of fire!
  Smile, as if those words should burn me,
Squeeze as lovers should—O kiss
  And in thy heart inurn me!
    O love me truly![1]

[1]From *The Complete Poems of Keats and Shelley,* (New York: The Modern Library, 1931), p. 284. Reprinted with permission of Random House, Inc.

The only difference between the three versions is the difference between the quality of the printing mechanisms.

Graphing

The weather at any particular place and time depends on many factors—the sun, the winds, the altitude, the seasons, the proximity to the sea or a mountain range, to mention just a few. The formulas used to predict weather are complicated, and even if we knew them precisely (which we do not), it would still be beyond our capacity to understand the delicate interplay between their parts. Some simpler form for presenting the results of the computations is needed. The most popular method is graphic; on maps, curves are drawn of equal temperature (isotherms), equal pressure (isobars), and so on. While the concepts we shall present may be used to draw weather maps, we limit ourselves to a much simpler illustration.

Of the various functions that pervade mathematics and the natural and social sciences, two that are frequently met are the sine and cosine.[2] The most familiar property of these functions is their periodicity—the fact that their values repeat themselves at regular intervals. By graphing these functions for one period, we can grasp what they look like for all values of the argument. To illustrate another application of the TAB function, we shall use it to plot SIN(X) and COS(X).

For the functions SIN(X) and COS(X), the argument, X, is assumed to be in radians, where one radian equals about 57.3 degrees. The conversion from degrees, Y, to radians, X, is given by the formula

$$X_{rad} = \frac{\pi}{180} Y^\circ$$

where π = 3.14159265358979323846 2643. . . , is given to greater accuracy than needed for most problems. We want to plot the graph of SIN(X) for $0 \leq X \leq 2\pi$ and choose $0 \leq X \leq 6.4$ to ensure one full period. The values of the SIN function lie between -1 and $+1$, and since the width of the paper is 72 columns, the zero line is set at position 40 (the first 8 positions are for the values of X). The height of the curve is scaled so that 30 print positions are equal to one unit, that is, the argument for the TAB function is chosen to be (40 + 30 * SIN X). The program and printout are given on the next page.

If the graphs of two or more functions, say SIN(x) and COS(X), are to be plotted together, the program must be modified. Because the print mechanism on the terminal does not backspace, we need to know which number, COS(X) and SIN(X), is smaller, that is, should be printed first. In the program and graphs shown on the upper half of page 182, this is accomplished in line 30. Once this accommodation is made, the program is straightforward.

The flat appearance of the sin curve for values of X between 1.4 and 1.8 and of the cosine curve for X between 3.0 and 3.4 is attributable to the fact that there are only 72 print positions on a line. On a terminal with 132 print positions, greater resolution is possible and the flatness disappears.

Bar Graphs

As a final application, we shall use the TAB function to draw both horizontal and vertical bar graphs.

Polly Quinter's staff (see Chapter 9, pages 148-51) prepared a surprise for her. Although she had shown them both a bar graph and a table giving the distribution, by property values, of homes in their state she had asked only that a computer program be written that would produce a comparable table for the homes in Yoknapatawpha County. The staff felt that they could have the computer produce the comparable bar graph also. Accordingly, they wrote and ran the program shown on the bottom half of page 182.

---

[2]For a definition and description of these functions, refer to a standard textbook on trigonometry.

```
10 ; & ;
20 PRINT TAB(4) "X" TAB(37) "SIN(X)"
30 ; & ;
40 FOR X=0 TO 6.4 STEP .2
50 PRINT X "" TAB(40+30*SIN(X)) "*"
60 NEXT X
```

```
   X                               SIN(X)

0                                     *
.200000                                    *
.400000                                         *
.600000                                              *
.800000                                                   *
1.00000                                                       *
1.20000                                                         *
1.40000                                                           *
1.60000                                                           *
1.80000                                                           *
2.00000                                                         *
2.20000                                                      *
2.40000                                                  *
2.60000                                             *
2.80000                                        *
3.00000                                   *
3.20000                             *
3.40000                       *
3.60000                 *
3.80000            *
4.00000        *
4.20000    *
4.40000  *
4.60000 *
4.80000 *
5.00000  *
5.20000    *
5.40000       *
5.60000            *
5.80000                 *
6.00000                      *
6.20000                            *
6.40000                                 *
```

Recognizing that the program should be sufficiently general to be able to handle fewer or more than 21 classes, they let the number of classes be a variable, lines 110–190. To adapt the program to other situations, they could either change the data in lines 150–190, or replace READ in line 130 by an INPUT instruction.

They quickly recognized that a major problem would be the size of the graph. After discussing this among themselves, they compromised on a scale whereby the largest entry in the graph would occupy 30 print positions. Obviously, the program first needed to discover the largest class; this is done in lines 200–330. Each class size is then scaled proportionately, the largest being allocated 30 print positions. For any other scaling, the programers recognized that they should replace the number 30 in line 380 by the desired scale factor. For example, if they want to scale the graph so that the largest class is allocated 40 spaces, they need only rewrite line 380 as follows:

```
380 S(I)=INT(40*F(I)/K+.5)
```

One row of the graph is drawn in lines 470–500; the number of asterisks that appear in a row equals S(I), the appropriately scaled value of F(I). The drawing of successive lines is done in the loop, lines 460–520.

```
10 ; & ;
20 FOR X=0 TO 6.4 STEP .2
30 IF COS(X)<=SIN(X) THEN 60
40 PRINT X "" TAB(40+30*SIN(X)) "*" TAB(40+30*COS(X)) "+"
50 GOTO 70
60 PRINT X "" TAB(40+30*COS(X)) "+" TAB(40+30*SIN(X)) "*"
70 NEXT X
```

```
0                                     *                             +
.200000                                    *                       +
.400000                                          *               +
.600000                                               *       +
.800000                                                   +*
1.00000                                               +        *
1.20000                                         +                *
1.40000                                    +                       *
1.60000                              +                             *
1.80000                        +                                   *
2.00000                  +                                       *
2.20000             +                                         *
2.40000        +                                          *
2.60000     +                                        *
2.80000  +                                      *
3.00000 +                                 *
3.20000 +                           *
3.40000 +                     *
3.60000    +            *
3.80000       +    *
4.00000        *  +
4.20000    *           +
4.40000  *                  +
4.60000 *                         +
4.80000 *                               +
5.00000  *                                    +
5.20000    *                                        +
5.40000       *                                          +
5.60000            *                                         +
5.80000                 *                                       +
6.00000                      *                                    +
6.20000                            *                               +
6.40000                                  *                         +
```

```
10 ********************
20 REM: THE PURPOSE OF THIS PROGRAM IS TO ILLUSTRATE
30 REM: THE USE OF THE TAB FUNCTION IN THE PREPARATION
40 REM: OF BAR GRAPHS.
50 ********************
60 REM: THE FIRST STEP IS TO SPECIFY THE VALUES OF
70 REM: THE FUNCTION. FOR THIS PURPOSE, WE USE THE
80 REM: VALUES GIVEN FOR THE NUMBER OF HOMES IN THE
90 REM: ILLUSTRATION ON PROPERTY VALUES AND TALLYING IN CHAPTER 9.
100 DIM F(25),S(25)
110 PRINT "HOW MANY PROPERTY CLASSES"; & INPUT C
120 FOR I=1 TO C
130 READ F(I)
140 NEXT I
150 DATA 90215, 78567, 70111,62345, 76327
160 DATA 72107, 69820, 59272, 53897, 46227
170 DATA 41648, 39787, 36274, 28132, 24812
180 DATA 20010, 18567, 17456, 9864, 6196
190 DATA 13456
200 ********************
210 REM: SINCE THE NUMBER OF HOMES IN EACH CATEGORY IS TOO
220 REM: LARGE TO PRODUCE A GRAPH OF REASONABLE SIZE,
230 REM: THESE NUMBERS ARE SCALED BY DIVIDING EACH BY THE
```

```
240 REM: MAXIMUM OF THE NUMBER OF HOMES IN EACH CATEGORY,
250 REM: THAT IS, BY THE MAXIMUM OF THE SEVERAL F(I).
260 REM: THIS PRODUCES VALUES THAT LIE BETWEEN Ø AND 1.
270 ********************
280 REM: THE MAXIMUM OF THE F(I) IS DENOTED BE 'K'.
290 K=F(1)
300 FOR I=2 TO C
310 IF F(I)<=K THEN 330
320 K=F(I)
330 NEXT I
340 ********************
350 REM: SINCE A REASONABLE HEIGHT FOR THE MAXIMUM ENTRY IS THIRTY UNITS,
360 REM: EACH VALUE IS SCALED AND ROUNDED SO THAT THE MAXIMUM EQUALS 30.
370 FOR I=1 TO C
380 S(I)=INT(30*F(I)/K+.5)
390 NEXT I
400 ********************
410 REM: THE GRAPH OF THE FUNCTION F(I) IS DRAWN.
420 PRINT
430 PRINT TAB(10) "CLASS NUMBER" TAB(35) "EACH * REPRESENTS"
440 PRINT TAB(31) "APPROXIMATELY" INT(K/30+.5) " HOMES."
450 PRINT
460 FOR I=1 TO C
470 PRINT TAB(15);I;
480 FOR J=1 TO S(I)
490 PRINT TAB(J+29) "*" TAB(Ø)
500 NEXT J
510 PRINT
520 NEXT I
530 ********************
540 REM: THE GRAPH IS ROTATED THROUGH 90 DEGREES.
550 PRINT & PRINT
560 PRINT TAB(4) "VALUE" TAB(23) "MULTIPLE THE VALUE BY" INT(K/30+.5) " TO"
570 PRINT TAB(23) "DETERMINE THE NUMBER OF HOMES."
580 PRINT TAB(23) "-----------------------------"
590 FOR W=31 TO 1 STEP -1
600 PRINT TAB(3) ; W ; TAB(Ø)
610 FOR I=1 TO C
620 IF S(I)<W THEN 640
630 PRINT TAB(3*I+8) "**" TAB(Ø)
640 NEXT I
650 PRINT
660 NEXT W
670 FOR I=1 TO 72
680 PRINT TAB(I) "-" TAB(O)
690 NEXT I
700 PRINT
710 FOR I=1 TO C
720 PRINT TAB(3*I+7) ""I"" TAB(Ø)
730 NEXT I
740 PRINT
750 PRINT TAB(28) "CLASS NUMBER"
760 END
```

```
HOW MANY PROPERTY CLASSES   ?21

         CLASS NUMBER              EACH * REPRESENTS
                               APPROXIMATELY 3007 HOMES.

               1              ******************************
               2              **************************
               3              ***********************
               4              *********************
               5              *************************
               6              ************************
               7              ***********************
               8              ********************
```

```
9            ******************
10           ***************
11           **************
12           *************
13           ************
14           *********
15           ********
16           *******
17           ******
18           ******
19           ***
20           **
21           ****
```

```
VALUE                MULTIPLE THE VALUE BY 3007 TO
                     DETERMINE THE NUMBER OF HOMES.
                     ------------------------------

31
30      **
29      **
28      **
27      **
26      ** **
25      ** **       **
24      ** **       ** **
23      ** ** **    ** ** **
22      ** ** **    ** ** **
21      ** ** ** ** ** ** **
20      ** ** ** ** ** ** ** **
19      ** ** ** ** ** ** ** **
18      ** ** ** ** ** ** ** ** **
17      ** ** ** ** ** ** ** ** **
16      ** ** ** ** ** ** ** ** **
15      ** ** ** ** ** ** ** ** ** **
14      ** ** ** ** ** ** ** ** ** ** **
13      ** ** ** ** ** ** ** ** ** ** ** **
12      ** ** ** ** ** ** ** ** ** ** ** ** **
11      ** ** ** ** ** ** ** ** ** ** ** ** **
10      ** ** ** ** ** ** ** ** ** ** ** ** **
9       ** ** ** ** ** ** ** ** ** ** ** ** ** **
8       ** ** ** ** ** ** ** ** ** ** ** ** ** ** **
7       ** ** ** ** ** ** ** ** ** ** ** ** ** ** ** **
6       ** ** ** ** ** ** ** ** ** ** ** ** ** ** ** ** ** **
5       ** ** ** ** ** ** ** ** ** ** ** ** ** ** ** ** ** **
4       ** ** ** ** ** ** ** ** ** ** ** ** ** ** ** ** ** **       **
3       ** ** ** ** ** ** ** ** ** ** ** ** ** ** ** ** ** ** **    **
2       ** ** ** ** ** ** ** ** ** ** ** ** ** ** ** ** ** ** ** ** **
1       ** ** ** ** ** ** ** ** ** ** ** ** ** ** ** ** ** ** ** ** **
-----------------------------------------------------------------------
         1  2  3  4  5  6  7  8  9 10 11 12 13 14 15 16 17 18 19 20 21
                          CLASS NUMBER
```

The caption of the graph is geared to the choice of 30 units representing the maximum of the several S(I). If another choice is made, say 40, then the expression INT(K/30+.5) that appears in line 440 should be changed to INT(K/40+.5). The horizontal bar graph is the output of lines 410–520.

Since the state's graph was a vertical bar graph, Polly's staff decided to rotate the horizontal bar graph through 90 degrees to produce a vertical one. This is done in lines 540–660. Again, if they had chosen to scale the graph so that the maximum S(I) was 40, they would have modified the formula in line 560 from INT(K/30+.5) to INT(K/40+.5) and, at line 590, changed the number 31 to 41. Otherwise, the actual drawing of the graph is done in lines 590–660. Lines 670–690 draw a horizontal line below the graph, and lines 710–750 enter the class number and provide a caption.

Exercises

10.1 Using the TAB function, write a program that prints your name on one line beginning in column 30, your address on the next beginning in column 32, the city or town on the third beginning in position 34, and the state and zip code on the fourth beginning at position 36.

10.2 Before running the programs, determine the output from each of the following:

(a)

```
10 FOR X = 1 TO 5
20 PRINT TAB(2*X - 1);X
30 NEXT X
40 END
```

(b)

```
10 FOR I = 1 TO 5
20 PRINT TAB(I^2)"*"
30 NEXT I
40 END
```

Check your answers by comparing them with the output obtained by running the programs on your computer.

10.3 Using the TAB function, write a program that will produce the following table. The entries to the table are to be made using the INPUT instruction.

```
10   20   30   40   50   60
11   21   31   41   51   61
12   22   32   42   52   62
13   23   33   43   53   63
14   24   34   44   54   64
15   25   35   45   55   65
16   26   36   46   56   66
```

10.4 Write programs that will produce the following designs:

```
123456789012345678901234567890123456789012345678901234567890

                    *************************
                      *********************
                        *****************
                          *************
                            *********
                              *****
                                *

GEORGE                  111111111                  *
  MARTHA                 2222222                  ***
    GEORGE                33333                  *****
      MARTHA               444                  *******
        GEORGE              5                  *********
          MARTHA           666                ***********
            GEORGE        77777              *************
              MARTHA     8888888            ***************
                        999999999                 ***
                                                  ***
                                                  ***
                                                  ***
```

10.5 In the printout at the bottom of page 176, the numbers are left-justified, creating a visual display contrary to the way we normally expect to see a column of numbers. Write a computer program that will produce the following table:

NUMBER	SQUARE	CUBE
1	1	1
2	4	8
3	9	27
4	16	64
5	25	125
6	36	216
7	49	343
8	64	512
9	81	729
10	100	1000

10.6 Plot the curve $y = 4x^2$ (a parabola) for values of x between $x = -3.5$ and $x = 3.5$, using .25 as the size of the interval between successive values of x. Can you discover an interval size that produces a graph more pleasing to the eye?

10.7 Plot the curve $y = x^3$ for values of x between -3.0 and 3.0. Choose a size for the interval between successive values of x that produces a graph pleasing to the eye.

10.8 Modify the program given in the text that produces bar graphs (pages 183-84) so that each asterisk represents approximately 2250 homes. Run your modified program and compare the output with that given in the text.

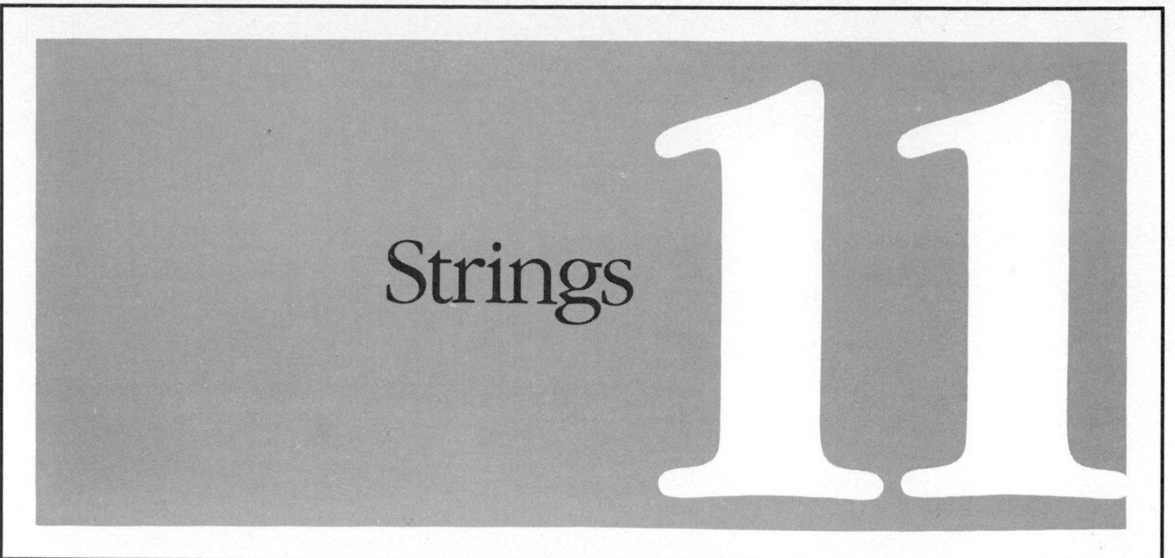

Strings 11

Until now, we have considered only variables that assume numeric values. In BASIC, however, it is possible to assign a string of nonnumeric characters to a variable; such a variable is called a "string variable." Typical examples of a string are a word, a phrase, a sentence, an address, and a telephone number.

Many of the properties of numerical variables apply, with the obvious changes, to string variables. We used three BASIC statements, LET, INPUT, and READ/DATA, to assign numbers to numerical variables. These same three instructions may be applied to strings. The plus (+) sign is used to add numbers; it may be used also for concatenation of strings. The arithmetic relations "less than" (<), "greater than" (>), and "equal to" (=), used to compare the relative size or the equality of two numbers, are used also to compare the precedence or equality of two strings. One string is "less than" a second, or more familiarly, precedes the second, if the first comes before the second alphabetically. Two strings are "equal" if, character by character, they are identical.

One characteristic of strings not shared exactly with numbers is that substrings exist within a given string. In this chapter, we shall also discuss locating and manipulating substrings for various purposes.

We shall introduce three new BASIC instructions. One, LEN, specifies the number of characters in a string. VAL and STR relate strings of digits and numbers. A number may be considered a string of digits, and on occasion, it may be convenient to do so; similarly, a string of digits may be thought of as a number. VAL converts a string of digits to a number, STR converts a number to a string of digits.

All the fundamental operations on strings as well as the string functions will be used in illustrative examples.

A Personalized Letter

How many such personalized form letters, spewed from a computer, have you received? The ability to manipulate strings of data, your name, your birthdate, your hair color, and so on, and have the final product look like it has been composed for you alone, can greatly influence your attitude toward the product being offered. Each of us likes to feel that somebody took the time to prepare a personal letter; we are less inclined to be receptive if we realize that the letter was prepared by a computer.

How does the computer do this? We shall now attempt to strip away some of the mystery.

Unified Distributing Company
17911 Kings Lane Park
Boridae, Kansas 12345

January 31, 1982

Ms. Sara Ringlette
1122 Lori Drive
South Springs, North Dakota 54321

Dear Ms. Ringlette:

We are pleased to inform you, Ms. Ringlette, that the Amalgamated Automobile Company has selected you as a potential winner of its Armadillo Touring Car. The criteria used for your selection were your birthdate, August 7th, the color of your hair, brown, your participation in the South Springs Community Choir, and the number of your driver's license, ND389127, which ends in a 7.

If you will sign the enclosed card, dear Sara, and return it to us, we shall enter it into our random selector drum, from which the lucky winner will be drawn.

Sincerely yours,

G. M. Barton

G. M. Barton
Vice-president

String Variables

So far, the use of strings—alphabetic information distinguished from numeric—has been limited to PRINT statements. Until now, whenever a string of alphabetic characters was to be printed, it had to be explicitly given, enclosed within quotation marks in a PRINT statement. It may be more convenient, however, to assign an alphabetic string to a variable and then manipulate this variable in a fashion similar to the way numeric variables are manipulated.

The computer can sort a list of numbers; it can also alphabetize a list of names. It can help you look up words in a dictionary, even when you cannot spell perfectly; it can serve as a tutor in a foreign language. Some people like to play word games; others like to try their hands at codes and ciphers. In all these ways and many more, words and phrases are manipulated. The variety of application seems endless. But before you can use them, you must learn about string variables.

Corresponding to the generic numeric variable X, there is the string variable X$. Whereas the designation of a numeric variable may be either a letter or a letter followed by a digit, such as X or X7, the designation of a string variable is limited to a single letter followed by a $. Thus, the number of string variables available is only 26.[1]

Numbers are assigned to numeric variables by way of a LET statement, an INPUT, or READ/DATA instructions. We may use these same three ways to assign strings to string variables, although the conventions for doing so may seem more restricted.

Assignment of String Variables

Let In explicit assignment statements, that is, when LET is expressed or implied, quotation marks must be used. For example, if we wish to assign the string OKLAHOMA to the variable X$, OKLAHOMA must be in quotes. If the quotes are omitted, an error message occurs:

```
>10 X$ = OKLAHOMA
 10 BAD FORMAT
>10 X$ = 'OKLAHOMA'
>
```

Note that Oklahoma is enclosed in single, rather than double, quotation marks. Many computer systems accept both types. We shall use both interchangeably.

Input When we use INPUT to assign strings to variables, the format for responding to the prompting ? (the request for INPUT) may vary from one computer to the next. In what follows, we shall describe the required responses for two computers; you will have to discover for yourself how BASIC has been implemented in your system.

As a first observation, note that quotation marks are not required on either computer. When they are used, however, everything between the quotation marks is taken as a single string.

```
     COMPUTER A

>10 INPUT X$,Y$
>20 PRINT X$,Y$

>RUN

?"ABLE BAKER,CHARLIE","HOW,ARE,YOU,?"

ABLE BAKER,CHARLIE          HOW,ARE,YOU,?
```

```
     COMPUTER B

*10 INPUT X$,Y$
*20 PRINT X$,Y$

*RUN

?"ABLE BAKER,CHARLIE","HOW,ARE,YOU,?"

ABLE BAKER,CHARLIE             HOW,ARE,YOU,?
```

Both computers accept numeric input as string variables, treating the input as strings, not numbers. The program is the one used above; the output is as follows.

---

[1]Some systems permit a letter followed by a digit followed by $, in which case 286 string variables are available.

```
      COMPUTER A

>RUN

?12345678901234567890,09876543210987654321
12345678901234567890          09876543210987654321
```

```
      COMPUTER B

*RUN

?12345678901234567890,09876543210987654321
12345678901234567890            09876543210987654321
```

Mixed input, a combination of alphabetic and numeric, is also acceptable by both computers.

```
      COMPUTER A

>RUN

?A7,5G
A7            5G
```

```
      COMPUTER B

*RUN

?A7,5G
A7              5G
```

In the preceding three illustrations, a comma was used to separate the two strings; this works on both computers. Here the similarities end, and the differences begin. On computer A, a space also will separate two strings; not so on computer B.

```
      COMPUTER A

>RUN

?ABLE BAKER
ABLE          BAKER
```

```
      COMPUTER B

*RUN

?ABLE BAKER

illegal input, retype?TWO INPUTS ARE NEEDED,HERE

TWO INPUTS ARE NEEDED          HERE
```

Input Phrases The difference between these two computers has certain consequences. On computer B, any phrase not containing a comma is entered as a single string. If the phrase contains a comma, we will need to use quotation marks if we wish to enter it as a single string. On computer A, a space between two words is also considered a delimiter, which might be an inconvenience if we want to enter a phrase as a single string. In this case, we can also use quotation marks.

Recognizing this limitation, the manufacturer of computer A augmented the BASIC interpreter with a specific command that informs the computer that strings are expected. The particular method is to issue the BASIC command INPUT = $. This command may be issued either inside a program or directly to the interpreter. In the first case, it might be

```
>75 INPUT = $
```

In the second, the line number is omitted,

```
> INPUT = $
```

Once INPUT = $ is issued, the computer treats everything between a ? prompt and the next <CR> as a single string. In the illusion that follows, the first part attempts to assign ABLE BAKER CHARLIE to X$, and HOW ARE YOU? to Y$. The space between ABLE and BAKER serves as a delimiter, however, and ABLE is assigned to X$ and BAKER to Y$.

In the second part, the INPUT = $ command was issued to the interpreter outside the program. When run, the entire phrase ABLE BAKER CHARLIE, HOW ARE YOU? was understood to be one phase because it followed the prompt ? and preceded the <CR>. When the <CR> was struck, a second prompt ? appeared, asking for the second input. In response to this, we typed NEEDS ANOTHER INPUT <CR>.

```
     COMPUTER A


>10 INPUT X$,Y$
>20 PRINT X$,Y$

>RUN

?ABLE BAKER CHARLIE,HOW ARE YOU?
ABLE           BAKER

>INPUT=$

>RUN

?ABLE BAKER CHARLIE,HOW ARE YOU?
?NEEDS ANOTHER INPUT
ABLE BAKER CHARLIE,HOW ARE YOU?           NEEDS ANOTHER INPUT

>INPUT=A
```

Once set, the INPUT = $ command will remain operative until explicitly countermanded. To countermand INPUT = $, we use the command INPUT = A, where A is any character different from $. INPUT = A may be used either inside a program or as a direct command to the interpreter.[2]

As implemented on the two machines, there is one final difference between the BASIC interpreters. On the first, a string, provided it contains no more than six characters, may be input to a *numeric* variable; on the second, numeric variables accept only numeric data. This is illustrated in the following printouts.

---

[2]Some computers accept the instruction

```
10 LINPUT A$
```

when a string containing such characters as quotation marks, commas, and blanks is to be entered. In this case, each character between the initial prompt ? and the ensuing <CR> is assigned to A$. LINPUT is an abbreviation for "line input."

```
COMPUTER A

>10 INPUT X,Y
>20 PRINT X,Y

>RUN

?ABLE,BAKER
ABLE           BAKER

>RUN

?CHARLIE,WASHINGTON
    CHARLIE,WASHINGTON
   RETYPE^
?CHARLI,WASHINGTON
       RETYPE^
?WASHIN
CHARLI     WASHIN


COMPUTER B

*10 INPUT X,Y
*20 PRINT X,Y

*RUN

?ABLE,BAKER
illegal input, retype?
```

READ/DATA A similar, but not identical, scenario may be written for the READ/DATA instructions for assigning strings to string variables. For both computer A and computer B, when quotation marks are used, there is no ambiguity; everything between the quotation marks is assigned to a single string variable. (This is the same as when INPUT is used.)

```
COMPUTERS A AND B

10 READ X$,Y$
20 DATA "ABLE BAKER,CHARLIE","HOW,ARE,YOU?"

RUN

ABLE BAKER,CHARLIE         HOW,ARE,YOU?
```

Neither computer will read numeric data and assign them to string variables. When quotation marks are used, however, the numbers are considered strings and are accepted as such. Recall, however, that when INPUT is used, quotation marks are not necessary (see the program runs on the top of page 190).

```
COMPUTER A

>10 READ X$,Y$
>20 DATA 12345678901234567890,09876543210987654321
>30 PRINT X$,Y$

>RUN
     10 DATA MIX-UP,$TRING VS NUMERIC
```

```
>10 READ X$,Y$
>20 DATA "1","2"
>30 PRINT X$,Y$

>RUN

1              2
```

COMPUTER B

```
*10 READ X$,Y$
*20 DATA 12345678901234567890,09876543210987654321
*30 PRINT X$,Y$

*RUN

out of data in 10

*10 READ X$,Y$
*20 DATA "1","2"
*30 PRINT X$,Y$

*RUN

1                2
```

When a string that contains both alphabetic and numeric characters is to be read, the first computer accepts the string if the leading character is alphabetic. If the leading character is numeric, the interpreter will not let you enter the DATA line into the program. The second computer also accepts the string if the leading character is alphabetic and rejects it if the leading character is numeric. The difference between the two computers is that the rejection occurs in the second computer after RUN <CR> has been typed, during the compiling phase. Recall that when INPUT is used, a combination of alphabetic and numeric input is acceptable (see the middle of page 190).

COMPUTER A

```
>10 READ X$,Y$
>20 DATA A7
>30 PRINT X$,Y$

>RUN

      10 OUT OF DATA

>20 DATA A7,5G
 20 BAD CONST
```

COMPUTER B

```
*10 READ X$,Y$
*20 DATA A7,5G
*30 PRINT X$,Y$

*RUN

20 DATA A7,5G
           ^
statement error
```

If a sequence of characters contains a comma but no space within it, the comma separates it into two strings. This is the same as for INPUT (page 189). If the string contains a space within it, the first computer treats it as two strings, the second treats it as a single phrase. The second computer, expecting two data elements and finding only one when no comma is used, reports the deficiency as an error statement. This is similar to INPUT (see page 189).

COMPUTER A

```
>10 READ X$,Y$
>20 DATA ABLE,BAKER
>30 PRINT X$,Y$

>RUN

ABLE          BAKER
```

```
>10 READ X$,Y$
>20 DATA ABLE BAKER
>30 PRINT X$,Y$

>RUN

ABLE          BAKER
```

COMPUTER B

```
*10 READ X$,Y$
*20 DATA ABLE,BAKER
*30 PRINT X$,Y$

*RUN

ABLE            BAKER
```

```
*10 READ X$,Y$
*20 DATA ABLE BAKER
*30 PRINT X$,Y$

*RUN

out of data in 10
```

Computer A has no provision comparable to INPUT = $ for reading phrases. We must therefore use quotation marks to surround a phrase if that phrase is to be read as a single string and assigned to a string variable. For computer B, as before, only a comma serves as a delimiter; spaces do not divide data elements.

COMPUTER A

```
>10 READ X$,Y$
>20 DATA ABLE BAKER CHARLIE,HOW ARE YOU?
>30 PRINT X$,Y$

>RUN

ABLE          BAKER
```

COMPUTER B

```
*10 READ X$,Y$
*20 DATA ABLE BAKER CHARLIE,HOW ARE YOU?
*30 PRINT X$,Y$

*RUN

ABLE BAKER CHARLIE              HOW ARE YOU?
```

Finally, as for INPUT, computer A will accept alphabetic data and assign them to a numeric variable, provided the length of the string does not exceed six characters; computer B accepts only numeric data for numeric variables.

```
     COMPUTER A

>10 READ X,Y
>20 DATA CHARLIE,WASHINGTON
>30 PRINT X,Y

>RUN

      10 DATA MIX-UP,$TRING VS NUMERIC

>20 DATA CHARLI,WASHIN

>RUN

CHARLI         WASHIN

>10 READ X,Y
>20 DATA ABLE,BAKER
>30 PRINT X,Y

>RUN

ABLE           BAKER


     COMPUTER B

*10 READ X,Y
*20 DATA ABLE,BAKER
*30 PRINT X,Y

*RUN

out of data in 10
```

While most BASIC interpreters handle numeric variables and data similarly, there is greater variability when handling strings. The preceding examples illustrate how string variables and strings are handled by two different computing systems. You will have to do a little exploring to discover how your system works. By repeating these illustrations on your equipment, you should be able to uncover the peculiarities of your system.

A String Operation: Concatenation

Once entered into the computer, strings may be manipulated in a variety of ways. The simplest is to concatenate them. Consider the following:

```
     COMPUTER A

>10 READ X$,Y$
>20 DATA "HAPPY DAYS"
>30 DATA "ARE HERE AGAIN"
>40 PRINT X$ Y$
>50 PRINT X$Y$
>60 Z$=X$+Y$
>70 PRINT Z$

>RUN

HAPPY DAYSARE HERE AGAIN
HAPPY DAYSARE HERE AGAIN
HAPPY DAYSARE HERE AGAIN
```

COMPUTER B

```
*10 READ X$,Y$
*20 DATA HAPPY DAYS
*30 DATA ARE HERE AGAIN
*40 PRINT X$ Y$
*50 PRINT X$Y$
*60 Z$=X$&Y$
*70 PRINT Z$

*RUN

HAPPY DAYSARE HERE AGAIN
HAPPY DAYSARE HERE AGAIN
HAPPY DAYSARE HERE AGAIN
```

Each of the three print lines produces the same output, although the instructions to the computer are different. One difference appears in lines 20 and 30. For computer A, each phrase must be enclosed within quotation marks; for computer B, each data line consists of one phrase and quotation marks are not needed. Lines 40 and 50 are direct print statements operating on the two different string variables X$ and Y$. In line 60, however, the two strings are concatenated, and a new string, denoted by the variable name Z$ and having an independent existence, is created. It is this string, Z$, that is printed in line 70. Some computers use the ampersand (&) for concatenation (computer B); others use the plus sign (+) (computer A).

When two strings are concatenated, the first character of the second string follows immediately after the last character of the first string. Thus, there is no space between DAYS and ARE. To insert a blank space between DAYS and ARE, we must enclose the phrase ARE HERE AGAIN within quotation marks, making sure that a space follows the opening quote and preceds "ARE." The following program illustrates this.

COMPUTER A

```
>10 READ X$,Y$
>20 DATA "HAPPY DAYS"
>30 DATA " ARE HERE AGAIN"
>40 PRINT X$ Y$
>50 PRINT X$Y$
>60 Z$=X$+Y$
>70 PRINT Z$

>RUN

HAPPY DAYS ARE HERE AGAIN
HAPPY DAYS ARE HERE AGAIN
HAPPY DAYS ARE HERE AGAIN
```

COMPUTER B

```
*10 READ X$,Y$
*20 DATA HAPPY DAYS
*30 DATA " ARE HERE AGAIN"
*40 PRINT X$ Y$
*50 PRINT X$Y$
*60 Z$=X$&Y$
*70 PRINT Z$

*RUN

HAPPY DAYS ARE HERE AGAIN
HAPPY DAYS ARE HERE AGAIN
HAPPY DAYS ARE HERE AGAIN
```

Illustration: A Form Letter

With what you have learned thus far, you should be able to write a personalized form letter, good for catching up on your correspondence. For example, consider the following program.

```
10 INPUT=$
20 REM: THIS IS A PERSONALIZED FORM LETTER, GOOD FOR WRITING TO
30 REM: RELATIVES, FRIENDS AND BUSINESS ASSOCIATES.
40 PRINT
50 PRINT "  THIS LETTER TAKES THE FOLLOWING FORM:"
60 PRINT
70 PRINT "DEAR [**],"
80 PRINT "      I HAVE [**] MY [**] CLASS [**] TIMES THIS SEMESTER."
90 PRINT "I REALLY [**] THIS PLACE CALLED [**]; MAYBE ITS" TAB(0)
100 PRINT " THE [**]." TAB(0)
110 PRINT "ENCLOSED YOU WILL FIND MY [**]." TAB(0)
120 PRINT "  I AM FEELING [**]." TAB(0)
130 PRINT "PLEASE WRITE SOON."
140 PRINT
150 PRINT TAB(30) "YOUR [**]"
160 PRINT TAB (30) "[**]"
170 ;\; "INSERT APPROPRIATE WORDS OR PHRASES IN THE PLACES WHERE"
180 ; "THE [**] APPEAR."
190 ;
200 PRINT "DEAR[**]"\INPUT A$
210 PRINT "I HAVE [**]"\INPUT B$
220 PRINT "MY [**]"\INPUT C$
230 PRINT "CLASS [**]"\INPUT D$
240 PRINT "I REALLY [**]"\INPUT E$
250 PRINT "THIS PLACE CALLED[**]"\INPUT F$
260 PRINT "MAYBE ITS THE [**]"\INPUT G$
270 PRINT "FIND MY[**]"\INPUT H$
280 PRINT "I AM FEELING [**]"\INPUT I$
290 PRINT "YOUR [**]"\INPUT J$
300 PRINT "YOUR NAME"\INPUT K$
310 ;&;
320 PRINT "DEAR "A$","
330 ;
340 PRINT TAB(5) "I HAVE "B$" MY "C$" CLASS "D$" TIMES THIS SEMESTER."
350 PRINT "I REALLY "E$" THIS PLACE CALLED "F$"; MAYBE ITS THE "
360 PRINT G$".   ENCLOSED YOU WILL FIND MY "H$".   I AM"
370 PRINT "FEELING "I$".  PLEASE WRITE SOON."
380 PRINT
390 PRINT TAB(30) "YOUR "J$","
400 PRINT TAB(30) K$
```

The first part of the program, lines 70–180, consists of instructions to the person writing the letter concerning its format as well as instructions about appropriate input. The middle part, lines 200–300, requests the input. The letter itself is printed in lines 320–400.

Because the computer on which this program was written and run uses both the comma and the space as separators between words, the INPUT = $ instruction was used at line 10. The instruction was issued in anticipation that phrases, rather than single words, would be inserted.

The program was run twice with the following outcomes.

```
  THIS LETTER TAKES THE FOLLOWING FORM:

DEAR [**],
     I HAVE [**] MY [**] CLASS [**] TIMES THIS SEMESTER.
I REALLY [**] THIS PLACE CALLED [**]; MAYBE ITS THE [**].
ENCLOSED YOU WILL FIND MY [**].  I AM FEELING [**].PLEASE WRITE SOON.

                              YOUR [**]
                              [**]
```

```
INSERT APPROPRIATE WORDS OR PHRASES IN THE PLACES WHERE
THE [**] APPEAR.

DEAR[**]
?JEANNE AND JIM
I HAVE [**]
?GONE TO
MY [**]
?PSYCH
CLASS [**]
?ONLY 5
I REALLY [**]
?DO NOT ENJOY
THIS PLACE CALLED[**]
?SUNNY ARIZONA
MAYBE ITS THE [**]
?WEATHER
FIND MY[**]
?CHECK FOR $10
I AM FEELING [**]
?DRAGGED OUT
YOUR [**]
?BUDDY
YOUR NAME
?BILL


DEAR JEANNE AND JIM,

    I HAVE GONE TO MY PSYCH CLASS ONLY 5 TIMES THIS SEMESTER.
I REALLY DO NOT ENJOY THIS PLACE CALLED SUNNY ARIZONA; MAYBE ITS THE
WEATHER.  ENCLOSED YOU WILL FIND MY CHECK FOR $10.  I AM
FEELING DRAGGED OUT.  PLEASE WRITE SOON.

                             YOUR BUDDY,
                             BILL



  THIS LETTER TAKES THE FOLLOWING FORM:

DEAR [**],
     I HAVE [**] MY [**] CLASS [**] TIMES THIS SEMESTER.
I REALLY [**] THIS PLACE CALLED [**]; MAYBE ITS THE [**].
ENCLOSED YOU WILL FIND MY [**].  I AM FEELING [**].PLEASE WRITE SOON.

                             YOUR [**]
                             [**]

INSERT APPROPRIATE WORDS OR PHRASES IN THE PLACES WHERE
THE [**] APPEAR.

DEAR[**]
?MOTHER
I HAVE [**]
?FAILED TO GO TO
MY [**]
?PHYS ED
CLASS [**]
?17
I REALLY [**]
?DO ENJOY
THIS PLACE CALLED[**]
?CLARKLY
MAYBE ITS THE [**]
?TOWN OR MAYBE THE PEOPLE
FIND MY[**]
?DIRTY LAUNDRY AND A BOOK OF POETRY
I AM FEELING [**]
?JUST GREAT AND HAVE LOST THREE POUNDS
YOUR [**]
?LOVING DAUGHTER
YOUR NAME
?SONJA
```

```
DEAR MOTHER,

    I HAVE FAILED TO GO TO MY PHYS ED CLASS 17 TIMES THIS SEMESTER.
I REALLY DO ENJOY THIS PLACE CALLED CLARKLY; MAYBE ITS THE
TOWN OR MAYBE THE PEOPLE.   ENCLOSED YOU WILL FIND MY
DIRTY LAUNDRY AND A BOOK OF POETRY.  I AM
FEELING JUST GREAT AND HAVE LOST THREE POUNDS.  PLEASE WRITE SOON.

                              YOUR LOVING DAUGHTER,
                              SONJA
```

String Lists and Arrays

Previously, we extended the concept of a single numerical variable to numeric lists and arrays; similarly, string variables may be extended to string lists and string arrays. Any list of words may be considered a string list; one important application would be in alphabetizing the list. For example, when initially preparing the index for this book, all significant words and the pages on which they occurred were entered into the computer as a list of strings. This list was then sorted and the index prepared.

The utility of string arrays may be appreciated from the following illustration. When you register your car, among the pertinent information you must supply are (1) the owner's name, (2) the owner's address, (3) make of car, (4) model, (5) year, and (6) the car's identification number. You are then issued (7) a license number. These seven bits of information make up the seven columns in an array. Each row in the array refers to a different owner, different car, and so on. There are as many rows in the array as there are cars registered. If a car is found abandoned, by searching the array for the car's identification number or license plate number, the name and address of the owner may be found. If you are stopped for a traffic violation, the police determine if the car you are driving has been reported stolen. The widespread use of string arrays and their extension to files and data bases, about which we shall say more later, is inexorably leading us toward a society in which our every action may be scrutinized. But that leads us to another facet of computers in society. We return to our central theme.

Although some computers do not require a DIM statement for a numeric list or array if the range of subscripts does not exceed 10, a DIM statement is usually required for all subscripted string variables, no matter what the range.

Alphabetizing: String Lists

A string list is a subscripted list of string variables A\$(1), A\$(2), . . . , A\$(N). To illustrate the application of string lists, consider the problem of alphabetizing a list of names. The bubble sort routine, which we used in Chapter 9 to arrange a sequence of numbers in order, is easily adapted for this purpose. All that is required is to replace the numeric list by a string list. The following program parallels the one on pages 146-47.

```
10 INPUT = $
20 DIM A$(25)
30 PRINT "HOW MANY NAMES ARE IN THE LIST";\INPUT N\;
40 FOR I=1 TO N
50 INPUT A$(I)
60 NEXT I
70 FOR I=1 TO N-1
80 FOR J=1 TO N-I
90 IF A$(J)<A$(J+1) THEN 140
100 X$=A$(J)
110 Y$=A$(J+1)
120 A$(J)=Y$
130 A$(J+1)=X$
140 NEXT J
150 NEXT I
160 PRINT
170 FOR I=1 TO N
180 PRINT A$(I)
190 NEXT I
200 INPUT =1
```

A minor difference between the two programs is that here the data, the names, are assigned by way of INPUT statements: MARY SMITH to A$(1), DAVID CONRAY to A$(2), . . . , SHERRY MARTIN to A$(10), whereas in the original problem the numbers were randomly generated. The significant difference is that for sorting numeric data, numeric variables are used; for sorting (alphabetizing) alphabetic data, string variables are used.

The arithmetic relation $A < B$ states that the number assigned to the variable A is numerically less than the number denoted by the variable B. The same symbol, $<$, when used with two string variables A$ and B$ in the string relation $A\$ < B\$$ states that, lexicographically, the string represented by the variable A$ precedes the string denoted by the variable B$. The computer's ability to decide which of two strings comes first alphabetically, line 90, is crucial to the program. The run appears as follows.

```
HOW MANY NAMES ARE IN THE LIST  ?10

?SMITH, MARY
?CONRAY, DAVID
?JONES, WILLIAM
?SINTER, RICHARD
?SPERRY, JOHN
?SMITH, HARRY
?LOWMAN, SCOTT
?EARNLEY, BRETT
?JONES, MARGE
?MARTIN, SHERRY

CONRAY, DAVID
EARNLEY, BRETT
JONES, MARGE
JONES, WILLIAM
LOWMAN, SCOTT
MARTIN, SHERRY
SINTER, RICHARD
SMITH, HARRY
SMITH, MARY
SPERRY, JOHN
```

An Application: String Arrays

The Clear River police department requires all residents owning bicycles to register them and get a license number and tag. The purpose is to discourage loss by theft and to provide rapid identification of unclaimed bicycles. A string array, $N \times 4$, with N rows, one for each of the N bicycles registered and 4 columns—one each for name, address, phone number, and license number—is constructed. By querying this array, we can discover if a given person has registered a bicycle and, conversely, for a given license number, who owns the bike.

```
10 INPUT = $
20 DIM A$(25,4)
30 FOR I=1 TO 10
40 FOR J=1 TO 4
50 READ A$(I,J)
60 NEXT J
70 NEXT I
80 ;
90 PRINT "DO YOU KNOW THE NAME OR LICENSE NUMBER?"
100 PRINT "RESPOND EITHER NAME OR NUMBER"; & INPUT X$
110 IF X$= "NAME" THEN 150
120 IF X$= "NUMBER" THEN 260
130 PRINT "PLEASE RESPOND WITH NAME OR NUMBER ONLY" & GOTO 80
140 ;
150 PRINT "WHAT IS THE NAME? ENTER LAST NAME, THEN COMMA, THEN SPACE"
160 PRINT "THEN FIRST NAME";\INPUT K$
170 FOR I=1 TO 10
180 IF K$=A$(I,1) THEN 360
190 NEXT I
```

```
200 ;
210 PRINT "THE NAME "K$" IS NOT IN THE FILE"
220 PRINT
230 PRINT "ARE THERE OTHER SEARCHES"; & INPUT Y$
240 IF Y$="YES" THEN 80
250 STOP
260 PRINT "WHAT IS THE LICENSE NUMBER";\INPUT K$
270 FOR I=1 TO 10
280 IF K$=A$(I,4) THEN 360
290 NEXT I
300 ;
310 PRINT "THE LICENSE NUMBER "K$" IS NOT IN THE FILE."
320 PRINT
330 PRINT "ARE THERE OTHER SEARCHES"; & INPUT Y$
340 IF Y$="YES" THEN 80
350 STOP
360 ;
370 PRINT "THE COMPLETE FILE YOU ARE SEEKING IS AS FOLLOWS:"
380 PRINT "THE NAME IS" TAB(25) A$(I,1)
390 PRINT "THE ADDRESS IS" TAB(25) A$(I,2)
400 PRINT "THE PHONE NUMBER IS" TAB(25) A$(I,3)
410 PRINT "THE LICENSE NUMBER IS" TAB(25) A$(I,4)
420 PRINT
430 GOTO 330
440 DATA "SMITH, MARY", "23 SOUTH STREET","764-1234","AJ-34"
450 DATA "CONRAY, DAVID","8 QUE PLACE","789-5749","B-753"
460 DATA "JONES, WILLIAM","85 W. 9TH ST.","724-8271","34-A-43"
470 DATA "SINTER, RICHARD","1002 43RD STREET","543-5678","1234"
480 DATA "SPERRY, JOHN","4 WILLIAMS ROAD","677-5433","ABCD"
490 DATA "SMITH, HARRY","105 EAST PEACE","234-9876","GH-6-PLR"
500 DATA "LOWMAN, SCOTT","300 FORT LANE","456-5522","ASD-123"
510 DATA "EARLNFY, BRETT","455 WASHINGTON ROAD","997-4457","67-A"
520 DATA "JONES, MARGE","1007 ANDERSON AVE.","556-6543","67-AA"
530 DATA "MARTIN, SHERRY","15 TRAIL ROAD","631-4628","A-3-F-6"
```

In this illustration, the data are read. The data in lines 440–530 are arranged in array form: Each of the ten rows (think of each row as a record) contains four fields. The first field is for the name, the second the address, the third the phone number, and the fourth the registration tag number. Visualize the array of string variables A$(I,J) as consisting of ten rows and four columms, as follows:

```
A$(1,1)     A$(1,2)     A$(1,3)     A$(1,4)
A$(2,1)     A$(2,2)     A$(2,3)     A$(2,4)
                ...
A$(10,1)    A$(10,2)    A$(10,3)    A$(10,4)
```

The assignment of each phrase to its appropriate string variable is then obvious: The phrase in the Ith row and Jth column is assigned to the variable A$(I,J). When we refer to an element of an array, the first index, I, denotes the row and the second index, J, denotes the column. To ensure that the entire phrase is assigned to the string variable, each phrase is enclosed within quotation marks. Thus, SMITH, MARY is assigned to A$(1,1), 1002 43RD STREET to A$(4,2), 456-5522 to A$(7,3) and ABCD to A$(5,4). Similarly, the other phrases are assigned to the appropriate elements of the array A$(I, 124

Suppose the double loop, lines 30–70, had been written

```
30 FOR J= 1 TO 4
40 FOR I= 1 to 10
50 READ A$(I,J)
60 NEXT I
70 NEXT J
```

It would have been necessary then to prepare the data as a list of ten names, followed by a list of ten addresses, followed by a list of phone numbers, followed by a list of license tag numbers. Care and consistency are important when preparing the data.

In the first line of the program, INPUT = $ was set in anticipation that the data to be entered would be a phrase, because the object of the program is to enter a name (or license number) and discover if the name (or license number) is in the array. If it is, the name, address, telephone number, and license number are to be printed; if it is not in the array, a message to that effect is to be printed.

Note in the above program the use of the equal sign to compare strings. In lines 110, 120, 240, and 340, a string variable is compared with a fixed string. The computer makes this comparison on a character-by-character basis. For the computer to recognize that the strings on the two sides of the equal sign are the same, there must be no misspelling, no punctuation differences, no extra spaces, nor any other differences.

At line 180, the computer compares the string represented by K$ with the string represented by A$(I,1). This is done within a loop, I = 1 to N, and a search of all names in the list is being made. If a string A$(I,1) is found that is identical to K$, character by character, the program goes to line 360, where the desired information is printed.

The other possibility, that we know the license number, leads to the search made in lines 270–290. Again, if a match is found, the pertinent information is printed beginning at line 360.

In both searches, if a match is found, two things happen. The more obvious one is that control is transferred to line 360. Less obvious, but crucial, is that the value of I for which the match was found is known and is used to select the proper record for printing. Thus, for example, if we are searching for the name Sinter, Richard, K$ as input at line 160, the computer would set I = 1 and compare Sinter, Richard to Smith, Mary, A$(1,1). Since these do no match, I is set equal to 2 and Sinter, Richard is compared to Conray, David, A$(2,1). Again there is no match. It is only when I = 4 that Sinter, Richard (K$) is compared to Sinter, Richard (A$(4,1)) and we see that K$=A$(4,1). At this point, the computer retains the information that I = 4 and uses this to select the proper record for printing, lines 370–410.

```
DO YOU KNOW THE NAME OR LICENSE NUMBER?
RESPOND EITHER NAME OR NUMBER   ?NEITHER
PLEASE RESPOND WITH NAME OR NUMBER ONLY

DO YOU KNOW THE NAME OR LICENSE NUMBER?
RESPOND EITHER NAME OR NUMBER   ?NAME
WHAT IS THE NAME? ENTER LAST NAME, THEN COMMA, THEN SPACE
THEN FIRST NAME   ?SPERRY, JOHN

THE COMPLETE FILE YOU ARE SEEKING IS AS FOLLOWS:
THE NAME IS             SPERRY, JOHN
THE ADDRESS IS          4 WILLIAMS ROAD
THE PHONE NUMBER IS     677-5433
THE LICENSE NUMBER IS   ABCD

ARE THERE OTHER SEARCHES  ?YES

DO YOU KNOW THE NAME OR LICENSE NUMBER?
RESPOND EITHER NAME OR NUMBER   ?NUMBER
WHAT IS THE LICENSE NUMBER  ?67-AA

THE COMPLETE FILE YOU ARE SEEKING IS AS FOLLOWS:
THE NAME IS             JONES, MARGE
THE ADDRESS IS          1007 ANDERSON AVE.
THE PHONE NUMBER IS     556-6543
THE LICENSE NUMBER IS   67-AA

ARE THERE OTHER SEARCHES  ?YES

DO YOU KNOW THE NAME OR LICENSE NUMBER?
RESPOND EITHER NAME OR NUMBER   ?NAME
WHAT IS THE NAME? ENTER LAST NAME, THEN COMMA, THEN SPACE
THEN FIRST NAME   ?SMITH, MARTY

THE NAME SMITH, MARTY IS NOT IN THE FILE
```

```
ARE THERE OTHER SEARCHES   ?YES

DO YOU KNOW THE NAME OR LICENSE NUMBER?
RESPOND EITHER NAME OR NUMBER   ?NUMBER
WHAT IS THE LICENSE NUMBER  ?234

THE LICENSE NUMBER 234 IS NOT IN THE FILE.

ARE THERE OTHER SEARCHES   ?NO
```

We have introduced string variables, string lists, and string arrays. The BASIC instructions LET, INPUT, and READ/DATA were used to assign alphabetic information to string variables. Once phrases are assigned to string variables, they can be used to prepare form letters; the needed operation is concatenation. Strings may be compared and manipulated to produce alphabetized lists, that is, the symbols < and > have the expected lexicographical meanings. Two strings may be compared to determine if they are identical. In that case, the equal symbol = is used; it was applied to searching a list.

We shall now turn to some other operations that may be performed on strings.

Substrings

Text editing offers a prime example of the need to manipulate strings and substrings. During the preparation of a manuscript, for example, the initial writing and editing may be done by hand or on a typewriter rather than as input to a computer. In the final phase, however, after a reasonable draft has been prepared (actually entered into a computer that controls a typesetting machine), changes to the text are made using computer instructions. Generally, these instructions, designed for and provided to the more specialized word processing and typesetting computers, are quite complex in that they consist of many simpler ones combined in some agreed-upon preprogramed sequence: Locate a substring, move it from one place in a paragraph to another, insert a new sentence, change font to italics, insert a footnote, and so on. At the basis of all this, however, are a few fundamental instructions and programs utilizing them. While BASIC is not a specialized text editing language, it does have some limited capabilities in this area. As we shall see, it is possible to locate a substring within a given string, to copy a substring, and to replace one substring with another. Using these, the instruction repertoire of the more specialized text editing computers may be mimicked.

Suppose we want to copy from the string variable A$ that substring of A$ that begins with the seventh character and contains nine characters. We use A$(:7,9). A$(:7,9) may be handled directly within a program or may be used to define a new string variable by an assign statement: B$=A4(:7,9).

If we write A$(:7), omitting the ,9, the computer will interpret this as the substring that begins with the seventh character and contains all the remaining characters in the original string. The following program shows how this works.

```
10 A$="ABCDEFGHIJKLMNOPQRSTUVWXYZ"
20 B$=A$(:7,9)
30 C$=A$(:7)
40 PRINT A$
50 PRINT B$
60 PRINT C$
70 PRINT A$(:7,9)
80 PRINT A$(:7)
```

```
ABCDEFGHIJKLMNOPQRSTUVWXYZ
GHIJKLMNO
GHIJKLMNOPQRSTUVWXYZ
GHIJKLMNO
GHIJKLMNOPQRSTUVWXYZ
```

If too few characters exist in the original string, the computer truncates after the last character.

```
10 A$="ABCDEFGHIJKLMNOPQRSTUVWXYZ"
20 B$=A$(:20,15)
30 PRINT A$
40 PRINT B$
50 PRINT A$(:20,15)
60 PRINT A$(:20)
```

```
ABCDEFGHIJKLMNOPQRSTUVWXYZ
TUVWXYZ
TUVWXYZ
TUVWXYZ
```

The above comments on the copying substrings from string variables apply, with the necessary changes, to string lists and string arrays. For these cases, if A$(I) is a string list and B$(I,J) a string array, then for each variable of the list and array, beginning in position L, the remaining characters may be copied by using

A$(I:L) and B$(I,J:L)

Paralleling copying a substring containing characters that occur in the middle of the string, we have the following forms, for string lists and string arrays, respectively:

A$(I:L,K) and B$(I,J:L,K)

For a given string A$, the positions denoted by (:L,K) may be modified under program control. The following program illustrates these instructions.

```
10 A$="ABCDEFGHIJKLMNOPQRSTUVWXYZ"
20 FOR I=5 TO 10
30 FOR J=2 TO 4
40 PRINT A$(:I,I-J)
50 NEXT J
60 NEXT I
```

```
EFG
EF
E
FGHI
FGH
FG
GHIJK
GHIJ
GHI
HIJKLM
HIJKL
HIJK
IJKLMNO
IJKLMN
IJKLM
JKLMNOPQ
JKLMNOP
JKLMNO
```

The symbols used in this program to instruct the computer to copy a substring from a given string are not universal. On some computers, a special three argument function performs this operation. We shall use the abbreviation EXT for the name of the function. Again, assume we begin with the string variable A$ = ABCDEFGHIJKL-MNOPQRSTUVWXYZ and let B$ = EXT(A$,L,K). The first position of the EXT function directs the computer's attention to the string variable A$; if we wish to extract a substring from a different string variable, for example, Y$, then that first position would be occupied by Y$. The first character of B$ will be that character of A$ that occupies position number L in A$. In all, the sequence of K consecutive characters of A$ makes up B$. For B$ = EXT(A$,7,5), B$ = GHIJK, since G is the seventh character of A$ and five consecutive characters are to be copied. The verb EXT may be different on different computers; your manual should provide the exact spelling used.

We should make one final observation concerning the copying operation. As described above, the original string from which the substring is obtained is *not* altered; the string variable A$ remains as originally given.

Modification of Strings

Rather than copying a substring from a given string, suppose we want to modify a given string by replacing specified characters within it. For example, we start with a string H$ and replace L characters in it, starting at position K, by L characters of another string, A$. Assume H$ = 12345678901234567890, A$ = JKLMN, and we want to replace characters 6 through 10 of H$ by those of A$ to produce a new H$ = 12345JKLMN1234567890. To accomplish this, we use:

```
H$(:6,5) = A$
```

The characters of the string A$ will replace those of H$ that occupy positions, 6, 7, 8, 9, and 10. Other possibilities are available; the point to remember is that the string whose characters are being replaced is to the left of the equal sign, the string from which the characters are taken is to the right.

The following program illustrates various possibilities that may arise. The string B$ is the alphabet; the string A$ is the set of digits 1, 2, . . . , 9,0, repeated once.

```
10 DIM H$(10)
20 A$="12345678901234567890"
30 B$="ABCDEFGHIJKLMNOPQRSTUVWXYZ"
40 PRINT
50 PRINT A$
60 PRINT B$
70 REM: FOR FUTURE USE, 8 COPIES OF A$ ARE MADE
80 FOR I=1 TO 8
90 H$(I)=A$
100 NEXT I
110 PRINT
120 H$(1:6)=B$
130 PRINT "H$(1)="H$(1)
140 PRINT
150 H$(2:6)=B$(:10)
160 PRINT "H$(2)="H$(2)
170 PRINT
180 H$(3:6)=B$(:10,5)
190 PRINT "H$(3)="H$(3)
200 PRINT
210 H$(4:6,8)=B$
220 PRINT "H$(4)="H$(4)
230 PRINT
240 H$(5:6,8)=B$(:10)
250 PRINT "H$(5)="H$(5)
260 PRINT
270 H$(6:6,8)=B$(:10,5)
280 PRINT "H$(6)="H$(6)
290 PRINT
300 H$(7:6,5)=B$(:10,5)
310 PRINT "H$(7)="H$(7)
```

```
320 PRINT
330 H$(8:6,2)=B$(:10,5)
340 PRINT "H$(8)="H$(8)
```

```
12345678901234567890
ABCDEFGHIJKLMNOPQRSTUVWXYZ

H$(1)=12345ABCDEFGHIJKLMNOPQRSTUVWXYZ

H$(2)=12345JKLMNOPQRSTUVWXYZ

H$(3)=12345JKLMN

H$(4)=12345ABCDEFGH4567890

H$(5)=12345JKLMNOPQ4567890

H$(6)=12345JKLMN   4567890

H$(7)=12345JKLMN1234567890

H$(8)=12345JK8901234567890
```

In line 120, the whole alphabet is inserted into H$(1), beginning at position 6. The outcome is H$(1) in the printout. In line 150, that subset of the alphabet beginning with the tenth letter, which is J, is inserted into H$(2) beginning in position 6. The result is given as H$(2) in the printout. At line 180, five characters, JKLMN, are copied from B$ and inserted, beginning in position 6 in H$(3); H$(3) indicates the result. In these three examples, the end of H$ was deleted (everything from the sixth character to the end of the string), and the appropriate string, represented by the symbols to the right of the equal sign, was tacked on.

If we want to replace only some of the interior characters of H$, the instruction is:

```
H$(:6,8) = B$
```

In this case, as called for in line 210 of the program, the eight characters 6, 7, 8, 9, 0, 1, 2, 3 of H$(4) are replaced by the first eight characters of B$, namely, ABCDEFGH. The new H$ is as given in the printout, H$(4).

If the characters to be replaced in H$ are not the first ones of B$, but those beginning with the tenth character of B$, J, then the right-hand side must be modified to become B$(:10). This is done in line 240 and the new H$ is printed as H$(5).

If too few characters are copied from B$ then "spaces" are used to fill out the number of characters needed for the replacement in H$. See line 270 and the printout, H$(6).

If exactly the correct number is extracted and inserted, the result is as expected; see line 300 and H$(7).

If five characters are extracted from B$ but only two spaces are to be modified in H$, only the first two of those extracted are used. This is programed in line 330 and shown as H$(8).

The symbols used to describe string modification are not universal. On some computers, a three argument function is used to replace characters within one string by characters from a second string. We shall use the abbreviation INS for the name of this function. (If this operation is available on your computer, your manual will indicate the appropriate name.) The following example illustrates the use of INS:

```
10 H$ = "ABCDEFGHIJKLMNOPQRSTUVWXY"
20 A$ = "12345"
30 H$ = INS (A$,5,0)
40 PRINT H$
```

ABCD12345EFGHIJKLMNOPQRSTUVWXYZ

The program instructs the computer to start in the 5th position of H$ (indicated by the 5 in the argument list of INS) and insert all of A$, deleting zero positions from H$ (the 0 in the argument list of INS).

If we want to replace part of H$, we use the following:

```
10 H$ = "ABCDEFGHIJKLMNOPQRSTUVWXYZ"
20 A$ = "12345"
30 H$ = INS (A$,8.3)
40 PRINT H$
```

ABCDEFG12345KLMNOPQRSTUVWXYZ

Three characters of H$, those beginning in position 8 (HIJ) are removed, and the five characters of A$ are inserted. The number of characters in H$ has been increased by two.

An Application: Graphing

We shall now apply this newly gained information to a problem already solved, that of graphing the mathematical function SIN(X). This time, instead of printing an asterisk on white paper to indicate the function value, we create black paper and use a white symbol, O, to represent the function value. In the following program, a line H$ containing 72 asterisks is constructed by concatenation, lines 30 through 60. The curve is centered as before, and the location of the function value is determined, also as before. Now, at line 80, the one asterisk that occupies the function position I is replaced by O. The modified H$ is then printed, line 90. The program follows. The graph appears in Fig. 11-1.

```
10 ;&;&;
20 FOR X=0 TO 6.4 STEP .2
30 H$=""
40 FOR I=1 TO 72
50 H$=H$+"*"
60 NEXT I
70 I=INT(40+30*SIN(X))
80 H$(:I,1)="O"
90 PRINT H$
100 NEXT X
```

If we don't like all the asterisks, we may modify line 50 by deleting the asterisk and replacing it with a space. The modified program follows. The resulting graph appears in Fig. 11-2.

```
10 ;&;&;
20 FOR X=0 TO 6.4 STEP .2
30 H$=""
40 FOR I=1 TO 72
50 H$=H$+" "
60 NEXT I
70 I=INT(40+30*SIN(X))
80 H$(:I,1)="O"
90 PRINT H$
100 NEXT X
```

Locating a Substring

Some BASIC interpreters provide a three argument function that can be used to locate a substring within a given string. We shall use the abbreviation POS to designate the function; two of its arguments are string variables, the third is numeric. The use of POS is illustrated in the following example. Consider the string

A$= IF YOU DO NOT EXPECT THE UNEXPECTED, YOU WILL NOT FIND IT.

Within this string we want to find the substring

B$= OU

Written in a program, the statement takes the form

X = POS (A$,B$,1)

The computer begins searching, starting with the first characters of A$ (this is the significance of the number 1 as the third argument of POS) for the two character string "OU." Because OU occupies positions 5 and 6 in A$, the value of X is 5.

If we write

X = POS (A$,B$,6)

the computer begins its search with position 6. In this case, X=39.

If the function POS is not available on your computer, the situation is not calamitous. The following program may be used instead.

```
10 DIM A$(5),B(5)
20 A$(1)="IF YOU DO NOT EXPECT THE UNEXPECTED, YOU WILL NOT FIND IT;"
30 A$(2)="FOR IT IS HARD TO BE SOUGHT OUT, AND DIFFICULT."
40 PRINT
50 FOR I=1 TO 2
60 PRINT A$(I)
70 B(I)=LEN(A$(I))
80 NEXT I
```

FIGURE 11-1

```
***************************************O********************************
********************************************O***************************
**************************************************O*********************
*******************************************************O****************
************************************************************O***********
****************************************************************O*******
******************************************************************O*****
********************************************************************O***
********************************************************************O***
********************************************************************O***
******************************************************************O*****
***************************************************************O********
***********************************************************O************
******************************************************O*****************
*************************************************O**********************
*******************************************O****************************
*************************************O**********************************
*******************************O****************************************
*************************O**********************************************
********************O***************************************************
****************O*******************************************************
************O***********************************************************
**********O*************************************************************
*********O**************************************************************
*********O**************************************************************
**********O*************************************************************
************O***********************************************************
***************O********************************************************
********************O***************************************************
*************************O**********************************************
******************************O*****************************************
************************************O***********************************
******************************************O*****************************
```

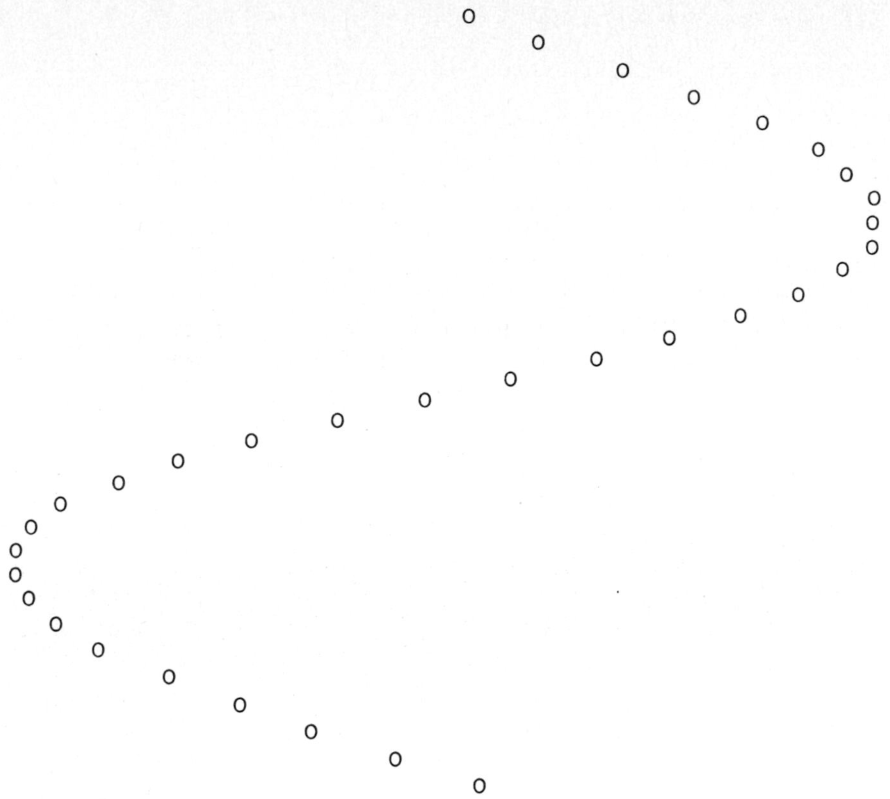

```
                               O
                                    O
                                          O
                                               O
                                                   O
                                                       O
                                                         O
                                                           O
                                                           O
                                                           O
                                                         O
                                                      O
                                                  O
                                             O
                                        O
                                  O
                            O
                      O
                O
           O
       O
   O
 O
O
O
 O
   O
     O
          O
               O
                    O
                          O
                                O
```

FIGURE 11-2

```
 90 PRINT
 100 PRINT "WHAT SUBSTRING DO YOU WANT TO SEARCH FOR"; \ INPUT C$
 110 PRINT
 120 C=LEN(C$)
 130 FOR J=1 TO 2
 140 FOR I=1 TO B(J)
 150 IF C$=A$(J:I,C) THEN 220
 160 NEXT I
 170 NEXT J
 180 PRINT
 190 PRINT "ANOTHER SEARCH? ANSWER YES OR NO."; \ INPUT D$
 200 IF D$="YES" THEN 90
 210 STOP
 220 PRINT "THE POSITION OF THE SUBSTRING "C$" IN STRING"J" IS"I
 230 GOTO 160
 240 END
```

```
IF YOU DO NOT EXPECT THE UNEXPECTED, YOU WILL NOT FIND IT;
FOR IT IS HARD TO BE SOUGHT OUT, AND DIFFICULT.

WHAT SUBSTRING DO YOU WANT TO SEARCH FOR  ?Y

THE POSITION OF THE SUBSTRING Y IN STRING 1 IS 4
THE POSITION OF THE SUBSTRING Y IN STRING 1 IS 38

ANOTHER SEARCH? ANSWER YES OR NO.   ?YES

WHAT SUBSTRING DO YOU WANT TO SEARCH FOR  ?OU

THE POSITION OF THE SUBSTRING OU IN STRING 1 IS 5
THE POSITION OF THE SUBSTRING OU IN STRING 1 IS 39
THE POSITION OF THE SUBSTRING OU IN STRING 2 IS 23
THE POSITION OF THE SUBSTRING OU IN STRING 2 IS 29
```

```
ANOTHER SEARCH? ANSWER YES OR NO.    ?YES

WHAT SUBSTRING DO YOU WANT TO SEARCH FOR  ?FIND

THE POSITION OF THE SUBSTRING FIND IN STRING 1 IS 51

ANOTHER SEARCH? ANSWER YES OR NO.    ?NO
```

The strings to be searched (the quotation is from Heraclitus) are given in lines 20 and 30. In lines 50–80, the length of each string is found and assigned to the subscripted variable B(I). The LEN function is explained in the next section. At line 100, we are asked to identify the substring sought. The search takes place in lines 130–170; whenever a match is found, the result is printed, line 220, and the search continues, line 230.

String Functions

The Length of a String

In the last program we used a function to find the length of a string. BASIC provides an intrinsic function LEN(A$), the argument of which is the generic string variable A$. The output of LEN(A$) is an integer, which is the number of characters in A$. The following program illustrates the use of LEN(A$) and reviews the copying of substrings from a given string. Thus, A$(:I,I-J) will copy, beginning in the Ith position of the string A$, (I-J) consecutive characters; LEN(A$(:I,I-J)) finds the length of the substring.

```
10 A$="ABCDEFGHIJKLMNOPQRSTUVWXYZ"
20 FOR I=5 TO 10
30 FOR J=2 TO 4
40 B=LEN(A$(:I,I-J))
50 PRINT B,
60 PRINT A$(:I,I-J)
70 NEXT J
80 NEXT I
```

```
3          EFG
2          EF
1          E
4          FGHI
3          FGH
2          FG
5          GHIJK
4          GHIJ
3          GHI
6          HIJKLM
5          HIJKL
4          HIJK
7          IJKLMNO
6          IJKLMN
5          IJKLM
8          JKLMNOPQ
7          JKLMNOP
6          JKLMNO
```

We have previously discussed the concatenation of strings. In the following program, we use concatenation to juxtapose single words into a phrase. The concatenation of A$(1) and A$(2) is the string IAM; we really want I AM. By assigning the character "space" to R$ at line 70 and executing lines 80–100, we add a blank space at the end of each of the first four words. With this done, all five words are joined into one phrase, lines 120–140. Note that B$ is initialized in line 110 to be an empty string; remember, there is a distinction between an empty string, line 110, and a string consisting of a "space" or "spaces," line 70. The length of the final string is determined at line 150; verify that the length is indeed 21. In lines 160–190, the leading character is stripped away, one at a time, until nothing but the grin is left.

```
10 DIM A$(10)
20 A$(1)="I"
30 A$(2)="AM"
40 A$(3)="THE"
50 A$(4)="CHESHIRE"
60 A$(5)="CAT"
70 R$=" "
80 FOR I=1 TO 4
90 A$(I)=A$(I)+R$
100 NEXT I
110 B$=""
120 FOR I=1 TO 5
130 B$=B$+A$(I)
140 NEXT I
150 B=LEN(B$)
160 FOR I=1 TO B+1
170 K=LEN(B$(:I))
180 PRINT"MY LENGTH IS="K,B$(:I)
190 NEXT I
200 PRINT "ONLY MY GRIN IS LEFT"
```

```
MY LENGTH IS= 21          I AM THE CHESHIRE CAT
MY LENGTH IS= 20           AM THE CHESHIRE CAT
MY LENGTH IS= 19          AM THE CHESHIRE CAT
MY LENGTH IS= 18          M THE CHESHIRE CAT
MY LENGTH IS= 17           THE CHESHIRE CAT
MY LENGTH IS= 16          THE CHESHIRE CAT
MY LENGTH IS= 15          HE CHESHIRE CAT
MY LENGTH IS= 14          E CHESHIRE CAT
MY LENGTH IS= 13           CHESHIRE CAT
MY LENGTH IS= 12          CHESHIRE CAT
MY LENGTH IS= 11          HESHIRE CAT
MY LENGTH IS= 10          ESHIRE CAT
MY LENGTH IS= 9           SHIRE CAT
MY LENGTH IS= 8           HIRE CAT
MY LENGTH IS= 7           IRE CAT
MY LENGTH IS= 6           RE CAT
MY LENGTH IS= 5           E CAT
MY LENGTH IS= 4            CAT
MY LENGTH IS= 3           CAT
MY LENGTH IS= 2           AT
MY LENGTH IS= 1           T
MY LENGTH IS= 0
ONLY MY GRIN IS LEFT
```

VAL and STR

When working with a string containing as a substring the symbols 0,1,2, . . . , 9, we may, on occasion, need to convert the numeric part of the string to its corrresponding number. We may also, on occasion, need to treat a number as if it were a string of characters. To illustrate these situations, consider the problem of constructing a record that consists of a single string containing a student's social security number, name, and scores on several examinations. The record is built by entering the student's social security number, last name, first name, and middle initial (NMI if there is none). This information is concatenated, and the length of the string is determined. This length is prefixed to the record. Initially, a typical record looks like this:

```
27145378945WILLBERRY,MARY,E
```

The two-character substring 27 indicates the number of characters from the initial 2 to the final E, and the substring 145378945 is the student's nine-digit social security number.

An intermediate form of the record, after two examination scores have been entered might be:

```
27145378945WILLBERRY,MARY,E085000
```

indicating that she scored 85 on the first exam and 0 on the second. The numbers 85 and 0 were converted to the strings 085 and 000, respectively, and concatenated with the initial string.

The final form of her record, after scoring 79, 100, and 9 on the next three exams is:

```
27145878945WILLBERRY,MARY,E085000079100009
```

At the end of the semester, Mary's record is entered into the computer, the several substrings that constitute her examination scores are copied and converted to numbers, and her final average score is calculated and printed. Before presenting and discussing a simplified form of this problem, however, we present and discuss two BASIC functions, STR (for "string") and VAL (for "value").

If A$ is a numeric string, then VAL(A$) will be the corresponding number and can be assigned to a numeric variable. For example, if the string A$ = "6789" then B = VAL(A$) is the positive number 6789. Conversely, if C is the number −1234, then D$ = STR(C) is the string "−1234". If C had been the positive number 1234, the D$ would be the string " 1234", the blank space preceding the 1 being reserved for the understood, but not printed, plus sign.

The following program demonstrates how VAL and STR operate.

```
10 DIM R$(10),S$(10),T(10)
20 N=8
30 R$(1)="123"
40 R$(2)=" 456"
50 R$(3)="1.23"
60 R$(4)=" 1.23"
70 R$(5)="1.23000"
80 R$(6)=" 1.23000"
90 R$(7)="12.3456"
100 R$(8)=" 12.3456"
110 FOR I=1 TO N
120 T(I)=VAL(R$(I))
130 S$(I)=STR(T(I))
140 NEXT I
150 FOR I=1 TO N
160 IF R$(I)=S$(I) THEN 290
170 PRINT "I="I, R$(I) " <> "S$(I)
180 NEXT I
190 PRINT
200 PRINT R$(1),R$(2),R$(3),R$(5)
210 PRINT T(1),T(2),T(3),T(5)
220 PRINT S$(1),S$(2),S$(3),S$(5)
230 PRINT
240 PRINT R$(1)+R$(2)+R$(3)+R$(5)
250 PRINT T(1)+T(2)+T(3)+T(5)
260 PRINT S$(1)+S$(2)+S$(3)+S$(5)
270 PRINT
280 STOP
290 PRINT "I="I, R$(I) " = "S$(I)
300 GOTO 180
```

```
I= 1           123 <>  123
I= 2            456 =  456
```

```
I= 3              1.23 <>   1.23000
I= 4               1.23 <>   1.23000
I= 5              1.23000 <>   1.23000
I= 6               1.23000 =   1.23000
I= 7              12.3456 <>   12.3456
I= 8               12.3456 =   12.3456

123               456            1.23              1.23000
 123              456             1.23000           1.23000
 123              456             1.23000           1.23000

123 4561.231.23000
 581.460
 123 456 1.23000 1.23000
```

The program starts with eight strings, R$(1), . . . , R$(8), (lines 30–100) and converts these to numbers that are assigned to the numeric variables T(1), . . . ,T(8), line 120. These eight numbers are then transformed back to strings and assigned to the string variables S$(I), I=1, . . . , 8 (line 130). Each original string R$(I) is compared with its final counterpart, S$(I), and the result of this comparison is printed. By comparing R$(1) and R$(2) to S$(1) and S$(2), respectively, we see that R$(1) and S$(1) are different, whereas R$(2) and S$(2) are the same. The reason is that when the string "123" is converted to the number 123, the computer automatically prefixes the number with a blank space to allow for the unprinted plus sign. When the number 123, including the prefixed blank space, is transformed back into a string, that blank space becomes part of the new string S$(1). Note, however, that when the string " 456" is converted to a number, the first character, a blank, is included in the conversion. Now, when that number is transformed back to a string, the blank space occupies the first position of that string, and thus, S$(2) is identical to R$(2).

When "1.23" and " 1.23", R$(3) and R$(4), are converted to numbers, they are decimal numbers and include the trailing zeros. When these decimal numbers are transformed to strings, the trailing zeros become part of the newly constructed strings. We can see, then, why R$(3) ≠ S$(3) and R$(4) ≠ S$(4).

When R$(5) and R$(6) are converted to numbers, both become 1.23000, and the leading position of both is a blank for the nonprinted plus sign. When this number is transformed back to a string, that string contains eight characters. But R$(5) has only seven characters and thus differs from S$(5); clearly, R$(6) = S$(6). Similar comments apply to R$(7) and R$(8); the characters used were changed to enhance the visibility.

The prefixing of a blank to a string of digits when (1) that string does not have a blank to begin with and (2) when the string is then converted to a number may also be readily seen by looking at the four columns printed by lines 200, 210, and 220. Finally, the concatenated string R$(1)+R$(2)+R$(3)+R$(5) is compared to the string S$(1)+S$(2)+S$(3)+S$(5), lines 240 and 260. Line 250 prints a number, the arithmetic sum of T(1)+T(2)+T(3)+T(5).

In the above illustration, we started with a string variable, converted it to a number, and then transformed that number back to a string. In the following illustration, we start with a number, convert it to a string, and then back to a number. Note that the precise way that the numbers are assigned to the variables S(I) parallels the way that the strings were assigned in the previous illustration to the string variables R$(I).

```
10 DIM R$(10),S(10),T(10)
20 N=8
30 S(1)=123
40 S(2)= 456
50 S(3)=1.23
60 S(4)= 1.23
70 S(5)=1.23000
80 S(6)= 1.23000
90 S(7)=12.3456
100 S(8)= 12.3456
```

```
110 FOR I=1 TO N
120 R$(I)=STR(S(I))
130 T(I)=VAL(R$(I))
140 NEXT I
150 FOR I=1 TO N
160 IF S(I)=T(I) THEN 290
170 PRINT "I="I, S(I) " <> "T(I)
180 NEXT I
190 PRINT
200 PRINT S(1),S(2),S(3),S(5)
210 PRINT R$(1),R$(2),R$(3),R$(5)
220 PRINT T(1),T(2),T(3),T(5)
230 PRINT
240 PRINT S(1)+S(2)+S(3)+S(5)
250 PRINT R$(1)+R$(2)+R$(3)+R$(5)
260 PRINT T(1)+T(2)+T(3)+T(5)
270 PRINT
280 STOP
290 PRINT "I="I, S(I) " = "T(I)
300 GOTO 180
```

```
I= 1            123 =   123
I= 2            456 =   456
I= 3            1.23000 =   1.23000
I= 4            1.23000 =   1.23000
I= 5            1.23000 =   1.23000
I= 6            1.23000 =   1.23000
I= 7            12.3456 =   12.3456
I= 8            12.3456 =   12.3456

 123            456            1.23000          1.23000
 123            456            1.23000          1.23000
 123            456            1.23000          1.23000

 581.460
 123 456 1.23000 1.23000
 581.460
```

In this example, each number, irrespective of how it was presented to the computer, is automatically prefixed with a single blank character for the understood plus sign. Thus, when the number is converted to a string and then back to a number, that leading blank character is carried along. The final number, in each case, is identical to the original. In the program, the conversion from number to string and then back to number is done in lines 120 and 130. The equality is obvious from the printout, lines 160 and 290. Paralleling the printout of the preceding illustration, the values of S(1), S(2), S(3), and S(5), R$(1), R$(2), R$(3), and R$(5), and T(1), T(2), T(3), and T(5) are given by lines 200, 210, and 220, respectively. Finally, the sum S(1)+S(2)+S(3)+S(5) and T(1)+T(2)+T(3)+T(5) are printed by lines 240 and 260. The concatenated string R$(1)+R$(2)+R$(3)+R$(5) is printed by line 250.

We turn now to the problem posed at the beginning of this section, namely, that of constructing a student's record as a single string and then using information from this record to compute a final average grade. As presented in the following program, that part of the record consisting of the student's social security number and name is constructed first and printed. Then, for each student, the several grades scored during the semester are appended, and this total record is printed. Finally, each record is examined, the various exam scores extracted, and the final average score is calculated and printed. The details will be explained as the lines of the program are discussed.

```
10 INPUT=$
20 DIM R$(50)
30 REM: THIS SECTION CONSTRUCTS THE CLASS LIST.
40 PRINT "HOW MANY STUDENTS IN THE CLASS"; & INPUT N
50 FOR I=1 TO N
```

```
60 PRINT
70 PRINT "STUDENT'S LAST NAME"; & INPUT L$
80 PRINT "FIRST NAME"; & INPUT F$
90 PRINT "MIDDLE INITIAL"; & INPUT M$
100 PRINT "SOCIAL SECURITY NUMBER"; & INPUT S$
110 LET R$(I)=S$+L$+","+F$+","+M$
120 L=LEN(R$(I))
130 L=L+2
140 IF L<51 THEN 170
150 R$(I)=R$(I:1,48)
160 L=50
170 K$=STR(L)
180 T$=K$(:2)
190 R$(I)=T$+R$(I)
200 IF L<51 THEN 220
210 R$(I)=R$(I:1,50)
220 NEXT I
230 REM: THE LIST IS PRINTED TO VERIFY THE DATA
240 PRINT
250 FOR I=1 TO N & PRINT R$(I) & NEXT I
260 PRINT
270 PRINT "HOW MANY GRADES ARE TO ENTERED FOR EACH STUDENT"; & INPUT N1
280 FOR I=1 TO N
290 PRINT
300 PRINT "ENTER GRADES FOR "R$(I:12) ".  ENTER ONLY ONE GRADE AT A TIME."
310 FOR K=1 TO N1
320 INPUT G
330 G$=STR(G) & G$=G$(:2)
340 IF G=0 THEN 420
350 IF G<10 THEN 400
360 IF G<100 THEN 380
370 GOTO 430
380 G$="0"+G$
390 GOTO 430
400 G$="00"+G$
410 GOTO 430
420 G$="000"
430 R$(I)=R$(I)+G$
440 NEXT K
450 NEXT I
460 REM: THE NEW STRINGS ARE PRINTED TO VERIFY THAT THE DATA ARE CORRECT.
470 PRINT
480 FOR I=1 TO N & PRINT R$(I) & NEXT I
490 PRINT
500 REM: THE AVERAGE SCORE FOR EACH STUDENT IS DETERMINED AND PRINTED.
510 FOR I=1 TO N
520 D$=R$(I:1,2)
530 D=VAL(D$)
540 R=LEN(R$(I))
550 V=0
560 FOR J=1 TO N1
570 U=VAL(R$(I:D+1+3*(J-1),3))
580 V=V+U
590 NEXT J
600 V=V/N1
610 PRINT "AVERAGE GRADE FOR "R$(I:12,D-11) " IS ="V
620 PRINT
630 NEXT I
640 END
```

```
HOW MANY STUDENTS IN THE CLASS  ?3

STUDENT'S LAST NAME   ?NEWBERRY
FIRST NAME  ?CATHERINE
MIDDLE INITIAL  ?K
SOCIAL SECURITY NUMBER  ?123123123

STUDENT'S LAST NAME   ?GORDON
FIRST NAME  ?BILLY
MIDDLE INITIAL  ?NMI
SOCIAL SECURITY NUMBER  ?456456456
```

```
STUDENT'S LAST NAME   ?PIKE
FIRST NAME  ?JEAN
MIDDLE INITIAL  ?S
SOCIAL SECURITY NUMBER  ?789878987

31123123123NEWBERRY,CATHERINE,K
27456456456GORDON,BILLY,NMI
22789878987PIKE,JEAN,S

HOW MANY GRADES ARE TO ENTERED FOR EACH STUDENT   ?5

ENTER GRADES FOR NEWBERRY,CATHERINE,K.  ENTER ONLY ONE GRADE AT A TIME.
?100
?90
?80
?0
?50

ENTER GRADES FOR GORDON,BILLY,NMI.  ENTER ONLY ONE GRADE AT A TIME.
?50
?60
?5
?35
?95

ENTER GRADES FOR PIKE,JEAN,S.  ENTER ONLY ONE GRADE AT A TIME.
?100
?100
?90
?90
?85

31123123123NEWBERRY,CATHERINE,K100090080000050
27456456456GORDON,BILLY,NMI050060005035095
22789878987PIKE,JEAN,S100100090090085

AVERAGE GRADE FOR NEWBERRY,CATHERINE,K IS = 64

AVERAGE GRADE FOR GORDON,BILLY,NMI IS = 49

AVERAGE GRADE FOR PIKE,JEAN,S IS = 93
```

A class of potentially 50 students is envisaged; the precise number is specified as input, line 40. The relevant data for each student is collected as input, lines 70–100. At line 110, these data are concatenated into a single string, with social security number first, followed by last name, first name, and middle initial. The last and first names are separated by a comma, as are the first name and the middle initial. It is assumed that if no middle initial is known, NMI will be entered.

The length of this string is then determined, line 120, and 2 added to this number, line 130. If this total length exceeds 50, only the first 48 characters of the record are retained; that should be more than enough to identify the student. This length, a number, is converted to a string, line 170, and the leading blank stripped away, line 180. This two-character string is then prefixed to the record, line 190. Now, if we look at the student's record, the first two characters tell us how many characters of the record are for identification; everything that follows is assumed to refer to grades. The records for the class are printed for you to see, line 250.

At this point, the grades for each student are to be entered.[3] As each grade is entered, the number is converted to a string and the leading blank space stripped away, lines 320–330. Because grades vary from 0 to 100, three characters are needed to cover all possibilities. Thus, the grade 0 is made to correspond to the string '000'; a grade less

---

[3]Normally, this would be done at different times during the semester. A program to accommodate this nicety, however, would require a knowledge of *files,* which are not discussed until Chapter 17.

than 10, say 8, is made to correspond to '008'; a grade less than 100, say 75, is made to correspond to the string '075'; and 100, of course, to '100'. This is done in lines 340–420. This three-character string is then attached at the end of the student's record, line 430. This process is repeated for each grade; the loop begins at line 310 and ends at line 440.

The final strings, the result of this process, are printed for you to see, line 480.

Thus far, the string function LEN was used at line 120 and STR at lines 170 and 330. LEN will be used again at line 540 and VAL at lines 530 and 570.

The record for each student is complete. We now want the computer to read this record, particularly the grades for the several examinations, compute the average, and print it. At lines 520 and 530, the length of the identification part of the record is determined; everything that follows pertains to grades. At 540, the total length of the record is found. The difference, R–D, an integer divisible by 3, is the number of characters allocated for the scores. Starting at position D + 1, three characters are copied from R$(I), see the right-hand side of line 570, with J = 1. This string is converted to a number and assigned to the numeric variable U. The program goes back to line 570 and now, for J = 2—that is, for position D + 1 + 3—repeats this process. At each step, the values assigned to U are accumulated in the numeric variable V. After all grades for the one student have been added together, the average is calculated at line 600. At line 610, the full name of the student is copied from the record and printed along with the average score. This process is repeated for each student; that loop starts at line 510 and ends at line 630.

Summary

In this chapter we introduced the concept of a substring of a given string. We showed how a substring could be copied from a string. A string may be modified by altering a substring within it; we illustrated how this is done on two different computer systems. At times it is desirable to locate a given substring within a given string. For some computer systems an intrinsic BASIC function locates the substring, for others it may be necessary to write a program.

We introduced and demonstrated three intrinsic BASIC string functions—LEN, VAL, and STR. As with all BASIC functions, their utility depends on the problems we need to solve.

Exercises

11.1 Write and program your own personalized form letter.

11.2 Recall the program on pages 200–201. Observe that when a match is found, the output is given in one set of instructions, lines 370–410. If a match is not found when the names are searched, the next section of the program used is given in lines 210–250. If a match is not found when the registration number is given, the section of the program used is given in lines 310–350. Because these two sections of the program are almost identical, there is an obvious redundancy.

Modify the program so that it continues to function as before as far as input and output are concerned but with the redundancy eliminated.

11.3 The telephone company produces a phone book that lists each subscriber alphabetically and then gives the address and phone number. A copy of this book is given to each subscriber. The company also prepares a book that lists phone numbers sequentially so that if you want to know the name and address to which a given phone number is assigned, you can find this information quite readily from this second book. (This book is generally not made available to subscribers.)

Write a program that will take the data name, address, and phone number either from INPUT or READ/DATA and prepare the two books. The data are to be entered randomly, that is, not already sorted by either name or phone number.

11.4 Draw a flow chart and write a program that carries out the following task. From an arbitrary set of twenty-five different words, assign ten to a list L$(I) and the remaining fifteen to a list K$(I). Print each list. Alphabetize each of the two lists separately. Print the two alphabetized lists. Merge the two alphabetized lists into one list M$(I) of twenty-five words so that the final list M$(I) is automatically alphabetized, that is, it should not be necessary to alphabetize M$(I).

For example, suppose the list L$(I) is: L$(1) = forty, L$(2) = cilia, L$(3) = knave, L$(4) = post, L$(5) = duet, L$(6) = voice, L$(7) = apple, L$(8) = food, L$(9) = adopt, L$(10) = parrot. The first task to alphabetize L$(I); after L$(I) is alphabetized, it reads: L$(1) = adopt, L$(2) = apple, L$(3) = cilia, L$(4) = duet, L$(5) = food, L$(6) = forty, L$(7) = knave, L$(8) = parott, L$(9) = post, L$(10) = voice. The list K$(I) is also initially given unalphabetized; when alphabetized it reads as follows: K$(1) = allegro, K$(2) = alter, K$(3) = brain, K$(4) = caster, K$(5) = cope, K$(6) = cork, K$(7) = disturb, K$(8) = erupt, K$(9) = guest, K$(10) = host, K$(11) = indigo, K$(12) = kilogram, K$(13) = marshy, K$(14) = parity, K$(15) parking.

The new list M$(I) is now obtained in the following way. Examine L$(1) = adopt and K$(1) = allegro. Since "adopt"precedes "allegro" alphabetically, assign "adopt" to M$(1). Next examine L$(2) = apple and K$(1) = allegro. Since "allegro" precedes "apple" alphabetically, assign "allegro" to M$(2). Next, examine L$(2) = apple and K$(2) = alter. Since "alter" precedes "apple," let M$(3) = alter and continue. Examine L$(2) = apple and K$(3) = brain. Since "apple" precedes "brain," assign "apple" to M$(4). Proceed in this fashion through both lists. At some point, one of the lists will be exhausted; in this example, the K$ list is exhausted when "parking" is assigned to M$(22). Three words remain in the L$ list; these are to be added on at the end of the M$ list as M$(23) = parrot, M$(24) = port, and M$(25) = voice. Print the alphabetized list M$.

11.5 A positive integer may be expressed in words. For example, "three thousand six hundred and seventy-four" is one way to express "3,674." Draw a flow chart and write a program that accepts as input a positive integer expressed in words and prints that number as a sequence of digits. You may limit the program by restricting the largest integer to be considered to "nine hundred and ninety-nine thousand nine hundred and ninety-nine."

11.6 Draw a flow chart and write a program that accepts as input one of the positive integers; 1, 2, 3, . . . , 999,999 and prints as output that integer expressed in words. Thus, if the input is 47,896, the output should be FORTY-SEVEN THOUSAND EIGHT HUNDRED AND NINETY-SIX.

11.7 A word or phrase is a "palindrome" if it is spelled the same forwards and backwards. Neglecting punctuation, two well known palindromes are: (1) MADAM I'M ADAM, and (2) ABLE WAS I ERE I SAW ELBA. Draw a flow chart and write a program that will test a given phrase and determine if it is a palindrome.

11.8 Assume that two lists, V$(I), I = 1 to 13 and S$(I), I = 1 to 4 are stored in your program. V$(1) = ACE, V$(2) = TWO, V$(3) = THREE,..., V$(10) = TEN, V$(11) = JACK, V$(12) = QUEEN, V$(13) = KING; S$(1) = CLUBS, S$(2) = DIAMONDS, S$(3) = HEARTS, S$(47) = SPADES. The totality of pairs (V$(I), S$(J)) represent the fifty-two cards in a standard deck.

(a) Using the random number generator, have the computer select and display a poker hand, that is a hand consisting of five cards. Show both a flow chart and a program.

(b) Have the computer select five cards at random and then decide if there is no pair in the hand, one pair, two pair, three of a kind, a full-house (three of one kind and a pair), or four of a kind. Show a flow chart and a program.

(c) Extend the program to require that the computer decide if the hand contains a flush (five cards of the same suit) or a straight (five cards in sequence without regard to suit.)

11.9 The word "Columbians" contains ten different letters. Consider all two-letter words that can be constructed from these ten letters using one vowel and one consonant; there are forty-eight possibilities in all. Find them and decide which are proper English words. For example, AN and IS would qualify, OC would not. Store those that quality in a list K$(I). Next, consider all three-letter combinations that may be constructed from the ten letters using either two different vowels and a consonant or two different consonants and a vowel. There are 576 of these. Of these 576 possibilities, determine those that contain one of the elements of the K$(I) list as a substring. For example, BAN contains AN, as does MAN; SIN contains IN. CAB does not contain a two-letter word as a substring. Of the 576 possibilities, determine those that contain a two-letter word as a substring.

Draw a flow chart and write a program that carries out this task.

11.10 Using a foreign language with which you are familiar, prepare a double dictionary of twenty-five pairs of equivalent words, one from each language. If, for example, the second language is German, typical entries might be (YOUNG, JUNG), (MAN, MANN), (TEACHER, LEHRER), (OLD, ALT). Draw a flow chart and write a tutorial program that accomplishes the following. First, the program randomly selects a word pair and prints the English word. It then waits for the student to supply the German equivalent. If the student gives the correct answer on the first try, score that as 5; if not, indicate that the answer is an error and give the student a second chance. If the correct answer is given on the second try, score that as 3; if not, score that as 0, tell the student that the second try was wrong also, and supply the correct answer.

After ten different words have been presented, repeat the process for another set of ten different words. This time, however, have the computer print the German word and have the student give the English equivalent. Score as before.

When the second part of the tutorial session is finished, print the student's score as a number between 0 and 100.

12 Functions and Subroutines

If you were given the two sides of a right triangle, say 3 and 4, you could quickly find, using the Pythagorean theorem, that the third side is 5. To obtain this result, you would perform two multiplications, 3×3 and 4×4, one addition, $9 + 16$, and extract a square root, $\sqrt{25}$. In the computer, only the simpler arithmetic operations—the multiplications and the addition—would be done in the electronic circuitry in the CPU. The square root operation would be done by a program supplied by the manufacturer of your computer as part of a collection of more complex mathematical operations called *scientific subroutines.*

Clearly, to build electronic circuitry to evaluate a variety of complicated mathematical functions is too expensive and too uncertain; the many uses the computer will be put to are unpredictable. Nevertheless, certain mathematical functions occur repeatedly; the square root operation is but one example. The intrinsic mathematical functions supplied by the manufacturer are nothing more than programs similar to ones you have written. When you write a program using one of these intrinsic functions, you need only refer to it by name. The computer will make that subprogram part of your program.

At times, because the intrinsic functions do not suffice, you will want to write subprograms of your own. While not with the same degree of generality that the intrinsic functions provide, BASIC does allow you to write your own subroutines. For the more mathematical subroutines, the instructions are DEF FN* (where the asterisk is to be replaced by one of the twenty-six letters of the alphabet) and at times, FNEND. In more general cases, the instructions are GOSUB and RETURN. In this chapter, we shall define these instructions and illustrate their use.

The Intrinsic Functions

In BASIC, mathematical functions are handled in a variety of ways. We have already used several of the intrinsic functions, the ones supplied within the language. Table 12-1 is a fairly inclusive list of intrinsic functions. While not all BASIC systems supply all of these, the ones marked with an asterisk should be available; the others are optional. Some systems include these and others; the designers of the interpreter decide which functions to include.

TABLE 12-1
The Intrinsic BASIC Functions

The Trigonometric Functions:		
SIN(X)	The sine of X	*
COS(X)	The cosine of X	*
TAN(X)	The tangent of X	*
CSC(X)	The cosecant of X	Optional
SEC(X)	The secant of X	Optional
COT(X)	The cotangent of X	*
The Inverse Trigonometric Functions:		
ASN(X)	The arcsine of X	Optional
ACS(X)	The arccosine of X	Optional
ATN(X)	The arctangent of X	*
The Exponential and Logarithmic Functions:		
EXP(X)	The number e to the power X	*
LOG(X)	The logarithm of X to the base e	*
LGT(X)	The logarithm of X to the base 10	Optional
LTW(X)	The logarithm of X to the base 2	Optional
The Hyperbolic Functions:		
HSN(X)	The hyperbolic sine of X	Optional
HCS(X)	The hyperbolic cosine of X	Optional
HTN(X)	The hyperbolic tangent of X	Optional
The Maximum and Minimum Functions:		
MAX (X(1),X(2), . . . ,X(N))	The maximum of the numbers X(1), X(2), . . . ,X(N)	Optional
MIN(X(1),X(2), . . . ,X(N))	The minimum of the numbers X(1), X(2), . . . ,X(N)	Optional
Other Functions:		
ABS(X)	The absolute value of X	*
INT(X)	The integer part of X	*
SQR(X)	The square root of X	*
SGN(X)	The sign of X	*
RND(X)	The random number generator	*

Any standard text on trigonometry will define and describe the six trigonometric functions and the three inverse trigonometric functions listed above. The exponential function, EXP(X), and the natural logarithm, LOG(X), are defined and their properties given in first texts on the calculus. These functions depend on the number e = 2.718282. . . ; EXP(X) = e^x. LOG(X), the inverse function of EXP(X), is the natural logarithm of X.

Some BASIC interpreters are supplied with LGT(X), which is the log of X to the base 10. This is the common logarithm and was used extensively in simplifying calculations before the advent of the hand calculator and the electronic digital computer. LTW(X) is the log function to the base 2.

The functions HSN(X), HCS(X), and HTN(X) are, respectively, the hyberbolic sine, the hyperbolic cosine, and the hyperbolic tangent. These three functions are most easily defined in terms of the exponential function, EXP(X). A first text on the calculus will define and describe these functions.

MAX(X(1),X(2), . . . ,X(N)) will return the maximum value of the arguments X(I), I=1, . . . ,N; MIN(X(1), . . . ,X(N)) will return the minimum.

Of the five functions listed under "Other Functions," only SQR(X) has not been discussed. SQR(X) is the square root of X and is defined only for nonnegative values of X. If we attempt to find the square root of a negative number, an error message will be generated.

Elementary Constructions

The functions MAX(X(1),X(2), . . . ,X(N)) and MIN(X(1),X(2), . . . ,X(N)) are quite useful. If they are not available on your system, you can construct them from programs you have seen. Similarly, although SQR(X) is a convenience, (X)^.5 does the same thing. LGT(X) is also nice to have; if it were not available, we could use the formula

```
LGT(X) = LOG (X)/LOG(10).
```

This is true also of the others; for example,

```
HSN(X) = (EXP(X) - EXP(- X))/2.
```

From a minimum set of intrinsic functions, together with the arithmetic operations addition, subtraction, multiplication, division, and exponentiation, many other functions can be constructed. If $X \geqslant 0$, then the Nth root of X may be found from (X)^(1/N). Care must be exercised, however; if X is negative, an error message should be expected. It is your responsibility to rewrite an expression such as (−3)^(1/3) as −(3)^(1/3). For complex numbers, such as (−3)^(1/2), again an error message will be printed. BASIC, as yet, does not have the capability to handle complex numbers directly; if this situation arises, you will have to discover a way around the difficulty.

Obviously, more complicated explicit functions of one or several variables may be programed as easily. The equation

```
Y=SIN(X)/X
```

is that for a damped sine function; its graph is given in Figure 12-1. The frequency function for the normal probability distribution with mean M, and standard deviation S is given by

```
F=EXP(-(X-M)^2/(2*S^2))/S/SQR(2*3.1415926)
```

FIGURE 12-1

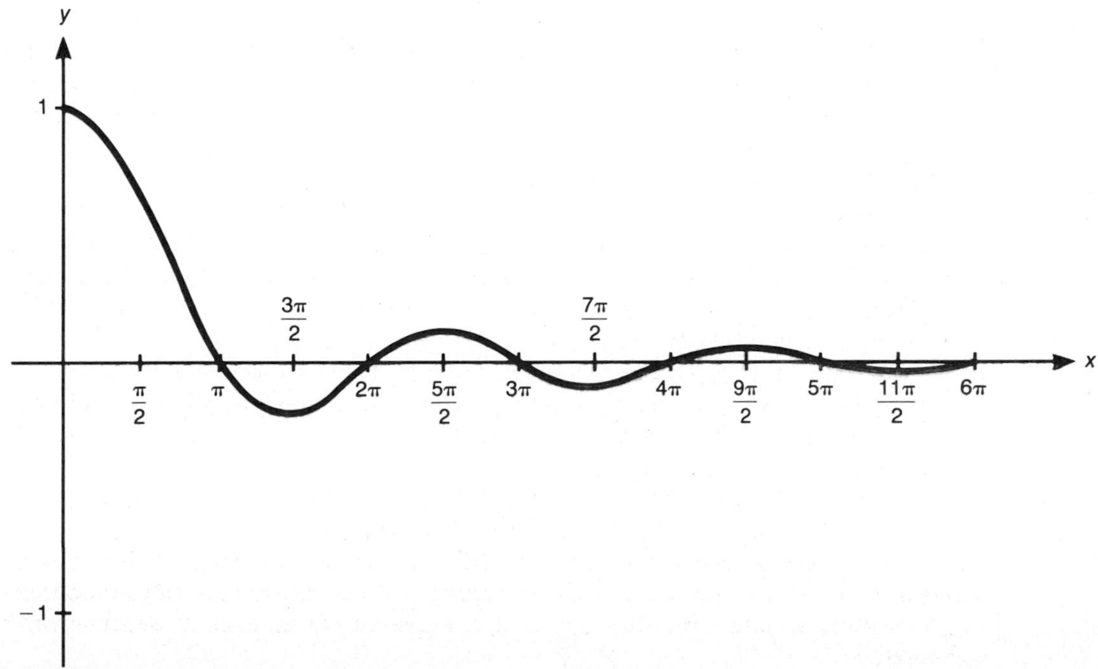

The DEF FN Statement

In addition to allowing us to write functions as expressions, BASIC provides a means of defining functions within a program. The format is given in the following example:

```
>100 DF FNA(X,Y,Z) = X^2 + (Y-Z)^3
```

The DEF following the line number stands for define. This is followed by FNA, where the FN is required but the A could have been any other letter of the alphabet (providing 26 different possibilities and 26 different functions). At least one explicit variable is required. In the example there are three—X, Y, and Z. To the right of the equal sign, we find the explicit function that will, henceforth in the program, be referred to as FNA(X,Y,Z). Consider the following:

```
10 DEF FNA(A,B,C)=(A-B)^2+(B-C)^4+(C-A)^6
20 DEF FNB(U,V,W)=U+V^2+W^3
30 PRINT " X"," Y"," Z" TAB(41) "FUNCTION"
40 PRINT
50 FOR X=1 TO 5
60 FOR Y=1 TO X
70 FOR Z=1 TO Y
80 IF FNA(X,Y,Z)<10 THEN 130
90 NEXT Z
100 NEXT Y
110 NEXT X
120 STOP
130 PRINT X,Y,Z,FNB(FNA(X,Y,Z),FNA(Y,Z,X),FNA(Z,X,Y))
140 GOTO 90
```

X	Y	Z	FUNCTION
1	1	1	0
2	1	1	14
2	2	1	14
2	2	2	0
3	2	2	14
3	3	2	14
3	3	3	0
4	3	3	14
4	4	3	14
4	4	4	0
5	4	4	14
5	5	4	14
5	5	5	0

The two functions FNA and FNB are each defined only once. Their position in the program precedes their use. Note that in the PRINT statement, line 130, the values of X, Y, and Z in FNA are permuted and that the arguments of FNB are the three values of FNA. Writing line 130 directly would be possible but horrendous. In fact, the degree of potential complexity is almost limitless. The following illustration differs from the preceding one only in that the arguments of FNB in line 130 are themselves values obtained by prior evaluations of FNB.

```
10 DEF FNA(A,B,C)=(A-B)^2+(B-C)^4+(C-A)^6
20 DEF FNB(U,V,W)=U+V^2+W^3
30 PRINT  " X"," Y"," Z" TAB(41) "FUNCTION"
40 PRINT
50 FOR X=1 TO 5
60 FOR Y=1 TO X
70 FOR Z=1 TO Y
80 IF FNA(X,Y,Z)<10 THEN 130
90 NEXT Z
100 NEXT Y
110 NEXT X
120 STOP
130 PRINT X,Y,Z,FNB(FNB(X,Y,Z),FNB(Y,Z,X),FNB(Z,Y,X))
140 GOTO 90
```

```
X              Y              Z              FUNCTION

1              1              1                39
2              1              1                1104
2              2              1                2325
2              2              2                2954
3              2              2                37041
3              3              2                56048
3              3              3                60879
4              3              3                444792
4              4              3                577763
4              4              4                599844
5              4              4                3069735
5              5              4                3673674
5              5              5                3748055
```

When defining functions, we must be careful to avoid circular definitions. For example,

```
100 DEF FNW(X) = X*FNW(X)
```

is a circular definition because the function is defined in terms of itself.

```
200 DEF FNW(A) = A*(FNX(A)
210 DEF FNX(A) = (FNY(A))^A
210 DEF FNY(A) = FNW(A)/A
```

is also circular because FNW is defined in terms of FNX, which is defined in terms of FNY, which in turn is defined in terms of FNW.

Illustration: Arithmetic Sum

Early in your mathematical education you learned that the sum

$$1 + 2 + \ldots + N$$

is equal to N(N + 1)/2. Suppose you didn't know this and you were asked to show that the functions

$$S(N) = 1 + 2 + \ldots + N$$

and

$$FNK(N) = \frac{N(N + 1)}{2}$$

were equal for $100 \leq N \leq 200$. Using the computer to evaluate FNK(N) for $100 \leq N \leq 200$ offers no problem. S(N) is computed in lines 40–60 in the following program:

```
10 DEF FNK(X)=X*(X+1)/2
20 FOR N=100 TO 200
30 S=0
40 FOR I=1 TO N
50 S=S+I
60 NEXT I
70 PRINT S,FNK(N)
80 NEXT N
```

The output, line 70, will show that the values for S(N) and FNK(N) are the same.

The question might be raised: Is it necessary each time to add 1 + 2 + . . . + 99?; cannot this be done once and then each successive N added to the previous sum to yield the new sum? The following modification does this.

```
10 DEF FNK(X)=X*(X+1)/2
20 S=0
30 FOR I=1 TO 99
40 S=S+I
50 NEXT I
60 FOR N=100 TO 200
70 S=S+N
80 PRINT S,FNK(N)
90 NEXT N
```

There are different ways to formulate the solution to a problem and, consequently, different programs will produce the solution. The lesson to be learned here is that a program is as much a solution to a problem as is a formula.

Multi-line Functions

Some BASIC interpreters permit us to define a multi-line function. In the following program, find the maximum of a set of numbers:

```
10 DEF FNM(A,B)
20      FNM=A
30      IF A>=B THEN 50
40      FNM=B
50 FNEND
60 PRINT"              X","              Y","             MAX"
70 READ X
80 FOR I=1 TO 9
90 READ Y
100 PRINT X,Y,FNM(X,Y)
110 X=FNM(X,Y)
120 NEXT I
130 PRINT"THE MAXIMUM OF THE SET ="FNM(X,Y)
140 DATA -5,6,0,3,-32,14,12,9,-4,2
```

```
               X                 Y                MAX
              -5                 6                  6
               6                 0                  6
               6                 3                  6
               6               -32                  6
               6                14                 14
              14                12                 14
              14                 9                 14
              14                -4                 14
              14                 2                 14
THE MAXIMUM OF THE SET =   14
```

If the set had consisted of only three numbers, the following would have sufficed:

```
10 DEF FNM(A,B)
20      FNM=A
30      IF A>=B THEN 50
```

```
40       FNM=B
50 FNEND
60 PRINT"           X","               Y","              Z","            MAX"
70 READ X,Y,Z
80 DATA -5,23,14
90 PRINT X,Y,Z,FNM(X,FNM(Y,Z))

         X              Y              Z              MAX
        -5              23             14              23
```

Note in the examples that DEF and the function name FNM with its arguments A and B open the definition. The definition is terminated by the new statement FNEND. All lines between DEF FNM(A,B) and FNEND, which constitute a program, make up the definition.

Subroutines

One reason why some BASIC interpreters do not include the multi-line function definition may be that it can be subsumed by another concept, the subroutine. The following fable sets the stage for subroutines.

A Fable

In the province of S—,those who question the state are banished to P—, a small island in the center of a large circular lake, the radius of which is 40 miles. Because the currents in the lake are swift and unpredictable and fog limits visibility to a few feet, there is no need for guards. To build a boat with the thought of escaping to civilization is difficult. It can be done, but since there are no tools, the vessel is at best crude and, when launched, difficult to handle in the tricky currents.

Ahmil, Bemil, Cahmil, and Peck are four revolutionaries whom fortune and the state have thrown together on P—. While each is opposed to the current regime, there is little else they agree on. In their present predicament, however, they can and do agree on the necessity of building a boat and attempting to escape.

The day of escape finally arrives: The boat is launched and they embark. Because they cannot agree on who shall be captain, they resolve to choose a captain each day by drawing straws. The captain for the day sets the course. When Ahmil is captain, Bemil and Cahmil row and Peck is the helmsman. Under the most favorable conditions they can cover a distance of 1 mile; with the currents and the fog, the actual distance may be anywhere from 0 to 1 mile. When Bemil is captain, he picks Cahmil as helmsman and leaves the rowing to Ahmil and Peck. On these days, they can travel at most 2 miles. When Cahmil is captain, he chooses Peck for helmsman and assigns Ahmil and Bemil to the oars; with perfect luck they can cover 3 miles. When it is Peck's turn to be captain, he takes the helm himself and rotates Ahmil, Bemil, and Cahmil at the oars. On the best of these days, they can go 5 miles.

How long, if ever they do, does it take them to escape? How many days was each one captain? What was the name of the captain on the day they regained their freedom?

We cannot be certain of all the events that occurred; at best, we can try to simulate the voyage and see if the results of the simulation agree with their recollections. After seemingly endless discussion, they reluctantly agree on the flow chart given in Figure 12-2 and the following program.

```
10 REM: (A1,A2) ARE COORDINATES OF THE BOAT ON DAY N.
20 A1=0,A2=0,N=0
30 REM: M$(I) ARE FOR THEIR NAMES, D(I) FOR THE NUMBER OF DAYS EACH WAS CAPTAIN
40 DIM M$(4),D(4)
50 FOR I=1 TO 4
60 READ M$(I),D(I)
70 NEXT I
80 DATA "AHMIL",0,"BEMIL",0,"CAHMIL",0,"PECK",0
```

```
90 REM: THE CAPTAIN FOR THE DAY IS CHOSEN.
100 F1=INT(4*RND(1))+1
110 D(F1)=D(F1)+1
120 ON F1 GOTO 130,180,230,280
130 GOSUB 330
140 X1=C1
150 X2=C2
160 GOSUB 400
170 GOTO 100
180 GO SUB 330
190 X1=2*C1
200 X2=2*C2
210 GOSUB 400
220 GOTO 100
230 GOSUB 330
240 X1=3*C1
250 X2=3*C2
260 GOSUB 400
270 GOTO 100
280 GOSUB 330
290 X1=5*C1
300 X2=5*C2
310 GOSUB 400
320 GOTO 100
330 REM: THIS SUBROUTINE SETS PARAMETERS NEEDED TO DETERMINE
340 REM: THE DISTANCE TRAVELED THAT DAY.
350 F2=RND(1)
360 T=2*3.1415926*RND(1)
370 C1=F2*COS(T)
380 C2=F2*SIN(T)
390 RETURN
400 REM: WE KNOW THE DISTANCE TRAVELED. WE WANT TO FIND OUT
410 REM: IF THEY HAVE LANDED.
420 A1=A1+X1
430 A2=A2+X2
440 IF A1^2+A2^2>40^2 THEN 480
450 N=N+1
460 RETURN
470 REM: WE NOW HAVE ALL THE INFORMATION WE NEED TO PRINT THE REPORT ON THE VOYAGE
480 PRINT \ PRINT
490 PRINT"  FREE AT LAST, AFTER"N" DAYS IN THE BOAT."
500 FOR I=1 TO 4
510 PRINT "  "M$(I)" WAS CAPTAIN FOR"D(I)" DAYS."
520 NEXT I
530 PRINT "  "M$(F1)" WAS CAPTAIN THE DAY THEY LANDED."
540 END
```

The lines of interest in the program are those in which GOSUB and RETURN occur. A1 and A2 are the coordinates of the boat; initially they coincide with the coordinates of the island. N is the number of days since the prisoners left the island. At line 100, the captain for the day is chosen: 1 is Ahmil, 2 is Bemil, 3 Cahmil, and 4 Peck. After the choice is made and recorded (line 110), the program goes to the appropriate line. At this point, the parameters needed to determine how far and in what direction the prisoners traveled that day are found by going to line 330. Since these parameters are needed independent of who the captain is, there are four places where GOSUB 330 occurs, one for each captain. GOSUB 330 is similar to GOTO 330; the difference is that when GOSUB 330 is executed, the computer *remembers* the line number of the GOSUB 330 instruction before transferring control to line 330.

A subroutine is entered at line 330. The calculations performed in lines 350–380, while essential to the program, are ancillary and would normally be done on a piece of scratch paper on the side. They are to be used in the calculation of the distance traveled that day.

Examine the geometry in Figure 12-3. The origin of the coordinate system is the island P—; the circumference of the circle represents freedom. The location of the boat on the morning of the Nth day is Q_N; recall that the captain for the day has been picked. Randomly select a direction in which they are to travel that day; this is done at line 360

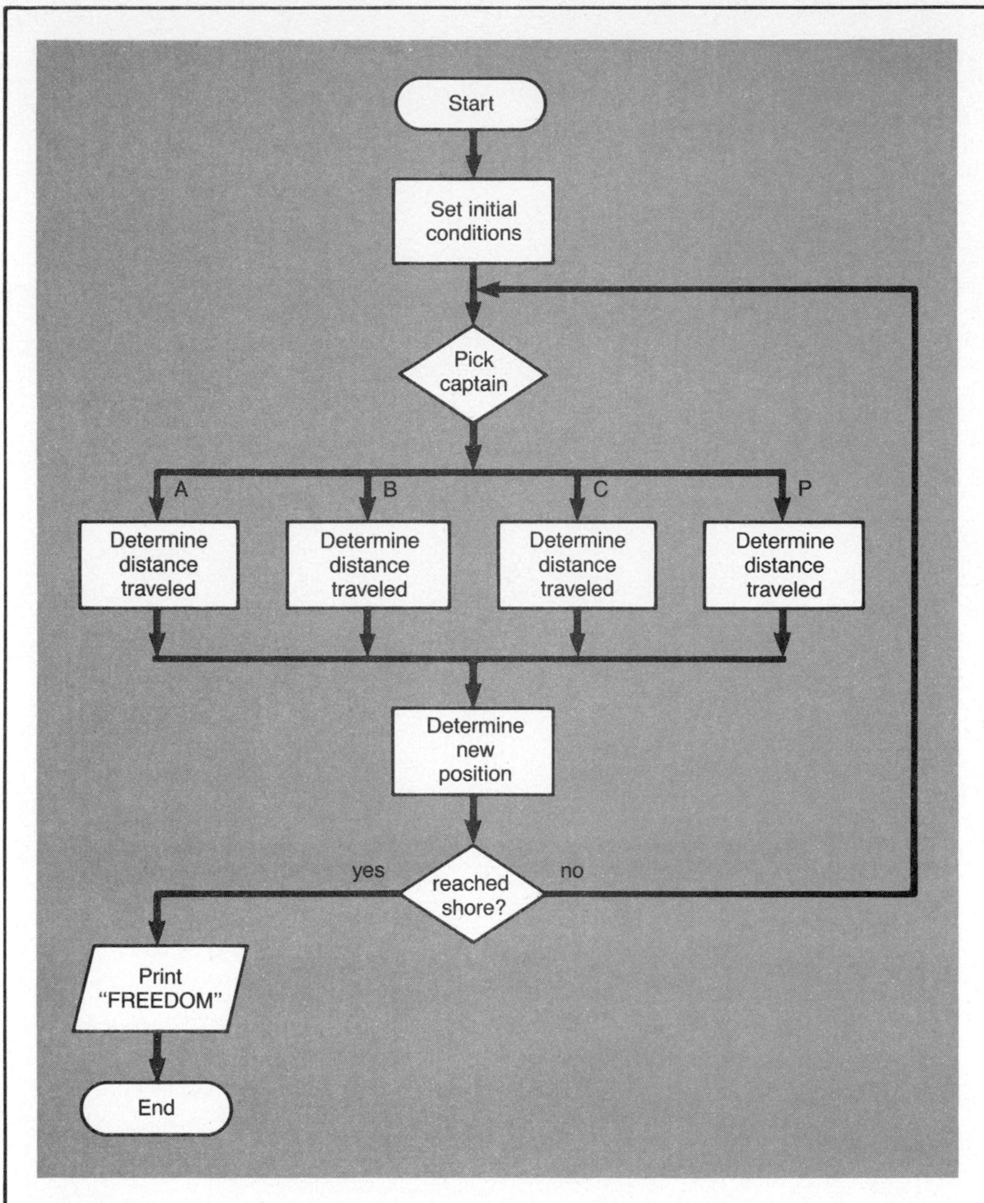

FIGURE 12-2

in the program; T is a random number between 0 and 2π. At line 350, F2 is selected as a random number between 0 and 1. At line 370, C1 is the *unadjusted* randomly obtained distance that is traveled in the X_1 direction that day. At line 380, C2 is the *unadjusted* randomly generated distance traveled in the X_2 direction that day. C1 and C2 are thought of as *unadjusted* because the actual distance traveled depends on who is captain.

When, at line 390, RETURN is encountered, the computer, remembering the line number where it was before control was transferred to the subroutine (which depends on who is captain), returns to the next line in the program and continues.

The components of the distance traveled that day, X1,X2, are then computed. GOSUB 400 is next. At lines 420–430, the coordinates of the escapees' new position are determined.

The crucial question is asked at line 440: Have they reached shore? Since their current position has coordinates A1 and A2, they will still be afloat if A1^2 + A2^2 < 40^2, and this is exactly the question asked at line 440. If they are, the fact that they have

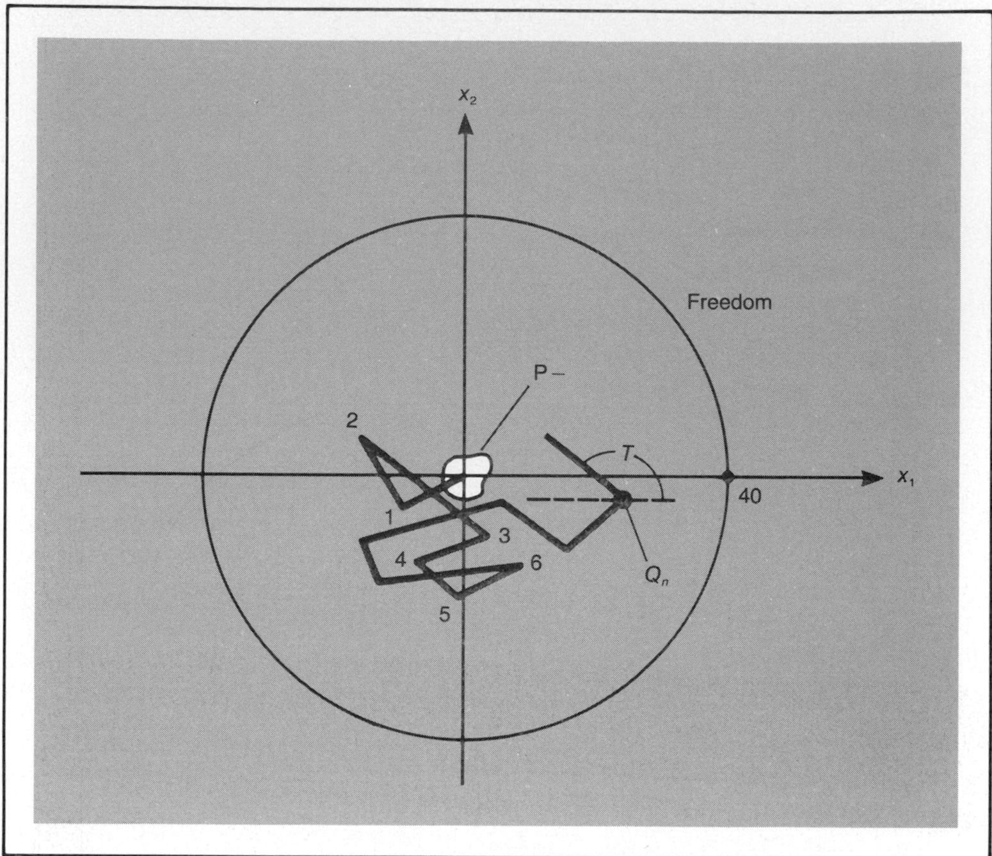

FIGURE 12-3

survived another day is recorded, N=N+1, and at line 460 RETURN is executed. The program returns to the line following the GOSUB 400 from which it had come. In all four cases, control is then transferred to line 20 and another day begins.

When the program was run, the following printout was obtained.

```
FREE AT LAST, AFTER 340 DAYS IN THE BOAT.
AHMIL WAS CAPTAIN FOR 100 DAYS.
BEMIL WAS CAPTAIN FOR 88 DAYS.
CAHMIL WAS CAPTAIN FOR 68 DAYS.
PECK WAS CAPTAIN FOR 85 DAYS.
PECK WAS CAPTAIN THE DAY THEY LANDED.
```

Ahmil, on seeing it, said, "Perfect. It describes the voyage exactly." He was voted down 3 to 1. The program was run again.

```
FREE AT LAST, AFTER 992 DAYS IN THE BOAT.
AHMIL WAS CAPTAIN FOR 260 DAYS.
BEMIL WAS CAPTAIN FOR 261 DAYS.
CAHMIL WAS CAPTAIN FOR 249 DAYS.
PECK WAS CAPTAIN FOR 223 DAYS.
CAHMIL WAS CAPTAIN THE DAY THEY LANDED.
```

This time, Bemil asserted, "Yes, Yes. That's it!" The others replied, "No, No. It's not!"

The program was run twice more; record one yes vote for Cahmil on run 3 and one for Peck on run 4. When last heard from, they were still running the program. As might be expected, they could not agree on the exact circumstances of the voyage.

Lines 400–460 need not have been a subroutine. The sequence GOSUB 400, 460 RETURN, and GOTO 100 could just as easily have been GOTO 400 replacing GOSUB 400,

460 GOTO 100 replacing 460 RETURN and deleting the GOTO 100 at lines 170, 220, 270 and 320. It is a matter of choice and preferred style. The modified version would run faster; the original has greater flexibility for possibile modification.

The use of the instructions GOSUB and RETURN is preferred when an ancillary calculation, outside the main stream of the program, must be made. It is particularly useful when this calculation is required at different points in the program. The main advantage of GOSUB is that the computer *remembers* the line number it came from and RETURN carries the program back to the next line.

An Illustration: Truth-Tables

To further illustrate the use of subroutines, we shall use the computer to print truth-tables for simple logical propositions. First, a few words about truth-tables. A proposition P is a statement that is either true (T) or false (F) but not both simultaneously. Thus, "Yesterday's rainfall exceeded one inch" is a proposition P that is either true or false, but obviously not both. Also, with a proposition P, we may associate the number 1 when P is true and the number 0 when P is false.

For any proposition P, we may consider its negation, not-P. In the example, not-P would be the proposition "It is not true that yesterday's rainfall exceeded one inch." Clearly, if P is true, not-P is false, and if P is false, then not-P is true. This relationship between P and not-P is exhibited in the table:

P	not-P
T	F
F	T

Each entry in the column under "not-P" gives the truth value of not-P that corresponds to truth value of P in that row. In general then, a truth table is a systematic tabulation of all possible combinations that may arise in a complex logical proposition. We shall illustrate with additional examples. Before we do, however, observe that the arithmetic function 1 − P yields the correct numerical values for the proposition not-P, that is, 1 − P is 0 when P is 1 and 1 − P is 1 when P is 0.

If there are two propositions P and Q, the logical conjunction P AND Q is a new proposition that is true only when P is true and Q is true. The truth-table for P AND Q is:

P	Q	P AND Q
T	T	T
T	F	F
F	T	F
F	F	F

For the conjunction, the arithmetic function P*Q equals 1 only when both P and Q are equal to 1, and therefore P*Q can serve to represent P AND Q.

The logical disjunction P OR Q[1] is a new proposition that is false only when both P is false and Q is false. The truth-table for P OR Q is

P	Q	P OR Q
T	T	T
T	F	T
F	T	T
F	F	F

[1]This is the inclusive OR. P OR Q is true when (P is true, Q is true), (P is true, Q is false) or (P is false,

The mathematical function SGN(P + Q) can serve to represent P OR Q since it is zero only when both P and Q are zero; it is one otherwise.

With these conventions, the following program illustrates how a computer may be programed to print truth-tables. The program prints the truth-table associated with the four propositions P, Q, P AND Q, and P OR Q. The TAB function is used only to enhance the graphic quality of the output; the output itself is printed using a subroutine, lines 190–230.

```
10 ;&;
20 PRINT" P" TAB(12)"Q" TAB(20)"P AND Q" TAB(30)"P OR Q"
30 ;
40 FOR P=1 TO 0 STEP-1
50 FOR Q=1 TO 0 STEP-1
60 N=0
70 X=P,N=N+1
80 GOSUB 190
90 X=Q,N=N+1
100 GOSUB 190
110 X=P*Q,N=N+1
120 GOSUB 190
130 X=SGN(P+Q),N=N+1
140 GOSUB 190
150 PRINT
160 NEXT Q
170 NEXT P
180 END
190 IF X=0 THEN 220
200 PRINT TAB(10*(N-1))"TRUE";
210 RETURN
220 PRINT TAB(10*(N-1))"FALSE";
230 RETURN
```

```
 P          Q          P AND Q     P OR Q

TRUE       TRUE       TRUE        TRUE
TRUE       FALSE      FALSE       TRUE
FALSE      TRUE       FALSE       TRUE
FALSE      FALSE      FALSE       FALSE
```

Illustration: The Greatest Common Divisor

A subroutine may be used also in place of a multi-line defined function. We shall illustrate this with the following problem: Find the greatest common divisor (GCD) of several given numbers.

Q is true). P OR Q is false only when (P is false, Q is false). As an example of its use in ordinary speech, consider the proposition "She is rich or she is bright." This proposition does not exclude the possibility that she is both rich and bright.

There is an exclusive OR that we shall represent by the symbol P⊕Q. As an example of its use in everyday speech, consider the proposition "This afternoon, I shall go to the beach or I shall go to the library." Clearly, I cannot do both simultaneously. Thus P⊕Q is true only when (P is true, Q is false) or when (P is false, Q is true). If you were to learn that P is false and that Q is false, you would conclude that P⊕Q is false; if you were to learn that P is true and Q is true, you would know that P⊕Q is false. The truth-table for P⊕Q is

P	Q	P⊕Q
T	T	F
T	F	T
F	T	T
F	F	F

The arithmetic function 1 − ABS(P + Q − 1) can serve to represent P⊕Q.

The greatest common divisor of two integers, each greater than 1, is the largest integer that divides each with no remainder. The greatest common divisor of 9 and 12 is 3. If the two integers are such that only 1 divides both exactly, the two are said to be relatively prime. The numbers 6 and 35, for example, are relatively prime.

A procedure for finding the greatest common divisor of two integers X and Y is credited to Euclid and is based on the following considerations. If the two numbers are equal, then the number itself is the greatest common divisor. If they are not equal, suppose Y > X; divide Y by X to get a quotient Q and a remainder R. If R = 0, then X is the greatest common divisor of X and Y. If R ≠ 0, write:

$$Y = Q*X+R$$

The greatest common divisor of X and Y divides Y−Q*X evenly (that is, the remainder equals 0) since it divides both X and Y evenly. Thus, the greatest common divisor must divide R=Y−Q*X evenly. Also, R is less than X. Therefore, to find the greatest common divisor of X and Y, we need only find the greatest common divisor of X and R, and these numbers are smaller than Y and X, respectively. We repeat for X and R, knowing the process must terminate since the magnitudes become less after each iteration. Eventually, we must find either R = 1 or R = 0. If R = 1, the original numbers are relatively prime; if R = 0, the preceding value of R is the greatest common divisor.

The following program finds the greatest common divisor of two numbers X and Y:

```
10 ;
20 ;"ENTER TWO POSITIVE INTEGERS"; & INPUT X,Y
30 ;
40 A=X,B=Y
50 Q=INT(Y/X)
60 R=Y-X*Q
70 IF R=0 THEN 110
80 IF R=1 THEN 170
90 Y=X,X=R
100 GOTO 50
110 ;"THE GCD OF"A" AND"B" IS"X
120 ;
130 ;"DO YOU WANT TO TEST OTHER NUMBERS"; & INPUT S$
140 PRINT
150 IF S$="YES" THEN 20
160 STOP
170 ; "THE TWO NUMBERS"A" AND"B" ARE RELATIVELY PRIME."
180 ;
190 GOTO 130
```

```
ENTER TWO POSITIVE INTEGERS   ?855,1840

THE GCD OF 855 AND 1840 IS 5

DO YOU WANT TO TEST OTHER NUMBERS   ?YES

ENTER TWO POSITIVE INTEGERS   ?2142,2070

THE GCD OF 2142 AND 2070 IS 18

DO YOU WANT TO TEST OTHER NUMBERS   ?YES

ENTER TWO POSITIVE INTEGERS   ?35,9

THE TWO NUMBERS 35 AND 9 ARE RELATIVELY PRIME.

DO YOU WANT TO TEST OTHER NUMBERS   ?NO
```

Line 40 "remembers" the two numbers being tested; this information is used in the output, lines 110 and 170. The Euclidean algorithm is contained in lines 50–100· the outcome must be either R=0 or R=1.

Suppose we extend the problem to find the greatest common divisor of three numbers. Can we write a routine that contains as a subroutine the Euclidean algorithm for finding the greatest common divisor of two numbers? The following program does this; it is based on the fact that the greatest common divisor of three numbers can be found by first finding the greatest common divisor of two numbers and then the greatest common divisor of that result and the third number.

```
10 PRINT
20 PRINT "ENTER THREE POSITIVE INTEGERS"; \ INPUT X,Y,Z
30 A1=X,A2=Y,A3=Z
40 REM: THE VARIABLES A AND B ARE USED TO CARRY VALUES TO THE SUBROUTINE.
50 A=X,B=Y
60 GOSUB 210
70 REM: WHEN THE PROGRAM RETURNS, W IS THE GCD OF THE FIRST TWO NUMBERS
80 A=Z,B=W
90 GOSUB 210
100 REM: WHEN THE PROGRAM RETURNS, W IS THE GCD OF THE THREE NUMBERS.
110 IF W<>1 THEN 150
120 PRINT "THE INTEGERS"A1","A2" AND"A3" ARE RELATIVELY PRIME."
130 PRINT
140 GOTO 170
150 PRINT "THE GCS OF"A1","A2" AND"A3" IS"W
160 PRINT
170 PRINT "ANY MORE TRIPLES"; \ INPUT S$
180 PRINT
190 IF S$="YES" THEN 20
200 STOP
210 X=A, Y=B
220 Q=INT(Y/X)
230 R=Y-X*Q
240 IF R=0 THEN 280
250 IF R=1 THEN 300
260 Y=X,X=R
270 GOTO 220
280 W=X
290 RETURN
300 W=R
310 RETURN
```

```
ENTER THREE POSITIVE INTEGERS   ?21,33,45
THE GCS OF 21, 33 AND 45 IS 3

ANY MORE TRIPLES  ?YES

ENTER THREE POSITIVE INTEGERS   ?1764
?414
?918
THE GCS OF 1764, 414 AND 918 IS 18

ANY MORE TRIPLES  ?YES

ENTER THREE POSITIVE INTEGERS   ?907,1423,3416
THE INTEGERS 907, 1423 AND 3416 ARE RELATIVELY PRIME.

ANY MORE TRIPLES  ?YES

ENTER THREE POSITIVE INTEGERS   ?28812,30870,19698
THE GCS OF 28812, 30870 AND 19698 IS 294

ANY MORE TRIPLES  ?NO
```

The three integers are "remembered" in line 30, and this information is used in the output, lines 120 and 150. The major difference between the subroutine of this program and the previous program is the introduction of the intermediate variable W, which is the greatest common divisor of the numbers being tested in the subroutine. W is calculated the first time for two reasons: (1) it is the greatest common divisor of the first two numbers, and (2) it is needed as input to the subroutine for the second pass through.

Sorting and Merging

In Chapter 9 we saw that the bubble sort uses [N(N − 1)]/2 comparisons to sort a list of N elements. If the list is divided into two lists, each of N/2 elements, then the number of comparisons needed to bubble sort these two lists separately is 2(N/2)[(N/2) − 1]/2 = [N(N − 2)]/4, less than half the number needed to sort the original N elements. The problem remains of merging the two sublists into one sorted list. This is done in the following way.

Denote two sorted sublists by A(I) and B(J), the final sorted list by C(K). Compare the first entries of A and B and assign the smaller of these two values to C. Thus, C(1) = smaller of A(1) and B(1). Whichever one is chosen, the next step is to compare the second entry from that list to the first entry of the other list. The smaller of these two values is assigned to C(2). This process continues until all entries from one list are used, at which time all the remaining entries from the other list are tacked on to the end of the C(K) list. Suppose we have two sorted lists A: −8, 5, 12, 17, and B: −4, 6, 7, 9, 11. We begin by comparing A(1) = −8 and B(1) = −4. Since −8 < −4, C(1) = A(1) = −8, and we next compare A(2) = 5 and B(1) = −4. Since −4 < 5, C(2) = B(1) = −4, and we next compare A(2) = 5 and B(2) = 6. We continue until we find that B(5) = 11 is assigned to C(7) and that the B list is exhausted. Then set C(8) = 12 and C(9) = 17, and we exhaust the A list. The two sorted list A(I) and B(J) have been merged into the one sorted list C(K): −8, −4, 5, 6, 7, 9, 11, 12, 17.

The minimum number of comparisons occurs when the smallest element of one list is greater than the largest element of the other. In this case, the number of comparisons is N/2 since, for example, A(1) is compared to B(1), B(2), . . . , B(N/2).

The maximum number of comparisons occurs when each successive element of the A list interleaves two successive elements of the B list. We would compare:

A(1) : B(1)
A(1) : B(2)
A(2) : B(2)
A(2) : B(3)
. . .

$$A\left(\frac{N}{2}-1\right) : B\left(\frac{N}{2}-1\right)$$
$$A\left(\frac{N}{2}-1\right) : B\left(\frac{N}{2}\right)$$
$$A\left(\frac{N}{2}\right) : B\left(\frac{N}{2}\right)$$

The number of comparisons is 2[(N/2) − 1] + 1 = N − 1.

The maximum number of comparisons for the two sorts and the merge is [$\frac{1}{4}N^2$ − (N/2)] + (N − 1) = $\frac{1}{4}N^2$ + (N/2) − 1. For large N, this is only slightly more than half the number needed to bubble sort the original list.

The following program is only a little more general in that the two lists need not be of equal length. A subroutine is used to sort the two lists, which are then merged by the main body of the program. A flow chart describing the process appears in Figure 12-4. The following program is based on the flow chart.

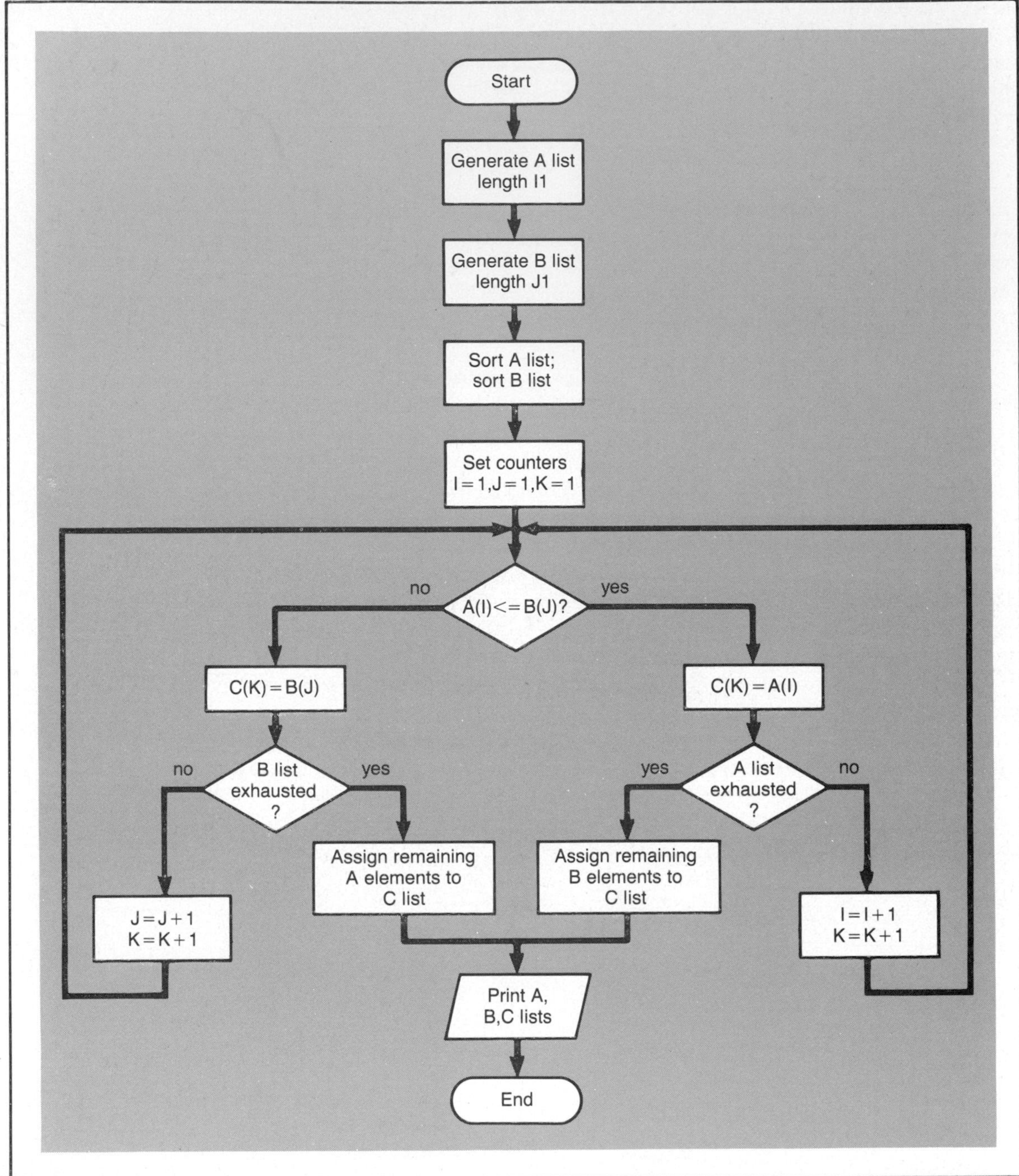

FIGURE 12-4

```
10 REM: THIS PROGRAM STARTS WITH TWO UNSORTED LISTS, THEN USING A
20 REM: SUBROUTINE, PRODUCES TWO ORDERED LISTS. FINALLY, THE TWO
30 REM: SORTED LISTS ARE MERGED INTO ONE SORTED LIST.
40 DIM A(100),B(100),C(200),D(100)
50 PRINT "HOW MANY ELEMENTS IN FIRST LIST"; \ INPUT I1
60 PRINT "HOW MANY ELEMENTS IN THE SECOND LIST"; \ INPUT J1
70 REM: THE TWO LISTS ARE GENERATED RANDOMLY
80 FOR S=1 TO I1
90 A(S)=INT(RND(1)*201)-100
100 NEXT S
110 FOR S=1 TO J1
120 B(S)=INT(RND(1)*201)-100
```

```
130 NEXT S
140 REM: A SUBROUTINE HAS BEEN SET UP TO SORT THE TWO LISTS.
150 REM: VARIABLES ARE SET TO USE THE SUBROUTINE
160 FOR I=1 TO I1
170 D(I)=A(I)
180 NEXT I
190 G=I1
200 GOSUB 680
210 FOR I=1 TO I1
220 A(I)=D(I)
230 NEXT I
240 FOR I=1 TO J1
250 D(I)=B(I)
260 NEXT I
270 G=J1
280 GOSUB 680
290 FOR I=1 TO J1
300 B(I)=D(I)
310 NEXT I
320 REM: THE ELEMENTS OF THE TWO SORTED LISTS ARE COMPARED. THE SMALLER
330 REM: ELEMENT IS ASSIGNED TO THE THIRD LIST
340 REM: WE HAVE TO KEEP TRACK OF WHEN EITHER LIST IS EXHAUSTED
350 I=1,J=1,K=1
360 IF A(I)<=B(J) THEN 410
370 C(K)=B(J)
380 IF J=>J1 THEN 450
390 J=J+1 ,K=K+1
400 GOTO 360
410 C(K)=A(I)
420 IF I=>I1 THEN 500
430 I=I+1,K=K+1
440 GOTO 360
450 REM: THE B LIST IS EXHAUSTED; THERE REMAIN I1-I+1 ELEMENTS IN THE A LIST
460 FOR S=1 TO I1-I+1
470 C(K+S)=A(I+S-1)
480 NEXT S
490 GOTO 540
500 REM: THE A LIST IS EXHAUSTED; THERE REMAIN J1-J+1 ELEMENTS IN THE B LIST
510 FOR S=1 TO J1-J+1
520 C(K+S)=B(J+S-1)
530 NEXT S
540 FOR I=1 TO I1
550 PRINT A(I);
560 NEXT I
570 PRINT \ PRINT
580 FOR I=1 TO J1
590 PRINT B(I);
600 NEXT I
610 PRINT \ PRINT
620 FOR I=1 TO I1+J1
630 PRINT C(I);
640 NEXT I
650 PRINT \ PRINT
660 STOP
670 REM: THE SUBROUTINE TO SORT THE ORIGINAL LISTS
680 FOR S=1 TO G-1
690 FOR T=1 TO G-S
700 IF D(T)<=D(T+1) THEN 740
710 X=D(T)
720 D(T)=D(T+1)
730 D(T+1)=X
740 NEXT T
750 NEXT S
760 RETURN
```

```
HOW MANY ELEMENTS IN FIRST LIST   ?5
HOW MANY ELEMENTS IN THE SECOND LIST  ?20

-69    13    56    73    81

-90   -87   -87   -85   -66   -56   -34   -33   -27   -22   -17   -3
 19    31    36    38    50    70    73    95

-90   -87   -87   -85   -69   -66   -56   -34   -33   -27   -22   -17
-3   13    19    31    36    38    50    56    70    73    73    81
 95


HOW MANY ELEMENTS IN FIRST LIST   ?20
HOW MANY ELEMENTS IN THE SECOND LIST  ?5

-88   -86   -46   -36   -33   -32   -31   -30   -16   -8    23    49
 57    62    66    72    75    82    85    89

-64   -31    12    23    46

-88   -86   -64   -46   -36   -33   -32   -31   -31   -30   -16   -8
 12    23    23    46    49    57    62    66    72    75    82    85
 89


HOW MANY ELEMENTS IN FIRST LIST   ?12
HOW MANY ELEMENTS IN THE SECOND LIST  ?12

-93   -73   -54   -51   -13   -5  -3   4    23    66    90    92

-92   -89   -83   -41   -16   -11    13    25    28    54    55    90


-93   -92   -89   -83   -73   -54   -51   -41   -16   -13   -11   -5  -3
 4   13    23    25    28    54    55    66    90    90    92
```

Nested GOSUBS

GOSUB statements may be nested. Consider:

```
500 GOSUB 600
510 -----
520 -----
530 -----
. . .
590 -----
600 XXXXX
610 XXXXX
620 XXXXX
. . .
650 GOSUB 800
660 XXXXX
. . .
690 RETURN
700 ZZZZZ
710 ZZZZZ
. . .
790 ZZZZZ
800 YYYYY
810 YYYYY
. . .
```

Answers to numerical cryptogram posed on page 93:

9376	9386	9476	9486
1086	1076	1086	1076
10462	10462	10562	10562

```
870 RETURN
880 WWWWW
...
```

When line 500 is executed, control immediately goes to line 600, where the subroutine XXXXX begins. During the course of executing this subroutine, which is assumed to use lines 600–690, a GOSUB command is encountered at line 650. When line 650 is executed, control is transferred to line 800. This second subroutine, YYYYY, is written in lines 800–870, so that when the RETURN in line 870 is executed, control returns to line 660, which is executed, followed by lines 670 and 680. When line 690 is reached, control returns to line 510 and the main program continues. Lines 700–790 and 880 were inserted to indicate other instructions that may exist in the program.

The nesting may be several layers deep; on some computers the program may execute as many as 20 GOSUB statements before a RETURN is necessary.

Summary of Subroutines

With the illustrations as models, we can formulate general rules for using subroutines. A subroutine directs the program to some subsection where a specific task is to be performed, generally several times. Frequently, this task is considered to be outside the main stream of the program; the subroutine may be thought of as scratch paper on which a needed side calculation is performed, time and again, for the main computation. The form of the subroutine is:

```
(line number) GOSUB (line)
(line number) RETURN
```

where RETURN is the last executed statement of the subroutine. We have seen that GOSUB to a specific line can originate from different places in the program and that more than one RETURN is possible from a subroutine. When RETURN is encountered control is directed to the statement immediately following the GOSUB statement last executed.

Exercises

12.1 Modify the program

```
10 FOR X=1 to 10
20 FOR Y=1 to 10
30 PRINT X^Y
40 NEXT Y
50 NEXT X
```

by eliminating line 30 and using a defined function FNA(X,Y), so that the output remains the same.

12.2 Consider the function FNS(X) = X−X^3/6 + X^5/120 − X^7/5040, which is an approximation to the function SIN(X) for small values of X. How large may X be before the difference between FNS(X) and SIN(X) is detected in the 4th decimal place?

12.3 Find those values of $X \geqslant 0$ for which the function EXP(ATN(X)) and the sum of terms

$$1 + X + \frac{X^2}{2!} - \frac{X^3}{3!} - \frac{7X^4}{4!} + \frac{5X^5}{5!}$$

agree to 5 decimal places.

12.4 Consider the sum of terms

$$S(N) = 1^4 + 2^4 + \ldots + N^4$$

and the function

$$FNK(N) = \frac{N}{30}(6N^4 + 15N^3 + 10N^2 - 1)$$

Write a program that will show that S(N) = FNK(N) for all integer values of N = 1, 2, . . . , 10.

12.5 The mathematical function associated with the negation of a proposition, −P, is 1−P. Modify the program on page 232 to produce the truth table for P, Q, −P, −Q, −P AND Q, P OR −Q.

12.6 The truth table for the conditional P → Q (P implies Q) is

P	Q	P ↔ Q
T	T	T
T	F	F
F	T	T
F	F	T

The conditional P → Q has the same truth table as (−P) OR Q. The biconditional P ↔ Q (P implies Q and Q implies P) has the truth table

P	Q	P ↔ Q
T	T	T
T	F	F
F	T	F
F	F	T

Write a program that will produce the truth table for the following: P, Q, −P, −Q, (P AND Q) OR (−P AND −Q) (P → Q) AND (Q → P). What do you notice about this truth table? What does this imply?

12.7 Modify the program on page 234 so that if the first two numbers tested are relatively prime, that is, if W = 1 when the program returns from its first trip to the subroutine, then the second trip to the subroutine is not made. The modification should include a message that the first two numbers are relatively prime and that testing halted after that was discovered. Otherwise, the modified program is to continue as the original one.

12.8 Write a program that will find the greatest common divisor of four numbers.

12.9 Write a program that finds the greatest common divisor of a string of N numbers, where the number N is entered as input.

12.10 Each terminating decimal number has a rational equivalent. For example, 0.375 = 375/1000 = 3/8. Write a program that asks for a decimal number as input and produces its rational equivalent, numerator and denominator relatively prime, as output.

13 On Representing Numbers

This chapter provides the background ideas and vocabulary for material to be presented in subsequent chapter. To understand how a computer operates, it is necessary to know how the various characters—numbers, letters, and punctuation marks—are represented within the machine. Because almost all computers operate in the binary system and we are brought up to think in the decimal system, we must develop more than a cursory familiarity with the binary system if we are to fully appreciate what is going on in the computer. As you will see, however, numbers written in binary are tedious both to write and to manipulate. We shall introduce the octal and hexadecimal number systems, which overcome these shortcomings.

Files are discussed in Chapters 17–21. Internally, data are stored in two ways: One is binary; the second representation is called binary coded decimal, or BCD. The BCD system will be described also.

The binary system is important because computers operate on currents flowing in electric circuits. The flow is controlled by switches, and in the simplest terms, a switch is either open or closed. The state of a switch being either open or closed is translated into the binary system, say, 1 for closed and 0 for open. Thus, the state of the computer at any instant in time may be described by a sequence of ones and zeros, indicating those switches that are closed and those that are open and thus, those circuits that are energized and those that are not. The computer solves problems by changing its state. Intermediate states correspond to intermediate steps in the solution. The answer to a problem is given by the computer translating its final state for us from its natural, binary language into our decimal language. If for some reason we suspect that the answer is not correct, and yet we are sure that the program we entered is mathematically and logically correct, we will have to look more deeply into what the computer is doing at various steps during the solution process. Ultimately, we must learn the computer's language, a language based on the binary number system.

Many newspaper stories have appeared concerning computer mistakes. Although the headlines usually point to the computer as being at fault, the story usually indicates that it was the programer who erred. This does not mean that the computer cannot fail; indeed, it can. There are at least three ways that a computer may fail. One is when a component fails because of some outside influence, such as being damaged by cosmic rays.[1] Although most manufacturers test the design of their computers to ensure logical consistency, rare circumstances have been known to arise in which incorrect results have been traced to a faulty design. The third type of error is inherent in the mathematical relationship between the binary and the decimal number systems and may surface, for example, when the INT(X) function is used. Knowing how this may arise should forestall future anxieties concerning programs that are mathematically correct but produce computationally incorrect results. We shall describe and illustrate one such situation involving the INT(X) function.

Digits and Integers, Positional Notation

An integer has an existence independent of the symbol that may be used to represent it. For the integer that in English is called "five," in German "funf," and for which the Romans used the symbol "V," our symbol is "5." While it would be possible to create a special symbol for each number, such a scheme would soon tax our memory and at the same time prove impractical for computational purposes. Over the last thousand years, Western civilization has come to adopt symbols for ten different digits and a method for arranging them so that integers of any magnitude may be written. The arrangement convention is called *positional notation;* the symbols are 0, 1, 2, 3, 4, 5, 6, 7, 8, and 9. You have been exposed to these symbols and to positional notation for so long that it is difficult to imagine that these are a creation of the human mind and, at that, not too old in the scale of history. Our method for writing integers is called the decimal system.

The decimal number system has base, or radix, ten because ten different symbols are used to write all the numbers. Although number systems to other bases have been known, studied, and used for centuries, it was only with the advent of the electronic digital computer that certain of these gained practical importance, specifically, the binary, the binary coded decimal, the octal, and the hexadecimal systems.

Fundamental to all these number systems is the idea of positional notation. In the decimal system, the symbol for the integer ten is 10, for one hundred it is 10^2, or 100, for one thousand it is 10^3, or 1000, and so on. In decimal notation, 2743 means $2 \cdot 10^3 + 7 \cdot 10^2 + 4 \cdot 10 + 3$ or equivalently: $2 \cdot 1000 + 7 \cdot 100 + 4 \cdot 10 + 3$. The position of the digit 2 tells us that it represents two thousand, the position of the digit 7 tells us it represents seven hundred, the position of the 4 that it represents four tens (also called forty), and the position of the 3 that it represents the integer three.

The Binary System

In the binary system, the radix, or base, is two and only the symbols 0 and 1 are used. These two symbols correspond to the integers in the following way: zero, 0; one, 1; two, 10; three, 11; four, 100; five, 101; six, 110; seven, 111; eight, 1000; nine, 1001; ten, 1010; eleven, 1011; twelve, 1100; thirteen, 1101; fourteen, 1110; fifteen, 1111; and so on. The binary number 11001101 means

$$1 \cdot 10^{111} + 1 \cdot 10^{110} + 0 \cdot 10^{101} + 0 \cdot 10^{100} + 1 \cdot 10^{11} + 1 \cdot 10^{10} + 0 \cdot 10^{1} + 1 \cdot 10^{0}$$

or, equivalently:

$$1 \cdot 10000000 + 1 \cdot 1000000 + 0 \cdot 100000 + 0 \cdot 10000 + 1 \cdot 1000 + 1 \cdot 100 + 0 \cdot 10 + 1$$

By its position, the leftmost 1 means one (one hundred and twenty-eight), the next 1 means one (sixty-four), the next symbol, 0, means zero (thirty-two), the next 0 means zero (sixteen), the following 1 means one (eight), then one (four), then zero (two), and finally one (one).

[1] J. F. Ziegler and W. A. Lanford, "Effect of Cosmic Rays on Computer Memories," *Science,* Vol. 206, 16 Nov. 1979, pp. 776–88.

The awkwardness of both the notation and the manner in which we must refer to the numbers is apparent. To overcome some of this, we shall introduce a hybrid notation. For the radix integer two, written 10 in binary, we substitute the decimal symbol 2, and for the exponents also we use the equivalent decimal symbol. In this hybrid notation, 11001101 is written as

$$1{\cdot}2^7 + 1{\cdot}2^6 + 0{\cdot}2^5 + 0{\cdot}2^4 + 1{\cdot}2^3 + 1{\cdot}2^2 + 0{\cdot}2^1 + 1{\cdot}2^0$$

We shall be using this form of binary notation, which is standard in the literature, in the text that follows.

Converting from Binary to Decimal

If we recognize the pattern, we should find it easy to convert a number written in binary to its decimal equivalent. Returning to the above illustration:

$$\begin{aligned}
1{\cdot}2^7 &= 1{\cdot}128_{dec}\\
1{\cdot}2^6 &= 1{\cdot}64_{dec}\\
0{\cdot}2^5 &= 0{\cdot}32_{dec}\\
0{\cdot}2^4 &= 0{\cdot}16_{dec}\\
1{\cdot}2^3 &= 1{\cdot}8_{dec}\\
1{\cdot}2^2 &= 1{\cdot}4_{dec}\\
0{\cdot}2^1 &= 0{\cdot}2_{dec}\\
1{\cdot}2^0 &= 1{\cdot}1_{dec}
\end{aligned}$$

If we sum the left-hand and the right-hand sides of these equations, we get

$$1{\cdot}2^7 + 1{\cdot}2^6 + 0{\cdot}2^5 + 0{\cdot}2^4 + 1{\cdot}2^3 + 1{\cdot}2^2 + 0{\cdot}2^1 + 1{\cdot}2^0 = 128 + 64 + 8 + 4 + 1$$

$$11001101_{bin} = 205_{dec}$$

An Alternative Method

An alternative conversion method uses the procedure for evaluating polynomials. The polynomial

$$a_0x^7 + a_1x^6 + a_2x^5 + \ldots + a_6x + a_7$$

may be evaluated using the following iterative sequence of steps:

a_0
$a_0{\cdot}x$
$a_0{\cdot}x + a_1$
$(a_0{\cdot}x + a_1){\cdot}x$
$(a_0{\cdot}x + a_1){\cdot}x + a_2$
preceding line·x
preceding line + a_3
preceding line·x
preceding line + a_4
preceding line·x
preceding line + next coefficient
. . .
preceding line + last coefficient.

When applied to numbers written in binary, each a_i is either 0 or 1 and $x = 2$. For the example 11001101, $a_0 = 1$, $a_1 = 1$, $a_2 = 0$, $a_3 = 0$, $a_4 = 1$, $a_5 = 1$, $a_6 = 0$, $a_7 = 1$.

Applying the algorithm:

$a_0 = 1$
$a_0x = 1{\cdot}2 = 2$
$a_0x + a_1 = 2 + 1 = 3$
$(a_0x + a_1)x = 3{\cdot}2 = 6$

$(a_0x + a_1)x + a_2 = 6 + 0 = 6$
preceding line $\cdot$ x = $6{\cdot}2 = 12$
preceding line + $a_3 = 12 + 0 = 12$
preceding line $\cdot$ x = $12{\cdot}2 = 24$
preceding line + $a_4 = 24 + 1 = 25$
preceding line $\cdot$ x = $25{\cdot}2 = 50$
preceding line + $a_5 = 50 + 1 = 51$
preceding line $\cdot$ x = $51{\cdot}2 = 102$
preceding line + $a_6 = 102 + 0 = 102$
preceding line $\cdot$ x = $102{\cdot}2 = 204$
preceding line + $a_7 = 204 + 1 = 205$

Therefore, the binary number 11001101 is equivalent to 205 in decimal notation.

Converting from Decimal to Binary

It is equally simple to convert an integer written in decimal notation to its binary representation. Consider 392_{dec}. First, find the greatest power of 2 that is less than or equal to 392. This is $2^8 = 256$. Subtract 256 from 392 to get 136. Find the greatest power of 2 less than or equal to 136; this is 2^7 or 128. Subtract: $136 - 128 = 8$ Find the greatest power of 2 less than or equal to 8; this is $2^3 = 8$. $8 - 8 = 0$. Using the symbol 1 as the coefficient for each power of 2 that is used in the process and the symbol 0 for the coefficients of those powers of 2 that are not used, we have:

$$\begin{aligned} 392_{dec} &= 1{\cdot}2^8 + 1{\cdot}2^7 + 0{\cdot}2^6 + 0{\cdot}2^5 + 0{\cdot}2^4 + 1{\cdot}2^3 + 0{\cdot}2^2 + 0{\cdot}2^1 + 0{\cdot}2^0 \\ &= 110001000_{bin} \end{aligned}$$

An Alternative Method

The method for evaluating polynomials provides an alternative for converting a number written in decimal notation to its binary equivalent. Before describing it, we shall review the addition and multiplication of binary numbers. These operations are most easily understood when seen in tabular form, as follows.

+	0	1
0	0	1
1	1	10

×	0	1
0	0	0
1	0	1

Note that when 1_{bin} and 1_{bin} are added, there is a carry of 1_{bin} to the next most significant place. At some point, $1_{bin} + 1_{bin} + 1_{bin}$ will be needed; the answer is 11_{bin}.

To multiply two binary numbers, arrange them as you would decimal numbers:

```
1010
1101
----
```

Write the intermediate steps, as follows:

```
   1010
   1101
   ----
   1010
  0000
 1010
1010
-------
```

Next, add the columns, carrying where appropriate. The answer is

10000010

You may wish to verify that $1010_{bin} = 10_{dec}$, $1101_{bin} = 13_{dec}$, and $10000010_{bin} = 130_{dec}$.

To convert 392_{dec} to binary, write

$$392 = 3{\cdot}10^2 + 9{\cdot}10 + 2 = (3{\cdot}10 + 9){\cdot}10 + 2$$

We have seen previously that: $2_{dec} = 10_{bin}$, $3_{dec} = 11_{bin}$, $9_{dec} = 1001_{bin}$, and $10_{dec} = 1010_{bin}$. Therefore,

$$3 \cdot 10_{dec} = (11 \cdot 1010)_{bin}$$

Multiply:

```
   1010
     11
   ----
   1010
  1010
  -----
  11110
```

$$((3 \cdot 10) + 9)_{dec} = (11110 + 1001)_{bin}$$

Add:

```
  11110
   1001
 ------
 100111
```

$$(3 \cdot 10 + 9)_{dec} = (100111)_{bin}$$
$$(3 \cdot 10 + 9) \cdot 10_{dec} = (100111 \cdot 1010)_{bin}$$

Multiply:

```
      100111
        1010
   ---------
      000000
     100111
    000000
   100111
   ---------
   110000110
```

$$(3 \cdot 10 + 9) \cdot 10_{dec} = (110000110)_{bin}$$

Add: $((3 \cdot 10 + 9) \cdot 10 + 2)_{dec} = (110000110 + 10)_{bin} = (1100010000)_{bin}$

Finally: $392_{dec} = 110001000_{bin}$

Binary Coded Decimals

Arithmetic operations in the binary system, because they are unfamiliar, remain awkward and tedious. Also, the number of places needed to represent a number in binary is excessive compared with the decimal system; 392_{dec} requires 3 places, 110001000_{bin} requires 9. For these reasons, a compromise system, known as BCD, or binary coded decimal, was invented.

In the decimal system, there are 10 digits, 0, 1, . . . ,9; we have given the binary equivalent of each. In BCD, the equivalence is: 0, 0000; 1, 0001; 2, 0010; 3, 0011; 4, 0100; 5, 0101; 6, 0110; 7, 0111; 8, 1000; and 9, 1001. To represent a decimal number in BCD, replace each digit in that decimal number with its BCD equivalent. Thus, 7205_{dec} becomes 0111001000000101_{BCD}, since $7_{dec} = 0111_{bin}$, $2_{dec} = 0010_{bin}$, $0_{dec} = 0000_{bin}$, and $5_{dec} = 0101_{bin}$. Graphically, the conversion may be represented by the following scheme:

```
   7        2        0        5
   ↓        ↓        ↓        ↓
  0111     0010     0000     0101
     ↘        ↘      ↙      ↙
      0111 0010 0000 0101 BCD
```

Although there are sixteen possible four-digit combinations of 0 and 1, only ten of them are used. To convert a BCD number to decimal, break it up into sets of four, starting with the least significant place, that is, at the right end. If the number of places is not a multiple of four, add the required number of zeros at the left end. For example, suppose the number is 10101100101110010_{BCD}. Because the number of places is not a multiple of 4, 3 high order zeros are added on the left.

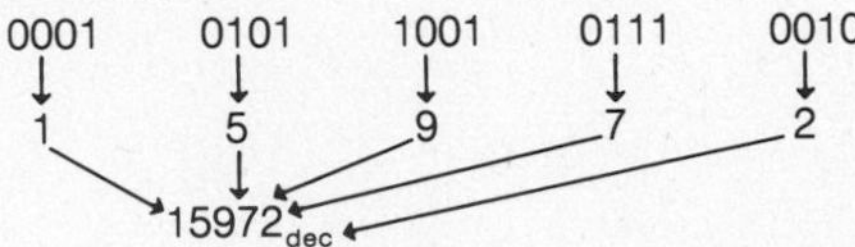

One advantage of looking at numbers written in BCD is the relative ease of converting them to decimals.

The Octal System

In the octal system, the radix, or base, is eight and the symbols 0, 1, 2, 3, 4, 5, 6, and 7 are used. Conversion from octal to decimal or from decimal to octal is similar to conversion of binary to decimal and decimal to binary. We shall illustrate the conversion with two examples.

To convert from octal to decimal:

$$\begin{aligned} 375_{oct} &= 3 \cdot 8^2 + 7 \cdot 8 + 5 \\ &= (3 \cdot 8 + 7) \cdot 8 + 5 \\ &= (31) \cdot 8 + 5 \\ &= 248 + 5 \\ &= 253_{dec} \end{aligned}$$

To convert from decimal to octal, first, find the largest power of 8 that is less than or equal to the decimal number. Divide the decimal number by eight to this power; record the quotient and the remainder. Repeat the process with the remainder. For example, to convert 489_{dec} to octal:

$8^0 = 1,\ 8^1 = 8,\ 8^2 = 64,\ 8^3 = 512$
INT(489/64) = 7
Remainder = 489 − 7·64 = 41
INT (41/8) = 5
Remainder = 41 − 5·8 = 1
Answer: $489_{dec} = 751_{oct}$

Additional and multiplication tables for octal arithmetic, Table 13-1, are useful if the conversion method is based on the polynominal representation of the numbers.

TABLE 13-1
Addition and Multiplication Tables for the Octal System

Octal Addition

+	0	1	2	3	4	5	6	7
0	0	1	2	3	4	5	6	7
1	1	2	3	4	5	6	7	10
2	2	3	4	5	6	7	10	11
3	3	4	5	6	7	10	11	12
4	4	5	6	7	10	11	12	13
5	5	6	7	10	11	12	13	14
6	6	7	10	11	12	13	14	15
7	7	10	11	12	13	14	15	16

Octal Multiplication

x	0	1	2	3	4	5	6	7
0	0	0	0	0	0	0	0	0
1	0	1	2	3	4	5	6	7
2	0	2	4	6	10	12	14	16
3	0	3	6	11	14	17	22	25
4	0	4	10	14	20	24	30	34
5	0	5	12	17	24	31	36	43
6	0	6	14	22	30	36	44	52
7	0	7	16	25	34	43	52	61

By way of illustration, 489_{dec} is converted to its octal equivalent as follows. Since the polynomial representation of 489_{dec} is:

$$489_{dec} = (4 \cdot 10 + 8) \cdot 10 + 9$$

we shall need the octal equivalents of 4, 8, 9, and 10. These are: $4_{dec} = 4_{oct}$, $8_{dec} = 10_{oct}$, $9_{dec} = 11_{oct}$, and $10_{dec} = 12_{oct}$. Then:

$$(4 \cdot 10)_{dec} = (4 \cdot 12)_{oct}$$

and from Table 13-1,

$$= 50_{oct}$$

Also,

$$(4 \cdot 10 + 8)_{dec} = 50_{oct} + 10_{oct}$$

and, again from the table,

$$= 60_{oct}$$
$$(4 \cdot 10 + 8) \cdot 10_{dec} = (60 \cdot 12)_{oct}$$

and from the table,

$$= 740_{oct}$$

Finally,

$$[(4 \cdot 10 + 8) \cdot 10 + 9]_{dec} = 740_{oct} + 11_{oct}$$
$$= 751_{oct}$$

Binary to Octal Conversion

The relationship between binary and octal representation of integers is quite simple. To each octal digit, we associate a three-place binary number and vice-versa.

Octal	Binary
0	000
1	001
2	010
3	011
4	100
5	101
6	110
7	111

Given a binary number, if the number of places in it is not exactly divisible by 3, at the high end of the number, at the left, insert one or two zeros, as needed.

Although the situations in which you may encounter numbers written in octal are rare, parts of some computer systems use the representation.

The Hexadecimal System

The final number system that we shall consider is the hexadecimal system. The radix, or base, is sixteen and sixteen symbols are used: 0, 1, 2, 3, 4, 5, 6, 7, 8, 9, A, B, C, D, E, F. These correspond to the integers as follows: zero, 0; one, 1; two, 2; three, 3; four, 4; five, 5; six, 6; seven, 7; eight, 8; nine, 9; ten, A; eleven, B; twelve, C; thirteen, D; fourteen, E; and fifteen, F. Using positional notation: sixteen, 10_x; seventeen, 11_x; eighteen, 12_x; nineteen, 13_x; twenty, 14_x . . . two hundred and fifty-five, FF_x, where the subscript x indicates that the number is written in the hexadecimal system.

Converting from Hexadecimal to Decimal and from Decimal to Hexadecimal

Converting from hexadecimal to decimal and conversely is similar to converting from binary to decimal and conversely. The conversion is illustrated in two examples. First, to convert from hexadecimal to decimal:

$$\begin{aligned} 3AF4_x &= 3 \cdot 16^3 + A \cdot 16^2 + F \cdot 16^1 + 4 \cdot 16^0 \\ &= ((3 \cdot 16 + A) \cdot 16 + F) \cdot 16 + 4 \\ &= ((3 \cdot 16 + 10) \cdot 16 + 15) \cdot 16 + 4 \\ &= 15092_{dec} \end{aligned}$$

To convert a decimal number to hexadecimal, first find the largest power of 16 that is less than or equal to the decimal number. Divide the original number by 16 to this power; record the quotient and the remainder. Then, repeat the process with the remainder. For example, to convert 3274980_{dec} to hexadecimal:

$$\begin{aligned} &16^1 = 16,\ 16^2 = 256,\ 16^3 = 4096,\ 16^4 = 65536,\ 16^5 = 1048576 \\ &\text{INT}(3274980/1048576) = 3, \\ &\text{Remainder} = 3274980 - 3(1048576) = 129252 \\ &\text{INT}(129252/65536) = 1 \\ &\text{Remainder} = 129252 - 65536 = 63716 \\ &\text{INT}(63716/4096) = F \\ &\text{Remainder} = 63716 - F(4096) = 2276 \\ &\text{INT}(2276/256) = 8 \\ &\text{Remainder} = 2276 - 8(256) = 228 \\ &\text{INT}(228/16) = E \\ &\text{Remainder} = 228 - E(16) = 4 \end{aligned}$$

Therefore, $3274980_{dec} = 31F8E4_x$

An Alternative Method

The polynominal evaluation technique may also be used to convert a numer from the decimal to the hexadecimal system. Tables 13-2 and 13-3 are the hexadecimal addition and multiplication tables. Assume, for example, that we want to convert 3274980_{dec} to the hexadecimal system.

$$\begin{aligned} 3274980_{dec} &= (((((3 \cdot 10 + 2) \cdot 10 + 7) \cdot 10 + 4) \cdot 10 + 9) \cdot 10 + 8) \cdot 10 + 0 \\ &= (((((3 \cdot A + 2) \cdot A + 7) \cdot A + 4) \cdot A + 9) \cdot A + 8) \cdot A + 0 \end{aligned}$$

TABLE 13-2
Addition Table for the Hexadecimal System

+	1	2	3	4	5	6	7	8	9	A	B	C	D	E	F	10
1	02	03	04	05	06	07	08	09	0A	0B	0C	0D	0E	0F	10	11
2	03	04	05	06	07	08	09	0A	0B	0C	0D	0E	0F	10	11	12
3	04	05	06	07	08	09	0A	0B	0C	0D	0E	0F	10	11	12	13
4	05	06	07	08	09	0A	0B	0C	0D	0E	0F	10	11	12	13	14
5	06	07	08	09	0A	0B	0C	0D	0E	0F	10	11	12	13	14	15
6	07	08	09	0A	0B	0C	0D	0E	0F	10	11	12	13	14	15	16
7	08	09	0A	0B	0C	0D	0E	0F	10	11	12	13	14	15	16	17
8	09	0A	0B	0C	0D	0E	0F	10	11	12	13	14	15	16	17	18
9	0A	0B	0C	0D	0E	0F	10	11	12	13	14	15	16	17	18	19
A	0B	0C	0D	0E	0F	10	11	12	13	14	15	16	17	18	19	1A
B	0C	0D	0E	0F	10	11	12	13	14	15	16	17	18	19	1A	1B
C	0D	0E	0F	10	11	12	13	14	15	16	17	18	19	1A	1B	1C
D	0E	0F	10	11	12	13	14	15	16	17	18	19	1A	1B	1C	1D
E	0F	10	11	12	13	14	15	16	17	18	19	1A	1B	1C	1D	1E
F	10	11	12	13	14	15	16	17	18	19	1A	1B	1C	1D	1E	1F
10	11	12	13	14	15	16	17	18	19	1A	1B	1C	1D	1E	1F	20

TABLE 13-3
Multiplication Table
for the Hexadecimal System

×	2	3	4	5	6	7	8	9	A	B	C	D	E	F	10
2	04	06	08	0A	0C	0E	10	12	14	16	18	1A	1C	1E	20
3	06	09	0C	0F	12	15	18	1B	1E	21	24	27	2A	2D	30
4	08	0C	10	14	18	1C	20	24	28	2C	30	34	38	3C	40
5	0A	0F	14	19	1E	23	28	2D	32	37	3C	41	46	4B	50
6	0C	12	18	1E	24	2A	30	36	3C	42	48	4E	54	5A	60
7	0E	15	1C	23	2A	31	38	3F	46	4D	54	5B	62	69	70
8	10	18	20	28	30	38	40	48	50	58	60	68	70	78	80
9	12	1B	24	2D	36	3F	48	51	5A	63	6C	75	7E	87	90
A	14	1E	28	32	3C	46	50	5A	64	6E	78	82	8C	96	A0
B	16	21	2C	37	42	4D	58	63	6E	79	84	8F	9A	A5	B0
C	18	24	30	3C	48	54	60	6C	78	84	90	9C	A8	B4	C0
D	1A	27	34	41	4E	5B	68	75	82	8F	9C	A9	B6	C3	D0
E	1C	2A	38	46	54	62	70	7E	8C	9A	A8	B6	C4	D2	E0
F	1E	2D	3C	4B	5A	69	78	87	96	A5	B4	C3	D2	E1	F0
10	20	30	40	50	60	70	80	90	A0	B0	C0	D0	E0	F0	100

3 · A = 1E
3 · A + 2 = IE + 2 = 20
(3 · A + 2) · A = (20) · A = 140
(3 · A + 2) · A + 7 = 140 + 7 = 147
(preceding line · A = (147) · A = CC6
preceding line + 4 = CC6 + 4 = CCA
(preceding line) · A = (CCA) · A = 7FE4
preceding line + 9 = 7FE4 + 9 = 7FED
(preceding line) · A = (7FED) · A = 4FF42
preceding line + 8 = 4FF42 + 8 = 4FF4A
(preceding line) · A = (4FF4A) · A = 31F8E4
preceding line + 0 = 31F8E4 + 0 = 31F8E4
$3274980_{dec} = 31F8E4_{x}$

Binary-Hexadecimal Conversion

The relationship between the binary and hexadecimal representations of numbers is straightforward. Every hexadecimal digit corresponds to a four-place binary number and vice-versa. The correspondence is as follows:

Hexadecimal	Binary
0	0000
1	0001
2	0010
3	0011
4	0100
5	0101
6	0110
7	0111
8	1000
9	1001
A	1010
B	1011
C	1100
D	1101
E	1110
F	1111

When we convert to hexadecimal, if the number of places in the binary number is not exactly divisible by 4, at the high end of the number, at the left, we insert one, two, or three zeros as needed. While the computer can describe its state to us in binary, to do so requires excessively long strings of zeros and ones. It has been found that by converting a binary string to its hexadecimal equivalent, the information contained in the string is more easily managed and understood.

We leave now the mechanics of the conversions between the several number systems and turn to the specific ways symbols we use in communicating—letters of the alphabet, numbers, punctuation—are represented within the computer.

Bits, Bytes, and Characters

A binary integer having only one place is called a "bit"; it may take only the values 0 and 1. A byte is a binary integer consisting of eight bits;[2] a byte may have 2^8, or 256 different values. With this number of different values available, it is possible to associate each of the ten digits, the 26 upper case and 26 lower case letters of the alphabet, as well as the various punctuation symbols, with different bytes. Generally, on those terminals with upper case only, there are at least 63 printable characters and one unprintable one, the "space." On those terminals that can print both upper and lower case, there would be at least 89 printable characters plus the "space." Control characters, for example, <CR> and ESC, account for at least 32 more. The DELETE key, which is considered neither a graphic nor a control character, is to be included also.

ASCII and EBCDIC

There are two standard methods for setting up a correspondence between a bit configuration and the control, graphic, and DELETE characters. Of these, the older uses seven bits; it is called ASCII, American Standards Code for Information Interchange, although it has become an international standard. Table 13-4 gives this correspondence. The first thirty-two positions in the table, those whose decimal values are 0–31, are for controls. Their meanings are as follows:

0	NUL	Null
1	SOH	Start of Heading
2	STX	Start of Text
3	ETX	End of Text
4	EOT	End of Transmission
5	ENQ	Enquiry
6	ACK	Acknowledge
7	BEL	Bell (an audible signal)
8	BS	Backspace
9	HT	Horizontal Tab
10	LF	Line Feed
11	VT	Vertical Tab
12	FF	Form Feed
13	CR	Carriage Return
14	SO	Shift Out
15	SI	Shift In
16	DLE	Data Link Escape
17	DC1	Device Control 1
18	DC2	Device Control 2
19	DC3	Device Control 3
20	DC4	Device Control 4
21	NAK	Negative Acknowledge
22	SYN	Synchronous Idle
23	ETB	End of Transmission Block
24	CAN	Cancel
25	EM	End of Medium
26	SUB	Substitute

[2]Some authors refer to a binary number with K bits as a K-byte number.

TABLE 13-4
ASCII Character Set

Decimal Value	Symbol	Decimal Value	Symbol	Decimal Value	Symbol	Decimal Value	Symbol
0	NUL	32	SP	64	@	96	`
1	SOH	33	!	65	A	97	a
2	STX	34	"	66	B	98	b
3	ETX	35	#	67	C	99	c
4	EOT	36	$	68	D	100	d
5	ENQ	37	%	69	E	101	e
6	ACK	38	&	70	F	102	f
7	BEL	39	'	71	G	103	g
8	BS	40	(	72	H	104	h
9	HT	41	)	73	I	105	i
10	LF	42	*	74	J	106	j
11	VT	43	+	75	K	107	k
12	FF	44	,	76	L	108	l
13	CR	45	–	77	M	109	m
14	SO	46	.	78	N	110	n
15	SI	47	/	79	O	111	o
16	DLE	48	0	80	P	112	p
17	DC1	49	1	81	Q	113	q
18	DC2	50	2	82	R	114	r
19	DC3	51	3	83	S	115	s
20	DC4	52	4	84	T	116	t
21	NAK	53	5	85	U	117	u
22	SYN	54	6	86	V	118	v
23	ETB	55	7	87	W	119	w
24	CAN	56	8	88	X	120	x
25	EM	57	9	89	Y	121	y
26	SUB	58	:	90	Z	122	z
27	ESC	59	;	91	[	123	{
28	FS	60	<	92	\	124	|
29	GS	61	=	93	]	125	}
30	RS	62	>	94	^	126	~
31	US	63	?	95	_ or ←	127	DEL

27 ESC Escape
28 FS File Separator
29 GS Group Separator
30 RS Record Separator
31 US Unit Separator

Position 32 is for "SPACE" and 127 is for "DELETE."

The other method associates an eight bit configuration with the various characters and functions. It is called the Extended Binary Coded Decimal Interchange Code (EBCDIC) and is given in Table 13-5. The unassigned values are for future definition. Although there are other schemes for setting up a correspondence between the control, graphic, and delete characters and bit patterns, we shall limit our presentation to these two. All future references in this book will be to either ASCII or EBCDIC machines.

The Internal Representation of Numbers

To this point it has been shown how the various graphic characters, as well as the control functions and the rubout may be represented internally by bit patterns, either as seven bit patterns in ASCII machines or as eight bit patterns in EBCDIC machines. We shall now show how numbers can be represented internally.

Representation of Positive Integers and Zero

Computer integers differ from ordinary integers in only one way. The familiar integers of arithmetic are infinite in number—there is no largest positive integer and no smallest negative one. A computer, however, has only a finite number of parts, and thus, only a finite number of bits can be used to represent an integer. Consequently, there must be a largest positive integer and a smallest negative one. The magnitude of these two computer integers is determined by the number of bits that the manufacturer allows for their representation. We shall discuss the case in which thirty-two bits are available in the machine for all computer integer representations, both positive and negative. The extension to the case to one in which more than thirty-two bits are available or the restriction to the case in which fewer than thirty-two bits are available will be obvious.

The thirty-two bits are thought of as consisting of four bytes; we shall refer to a group of four bytes as a "word." Imagine the thirty-two bits strung out on a line from left to right. The leftmost bit determines the sign of the integer; if the sign bit is 0, the number is positive, if it is 1, the number is negative. The remaining thirty-one bits are used to represent the integer. The four bytes representing the integer "zero" consist of thirty-two zeros.

Start with an arbitrary positive integer and write it in binary. If more than thirty-one bits are needed, the number is too large to be written as an integer in the machine we are using as a model. Therefore, we are limited to thinking only of positive integers that, when written in binary, do not require more than thirty-one bits for their representation. If fewer than thirty-one bits are required, at the lefthand side, add enough zeros to fill out thirty-one places. For example, the integer $3{,}274{,}980_{dec}$, which has the hexadecimal representation $31F8E4_X$, would have the binary representation $0011000111111000011100100_{bin}$, and the machine representation: 00000000 00110001 1111000 11100100. Note that when writing the number as a machine word, we separated the word into its four bytes for clarity. The largest positive integer in this computer would have the representation

01111111 11111111 11111111 11111111

In decimal form, this number is $2^{31} - 1 = 2{,}147{,}483{,}647$.

Negative Integers and Two's Complement

We have said that negative numbers will have a 1 in the leftmost bit but have not otherwie defined their representation. The representation of negative integers is based on a technique called two's complement. Every positive machine integer is represented by a sequence of zeros and ones. If we construct a new computer integer by changing each

TABLE 13-5
Internal Representation of Numbers

EBCDIC VALUE	CHARACTER	MEANING	EBCDIC VALUE	CHARACTER	MEANING
0	NUL	null	8	BS or EOM	backspace or end of message
1	SOH	start of header	9	ENQ	enquiry
2	STX	start of text	10	NAK	negative acknowledge
3	ETX	end of text	11	VT	vertical tab
4	EOT	end of transmission	12	FF	form feed
5	HT	horizontal tab	13	CR	carriage return
6	ACK	acknowledge (positive)	14	SO	shift out
7	BEL	bell	15	SI	shift in

TABLE 13-5 (continued)

EBCDIC VALUE	CHARACTER	MEANING	EBCDIC VALUE	CHARACTER	MEANING
16	DLE	data link escape	76	<	less than
17	DC1	device control 1	77	(	left parenthesis
18	DC2	device control 2	78	+	plus
19	DC3	device control 3	79	| or ¦	vertical or broken bar
20	DC4	device control 4	80	&	ampersand
21	LF or NL	line feed or new line	81		
22	SYN	synchronous idle	82		
23	ETB	end of transmission block	83		
24	CAN	cancel	84		
25	EM	end of medium	85		
26	SUB	substitute	86		
27	ESC	escape	87		
28	FS	file separator	88		
29	GS	group separator	89		
30	RS	record separator	90	!	exclamation point
31	US	unit separator	91	$	dollars
32	LF only	line feed only	92	*	asterisk
33	FS		93	)	right parenthesis
34	GS		94	;	semicolon
35	RS		95	~ or ¬	tilde or logical not
36	US		96	–	minus, dash, hyphen
37	EM		97	/	slash
38	/		98		
39	↑		99		
40	=		100		
41	CR only	carriage return only	101		
42	EOT		102		
43	BS		103		
44	)		104		
45	HT	tab code only	105		
46	LF only	line feed only	106		circumflex
47	SUB		107	,	comma
48	ESC F	end of file	108	%	percent
49	CANCEL	delete all input and output	109	___	underline
50	ESC X	delete input line	110	>	greater than
51	ESC P	toggle half-duplex paper tape mode	111	?	question mark
52	ESC U	toggle restrict upper case	112		
53	ESC (	upper case shift	113		
54	ESC)	lower case shift	114		
55	ESC T	toggle tab simulation mode	115		
56	ESC S	toggle space insertion mode	116		
57	ESC E	toggle echo mode	117		
58	ESC C	toggle tab relative mode	118		
59	ESC LF	line continuation	119		
60	X-ON	start paper tape	120		
61	X-OFF	stop paper tape	121		
62	ESC R	retype	122	:	colon
63	ESC CR	line continuation	123	#	number
64	SP	blank	124	@	at
65			125	'	apostrophe (single quote)
66			126	=	equals
67			127	"	quotation mark
68			128		
69			129	a	
70			130	b	
71			131	c	
72			132	d	
73			133	e	
74	¢ or `	cent or `	134	f	
75	.	period	135	g	

TABLE 13-5 *(continued)*

EBCDIC VALUE	CHARACTER	MEANING	EBCDIC VALUE	CHARACTER	MEANING
136	h		196	D	
137	i		197	E	
138			198	F	
139			199	G	
140			200	H	
141			201	I	
142			202		
143			203		
144			204		
145	j		205		
146	k		206		
147	l		207		
148	m		208		
149	n		209	J	
150	o		210	K	
151	p		211	L	
152	q		212	M	
153	r		213	N	
154			214	O	
155			215	P	
156			216	Q	
157			217	R	
158			218		
159			219		
160			220		
161			221		
162	s		222		
163	t		223		
164	u		224	–	minus
165	v		225		
166	w		226	S	
167	x		227	T	
168	y		228	U	
169	z		229	V	
170			230	W	
171			231	X	
172			232	Y	
173			233	Z	
174			234		
175	|	logical and	235		
176			236		
177	\	backslash	237		
178	{	left brace	238		
179	}	right brace	239		
180	[	left bracket	240	0	
181	]	right bracket	241	1	
182			242	2	
183			243	3	
184			244	4	
185			245	5	
186			246	6	
187			247	7	
188	[	left bracket	248	8	
189	]	right bracket	249	9	
190	lost data	lost data	250		
191	¬	logical not	251		
192	SP	blank	252		
193	A		253		
194	B		254		
195	C		255		delete

From Xerox *BASIC, Sigma 5–9 Computers, Language and Operations Reference Manual: 90-15-46G*, pp. 67–71.

zero to a one and each one to a zero, the result is called the one's complement of the original integer. Thus, the one's complement of

0000 0000 0011 0001 1111 1000 1110 0100

is

1111 1111 1100 1110 0000 0111 0001 1011

The sum of any integer and its one's complement consists of a string of 32 ones.

The two's complement of the original number is equal to its one's complement plus 1. Thus, taking the machine representation of 3,274,980, the two's complement of

0000 0000 0011 0001 1111 1000 1110 0100

is

1111 1111 1100 1110 0000 0111 0001 1100

This is the machine representation of $-3,274,980$.

A reason for choosing this representation is based on the arithmetic equation that for any number x, $x+(-x)=0$. You have seen that when a number and its one's complement are added, the result, in binary, is 32 ones. If 1 is added to this, the result would be a 1 in the 33rd position and 0 in the remaining 32 positions. The hardware, where the addition takes place, however, has only 32 positions. Because addition proceeds from right to left, the 32 positions are filled with zeros, and the 1 that would normally go into the 33rd position drops off the high end and is lost. The result, because of the way the computer circuitry is constructed, is zero.

The Representation of Floating-Point Numbers

Floating-point numbers are those that are not computer integers. A number would be floating-point if it contained a decimal point, for example, 2.719, -34.6, .000671, or because, although it is an integer in the mathematical sense, it is too large to be accommodated in computer integer form, for example, 2.65×10^{47}.

Floating-Point Numbers Compared with Rational Numbers

The arithmetic of floating-point numbers differs from the arithmetic of rational numbers in several ways. For the moment, consider only the nonnegative rationals. One difference is that the magnitude of the rational numbers is unbounded, whereas because there must be a finite number of bits in a computer word, the magnitude of the largest positive computer number must be bounded.

Both the rationals and the computer rationals include zero. For the computer, however, there is a smallest positive floating-point number; for any positive rational *r*, no matter how small, there are infinitely many positive rationals less than *r*.

Another difference is that for the computer, and except for the largest number, every floating-point number has an immediate successor, the next largest floating-point number that can be accommodated in the finite number of storage places available. For any arithmetic rational *r*, there is no next larger rational.

A Computer Model for Representing Floating-Point Numbers

When discussing computer integers, we used as our model a computer that set aside one word to represent them. Now that we are to discuss floating-point numbers, we shall use as our model a computer that sets aside two words, sixty-four bits, to represent them.

Writing a string of sixty-four zeros and ones is tedious. Instead, wherever possible, we shall use hexadecimal notation and switch back and forth between it and binary as needed.[3] Thus, the two computer words, the sixty-four bits, will be represented by sixteen hexadecimal digits. A typical floating-point number will look like: $\underline{\alpha_1\alpha_2}\beta1\beta2\beta3\beta4\beta5\beta6\beta7\beta8\beta9\beta10\beta11\beta12\beta13\beta14$, where the α_i and β_i are hexadecimal digits. We shall always underline the first two digits.

The floating-point number "zero" is represented by $\underline{00}000000\ 00000000_x$. (Remember, each $0_x = 0000_{bin}$.) A positive floating-point number will always have a 0_{bin} as its first bit. Thus, all positive floating-point numbers can start only with one of the hexadecimal digits 0, 1, 2, 3, 4, 5, 6, 7, since their binary representations are 0000, 0001, 0010, 0011, 0100, 0101, 0110, and 0111, respectively. These first two hexadecimal numbers, $\underline{\alpha_1\alpha_2}$, which range from $\underline{00}_x$ to $\underline{7F}_x$, are to be correlated with the exponent in some power of 16_{dec}.[4]

The manufacturer of the computer we are using as a model chose to set up this correspondence in the following way. Convert the hexadecimal integer $\underline{\alpha_1\alpha_2}$ into its equivalent decimal form. This will be an integer in the range 0, 1, . . . , 127. Subtract 65 from this integer; this result is an integer in the range $-65, -64, \ldots, 62$. Call a typical integer in this range K. The hexadecimal integer $\underline{\alpha_1\alpha_2}$ is to be associated with the decimal number 16^K. Typically, $\underline{00}_x \to 16^{-65}$, $\underline{01}_x \to 16^{-64}, \ldots, \underline{40}_x \to 16^{-1}$, $\underline{41}_x \to 16^0$, $\underline{42}_x \to 16^1, \ldots, \underline{4F}_x \to 16^{14}$, $\underline{50}_x \to 16^{15}$, $\underline{5F}_x \to 16^{30}$, $\underline{6F}_x \to 16^{46}$, and finally, $\underline{7F}_x \to 16^{62}$.

Continuing with the scheme chosen to represent floating-point numbers, the third hexadecimal digit, β_1, is never 0_x; it must be one of the digits $1_x, 2_x, \ldots, F_x$. Consider now the special floating-point number

$$\underline{\alpha_1\alpha_2}\beta_1 00000\ 00000000$$

where $\beta_2 = \ldots = \beta_{14} = 0_x$. To translate this number into its decimal equivalent, first find the decimal equivalent of β_1 and call it γ_1. Then, multiply γ_1 by 16^K. This result is the answer. For example, if the computer representation of a floating-point number X_x is $\underline{00}100000\ 00000000_x$, then $\underline{00}_x \to 16^{-65}$ and $1_x \to 1_{dec}$ and the decimal equivalent of X. is $1 \cdot 16^{-65}$. Other examples are:

$$\begin{array}{lcl} \underline{0F}900000\ 00000000_x & \to & 9 \cdot 16^{-50} \\ \underline{40}B00000\ 00000000_x & \to & 11 \cdot 16^{-1} \\ \underline{41}F00000\ 00000000_x & \to & 15 \cdot 16^{0} = 15 \\ \underline{50}700000\ 00000000_x & \to & 7 \cdot 16^{15} \\ \underline{7F}F00000\ 00000000_x & \to & 15 \cdot 16^{62} \end{array}$$

Suppose we consider next a case in which the fourth hexadecimal digit, $\beta_2 \neq 0_x$, but $\beta_3 = \beta_4 = \ldots = \beta_{14} = 0_x$, $X_x = \underline{\alpha_1\alpha_2}\beta_1\beta_2 0000\ 00000000$. We would begin as before; first find K and γ_1. Next we would determine γ_2, the decimal equivalent of β_2. Then the decimal form of the number X, whose floating-point representation is given above, is $X_{dec} = \gamma_1 \cdot 16^K + \gamma_2 \cdot 16^{K-1}$. For example:

$$\underline{00}120000\ 0000\ 0000_x \to 1 \cdot 16^{-65} + 2 \cdot 16^{-66}$$

Other examples are:

$$\begin{array}{lcrcl} \underline{0F}9A0000\ 00000000_x & \to & 9 \cdot 16^{-50} & + & 10 \cdot 16^{-51} \\ \underline{40}BC0000\ 00000000_x & \to & 11 \cdot 16^{-1} & + & 12 \cdot 16^{-2} \\ \underline{41}F70000\ 00000000_x & \to & 15 \cdot 16^{0} & + & 7 \cdot 16^{-1} \\ \underline{50}7F0000\ 00000000_x & \to & 7 \cdot 16^{15} & + & 15 \cdot 16^{14} \\ \underline{7F}FF0000\ 00000000_x & \to & 15 \cdot 16^{62} & + & 15 \cdot 16^{61} \end{array}$$

---

[3]For the relationship between these two systems, see page 249.

[4]This representation of floating-point numbers is analogous to the representation of the logarithm of a number. The integer part of the log of a number represents an integer power of the base (for the common log, some power of 10); the underscored part of our hexadecimal number represents some power of 16.

The decimal equivalent of the floating-point number X = $\underline{\alpha_1\alpha_2}\beta_1\beta_2\beta_3\beta_4\beta_5\beta_6\beta_7\beta_8\beta_9\beta_{10}\beta_{11}\beta_{12}\beta_{13}\beta_{14}$ is found in three steps: first, find the decimal integer K associated with the hexadecimal integer $\underline{\alpha_1\alpha_2}$; second, find γ_i, the decimal equivalents of the hexadecimal numbers, β_i, for $i = 1,2,\ldots, 14$; third, form the sum:

$$\gamma_1 \cdot 16^{K} + \gamma_2 \cdot 16^{K-1} + \gamma_3 \cdot 16^{K-2} + \ldots + \gamma_{14} \cdot 16^{K-13}$$

This sum, in decimal form, is the decimal equivalent of X_x. For example, the decimal equivalent of $\underline{3F}$52A7BE FDA060CO$_X$ would be found by remembering that $\underline{3F}_x \rightarrow -2$ and writing $X_{dec} = 5\cdot16^{-2} + 2\cdot16^{-3} + 10\cdot16^{-4} + 7\cdot16^{-5} + 11\cdot16^{-6} + 14\cdot16^{-7} + 15\cdot16^{-8} + 13\cdot16^{-9} + 10\cdot16^{-10} + 0\cdot16^{-11} + 6\cdot16^{-12} + 0\cdot16^{-13} + 12\cdot16^{-14} + 0\cdot16^{-15}$. Once the highest power of 16 is known, that is, once K is known, and the decimal equivalents of the hexadecimal digits are memorized, the expansion of X_{dec} can be read directly from the floating-point representation of X_x. Based on this correspondence, the smallest positive floating-point number, X = $\underline{00}$100000 00000000$_x$ is equivalent to the decimal number $1\cdot16^{-65}$; the largest floating point number, $\underline{7F}$FFFFFF FFFFFFFF$_x$ is equal to, in decimal notation,

$$15(16^{62} + 16^{61} + \ldots + 16^{49}) = 16^{49}(16^{14} - 1)$$

The smallest positive number is approximately $5.397605346934026 \times 10^{-79}$ and the largest is approximately $7.237005577332259 \times 10^{75}$.

Again, note that for all hexadecimal integers beween 00_x and $7F_x$ (the first two hexadecimal integers used to represent the highest power of 16 in a given positive, floating-point number), the leading bit in their binary representations is a 0. This is consistent with the convention described above for writing positive integers.

The Representation of Negative Floating-Point Numbers

Negative numbers are represented as a two's complement. For example, since the decimal number 5.0 is represented in the machine as 41500000 00000000, the decimal number −5.0 would be represented by BEB00000 00000000. If these two machine numbers are added, we get

```
  41500000 00000000
  BEB00000 00000000
1 00000000 00000000
```

In the answer, the digit 1 occurs in the 17th hexadecimal position, counting from right to left, but the computer sees only the first 16 hexadecimal digits, and these are all 0.

Fractions in Binary Notation

You have seen that, in a finite number of steps, it is possible to convert a decimal integer to a binary integer and conversely. For fractions, the situation is more complicated. In decimal notation, some fractions are represented by a finite number of symbols, for example, 1/2 = .5, 117/256 = .45703125; some are not, 1/3 = .333 . . . . Those fractions that can be represented with a finite number of symbols in decimal notation are written as:

$$.a_1\, a_2\, a_3 \ldots a_n, \text{ which means } \frac{a_1}{10} + \frac{a_2}{10^2} + \frac{a_3}{10^3} + \ldots + \frac{a_n}{10^n}$$

The representation of fractions in binary notation parallels that for decimal notation. In binary notation, the fraction $(1/2)_{dec} = .1_{bin}$, the fraction $(1/4)_{dec} = .01_{bin}$, $(3/4)_{dec} = .11_{bin}$, and so on. Those binary fractions that can be written with a finite number of symbols will appear as $.a_1a_2a_3 \ldots a_n$, where each a_i is either 0 or 1. Think of this in a form paralleling the decimal notation used above:

$$.a_1a_2a_3 \ldots a_n = \frac{a_1}{2} + \frac{a_2}{2^2} + \frac{a_3}{2^3} + \ldots + \frac{a_n}{2^n}$$

Because each term on the right-hand side can be written in decimal notation with a finite number of places, for example, $1/2 = .5$, $1/2^3 = .125$, $1/2^8 = .00390625$, a binary fraction with a finite number of places will always convert to a decimal fraction with a finite number of places. Furthermore, this conversion is unique.

Going from a decimal fraction with a finite number of places to its binary representation may require an infinite number of places. For example:

$$\frac{1}{10_{dec}} = .1_{dec}$$

whereas, in binary,

$$\begin{aligned} \frac{1}{10_{dec}} &= \frac{0}{2^1} + \frac{0}{2^2} + \frac{0}{2^3} + \frac{1}{2^4} + \frac{1}{2^5} + \frac{0}{2^6} + \frac{0}{2^7} + \frac{1}{2^8} + \frac{1}{2^9} + \ldots \\ &= .00011001100110011 \ldots_{bin} \end{aligned}$$

It is this last conversion that may cause difficulty in a specific numerical problem. When a number like $.1_{dec}$ (which we think of as a decimal) is entered into the computer, it is represented in binary form. However, since there are only a finite number of places available within the double word for storing the bits and an infinite number are needed, the correspondence between the binary and the decimal representations is not exact. Occasionally, this will produce a wrong answer, particularly when INT(X) is used. The following situation is illustrative.

```
10 REM: THIS PROGRAM REQUESTS THAT YOU INPUT, IN
20 REM: TERMS OF DOLLARS AND CENTS, AN AMOUNT OF
30 REM: MONEY.  THE PROGRAM THEN PRINTS OUT, IN TWO
40 REM: WAYS, FIRST AVOIDING THE USE OF THE INT(X)
50 REM: FUNCTION, AND THEN USING IT, THE NUMBER OF CENTS,
60 REM: EXCLUDING THE DOLLAR AMOUNT, THAT YOU HAD
70 REM: ORIGINALLY ENTERED.
80 REM: ITS SIGNIFICANCE LIES IN THE UNEXPECTED ERROR THAT MAY OCCUR
90 REM: WHEN THE INT(X) FUNCTION IS USED.
100 PRINT
110 PRINT "INPUT THE AMOUNT OF MONEY"; \ INPUT X
120 REM: THE NUMBER OF DOLLARS IS DETERMINED.
130 Y=INT(X)
140 REM: IN THE NEXT TWO LINE THE NUMBER OF CENTS IS DETERMINED.
150 W=100*X
160 Z=W-100*Y
170 REM: WE WOULD NORMALLY EXPECT THAT Z IS AN INTEGER.
180 REM: AS WE SHALL SEE, IT MAY NOT BE.
190 PRINT
200 PRINT "THE NUMBER OF CENTS AS DETERMINED:"
210 PRINT "WITHOUT THE INTEGER VALUE FUNCTION IS ="  Z
220 PRINT "WITH THE INTEGER VALUE FUNCTION IS ="  INT(Z)
```

```
INPUT THE AMOUNT OF MONEY   ?65.35

THE NUMBER OF CENTS AS DETERMINED:
WITHOUT THE INTEGER VALUE FUNCTION IS = 35
WITH THE INTEGER VALUE FUNCTION IS = 35



INPUT THE AMOUNT OF MONEY   ?65.36

THE NUMBER OF CENTS AS DETERMINED:
WITHOUT THE INTEGER VALUE FUNCTION IS = 36.0000
WITH THE INTEGER VALUE FUNCTION IS = 35
```

```
INPUT THE AMOUNT OF MONEY    ?65.37

THE NUMBER OF CENTS AS DETERMINED:
WITHOUT THE INTEGER VALUE FUNCTION IS = 37
WITH THE INTEGER VALUE FUNCTION IS = 37


INPUT THE AMOUNT OF MONEY    ?65.38

THE NUMBER OF CENTS AS DETERMINED:
WITHOUT THE INTEGER VALUE FUNCTION IS = 38.0000
WITH THE INTEGER VALUE FUNCTION IS = 37


INPUT THE AMOUNT OF MONEY    ?.01

THE NUMBER OF CENTS AS DETERMINED:
WITHOUT THE INTEGER VALUE FUNCTION IS = 1
WITH THE INTEGER VALUE FUNCTION IS = 1


INPUT THE AMOUNT OF MONEY    ?.02

THE NUMBER OF CENTS AS DETERMINED:
WITHOUT THE INTEGER VALUE FUNCTION IS = 2
WITH THE INTEGER VALUE FUNCTION IS = 2


INPUT THE AMOUNT OF MONEY    ?.03

THE NUMBER OF CENTS AS DETERMINED:
WITHOUT THE INTEGER VALUE FUNCTION IS = 3.00000
WITH THE INTEGER VALUE FUNCTION IS = 2
```

When the program was run the first, third, fifth, and sixth times, the answers agreed, as we would expect. They disagreed on the other runs, however. In those three cases, notice that the answers contain zeros trailing the decimal point. This is a warning that the value of Z being printed is *not* an integer. Actually, the value of Z as determined at line 160 is very close to, but just ever so slightly less than, the correct integer value.

Summary

The detailed exposition on the internal representation of integers and floating-point numbers given in this chapter will provide background for material yet to be presented, particularly as it pertains to the creation and handling of files. To a lesser extent, the information should give you a deeper understanding of the operation of the BASIC instruction CHANGE, which we shall discuss in the next chapter. While it may have come as an unpleasant shock, you are now aware that computers can make mistakes, that is, they can give answers that differ from the expected and correct one. This is particularly true for the function INT(X) when the argument X is close to an integer.

Exercises

13.1 Using the representation $392 = 3{\cdot}10{\cdot}10 + 9{\cdot}10 + 2$, convert 392_{dec} to binary. First multiply the binary equivalents of 10·10, then multiply this result by the binary equivalent of 3. Next, multiply the binary equivalents of 9 and 10. Then, add these two results and the binary equivalent of 2.

13.2 The largest integer that can be represented using only two decimal digits is 9^9; the largest integer that can be represented using two hexadecimal digits is F^F. What is the decimal equivalent of F^F?

13.3 Give the machine representation of the following integers:
(a) 1 and −1
(b) 61 and −61
(c) 742961
(d) −43596

13.4 Given that $\underline{41}100000\ 00000000_x$ is the machine representation for the floating-point number +1, what is the machine representation for the floating-point number −1?

13.5 What is the machine representation for the floating-point numbers −256, −273?

13.6 What is the decimal equivalent of $40100000\ 00000000_x$?

13.7 What is the decimal equivalent of $40110000\ 00000000_x$?

13.8 Show that BFF00000 0000000 = − 1/16, COF00000 00000000 = $-(1/16)^2$ and BFEF0000 00000000 = $-(1/16) - (1/16)^2$.

14 The Change Instruction

The need for codes and ciphers to safeguard information permeates both business and government. In business, company data must be kept from competitors to ensure the viability of the firm. To safeguard national interests, the ability to exchange confidential information without having it intercepted and disseminated to malevolent parties is of utmost importance. Notwithstanding the classic remark "Gentlemen do not read other people's mail," the gentility of others must be continually questioned.

We can imagine a scheme whereby each graphic character—a letter of the alphabet, a punctuation mark, or a digit—corresponds to an integer. Two such associations have been noted, ASCII and EBCDIC; the details of the correspondence were given in Tables 13-4 and 13-5. In this chapter, we shall use the computer to explore these correspondences more fully.

Some computers use ASCII, others use EBCDIC. We shall present the programs in the examples twice, once for each of the two standards.

The CHANGE Statement

The fundamental BASIC instruction CHANGE is used in the following fashion. Start with an arbitrary string of symbols: A$="THIS IS AN EXAMPLE OF A STRING." By using the instruction B=LEN(A$), we can have the computer determine its length. Dimension a list X(I) with a least B subscripts. Under the statement:

```
CHANGE A$ TO X
```

the machine will look up the ASCII or EBCDIC equivalent of T and assign that number to X(1), the equivalent of H and assign that number to X(2), . . . , the equivalent of the period and assign that number to X(31). Note that in the CHANGE statement, X appears without a subscript.

Change in ASCII

The program that follows makes the above change for the ASCII code.

```
10 DIM X(100)
20 A$="THIS IS AN EXAMPLE OF A STRING."
30 PRINT A$
40 PRINT
50 B=LEN(A$)
60 PRINT "LENGTH OF STRING ="B
70 PRINT
80 CHANGE A$ TO X
90 FOR I=1 TO B
100 C$=SST(A$,I,1)
110 PRINT C$"="X(I)
120 NEXT I
130 PRINT \ PRINT
140 CHANGE X TO D$
150 PRINT D$
```

```
THIS IS AN EXAMPLE OF A STRING.

LENGTH OF STRING =   31

T=   84
H=   72
I=   73
S=   83
 =   32
I=   73
S=   83
 =   32
A=   65
N=   78
 =   32
E=   69
X=   88
A=   65
M=   77
P=   80
L=   76
E=   69
 =   32
O=   79
F=   70
 =   32
A=   65
 =   32
S=   83
T=   84
R=   82
I=   73
N=   78
G=   71
.=   46


THIS IS AN EXAMPLE OF A STRING.
```

In line 80, the ASCII equivalent of each character is assigned to successive elements of the subscripted list X(I). Unknown to us, the length of the string is assigned to the variable X(0). The extract substring command[1] is used in line 100. For the specific machine on which this program was run, the extract verb takes the form SST. Of the three arguments of SST(A$,I,1), the first is for the name of the string from which the extraction is to be made, the second for the position in the string from which the first character of

[1]Although we use the verb "extract," the machine actually only copies the indicated substring, leaving the original string untouched.

the substring is obtained and the third is for the number of characters to be extracted. The appropriate character from A$ is extracted, assigned to C$, and is used to display the ASCII correspondence.

CHANGE in EBCDIC

The modification needed to run the same program on an EBCDIC machine consists of changing line 100 to the form required by the other computer, which is:

```
100 C$=A$(:I,1)
```

The program follows.

```
10 DIM X(100)
20 A$="THIS IS AN EXAMPLE OF A STRING."
30 PRINT A$
40 PRINT
50 B=LEN(A$)
60 PRINT "LENGTH OF STRING ="B
70 PRINT
80 CHANGE A$ TO X
90 FOR I=1 TO B
100 C$=A$(:I,1)
110 PRINT C$"="X(I)
120 NEXT I
130 PRINT \ PRINT
140 CHANGE X TO D$
150 PRINT D$
```

```
THIS IS AN EXAMPLE OF A STRING.

LENGTH OF STRING = 31

T= 227
H= 200
I= 201
S= 226
 = 64
I= 201
S= 226
 = 64
A= 193
N= 213
 = 64
E= 197
X= 231
A= 193
M= 212
P= 215
L= 211
E= 197
 = 64
O= 214
F= 198
 = 64
A= 193
 = 64
S= 226
T= 227
R= 217
I= 201
N= 213
G= 199
.= 75

THIS IS AN EXAMPLE OF A STRING.
```

From EBCDIC to Characters

In the preceding examples, we started with a string and found the associated ASCII or EBCDIC values. At the end of the program, line 140, the numeric list X(I) was changed to a new string D$ that was seen to be identical to the original.

If we attempt to start with a list of numerical values, each an ASCII or EBCDIC equivalent of a graphic symbol or command or one that is perhaps as yet unassigned, should there be any difficulty in determining the corresponding symbol or control character? Some care is required.

The subscripted list cannot be too long. On many computers, the length of a string is limited to 72 characters, the length of a print line.[2] Thus, if the original list is too long, it will have to be subdivided into lists whose lengths are within acceptable limits. In the following program, a subscripted list, 256 elements long, is defined by the relationship

$$X(I) = I - 1$$

This assigns to each variable of the list a legitimate EBCDIC value. Since the list is too long to be converted at one time, it is divided into four sublists, each 64 elements long. Each of the sublists, in turn, is changed. The EBCDIC value and the corresponding symbol, control character, and so on, are then displayed. In the actual printout, the result of applying this procedure to the first 64 elements of the original list X(I) is omitted because there is no graphic symbol in that group. If you wish to experiment with the program, delete line 120. Among the effects you will notice is that a bell rings[3] (EBCDIC value = 7).

```
10 DIM X(256),Y(64)
20 FOR I=1 TO 256
30 X(I)=I-1
40 NEXT I
50 FOR K=0 TO 3
60 FOR I=1 TO 64
70 Y(I)=X(I+K*64)
80 NEXT I
90 CHANGE Y TO A$
100 FOR I= 1 TO 64
110 C$=A$(:I,1)
120 IF Y(I)<64 THEN 140
130 PRINT Y(I)"="C$,
140 NEXT I
150 NEXT K
```

```
64=          65=          66=#         67=          68=#
69=#         70=          71=          72=#         73=#
74=`         75=.         76=<         77=(         78=+
79=|         80=&         81=          82=          83=#
84=          85=#         86=#         87=#         88=#
89=#         90=!         91=$         92=*         93=)
94=;         95=~         96=-         97=/         98=#
99=#         100=#        101=#        102=#        103=#
104=#        105=#        106=^        107=,        108=%
109=_        110=>        111=?        112=#        113=#
114=#        115=#        116=#        117=#        118=#
119=#        120=#        121=#        122=:        123=#
```

[2]There are computers that accept strings thousands of characters in length. On these, the descriptions that follow would apply only in principle. On some computers a switch in BASIC controls string length. The default value, the length automatically assigned by the interpreter when we log on, is 72; it can be changed to a maximum of 132 characters. On those terminals that have 132 print positions, the longer string length may be desirable. On one computer, the switch, activated outside of the program is: SET $ = number, where the number can be any integer not exceeding 132. You should expect some variation on other computers.

[3]Every terminal should have a bell or some other device for making an audible sound. The bell is activated when the proper signal is received from the computer. In both ASCII and EBCDIC, the decimal value of that signal is 7. See Tables 13-4 and 13-5.

```
124=@      125='      126==      127="      128=#
129=a      130=b      131=c      132=d      133=e
134=f      135=g      136=h      137=i      138=#
139=#      140=#      141=#      142=#      143=#
144=#      145=j      146=k      147=l      148=m
149=n      150=o      151=p      152=q      153=r
154=#      155=#      156=#      157=#      158=#
159=#      160=#      161=#      162=s      163=t
164=u      165=v      166=w      167=x      168=y
169=z      170=#      171=#      172=#      173=#
174=#      175=|      176=       177=\      178={
179=}      180=[      181=]      182=       183=#
184=#      185=#      186=#      187=#      188=[
189=]      190=       191=~      192=       193=A
194=B      195=C      196=D      197=E      198=F
199=G      200=H      201=I      202=#      203=#
204=#      205=#      206=#      207=#      208=#
209=J      210=K      211=L      212=M      213=N
214=O      215=P      216=Q      217=R      218=#
219=#      220=#      221=#      222=#      213=#
224=-      225=#      226=S      227=T      228=U
229=V      230=W      231=X      232=Y      233=Z
234=#      235=#      236=#      237=#      238=#
239=#      240=0      241=1      242=2      243=3
244=4      245=5      246=6      247=7      248=8
249=9      250=#      251=#      252=#      253=#
254=#      255=
```

The output shown here may not be the same as you will see if you run the program. There are three reasons for the differences. First, since many values are not assigned and, therefore are not standard, different computers may send different signals to your terminal, eliciting different responses. For example, a blank or # may be replaced by another character. Second, when this program was run on the same computer but from two different terminals, other differences appeared. For example, the signal FF (form feed), decimal value 176 was ignored by one but not the other. Finally, on those terminals that have interchangeable type, differences on ostensibly identical balls or wheels may be seen.

From ASCII to Characters

On an ASCII machine, there is one additional requirement. First, remember that the subscripts of the list X(I) go only from 1 to 128. Again, the list is broken into two lists, each 64 elements long. Before the CHANGE instruction will function, the machine needs to know the exact length of the X(I) list. Equivalently, what is the length of the string to be created? In this illustration, the length is 64; it is stored in the Y(0) element of the list. (On ASCII machines, when any list Z is dimensioned, the computer automatically assigns one extra element, Z(0).) The program follows:

```
10 DIM X(128),Y(64)
20 FOR I=1 TO 128
30 X(I)=I-1
40 NEXT I
50 FOR K=0 TO 1
60 FOR I=1 TO 64
70 Y(I)=X(I+K*64)
80 NEXT I
85 Y(0)=64
90 CHANGE Y TO A$
100 FOR I=1 TO 64
110 C$=SST(A$,I,1)
120 IF Y(I)<32 THEN 140
130 PRINT Y(I)" = "C$,
140 NEXT I
150 NEXT K
```

```
 32 =       33 = !      34 = "      35 = #      36 = $
 37 = %     38 = &      39 = '      40 = (      41 = )
 42 = *     43 = +      44 = ,      45 = -      46 = .
 47 = /     48 = 0      49 = 1      50 = 2      51 = 3
 52 = 4     53 = 5      54 = 6      55 = 7      56 = 8
 57 = 9     58 = :      59 = ;      60 = <      61 = =
 62 = >     63 = ?      64 = @      65 = A      66 = B
 67 = C     68 = D      69 = E      70 = F      71 = G
 72 = H     73 = I      74 = J      75 = K      76 = L
 77 = M     78 = N      79 = O      80 = P      81 = Q
 82 = R     83 = S      84 = T      85 = U      86 = V
 87 = W     88 = X      89 = Y      90 = Z      91 = [
 92 = \     93 = ]      94 = ^      95 = ←      96 = `
 97 = a     98 = b      99 = c     100 = d     101 = e
102 = f    103 = g     104 = h     105 = i     106 = j
107 = k    108 = l     109 = m     110 = n     111 = o
112 = p    113 = q     114 = r     115 = s     116 = t
117 = u    118 = v     119 = w     120 = x     121 = y
122 = z    123 = {     124 = |     125 = }     126 = ~
127 =
```

The changes from the first program to the second are the obvious ones: 256 was changed to 128 and line 50 was changed from:

FOR K=0 TO 3

to

FOR K=0 TO 1.

In line 120, 64 was changed to 32 since there is no printable character in ASCII less than 33. The major modification is the insertion of line 85, where the length of the list to be converted is stored in Y(0).

An Illustration: The Caesar Cipher

It is recorded that Julius Caesar wrote in cipher to his commanders in the field. By modern standards the cipher was simple: Each letter in the clear message was replaced by a letter further along in the alphabet. If the shift is 2, A is replaced by C, M by O, X by Z. The letters Y and Z wrap around to the beginning of the alphabet so that the Y is replaced by A and Z by B.

```
Replace     A B C D E F G H I J K L M N O P Q R S T U V W X Y Z
            ↓ ↓                                             ↓ ↓
by          C D E F G H I J K L M N O P Q R S T U V W X Y Z A B
```

Using the CHANGE instruction, it is relatively easy to write a program that will encipher and decipher any message written using Caesar's method.

```
10 DIM X(50),Y(50),Z(50),U(50)
20 ***** ALL VARIABLES ARE INITIALIZED TO ZERO OR BLANK
30 A$="",B$=""
40 FOR I=1 TO 50
50 X(I)=0,Y(I)=0,Z(I)=0,U(I)=0
60 NEXT I
70 INPUT =$
80 PRINT "WHAT IS YOUR CLEAR MESSAGE"
90 INPUT A$
100 ***** THE STRING IS CHANGED TO A VECTOR
110 CHANGE A$ TO X
120 L=LEN(A$)
130 ***** SINCE THE EBCDIC NUMBERS ASSOCIATED WITH THE ALPHABET
```

```
140 ***** ARE NOT CONSECUTIVE, WE WANT TO REMOVE THE GAPS
150 FOR I=1 TO L
160 IF (X(I)-209)*(217-X(I))>=0 THEN 510
170 IF (X(I)-226)*(233-X(I))>=0 THEN 530
180 Y(I)=X(I)
190 NEXT I
200 ***** THE AMOUNT OF SHIFT = K
210 PRINT "WHAT IS THE SHIFT"; & INPUT K
220 ***** FIRST, IF A CHARACTER IS NOT A LETTER, WE WANT IT TO REMAIN
230 ***** AS IT IS. SECONDLY, IF IT IS A LETTER, WE WANT
240 ***** TO SHIFT IT K PLACES TO THE RIGHT IN THE ALPHABET.
250 ***** FINALLY, IF WE HAVE SHIFTED PAST 'Z', WE WANT TO WRAP
260 ***** AROUND TO THE BEGINNING OF THE ALPHABET
270 FOR I=1 TO L
280 IF (Y(I)-193)*(218-Y(I))<0 THEN 550
290 Z(I)=Y(I)+K
300 IF Z(I)>218 THEN 570
310 NEXT I
320 ***** EVERY LETTER HAS NOW BEEN SHIFTED. HOWEVER, WE HAVE TO GET
330 ***** BACK TO THE FORM THAT THE COMPUTER RECOGNIZES, I.E. WE HAVE
340 ***** TO REINTRODUCE THE GAPS SO THAT THE EBCDIC
350 ***** CORRESPONDENCE WILL BE AVAILABLE
360 FOR I=1 TO L
370 IF(Z(I)-202)*(210-Z(I))>=0 THEN 590
380 IF (Z(I)-211)*(218-Z(I))>=0 THEN 610
390 U(I)=Z(I)
400 NEXT I
410 ***** THE VECTOR U NOW CONTAINS THE EBCDIC VALUES THAT WE WANT
420 ***** TO TRANSLATE BACK INTO ALPHABETIC
430 CHANGE U TO B$
440 ***** THE FINAL OUTPUT
450 PRINT"YOUR CLEAR MESSAGE IS"
460 PRINT A$
470 PRINT "YOUR ENCIPHERED MESSAGE IS"
480 PRINT B$
490 INPUT =1
500 STOP
510 Y(I)=X(I)-7
520 GOTO 190
530 Y(I)=X(I)-15
540 GOTO 190
550 Z(I)=Y(I)
560 GOTO 300
570 Z(I)=Z(I)-26
580 GOTO 300
590 U(I)=Z(I)+7
600 GOTO 400
610 U(I)=Z(I)+15
620 GOTO 400
```

In the program, we assume messages of no more than 50 characters so that the number of components of the various vectors to be used is limited to 50. A$ is used for the input message and B$ for the output. All vectors and strings are initialized to zero or blank in lines 30–60.

As you can see from the run on pages 264–65 or from Table 13–5, the EBCDIC numbers corresponding to the letters A through Z are not consecutive, there are two gaps. We can remove the gaps by mapping the EBCDIC values of the alphabet into 26 consecutive integers, beginning at 193, the EBCDIC value for A.

EBCDIC value	193 ... 201			209 ... 217			226 ... 233		
	↕		↕	↕		↕	↕		↕
Letter	A	...	I	J	...	R	S	...	Z
	↕		↕	↕		↕	↕		↕
Corresponding value	193	...	201	202	...	210	211	...	218

The X vector, which contains the EBCDIC values of the input message, will then be mapped into the Y vector, which will contain the newly constructed equivalents of the alphabet. This was accomplished in lines 150–190 and 510–540. This mapping does not modify the EBCDIC value for any punctuation since the values for punctuation lie outside the interval for the modified numbers.

The next section of the program applies the shift K to the letters; punctuation is not to be affected. The Y vector is mapped into a Z vector. If any Y(I) lies outside the interval 193–218, it is not a letter; these values are assigned to the corresponding variables Z(I), lines 280 and 550. For values of Y(I) that lie within the interval 193–218, the corresponding value of Z(I) is increased by K. If any Z(I) > 218, it must be reduced by 26; this is done in lines 300 and 570.

The numbers that are the components of the vector Z are not EBCDIC values for the alphabet; to get back to EBCDIC values, the inverse of the transformation described above (from X to Y) is used. This is done in lines 360–400, 590, and 610. Thus, the Z vector is mapped into the U vector. The values of the U vector are EBCDIC values.

In line 430 the U vector is changed to the string B$ and the clear and ciphered messages are printed. A typical run follows:

```
WHAT IS YOUR CLEAR MESSAGE
?ET TU, BRUTUS?
WHAT IS THE SHIFT    ?18
YOUR CLEAR MESSAGE IS
ET TU, BRUTUS?
YOUR ENCIPHERED MESSAGE IS
WL LM, TJMLMK?
```

Deciphering a Caesar Cipher

Because a shift of 26 does not alter a message, the same program may be used to decipher a message. If a message is enciphered using a shift of 18, the resulting message, when entered as an original and then enciphered using a shift of 8 (8 + 18 = 26), will produce a doubly enciphered message identical to the original. The following runs illustrate this as well as the fact that a shift of 0 or 26 returns the original message.

```
WHAT IS YOUR CLEAR MESSAGE
?WL LM, TJMLMK?
WHAT IS THE SHIFT    ?8
YOUR CLEAR MESSAGE IS
WL LM, TJMLMK?
YOUR ENCIPHERED MESSAGE IS
ET TU, BRUTUS?
```

```
WHAT IS YOUR CLEAR MESSAGE
?ET TU, BRUTUS?
WHAT IS THE SHIFT    ?0
YOUR CLEAR MESSAGE IS
ET TU, BRUTUS?
YOUR ENCIPHERED MESSAGE IS
ET TU, BRUTUS?
```

```
WHAT IS YOUR CLEAR MESSAGE
?ET TU, BRUTUS?
WHAT IS THE SHIFT    ?26
YOUR CLEAR MESSAGE IS
ET TU, BRUTUS?
YOUR ENCIPHERED MESSAGE IS
ET TU, BRUTUS?
```

Finally, the program, as written, does not take into account the possibility of a negative shift. This was tried with the following outcome.

```
WHAT IS YOUR CLEAR MESSAGE
?ET TU, BRUTUS?
WHAT IS THE SHIFT   ?-7
YOUR CLEAR MESSAGE IS
ET TU, BRUTUS?
YOUR ENCIPHERED MESSAGE IS
M MN, #KNMNL?
```

Enciphering and Deciphering on an ASCII Computer

The corresponding program for ASCII machines is simpler since in ASCII the 26 alphabetic characters occupy consecutive places, 65 through 90. The essential difference between the two programs is that the gaps that appear in the EBCDIC code do not have to be removed and then reinserted. The program for an ASCII computer follows.

```
10 DIM X(50),Y(50)
20 REM: ALL VARIABLES ARE INITIALIZED TO ZERO OR BLANK
30 A$="" \ B$=""
40 FOR I=1 TO 50
50 X(I)=0 \ Y(I)=0
60 NEXT I
70 PRINT "ENTER YOUR CLEAR MESSAGE"
80 INPUT A$
90 REM: THE STRING IS CHANGED TO A LIST (VECTOR)
100 CHANGE A$ TO X
110 L=X(0)
120 REM: THE AMOUNT OF THE SHIFT
130 PRINT" WHAT IS THE SHIFT"; \ INPUT K
140 REM: WE SHALL SHIFT ONLY ALPHABETIC CHARACTERS. IF, AS A RESULT OF THE
150 REM: SHIFT A VALUE IN EXCESS OF 90 IS OBTAINED, IT IS REDUCED BY 26.
160 FOR I=1 TO L
170 IF (X(I)-65)*(90-X(I))<0 THEN 290
180 Y(I)=X(I)+K
190 IF Y(I)<91 THEN 210
200 Y(I)=Y(I)-26
210 NEXT I
220 REM: THE VECTOR Y IS CHANGED TO THE STRING B$
230 Y(0)=L
240 CHANGE Y TO B$
250 PRINT "YOUR CLEAR MESSAGE IS"
260 PRINT A$
265 PRINT "YOUR ENCIPHERED MESSAGE IS"
270 PRINT B$
280 STOP
290 Y(I)=X(I)
300 GOTO 210
```

Random Number Ciphers

Once a set of symbols used in communicating, such as letters of an alphabet, numbers, or punctuation, is mapped into a set of integers, then all the power of mathematics can be brought to bear to transform lists of these integers into other lists. The random number generator is one such powerful tool that can be used to safeguard information. In the following example, only the letters of the alphabet are enciphered; to simplify the discussion, the integers and punctuation are left unaltered. The program is for an ASCII machine; the modification for an EBCDIC machine is left as an exercise. The program uses a random sequence that can be replicated as needed. To provide one level of enciphering security, the starting place in that random sequence is left to the encoder. A second option for the encoder is the range of random numbers to be chosen. In the list that follows, the first column is a list of random numbers, RND(0), that can be repeated, the second is INT(10*RND(0)) and the third is INT(75*RND(0)).

```
.445282        4      33
.353333        3      26
.112460        1      8
.494758        4      37
.956412        9      71
.285648        2      21
.106182        1      7
6.62574E-02    0      4
.441906        4      33
5.51176E-02    0      4
.353555        3      26
.625270        6      46
.569627        5      42
.790333        7      59
.615352        6      46
.579120        5      43
.936548        9      70
.407208        4      30
1.43185E-02    0      1
.421038        4      31
.397360        3      29
.594821        5      44
.992685        9      74
.602720        6      45
.682154        6      51
.668440        6      50
.871255        8      65
.211575        2      15
.428152        4      32
.664736        6      49
.135047        1      10
.827656        8      62
.750516        7      56
5.41902E-02    0      4
.570499        5      42
.935282        9      70
.477204        4      35
.445679        4      33
.379244        3      28
.264349        2      19
.172899        1      12
.658255        6      49
.393437        3      29
.436322        4      32
7.70005E-02    0      5
.535109        5      40
.517650        5      38
.289920        2      21
8.06676E-02    0      6
.874724        8      65
```

Using the table with the range of 0 to 9 and starting at the 5th entry, 9, the message WELCOME TO BASIC would be enciphered as follows.

W + 9 = F		B + 7 = I
E + 2 = G		A + 6 = G
L + 1 = M	T + 6 = Z	S + 5 = X
C + 0 = C	O + 5 = T	I + 9 = R
O + 4 = S		C + 4 = G
M + 0 = M		
E + 3 = H		

The enciphered message is of no value unless we also have the following information: (1) the sequence of random numbers, (2) the starting point for enciphering in that sequence, and (3) the range of integers used in the scheme. Without this information, the cipher is practically unbreakable. The following enciphering and deciphering program, written for ASCII machine, uses these ideas.

```
10 DIM X(100),Y(100)
20 PRINT"ENTER MESSAGE" \ INPUT A$
30 CHANGE A$ TO X
40 L=LEN(A$)
50 PRINT "STARTING PLACE FOR RANDOM NUMBERS" \ INPUT A
60 FOR I=1 TO A-1
70 J=RND(0)
80 NEXT I
90 PRINT"RANGE OF RANDOM NUMBERS" \ INPUT R
100 PRINT "ENCIPHER OR DECIPHER" \ INPUT B$
110 IF B$="ENCIPHER" THEN 140
120 IF B$="DECIPHER" THEN 250
130 GOTO 100
140 REM:ENCIPHERING SECTION
150 FOR I=1 TO L
160 REM: TEST FOR PUNCTUATION, NUMBERS, ETC.
170 IF (X(I)-65)*(90-X(I))<0 THEN 220
180 Y(I)=X(I)+INT(R*RND(0))
190 IF Y(I)<91 THEN 230
200 Y(I)=Y(I)-26
210 GOTO 190
220 Y(I)=X(I)
230 NEXT I
240 GOTO 350
250 REM: DECIPHERING SECTION
260 FOR I=1 TO L
270 REM: TEST FOR PUNCTUATION, ETC.
280 IF (X(I)-65)*(90-X(I))<0 THEN 330
290 Y(I)=X(I)-INT(R*RND(0))
300 IF Y(I)>64 THEN 340
310 Y(I)=Y(I)+26
320 GOTO 300
330 Y(I)=X(I)
340 NEXT I
350 Y(0)=L
360 CHANGE Y TO C$
370 PRINT A$
380 PRINT C$
```

```
ENTER MESSAGE
?"WELCOME TO BASIC"
STARTING PLACE FOR RANDOM NUMBERS
?1234
RANGE OF RANDOM NUMBERS
?5678
ENCIPHER OR DECIPHER
?ENCIPHER
WELCOME TO BASIC
VOHSYBN KM IVZLW


ENTER MESSAGE
?VOHSYBN KM IVZLW
STARTING PLACE FOR RANDOM NUMBERS
?1234
RANGE OF RANDOM NUMBERS
?5678
ENCIPHER OR DECIPHER
?DECIPHER
VOHSYBN KM IVZLW
WELCOME TO BASIC


ENTER MESSAGE
?"12345!@#$%"
STARTING PLACE FOR RANDOM NUMBERS
?27
RANGE OF RANDOM NUMBERS
?123456
```

```
ENCIPHER OR DECIPHER
?ENCIPHER
12345!@#$%
12345!@#$%


ENTER MESSAGE
?"12345!@#$%"
STARTING PLACE FOR RANDOM NUMBERS
?27
RANGE OF RANDOM NUMBERS
?123456
ENCIPHER OR DECIPHER
?DECIPHER
12345!@#$%
12345!@#$%
```

The section in lines 60–80, discards the first A-1 random numbers, making the Ath number the first available for the enciphering process. The two sections, one for enciphering, the other for deciphering, while similar, are written separately for clarity. Since the value chosen for R may be large, Y(1) may be large (line 180) and may have to be reduced repeatedly by 26 to bring it within the specified limits, 65 through 90; this is done in lines 190–210. Similar shifting in the deciphering section is done in lines 300–320. Once the components of Y are known, the corresponding string is found, line 350–360.

The CHR$(N) and ASC("STRING") Statements

Although, using the CHANGE command, a string of characters can be generated from a list of numbers (and vice versa) provided these are the ASCII or EBCDIC equivalents of characters, some systems provide separate functional instructions for converting a single number and a single character. Thus, you may find that a function such as CHR$(N) will return a character for appropriate values of N; for example, if N=65, CHR$(65)=A. The inverse function may also exist; there may be a function ASC(A$) that will return the ASCII number for the first character in A$. For example, ASC(XYZ)=88.

How a Computer Alphabetizes

We now have sufficient information to answer how a computer "alphabetizes" a list of symbols such as numbers, letters, and punctuation marks. It uses its ASCII or EBCDIC code and sorts according to these values. The two programs that follow show that "1" precedes "A" on an ASCII machine and "A" precedes "1" on an EBCDIC machine, consistent with the ordering of the symbols in the two codes.

EBCDIC

```
10 A$="1"
20 B$="A"
30 IF A$<B$ THEN 60
40 PRINT B$"<"A$
50 STOP
60 PRINT A$"<"B$


A<1
```

ASCII

```
10 A$="1"
20 B$="A"
30 IF A$<B$ THEN 60
40 PRINT B$"<"A$
50 STOP
60 PRINT A$"<"B$


1<A
```

Summary

The proliferation of electronic communications has been accompanied by serious problems of security. Medical records, legitimate financial transactions, and credit ratings are but a few areas in which data should not be readily available. One way suggested to discourage eavesdropping and forgery is to encipher such information so that only those knowing the key have access to it. Older enciphering methods, those derived from substitutions and transpositions, have proved to be somewhat insecure; methods based on random numbers offer more security. There is, however, a serious drawback to random number ciphers: Both sender and receiver must know the key.

The burden placed on the postal system, doing business in the same old way, handling written material in sealed envelopes, is ever increasing, with a concomitant slowdown in delivery. One proposed solution to this problem is electronic mail, an elaborate version of a service offered by Western Union. A letter is transcribed into electronic signals, similar to what happens when you type at your terminal keyboard, and the signals are sent to the computer. The signals are then transmitted to the addressee, where a device deciphers them into comprehensible language; again, a process similar to that which takes place when your computer sends a message to you.

The glaringly undesirable feature is the loss of privacy. Ciphers are an obvious way to overcome this. The difficulty mentioned above, however, that both sender and receiver must know the key, as well as the enormous number of combinations of senders and receivers, present seemingly insurmountable obstacles. In recent years, however, alternative methods, known as public-key cryptograms[4], for enciphering messages have been proposed.

All ciphering schemes can be reduced to mapping the communication symbols—letters, digits, punctuation marks—onto a set of numbers and then using mathematical techniques to render this set unintelligible to all except those who know the details of the technique. It is hoped that this latter group would consist only of the addressee. Two such computer mappings were described, one called ASCII, the other EBCDIC. Other mapping schemes have been implemented. All, however, share the common feature of the CHANGE instruction; each is a mapping from the communication symbols into a set of numbers.

Exercises

14.1 Neither of the programs on pages 266–67 and on page 269 takes into account a negative shift, for example, K = −5. Make the necessary changes to the program so that negative values for the shift will still change alphabetic characters into alphabetic characters.

14.2 Consider the following enciphering scheme. The letters in the alphabet A through Z are assigned the numbers 1 through 26 consecutively. Each number is then doubled. If a number X is less than 27, it remains; if a number X is greater than 27, it is replaced by the number X − 27. Thus, 22 would remain 22, 42 would become 42 − 27 = 15.

Hint: The correspondence between letters is given by

```
A B C D E F G H I J K L M N O P Q R S T U V W X Y Z
↓ ↓                                             ↓
B D F H J L N P R T V X Z A C E G I K M O Q S U W Y
```

Write a program that uses this scheme to encipher an arbitrary message.

14.3 Write a program that will decipher a message written in the cipher described in Exercise 14.2.

---

[4]A readable account of two methods may be found in: Martin E. Hellman, "The Mathematics of Public-Key Cryptography," *Scientific American*, Vol. 241, No. 2, Aug. 1979, pp. 146–157.

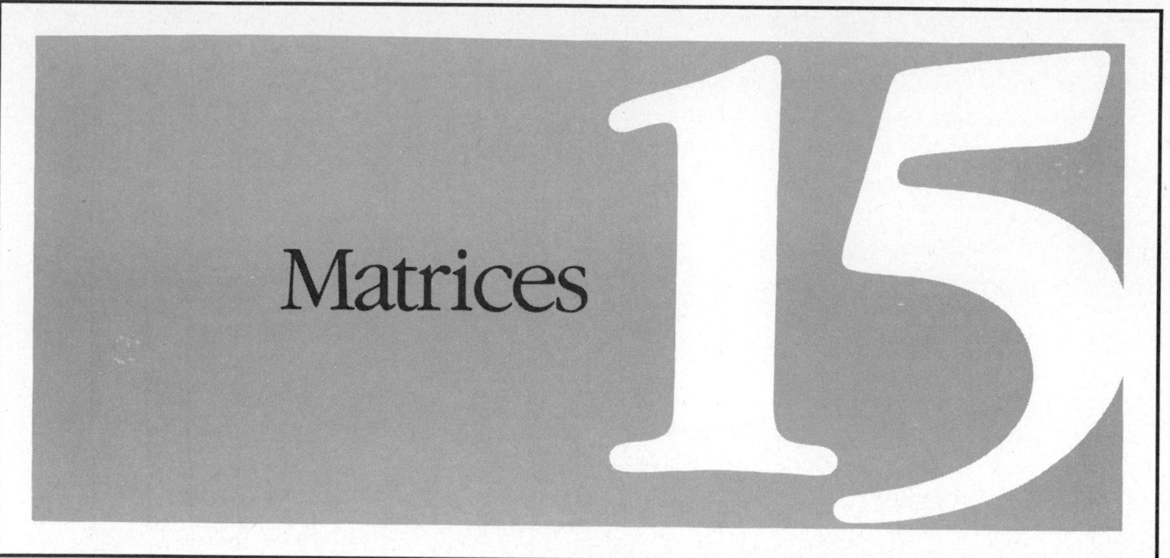

Matrices

The significance of mathematics as an intellectual activity has been recognized for centuries. Until recently, however, its applicability had been limited primarily to the physical sciences, gambling, and surveying. Surveying, and the geometry it gave rise to, can be traced back to the Egyptians. The origins of probability lie in the analysis of games. The growth of the physical sciences rests heavily on the calculus. About fifty years ago, a branch of mathematics called linear algebra came to be recognized as applicable to a wide variety of problems. Linear algebra became an important tool in economic modeling, sociology, forestry, genetics, personnel assignment, and job scheduling.

The theoretical basis of linear algebra lies in the subject matter known as "linear vector spaces." Although it would be too much of a digression to discuss this adequately here, at the base of the manipulative aspects of linear algebra are vectors and matrices, which are simply different names for concepts you are already familiar with, namely, lists and arrays.

The rules for manipulating matrices are easily enough understood and have been incorporated into BASIC. This chapter has two purposes: (1) to expound the rules of matrix algebra and the BASIC instructions that carry out these operations and (2) to illustrate the use of matrices in several disciplines.

There are BASIC instructions that both input and read values into matrices; similarly, there is the companion PRINT statement. Matrices can be added, subtracted, and multiplied. Matrix addition is commutative, that is, $A + B = B + A$; multiplication need not be, that is, in general: $AB \neq BA$. In ordinary arithmetic, the inverse of addition is subtraction; subtraction of matrices is handled in BASIC. The inverse of multiplication in ordinary arithmetic is division; remember, the one exceptional case is that you cannot divide by zero. The inverse of a matrix is also handled in BASIC; you will have to be careful when working with the corresponding exceptional case. There are several useful ancillary BASIC statements, which will be presented at the appropriate places in the text.

Matrices and Arrays, Vectors and Lists

Arrays and lists were discussed and illustrated with several examples. The spectrum of problems to which they apply, however, is so great that a set of special instructions devoted to them is implemented in BASIC. First, there is a change of terminology. An array will be called a matrix and a list a vector. Just as a list is an $n \times 1$ or $1 \times n$ array, a vector is an $n \times 1$ or $1 \times n$ matrix. The matrix $A(3,6)$ has three rows and six columns and there is no ambiguity. If we write the vector B(7), it is not clear whether this means a vector of one row and seven columns that we would think of as $(b_1, b_2, b_3, b_4, b_5, b_6, b_7)$ or a vector of seven rows and one column that we would think of as:

$$\begin{pmatrix} b_1 \\ b_2 \\ b_3 \\ b_4 \\ b_5 \\ b_6 \\ b_7 \end{pmatrix}$$

In each specific problem, it is your responsibility to keep this distinction straight in your mind and in your instructions to the computer. Unfortunately, to conserve paper, the computer will print a row vector and a column vector as if both were a row vector, that is: $(b_1, b_2, \ldots, b_7)$.

The MAT READ Statement

The first two programs below illustrate the MAT READ statement. In the first one, 18 numbers are read into an array that is then printed; in the second, the loop instructions, lines 20, 30, 50, and 60, are deleted and the instruction MAT READ A is substituted for READ A(I,J) in line 40. Clearly, the one line 40 in the second program does everything that lines 20–60 do in the first. In particular, note that the READ A(I,J) loop was set to read the first row, then the second, then the third row; the MAT READ A instruction also reads and assigns numbers by first filling the first row, then the second, and so on.

```
10 DIM A(3,6)
20 FOR I=1 TO 3
30 FOR J=1 TO 6
40 READ A(I,J)
50 NEXT J
60 NEXT I
70 DATA 1,2,3,4,5,6,7,8,9,10,11
80 DATA 12,13,14,15,16,17,18
100 FOR I=1 TO 3
110 FOR J=1 TO 6
120 PRINT A(I,J);
130 NEXT J
140 PRINT
150 NEXT I


1  2  3  4  5  6
7  8  9  10  11  12
13  14  15  16  17  18
```

```
10 DIM A(3,6)
40 MAT READ A
70 DATA 1,2,3,4,5,6,7,8,9,10,11
80 DATA 12,13,14,15,16,17,18
100 FOR I=1 TO 3
110 FOR J=1 TO 6
120 PRINT A(I,J);
130 NEXT J
140 PRINT
150 NEXT I


1  2  3  4  5  6
7  8  9  10  11  12
13  14  15  16  17  18
```

The MAT PRINT Statement

Just as MAT READ shortens the progrm that assigns values to the elements of the matrix, MAT PRINT reduces the number of statements needed to print the matrix A. We can modify the second program above by deleting lines 100, 110, 130, 140, and 150 and rewriting line 120 as MAT PRINT A:

```
10 DIM A(3,6)
40 MAT READ A
70 DATA 1,2,3,4,5,6,7,8,9,10,11
80 DATA 12,13,14,15,16,17,18
120 MAT PRINT A
```

```
1             2             3             4             5             6

7             8             9             10            11
12

13            14            15            16            17
18
```

In addition to MAT PRINT A, there are the two instructions MAT PRINT A, (with a comma) and MAT PRINT A; (with a semicolon). The following printouts show the effects produced by these instructions.

```
10 DIM A(3,6)
40 MAT READ A
70 DATA 1,2,3,4,5,6,7,8,9,10,11
80 DATA 12,13,14,15,16,17,18
120 MAT PRINT A,


1             2             3             4             5             6


7             8             9             10            11
12

13            14            15            16            17
18


10 DIM A(3,6)
40 MAT READ A
70 DATA 1,2,3,4,5,6,7,8,9,10,11
80 DATA 12,13,14,15,16,17,18
120 MAT PRINT A;


1  2  3  4  5  6

7  8  9  10  11  12

13  14  15  16  17  18
```

As you will recall, the effect of the comma is to print the next number in the next available field; the effect of the semicolon is to print the numbers packed as closely as possible.

The MAT INPUT Statement

The MAT INPUT instruction permits data to be entered from the keyboard. The following example further illustrates that if data are input to two matrices, the first set of data is assigned to the first matrix and the second set to the second matrix. The MAT PRINT command may also be given to more than one matrix per instruction line; the matrix print formats associated with the use of the comma and semicolon are further illustrated.

```
10 DIM A(2,2),B(3,3)
20 MAT INPUT A,B
30 MAT PRINT A,B
40 MAT PRINT A;B
50 MAT PRINT A,B;
60 MAT PRINT A;B;
```

```
?1,2,3,4,11,12,13,14,15,16,17,18,19
 1              2

 3              4

 11             12             13

 14             15             16

 17             18             19

 1  2

 3  4

 11             12             13

 14             15             16

 17             18             19

 1              2

 3              4

 11     12     13

 14     15     16

 17     18     19

 1  2

 3  4

 11     12     13

 14     15     16

 17     18     19
```

Matrix Addition and Subtraction

The addition and subtraction of matrices is similar to that of numbers. Before two matrices can be added or subtracted, however, both must have the same number of rows and the same number of columns. If that is the case, the instruction is MAT C = A + B or, in the case of subtraction, MAT C = A − B. The result is that the element in the *i*th row and *j*th column of *C* is the sum (or the difference) of the elements in the *i*th row and *j*th column of the two matrices *A* and *B*. This is illustrated in the following program:

```
10 DIM A(2,3),B(2,3)
20 DIM C(2,3),D(2,3)
30 MAT READ A,B
40 DATA 1,2,3,4,5,6
50 DATA 11,22,33,44,55,66
60 PRINT
70 PRINT "MATRIX A"
80 MAT PRINT A;
90 PRINT
100 PRINT "MATRIX B"
110 MAT PRINT B;
120 MAT C=A+B
130 MAT D=B-A
140 PRINT
150 PRINT "MATRIX A+B"
160 MAT PRINT C;
170 PRINT
```

```
180 PRINT "MATRIX B-A"
190 MAT PRINT D;
```

```
MATRIX A

 1   2   3

 4   5   6

MATRIX B

 11     22     33

 44     55     66

MATRIX A+B

 12     24     36

 48     60     72

MATRIX B-A

 10     20     30

 40     50     60
```

Multiplication by a Scalar

A matrix may be multiplied by a scalar, that is, an ordinary number. The format of the instruction is MAT B = (K)*A, where *A* is the original matrix and *K* is the scalar. The parentheses around *K* are necessary. By definition, each element of the matrix *B* is obtained by multiplying each element of the matrix *A* by the number *K*. The following program illustrates this for $K = -3$:

```
10 DIM A(3,4),B(3,4)
20 MAT READ A
30 DATA 10,11,12,13,14,15,16,17,18,19,20,21
40 K=-3
50 MAT B=(K)*A
60 PRINT
70 PRINT "MATRIX A"
80 MAT PRINT A;
90 PRINT
100 PRINT "MATRIX B"
110 MAT PRINT B;
```

```
MATRIX A

 10     11     12     13

 14     15     16     17

 18     19     20     21

MATRIX B

-30    -33    -36    -39

-42    -45    -48    -51

-54    -57    -60    -63
```

Transpose of a Matrix

The transpose of matrix *A* is defined as the matrix *B* for which the element in the *i*th row and the *j*th column of the *A* matrix becomes the element in the *j*th row and the *i*th column of the *B* matrix. In effect, rows and columns are interchanged. The BASIC statement, MAT B = TRN(A), appears in line 30 below. The program illustrates the transpose of a matrix.

```
10 DIM A(2,5),B(5,2)
20 MAT READ A
30 MAT B=TRN(A)
40 PRINT
50 PRINT "MATRIX A"
60 MAT PRINT A;
70 PRINT
80 PRINT "A TRANSPOSE"
90 MAT PRINT B;
100 DATA 10,11,12,13,14,15,16,17,18,19
```

```
MATRIX A

 10     11     12     13     14

 15     16     17     18     19

A TRANSPOSE

 10     15

 11     16

 12     17

 13     18

 14     19
```

Copying a Matrix

During the writing of a program, we may want to copy a matrix. Such a situation arises, for example, when we intend to alter the elements of the matrix and we want to save a copy of the original. BASIC provides a simple copy statement:

```
MAT B = A
```

A copy of the matrix *A*, now labeled *B*, is made.

In the program that follows, lines 20, 30, 40, 60, and 70 create a matrix *A* for test purposes without using either READ or INPUT. Although it is not necessary to effect the copy instruction, each element of the original matrix *B* is set equal to zero (line 50). The rest of the program, aside from line 140, where the copy of the matrix *A* is made, deals with the printout and is intended only for verification.

```
10 DIM A(5,4),B(5,4)
20 FOR I=1 TO 5
30 FOR J=1 TO 4
40 A(I,J)=I^2-J
50 B(I,J)=0
60 NEXT J
70 NEXT I
80 PRINT
90 PRINT "THE ORIGINAL MATRIX A"
```

```
100 MAT PRINT A
110 PRINT
120 PRINT "THE ORIGINAL MATRIX B"
130 MAT PRINT B
140 MAT B=A
150 PRINT
160 PRINT "THE COPIED MATRIX"
170 MAT PRINT B
```

```
THE ORIGINAL MATRIX A

0          -1          -2          -3

3           2           1           0

8           7           6           5

15          14          13          12

24          23          22          21

THE ORIGINAL MATRIX B

0           0           0           0

0           0           0           0

0           0           0           0

0           0           0           0

0           0           0           0

THE COPIED MATRIX

0          -1          -2          -3

3           2           1           0

8           7           6           5

15          14          13          12

24          23          22          21
```

The Zero Matrix

The need to set all elements of a matrix equal to zero arises frequently, and writing several lines of code to do this each time becomes tedious. To overcome this, BASIC provides the single instruction:

```
MAT B = ZER
```

This instruction is illustrated in the following program and run.

```
10 DIM B(5,4)
20 FOR I=1 TO 5
30 FOR J=1 TO 4
40 B(I,J) = I^J
50 NEXT J
60 NEXT I
70 PRINT
80 PRINT "THE ORIGINAL MATRIX"
90 MAT PRINT B
100 MAT B=ZER
```

```
110 PRINT
120 PRINT "THE ZERO MATRIX"
130 MAT PRINT B
```

```
THE ORIGINAL MATRIX

1              1              1              1

2              4              8              16

3              9              27             81

4              16             64             256

5              25             125            625

THE ZERO MATRIX

0              0              0              0

0              0              0              0

0              0              0              0

0              0              0              0

0              0              0              0
```

Again, lines 20–60 set up a test matrix B and line 100 sets each element of B equal to zero. The remaining statements are for the printout and verification.

The Constant Matrix

Each element of a matrix B will be set equal to 1, instead of zero, if we use the instruction:

```
MAT B = CON
```

In fact, the following program differs from the preceding one only by the change in line 100 of the word ZER to the word CON, for constant, and the appropriate change in the designation of the final result in line 120.

```
10 DIM B(5,4)
20 FOR I=1 TO 5
30 FOR J=1 TO 4
40 B(I,J) = I^J
50 NEXT J
60 NEXT I
70 PRINT
80 PRINT "THE ORIGINAL MATRIX"
90 MAT PRINT B
100 MAT B= CON
110 PRINT
120 PRINT "THE CON MATRIX"
130 MAT PRINT B
```

```
THE ORIGINAL MATRIX

1              1              1              1

2              4              8              16

3              9              27             81

4              16             64             256

5              25             125            625
```

```
THE CON MATRIX

1            1            1            1

1            1            1            1

1            1            1            1

1            1            1            1

1            1            1            1
```

Having constructed a matrix the elements of which are 1, we can easily use scalar multiplication to construct a matrix for which all the elements are a given constant. The following illustrates this for $K=7$; we add line 105 to the previous program and change the description at line 120.

```
10 DIM B(5,4)
20 FOR I=1 TO 5
30 FOR J=1 TO 4
40 B(I,J) = I^J
50 NEXT J
60 NEXT I
70 PRINT
80 PRINT "THE ORIGINAL MATRIX"
90 MAT PRINT B
100 MAT B= CON
105 MAT B=(7)*B
110 PRINT
120 PRINT "THE MODIFIED MATRIX"
130 MAT PRINT B
```

```
THE ORIGINAL MATRIX

1            1            1            1

2            4            8            16

3            9            27           81

4            16           64           256

5            25           125          625

THE MODIFIED MATRIX

7            7            7            7

7            7            7            7

7            7            7            7

7            7            7            7

7            7            7            7
```

The Identity Matrix

One other special matrix, called the identity matrix, may be obtained using a single BASIC statement. Whereas ZER and CON may apply to any matrix, IDN must refer to a square matrix, one for which the number of rows is equal to the number of columns. The instruction

```
MAT A = IDN
```

produces a square matrix A that has 1 for each entry on the main diagonal and 0 everywhere else. (The main diagonal is made up of those elements whose positions in the array are (1,1), (2,2), . . . , (n,n).)

```
10 DIM A(5,5)
20 MAT A=IDN
30 MAT PRINT A;
```

```
1  0  0  0  0

0  1  0  0  0

0  0  1  0  0

0  0  0  1  0

0  0  0  0  1
```

Matrix Multiplication

The rationale for calling a square matrix that has 1 for each entry on the main diagonal the identity matrix will become apparent when we define matrix multiplication. It will be seen that, when used in matrix multiplication, IDN behaves as does the number 1 in ordinary multiplication: If A is any matrix, IDN*A = A.

To define matrix multiplication, we first define the scalar product of two vectors.[1] If $S = (s_1, s_2, \ldots, s_n)$ and $T = (t_1, t_2, \ldots, t_n)$ are two vectors of the same length, n, then the scalar product $S{\cdot}T$ is obtained by multiplying s_1 by t_1, s_2 by t_2, . . . , s_n by t_n, and adding these products. Thus, $S{\cdot}T = s_1t_1 + s_2t_2 + \ldots + s_nt_n$. Note that while S and T are vectors, $S{\cdot}T$ is a scalar.

Let A be an $m \times n$ matrix; A has m rows and n columns.[2]

$$A = \left(\begin{array}{cccccc} a_{11} & a_{12} & \cdots & a_{1k} & \cdots & a_{1n} \\ a_{21} & a_{22} & \cdots & a_{2k} & \cdots & a_{2n} \\ & & \cdots\cdots & & & \\ \hline a_{i1} & a_{i2} & \cdots & a_{ik} & \cdots & a_{in} \\ \hline & & \cdots\cdots & & & \\ a_{m1} & a_{m2} & \cdots & a_{mk} & \cdots & a_{mn} \end{array} \right)$$

Let B be an $n \times p$ matrix; B has n rows and p columns.

$$B = \left(\begin{array}{ccc|c|cc} b_{11} & b_{12} & \cdots & b_{1j} & \cdots & b_{1p} \\ b_{21} & b_{22} & \cdots & b_{2j} & \cdots & b_{2p} \\ & & \cdots & \cdots & & \\ b_{k1} & b_{k2} & \cdots & b_{kj} & \cdots & b_{kp} \\ & & \cdots & \cdots & & \\ b_{n1} & b_{n2} & \cdots & b_{nj} & \cdots & b_{np} \end{array} \right)$$

[1]Also called the dot product and the inner product.
[2]Large parentheses are used to indicate a matrix.

The product $C = A*B$ is an $m \times p$ matrix; C has m rows and p columns.

$$C = \begin{pmatrix} c_{11} & c_{12} & \cdots & c_{1j} & \cdots & c_{1p} \\ c_{21} & c_{22} & \cdots & c_{2j} & \cdots & c_{2p} \\ & & \cdots & \cdots & & \\ c_{i1} & & \cdots & \boxed{c_{ij}} & \cdots & c_{ip} \\ c_{m1} & & \cdots & c_{mj} & \cdots & c_{mp} \end{pmatrix}$$

The element c_{ij} that occupies the position in the ith row and jth column is obtained by considering the n elements in the ith row of the A matrix as a vector $(a_{i1}, a_{i2}, \ldots, a_{ik}, \ldots, a_{in})$ and the n elements in the jth column of the B matrix as a vector $(b_{1j}, b_2, \ldots, b_{kj} \ldots, b_{nj})$ and forming the scalar product of these two vectors. Thus, $c_{ij} = a_{i1}b_{1j} + a_{i2}b_{2j} + \ldots + a_{ik}b_{kj} + \ldots + a_{in}b_{nj} = \sum_{k=1}^{n} a_{ik}b_{kj}$. This is done for each of the m times p elements of the C matrix.

To form the product A*B, the number of columns in A must be equal to the number of rows in B; if not, the product is not defined.

```
10 DIM A(3,2),B(2,4),C(3,4)
20 MAT READ A
30 DATA 1,2,3,4,5,6
40 MAT READ B
50 DATA 11,12,13,14,15,16,17,18
60 MAT C=A*B
70 PRINT
80 PRINT "THE MATRIX A"
90 MAT PRINT A
100 PRINT
110 PRINT"THE MATRIX B"
120 MAT PRINT B
130 PRINT
140 PRINT"THE PRODUCT A*B"
150 MAT PRINT C
```

```
THE MATRIX A

 1             2

 3             4

 5             6

THE MATRIX B

 11            12            13            14

 15            16            17            18

THE PRODUCT A*B

 41            44            47            50

 93            100           107           114

 145           156           167           178
```

In the program, the elements of C are obtained from those of A and B by the specified rule: For example:

$$\begin{aligned} c_{23} &= \sum_{k=1}^{2} a_{2k}b_{k3} \\ &= a_{21} \cdot b_{13} + a_{22} \cdot b_{23} \\ &= 3 \cdot 13 + 4 \cdot 17 = 107 \end{aligned}$$

Two matrices X and Y are equal, written $X = Y$, if and only if each element of X is equal to the corresponding element of Y. In general, matrix multiplication is not commutative, that is: $A*B<>B*A$, as the following example shows:

```
10 DIM A(3,3),B(3,3),C(3,3),D(3,3)
20 MAT READ A
30 DATA 1,2,3,4,5,6,7,8,9
40 MAT READ B
50 DATA 21,32,43,54,65,76,87,98,25
60 MAT C=A*B
70 MAT D=B*A
80 PRINT
90 PRINT "THE MATRIX A"
100 MAT PRINT A
110 PRINT
120 PRINT "THE MATRIX B"
130 MAT PRINT B
140 PRINT
150 PRINT "THE PRODUCT A*B"
160 MAT PRINT C
170 PRINT
180 PRINT "THE PRODUCT B*A"
190 MAT PRINT D
```

```
THE MATRIX A

 1              2              3

 4              5              6

 7              8              9

THE MATRIX B

 21             32             43

 54             65             76

 87             98             25

THE PRODUCT A*B

 390            456            270

 876            1041           702

 1362           1626           1134

THE PRODUCT B*A

 450            546            642

 846            1041           1236

 654            864            1074
```

Thus far, the arithmetic operations of addition, subtraction, and multiplication of matrices and the multiplication of a matrix by a scalar have been discussed. We shall discuss matrix inversion next.

Inverse of a Matrix

The inverse of a real number a different from zero is found by solving either of the equations $a \cdot x = 1$ or $x \cdot a = 1$ for x. Because multiplication of real numbers is commutative, the same value for the inverse is obtained. Frequently, the inverse is written a^{-1}.

The analogous problem for square matrices is more complex. The condition corresponding to $a \neq 0$ is that the determinant[3] of the square matrix A is different from zero, det(A) $\neq$ 0. Although, matrix multiplication is not commutative, it can be shown that the solutions of the two equations A*X = IDN and X*A = IDN are equal, that is, the inverse of A, written A^{-1}, is unique.

The BASIC instruction MAT C = INV(A,X) simultaneously calculates A^{-1} and det(A). C is A^{-1} and the numerical value assigned to the variable X is the value of the determinant.

The following program is straightforward.

```
10 DIM A(3,3)
20 DIM B(10,10),C(10,10),D(10,10),E(10,10)
30 MAT READ A
40 DATA 1,1,1,1,2,2,4,5,6
50 PRINT
60 PRINT"THE ORIGINAL MATRIX-A"
70 MAT PRINT A
80 REM: THE MATRIX B IS A COPY OF THE MATRIX A
90 MAT B=A
100 PRINT
110 PRINT "THE INVERSE MATRIX - C"
120 MAT C=INV(A,X)
130 MAT PRINT C
140 PRINT
150 PRINT "THE VALUE OF DET(A) ="X
160 PRINT
170 PRINT "LOOK WHAT HAPPENED TO THE ORIGINAL MATRIX - A"
180 MAT PRINT A
190 REM: BOTH B*C AND C*B SHOULD BE THE IDENTITY MATRIX IDN
200 PRINT
210 MAT D=B*C
220 PRINT "THE PRODUCT OF A*INV(A)"
230 MAT PRINT D
240 PRINT
250 PRINT "THE PRODUCT OF INV(A)*A"
260 MAT E=C*B
270 MAT PRINT E
280 PRINT
```

```
THE ORIGINAL MATRIX-A

 1              1              1

 1              2              2

 4              5              6

THE INVERSE MATRIX - C

 2             -1             -2.77556E-17

 2.00000        2.00000       -1.00000

-3.00000       -1.00000        1.00000

THE VALUE OF DET(A) = 1

LOOK WHAT HAPPENED TO THE ORIGINAL MATRIX - A

 0              1.25000        .666667

 1              0              .666667

 1             -.250000        0
```

[3]Most secondary texts on algebra define and discuss determinants.

```
THE PRODUCT OF A*INV(A)

 1.00000        -8.32667E-17   0

-4.44089E-16     1             2.22045E-16

 0              -2.22045E-16   1

THE PRODUCT OF INV(A)*A

 1              -1.38778E-16  -1.66533E-16

 0               1.00000       0

 0               0             1
```

Lines 10–20 are dimension statements for the matrices; line 30–40 read the elements of the matrix A, which for verification is printed, lines 60–70. In case the need should arise, a copy of matrix A is made for future use, line 90. The core of the inverse instruction is line 120, where the inverse of the matrix A is assigned to the matrix C. As written, the inverse instruction is a function of two arguments, A, the matrix to be inverted and a numerical variable X. The value of det(A) is assigned to X. A line 130, the inverse matrix is printed; the value of the determinant is given at line 150.

On some computers, when the inverse of a matrix is determined, the entries in the original matrix are modified, with the result that they and the matrix itself are lost. The copy B, made at line 90, is available for possible future use. There is no significance to the modified A matrix. We have included it in the printout to show that the original elements are altered.

The simplest test that C is the inverse of A is to show that both A*C = IDN and C*A = IDN. These multiplications are done at lines 210 and 260; the results are printed at lines 230 and 270, respectively.

Calculating the inverse of a matrix requires many basic arithmetic operations. Remembering that decimal numbers may not be exactly represented internally in the machine, it should not be too surprising that small errors in the computation may accumulate. The fact that some entries of C are integers and some are floating-point numbers should alert you to this. The correct inverse of the matrix A is

$$A^{-1} = \begin{pmatrix} 2 & -1 & 0 \\ 2 & 2 & -1 \\ -3 & -1 & 1 \end{pmatrix}$$

This may be verified by applying the rule for matrix multiplication.

It is your responsibility to decide whether a number such as $-2.77556\text{E-}17$ should be interpreted as zero (as it should in this case) or whether it has significance for the problem at hand.[4] In this particular case, the question is easily resolved since we can write a program to compute A*INV(A) and INV(A)*A, where for A we use the original matrix $\begin{pmatrix} 1 & 1 & 1 \\ 1 & 2 & 2 \\ 4 & 5 & 6 \end{pmatrix}$ and for INV(A) we first use the value of the inverse as given by the computer $\begin{pmatrix} 2 & -1 & -2.77556\text{E}-17 \\ 2.00000 & 2.00000 & -1.00000 \\ -3.00000 & -1.00000 & 1.00000 \end{pmatrix}$

[4] If you are interested in pursuing this matter further, see S. D. Conte, *Elementary Numerical Analysis* (New York: McGraw-Hill, 1965), L. Fox, *An Introduction to Numerical Linear Algebra* (New York: Oxford, 1965), *R. W. Hamming,* Introduction to Applied Numerical Analysis (N.Y.: McGraw-Hill, 1971).

and then as we might guess it to be $\begin{pmatrix} 2 & -1 & 0 \\ 2 & 2 & -1 \\ -3 & -1 & 1 \end{pmatrix}$

The results are given below. The conclusion is obvious: The computer-generated inverse is correct only to within the arithmetic capabilities of the machine; the true inverse is A^{-1}, as given above. Remember, however, that the guessed values probably could not have been found without first knowing the values given by the computer.

```
10 DIM A(3,3),B(3,3),C(3,3),D(3,3)
20 MAT READ A,B
30 DATA 1,1,1,1,2,2,4,5,6
40 DATA 2,-1,-2.77556E-17,2,2,-1,-3,-1,1
50 MAT C=A*B
60 PRINT
70 PRINT "A*INV(A) AS GIVEN BY COMPUTER"
80 MAT PRINT C
90 PRINT
100 MAT D=B*A
110 PRINT "INV(A)*A AS GIVEN BY THE COMPUTER"
120 MAT PRINT D
```

```
A*INV(A) AS GIVEN BY COMPUTER

1              0              0

0              1              0

0              0              1

INV(A)*A AS GIVEN BY THE COMPUTER

1              -1.38778E-16   -1.66534E-16

0              1              0

0              0              1
```

```
10 DIM A(3,3),B(3,3),C(3,3),D(3,3)
20 MAT READ A,B
30 DATA 1,1,1,1,2,2,4,5,6
40 DATA 2,-1,0,2,2,-1,-3,-1,1
50 MAT C=A*B
60 PRINT
70 PRINT "A*INV(A) USING GUESSED VALUES FOR INV(A)"
80 MAT PRINT C
90 PRINT
100 MAT D=B*A
110 PRINT "INV(A)*A USING GUESSED VALUES FOR INV(A)"
120 MAT PRINT D
```

```
A*INV(A) USING GUESSED VALUES FOR INV(A)

1              0              0

0              1              0

0              0              1
```

```
INV(A)*A USING GUESSED VALUES FOR INV(A)

1           0           0

0           1           0

0           0           1
```

The DET Function

On some computers, the matrix inversion instruction is:

```
MAT C = INV(A)
```

We should still expect, however, that the determinant is calculated and available. A simplified version of the preceding program, run on another computer, gave the following result.

```
10 DIM A(3,3)
20 DIM C(10,10)
30 MAT READ A
40 DATA 1,1,1,1,2,2,4,5,6
50 PRINT
60 PRINT "THE ORIGINAL MATRIX - A"
70 MAT PRINT A
80 PRINT
90 PRINT "THE INVERSE MATRIX - C"
100 MAT C=INV(A)
110 MAT PRINT C
120 X=DET(1)
130 PRINT "DET(A)="X
140 PRINT
```

```
THE ORIGINAL MATRIX - A

           1              1              1

           1              2              2

           4              5              6


THE INVERSE MATRIX - C

           2             -1              0

           2              2             -1

          -3             -1              1

DET(A)=    1
```

At line 100, the inverse of A is determined; at line 120 the DET function (the argument may be any constant or variable)[5] assigns the value of det(A) to the variable X. Since the mathematical algorithm for calculating the inverse of a matrix may be different on different computers, the inverse as calculated here does not exhibit the accumulation of small errors.

[5]On other computers DET with no argument is sufficient.

A Singular Matrix

When the determinant of a matrix is different from zero, the matrix has an inverse. When the determinant is zero, the matrix does not have an inverse; such a matrix is called "singular." The matrix $\begin{pmatrix} 1 & 2 & 3 \\ 4 & 5 & 6 \\ 7 & 8 & 9 \end{pmatrix}$ is singular.

Nevertheless, we can see what happens when we use the computer to try to find the inverse. With the appropriate change in the data in line 40 of the program on page 287, that program was rerun with the following outcome.

```
10 DIM A(3,3)
20 DIM B(10,10),C(10,10),D(10,10),E(10,10)
30 MAT READ A
40 DATA 1,2,3,4,5,6,7,8,9
50 PRINT
60 PRINT"THE ORIGINAL MATRIX-A"
70 MAT PRINT A
80 REM: THE MATRIX B IS A COPY OF THE MATRIX A
90 MAT B=A
100 PRINT
110 PRINT "THE INVERSE MATRIX - C"
120 MAT C=INV(A,X)
130 MAT PRINT C
140 PRINT
150 PRINT "THE VALUE OF THE DETERMINANT ="X
160 PRINT
170 PRINT "LOOK WHAT HAPPENED TO THE ORIGINAL MATRIX - A"
180 MAT PRINT A
190 REM: BOTH B*C AND C*B SHOULD BE THE IDENTITY MATRIX IDN
200 PRINT
210 MAT D=B*C
220 PRINT "THE PRODUCT OF A*INV(A)"
230 MAT PRINT D
240 PRINT
250 PRINT "THE PRODUCT OF INV(A)*A"
260 MAT E=C*B
270 MAT PRINT E
280 PRINT
```

```
THE ORIGINAL MATRIX-A

 1              2              3

 4              5              6

 7              8              9

THE INVERSE MATRIX - C

-1.33333        0              .333333

 1.16667        0             -.166667

-.500000        1             -.500000

THE VALUE OF THE DETERMINANT = 0

LOOK WHAT HAPPENED TO THE ORIGINAL MATRIX - A

 0              1.14286       -1.00000

 4              0              2.00000

 1              .428571        9.71445E-17
```

```
THE PRODUCT OF A*INV(A)
-.500000        3       -1.50000
-2.50000        6       -2.50000
-4.50000        9       -3.50000
THE PRODUCT OF INV(A)*A
 1.00000        0       -1.00000
 2.22045E-16    1        2
 2.22045E-16    0        0
```

While the computer produced a matrix, C, it is not the inverse of A. A has no inverse because the determinant of A is zero. If we were not aware that the matrix C is not A^{-1}, we could be led to an incorrect conclusion. We must be sure to look at the value of the determinant of A and decide if it is sufficiently large so that INV(A) is meaningful.

In this program, the form used to calculate the inverse of A was (line 120)

```
MAT C = INV(A,X)
```

where the presence of the second argument, X, alerted the computer of our awareness that the determinant will be inspected. On this same computer, another form for finding the inverse that omits the second argument is:

```
MAT C = INV(A)
```

When this form is used, the computer prints an error message when the matrix A is singular. Thus, with the only change in the program being from

```
120 MAT C = INV(A,X)
```

to

```
120 MAT C = INV(A)
```

the new output is:

```
THE ORIGINAL MATRIX-A
 1          2          3
 4          5          6
 7          8          9
THE INVERSE MATRIX - C
    120 SINGULAR MATRIX
```

The error message indicates that the computer detected a singular matrix when it tried to execute line 120.

When this same singular matrix was tried on another computer, a meaningless matrix C was determined. Unfortunately, on this second computer, there is no warning that the matrix A is singular. It is only after we see $\det(A) = 0$ that we realize that A has no inverse.

```
10 DIM A(3,3)
20 DIM C(10,10)
30 MAT READ A
40 DATA 1,2,3,4,5,6,7,8,9
50 PRINT
60 PRINT "THE ORIGINAL MATRIX - A"
70 MAT PRINT A
80 PRINT
90 PRINT "THE INVERSE MATRIX - C"
100 MAT C=INV(A)
110 MAT PRINT C
120 X=DET(1)
130 PRINT "DET(A)="X
140 PRINT
```

```
THE ORIGINAL MATRIX - A

         1              2              3

         4              5              6

         7              8              9


THE INVERSE MATRIX - C

  .6666667      -.1666667            -.5

        -1             .5            -.5

        -1              2              0


DET(A)=    0
```

A System of Linear Equations

You first met the problem of finding the solution of a system of linear equations in elementary algebra. For the case of two equations in two unknowns, the geometric interpretation is to find the point of intersection of two lines in a plane; for three equations in three unknowns, the problem is to find the point of intersection of three planes in space.

Exceptional cases may arise. If two distinct lines in a plane are to have a point of intersection, they cannot be parallel. Three distinct planes in space can fail to have a point of intersection for several reasons: (1) all three planes are parallel, (2) two planes are parallel, (3) all three intersect in a common line and (4) each pair of planes intersect in a line but all three lines are parallel.

The solution of a system of linear equations is intimately related to matrix operations. We shall establish this relationship with an example. A solution of a system of equations exists only if the determinant of a certain matrix is different from zero.

Solve the system of equations:

$$\begin{aligned} 3X + 2Y - 6Z &= -10 \\ -X - 3Y + 4Z &= 14 \\ 2X - Y + Z &= 13 \end{aligned}$$

We may think of the left-hand side of these equations as being obtained from the product of the coefficient matrix $A = \begin{pmatrix} 3 & 2 & -6 \\ -1 & -3 & 4 \\ 2 & -1 & 1 \end{pmatrix}$ and the vector $V = \begin{pmatrix} X \\ Y \\ Z \end{pmatrix}$.

With this notation, the left-hand side may be written

$A*V$

Similarly, the right-hand side of the equations may be thought of as a vector $M = \begin{pmatrix} -10 \\ 14 \\ 13 \end{pmatrix}$. We can then write the matrix equation

$A*V = M$

If we can find the inverse of the matrix A, call it B, then we can multiply both sides of this matrix equation by B and get:

$B*(A*V) = B*M$

Because matrix multiplication is associative, that is: $B*(A*V) = (B*A)*V$, we have:

$(B*A)*V = B*M$

Also, because B is the inverse of A, $B*A$ = IDN and IDN$*V = V$. Thus, we finally have:

$V = B*M$

and we have solved the equations for X, Y, and Z.

The following program carries out the several steps, solving this system of equations:

```
10 DIM A(3,3),B(3,3),M(3),V(3)
20 MAT READ A
30 DATA 3,2,-6,-1,-3,4,2,-1,1
40 MAT READ M
50 DATA -10,14,13
60 MAT B=INV(A,D)
70 IF D=0 THEN 110
80 MAT V=B*M
90 MAT PRINT V
100 STOP
110 PRINT "DET(A) = 0"
```

```
4.00000        -2.00000        3.00000
```

The SIM Statement

As straighforward as the above solution is, some BASIC interpreters provide a simpler solution. Using the same notation as before, we would still write lines 10–50. Line 80 would be omitted, however, and line 60 replaced by

```
60 MAT M = SIM(A,D)
```

(SIM stands for simultaneous.) Line 70 remains, line 90 is changed to MAT PRINT M. It is important to recognize that the vector M used in line 60 to store the final answer must be the *same* vector M used in lines 40 and 50 to store the values found on the right-hand side of the equations. With these changes, we have:

```
10 DIM A(3,3),B(3,3),M(3),V(3)
20 MAT READ A
30 DATA 3,2,-6,-1,-3,4,2,-1,1
40 MAT READ M
50 DATA -10,14,13
60 MAT M=SIM(A,D)
70 IF D=0 THEN 110
90 MAT PRINT M
100 STOP
110 PRINT "DET(A)  = 0"
```

```
4.00000        -2.00000        3
```

Just as it is not necessary when finding the inverse of a matrix A to ask for the determinant of A (we can write INV(A) instead of INV(A,D)), we need not ask for the determinant of the matrix A in SIM(A,D). Line 60 could have been written:

```
60 MAT M = SIM(A)
```

and this would have precluded the need for lines 70, 100, and 110.

The SIM(A) and SIM(A,D) instructions suffer the same drawback as the INV(A) and INV(A,D) instructions, namely, results obtained may be only approximate, and after the execution of the instruction, the matrix A is altered and meaningless.

Repeated Solutions of a System of Equations

At times it is necessary to solve the same system of linear equations, that is, invert the same coefficient matrix A, for different vectors M. For example, we may want to solve the same system of equations for five different sets of values for M, $M_1 = (-10, 14, 13)$ as before, $M_2 = (17, -12, -1)$, $M_3 = (37, -23, 5)$, $M_4 = (9, -12, -6)$, and $M_5 = (-2, 0, 4)$. While we could run the previous program five times, once for each different M_i, BASIC offers a faster technique. Construct the 3×5 matrix

$$
\begin{array}{c} \\ M = \end{array}
\begin{array}{c}
\begin{array}{ccccc} M_1 & M_2 & M_3 & M_4 & M_5 \end{array} \\
\hline
\begin{pmatrix} -10 & 17 & 37 & 9 & -2 \\ 14 & -12 & -23 & -12 & 0 \\ 13 & -1 & 5 & -6 & 4 \end{pmatrix}
\end{array}
$$

where each column vector consists of the entries in one of the five vectors, M_1, $M_2, \ldots, M_5$.

Previously, we thought of V as a 3×1 matrix (a vector); now we think of V as a 3×5 matrix. We would still write:

$$A^*V = M$$

Again, if B = INV(A), then

$$B^*(A^*V) = B^*M$$

and finally,

$$V = B^*M$$

The following program, which is a modification of the program on page 294, carries out the computation.

```
10 DIM A(3,3),B(3,3),M(3,5),V(3,5)
20 MAT READ A
30 DATA 3,2,-6,-1,-3,4,2,-1,1
40 MAT READ M
50 DATA -10,17,37,9,-2
51 DATA 14,-12,-23,-12,0
52 DATA 13,-1,5,-6,4
60 MAT B=INV(A)
80 MAT V=B*M
90 MAT PRINT V
```

```
 4.00000        1.00000        5.00000       -1.00000        2.00000

-2.00000        1              2.00000        3.00000        2.00000

 3.00000       -2             -3             -1.00000        2.00000
```

The modification consists of redimensioning the vectors V and M and inserting the additional data for M. Note that in the three data statements, lines 50–52, the data for M are arranged as we need them in the computer. Observe also that the five solution vectors $V_1, V_2, \ldots, V_5$ are arranged vertically, as might be expected, and match the order in which the elements of the matrix M are arranged. Thus, the solution vector $V_1 = (4, -2, 3)$ corresponds to the vector $M_1 = (-10, 14, 13)$; the solution vector $V_2 = (1, 1, -2)$ corresponds to the vector $M_2 = (17, -12, -1)$; the solution vector $V_3 = (5, 2, -3)$ corresponds to $M_3 = (37, -23, 5)$; $V_4 = (-1, 3, -1)$ corresponds to $M_4 = (9, -12, -6)$; and $V_5 = (2, 2, 2)$ corresponds to $M_5 = (-2, 0, 4)$. Lines 70, 100, and 110 are deleted.

The SIM instruction works as well. Line 60 is replaced by

```
60 MAT M = SIM(A)
```

and line 80 is deleted. Line 90, the print statement, is modified accordingly.

```
10 DIM A(3,3),M(3,5)
20 MAT READ A
30 DATA 3,2,-6,-1,-3,4,2,-1,1
40 MAT READ M
50 DATA -10,17,37,9,-2
51 DATA 14,-12,-23,-12,0
52 DATA 13,-1,5,-6,4
60 MAT M=SIM(A)
90 MAT PRINT M
```

```
 4.00000        1.00000        5.00000       -1.00000        2.00000

-2.00000        1.00000        2              3.00000        2.00000

 3             -2.00000       -3             -1.00000        2
```

The MAT SIZE Statement

You may have observed that in some of the illustrations great care was not directed to the dimensions of the matrices; all that was needed was that these dimensions were large enough for the problem at hand. The computer adjusted the size of the matrix as needed. The following program is an example:

```
10 DIM A(2,3),B(10,10)
20 MAT READ A
30 DATA 1,2,3,4,5,6
40 MAT B=A
50 MAT PRINT B



1             2             3

4             5             6
```

The remaining elements of *B* are not lost and may be seen if we use the BASIC statement MAT SIZE. In this example, if the matrix *B* is to be 3 × 5, we would add 60 MAT SIZE B(3,5), and to show the result 70 MAT PRINT B.

```
10 DIM A(2,3),B(10,10)
20 MAT READ A
30 DATA 1,2,3,4,5,6
40 MAT B=A
50 MAT PRINT B
60 MAT SIZE B(3,5)
70 MAT PRINT B



1             2             3

4             5             6

1             2             3             0             0

4             5             6             0             0

0             0             0             0             0
```

If we try to increase the size of a matrix beyond that specified in the original DIM statement, we get an error message.

```
10 DIM A(2,3),B(10,10)
20 MAT READ A
30 DATA 1,2,3,4,5,6
40 MAT B=A
50 MAT PRINT B
60 MAT SIZE B(11,5)
70 MAT PRINT B



1             2             3

4             5             6

     60 DIM TOO BIG
```

When a matrix *A* is copied into a matrix *B*, the current dimensions of *A* become those of *B*. In the following, *B*, originally a 10 × 10 matrix (created and displayed in lines 60–120), had its current dimensions reduced to 2 × 3 when used in the copy statement, line 130. This reduced *B* is displayed, lines 140–150. The remaining entries of *B* are not altered, however, and may be seen by redimensioning *B*, per line 160, and displaying it, lines 170–180. MAT SIZE B(7, 7) was used to show the versatility of the instruction. Any two numbers—they need not be the same—up to and including 10 would do as well.

```
10 DIM A(2,3),B(10,10)
20 MAT READ A
30 DATA -11,-22,-33,-44,-55,-66
40 PRINT & PRINT "MATRIX A"
50 MAT PRINT A;
60 FOR I=1 TO 10
70 FOR J=1 TO 10
80 B(I,J)= 10+I+J
90 NEXT J
100 NEXT I
110 PRINT & PRINT "MATRIX B(10,10)"
120 MAT PRINT B;
130 MAT B=A
140 PRINT & PRINT "MATRIX B AS COPIED FROM A"
150 MAT PRINT B;
160 MAT SIZE B(7,7)
170 PRINT & PRINT "MATRIX B(7,7)"
180 MAT PRINT B;
```

```
MATRIX A

-11   -22   -33

-44   -55   -66

MATRIX B(10,10)

 12    13    14    15    16    17    18    19    20    21

 13    14    15    16    17    18    19    20    21    22

 14    15    16    17    18    19    20    21    22    23

 15    16    17    18    19    20    21    22    23    24

 16    17    18    19    20    21    22    23    24    25

 17    18    19    20    21    22    23    24    25    26

 18    19    20    21    22    23    24    25    26    27

 19    20    21    22    23    24    25    26    27    28

 20    21    22    23    24    25    26    27    28    29

 21    22    23    24    25    26    27    28    29    30

MATRIX B AS COPIED FROM A

-11   -22   -33

-44   -55   -66

MATRIX B(7,7)

-11   -22   -33    15    16    17    18

-44   -55   -66    16    17    18    19

 14    15    16    17    18    19    20

 15    16    17    18    19    20    21

 16    17    18    19    20    21    22

 17    18    19    20    21    22    23

 18    19    20    21    22    23    24
```

If, using the original 10 × 10 matrix *B* as in the previous example, we had wanted ZER in the 5 × 3 submatrix that constitutes the upper left-hand corner of *B,* we could have written:

```
10 DIM B(10,10)
20 FOR I=1 TO 10
30 FOR J=1 TO 10
40 B(I,J)= 10+I+J
50 NEXT J
60 NEXT I
70 PRINT & PRINT "MATRIX B(10,10)"
80 MAT PRINT B;
90 MAT B=ZER(5,3)
100 PRINT & PRINT "B(5,3) WITH ALL ZEROS"
110 MAT PRINT B;
120 MAT SIZE B(7,5)
130 PRINT & PRINT "MATRIX B(7,5)"
140 MAT PRINT B
```

```
MATRIX B(10,10)

 12    13    14    15    16    17    18    19    20    21

 13    14    15    16    17    18    19    20    21    22

 14    15    16    17    18    19    20    21    22    23

 15    16    17    18    19    20    21    22    23    24

 16    17    18    19    20    21    22    23    24    25

 17    18    19    20    21    22    23    24    25    26

 18    19    20    21    22    23    24    25    26    27

 19    20    21    22    23    24    25    26    27    28

 20    21    22    23    24    25    26    27    28    29

 21    22    23    24    25    26    27    28    29    30

B(5,3) WITH ALL ZEROS

 0   0   0

 0   0   0

 0   0   0

 0   0   0

 0   0   0

MATRIX B(7,5)

 0              0              0              15             16

 0              0              0              16             17

 0              0              0              17             18

 0              0              0              18             19

 0              0              0              19             20

 17             18             19             20             21

 18             19             20             21             22
```

At line 90, the desired ZER matrix is created. That the remaining entries in B are unaffected is shown at lines 120–140, where B is redimensioned and printed.

Illustrations

The matrix instructions introduced above suffice for the solution of a variety of problems. In the remainder of this chapter, we shall illustrate the use of these BASIC statements in programs to solve problems drawn from various disciplines.

Illustration: A Sales Problem

The management of Broadhurst Catechu Distributers, a company that produces and sells six different extracts, wishes to automate some of its clerical operations. For example, management needs to know, on a daily basis, the company's production needs, production costs, estimated profits, and so on. After studying these needs, the computer staff formulates the problem in the following terms.

The six extracts are labeled $P_1, P_2, \ldots, P_6$; the company's five salespersons are denoted by $Z_1, \ldots, Z_5$. Orders, compiled daily for the next day's production run, provide the input for an order matrix A. A typical day might produce the following matrix:

Salesperson \ Product	P_1	P_2	P_3	P_4	P_5	P_6
Z_1	75	69	123	149	23	45
Z_2	27	12	92	108	213	87
Z_3	38	91	19	58	82	73
Z_4	96	41	49	88	12	209
Z_5	47	55	37	45	78	85

The cost to produce one unit of P_1 is C_1, to produce one unit of P_2 is $C_2, \ldots,$ to produce one unit of P_6 is C_6. Similarly, the selling prices for the six items are $S_1, \ldots, S_6$. A typical set of unit costs might be (15, 20, 25, 20, 25, 30); a typical set of unit selling prices might be (25, 35, 45, 40, 40, 50). If the product $A*C$ is calculated, the result will be the cost, per salesperson, of producing the extracts ordered through that salesperson; the product $A*S$ will be the amount invoiced, per salesperson, for the extracts ordered. The difference, written either $A*S - A*C$ or $A*(S - C)$, will be the gross profit per salesperson.

If we use the vector $I = (1, 1, 1, 1, 1)$ and calculate $I*A$, we will get a new vector that gives the amount of each extract ordered that day. The product $(I*A)*C$ will give the total cost of the day's production, $(I*A)*S$ will give the total amount invoiced, and $(I*A)*(S - C)$ will be the total gross profit.

The computer staff wrote and ran the following program.

```
10 DIM A(5,6),I(5),C(6),S(6)
20 DIM X(5),Y(5),Z(5)
30 DIM U(6),V(1),W(1),Q(1)
40 MAT READ A
50 DATA 75,69,123,149,23,45
60 DATA 27,12,92,108,213,87
70 DATA 38,91,19,58,82,73
80 DATA 96,41,49,88,12,209
90 DATA 47,55,37,45,75,85
100 MAT I=CON
110 MAT READ C
120 DATA 15,20,25,20,25,30
130 MAT READ S
140 DATA 25,35,45,40,40,50
150 MAT X=A*C
```

```
160 PRINT & PRINT "COST, PER SALESPERSON, FOR FILLING THAT PERSON'S ORDER"
170 MAT PRINT X
180 MAT Y=A*S
190 PRINT & PRINT "AMOUNT INVOICED PER SALESPERSON"
200 MAT PRINT Y
210 PRINT & PRINT "GROSS PROFIT PER SALESPERSON"
220 MAT Z=Y-X
230 MAT PRINT Z
240 PRINT & PRINT "AMOUNT, BY ITEM, ORDERED THIS DAY"
250 MAT U=I*A
260 MAT PRINT U;
270 PRINT & PRINT "TOTAL COST OF THE DAY'S ORDER"
280 MAT V=I*X
290 MAT PRINT V
300 PRINT & PRINT "TOTAL AMOUNT TO BE INVOICED FOR THAT DAY"
310 MAT W=I*Y
320 MAT PRINT W
330 PRINT & PRINT "GROSS PROFIT FOR THE DAY"
340 MAT Q=W-V
350 MAT PRINT Q
```

```
COST, PER SALESPERSON, FOR FILLING THAT PERSON'S ORDER

 10485          13040          8265           11815          8055

AMOUNT INVOICED PER SALESPERSON

 18955          22425          14240          20490          13815

GROSS PROFIT PER SALESPERSON

 8470           9385           5975           8675           5760

AMOUNT, BY ITEM, ORDERED THIS DAY

 283   268   320   448   405   499

TOTAL COST OF THE DAY'S ORDER

 51660

TOTAL AMOUNT TO BE INVOICED FOR THAT DAY

 89925

GROSS PROFIT FOR THE DAY

 38265
```

In the program, lines 10–140 are basically housekeeping, that is, setting the dimensions of the various vectors and matrices and loading into them the appropriate values.

At line 150, the vector X is calculated; each component of X is the cost of filling one salesperson's order. At line 180, the vector Y is calculated; each component of Y is the amount, per salesperson, to be invoiced. The difference between these two vectors, $Y - X$, is the vector Z that gives the gross profit, per salesperson, to be realized from the day's business, line 220.

As a cross-tabulation, the total of each item ordered that day is calculated in line 250. In line 280, the total cost of the day's order, calculated as the product of the vectors I and X, is assigned to the variable V. Since I and X are vectors, however, we must treat V as a vector. The same applies to W in line 310, the total amount to be invoiced that day.

Although W and V are each single numbers, they are viewed by the computer as vectors, and if they are to be subtracted, matrix subtraction must be used. Therefore, to find the gross profit for the day, matrix subtraction is used at line 340.

Illustration: A Markov Process[6]

Four countries trade with one another. Their initial resources available for foreign trade, in billions of dollars, are 100, 200, 300, and 100. It has been observed that during any one year, funds are transferred from one country to another according to the matrix:

From \ To	G_1	G_2	G_3	G_4
G_1	0	.2	.5	.3
G_2	.1	0	.4	.5
G_3	.6	.3	0	.1
G_4	.4	.5	.1	0

The matrix implies that during a year, of all the resources of G_1 available for foreign trade, .2 go to G_2, .5 go to G_3, and .3 go to G_4. Similarly, to determine how the resources of any G_i are distributed, read across that row for which the first entry is G_i.

If the vector of initial resources is designated A and the matrix of transfers T, then at the end of one year, the resources available to each country G_i for trade for the next year is $A*T$. At the end of the second year, the funds available to each country G_i for trade for the third year is $(A*T)*T$. This process can be continued for an arbitrary number of years. The following program follows the course of this trade pattern for the first 10 years. The details are given in lines 130, 150, and 160, where $A*T$ is calculated and is called B (line 130), the result is printed (line 150), the initial vector for the next year is labeled A (line 160), and the process repeats.

```
10 DIM T(4,4)
20 DIM A(4),B(4)
30 MAT READ T
40 DATA 0,.2,.5,.3,.1,0,.4,.5,.6,.3,0,.1,.4,.5,.1,0
50 MAT READ A
60 DATA 100,200,300,100
70 PRINT & PRINT "THE INITIAL DISTRIBUTION OF RESOURCES IS"
80 MAT PRINT A
90 PRINT & PRINT "THE MATRIX OF TRANSFERS OF RESOURCES BETWEEN COUNTRIES IS"
100 MAT PRINT T
110 PRINT & PRINT "INPUT THE NUMBER OF CYCLES TO BE RUN"; & INPUT N
120 FOR I=1 TO N
130 MAT B=A*T
140 PRINT & PRINT "AT THE END OF CYCLE NUMBER"I" THE DISTRIBUTION OF RESOURCES IS"
150 MAT PRINT B
160 MAT A=B
170 NEXT I
```

```
THE INITIAL DISTRIBUTION OF RESOURCES IS

 100            200            300            100

THE MATRIX OF TRANSFERS OF RESOURCES BETWEEN COUNTRIES IS

 0              .200000        .500000        .300000

 .100000        0              .400000        .500000
```

[6]This example illustrates the property of a regular Markov process. See, for example, G. Owen and M. E. Munroe, *Finite Mathematics and Calculus* (Philadelphia: W. B. Saunders, 1971), pp. 504–508; H. Anton and B. Kolman, *Applied Finite Mathematics*, 2nd ed. (N.Y.: Academic Press, 1978), pp. 392–410.

```
 .600000        .300000        0              .100000

 .400000        .500000        .100000        0

INPUT THE NUMBER OF CYCLES TO BE RUN  ?10

AT THE END OF CYCLE NUMBER 1 THE DISTRIBUTION OF RESOURCES IS

 240.000        160.000        140.000        160

AT THE END OF CYCLE NUMBER 2 THE DISTRIBUTION OF RESOURCES IS

 164.000        170.000        200.000        166.000

AT THE END OF CYCLE NUMBER 3 THE DISTRIBUTION OF RESOURCES IS

 203.400        175.800        166.600        154.200

AT THE END OF CYCLE NUMBER 4 THE DISTRIBUTION OF RESOURCES IS

 179.220        167.760        187.440        165.580

AT THE END OF CYCLE NUMBER 5 THE DISTRIBUTION OF RESOURCES IS

 195.472        174.866        173.272        156.390

AT THE END OF CYCLE NUMBER 6 THE DISTRIBUTION OF RESOURCES IS

 184.006        169.271        183.321        163.402

AT THE END OF CYCLE NUMBER 7 THE DISTRIBUTION OF RESOURCES IS

 192.281        173.498        176.051        158.169

AT THE END OF CYCLE NUMBER 8 THE DISTRIBUTION OF RESOURCES IS

 186.248        170.356        181.357        162.039

AT THE END OF CYCLE NUMBER 9 THE DISTRIBUTION OF RESOURCES IS

 190.665        172.676        177.471        159.188

AT THE END OF CYCLE NUMBER 10 THE DISTRIBUTION OF RESOURCES IS

 187.425        170.968        180.322        161.285
```

From the printout, it appears that as time progresses, the funds available for trade become stabilized. In order to verify this without a huge printout, the code was modified to print results only for the end of each decade. The modification consists of inserting line 135 into the above program, as follows:

```
135 IF I<>INT(I/10)*10 THEN 160
```

The result follows.

```
THE INITIAL DISTRIBUTION OF RESOURCES IS

 100            200            300            100

THE MATRIX OF TRANSFERS OF RESOURCES BETWEEN GROUPS IS

 0              .200000        .500000        .300000

 .100000        0              .400000        .500000

 .600000        .300000        0              .100000

 .400000        .500000        .100000        0
```

```
INPUT THE NUMBER OF CYCLES TO BE RUN  ?70

AT THE END OF CYCLE NUMBER 10 THE DISTRIBUTION OF RESOURCES IS

 187.425       170.968       180.322       161.285

AT THE END OF CYCLE NUMBER 20 THE DISTRIBUTION OF RESOURCES IS

 188.734       171.659       179.170       160.437

AT THE END OF CYCLE NUMBER 30 THE DISTRIBUTION OF RESOURCES IS

 188.794       171.691       179.117       160.398

AT THE END OF CYCLE NUMBER 40 THE DISTRIBUTION OF RESOURCES IS

 188.797       171.692       179.115       160.397

AT THE END OF CYCLE NUMBER 50 THE DISTRIBUTION OF RESOURCES IS

 188.797       171.692       179.115       160.396

AT THE END OF CYCLE NUMBER 60 THE DISTRIBUTION OF RESOURCES IS

 188.797       171.692       179.115       160.396

AT THE END OF CYCLE NUMBER 70 THE DISTRIBUTION OF RESOURCES IS

 188.797       171.692       179.115       160.396
```

Stability is attained after 50 years.

Illustration: The Cayley-Hamilton Theorem

> It is difficult to give an idea of the vast extent of modern mathematics. The word "extent" is not the right one: I mean extent crowned with beautiful detail—not an extent of mere uniformity such as an objectless plain, but of a tract of beautiful country seen at first in the distance, but which will bear to be rambled through and studied in every detail of hillside and valley, stream, rock, wood, and flower. But, as for everything else, so for a mathematical theory—beauty can be perceived but not explained.[7]

From the hundreds of mathematical results discovered by Cayley, we present one gem of outstanding beauty, the Cayley-Hamilton theorem. We use it here to show that BASIC can be used to demonstrate a mathematical theorem of considerable complexity.

Let $A = (a_{ij})$ be a square $n \times n$ matrix. Consider the determinant of the matrix $(A - kI)$, where k is a variable. When this determinant is evaluated, the resulting expression is a polynomial in k, which we represent by $P(k)$. $P(k)$ is called the characteristic polynomial of the matrix A.

$$P(k) = (-1)^n(k^n + b_1k^{n-1} + b_2k^{n-2} + \ldots + b_{n-1}k + b_n)$$

where the b_i are numbers calculated from the a_{ij}. For example, let

$$A = \begin{pmatrix} 3 & 5 & 7 \\ 1 & -1 & -2 \\ 4 & -3 & 6 \end{pmatrix}$$

$$A - kI = \begin{pmatrix} 3-k & 5 & 7 \\ 1 & -1-k & -2 \\ 4 & -3 & 6-k \end{pmatrix}$$

[7]From Arthur Cayley's presidential address in 1883 to the British Association for the Advancement of Science as quoted in Eric Temple Bell, *Men of Mathematics* (N.Y.: Simon and Schuster, 1937), p. 378.

$$\det(A - kI) = \begin{vmatrix} 3-k & 5 & 7 \\ 1 & -1-k & -2 \\ 4 & -3 & 6-k \end{vmatrix}$$

$$P(k) = -k^3 + 8k^2 + 30k - 99$$

The polynomial $P(k)$ is the characteristic polynomial of the matrix A.

Since you know how to multiply matrices, you can form $A^2 = A*A$ and $A^3 = A*A^2$. Take the matrices A, A^2, and A^3, formally substitute them for k, k^2, and k^3, respectively, in $P(A)$: $P(A)$ $P(k)$, and multiply 99 by the identity matrix. The result is a matrix denoted $P(A)$: $P(A) = -A^3 + 8A^2 + 30A - 99I$. The details of the computation are as follows:

$$A^2 = \begin{pmatrix} 42 & -11 & 53 \\ -6 & 12 & -3 \\ 33 & 5 & 70 \end{pmatrix} \qquad A^3 = \begin{pmatrix} 327 & 62 & 634 \\ -18 & -33 & -84 \\ 384 & -50 & 641 \end{pmatrix}$$

$$P(A) = -\begin{pmatrix} 327 & 62 & 634 \\ -18 & -33 & -84 \\ 384 & -50 & 641 \end{pmatrix} + 8\begin{pmatrix} 42 & -11 & 53 \\ -6 & 12 & -3 \\ 33 & 5 & 70 \end{pmatrix} + 30\begin{pmatrix} 3 & 5 & 7 \\ 1 & -1 & -2 \\ 4 & -3 & 6 \end{pmatrix}$$

$$-99\begin{pmatrix} 1 & 0 & 0 \\ 0 & 1 & 0 \\ 0 & 0 & 1 \end{pmatrix}$$

The Cayley-Hamilton theorem states that the matrix $P(A)$ is the zero matrix.

In the following program, the computation for the specific matrix A is carried through and the theorem verified.

```
10 DIM A(3,3),B(3,3),C(3,3),D(3,3),E(3,3)
20 MAT READ A
30 DATA 3,5,7,1,-1,-2,4,-3,6
40 MAT B=A*A
50 MAT C=A*B
60 MAT E=(-1)*C
70 MAT D=(8)*B
80 MAT E=E+D
90 MAT D=(30)*A
100 MAT E=E+D
110 MAT B=IDN
120 MAT D=(-99)*B
130 MAT E=E+D
140 MAT PRINT E;
```

```
0   0   0

0   0   0

0   0   0
```

At lines 40 and 50, A^2 and A^3 are calculated. The several steps of the calculation are to be collected in the matrix E; at the first stage: $E = -A^3$ (lines 40–60). At line 70, $D = 8A^2$, and at line 80, $E = -A^3 + 8A^2$. At line 90, $D = 30A$, and at line 100, $E = -A^3 + 8A^2 + 30A$. Lines 110 and 120 produce $D = -99I$, and at line 130, $E = -A^3 + 8A^2 + 30A - 99I$. Line 140 prints the verification of the Cayley-Hamilton theorem.

The Minimal Polynomial

Every square matrix A satisfies its characteristic polynomial; that is the Cayley-Hamilton theorem. Sometimes, however, an $n \times n$ matrix A may satisfy a polynomial of degree less than n. The minimal polynomial $m(k)$ of an $n \times n$ matrix A is defined as the polynomial of lowest degree, with leading coefficient 1, such that $m(A)$ is the zero matrix.

Consider the matrix

$$A = \begin{pmatrix} -3 & -2 & 2 \\ -8 & -3 & 4 \\ -18 & -9 & 10 \end{pmatrix}$$

Its characteristic polynomial is

$$P(k) = -k^3 + 4k^2 - 5k + 2$$

and therefore:

$$P(A) = -A^3 + 4A^2 - 5A + 2I = \text{ZER}$$

There is a polynomial of lower degree, however, leading coefficient 1 (or -1) such that when A is substituted for the variable k in that polynomial, the zero matrix is obtained. There are two possibilities for the degree; it is either 1 or 2. If we examine an arbitrary polynomial of the first degree, $x - b$, we must decide if we can find one number b such that

$$A - bI = \begin{pmatrix} -3-b & -2 & 2 \\ 8 & -3-b & 4 \\ -18 & -9 & 10-b \end{pmatrix} = \begin{pmatrix} 0 & 0 & 0 \\ 0 & 0 & 0 \\ 0 & 0 & 0 \end{pmatrix}$$

Clearly, no such number b exists.

How about a second degree polynominal, $x^2 + bx + c$? Can we find two numbers b and c such that

$$A^2 + bA + cI = \text{ZER}$$

The left-hand side is

$$\begin{pmatrix} -11-3b+c & -6-2b & 6+2b \\ -24-8b & -11-3b+c & 12+4b \\ -54-18b & -27-9b & 28+10b+c \end{pmatrix}$$

If this is to be the zero matrix, then each element must be zero. If the elements in positions (1,1) and (1,2) are set equal to zero, we get two linear equations

$$\begin{aligned} -3b + c &= 11 \\ -2b \phantom{{}+c} &= 6 \end{aligned}$$

and we find $b = -3$ and $c = 2$. When these two values are substituted into the other elements of the matrix, each becomes zero. Therefore, there is a second degree polynomial, with leading coefficient equal to 1, namely $k^2 - 3k + 2$, such that $A^2 - 3A + 2I = \text{ZER}$. This polynomial is the minimal polynomial for the matrix A.

We stated that there are many methods for calculating the inverse of a matrix. Using the Cayley-Hamilton theorem, we shall demonstrate one.

Assume that the characteristic polynomial of the nonsingular matrix A is known. Then, using the theorem, we write

$$(-1)^n(A^n + b_1A^{n-1} + b_2A^{n-2} + \ldots + b_{n-1}A + b_nI) = \text{ZER}$$

Rewrite this equation as

$$I = -\frac{1}{b_n}(A^n + b_1A^{n-1} + \ldots + b_{n-1}A)$$

and multiply through by the as yet unknown A^{-1}. This gives

$$A^{-1} = -\frac{1}{b_n}(A^{n-1} + b_1A^{n-2} + \ldots + b_{n-1}I)$$

Evaluating the right-hand side, we get $A^{-1.}$

The coefficients b_i in the characteristic polynominal may be determined by the following algorithm.[8] First, we define the trace of a square matrix, denoted tr(A), as the sum of the diagonal elements, that is, tr(A) = $a_{11} + a_{22} + \ldots + a_{nn}$. The coefficients b_i are then calculated as follows:

$$\begin{array}{lll} A_1 = A & b_1 = -\mathrm{tr}(A_1) & B_1 = A_1 + b_1 I \\ A_2 = AB_1 & b_2 = -\frac{1}{2}\mathrm{tr}(A_2) & B_2 = A_2 + b_2 I \\ & \ldots\ldots\ldots\ldots\ldots & \\ A_{n-1} = AB_{n-2} & b_{n-1} = -\frac{1}{n-1}\mathrm{tr}(A_{n-1}) & B_{n-1} = A_{n-1} + b_{n-1} I \\ A_n = AB_{n-1} & b_n = -\frac{1}{n}\mathrm{tr}(A_n) & B_n = A_n + b_n I = \mathrm{ZER} \end{array}$$

From the last line in the algorithm, it is easy to see that A^{-1} is given by

$$A^{-1} = -\left(\frac{1}{b_n}\right)B_{n-1}$$

Illustration: The Orbit of a Satellite

In all experimental sciences, we seek to establish a relationship between several observed variables. If we can express this relationship in a mathematical formula and then draw verifiable conclusions from it, our understanding of the phenomenon is enhanced.

In astronomy, if the position of a satellite at various times is known, its orbit can be determined. Once the orbit is known, the satellite's position at future times can be predicted. The methods of matrix algebra will be applied to the first part of this problem, namely, given the coordinates of a satellite at five different times, determine the equation of its orbit. The underlying theory is Newtonian mechanics and, particularly, Kepler's first law, plus the mathematical fact that a conic is uniquely determined by five coplanar points.

An (x,y) coordinate system is set up in the plane of the orbit; five observations are made at five different times. The coordinates of the observed points are (20, 27.625), (22, 27.467), (26, 26.9281), (32, 25.565), and (40, 22.6777).

The general equation of an ellipse can be written

$$Ax^2 + Bxy + Cy^2 + Dx + Ey = 1 \qquad (1)$$

By substituting the pairs of values for the coordinates of the observed points into the equation, five linear equations in the unknowns A, B, C, D, E are obtained.

$$\begin{array}{rrrrrl} 400\,A\, + & 552.5\,B\, + & 763.14062\,C\, + & 20\,D\, + & 27.625\,E & = 1 \\ 484\,A\, + & 604.274\,B\, + & 754.43609\,C\, + & 22\,D\, + & 27.467\,E & = 1 \\ 676\,A\, + & 700.1306\,B\, + & 725.12256\,C\, + & 26\,D\, + & 26.9281\,E & = 1 \\ 1024\,A\, + & 818.08\,B\, + & 653.56922\,C\, + & 32\,D\, + & 25.565\,E & = 1 \\ 1600\,A\, + & 907.108\,B\, + & 514.27807\,C\, + & 40\,D\, + & 22.6777\,E & = 1 \end{array} \qquad (2)$$

Solving these five equations simultaneously will yield values for A, B, C, D, and E. The following program carries this out.

[8]D. K. Faddeev and V. N. Faddeeva, *Computational Methods of Linear Algebra* (San Francisco and London: W. H. Freeman & Co.), 1963, pp. 260–265. The method is credited to U.J.J. Leverrier.

```
10 DIM X(5),Y(5),M(5),S(5),Q(5,5),R(5,5)
20 FOR I=1 TO 5
30 M(I)=1
40 READ X(I),Y(I)
50 NEXT I
60 DATA 20,27.625,22,27.467,26,26.9281,32,25.565,40,22.6777
70 PRINT
80 PRINT "THE X VALUES ARE"
90 MAT PRINT X
100 PRINT
110 PRINT "THE Y VALUES ARE"
120 MAT PRINT Y
130 FOR I=1 TO 5
140 Q(I,1)=X(I)^2
150 Q(I,2)=X(I)*Y(I)
160 Q(I,3)=Y(I)^2
170 Q(I,4)=X(I)
180 Q(I,5)=Y(I)
190 NEXT I
200 MAT R=INV(Q,D)
210 PRINT
220 PRINT "DET="D
230 PRINT
240 MAT S=R*M
250 REM: WE DON'T KNOW THE SMALLEST VALUE OF THE S(I). WE FIND IT AND SCALE
260 REM: EVERY COEFFICIENT BY THAT VALUE
270 J=MIN(ABS(S(1)),ABS(S(2)),ABS(S(3)),ABS(S(4)),ABS(S(5)),1)
280 MAT S=(1/J)*S
290 REM: WE NEED TO SCALE M ACCORDINGLY
300 MAT M=(1/J)*M
310 PRINT "THE COEFFICIENTS OF THE CONIC ARE"
320 MAT PRINT S
330 PRINT
340 PRINT "THE CONSTANT TERM IS"
350 PRINT
360 PRINT M(1)
```

```
THE X VALUES ARE

 20              22              26              32              40

THE Y VALUES ARE

 27.6250         27.4670         26.9281         25.5650         22.6777

DET= 15917.2

THE COEFFICIENTS OF THE CONIC ARE

 2.44268         1.00000         2.95214        -110.035         70.8356

THE CONSTANT TERM IS

 3538.60
```

In the program, the unknown vector is labeled $S = (A,B,C,D,E)$. The coefficients of the variables $A, \ldots, E$ are stored in the matrix Q; the values of the elements of Q are determined in lines 130–190. The vector $M = (1,1,1,1,1)$. The vector S is found from the relation

S = INV(Q)*M

in lines 200 and 240.

Since the relative sizes of the coefficients $A, \ldots, E$ in equation (1) compared with the right-hand side of equation (1), the number 1, are not known to us at this time, it is wise to scale these coefficients so that the smallest number appearing is 1. This scaling retains the relative magnitudes of all five coefficients and might modify the right-hand side of equation (1). In the program, this new value for the right-hand side, which may no longer be 1, is called the "CONSTANT TERM." All this is done in lines 250–300.

A graph of the curve is given in Figure 15-1.

The technique illustrated can be used, when properly modified, to find the equation of a line through two points, of a plane through three noncollinear points, of a circle through three noncollinear points, and of a sphere through four noncoplanar points.

Illustration Family Influence

Our final illustration is drawn from sociology. A family unit consisting of a paternal grandfather and grandmother, a maternal grandmother, a father, mother, three daughters, and two sons relate to each other in a way described by the graph in Figure 15-2.

If a member can influence another, an arrow is drawn connecting the two; the direction of the arrow indicates the direction of the influence. Matrix A in Figure 15-3 corresponds to this directed graph. The matrix consists of zeros and ones; a one appears in position (α,β) if member α (in a row) influences member β (in a column).

The F $\rightarrow$ MGM relationship is an example of a one-step relationship; the father directly influences the maternal grandmother. The father cannot directly influence his oldest daughter, that is, the position (F,D_1) in the matrix has a zero entry. The father, however, can influence his oldest daughter indirectly through the maternal grandmother: F $\rightarrow$ MGM $\rightarrow$ D_1. This is called a two-step relationship. To discover all two-step relationships, we calculate the matrix A^2. Each entry will indicate the number of two-step relationships among the various family members. Similarly, the entries of A^3 will indicate the number of three-step relationships among the members of the family. The following program does this for this family; the output consists of the one-, two-, three-, and four-step relationships.

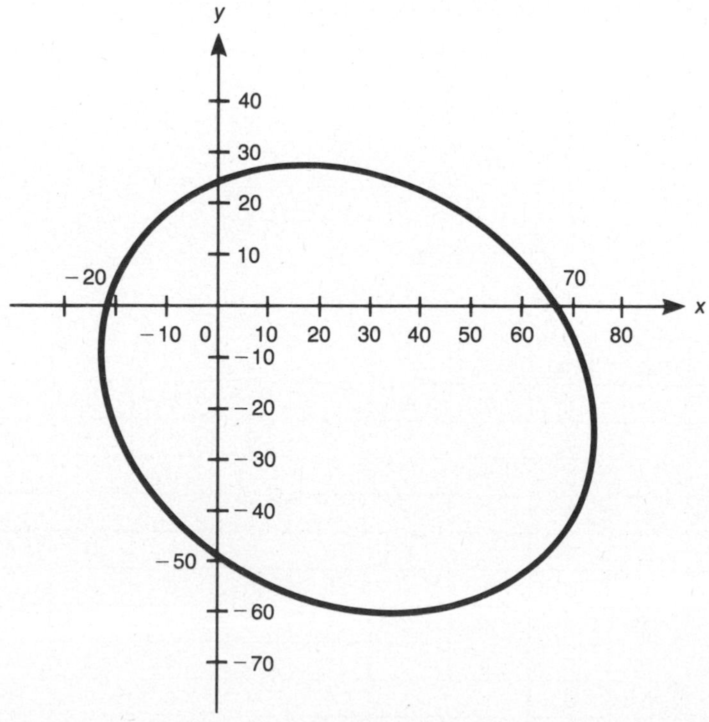

FIGURE 15-1

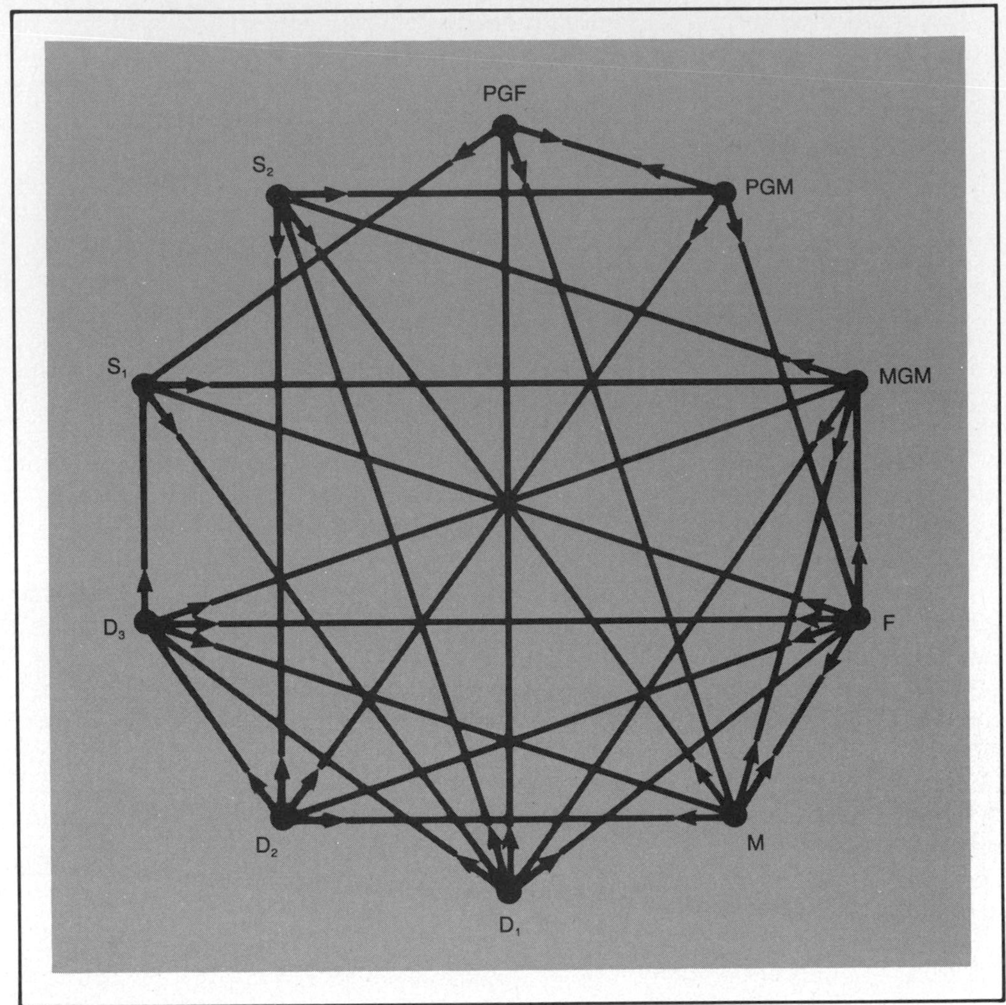

FIGURE 15-2

FIGURE 15-3

	PGF	PGM	MGM	F	M	D_1	D_2	D_3	S_1	S_2
PGF	0	1	0	0	1	0	0	0	1	0
PGM	1	0	0	1	0	0	1	0	0	0
MGM	0	0	0	0	1	1	0	0	0	1
F	0	0	1	0	1	0	1	1	1	0
M	0	0	1	1	0	0	1	0	0	1
D_1	1	0	0	1	0	0	0	1	0	1
D_2	0	1	0	0	1	0	0	1	0	1
D_3	0	0	1	1	1	0	0	0	1	0
S_1	0	0	1	0	0	1	0	0	0	0
S_2	0	1	0	0	1	0	1	0	0	0

```
10 DIM A(10,10),B(10,10),C(10,10)
20 MAT A=ZER
30 A(1,2)=1,A(1,5)=1,A(1,9)=1
40 A(2,1)=1,A(2,4)=1,A(2,7)=1
50 A(3,5)=1,A(3,6)=1,A(3,10)=1
60 A(4,3)=1,A(4,5)=1,A(4,7)=1,A(4,8)=1,A(4,9)=1
70 A(5,3)=1,A(5,4)=1,A(5,7)=1,A(5,10)=1
80 A(6,1)=1,A(6,4)=1,A(6,8)=1,A(6,10)=1
90 A(7,2)=1,A(7,5)=1,A(7,8)=1,A(7,10)=1
100 A(8,3)=1,A(8,4)=1,A(8,5)=1,A(8,9)=1
110 A(9,3)=1,A(9,6)=1
120 A(10,2)=1,A(10,5)=1,A(10,7)=1
130 PRINT "FIRST LEVEL"
140 MAT PRINT A;
150 MAT B=A*A
160 PRINT "SECOND LEVEL"
170 MAT PRINT B;
180 MAT C=A*B
190 PRINT "THIRD LEVEL"
200 MAT PRINT C;
210 MAT B=A*C
220 PRINT "FOURTH LEVEL"
230 MAT PRINT B;
```

```
FIRST LEVEL

    0    1    0    0    1    0    0    0    1    0

    1    0    0    1    0    0    1    0    0    0

    0    0    0    0    1    1    0    0    0    1

    0    0    1    0    1    0    1    1    1    0

    0    0    1    1    0    0    1    0    0    1

    1    0    0    1    0    0    0    1    0    1

    0    1    0    0    1    0    0    1    0    1

    0    0    1    1    1    0    0    0    1    0

    0    0    1    0    0    1    0    0    0    0

    0    1    0    0    1    0    1    0    0    0

SECOND LEVEL

    1    0    2    2    0    1    2    0    0    1

    0    2    1    0    3    0    1    2    2    1

    1    1    1    2    1    0    2    1    0    2

    0    1    3    2    3    2    1    1    1    3

    0    2    1    0    4    1    2    2    1    2

    0    2    2    1    4    0    2    1    3    0

    1    1    2    3    2    0    3    0    1    1

    0    0    3    1    2    2    2    1    1    2

    1    0    0    1    1    1    0    1    0    2

    1    1    1    2    1    0    2    1    0    2
```

```
THIRD LEVEL
    1     4     2     1     8     2     3     5     3     5
    2     2     7     7     5     3     6     1     2     5
    1     5     4     3     9     1     6     4     4     4
    3     4     7     7    10     4     9     5     3     9
    3     4     7     9     7     2     8     3     2     8
    2     2     9     7     6     5     7     3     2     8
    1     5     6     3    10     3     7     6     4     7
    2     4     5     5     9     4     5     5     2     9
    1     3     3     3     5     0     4     2     3     2
    1     5     4     3     9     1     6     4     4     4
FOURTH LEVEL
    6     9    17    19    17     5    18     6     7    15
    5    13    15    11    28     9    19    16    10    21
    6    11    20    19    22     8    21    10     8    20
    8    21    25    23    40    10    30    20    15    30
    6    19    21    16    38     9    28    19    15    24
    7    17    18    16    36    11    23    19    12    27
    8    15    23    24    30    10    25    13    10    26
    8    16    21    22    31     7    27    14    12    23
    3     7    13    10    15     6    13     7     6    12
    6    11    20    19    22     8    21    10     8    20
```

We know that not every member can influence directly every other member; the matrix A has many zeros. When we compute A^2, we are calculating the number of two-step relationships. If A and A^2 are added, then each positive entry indicates a one-step or two-step relationship; a zero entry continues to indicate no influence. If A^3 is added to $(A + A^2)$, then a positive entry in position (α,β) indicates the number of one-step, two-step, or three-step relationships existing in that position.

This process is carried out in the following program.

```
10 DIM A(10,10),B(10,10),C(10,10),D(10,10)
20 MAT A=ZER
30 A(1,2)=1,A(1,5)=1,A(1,9)=1
40 A(2,1)=1,A(2,4)=1,A(2,7)=1
50 A(3,5)=1,A(3,6)=1,A(3,10)=1
60 A(4,3)=1,A(4,5)=1,A(4,7)=1,A(4,8)=1,A(4,9)=1
70 A(5,3)=1,A(5,4)=1,A(5,7)=1,A(5,10)=1
80 A(6,1)=1,A(6,4)=1,A(6,8)=1,A(6,10)=1
90 A(7,2)=1,A(7,5)=1,A(7,8)=1,A(7,10)=1
100 A(8,3)=1,A(8,4)=1,A(8,5)=1,A(8,9)=1
110 A(9,3)=1,A(9,6)=1
120 A(10,2)=1,A(10,5)=1,A(10,7)=1
130 PRINT "FIRST LEVEL DOMINANCE"
140 MAT PRINT A;
150 MAT B=A*A
160 MAT C=A+B
170 PRINT "FIRST + SECOND LEVEL DOMINANCE"
```

```
180 MAT PRINT C;
190 MAT D=A*B
200 MAT D=D+C
210 PRINT "FIRST + SECOND + THIRD LEVEL DOMINANCE"
220 MAT PRINT D;
```

```
FIRST LEVEL DOMINANCE

   0   1   0   0   1   0   0   0   1   0

   1   0   0   1   0   0   1   0   0   0

   0   0   0   0   1   1   0   0   0   1

   0   0   1   0   1   0   1   1   1   0

   0   0   1   1   0   0   1   0   0   1

   1   0   0   1   0   0   0   1   0   1

   0   1   0   0   1   0   0   1   0   1

   0   0   1   1   1   0   0   0   1   0

   0   0   1   0   0   1   0   0   0   0

   0   1   0   0   1   0   1   0   0   0


FIRST + SECOND LEVEL DOMINANCE

   1   1   2   2   1   1   2   0   1   1

   1   2   1   1   3   0   2   2   2   1

   1   1   1   2   2   1   2   1   0   3

   0   1   4   2   4   2   2   2   2   3

   0   2   2   1   4   1   3   2   1   3

   1   2   2   2   4   0   2   2   3   1

   1   2   2   3   3   0   3   1   1   2

   0   0   4   2   3   2   2   1   2   2

   1   0   1   1   1   2   0   1   0   2

   1   2   1   2   2   0   3   1   0   2

FIRST + SECOND + THIRD LEVEL DOMINANCE

   2   5   4   3   9   3   5   5   4   6

   3   4   8   8   8   3   8   3   4   6

   2   6   5   5  11   2   8   5   4   7

   3   5  11   9  14   6  11   7   5  12

   3   6   9  10  11   3  11   5   3  11

   3   4  11   9  10   5   9   5   5   9

   2   7   8   6  13   3  10   7   5   9

   2   4   9   7  12   6   7   6   4  11

   2   3   4   4   6   2   4   3   3   4

   2   7   5   5  11   1   9   5   4   6
```

We can see from the printout that there are several places where two-step relationships do not exist. When three-step relationships are included, everybody can influence everybody else. Note, there is only one way that the younger son can influence his oldest sister. Can you find it?[9]

Exercises

15.1 Show that if A is an arbitrary $m \times n$ matrix and I is the $m \times m$ identity matrix, that $I*A=A$. Also, if I is the $n \times n$ identity matrix, that $A*I=A$. (This is not a computer exercise. It can be proved directly from the definition of matrix multiplication.)

15.2 Write a program that will solve the following system of linear equations:

$$\begin{aligned} 3X + 2Y - 6Z + 4W &= 29 \\ -X - 3Y + 4Z - 5W &= -40 \\ 2X - Y + Z - 3W &= -25 \\ -2X + 2Y - 4Z + W &= 28 \end{aligned}$$

15.3 Modify the program written for Exercise 15.2 so that it will solve the same system of equations when the values assigned to the right-hand side are:
(a) $-25, 13, 2, -9$
(b) $16, -27, -12, -3$
(c) $3, -5, -1, -3$

15.4 Using the same matrix B as in the illustration on page 298, modify the program to produce a final matrix B that has -10 in the 2×3 submatrix located in the upper left-hand corner.

15.5 Modify the program on page 302 so that at the end of each year, the funds available for distribution for the following year are increased by 10 percent. For the results printed, at the end of the first year the funds available were 240, 160, 140, and 160, but now $240 + 10\%(240) = 264$ will be available to G_1, $160 + 10\%(160) = 176$ will be available to G_2, $140 + 10\%(140) = 154$ will be available to G_3, and 176 will be available to G_4. Thus, the vector of starting values for the second year is (264, 176, 154, 176).

What are the short-range (first 10-years) implications of this arrangement? Is the system stable over the long range? What happens to the ratios G_i/G_j $(i \neq j)$ over the long range?

15.6 For each of the following matrices, find its characteristic equation.

(a)

2576	2512	2443	3077	2311	2088
-572	-555	-540	-686	-508	-456
-5533	-5398	-5247	-6614	-4963	-4482
-205	-200	-195	-242	-185	-168
5502	5366	5215	6581	4929	4446
-1796	-1752	-1702	-2150	-1608	-1449

[9] For the interested reader, two elementary references and an advanced one are offered: Chris Rorres and Howard Anton, *Application of Linear Algebra* (N.Y.: John Wiley and Sons,1977); Gareth Williams, *Computational Linear Algebra with Models*, Second Edition (Boston: Allyn and Bacon, 1978); and *Proceedings of the IBM Scientific Computing Symposium on Combinatorial Problems, March 16–18* (White Plains, N.Y.: IBM, Data Processing Division, 1964).

(b)

18792	21360	21614	23736	24438	25698
−4277	−4868	−4923	−5408	−5569	−5856
−40483	−46014	−46563	−51132	−52647	−55362
−1485	−1686	−1707	−1874	−1929	−2028
40432	45960	46508	51068	52586	55296
−13216	−15022	−15202	−16690	−17188	−18073

(c)

13291	11712	14798	12126	16302	18300
−3140	−2779	−3492	−2876	−3844	−4308
−28618	−25212	−31859	−26100	−35094	−39396
−1018	−896	−1134	−933	−1250	−1404
28680	25276	31922	26166	35161	39468
−9378	−8264	−10438	−8552	−11498	−12909

(d)

−29244	−32032	−31542	−37604	−33838	−33894
6601	7240	7119	8512	7637	7644
62951	68950	67895	80948	72835	72954
2317	2534	2499	2970	2681	2688
−62776	−68768	−67704	−80752	−72630	−72744
20510	22470	22120	26390	23730	23767

(e)

30826	34401	35204	38653	39584	41622
−7042	−7865	−8046	−8836	−9050	−9516
−66399	−74100	−75831	−83258	−85267	−89658
−2428	−2708	−2772	−3043	−3116	−3276
66336	74035	75764	83181	85194	89580
−21684	−24200	−24766	−27188	−27848	−29281

15.7 For each of the matrices in Exercise 15.6, find its minimal equation.

PRINTUSING 16

Our control over printing output has been limited to the use of the comma, the semicolon, and the TAB function. Control over the printing of strings is greater than control over the printing of numbers. Additional control over the printing of numbers may be obtained by converting them to strings and then printing the numbers as strongs—obviously, not a desirable procedure. Another BASIC printing instruction, however, applied to both alphabetic and numeric information and offers all the control we may reasonably need. This instruction, really a pair of instructions, is called PRINTUSING. Associated with each PRINTUSING statement is an image statement.

An Unresolved Problem

In Chapter 4, we discussed the question of investing $1000 for a period of two years in a bank paying 6 percent interest compounded quarterly. The formula for calculating the future value of the investment at the end of the period is:

$$A = 1000\left(1 + \frac{.06}{4}\right)^{2 \cdot 4}$$

and, in this case, A = 1126.49. The format for representing the number A seems quite reasonable. An integral part represents the dollars, and a decimal part represents the cents. Suppose, however, that we have invested only $100. In this case, the computer would print A = 112.649, and our aesthetic sense might balk. Of course, we can round A to 2 decimal places, but if we do, the computer will print A = 112.650, and there is still a trailing zero.

If we have invested $10,000, then the amount A is 11264.9, and while we can interpret the answer, we might wonder if the number of cents is 90, or 91, or anything else up to 99. We could find out easily enough by using extended precision, a concept we shall discuss in Chapter 22, in which case A = 11264.92586595306. While it answers the question (A = 11264.93 when rounded), we still cannot get the computer to print A = 11264.93.

If our deposit were $1,000,000, the answer would come back, in single precision, A = 1.12649E+06, clearly not the way to represent dollar amounts. If extended precision is used, A = 1126492.58659506, which we could round by eye to 1126492.59. The extended precision format will work if the amount deposited is $1,000,000,000,000,000 (one quadrillion dollars), quite a sizable sum. If 10 quadrillion is used, even in extended precision, the answer is given in floating-point notation.

We might ask another question: Is it possible to have the dollar sign printed in its proper position, so that $1126.49 would appear? The statement

```
PRINT "$"A
```

does not work because it leaves at least one blank space between the dollar sign and the first digit.

These problems can be circumvented by the following procedure. Calculate the amount A in extended precision, round to two decimal places, convert the number to a string variable, delete the first character (a blank), and then delete all characters to the right of the second position past the decimal point. Concatenate the dollar sign and this resulting string and print. Quite a job.

To circumvent the bother of writing a special program every time a special print format is needed, BASIC provides a fourth print option, PRINTUSING.[1]

The PRINTUSING Instruction

Like the READ statement that requires an accompanying DATA statement, PRINTUSING needs an "image" line. Whereas the computer automatically keeps track of which data have been read, we must explicitly indicate in the PRINTUSING statement the image line that is to be used. This is done by referring to it by its line number. An image line is further recognized by the fact that its leading character is a colon. We shall refer to the image line as :(image).

The general rules governing these two instructions will become apparent from the examples that follow. The guiding principle, however, is that all references to the data to be printed are made in the PRINTUSING line, whereas the details of how they are to be presented on the page are given in the :(image) line.

```
 10 PRINTUSING 50
 50 :     EXACTLY WHAT APPEARS HERE
>

     EXACTLY WHAT APPEARS HERE
```

In this example, think of mapping the image line, line 50, character by character, into a string S$. The first character of S$ is the first character following the colon in line 50; in this example, it is a blank. In fact, since the first five characters following the colon are blanks, the first five characters in S$ are to be blanks. The next 25 characters in both line 50 and S$, corresponding to positions 6 through 30, are "EXACTLY WHAT APPEARS HERE." The remaining characters in both are blanks. Then, printing line 50 is the same as printing S$ with the first character of the string appearing in the first print position on the line. In this example, EXACTLY WHAT APPEARS HERE occupies print positions 6 through 30. The prompt symbol > appears in the first print position.

Another example can be seen in the following program.

```
10 FOR X=1 TO 10
20 PRINT
30 PRINT "IF X="X", THEN"X^(1/3)" IS ITS CUBE ROOT"
40 PRINTUSING 60,X,X^(1/3),"CUBE ROOT"
50 NEXT X
60 :IF X=##, THEN #.### IS ITS #########
```

[1]On some computers, PRINTUSING and PRINT USING are equivalent.

```
IF X= 1, THEN 1 IS ITS CUBE ROOT
IF X= 1, THEN 1.000 IS ITS CUBE ROOT

IF X= 2, THEN 1.25992 IS ITS CUBE ROOT
IF X= 2, THEN 1.260 IS ITS CUBE ROOT

IF X= 3, THEN 1.44225 IS ITS CUBE ROOT
IF X= 3, THEN 1.442 IS ITS CUBE ROOT

IF X= 4, THEN 1.58740 IS ITS CUBE ROOT
IF X= 4, THEN 1.587 IS ITS CUBE ROOT

IF X= 5, THEN 1.70998 IS ITS CUBE ROOT
IF X= 5, THEN 1.710 IS ITS CUBE ROOT

IF X= 6, THEN 1.81712 IS ITS CUBE ROOT
IF X= 6, THEN 1.817 IS ITS CUBE ROOT

IF X= 7, THEN 1.91293 IS ITS CUBE ROOT
IF X= 7, THEN 1.913 IS ITS CUBE ROOT

IF X= 8, THEN 2 IS ITS CUBE ROOT
IF X= 8, THEN 2.000 IS ITS CUBE ROOT

IF X= 9, THEN 2.08008 IS ITS CUBE ROOT
IF X= 9, THEN 2.080 IS ITS CUBE ROOT

IF X= 10, THEN 2.15443 IS ITS CUBE ROOT
IF X=10, THEN 2.154 IS ITS CUBE ROOT
```

Observe the following difference between this example and the previous one. In the first, there was no reference to any data following the line number 50 in the PRINTUSING statement, line 10. In this example, at line 40 there are references to two numeric variables, X and X^(1/3), and to a string "CUBE ROOT." Exactly how these are to appear on the page is controlled by :(image), line 60. Using the analogy presented in the first example, line 60 is equivalent to a string S$ into which the familiar graphic symbols—the letters of the alphabet, the equal sign, the comma, and the decimal point—as well as the separating blank spaces, are to be mapped. But what about the number signs, the #'s?

From line 10, we see that the variable X assumed values from 1 to 10. This required at most 2 print positions and, if you look at line 60, there are two #'s following "IF X= " at positions 6 and 7. Each time the program executed the loop, the appropriate value of X was substituted for these two #'s. If we had wanted X to take on values between 100 and 999, we would have reserved three spaces; this would be done with ###.

The second numeric variable is X^(1/3) and is an integer for X equal to 1 and 8. Otherwise, for the X's being used, it is an infinite decimal whose integer part is either 1 or 2. The significant point is that the integer part needs only one print position. That is why, in line 60, only one # was written immediately preceding the decimal point. The integer part of X^(1/3) was inserted there each time the loop was executed.

The computer calculated the cube root of X to more places than we needed. For our illustration, we wanted to present the values rounded to three decimal places. We did this by using, in line 60, exactly three #'s following the decimal point. If we had wanted the answer rounded to two decimal places, we would have used only two #'s; if we had wanted four decimal places, we would have used four #'s, ####.

Finally, observe that the length of the string "CUBE ROOT" is nine and that there are nine #'s at the end of line 60. Each time the loop was executed, the string replaced these nine #'s and was printed instead.

The familiar print line 30 was inserted in the program to provide a basis for comparison. Observe that when the value of X was printed using line 30, the number was left justified;[2] when the same value was printed using lines 40 and 60, the number was right

[2]On some computers, the printed values of a variable are right justified.

justified. This is most clearly seen for X = 10. When the cube roots of 1 and 8, which are the integers 1 and 2, were calculated and printed using line 30, the numbers were printed as integers. When these same values are printed using lines 40 and 60, there are three trailing zeros. This is characteristic of PRINTUSING: When there are fewer digits in the decimal part of a number than are called for by the number of #'s in the :(image) line, the computer supplies trailing zeros.

That PRINTUSING right justifies numbers might be more easily seen from the following printout:

```
10 FOR I=1 TO 5
20 PRINTUSING 40,I,10^I
30 NEXT I
40 :       #      ######


     1         10
     2        100
     3       1000
     4      10000
     5     100000
```

Six #'s are needed because 10^5 requires six spaces.

When a number to be printed requires more print positions than we allotted, asterisks are generated to warn us. This is illustrated in the following:

```
10 PRINT TAB(6)"X"TAB(16)"2^X"TAB(29)"3^X"TAB(43)"5^X"
20 PRINT
30 FOR X=1 TO 15
40 PRINTUSING 60,X,2^X,3^X,5^X
50 NEXT X
60 :     ##          ####        #####         ######


     X         2^X          3^X           5^X

     1           2            3             5
     2           4            9            25
     3           8           27           125
     4          16           81           625
     5          32          243          3125
     6          64          729         15625
     7         128         2187         78125
     8         256         6561        390625
     9         512        19683        ******
    10        1024        59049        ******
    11        2048        *****        ******
    12        4096        *****        ******
    13        8192        *****        ******
    14        ****        *****        ******
    15        ****        *****        ******
```

PRINTUSING with Negative Numbers

In the preceding examples, only nonnegative data were chosen. The following program, in addition to illustrating how negative numbers are treated, introduces two modifications to the generic form #. . .# . #. . . # . One is + # . . . # . #, the other is − # . . . #. # . . . #.

```
10 FOR I=1 TO 3
20 READ X,Y,Z
30 PRINTUSING 40,X,Y,Z
40 : ##.##     +##.##     -##.##
50 NEXT I
```

```
60 DATA -12.345,-34.567,-56.789
70 DATA +12.345,+34.567,+56.789
80 DATA  12.345, 34.567, 56.789
```

```
-****       -34.57      -56.79
12.34       +34.57       56.79
12.34       +34.57       56.79
```

When ## . ## is used, a positive number, either with an explicit plus sign preceding it or with the plus sign only implied, is printed without the plus symbol. If the program is required to print a negative number, the result is flagged for our attention; the minus sign appears in the first position followed by asterisks in the remaining spaces that have been reserved. This can be seen in the first row of the first column of the printout.

If the convention print minus signs, leave plus signs blank is wanted, we would use − ## . ##. See the third column of the printout. Finally, if both plus and minus signs are to be printed, we would use + ## . ##. See the second column of the printout.

We said that when PRINTUSING is used the answer is rounded. In this last example, however, the number 12.345 appears to have been truncated, not rounded. The explanation was given earlier, pages 257–59. All internal arithmetic is done in binary, but the input and the printout are in decimal. The conversion of some decimal numbers with a finite number of places to their binary equivalents is only approximate. The error in the printout stems from the lack of perfect correspondence inside the computer between the decimal and binary representations of the number.

PRINTUSING with Floating-Point Numbers

Floating-point notation is also available in PRINTUSING. When floating point notation is wanted, we must provide for four places: the E, the plus or minus sign and the two digits. We signal this by using !!!!. If any other number of exclamation points is used, they will be printed, exactly as given, in the output. As an additional signal to the computer that floating point notation is being called for, a decimal point must appear in the field in :(image). All floating-point printout is independent of where we put the decimal point; in the printout, the decimal point will appear after the first digit. The number of digits printed equals the number of #'s used. The following program illustrates this.

```
10 FOR I=1 TO 10
20 X=INT(50*RND(1))
30 Y=10-20*RND(1)
40 Z=Y^X
50 PRINTUSING 70,X,Y,Z
60 NEXT I
70 :THE EXPONENT =##, THE BASE = -##.##!!!! AND THE ANSWER =+####.####!!!!
```

```
THE EXPONENT =20, THE BASE =  8.551E+00 AND THE ANSWER =+4.3638749E+18
THE EXPONENT =40, THE BASE =  6.646E+00 AND THE ANSWER =+7.9892209E+32
THE EXPONENT =38, THE BASE =  7.035E+00 AND THE ANSWER =+1.5685611E+32
THE EXPONENT =45, THE BASE =  8.297E+00 AND THE ANSWER =+2.2471858E+41
THE EXPONENT =19, THE BASE = -4.691E-01 AND THE ANSWER =-5.6752285E-07
THE EXPONENT =35, THE BASE = -5.073E-01 AND THE ANSWER =-4.8235067E-11
THE EXPONENT =39, THE BASE =  8.866E+00 AND THE ANSWER =+9.1479167E+36
THE EXPONENT = 8, THE BASE =  6.763E-01 AND THE ANSWER =+4.3758492E-02
THE EXPONENT =16, THE BASE = -5.970E+00 AND THE ANSWER =+2.6056250E+12
THE EXPONENT =39, THE BASE = -2.244E+00 AND THE ANSWER =-4.9356483E+13
```

In line 20, X is an integer 0 through 49 selected at random. In line 30, Y is a number between −10 and +10, also selected at random. Since both Y and Z can be either positive or negative, it was necessary to use either the plus or minus sign in the field for these numbers in the :(image), line 70.

Printing Strings

We have shown that text strings may be inserted in a field of the form ##...#. In addition, text strings may be inserted in fields containing plus or minus signs, a decimal point, and four exclamation points. A text string when inserted into any field is left justified, that is, the first character of the string is inserted in the first available position. If the length of the string is less than the available spaces, blanks are used as filler at the end. If the length of the string is greater than the available spaces, the string is truncated at the right.

```
10 :THE VALUE IS +##.########## , WHICH WAS ##########
20 FOR I=1 TO 10
30 X=100*RND(1)
40 IF X<50 THEN 70
50 PRINTUSING 10,X,'EXPECTED'
60 GOTO 80
70 PRINTUSING 10,'TOO SMALL','UNEXPECTED'
80 NEXT I
```

```
THE VALUE IS TOO SMALL      , WHICH WAS UNEXPECTED
THE VALUE IS TOO SMALL      , WHICH WAS UNEXPECTED
THE VALUE IS +64.9266886292 , WHICH WAS EXPECTED
THE VALUE IS TOO SMALL      , WHICH WAS UNEXPECTED
THE VALUE IS +97.1270627109 , WHICH WAS EXPECTED
THE VALUE IS TOO SMALL      , WHICH WAS UNEXPECTED
THE VALUE IS +89.2253513215 , WHICH WAS EXPECTED
THE VALUE IS TOO SMALL      , WHICH WAS UNEXPECTED
THE VALUE IS TOO SMALL      , WHICH WAS UNEXPECTED
THE VALUE IS +69.8968630051 , WHICH WAS EXPECTED
```

In the above program, the string "TOO SMALL" was inserted into the first field; it is clear that the letter T occupies the first available space. Since the total length of the allotted field (14 spaces) is more than 9 characters—the length of the string TOO SMALL—blanks fill the remaining 5 spaces. The second field allowed for 10 characters, and both EXPECTED and UNEXPECTED are accommodated.

The following program differs from the one above only in that the lengths of the two fields in line 10 were shortened to illustrate the truncation of the strings and the plus sign was changed to minus.

```
10 :THE VALUE IS -##.### ,WHICH WAS #######
20 FOR I=1 TO 10
30 X=100*RND(1)
40 IF X<50 THEN 70
50 PRINTUSING 10,X,'EXPECTED'
60 GOTO 80
70 PRINTUSING 10,'TOO SMALL','UNEXPECTED'
80 NEXT I
```

```
THE VALUE IS  75.514 ,WHICH WAS EXPECTE
THE VALUE IS  85.254 ,WHICH WAS EXPECTE
THE VALUE IS TOO SMA ,WHICH WAS UNEXPEC
THE VALUE IS TOO SMA ,WHICH WAS UNEXPEC
THE VALUE IS  57.580 ,WHICH WAS EXPECTE
THE VALUE IS TOO SMA ,WHICH WAS UNEXPEC
THE VALUE IS  52.625 ,WHICH WAS EXPECTE
```

```
THE VALUE IS  59.482 ,WHICH WAS EXPECTE
THE VALUE IS  83.270 ,WHICH WAS EXPECTE
THE VALUE IS  64.286 ,WHICH WAS EXPECTE
```

Too Few Data and Too Many Data

If, in a PRINTUSING statement, fewer data are given than there are fields in the :(image) line, those data that are available are printed. When data are called for to replace the next # and none are available, printing of the line halts. This may be seen in the following.

```
10 PRINTUSING 20,99,88
20 :AA  ##  BB  ##  CC  ##  DD
```

```
AA  99  BB  88  CC
```

Only two data elements are provided at line 10 although :(image) expects three. Printing stopped when the third ## was encountered.

If, in a PRINTUSING statement, more variables are specified than there are fields in the :(image) statement, the image statement is used repeatedly until all values are printed, at which point the printing stops at the first unused field in the image statement.

```
10 PRINTUSING 20,99,88,77,66,55,44,33
20 :AA  ##  BB  ##  CC  ##  DD
```

```
AA  99  BB  88  CC  77  DD
AA  66  BB  55  CC  44  DD
AA  33  BB
```

In the example, seven values are specified in the PRINTUSING statement but only three fields are indicated in the image. The first three values go to the first three fields; the next three are used when the image statement is reprinted. The seventh number then goes into the first field, and printing continues until the next field is reached. But there is no datum for this field and the printing stops.

Exercises

16.1 Let the initial value of an investment be $1,000. Calculate the future value of this investment when the interest rate is 14 percent, compounded monthly, and the money is left on deposit for 1, 2, . . . , 10 years. Print your answer so that the dollar sign immediately precedes the first digit and use a comma to separate the hundreds place from the thousands place. A typical line would look like (for 2 years)

$1,320.99

16.2 Using the same data as in Exercise 16.1, print your answer in the form $1,320AND99CTS.

16.3 Refer to Chapter 6, Exercise 6.2 (page 99). Rewrite your program so that the table generated is printed exactly like the one given on page 100.

16.4 Assume you are a printer preparing blank checks for the customers of several banks. Each bank uses a slightly different format for its checks. Also, each bank wants to imprint the name, address, city, and zip code for each of its customers. Some customers want their telephone number printed also; others do not.

You have a printing press that understands BASIC. Write one program that can be used to prepare the blank checks for several banks. Test your program for at least three different banks. Also, test it for different customers. Ignore the fact that the bank number and account numbers use MICA letters; use the terminal characters available to you.

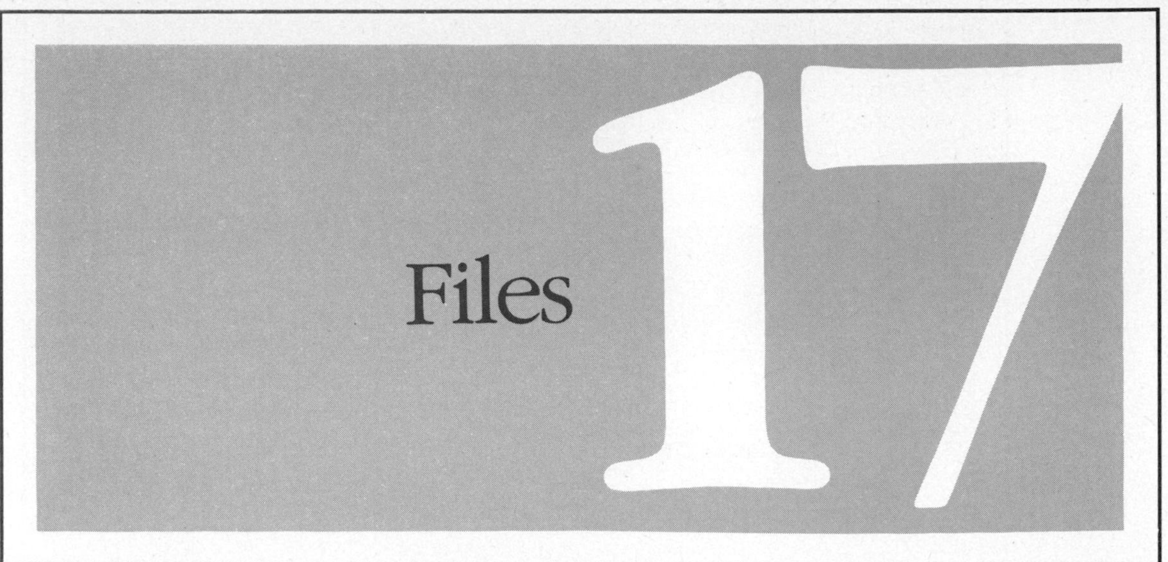

Files

17

Chapters 17 through 21 pertain to files—what they are and how to build, use, and modify them. Although not intended as an exhaustive treatise on files, these chapters will describe and illustrate a common type, known as keyed files. The information presented will be sufficient for you to understand how files in general are handled.

In this chapter we shall introduce those BASIC instructions needed to create new files, read old files, and modify existing ones. The files we shall describe are "keyed" because each record in the file has a key number associated with it. As we shall see, the key number is a useful device, which helps us to manipulate the file and its contents.

Stating the Problem

As a starting point, consider the problem of creating a personnel file for a group of people. With the information we already have, we can write a BASIC program using lists and arrays to produce such a file. This was demonstrated with the bicycle registration program.[1] If the file is needed for different purposes, we would have to modify the program to accommodate each additional need. The question then arises: Is it possible to create a file that has an existence of its own, independent of any specific program, and such that different programs, each of which may need only partial information from the file, can access it?

Suppose we teach a large class and we want to create a file containing each student's name, ID number, local address, and phone number. We expect that at future dates we will be entering grades for homework, exam grades, and a final grade. What we need is a file, stored somewhere in a cabinet, with perhaps one card per student, that contains this information. Using BASIC, we can construct an electronic equivalent.

The picture we want to keep before us consists of our terminal, a communication channel (or stream) between it and the computer, and several communication channels between the computer and the disk storage, as illustrated in Figure 17-1. The computer on which the programs here were written and run provides one channel between the

[1]See Chapter 11, pages 202–205.

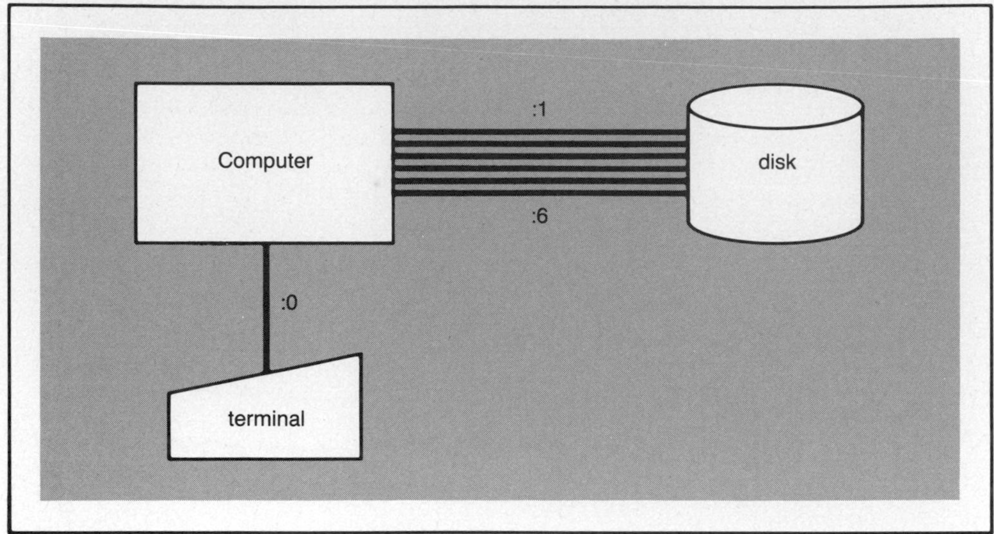

FIGURE 17-1

terminal and itself—this is designed by the symbol :0—and six channels between the disk and itself—these are denoted by :1,:2, . . . , :6. Each of the seven channels provides two way communication.

Creating a File

Because the file is to be kept in a general cabinet (on disk) with other files created by other programers, we need a means to identify it. Although having it under our account number is one level of classification, we may have several such files, one for each class we teach. The easiest way to identify a particular file would be to give it a name. In our example, we shall use MATH100.

A BASIC program that can be used to create a file follows. The BASIC program itself is called CREATE.[2]

```
      CREATE1

 1Ø OPEN "MATH1ØØ" TO :1, PRINT ON
 2Ø INPUT = $
 3Ø INPUT N$
 4Ø IF N$="" THEN 7Ø
 5Ø PRINT :1,N$
 6Ø GOTO 3Ø
 7Ø CLOSE :1
 8Ø END

 RUN

?JONES, WILLIAM
?ADAMS, DAVID
?SMITH, JOAN
?HAMBORT, ROGER
?
```

There are three unfamiliar BASIC instructions in the program, they are used in lines 10, 50, and 70. At line 10, the computer is instructed to create on disk a new file, named

[2]For most programs and printouts presented thus far, command words such as LIST and RUN were not printed because they added nothing to the continuity of the material. In what follows, they will appear when they enhance the continuity of the exposition.

'MATH100'; it is told that the information for this file will be transmitted from the computer to the disk via channel number :1 and that the only operation permitted is to put information into an *empty* file, PRINT ON. In response to the request for input, line 30, we enter the first record, JONES, WILLIAM (we assume in our example that we are initially creating a name file only), and at line 50, the name is sent from the computer to the file MATH100 via channel :1. Line 60 creates a loop, since more than one name is to be entered. After all names have been entered, we create an empty string by striking <CR>. This empty string is recognized at line 40 and control is transferred to line 70, where the communication link between the computer and the disk is closed. Actually, before the link is closed, a special record, called an end-of-file record, a non-printable control character, is placed into the file immediately after the last record we had entered.

Reading a File

Somewhere, in some distant place (actually, on disk), a file containing these four names has been created. Although we may feel a little uncomfortable because there is no tangible evidence that it exists, we need not worry.

The file is there. Using BASIC, we can write a program that retrieves the information from file MATH100 and displays it. We choose the name DISPLAY1 for this second program. A listing and run follow:

```
    DISPLAY1

10 OPEN "MATH100" TO :4, INPUT
20 ENDFILE :4,70
30 INPUT = $
40 INPUT :4,N$
50 PRINT N$
60 GOTO 40
70 CLOSE :4
80 END

RUN

JONES, WILLIAM
ADAMS, DAVID
SMITH, JOAN
HAMBORT, ROGER
```

This time, for variety, we use channel :4 to access MATH100. Any other channel would do as well. The word INPUT in line 10 means that a copy of the data in the file is to be made and brought to the main memory. The first record in the file is copied and brought into the computer, where it is assigned to the variable N$, line 40. This record is printed at our terminal, line 50. The second record is then copied from the disk and brought it, and the process repeats. Eventually, all records having pertinent data are brought in, printed at our terminal, and that special record, end-of-file (EOF), is encountered. When EOF is met, line 20 causes control to be transferred to line 70, channel :4 is closed, and the program ends.

Note that the words PRINT ON and INPUT when used in connection with files have the same operational intent as when used at a terminal. PRINT is an operation originated by the computer; the result appears at the terminal or on the disk. INPUT originates at the terminal or disk, and information is delivered to the computer.

An Alternative Method for Creating a File

Suppose the tutor for one of our classes, MATH101, when asked to create a file for that class, uses READ/DATA rather than INPUT in her program to create MATH101. She calls her program CREATE2.

```
     CREATE2

10 OPEN "MATH101" TO :1, PRINT ON
20 FOR I= 1 TO 4
30 READ N$
40 PRINT :1,N$
50 NEXT I
60 CLOSE :1
70 DATA "GRIFT, ANN","ZIMET, NANCY","WEST, ARTHUR","TRAINER, NED"
80 END

RUN
```

There is no difference between CREATE1 and CREATE2 as far as the creation of the file is concerned. Line 10 is the same in both; line 50 in CREATE1 corresponds to line 40 in CREATE2, and line 70 to line 60.

We can use the program DISPLAY1 to verify that the file MATH101 was properly constructed, provided the file name in line 100 is changed from MATH100 to MATH101. This was done and the program run.

```
     DISPLAY1

10 OPEN "MATH101" TO :4, INPUT
20 ENDFILE :4,70
30 INPUT = $
40 INPUT :4,N$
50 PRINT N$
60 GOTO 40
70 CLOSE :4
80 END

RUN

GRIFT, ANN
ZIMET, NANCY
WEST, ARTHUR
TRAINER, NED
```

A Numeric File

Thus far, we created two files, first by inputing information from the terminal and then by having the computer read prepared data. We could also create a file by having the computer perform a calculation and store the results in a file. For example, suppose we wanted to create a file consisting of the numbers 1 through 10, their squares, and their cubes. The name we chose for the file is TABLE; the program we wrote to create it, CALCULATE, is reproduced below.

```
     CALCULATE

10 OPEN "TABLE" TO :6, PRINT ON
20 FOR X=1 TO 10
30 PRINT :6,X
40 PRINT :6,X^2
50 PRINT :6,X^3
60 NEXT X
70 CLOSE :6
80 END

RUN
```

If we want to see what is in TABLE, the following program, called SHOW-TABLE, will return the data and print them.

```
        SHOW-TABLE

10 OPEN "TABLE" TO :3, INPUT
20 FOR I=1 TO 10
30 INPUT :3,A
40 INPUT :3,B
50 INPUT :3,C
60 PRINTUSING 90,A,B,C,A+B+C
70 NEXT I
80 CLOSE :6
90 :  ##            ###           ####           ####
100 END

RUN

  1             1             1              3
  2             4             8             14
  3             9            27             39
  4            16            64             84
  5            25           125            155
  6            36           216            258
  7            49           343            399
  8            64           512            584
  9            81           729            819
 10           100          1000           1110
```

At line 60, an additional wrinkle was introduced. Once the values of X, X^2, and X^3 are in the computer's main memory, they can be manipulated as needed and the results of this additional computation printed. In this example, the program also prints the sum X + X^2 + X^3.

End-of-File

Reexamine CREATE1, which is reproduced for convenience:

```
10 OPEN "MATH100" TO :1, PRINT ON
20 INPUT = $
30 INPUT N$
40 IF N$="" THEN 70
50 PRINT :1,N$
60 GOTO 30
70 CLOSE :1
80 END
```

The program was terminated when, in response to a request for additional input at line 30, we created an empty string by striking <CR>. When this empty string is recognized at line 40, control is transferred to line 70 and channel :1 is closed. Another procedure purposefully creates the end-of-file mark and accomplishes the same results. First, we delete line 40 and, second, insert line 15.

```
10 OPEN "MATH100" TO :1, PRINT ON
15 ENDFILE :0,70
20 INPUT = $
30 INPUT N$
50 PRINT :1,N$
60 GOTO 30
70 CLOSE :1
80 END
```

Recall that the :0 channel is the communication link between the terminal and the computer. Line 15 states that when an end-of-file signal is received from the keyboard, the program is to execute line 70 next. The word GOTO is not needed; the line number after the comma designates the location of the next instruction. The end-of-file signal is ESC F.[3]

To illustrate this procedure, we use this modified form of CREATE1. We call it CREATE3.

```
        CREATE3

 10 OPEN "MATH100" TO :1, PRINT ON
 15 ENDFILE :0,70
 20 INPUT = $
 30 INPUT N$
 50 PRINT :1,N$
 60 GOTO 30
 70 CLOSE :1
 80 END

 RUN

MATH100

      10 OLD FILE
```

Note that when CREATE3 was run an error message appeared. The FILE MATH100 has already been created, and the PRINT ON command in line 10 does not permit writing on an existing file. If MATH100 had been a new file, there would have been no such prohibition. To demonstrate the running of the program, we could either create a new file, say MATH102, or delete MATH100 and then recreate it. We chose the latter course; we deleted MATH100 and immediately ran the program.

```
 DELETE MATH100

 RUN

?JONES, WILLIAM
?ADAMS, DAVID
?SMITH, JOAN
?HAMBORT, ROGER
?F\
```

The F\ that appears after the fifth question mark is this particular terminal's way of printing ESC F.

Again, we use DISPLAY1 to verify that the file was created:

```
      DISPLAY1

 10 OPEN "MATH100" TO :4, INPUT
 20 ENDFILE :4,70
 30 INPUT = $
 40 INPUT :4,N$
 50 PRINT N$
 60 GOTO 40
 70 CLOSE :4
 80 END

 RUN

JONES, WILLIAM
ADAMS, DAVID
SMITH, JOAN
HAMBORT, ROGER
```

[3] Refer to the EBCDIC character code, pages 252–53. EBCDIC value 48,ESC F, is for end-of-file.

We have illustrated three ways to create a file; one used the interactive INPUT instruction, the second used the READ/DATA instructions, and the third stored calculated values. Using INPUT, two ways to indicate the end-of-file were given. One is based on the recognition of some special character specified by the programer; the other uses the ESC F command from the terminal. Also, we illustrated how the contents of a file can be read back into a BASIC program and used within that program.

Key Numbers

Although it is not apparent, the computer keeps track of the number of records entered into the file; in fact, it actually numbers each record as it is entered. Thus, not only are there four names in the file MATH100, but each has a key number associated with it, and the names in the file as well as their associated key numbers can be recalled. To do this, we modify the program DISPLAY1 by inserting line 45 and renaming it DISPLAY2.

```
      DISPLAY2

10 OPEN "MATH100" TO :4, INPUT
20 ENDFILE :4,70
30 INPUT = $
40 INPUT :4,N$
45 PRINT KEY(4);
50 PRINT N$
60 GOTO 40
70 CLOSE :4
80 END

RUN

1  JONES, WILLIAM
2  ADAMS, DAVID
3  SMITH, JOAN
4  HAMBORT, ROGER
```

As each record is read into the computer via channel :4, the associated key number is assigned to KEY (4). KEY (I) is a special subscripted variable; the I refers to the channel number being used. Line 45 prints the key number.

Locating a Record

If we know the key number, we can query the file for the specific item identified by that key. Suppose we want the data for which the key number is 3.

```
10 OPEN "MATH100" TO :1, INPUT
20 INPUT :1;3,N$
30 PRINT KEY(1);N$
40 CLOSE :1

RUN

3  SMITH, JOAN
```

The format is as follows: In line 20, when we ask for INPUT from the file via channel :1, the semicolon and the number 3 following the :1 signal the computer to search for that item for which the key number is 3 and to assign that record to the variable N$. At line 30, both the key number and the contents of the record are printed at our terminal.

The Length of a File

Suppose we have a file of unknown length, but we know it to contain fewer than ten thousand records and, for the purposes of the program we are writing, it is important to know exactly the number of records in the file. The following procedure, which is not a program,[4] will determine this. While still in BASIC, we type the first two unnumbered lines below:

```
OPEN "MATH100" TO :2, INPUT   <CR>
INPUT :2;9999,N$              <CR>

        KEY NOT FOUND

PRINT KEY(2)                  <CR>
4

CLOSE :2                      <CR>
```

After we pressed <CR> the second time, the computer responded that the key was not found. Internally, however, the computer has searched the file and found the key number associated with the last data record. Thus, when we type the fourth line, the computer responds with the key number for this last record found, in this case 4, the number of records in our file. Since it is good practice to keep all files closed when not in use, we close the file in the sixth line.

PRINT ON vs. PRINT OVER

When we created the file 'MATH100', we used the phrase PRINT ON in the OPEN statement, line 100 of CREATE1. Now that MATH100 exists, can we modify it? We can try by bringing the program CREATE1 from disk into memory and then attempting to run it. If we do, an error message results; MATH100 is an old file. The situation parallels that for the SAVE ON and SAVE OVER commands. When we write a *new* program and want to save it on disk, SAVE ON is appropriate. If we modify a program and want to save the new version, however, SAVE OVER is appropriate. Remember that when SAVE OVER is used, whatever previously existed on disk is wiped out and only the new version, the one currently in main memory, is stored. A similar effect occurs if the PRINT ON statement is replaced by PRINT OVER. We can write over the old file MATH100, but everything that was there previously is wiped out and only the new data are retained. The following sequence illustrates this.

```
     CREATE1

 LIST 10

 10 OPEN "MATH100" TO :1, PRINT ON

 RUN

MATH100

     10 OLD FILE
```

At this point, we are warned that MATH100 is an old file and PRINT ON is not appropriate. Accordingly, we modify line 10, replacing ON by OVER.

```
10 OPEN "MATH100" TO :1, PRINT OVER

LIST

10 OPEN "MATH100" TO :1, PRINT OVER
20 INPUT = $
30 INPUT N$
40 IF N$="" THEN 70
```

[4]This is done in the immediate mode, see Chapter 2.

```
 50 PRINT :1,N$
 60 GOTO 30
 70 CLOSE :1
 80 END

 RUN

?BAKER, ALICE
?FRICK, MARY
?


      DISPLAY1

 RUN

BAKER, ALICE
FRICK, MARY
```

To recapitulate, first, CREATE1 is loaded and its first line printed to refresh our memory. When we try to RUN it, the error message

```
10 OLD FILE
```

appears. We modify line 10 by replacing PRINT ON by PRINT OVER and then list this new version of CREATE1. We then RUN the program. Two names are entered, BAKER, ALICE, and FRICK, MARY, and the data entry terminated. The program DISPLAY1 is then loaded and run. The output of DISPLAY1 consists of the two names:

```
BAKER, ALICE
FRICK, MARY
```

The four names that previously were records in MATH100 are gone.

Updating a File

Having created an initial file, we should expect that we will want to modify it. Modifications may be made as follows. The appropriate BASIC instruction couples the OPEN statement with INPUT UPDATE; the format is:

```
10 OPEN 'MATH100' TO :1, INPUT UPDATE
```

INPUT UPDATE combines some of the features of PRINT ON (or OVER) and INPUT. When used, we can read selected records from a file and replace or add single records to a file.

The underlying mechanism may be visualized in the following terms. Imagine the file laid out before us, each record prefixed by its key number. Imagine a pointer that indicates the record currently being scrutinized. If we can discover a way to move the pointer to a desired location, we can then work with the record that is there. This is the approach taken in the following programs. There is one additional bit of information that must be known: Every time a file is opened, the pointer is set to the first record.

Adding New Records

The following program adds names to an existing file.

```
      CREATE4

10 OPEN "MATH100" TO :1, INPUT UPDATE
20 INPUT = $
30 ENDFILE :1,70
```

```
40 ENDFILE :0,120
50 INPUT :1,N$
60 GOTO 30
70 K=KEY(1)
80 INPUT N$
90 K=K+1
100 PRINT :1;K,N$
110 GOTO 80
120 CLOSE :1
```

In line 50, the program begins to read records into the computer from the file MATH100 (stored on disk) and continues to do so, line 60, until the end-of-file mark is encountered. When the end-of-file mark is detected, the computer knows the key number of the last data file. This key number is now assigned to the variable K, line 70. Line 80 transfers control to the keyboard and the program asks for the new, additional record. After we enter the new record and press <CR>, K is incremented by 1 and this new value of K becomes the key number to be associated with the new record as both are added to the file, line 100. Our INPUT from the keyboard continues until all additional records have been created and added to MATH100. On our signal from the keyboard, ESC F, channel :1 is closed and the program terminates.

What follows uses this program to add names to the file MATH100. First, DISPLAY2 is used to exhibit the contents of MATH100. The updating program, CREATE4, is then brought in, listed, and run. Two names, GRIFT, ANN, and ZIMET, NANCY, are added to MATH100. To verify that the data are actually present as expected, DISPLAY2 is brought in again and run. The augmented contents of MATH100 are printed.

```
    DISPLAY2

RUN

1  JONES, WILLIAM
2  ADAMS, DAVID
3  SMITH, JOAN
4  HAMBORT, ROGER


     CREATE4

LIST

10 OPEN "MATH100" TO :1, INPUT UPDATE
20 INPUT = $
30 ENDFILE :1,70
40 ENDFILE :0,120
50 INPUT :1,N$
60 GOTO 30
70 K=KEY(1)
80 INPUT N$
90 K=K+1
100 PRINT :1;K,N$
110 GOTO 80
120 CLOSE :1

RUN

?GRIFT, ANN
?ZIMET, NANCY
?F\


     DISPLAY2

RUN

1  JONES, WILLIAM
2  ADAMS, DAVID
```

```
3  SMITH, JOAN
4  HAMBORT, ROGER
5  GRIFT, ANN
6  ZIMET, NANCY
```

Changing a Record

We have already seen how to add new records to a file. At times, we may want to modify an existing record or even delete it. The following program enables us to do all three: change the contents of a record, delete a record, and add new records. The rationale of the program is as follows. As each record is read from the file and displayed at our terminal, we are asked if we want to retain it, change it, or delete it. If the record is to be changed, we input the new information from our keyboard and then transfer it to the file where it replaces the old. If the record is to be deleted, its contents in the file are replaced by an empty string. After all the records in the file have been examined, the computer tells us the EOF has been detected and asks if additional records are to be entered. If not, the program terminates; if new records are to be entered, they are added, starting at the next key number.

We start with the last version of the MATH100 class list given above. The program UPDATE1, which is used to accomplish these changes, follows

```
    UPDATE1

10 REM: THE PURPOSE OF THIS PROGRAM IS TO EXAMINE THE CONTENTS OF
20 REM: RECORDS IN A GIVEN FILE, AND TO MODIFY THEM ACCORDING
30 REM: TO CHANGING NEEDS. THUS, WE SHALL (A) DELETE RECORDS,
40 REM: (B) CHANGE INFORMATION IN THE RECORD AND (C) ADD NEW RECORDS.
50 OPEN 'MATH100' TO :1, INPUT UPDATE
60 ENDFILE :0,400
70 ENDFILE :1, 260
80 INPUT = $
90 REM: THIS SECTION EXHIBITS A RECORD AND ASKS IF IT IS TO BE CHANGED
100 INPUT :1,N$
110 K=KEY(1)
120 PRINT K;N$
130 PRINT"IS THIS RECORD TO BE CHANGED OR DELETED";
140 PRINT "TYPE 'YES' OR 'NO'"
150 INPUT C$
160 IF C$="NO" THEN 100
170 IF C$="YES" THEN 210
180 PRINT "WRONG RESPONSE. TRY AGAIN";
190 GOTO 140
200 REM: THIS SECTION IS FOR CORRECTING RECORDS IN THE FILE
210 PRINT "ENTER NEW RECORD OR STRIKE <CR> TO DELETE"
220 INPUT N$
230 PRINT :1;K,N$
240 GOTO 100
250 REM: THIS SECTION IS FOR THE ADDITION OF NEW RECORDS.
260 PRINT "END-OF-FILE REACHED";
270 PRINT "ANY ADDITIONAL RECORDS TO BE ENTERED? TYPE 'YES' OR 'NO'"
280 INPUT C$
290 IF C$= "NO" THEN 400
300 IF C$= "YES" THEN 330
310 PRINT "WRONG RESPONSE. TYPE 'YES' OR 'NO'"
320 GOTO 280
330 K=KEY(1)
340 K=K+1
350 PRINT "NEXT RECORD";
360 INPUT N$
370 PRINT :1;K,N$
380 GOTO 270
390 REM: THE FILE IS CLOSED AND THE RUN ENDED
400 CLOSE :1
410 END
```

Line 50 opens the file for change. For the moment, ignore lines 60 and 70. Lines 100–190 take a single record from the file (line 100), print it and its key number at the terminal (line 120), and inquire if there is to be a change (lines 130–180). If no change is needed, the next record is brought in; if a change is required, control is transferred to line 210 and the change incorporated (lines 210–240). After all records in the file have been examined and modified as required, the end-of-file mark is detected on MATH100, and line 70 takes over and directs control to line 260. That section of the program, from line 260 through line 380, permits the addition of new records. When there are no more new records, the variable C$ is assigned 'NO' (lines 280–290), and control is transferred to line 400 where channel :1 is closed and the program ends. (We shall explain line 60 shortly.)

```
 1  JONES, WILLIAM
IS THIS RECORD TO BE CHANGED OR DELETED   TYPE 'YES' OR 'NO'
?NO
 2  ADAMS, DAVID
IS THIS RECORD TO BE CHANGED OR DELETED   TYPE 'YES' OR 'NO'
?YES
ENTER NEW RECORD OR STRIKE <CR> TO DELETE
?DAVIDSON, ADAM
 3  SMITH, JOAN
IS THIS RECORD TO BE CHANGED OR DELETED   TYPE 'YES' OR 'NO'
?NO
 4  HAMBORT, ROGER
IS THIS RECORD TO BE CHANGED OR DELETED   TYPE 'YES' OR 'NO'
?Q
WRONG RESPONSE. TRY AGAIN   TYPE 'YES' OR 'NO'
?
WRONG RESPONSE. TRY AGAIN   TYPE 'YES' OR 'NO'
?YES
ENTER NEW RECORD OR STRIKE <CR> TO DELETE
?
 5  GRIFT, ANN
IS THIS RECORD TO BE CHANGED OR DELETED   TYPE 'YES' OR 'NO'
?NO
 6  ZIMET, NANCY
IS THIS RECORD TO BE CHANGED OR DELETED   TYPE 'YES' OR 'NO'
?NO
END-OF-FILE REACHED
ANY ADDITIONAL RECORDS TO BE ENTERED? TYPE 'YES' OR 'NO'
?YES
NEXT RECORD   ?FLAMBEE, RUTH
ANY ADDITIONAL RECORDS TO BE ENTERED? TYPE 'YES' OR 'NO'
?Q
WRONG RESPONSE. TYPE 'YES' OR 'NO'
?
WRONG RESPONSE. TYPE 'YES' OR 'NO'
?YES
NEXT RECORD   ?GARRNOR, EARL
ANY ADDITIONAL RECORDS TO BE ENTERED? TYPE 'YES' OR 'NO'
?NO
```

When the program was run, the first record was left unchanged and the second one was changed. The third record was unchanged; for the fourth record, unacceptable responses were given to the question asked. We did this to test the loop: Only YES or NO answers are permitted. Eventually, record 4 was deleted; records 5 and 6 were left unchanged. Two new records, to be numbered 7 and 8, were entered into the file. Again, before entering the 8th record, the response loop was tested.

We now have a new version of MATH100. Program DISPLAY2 exhibits it.

```
     DISPLAY2

RUN

1  JONES, WILLIAM
2  DAVIDSON, ADAM
3  SMITH, JOAN
4
```

```
5  GRIFT, ANN
6  ZIMET, NANCY
7  FLAMBEE, RUTH
8  GARRNOR, EARL
```

Return now to line 60 in UPDATE1. We shall explain its function by running UPDATE1 against this last version of MATH100.

```
      UPDATE1

RUN

 1  JONES, WILLIAM
IS THIS RECORD TO BE CHANGED OR DELETED   TYPE 'YES' OR 'NO'
?NO
 2  DAVIDSON, ADAM
IS THIS RECORD TO BE CHANGED OR DELETED   TYPE 'YES' OR 'NO'
?YES
ENTER NEW RECORD OR STRIKE <CR> TO DELETE
?DAVID, ADEMSEN
 3  SMITH, JOAN
IS THIS RECORD TO BE CHANGED OR DELETED   TYPE 'YES' OR 'NO'
?F\
```

The first record was brought in and left unchanged; the second record was brought in and changed. At this point, we decided that no more records were to be changed and we wanted the program to terminate. Therefore, in response to the question as to whether record number 3 is to be changed, neither YES nor NO was entered. Rather, we typed ESC F. At this time, line 60 became operative and program control was transferred to line 400, the file was closed, and the run ended. The result is shown using DISPLAY2.

```
     DISPLAY2

RUN

1  JONES, WILLIAM
2  DAVID, ADEMSEN
3  SMITH, JOAN
4
5  GRIFT, ANN
6  ZIMET, NANCY
7  FLAMBEE, RUTH
8  GARRNOR, EARL
```

Copying a File

Before we start to modify a file, it is good programing practice to make a copy of it so that if we inadvertently mess up the version we are working on, we will not have to reconstruct the original file from the beginning. Suppose initially we have a file, such as MATH100, and want to make a copy of it, calling the copy MATH100A. The following sequence demonstrates the several steps:

1. Using DISPLAY2, the contents of MATH100 are shown.
2. Although we are reasonably sure that MATH100A doesn't exist, to be on the safe side, we try using DISPLAY2, properly modified, to display its contents.
3. The computer tells us it cannot open MATH100A; this is equivalent to the computer saying that MATH100A does not exist.
4. A BASIC program, COPY1, is brought into main memory and listed. When COPY1 is executed, MATH100A is created. Effectively, when a record from MATH100 is read into the computer (line 50), it is immediately printed out into file MATH100A (line

60). When the EOF is detected on MATH100, both channels 1 and 2 are closed and the program terminated. MATH100A is now identical to MATH100.

5. Using DISPLAY2, properly modified, the contents of MATH100A are exhibited.

```
    DISPLAY2

LIST 10

10 OPEN "MATH100" TO :4, INPUT

RUN

1  JONES, WILLIAM
2  DAVID, ADEMSEN
3  SMITH, JOAN
4
5  GRIFT, ANN
6  ZIMET, NANCY
7  FLAMBEE, RUTH
8  GARRNOR, EARL

10 OPEN "MATH100A" TO :4, INPUT

RUN

MATH100A

   10 CANNOT OPEN

    COPY1

LIST

10 OPEN 'MATH100' TO :1, INPUT
20 OPEN 'MATH100A' TO :2, PRINT OVER
30 ENDFILE :1,80
40 INPUT = $
50 INPUT :1,N$
60 PRINT :2,N$
70 GOTO 50
80 CLOSE :1\CLOSE :2
90 END

RUN

    DISPLAY2

LIST 10

10 OPEN "MATH100" TO :4, INPUT
10 OPEN "MATH100A" TO :4, INPUT

RUN

1  JONES, WILLIAM
2  DAVID, ADEMSEN
3  SMITH, JOAN
4
5  GRIFT, ANN
6  ZIMET, NANCY
7  FLAMBEE, RUTH
8  GARRNOR, EARL
```

Having copied the file, we can now turn our attention to a disquieting feature that cropped up. When the copy was made, blank entries were carried over. It would be nice not only to copy the file but at the same time to remove all blank records. The insertion of one line:

```
55 IF N$ = '''' THEN 50
```

into COPY1 will do this. The following sequence of steps illustrates this process.

1. DELETE MATH100A from disk.
2. Use DISPLAY 2 to show the current form of MATH100.
3. Load the modified version of COPY1, called COPY2, and list and run it.
4. Load DISPLAY2, and modify line 10 so that MATH100 is replaced by MATH100A.
5. Run the modified DISPLAY2.

```
DELETE MATH1ØØA

     DISPLAY2

LIST 1Ø

1Ø OPEN "MATH1ØØ" TO :4, INPUT

RUN

1  JONES, WILLIAM
2  DAVID, ADEMSEN
3  SMITH, JOAN
4
5  GRIFT, ANN
6  ZIMET, NANCY
7  FLAMBEE, RUTH
8  GARRNOR, EARL

     COPY2

LIST

1Ø OPEN 'MATH1ØØ' TO :1, INPUT
2Ø OPEN 'MATH1ØØA' TO :2, PRINT OVER
3Ø ENDFILE :1,8Ø
4Ø INPUT = $
5Ø INPUT :1,N$
55 IF N$="" THEN 5Ø
6Ø PRINT :2,N$
7Ø GOTO 5Ø
8Ø CLOSE :1\CLOSE :2
9Ø END

RUN

     DISPLAY2

LIST 1Ø

1Ø OPEN "MATH1ØØ" TO :4, INPUT
1Ø OPEN "MATH1ØØA" TO :4, INPUT

RUN

1  JONES, WILLIAM
2  DAVID, ADEMSEN
3  SMITH, JOAN
4  GRIFT, ANN
5  ZIMET, NANCY
6  FLAMBEE, RUTH
7  GARRNOR, EARL
```

Keyed Records

Thus far, we have made little use of the key number associated with each record. The key is a useful tool that can be profitably used under certain circumstances.

Suppose a scheme exists whereby with each record we can associate an integer, one from the sequence 1, 2, . . . , 9,999,999. For example, each student may have an ID number that falls within this range. It may be possible to construct a file such that the ID number is the key of the record containing the student's name. This idea is carried through for the seven students who currently make up the records in the MATH100A file. Suppose that the ID numbers are as follows:

JONES, WILLIAM	2,164,100
DAVID, ADEMSEN	670,163
SMITH, JOAN	3,834,819
GRIFT, ANN	1,182,173
ZIMET, NANCY	4,433,093
FLAMBEE, RUTH	1,015,247
GARRNOR, EARL	959,954

The following program constructs a file for which the key number for a given name is the ID number associated with that name.

```
     KEYFILE1

1Ø OPEN "MATH1ØØB" TO :1, PRINT ON
2Ø FOR I=1 TO 7
3Ø READ N$,K
4Ø K=K/1ØØØ
5Ø PRINT :1;K,N$
6Ø NEXT I
7Ø CLOSE :1
8Ø DATA "JONES, WILLIAM",21641ØØ,"DAVID, ADEMSEN",67Ø163
9Ø DATA "SMITH, JOAN",3834819
1ØØ DATA "GRIFT, ANN", 1182173,"ZIMET, NANCY",44333Ø93
11Ø DATA "FLAMBEE, RUTH", 1Ø15247,"GARRNOR, EARL", 959954

RUN
```

The program itself should have no surprises save one. The impression given in the preceding paragraph was that all the key numbers are integers between 1 and 9,999,999. Actually, this is not correct. The key numbers in the file range from .001 to 9999.999. Therefore, in order to change the ID numbers into key numbers, it was necessary to divide each ID by 1000. This was done in line 40 and the program was run.

Again, DISPLAY2 was loaded and its first line, line 10, modified so that it would be operative on the file MATH100B. The printout is:

```
     DISPLAY2

LIST 1Ø

1Ø OPEN "MATH1ØØ" TO :4, INPUT
1Ø OPEN "MATH1ØØB" TO :4, INPUT

RUN

67Ø.163 DAVID, ADEMSEN
959.954 GARRNOR, EARL
1Ø15.25 FLAMBEE, RUTH
1182.17 GRIFT, ANN
2164.1Ø JONES, WILLIAM
3834.82 SMITH, JOAN
4433.Ø9 ZIMET, NANCY
```

A discerning eye will notice that although the key numbers for DAVID and GARRNOR as printed match the numbers entered into the file, those for the others do not. The fault, of course, lies with the limitation that the computer allocates only eight print positions for decimal numbers and nine are needed. By replacing lines 45 and 50 in DISPLAY2 by PRINTUSING and :(image) statements, we obtain output matching the input.

```
10 OPEN "MATH100B" TO :4, INPUT
20 ENDFILE :4,80
30 INPUT = $
40 INPUT :4,N$
45 PRINTUSING 50, KEY(4),N$
50 :    ####.###       ##########################################
60 GOTO 40
70 CLOSE :4
80 END

RUN

   670.163        DAVID, ADEMSEN
   959.954        GARRNOR, EARL
  1015.247        FLAMBEE, RUTH
  1182.173        GRIFT, ANN
  2164.100        JONES, WILLIAM
  3834.819        SMITH, JOAN
  4433.093        ZIMET, NANCY
```

ID numbers can be assigned in a variety of arbitrary ways. The scheme used above was to take the first six characters of the student's name as given—for example, for DAVID, ADEMSEN, we used DAVIDA—change each character to its EBCDIC equivalent, and subtract 190 from each number. The number corresponding to the first character was multiplied by 10^5, the number correspponding to the second by 10^4, . . . , the last number by 10^0, or 1. These six numbers were then added and used as the basis for selecting the key number.

An advantage of using this or any other algorithmic scheme, is that we can have the computer calculate the key numbers; a disadvantage is that if there are two people whose names yield the same key number, the assignment of unique ID's fails. For the scheme cited, the failure can occur in two ways: (1) the first six characters of two persons' names may be the same, that is, SMITH, JOAN and SMITH, JOHN will both produce the same key number: 3834.819, and (2) although the first six characters may be different, the same key number may be obtained. For example, PAPAPA and NNNNNN both produce 2555.553.

Searching a Keyed File

One advantage of a keyed file is illustrated by the following example. Suppose we have a lengthy *unkeyed* personnel file and we want information on one person. However the file is organized, whether alphabetized, by date of birth, or some other way, there must be an algorithm to search it for the needed record. No matter how efficient the algorithm may be, it will be time consuming and expensive in machine utilization. On the other hand, if a keyed file is used, then, when the name is entered, a program can determine the key, and the computer can immediately retrieve the record stored at the key number. The following program does this for the keyed file previously prepared.

```
10 REM: THIS PROGRAM ILLUSTRATES THE RETREVIAL OF INFORMATION FROM
20 REM: A KEYED FILE.
30 DIM B(6)
40 INPUT = $
50 PRINT "ENTER THE NAME OF THE INDIVIDUAL WHOSE FILE YOU WISH TO SEE."
60 PRINT "TYPE ONLY SIX CHARACTERS BEGINNING WITH THE LAST NAME,"
70 PRINT "THEN THE FIRST NAME, OMITTING ALL PUNCTUATION."
80 PRINT "WHEN YOU HAVE FINISHED USING THE FILE, TYPE 'DONE'"
90 PRINT "NAME PLEASE";
100 INPUT N$
110 M$=N$
120 IF N$="DONE" THEN 290
```

```
130 N=LEN(N$)
140 N$=N$(:1,6)
150 CHANGE N$ TO B
160 A=0
170 N=MIN(N,6)
180 FOR I=1 TO N
190 A=A+(B(I)-190)*10^(6-I)
200 NEXT I
210 A=A/1000
220 OPEN 'MATH100B' TO :1, INPUT
230 INPUT :1;A,N$
240 IF N$<>"" THEN 260
250 PRINT "NAME NOT FOUND IN FILE" \ CLOSE :1 \ GOTO 90
260 PRINTUSING 270,A,N$
270 :  KEY = ####.### NAME IS ##########################################
280 CLOSE :1 \ GOTO 90
290 END

RUN
```

```
ENTER THE NAME OF THE INDIVIDUAL WHOSE FILE YOU WISH TO SEE.
TYPE ONLY SIX CHARACTERS BEGINNING WITH THE LAST NAME,
THEN THE FIRST NAME, OMITTING ALL PUNCTUATION.
WHEN YOU HAVE FINISHED USING THE FILE, TYPE 'DONE'
NAME PLEASE   ?ZIMETN
  KEY = 4433.093 NAME IS ZIMET, NANCY
NAME PLEASE   ?JONESW
  KEY = 2164.100 NAME IS JONES, WILLIAM
NAME PLEASE   ?DONE


RUN

ENTER THE NAME OF THE INDIVIDUAL WHOSE FILE YOU WISH TO SEE.
TYPE ONLY SIX CHARACTERS BEGINNING WITH THE LAST NAME,
THEN THE FIRST NAME, OMITTING ALL PUNCTUATION.
WHEN YOU HAVE FINISHED USING THE FILE, TYPE 'DONE'
NAME PLEASE   ?FLAMBE
  KEY = 1015.247 NAME IS FLAMBEE, RUTH
NAME PLEASE   ?BURTON

     230 KEY NOT FOUND
```

In the program, the purpose of line 170 is to accept names with fewer than six characters. In order to search a file, the file first must be opened. During the time a file is open, a machine malfunction may destroy its contents. To minimize this possibility, the file is opened only as needed (line 220) and closed as soon thereafter as possible (line 250 or 280).

Two runs are presented. On the first, two names were entered and the records retrieved. When no more records were needed, "DONE" was entered and the program ended.

On the second run, a name known not to be in the file was entered. An unfortunate feature of the program is that if a name is entered for which no key number and record exist in the file, the program terminates after printing an error message. Line 250 is never executed. Generally, we want notification that the record does not exist, but the opportunity to continue searching for other names should not be precluded.

What happened internally is this: Not having found the key, the computer continued to the end of the file and stopped after printing the error message 230. To circumvent this, all that is necessary is to have the program go to line 250 if it reaches the end-of-file mark. A one-line insertion will do:

```
225 ENDFILE :1,250.
```

With this change in the program, when a name is entered and the key and record not found, program control goes to line 250. Thus, the program does not terminate but continues to request additional input. The modified program follows.

```
10 REM: THIS PROGRAM ILLUSTRATES THE RETREVIAL OF INFORMATION FROM
20 REM: A KEYED FILE.
30 DIM B(6)
40 INPUT = $
50 PRINT "ENTER THE NAME OF THE INDIVIDUAL WHOSE FILE YOU WISH TO SEE."
60 PRINT "TYPE ONLY SIX CHARACTERS BEGINNING WITH THE LAST NAME,"
70 PRINT "THEN THE FIRST NAME, OMITTING ALL PUNCTUATION."
80 PRINT "WHEN YOU HAVE FINISHED USING THE FILE, TYPE 'DONE'"
90 PRINT "NAME PLEASE";
100 INPUT N$
110 M$=N$
120 IF N$="DONE" THEN 290
130 N=LEN(N$)
140 N$=N$(:1,6)
150 CHANGE N$ TO B
160 A=0
170 N=MIN(N,6)
180 FOR I=1 TO N
190 A=A+(B(I)-190)*10^(6-I)
200 NEXT I
210 A=A/1000
220 OPEN 'MATH100B' TO :1, INPUT
225 ENDFILE :1,250
230 INPUT :1;A,N$
240 IF N$<>"" THEN 260
250 PRINT "NAME NOT FOUND IN FILE" \ CLOSE :1 \ GOTO 90
260 PRINTUSING 270,A,N$
270 :  KEY = ####.### NAME IS ##########################################
280 CLOSE :1 \ GOTO 90
290 END
```

```
ENTER THE NAME OF THE INDIVIDUAL WHOSE FILE YOU WISH TO SEE.
TYPE ONLY SIX CHARACTERS BEGINNING WITH THE LAST NAME,
THEN THE FIRST NAME, OMITTING ALL PUNCTUATION.
WHEN YOU HAVE FINISHED USING THE FILE, TYPE 'DONE'
NAME PLEASE   ?GARRNO
  KEY =  959.954 NAME IS GARRNOR, EARL
NAME PLEASE   ?BURTON
NAME NOT FOUND IN FILE
NAME PLEASE   ?GRIFTA
  KEY = 1182.173 NAME IS GRIFT, ANN
NAME PLEASE   ?DONE
```

A General Observation

The sequence of programs given above is intended to introduce the way keyed files may be used in BASIC. Unfortunately, there is no standard format; procedures will vary from one system to the next. For example, to open a file, we used

```
OPEN 'MATH100' TO :1, INPUT UPDATE
```

Another system may simply open the file with

```
FILE #1 :"MATH100"
```

Other differences abound. If you understand what it is you need to know, the manual supplied by the manufacturer of your computer system will be your ultimate source. It is hoped that the above presentation will help you more easily search out and understand the relevant sections in that manual.

Exercises

17.1 Assume you work for a small magazine that has a growing circulation. Each month, a mailing list is printed. An entry in the list consists of three lines: the subscriber's name, the street address, and the city, state, and zip code. The old equipment is wearing out and is very slow. The publisher decided to have the computer print the mailing list and assigned you to the task. (a) Write a program that allows you to create the file of subscribers. The file is to store the name in one record, the street address in the next, and the city, state, and zip code in a third. (b) The mailing list is to be printed on a printer that prints six lines per inch. Write a program that will read this file and print the labels so that there is 1 inch of space between each three lines of print. Test the programs on a list of at least 10 subscribers.

17.2 In the preceding exercise, the mailing list is being continually updated. There are new subscribers, those who do not renew, those who move from one location to another, and those who change their names. Write a program that, given the initial file created in Exercise 17.1, allows you to update it.

17.3 A seven-digit telephone number converts easily to a seven digit key number. For example, 567-1234 would become 5671.234. (a) Write a program that enables you to prepare a file in which the name of a subscriber is stored in the record whose key number is the telephone number. (b) Knowing the telephone number, it is easy to retrieve the name of the subscriber. (Also, see Chapter 11, Exercise 11.3.) Write a program that, given the telephone number, returns the subscriber's name.

17.4 You are to prepare a trilingual dictionary in English, French, and German. All the English words are to be entered into a file called ENGLISH, their French equivalents into a file called FRENCH, and the German equivalents into a file marked GERMAN. Your first task is to prepare these three files. Test your program on a list of at least 10 words.

The dictionary will be used in the following way. The user will indicate a language and then a specific word in that language. She will then specify a second language. The computer will print both the input word and its equivalent. For example, the original language is French, the word is *cinq,* and the target language is German. The computer should return:

```
FRENCH      GERMAN
CINQ        FUNF
```

Test your program on a list of at least 10 words.

17.5 It is relatively easy, using the files prepared for Exercise 17.4, to write a tutorial program. The student begins by indicating the two languages. The computer then selects a word from the first language, prints it, and asks the student to supply the equivalent word in the second language. The student's response is compared with the equivalent word stored in the second file. If it is correct, the computer selects a second word, and the process continues. If the response is wrong, the computer should give the student a second chance. A correct answer would again lead to a new word; if the answer is wrong the second time, the computer prints the correct word. A correct answer on the first trial is scored as 10; on the second trial, as 5. After 10 words, a final score is printed. Write the program and test it.

17.6 Imagine an unordered list so long that only part of it can fit into the computer's main memory at one time. The problem is to sort this list. For purposes of illustration, assume that the original list consists of 100 integers, selected at random, each between 1 and 10,000. These numbers are stored in a file F_1. (a) Prepare the file F_1.

Our second assumption is that the main memory can hold, in addition to a sort routine (such as the bubble sort), at most 10 elements from F_1. (b) Input 10 elements from F_1, sort them and store the sorted list in a file F_2. (c) Read into memory the second 10 elements from F_1, sort them and store this sorted list in a file F_3. (d) Using a merge routine (as described in Chapter 11, Exercise 11.4), merge the two lists from F_2 and F_3 and store the result in F_4. (e) Copy the file F_4 over the file F_3. (f) Read in the third set of 10 numbers from F_1, sort, and store in F_2. (g) Merge files F_2 and F_3 and store in F_4. (h) Copy F_4 over F_3. (i) Read in the next set of 10 numbers from F_1, sort, and store them in F_2. (j) Merge F_2 and F_3 and store in F_4. (k) Copy F_4 over F_3. Repeat this process until the list in file F_1 is exhausted. The final sorted list will be in file F_3. (l) Write a program that carries out this procedure and prints the final list.

17.7 Write a program that maps the letters of the alphabet into the integers 1 through 26. Then, using a method for calculating ID numbers similar to that described on page 341, produce a keyed file for the following names: Hamms, Gordon; Zernek, Helen; Archer, John; Spencer, Mary; Martin, Jefferson; Edwards, Pauline; and Velnork, Betty. Build into your program the following capabilities: (1) Given the first six characters of the name, the whole name is retrieved. (2) If a name not contained in the file is given, the program notifies you to that effect but does not terminate in an error message.

18 An Introduction to EDIT

Whenever a BASIC program is written and saved on disk, the program itself becomes a file on the disk. Using the familiar BASIC commands, we can have the program retrieved, modified, copied, resaved, and so on. If we want to, we can call it from the disk and look at it using LIST. By contrast, we were not able to create a data file directly; it was necessary to use a BASIC program to do so. Also, different BASIC programs are needed to look at a data file, to modify it, and to copy it. We cannot call it from the disk and LIST it as we would a program file. The following sequence illustrates the computer's responses if we try to LIST a data file. The three files MATH100, MATH100A, and MATH100B, which were previously created and currently reside on disk, can be brought from disk to main storage but cannot be listed. If we attempt to bring a nonexistent file, MATH100C, from disk to main storage, an error message, UNABLE TO OPEN, is generated.

```
>LOAD MATH100
>LIST
00000-00000 NO PROGRAM
>LOAD MATH100A
>LIST
00000-00000 NO PROGRAM
>LOAD MATH100B
>LIST
00000-00000 NO PROGRAM
>LOAD MATH100C
MATH100C
UNABLE TO OPEN
```

All of this raises the question: Is there a way to circumvent writing separate BASIC programs to perform these editing functions, to create, examine, modify, and copy data files? Is there an easier way than using BASIC to edit a file? On some computer systems the answer is yes.

Another Processor: EDIT

In what follows, we assume that the computer system available to you is sufficiently extensive to include another processor that can be used to edit files in general, not only data files but program files as well.[1] It is designed to let you easily create, look at, modify, and copy any file. The full power of this processor, which we shall refer to by the generic name EDIT, will not be described; rather, only those instructions pertinent to the four operations create, examine, modify, and copy will be discussed.

Calling EDIT

EDIT is a processor, just as BASIC is, under control of the operating system. Therefore, at the operating system level, when we see ! or SYSTEM? we type EDIT <CR>. A typical computer response is: EDIT HERE, followed by the prompt symbol for the EDIT processor. We shall use the symbol * for this purpose.

Building a File

Our first exercise is to construct a new file (to be called MATH100C) under EDIT. After the asterisk (*) prompt, we type:

```
BUILD MATH100C      <CR>
```

This informs the computer that a new file is to be created. If we happen to select an old file name, an error message

```
– FILE EXISTS; CAN'T BUILD
```

will be returned. The computer responds with the first sequence (key) number 1.000 and waits for our input. After the input and the <CR>, the computer prompts with the second sequence number. After the input and the <CR>, the computer prompts with the third sequence number, and the process continues. To signal that there is no more input, we strike <CR> and EDIT awaits our next instruction.

```
*BUILD MATH1ØØ
- FILE EXISTS; CAN'T BUILD

*BUILD MATH1ØØC
   1.ØØØ WARNER, HILDA
   2.ØØØ ANDERSON, CARL
   3.ØØØ JACOBS, ALBERT
   4.ØØØ HUNTER, BILLY
   5.ØØØ
```

There are variants of the BUILD command. If we used

```
BUILD MATH100D,17,4
```

17.000 would be the first sequence number and the numbers would increase by 4.

```
*BUILD MATH1ØØD ,17,4
   17.ØØØ HILDA WARNER
   21.ØØØ CARL ANDERSON
   25.ØØØ ALBERT JACOBS
   29.ØØØ BILLY HUNTER
   33.ØØØ
```

In the general case, BUILD fid,[2] n,i starts the sequence numbers at n and increases them by i.

[1]You may have to inquire of your computer facility manager if an EDIT-type processor exists on your computer. If one does, its name may be different. While the details and vocabulary of its command structure also may be different from the ones described in the text, its functions and operations will be similar. An understanding of what can be done using EDIT is fundamental to understanding all computing systems and, in particular, word processing systems.

[2]The fid stands for file name or file identification.

No Need for SAVE

Having created the file MATH100C under EDIT, we do not need to SAVE it on disk; this is done automatically. The contents of the file, whether meaningful or not, are stored on disk exactly as they were entered.

Undetected Errors

When building a program file, say a BASIC program, using BUILD, no error is detected until we attempt to load the program under the BASIC processor. In the following sequence, a BASIC program called ADDER is written in EDIT. Line 10 has two errors, PRONT should be PRINT, a quotation mark is needed after NUMBERS, and in line 30 LIT should be LET. Under EDIT, no error is reported; whatever is typed is accepted and stored permanently on the disk. When the program is loaded under BASIC, however, error messages appear.

```
 BUILD ADDER
   1.000 10 PRONT "THIS PROGRAM ADDS TWO NUMBERS.
   2.000 20 X=5,Y=7
   3.000 30 LIT Z=X+Y
   4.000 40 PRINT X,Y,Z
   5.000

*END

!BASIC

 LOAD ADDER
 10 BAD STMT
10 PRONT "THIS PROGRAM ADDS TWO NUMBERS.
 30 BAD STMT
30 LIT Z=X+Y

 LIST
 20 X=5,Y=7
 40 PRINT X,Y,Z
```

At this point, we listed the program and saw that only the correct lines, 20 and 40, were in memory. Still in BASIC, we retyped lines 10 and 30 correctly and listed the program.

```
10 PRINT "THIS PROGRAM ADDS TWO NUMBERS."
30 LET Z=X+Y

LIST
10 PRINT "THIS PROGRAM ADDS TWO NUMBERS."
20 X=5,Y=7
30 LET Z=X+Y
40 PRINT X,Y,Z
```

Satisfied with what we saw, we saved it over ADDER.

```
 SAVE OVER ADDER

 SYS

!EDIT
EDIT HERE
*EDIT ADDER
```

To see the effect of these changes as they would occur on the disk, we used the BASIC command SYS (for system) to exit from BASIC and then called EDIT.

```
*TY 1-4
    1.000 10 PRINT "THIS PROGRAM ADDS TWO NUMBERS."
    2.000 20 X=5,Y=7
    3.000 30 LET Z=X+Y
    4.000 40 PRINT X,Y,Z
```

We are now in EDIT and have called for the file named ADDER. To display the contents of the file, we typed TY 1 – 4 <CR>.

Exiting from EDIT

The above illustration focused on building a file under EDIT. Although we flipped from EDIT to BASIC and back again, the steps necessary to do so were not made explicit. Both BASIC and EDIT are processors called from the operating system level, TEL. In response to the operating system prompt, we would type either BASIC or EDIT. To go from one to the other, we must exit first from one processor, get to the operating system level, and then call the other. If we are in BASIC, there are several ways to get to the operating system level: Strike the BREAK key twice or use a specific command, such as SYS, to call the operating system. If we are in EDIT, a different exiting signal may be required to get us to the operating system level. In this book, we shall use X <CR> or END <CR>. A third way common to both BASIC and EDIT is to press Y while depressing the control key, CTRL.[3] We write this as Y^c.

The TY and TS Commands

In the illustration, we used one other EDIT command, TY. In BASIC, LIST displays the contents of a program; in EDIT, TY (for TYPE) does the same thing. The TY command, like LIST, can be used to exhibit one line, such as TY 7, a consecutive sequence, such as TY 3–7, or an entire file.

As the printout shows, the TY command also displays the sequence numbers. If we want to view the file without the sequence numbers, the command is TS, which stands for TYPE and SUPPRESS sequence numbers.

```
*TS 1-4
10 PRINT "THIS PROGRAM ADDS TWO NUMBERS."
20 X=5,Y=7
30 LET Z=X+Y
40 PRINT X,Y,Z
```

The DELETE Command

When in EDIT, an entire file may be deleted using the same command as is used in BASIC, namely

```
DELETE fid
```

where fid is the name of the file no longer needed. The command used to delete a record within a file is discussed below.

File Modification

The DE(lete) Command

We turn now to the modification of a file, that is, the deletion of records as well as the insertion of new ones. Consider the following file, called NAMEFILE1, consisting of 18 records. To delete a single record, simply type DE and the key number; to delete a sequence of records, type DE n-m, where n is the key number of the first record in the sequence to be deleted and m is the key number of the last. Note that after both deletions in the following example, the end-of-file remained after record number 18. When the last record is deleted, however, the end-of-file is adjusted to the last remaining record in the file.

---

[3] See page 76. These exiting signals may be expected to vary from one computer system to another.

```
 EDIT NAMEFILE1
*TY
    1.000 ALTER, JOHN
    2.000 BAILIE, MICHEAL
    3.000 COMMART, KAREN
    4.000 DELOW, MARY
    5.000 EBNER, SYLVIA
    6.000 FREANT, HELEN
    7.000 GEORGE, WILBER
    8.000 HAMMILL, PEGGY
    9.000 IRELY, MARTHA
   10.000 JACKSTONE, RICHARD
   11.000 KLISTON, ARON
   12.000 LAMPERT, ALAN
   13.000 MICHEALTON, MICHAEL
   14.000 NORCROST, ARNOLD
   15.000 OPALSKI, MADGE
   16.000 PHRAGER, OTIS
   17.000 QUORRIN, JAMES
   18.000 RAPHASON, LOUIS
--EOF HIT AFTER 18.
*DE 8
*TY
    1.000 ALTER, JOHN
    2.000 BAILIE, MICHEAL
    3.000 COMMART, KAREN
    4.000 DELOW, MARY
    5.000 EBNER, SYLVIA
    6.000 FREANT, HELEN
    7.000 GEORGE, WILBER
    9.000 IRELY, MARTHA
   10.000 JACKSTONE, RICHARD
   11.000 KLISTON, ARON
   12.000 LAMPERT, ALAN
   13.000 MICHEALTON, MICHAEL
   14.000 NORCROST, ARNOLD
   15.000 OPALSKI, MADGE
   16.000 PHRAGER, OTIS
   17.000 QUORRIN, JAMES
   18.000 RAPHASON, LOUIS
--EOF HIT AFTER 18.
*DE 10-16
        7 RECORDS DELETED
*TY
    1.000 ALTER, JOHN
    2.000 BAILIE, MICHEAL
    3.000 COMMART, KAREN
    4.000 DELOW, MARY
    5.000 EBNER, SYLVIA
    6.000 FREANT, HELEN
    7.000 GEORGE, WILBER
    9.000 IRELY, MARTHA
   17.000 QUORRIN, JAMES
   18.000 RAPHASON, LOUIS
--EOF HIT AFTER 18.
*DE 18
*TY
    1.000 ALTER, JOHN
    2.000 BAILIE, MICHEAL
    3.000 COMMART, KAREN
    4.000 DELOW, MARY
    5.000 EBNER, SYLVIA
    6.000 FREANT, HELEN
    7.000 GEORGE, WILBER
    9.000 IRELY, MARTHA
   17.000 QUORRIN, JAMES
--EOF HIT AFTER 17.
*
```

The IN(sert) Command

The IN(sert) command, as the name implies, is used to insert records into an existing file. Suppose we start with the last version of NAMEFILE1 and insert records into positions 8, 10–16, and 18, that is, we reconstruct a file of 18 records. The records to be entered will be different from those previously deleted. The first record is to be inserted in position 8. We type: IN 8 <CR>, and the computer responds with the key number 8.000. We type the name HAMILTON, JOSEPH, and press <CR>. At this point, the computer, recognizing that there is a record with key number 9.000, cautions the programer by ringing a bell and does *not* ask for additional records.

When records are to be inserted beginning at position 10, a slightly different sequence of events takes place. After we enter: IN 10 <CR>, the computer responds with 10.000 and awaits our entry. After the entry is made and <CR> pressed, the computer responds with 11.000 and again awaits our entry. This process continues until we complete the entry for which the key number is 16. Again, since there is a record with key number 17, the bell rings and *no* request is made for additional entries.

After we type: IN 18 <CR> and insert a record, the computer responds with the key number 19.000. Not wishing to add any more records, we press <CR> and the file is closed.

```
  TY
    1.000 ALTER, JOHN
    2.000 BAILIE, MICHEAL
    3.000 COMMART, KAREN
    4.000 DELOW, MARY
    5.000 EBNER, SYLVIA
    6.000 FREANT, HELEN
    7.000 GEORGE, WILBER
    9.000 IRELY, MARTHA
   17.000 QUORRIN, JAMES
--EOF HIT AFTER 17.
*IN 8
    8.000 HAMILTON, JOSEPH
*TY
    1.000 ALTER, JOHN
    2.000 BAILIE, MICHEAL
    3.000 COMMART, KAREN
    4.000 DELOW, MARY
    5.000 EBNER, SYLVIA
    6.000 FREANT, HELEN
    7.000 GEORGE, WILBER
    8.000 HAMILTON, JOSEPH
    9.000 IRELY, MARTHA
   17.000 QUORRIN, JAMES
--EOF HIT AFTER 17.
*IN 10
   10.000 JOLLY, ROGER
   11.000 KELLY, JAMES
   12.000 LEWIS, SADIE
   13.000 MORRIS, OLIE
   14.000 NOLLTON, WILMA
   15.000 OLLING, SARA
   16.000 PHILLIPS, DOUGLAS
*IN 18
   18.000 ROGERS, NELLIE
   19.000
*TY
    1.000 ALTER, JOHN
    2.000 BAILIE, MICHEAL
    3.000 COMMART, KAREN
    4.000 DELOW, MARY
    5.000 EBNER, SYLVIA
    6.000 FREANT, HELEN
    7.000 GEORGE, WILBER
    8.000 HAMILTON, JOSEPH
    9.000 IRELY, MARTHA
   10.000 JOLLY, ROGER
```

```
  11.000 KELLY, JAMES
  12.000 LEWIS, SADIE
  13.000 MORRIS, OLIE
  14.000 NOLLTON, WILMA
  15.000 OLLING, SARA
  16.000 PHILLIPS, DOUGLAS
  17.000 QUORRIN, JAMES
  18.000 ROGERS, NELLIE
--EOF HIT AFTER 18.
```

We can also use the IN command to replace one record by another. Starting with the last list, suppose we want to replace entries 7, 17, and 18. After the asterisk prompt, we type: IN 7 <CR>. The computer responds with the key number 7.000 and awaits the new record. The name GRANGER, WARREN is entered and <CR> is pressed. The bell rings (there is a record numbered 8), and the asterisk prompt appears. We type: IN 17 <CR>; the computer types 17.000. We enter the new record: QUARRLY, RICHARD <CR>. The bell rings and the prompt appears. We type: IN 18 <CR>; the computer responds 18.000. We enter ROLLAND, RACHAEL <CR>; since there is no record in 19.000, the computer responds with 19.000. Not having any more records to enter, we press <CR>.

```
 TY
   1.000 ALTER, JOHN
   2.000 BAILIE, MICHEAL
   3.000 COMMART, KAREN
   4.000 DELOW, MARY
   5.000 EBNER, SYLVIA
   6.000 FREANT, HELEN
   7.000 GEORGE, WILBER
   8.000 HAMILTON, JOSEPH
   9.000 IRELY, MARTHA
  10.000 JOLLY, ROGER
  11.000 KELLY, JAMES
  12.000 LEWIS, SADIE
  13.000 MORRIS, OLIE
  14.000 NOLLTON, WILMA
  15.000 OLLING, SARA
  16.000 PHILLIPS, DOUGLAS
  17.000 QUORRIN, JAMES
  18.000 ROGERS, NELLIE
--EOF HIT AFTER 18.
*IN 7
   7.000 GRANGER, WARREN
*IN 17
  17.000 QUARRLY, RICHARD
*IN 18
  18.000 ROLLAND, RACHAEL
  19.000
*TY
   1.000 ALTER, JOHN
   2.000 BAILIE, MICHEAL
   3.000 COMMART, KAREN
   4.000 DELOW, MARY
   5.000 EBNER, SYLVIA
   6.000 FREANT, HELEN
   7.000 GRANGER, WARREN
   8.000 HAMILTON, JOSEPH
   9.000 IRELY, MARTHA
  10.000 JOLLY, ROGER
  11.000 KELLY, JAMES
  12.000 LEWIS, SADIE
  13.000 MORRIS, OLIE
  14.000 NOLLTON, WILMA
  15.000 OLLING, SARA
  16.000 PHILLIPS, DOUGLAS
  17.000 QUARRLY, RICHARD
  18.000 ROLLAND, RACHAEL
--EOF HIT AFTER 18.
```

The original version of the file NAMEFILE1, which we have been modifying and which is reprinted below, happens to be alphabetized. Suppose that the additional records JONES, WILLIAM, JOHNSTON, BARRY, and JONTOWN, MILDRED are to be inserted into the file, retaining the alphabetical order. The first name, JONES, WILLIAM, is to be inserted between JACKSTONE and KLISTON. We type IN 10.5 and, when the computer responds, enter that name. The second name, JOHNSTON, should be entered between JACKSTONE and JONES. We type IN 10.25 and, when the computer responds, enter that name. Finally, JONTOWN should be between JONES and KLISTON, and we could use IN 10.9.

The final list is still alphabetized.

```
 EDIT NAMEFILE1
*TY
    1.000 ALTER, JOHN
    2.000 BAILIE, MICHEAL
    3.000 COMMART, KAREN
    4.000 DELOW, MARY
    5.000 EBNER, SYLVIA
    6.000 FREANT, HELEN
    7.000 GEORGE, WILBER
    8.000 HAMMILL, PEGGY
    9.000 IRELY, MARTHA
   10.000 JACKSTONE, RICHARD
   11.000 KLISTON, ARON
   12.000 LAMPERT, ALAN
   13.000 MICHEALTON, MICHAEL
   14.000 NORCROST, ARNOLD
   15.000 OPALSKI, MADGE
   16.000 PHRAGER, OTIS
   17.000 QUORRIN, JAMES
   18.000 RAPHASON, LOUIS
*IN 10.5
   10.500 JONES, WILLIAM
*TY 9-11
    9.000 IRELY, MARTHA
   10.000 JACKSTONE, RICHARD
   10.500 JONES, WILLIAM
   11.000 KLISTON, ARON
*IN 10.25
   10.250 JOHNSTON, BARRY
*TY 9-11
    9.000 IRELY, MARTHA
   10.000 JACKSTONE, RICHARD
   10.250 JOHNSTON, BARRY
   10.500 JONES, WILLIAM
   11.000 KLISTON, ARON
*IN 10.9
   10.900 JONTOWN, MILDRED
*TY
    1.000 ALTER, JOHN
    2.000 BAILIE, MICHEAL
    3.000 COMMART, KAREN
    4.000 DELOW, MARY
    5.000 EBNER, SYLVIA
    6.000 FREANT, HELEN
    7.000 GEORGE, WILBER
    8.000 HAMMILL, PEGGY
    9.000 IRELY, MARTHA
   10.000 JACKSTONE, RICHARD
   10.250 JOHNSTON, BARRY
   10.500 JONES, WILLIAM
   10.900 JONTOWN, MILDRED
   11.000 KLISTON, ARON
   12.000 LAMPERT, ALAN
   13.000 MICHEALTON, MICHAEL
   14.000 NORCROST, ARNOLD
   15.000 OPALSKI, MADGE
   16.000 PHRAGER, OTIS
   17.000 QUORRIN, JAMES
   18.000 RAPHASON, LOUIS
--EOF HIT AFTER 18.
```

Copying Files: COPY- ON- and COPY- OVER-

The procedure for copying a file is illustrated in the following examples:

```
*EDIT NAMEFILE1
*TY
    4.000 DELOW, MARY
    5.000 EBNER, SYLVIA
    6.000 FREANT, HELEN
   11.000 KLISTON, ARON
   12.000 LAMPERT, ALAN
   13.000 MICHEALTON, MICHAEL

 EDIT FILE1
-NO SUCH FILE

 COPY NAMEFILE1 ON FILE1
..COPYING
..COPY DONE

 EDIT FILE1
*TY
    4.000 DELOW, MARY
    5.000 EBNER, SYLVIA
    6.000 FREANT, HELEN
   11.000 KLISTON, ARON
   12.000 LAMPERT, ALAN
   13.000 MICHEALTON, MICHAEL


 COPY NAMEFILE1 OVER FILE1 ,7,3
..EDIT STOPPED
..COPYING
..COPY DONE

*EDIT FILE1
*TY
    7.000 DELOW, MARY
   10.000 EBNER, SYLVIA
   13.000 FREANT, HELEN
   16.000 KLISTON, ARON
   19.000 LAMPERT, ALAN
   22.000 MICHEALTON, MICHAEL
```

To illustrate the commands COPY ON and COPY OVER, we have used an abbreviated version of the file NAMEFILE1. It is brought in under EDIT and its contents exhibited. It is then shown that the file FILE1 does not exist. The copy command comes next:

COPY NAMEFILE1 ON FILE1.

The computer does the copying, and to verify that it has been successfully accomplished, the contents of FILE1 are exhibited. FILE1 is now identical to NAMEFILE1.

The copy command is invoked a second time; this time the format is

COPY NAMEFILE1 OVER FILE1 ,7,3

Initially, FILE1 did not exist and the COPY- ON- command was used. For this second case, FILE1 already exists, and what we want is to replace its contents with the contents of NAMEFILE1. To do this, the COPY- OVER- command is needed. Note also the ,7,3 at the end of the line; this tells the computer that the first record of the new file is to have key number 7 and that the increment between successive records is to be 3. The final TY exhibits the results.

A file may be copied over itself. A file of 21 records was created by inserting three names alphabetically into the existing file, NAMEFILE1. The increments between records are not uniform, and we want to copy this file over itself with the first record being assigned key number 1 and the increment between key numbers being 1. The command structure is

COPY NAMEFILE1 OVER NAMEFILE1 ,1,1 <CR>

The following printout illustrates this.

```
 EDIT NAMEFILE1
*TY
    1.000 ALTER, JOHN
    2.000 BAILIE, MICHEAL
    3.000 COMMART, KAREN
    4.000 DELOW, MARY
    5.000 EBNER, SYLVIA
    6.000 FREANT, HELEN
    7.000 GEORGE, WILBER
    8.000 HAMMILL, PEGGY
    9.000 IRELY, MARTHA
   10.000 JACKSTONE, RICHARD
   10.250 JOHNSTON, BARRY
   10.500 JONES, WILLIAM
   10.900 JONTOWN, MILDRED
   11.000 KLISTON, ARON
   12.000 LAMPERT, ALAN
   13.000 MICHEALTON, MICHAEL
   14.000 NORCROST, ARNOLD
   15.000 OPALSKI, MADGE
   16.000 PHRAGER, OTIS
   17.000 QUORRIN, JAMES
   18.000 RAPHASON, LOUIS

*COPY NAMEFILE1 OVER NAMEFILE1 ,1,1
..EDIT STOPPED
..COPYING
..COPY DONE

*TY
    1.000 ALTER, JOHN
    2.000 BAILIE, MICHEAL
    3.000 COMMART, KAREN
    4.000 DELOW, MARY
    5.000 EBNER, SYLVIA
    6.000 FREANT, HELEN
    7.000 GEORGE, WILBER
    8.000 HAMMILL, PEGGY
    9.000 IRELY, MARTHA
   10.000 JACKSTONE, RICHARD
   11.000 JOHNSTON, BARRY
   12.000 JONES, WILLIAM
   13.000 JONTOWN, MILDRED
   14.000 KLISTON, ARON
   15.000 LAMPERT, ALAN
   16.000 MICHEALTON, MICHAEL
   17.000 NORCROST, ARNOLD
   18.000 OPALSKI, MADGE
   19.000 PHRAGER, OTIS
   20.000 QUORRIN, JAMES
   21.000 RAPHASON, LOUIS
```

We may summarize these examples of copying under EDIT as follows: An existing file fid_1 can be copied ON a nonexistent file, fid_2 thereby creating a new file. The file fid_2 is identical to fid_1. An existing file fid_1 can be copied OVER an existing file fid_2. The file fid_2 is identical to fid_1. Both COPY commands offer the option of specifying the first key number of the second file fid_2 as well as the increment between records in it. The format is

$$\text{COPY fid}_1 \begin{Bmatrix} \text{ON} \\ \text{OVER} \end{Bmatrix} \text{fid}_2\text{,n,i}$$

where n is the key number of the first record in fid_2 and i is the increment between successive records. If n and i are not specified, fid_2 is identical to fid_1.

Concluding Remarks

It would be a quite minimal processor that had only the command structure given above. In general, EDIT should be expected to facilitate the modification of one or several records at a time. We might be interested in changing one or several fields in a record or a set of records; we might be interested in changing only one character in a given field. A reasonably sophisticated EDIT processor will have these capabilities and more. We have limited our presentation, however, to little more than those features of EDIT needed to facilitate an understanding of how BASIC handles files. It is hoped that your interest has been sufficiently whetted for you to examine the additional features of EDIT.

Exercises

18.1 While in BASIC, write a simple program. For example, write a program that asks for two numbers as input, adds them, and prints the answer. After you have tested the program and feel sure it is correct, save it on disk. Print a listing of the program. Exit from BASIC, call EDIT, and then call your program. Under EDIT, print a listing of the program. Verify that these two listings are identical.

18.2 Under EDIT, write a simple BASIC program. For example, repeat the program of Exercise 18.1. Print a listing of the program. Exit from EDIT, call BASIC, and load your program. If you have made no errors, your program will be in main memory and ready to run. Before running it, however, list the program and verify that this listing and the one obtained under EDIT are the same.

18.3 Repeat Exercise 18.2, except purposely make some errors. List your program under EDIT. Exit from EDIT, call BASIC, and try to load the program. Observe that those lines containing errors are flagged for you. List the program under BASIC. Observe that the lines that appear are only those that contain no errors; lines containing errors have been automatically deleted.

18.4 In the preceding chapter, we used the BASIC program CREATE1 to construct a name file, MATH100. We entered four names into MATH100: William Jones, David Adams, Joan Smith, and Roger Hambort. In order to verify that MATH100 existed and that the four names were really there, we wrote and ran a second BASIC program, DISPLAY1. Using EDIT, we do not need DISPLAY1. After we run CREATE1 and enter the four names, we can exit from BASIC, enter EDIT, and call for the file MATH100. If we ask for a list of the contents of MATH100, these four names will be printed. Perform these several steps on your computer.

18.5 In Chapter 17, the BASIC program CALCULATE created a file called TABLE whose records consisted of the numbers 1 through 10, their squares, and cubes. Using EDIT, display the contents of the file TABLE.

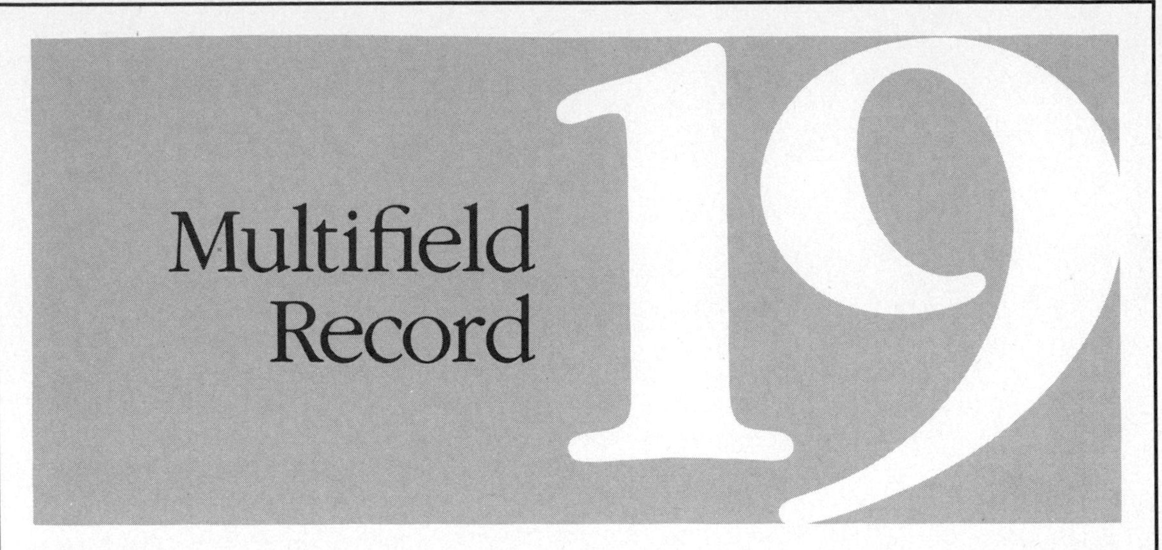

19 Multifield Record

Each record we created in Chapters 17 and 18 was treated as if it had only one entry, consisting of a person's name or a single number. Suppose we want to create a name and address file. We can do this by entering the name into one record and the corresponding address into the next as indicated in Exercise 17.1, Chapter 17. This file would be no different from the ones with which we have been working. On the other hand, we may want to create a record having two entries, two fields, one for the name, the second for the address.

There are two problems. The first is what the record looks like after it has been created; the second is how it can be retrieved for use in BASIC programs. We shall answer these two questions in this chapter.

Creating a Multifield Record

When a record is printed in a file, the arrangement of the characters in the record is the same as the arrangement would be if the record were printed at your terminal. This is shown in the following examples. Several of the PRINT formats that have been discussed are used. In the first example, the two strings, N$ and A$, are separated by a comma; the second time by a semicolon. The third time the program is run, the TAB function is used; the fourth time, PRINTUSING. Normally, each of the different printouts would have the program that produced it appended. Because only line 40 was changed to yield the first three exhibits, however, we have displayed the program only once. Since PRINTUSING requires a change in line 40 and an additional line, line 110, inserted, that program is reproduced. All four outputs are viewed under EDIT.

```
10 OPEN 'CLASS1' TO :1, PRINT OVER
20 FOR I=1 TO 4
30 READ N$,A$
40 PRINT :1,N$,A$
50 NEXT I
60 DATA 'JONES, WILLIAM','115 HARVARD STREET'
70 DATA 'ADAMS, DAVID','207 PLUM AVENUE'
80 DATA 'SMITH, JOAN','95 CENTER ROAD'
90 DATA 'HAMBORT, ROGER','8220 RIDGE LANE'
100 CLOSE :1

RUN
```

```
!EDIT CLASS1
EDIT HERE
*TY
   1.000 JONES, WILLIAM                 115 HARVARD STREET
   2.000 ADAMS, DAVID  207 PLUM AVENUE
   3.000 SMITH, JOAN   95 CENTER ROAD
   4.000 HAMBORT, ROGER                 8220 RIDGE LANE
```

The execution of line 40 assigns N$ to the first print field,[1] 14 characters wide. Since the string "JONES, WILLIAM" is exactly 14 characters long, the comma assigns the next string, "115 HARVARD STREET," not to the second print field but to the third; there must be at least one space between the two consecutive strings. The two strings "HAMBORT, ROGER" and "8220 RIDGE LANE" are treated similarly.

Because the string "ADAMS, DAVID" is only 12 characters long, "207 PLUM AVENUE" may begin in the second print field. The same is true for "SMITH, JOAN" and "95 CENTER ROAD."

At this point, the program is reloaded under BASIC and line 40 is changed so that a semicolon separates N$ and A$. The program is rerun and the results viewed again under EDIT. This time, the strings are printed using the packed format.

```
LIST 40
40 PRINT :1,N$,A$
40 PRINT :1,N$;A$

RUN
```

```
!EDIT CLASS1
EDIT HERE
*TY
   1.000 JONES, WILLIAM  115 HARVARD STREET
   2.000 ADAMS, DAVID  207 PLUM AVENUE
   3.000 SMITH, JOAN   95 CENTER ROAD
   4.000 HAMBORT, ROGER  8220 RIDGE LANE
```

The program is again reloaded and line 40 changed to read:

40 PRINT :1,N$""TAB(25)""A$

The program is rerun and the output viewed using EDIT.

```
LIST 40
40 PRINT :1,N$,A$
40 PRINT :1,N$""TAB(25)""A$

RUN
```

```
!EDIT CLASS1
EDIT HERE
*TY
   1.000 JONES, WILLIAM          115 HARVARD STREET
   2.000 ADAMS, DAVID            207 PLUM AVENUE
   3.000 SMITH, JOAN             95 CENTER ROAD
   4.000 HAMBORT, ROGER          8220 RIDGE LANE
```

---

[1]The word "field" has two different meanings. It has been used previously to indicate how the 72 print positions in a line are divided: five fields of 14 characters each and one field of 2 characters. To emphasize this meaning, we shall use the phrase "print field." The other meaning attached to field is any set of consecutive characters that we want to consider a unit. Thus, the name may be called a field; it may also be considered two fields, the last name being one and the first name the other. The intent will be clear from the context.

Finally, we used the PRINTUSING format. A listing of the program and the result of running it follow:

```
10 OPEN 'CLASS1' TO :1, PRINT OVER
20 FOR I=1 TO 4
30 READ N$,A$
40 PRINT :1,USING 110,N$,A$
50 NEXT I
60 DATA 'JONES, WILLIAM','115 HARVARD STREET'
70 DATA 'ADAMS, DAVID','207 PLUM AVENUE'
80 DATA 'SMITH, JOAN','95 CENTER ROAD'
90 DATA 'HAMBORT, ROGER','8220 RIDGE LANE'
100 CLOSE :1
110 :          ####################          ####################

RUN
```

```
!EDIT CLASS1
EDIT HERE
*TY
   1.000            JONES, WILLIAM                 115 HARVARD STREET
   2.000            ADAMS, DAVID                   207 PLUM AVENUE
   3.000            SMITH, JOAN                    95 CENTER ROAD
   4.000            HAMBORT, ROGER                 8220 RIDGE LANE
```

When we used PRINTUSING in the past, the output was always assumed to be directed to the terminal and it was not necessary to specify the channel, :0. When PRINTUSING is used to structure a record in a file, as in this last illustration, the channel between the CPU and the file must be made explicit. There are various options available for specifying the format. The manufacturer of the equipment on which these programs were written and run chose the following: PRINT :channel ; key ,USING :(image),variable, . . . ,variable. The inclusion of ; key is optional.

In summary, strings are "printed" as fields in a record exactly as if the file were a sheet of paper, each record a line on the sheet, and the characters in the strings subject to the PRINT instructions that would otherwise produce the output at the terminal.

Reading a Multifield Record

Multifield records are read from a file, using the file INPUT instruction, as data would be entered into the computer from a terminal using the more familiar INPUT statement. If the INPUT = $ switch is set, an entire record is entered and assigned to a single variable. If the INPUT = $ is not operative, data elements separated by a comma or a space are treated as different strings and assigned to successive variables.

In the several examples given in earlier chapters, the INPUT = $ switch was set and each record read from a file was assigned to a single variable. In the above examples, by contrast, each record created contains five fields: last name, first name, and a three-field address. Knowing that the record contains five fields allows us to write a program that brings each field into the computer and assigns it to a different variable. This is done in the following program.

```
10 DIM N$(5)
20 OPEN 'CLASS1' TO :1, INPUT
30 ENDFILE :1,110
40 FOR I=1 TO 5
50 INPUT :1,N$(I)
60 NEXT I
70 PRINT
80 PRINT "NAME IS "N$(1) ","N$(2)
```

```
90 PRINT "ADDRESS IS "N$(3)" "N$(4)" "N$(5)
100 GOTO 40
110 CLOSE :1

RUN
```

```
NAME IS JONES,WILLIAM
ADDRESS IS 115 HARVARD STREET

NAME IS ADAMS,DAVID
ADDRESS IS 207 PLUM AVENUE

NAME IS SMITH,JOAN
ADDRESS IS 95 CENTER ROAD

NAME IS HAMBORT,ROGER
ADDRESS IS 8220 RIDGE LANE
```

In the loop, lines 40–60, the five strings making up the first record are assigned to the five string variables N$(I). After they are printed at the terminal, the program brings in the next five strings (the second record in the file) and prints them at the terminal. The process continues until the file is exhausted.

If we know in detail the layout of each record, we can bring each, as a unit, in from the file and then separate the record into its component fields. In the following illustration, we use the file CLASS1, created using the PRINTUSING format. Each record begins with 10 spaces followed by positions for 20 characters, the name; this is then followed by 10 spaces followed by positions for 20 more characters, the address. This entire record is brought in and assigned to one string variable, N$. Under program control, the first 30 characters of N$ are then assigned to M$ and all characters from position 31 to the end of N$ assigned to A$. The effect is to create two string variables M$ and A$ that can be thought of as representing the two fields in the original record. The file CLASS1 is exhibited for reference.

```
!EDIT CLASS1
EDIT HERE
*TY
   1.000          JONES, WILLIAM               115 HARVARD STREET
   2.000          ADAMS, DAVID                 207 PLUM AVENUE
   3.000          SMITH, JOAN                  95 CENTER ROAD
   4.000          HAMBORT, ROGER               8220 RIDGE LANE
```

```
10 OPEN 'CLASS1' TO :1, INPUT
20 ENDFILE :1,110
30 INPUT =$
40 INPUT :1,N$
50 M$=N$(:1,30)
60 A$=N$(:31)
70 PRINT M$
80 PRINT A$
90 PRINT
100 GOTO 40
110 CLOSE :1

RUN

         JONES, WILLIAM
         115 HARVARD STREET

         ADAMS, DAVID
         207 PLUM AVENUE
```

```
SMITH, JOAN
95 CENTER ROAD

HAMBORT, ROGER
8220 RIDGE LANE
```

Numerical Records

In Chapter 17, using the program CALCULATE (see page 328), we illustrated how numerical data are entered into a file, each datum in a separate record. That program is more naturally written with the data elements X, X^2, and X^3 entered in one record. In the program SHOW-TABLE (page 329), these data are retrieved, one record at a time. Again, having written the three elements in one record, it is more natural to retrieve them as a group from that record and assign successive elements to the variables *A, B,* and *C.*

Accordingly, we rewrote CALCULATE by changing line 30 to read PRINT :6,X,X^2, X^3 and deleting lines 40 and 50. A listing of this revised program, now called CALCULATE1, follows.

```
    CALCULATE1

10 OPEN "TABLE1" TO :6, PRINT ON
20 FOR X=1 TO 10
30 PRINT :6,X,X^2,X^3
60 NEXT X
70 CLOSE :6
80 END

RUN
```

A similar modification is needed for SHOW-TABLE. In that program, we changed line 30 to INPUT :3,A,B,C and deleted lines 40 and 50. This new version follows.

```
     SHOW-TABLE1

10 OPEN "TABLE1" TO :3, INPUT
20 FOR I=1 TO 10
30 INPUT :3,A,B,C
60 PRINTUSING 90,A,B,C,A+B+C
70 NEXT I
80 CLOSE :6
90 :  ##           ###          ####          ####
100 END

RUN

  1          1            1             3
  2          4            8            14
  3          9           27            39
  4         16           64            84
  5         25          125           155
  6         36          216           258
  7         49          343           399
  8         64          512           584
  9         81          729           819
 10        100         1000          1110
```

At that time, we had not introduced EDIT and therefore could not look at TABLE directly. If we could have, we would have seen that it consisted of 30 lines, starting with: 1,1,1,2, . . . , and ending with: . . . , 10, 100, 1000. Each number occupied a separate line.

Now that EDIT is available to us, we may look at TABLE1. The printout follows.

```
!EDIT
EDIT HERE
*EDIT TABLE1
*TY
   1.000  1             1             1
   2.000  2             4             8
   3.000  3             9             27
   4.000  4             16            64
   5.000  5             25            125
   6.000  6             36            216
   7.000  7             49            343
   8.000  8             64            512
   9.000  9             81            729
  10.000  10            100           1000
```

Matrix Operations

For most examples in this chapter, the data are alphanumeric. If we are dealing with numerical data arranged in matrix form, the instructions for printing on or over files, input, and input update differ only slightly from the instructions we already know. We need only change PRINT to MATPRINT when we want to print a matrix on a file and INPUT to MAT INPUT when we want to input a matrix from a file. This is illustrated in the program MATPRINT given below.

```
      MATPRINT

10 DIM A(3,3),B(3,3)
20 A(1,1)=1,A(1,2)=2,A(1,3)=3
30 A(2,1)=21,A(2,2)=22,A(2,3)=23
40 A(3,1)=311,A(3,2)=322,A(3,3)=333
50 PRINT
60 PRINT "THE MATRIX A IS PRINTED AT THE TERMINAL"
70 MAT PRINT A
80 PRINT
90 PRINT "THE MATRIX A IS PRINT ON THE FILE 'MATFORM1'."
100 OPEN "MATFORM1" TO :1, PRINT ON
110 MAT PRINT :1,A
120 CLOSE :1
130 PRINT "CHANNEL :1 WAS CLOSED AND :2 IS OPENED FOR INPUT."
140 PRINT "THE CONTENTS OF 'MATFORM1' ARE ENTERED IN MATRIX B."
150 OPEN "MATFORM1" TO :2, INPUT
160 MAT INPUT :2,B
170 CLOSE :2
180 PRINT "MATRIX B IS PRINTED AT THE TERMINAL"
190 MAT PRINT B
200 END

RUN


THE MATRIX A IS PRINTED AT THE TERMINAL

1             2             3

21            22            23

311           322           333

THE MATRIX A IS PRINT ON THE FILE 'MATFORM1'.
CHANNEL :1 WAS CLOSED AND :2 IS OPENED FOR INPUT.
THE CONTENTS OF 'MATFORM1' ARE ENTERED IN MATRIX B.
MATRIX B IS PRINTED AT THE TERMINAL

1             2             3

21            22            23

311           322           333
```

Matrix *A* is defined in lines 20–40 and printed at the terminal, line 70. A file called MATFORM1 is opened at line 100 and matrix *A* is printed into it, line 110. The channel is immediately closed, line 120.

A second channel, :2, is then opened for input, line 150, and the contents of the file MATFORM1 are read into matrix *B* using the instruction MAT INPUT, line 160. Matrix *B* is printed at the terminal.

We have not yet seen how matrix *A* is laid out in the file MATFORM1. To do this, we exit from BASIC, call EDIT, and ask for MATFORM1. When printed, we see that, in form, it is identical to the form in which matrix *A* was printed at the terminal.

```
!EDIT MATFORM1
EDIT HERE
*TY
   1.000
   2.000  1              2              3
   3.000
   4.000  21             22             23
   5.000
   6.000  311            322            333
```

When we studied matrices in Chapter 15, we saw that there were two ways they could be printed. One is as above; the other is in packed format. The instruction to print in packed format requires a semicolon after the matrix name; in this case, we must replace A by A;, lines 70 and 110. We do this after deleting MATFORM1 from the disk; remember, we are using PRINT On at line 100. We did not change the way matrix *B* is to be printed. With the changes described, the program was rerun. The printout appears below.

```
 LIST 70

 70 MAT PRINT A
 70 MAT PRINT A;

 LIST 110

 110 MAT PRINT :1,A
 110 MAT PRINT :1,A;



 RUN


THE MATRIX A IS PRINTED AT THE TERMINAL

 1  2  3

 21    22    23

 311   322   333

THE MATRIX A IS PRINT ON THE FILE 'MATFORM1'.
CHANNEL :1 WAS CLOSED AND :2 IS OPENED FOR INPUT.
THE CONTENTS OF 'MATFORM1' ARE ENTERED IN MATRIX B.
MATRIX B IS PRINTED AT THE TERMINAL

 1             2             3

 21            22            23

 311           322           333
```

Again, we left BASIC, went to EDIT, and asked for MATFORM1. When printed, the layout of the data is identical to that of MAT PRINT A;.

```
!EDIT MATFORM1
EDIT HERE
*TY
   1.000
   2.000  1   2   3
   3.000
   4.000  21     22     23
   5.000
   6.000  311    322    333
```

The final illustration shows that these matrix operations function as well under INPUT UPDATE. Care must be taken, however, to ensure that when the file is updated, the pointer is moved to the desired starting position. The following program, MATPRINT1, is an extension of MATPRINT. As in MATPRINT, matrix *A* is printed in a file, now called MATFORM2. The contents of MATFORM2 are then read into the computer and assigned to matrix *B*. At this point, matrix *C* is created; its entries are twice those of *B*. We want to print matrix *C* into the file MATFORM2 such that its first row will go into the record immediately following the last record occupied by matrix *A*. We do this by assigning the first row of *C* to the next key number, KEY(2) + 1, line 230. Matrix *C* will follow matrix *A* in MATFILE2.

```
10 DIM A(3,3),B(3,3),C(3,3)
20 A(1,1)=1,A(1,2)=2,A(1,3)=3
30 A(2,1)=21,A(2,2)=22,A(2,3)=23
40 A(3,1)=311,A(3,2)=322,A(3,3)=333
50 PRINT
60 PRINT "THE MATRIX A IS PRINTED AT THE TERMINAL"
70 MAT PRINT A
80 PRINT
90 PRINT "THE MATRIX A IS PRINT ON THE FILE 'MATFORM2'."
100 OPEN "MATFORM2" TO :1, PRINT ON
110 MAT PRINT :1,A
120 CLOSE :1
130 PRINT "CHANNEL :1 WAS CLOSED AND :2 IS OPENED FOR INPUT UPDATE."
140 PRINT "THE CONTENTS OF 'MATFORM2' ARE ENTERED IN MATRIX B."
150 OPEN "MATFORM2" TO :2, INPUT UPDATE
160 MAT INPUT :2,B
170 PRINT "MATRIX B IS PRINTED AT THE TERMINAL"
180 MAT PRINT B
190 PRINT
200 PRINT "MAT C=(2)*B IS CREATED."
210 MAT C=(2)*B
220 MAT PRINT C
230 MAT PRINT :2;KEY(2)+1,C
240 CLOSE :2
250 PRINT
260 PRINT "MATRIX C IS PRINTED ON THE FILE 'MATFORM2',"
270 PRINT "BEGINNING IN THE RECORD IMMEDIATELY FOLLOWING"
280 PRINT "THE LAST RECORD OCCUPIED BY THE MATRIX A."
290 END
```

The program was run. The matrices were printed at the terminal. We exited from BASIC, called EDIT, and displayed the contents of MATFORM2.

```
 RUN

THE MATRIX A IS PRINTED AT THE TERMINAL

 1              2              3

 21             22             23

 311            322            333

THE MATRIX A IS PRINT ON THE FILE 'MATFORM2'.
CHANNEL :1 WAS CLOSED AND :2 IS OPENED FOR INPUT UPDATE.
```

```
THE CONTENTS OF 'MATFORM2' ARE ENTERED IN MATRIX B.
MATRIX B IS PRINTED AT THE TERMINAL

 1              2              3

 21             22             23

 311            322            333

MAT C=(2)*B IS CREATED.

 2              4              6

 42             44             46

 622            644            666

MATRIX C IS PRINTED ON THE FILE 'MATFORM2',
BEGINNING IN THE RECORD IMMEDIATELY FOLLOWING
THE LAST RECORD OCCUPIED BY THE MATRIX A.


!EDIT MATFORM2
EDIT HERE
*TY
   1.000
   2.000  1             2             3
   3.000
   4.000  21            22            23
   5.000
   6.000  311           322           333
   7.000
   8.000  2             4             6
   9.000
  10.000  42            44            46
  11.000
  12.000  622           644           666
```

Exercises

19.1 Assume you work for a distributing company that markets a thousand different products. These products are received from many sources and stored in a warehouse. All records of both incoming and shipped merchandise are kept on ledger cards, but with an increase in the volume of business and the desire to expand the product line, this procedure has become obsolete. The decision was made to computerize the inventory.

(a) Write a computer program that creates the initial inventory file. Assume that the inventory will be taken over a holiday when the warehouse is normally closed and that these values will be used to create the initial file.

(b) Write a program (which may contain the first program as a subset) that updates the inventory. The program is to warn the warehouse manager when a specific item is depleted or when the demand for it exceeds the number of units available.

(c) Prepare a printout of the inventory at the end of each working day.

Assume that each product is identified by a six character code word; an example might be WIDGET. Verify that your programs work by testing them on the following initial list of 10 different products.

ARBBET	257
BOLKEL	139
GIMBET	45
JOBSOB	192
MOXWEL	449
SMATIC	567
TRIPTE	157

WIDGET	547
WOLTIC	73
YOLDIL	630

19.2 The local supermarket is part of a regional chain and all prices are dictated by the regional office. The supermarket stocks more than two thousand items and each Wednesday morning receives notice of changes in prices that are to be effective the following day. Assume you work in the regional office and are responsible for preparing these notices. The scheme devised to handle the process is the following. First, an initial file of prices for all items stocked is created. This file is called "PRICE011282". The six digits indicate the file was created on Tuesday, January 12, 1982. Second, the following Tuesday morning, a written copy of the prices to be changed is delivered to you. You copy "PRICE011282" onto a file you call "PRICE011982". You then update "PRICE011982" by incorporating the changes. The computer then compares these two files, item by item, and prepares a third file, "TEMPO", that contains the names of those items whose prices were changed as well as the new prices. A printed copy of "TEMPO," as well as a printed copy of "PRICE011982," is sent to the several markets, arriving Wednesday. The temporary file "TEMPO" is expunged. The file "PRICE011982" is available to continue the process the next week.

Write the necessary programs to (a) create an original file of 10 items, (b) update this file, and (c) prepare the printed output. Run your programs so that the output for 4 weeks is available.

19.3 Assume you work for a distributing company that stores and ships one thousand different products from each of three warehouses—one in Texas, a second in Pennsylvania, and a third in Oregon. The master inventory record is kept on a computer in the main office, which happens to be in Florida.

A sales person, upon receipt of an order, uses a portable terminal to access the master file in order to verify that the quantity being ordered is in stock. If the items are, he calls the main office and places the order. At the main office, the clerk who receives his telephone call immediately accesses the master inventory to verify that the quantity being ordered is available, and if it is, reduces the number in inventory by the amount ordered.

Actually, the clerk decides how many of a given item to ship from each warehouse. Thus, if there are 250 GIMBOS in Texas, 457 in Pennsylvania, and 193 in Oregon, and the order is for 10 to be shipped to a customer in New York, the clerk would probably cut the order to ship all 10 from the Pennsylvania warehouse and reduce the number available there to 447. If the order were for 470 GIMBOS for a customer in Kansas, however, the clerk might decide to ship 100 from Texas, 300 from Pennsylvania, and the remaining 70 from Oregon. That would leave 150 in the warehouse in Texas, 157 in Pennsylvania, and 123 in Oregon.

(a) Write a program that will create the original master inventory list.

(b) Write a program that will allow a sales person to read this inventory list in order to see if the quantities of the needed items are available at the time the sales person is ready to place the order.

(c) Write a program that permits the clerk in the home office to update the inventory list as orders are accepted. This program should also allow the clerk to update the inventory as new merchandise is added to inventory.

(d) Test your program on the following list of 10 products.

PRODUCT	TEXAS	PENNSYLVANIA	OREGON
ARBBET	257	35	854
BOLKEL	139	467	183
GIMBET	45	72	56
JOBSOB	192	195	96
MOXWEL	449	234	85
SMATIC	567	290	486
TRIPTE	157	192	149
WIDGET	547	436	325
WOLTIC	73	85	40
YOLDIL	630	471	297

19.4 A county property file would contain, among other things, the following information for each taxable unit in the country.

(i) A master identification number
(ii) Current owner's name
(iii) Local address
(iv) Assessed value of the land
(v) Assessed value of all improvements

(a) Prepare a file that contains this information.

(b) Write a program that calculates the total assessed value of all the land in the county as of December 31, and the total assessed value of all improvements as of that date.

(c) During the year, the values change. Buildings are torn down or burn, new construction takes place, land is rezoned from one use to another. Also, parcels are subdivided and sold to different buyers, and multiple parcels are acquired by a single owner to be used for a single purpose. These actions, and others, require that the file be updated. This is done annually. Write a program that will update the file.

(d) The year-end files described above are kept indefinitely. However, you have access to these records only for the last 10 years. Write a program that accesses these 10 files and creates a new file that records the year-end data for the assessed value of the land and the assessed value of all improvements for that period.

19.5 At the beginning of this chapter, we showed how to prepare and access a name and address file. We turn now to the problem of working with a file that consists initially only of students' names and ID numbers. The ID consists of three alphabet characters followed by a three-digit number; a typical ID would be: CWM759.

(a) Create an alphabetized name and ID file for a class of 10 students and print a copy of it.

(b) At the end of the first month, an examination is given and graded on the scale 0 to 100. Update the file by appending the scores on this first examination and print a copy of the new file.

(c) At the end of the second month, a second examination is given and graded on the scale 0 to 50. Update the file created in (b) by appending the scores on this second examination and print a copy of this new file.

At the end of the semester, a final examination is given and graded on the scale 0 to 150. To arrive at a final score, the instructor weights the first exam 25, the second exam 35 and the final 40. Thus, if a student scores 70, 40, and 125, the final score would be calculated by the formula:

$$(.25)\times(1)\times(70)+(.35)\times(2)\times(40)+\left(\frac{2}{3}\right)(.40)(125) = 78.8$$

The final grade is assigned as follows: If the final score is at least 90, A; if the final score is at least 80 but less than 90, B; if the final score is at least 70 but less than 80, C; and if the final score is less than 70, F.

(d) Update the file created in (c) by entering the score on the final exam. Have the computer calculate the final score and the final grade and enter them at that time. When the file is completed, print a copy of it. At that time, also print two class lists, one for the registrar and the other for posting on the department's bulletin board. The list for the registrar is to be alphabetized by name and contain the ID number and final grade. The list for the bulletin board is to be alphabetized by ID number and is to contain the score on the final examination and the final grade. The students' names are not to appear on this list.

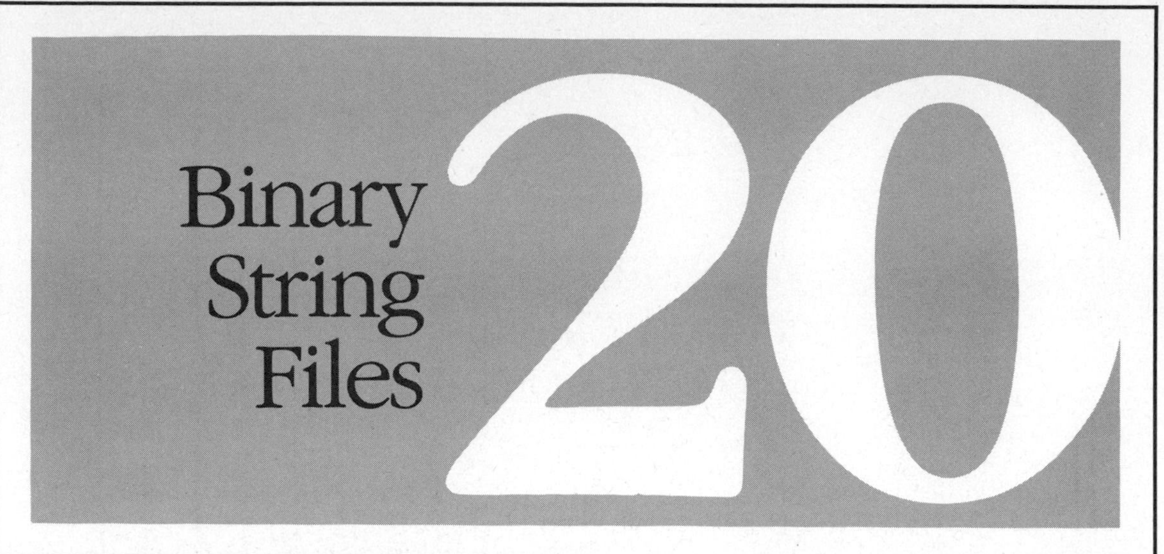

20 Binary String Files

In the previous chapters on files (Chapters 17 and 19), we encouraged you to think that each file resided on disk in much the same layout as we imagine the corresponding characters would appear on the printed page. This was done for pedagogical reasons: to introduce the subject in a natural way, to give you the experience and confidence in handling files, and to provide a basis on which to build your concept of files. The contents of a file actually are stored on disk in a more complex fashion, but we are not so concerned with how files are physically stored on disk or manipulated internally by the computer. We are more concerned with how the contents of a file appear to us.

The files we have studied thus far are called binary coded decimal (BCD) files, which appear to us in "print" form. There is a second file structure that we call **binary files.**[1] Because computers use binary numbers, both the BCD file and the binary file evolve from binary representations, but along different lines. The difference will be explained in this chapter.

We shall introduce binary files the same way we introduced BCD files: First we will create a binary file and then show how to read it. The programs we wrote to create and read the BCD file require only slight modification to create and read a binary file. We will then turn our attention to updating a binary file, which is procedurally similar to updating a BCD file.

In Chapter 18, we were able to examine a BCD file directly by using EDIT. The authors of EDIT, however, did not include it in the capability to examine binary files, as we shall see when we try to use EDIT to examine a binary file. There is another avenue: Under direct control of the operating system, the computer can exhibit a BCD file in the same layout as that produced under EDIT. A slight variation of this command produces the binary representation of both a BCD file and a binary file.

The material presented in the next two chapters presumes knowledge of hexadecimal notation and the EBCDIC representation. These concepts were discussed in Chapters 13 and 14 (pages 241–73).

---

[1]We shall use the phrase "binary file" as the name for the type of file decribed in this chapter. When the word "binary" is used, it will mean a bit—0 or 1.

Creating a Binary File

Paralleling the PRINT ON and PRINT OVER statements used to create or rewrite BCD files, the statements PUT,ON and PUT,OVER are used to create or rewrite binary files. The specific format to create a binary file called "ALPHA1" is

```
OPEN 'ALPHA1' to :1, PUT,ON
```

To write over the binary file ALPHA1, the format is:

```
OPEN 'ALPHA1' to :2, PUT,OVER
```

To illustrate the use of these instructions, we create a BCD file called ALPHA.

```
EDIT ALPHA
EDIT HERE
 TY
    1.000 A,AB,ABC,ABCD,ABCDE
    2.000 FGHIJ,FGHI,FGH,FG,F
    3.000 "KLM","KLMN","KLMNO","KLMNOP","KLMNOPQ"
    4.000 "XYR","XYRS","XYRST","XYRSTU","XYRSTUV"
    5.000 09876,098767,0987678,09876789,098767890
    6.000 12345,1234,123,12,1
```

ALPHA is a data file of strings containing alphabetic and numeric information and two punctuation characters—a quotation mark and a comma. We shall distinguish between files containing records whose contents are strings and files containing records whose contents are numbers. In what immediately follows, all data are considered to be strings; we shall examine in Chapter 21, the case in which the data are numeric.

The program BINFILE, below, will INPUT the contents of the BCD file ALPHA and create the binary file ALPHA1. There are 30 strings in ALPHA, K = 30 (line 10), and these strings are assigned to the vector string variable N$(I), lines 20 and 50–70. In line 130, the computer is told that a new binary file ALPHA1 is to be created. Line 90 is not essential to the program; it is inserted only to indicate that this section of the task has been completed. Similarly, lines 100–120 are not integral to the creation of the binary file; their purpose is to verify the data assigned to N$(I).

The binary file ALPHA1 is created in lines 140–160; line 190 tells us that the binary file ALPHA1 exists.

```
    BINFILE

10 K=30
20 DIM N$(50)
30 OPEN 'ALPHA' TO :1, INPUT
40 ENDFILE :1,80
50 FOR I=1 TO K
60 INPUT :1,N$(I)
70 NEXT I
80 CLOSE :1
90 PRINT "HAVE READ INTO N$" & PRINT
100 FOR I=1 TO K
110 PRINT N$(I),
120 NEXT I
130 OPEN 'ALPHA1' TO :2, PUT,ON
140 FOR I=1 TO K
150 PUT :2, N$(I)
160 NEXT I
170 CLOSE :2
180 PRINT & PRINT
190 PRINT "ALPHA1 BUILT"

RUN
```

```
HAVE READ INTO N$

A          AB          ABC          ABCD          ABCDE
FGHIJ      FGHI        FGH          FG            F
KLM        KLMN        KLMNO        KLMNOP        KLMNOPQ
XYR        XYRS        XYRST        XYRSTU        XYRSTUV
09876      098767      0987678      09876789      098767890
12345      1234        123          12            1

ALPHA1 BUILT
```

Now that the binary file exists, how do we want to use it? First, we may want to read it back into the computer to verify its contents or use them for other purposes. Second, we may want to update the contents. Third, out of curiosity and because it will be important at some future time, we want to know how the file is organized.

Reading a Binary File

After we create a BCD file, (using either a BASIC program or directly in EDIT), we need a second program that will read the contents of the file into the computer's main memory. Once there, the data may be manipulated for whatever purpose we wish, for example, simply printing them at our terminal. For the same reasons, having created a binary file, we need a second program to read its contents into the computer's memory. A program that reads binary files is given below. It is similar to the program DISPLAY1 (Chapter 17, page 327) that we used to read BCD files, except that the verb GET replaces INPUT.

```
10 OPEN 'ALPHA1' TO :1,GET
20 ENDFILE :1,60
30 GET :1,A$
40 PRINT A$,
50 GOTO 30
60 CLOSE :1
70 END

RUN

A          AB          ABC          ABCD          ABCDE
FGHIJ      FGHI        FGH          FG            F
KLM        KLMN        KLMNO        KLMNOP        KLMNOPQ
XYR        XYRS        XYRST        XYRSTU        XYRSTUV
09876      098767      0987678      09876789      098767890
12345      1234        123          12            1
```

Thus far, we have introduced three new instructions: PUT,ON and PUT,OVER to create binary files (ON for a new file, OVER for writing over an existing file) and GET to retrieve data from a binary file. The instruction GET UPDATE is comparable to INPUT UPDATE and is used to both read from and write onto an existing binary file.

How UPDATE Functions

The update operation provides an opportunity to see the difference between the structures of BCD files and binary files.

INPUT UPDATE

Again, we start with the BCD file ALPHA, consisting of 30 strings arranged in six records. A program is written to read the contents of ALPHA and write them out again, but this time on fifteen records of two fields each. The original ALPHA, the program, and the reconstructed BCD ALPHA appear below:

```
*EDIT ALPHA
*TY
   1.000 A,AB,ABC,ABCD,ABCDE
   2.000 FGHIJ,FGHI,FGH,FG,F
   3.000 "KLM","KLMN","KLMNO","KLMNOP","KLMNOPQ"
   4.000 "XYR","XYRS","XYRST","XYRSTU","XYRSTUV"
   5.000 09876,098767,0987678,09876789,098767890
   6.000 12345,1234,123,12,1
```

```
10 *********
20 REM: WE START WITH A FILE 'ALPHA' WHICH HAS A TOTAL OF 30 FIELDS
25 REM: IN 6 RECORDS, 5 FIELDS PER RECORD.
30 REM: WE WILL READ IT IN AND THEN WRITE IT OUT AGAIN ON 'ALPHA',
40 REM: THIS TIME THERE WILL BE 2 FIELDS IN 15 RECORDS.
50 *********
60 DIM N$(50)
70 OPEN 'ALPHA' TO :2, INPUT UPDATE
80 L=30
90 FOR I=1 TO L
100 INPUT :2,N$(I)
110 NEXT I
120 *********
130 REM: THE DATA ARE NOW PRINTED OUT ONTO 'ALPHA' BUT NOW 2 FIELDS TO A RECORD
140 **********
150 FOR I=1 TO 29 STEP 2
160 PRINT :2;INT(I/2)+1,N$(I);N$(I+1)
170 NEXT I
180 CLOSE :2

RUN
```

```
*EDIT ALPHA
*TY
   1.000 A    AB
   2.000 ABC    ABCD
   3.000 ABCDE    FGHIJ
   4.000 FGHI  FGH
   5.000 FG  F
   6.000 KLM    KLMN
   7.000 KLMNO    KLMNOP
   8.000 KLMNOPQ    XYR
   9.000 XYRS  XYRST
  10.000 XYRSTU   XYRSTUV
  11.000 09876    098767
  12.000 0987678    09876789
  13.000 098767890    12345
  14.000 1234  123
  15.000 12  1
```

Since ALPHA is being both read from and written on, INPUT UPDATE is needed, line 70. In lines 90–110, the strings are read from the file and assigned to the variable N$(1), . . . , N$(30). As this is being done, the pointer that locates the key number moves from key number 1 to key number 6, where it now is. The next line of significance is line 160. In particular, note :2;INT(I/2) + 1; . . . . If ;INT(I/2) + 1 were omitted and the line written :2,N$(I), . . . , then the next record entered into the file would have key number 7. Thus, when the 15 records were entered, the file would consist of 21 records: the original 6 plus the additional 15. This is not the intent, however; we want actually to expunge the original six records by writing over them. Thus, the pointer must be returned to the position for which the key number is 1. The method we have chosen to do this is to write each record with a key number, specifically, to use INT(I/2) + 1 to specify the key number.

A second point to notice is the use of the semicolon to specify the print format of the fields in each record. In BCD files, we may choose the comma, the semicolon, TAB, or PRINTUSING; in binary files, we are limited to the comma.

GET UPDATE

Suppose we try to mimic the above sequence of operations using a binary file. We have created ALPHA1, the binary counterpart of ALPHA. The program on page 372 is rewritten to handle binary files: ALPHA1 is substituted for ALPHA and GET UPDATE for INPUT UPDATE. The other change is to replace the semicolon separating the N$(I) and N$(I + 1) in line 160 with a comma.

With what we know thus far, it is impossible to exhibit the contents of ALPHA1 either before or after the change. Although EDIT cannot read binary files, we can use it to show that ALPHA1 consisted of three (not six) records before the execution of the program and 15 after. It is the contents of the records that cannot be shown.

In the following printout, EDIT initially tries to read ALPHA1, cannot interpret it, prints a message, and proceeds to list the three key numbers with meaningless symbols following each key number. After our revised program is run, EDIT is again invoked and it attempts to read the reconstructed ALPHA1. (Note that 15 records are indicated.) EDIT has tried to interpret what it found in ALPHA1. The line TAB CHAR. . . .SIMULATION is totally meaningless in our context. While not an error message *for us,* it does indicate that something is awry.

```
*EDIT ALPHA1
--TAB CHAR. FOUND; 'TA' NEEDED FOR COL. SIMULATION
*TY
--TAB CHAR. FOUND; 'TA' NEEDED FOR COL. SIMULATION
   1.000 Z
   2.000 #
   3.000 >
```

```
 10 *********
 20 REM: WE START WITH A FILE 'ALPHA1' WHICH IS THE BINARY COUNTERPART OF 'ALPHA'
 30 REM: WE WILL READ IT IN AND THEN WRITE IT OUT AGAIN ON 'ALPHA1',
 40 REM: THIS TIME CONSISTING OF 15 RECORDS CONTAINING 2 FIELDS EACH."
 50 *********
 60 DIM N$(50)
 70 OPEN 'ALPHA1' TO :2, GET UPDATE
 80 L=30
 90 FOR I=1 TO L
 100 GET :2,N$(I)
 110 NEXT I
 120 **********
 130 REM: THE DATA ARE PRINTED OUT ON 'ALPHA1' BUT NOW 2 FIELDS TO A RECORD.
 140 **********
 150 FOR I=1 TO 29 STEP 2
 160 PUT :2;INT(I/2)+1,N$(I),N$(I+1)
 170 NEXT I
 180 CLOSE :2

 RUN
```

```
*EDIT ALPHA1
--TAB CHAR. FOUND; 'TA' NEEDED FOR COL. SIMULATION
*TY
--TAB CHAR. FOUND; 'TA' NEEDED FOR COL. SIMULATION
   1.000 O
   2.000 X
   3.000 r
   4.000
```

```
 5.000 Z
 6.000 #
 7.000 ~
 8.000 #
 9.000
10.000 [
11.000
12.000 )
13.000 #
14.000
15.000 #
```

The following diagram indicates the order of creation of the four files in ALPHA and ALPHA1.

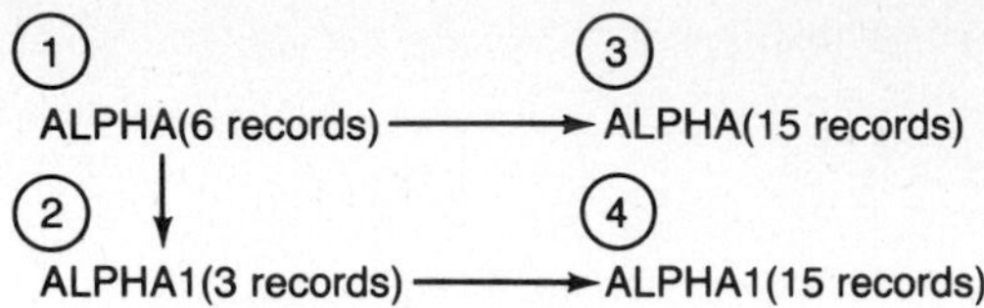

The Structure of a Binary Record

The following digression should help you understand what is happening. On the computer on which these programs were run, a binary record normally consists of 120 bytes, arranged as follows: The first four and last four bytes are reserved for record keeping, that is, the start of a record, the end of a record, and so on. The remaining 112 bytes are grouped into 28 fields of 4 bytes each. As data arrive, elements are entered into four-byte fields until all 28 fields are filled, at which time the next record is opened and its 28 fields are filled. This process repeats until all the data have been read into the file and the last record is closed.

Recall that a symbol we would normally think of as a character (the letter P, the digit 5, the punctuation mark ,) is represented internally in the computer by its EBCDIC value (one of the decimal numbers: 0, 1, 2, . . . , 255). When written in hexadecimal notation, the EBCDIC value requires two places. Thus, the space required for one character is two hexadecimal digits, or one byte. In terms of binary records, each record contains 112 informational characters.

A BCD Record in Binary

If we are to study the internal binary representation of the data in a BCD file such as ALPHA, there must be an instruction that exhibits it to us. As we said, EDIT was never intended to have this capability; the needed instruction is available only at the operating system level. On the computer we have used to illustrate our examples, this instruction is

```
! COPY fid TO ME (X)      <CR>
```

When used, for example, with the BCD file ALPHA, the binary representation of ALPHA will be printed.

The "print" form of a BCD file can also be printed by an instruction at the operating system. The instruction is simply

```
! COPY fid TO ME      <CR>
```

Having this facility precludes the need to go to EDIT every time we want to view a BCD file. In the figure that follows, both of these instructions are applied to the BCD file ALPHA.

```
!COPY ALPHA TO ME

A,AB,ABC,ABCD,ABCDE
FGHIJ,FGHI,FGH,FG,F
"KLM","KLMN","KLMNO","KLMNOP","KLMNOPQ"
"XYR","XYRS","XYRST","XYRSTU","XYRSTUV"
09876,098767,0987678,09876789,098767890
12345,1234,123,12,1

!COPY ALPHA TO ME (X)


KEY =X'0003E8'  -   19 BYTES

00000   C16BC1C2  6BC1C2C3  6BC1C2C3  C46BC1C2    A,AB,ABC,ABCD,AB
00004   C3C4C5                                    CDE

KEY =X'0007D0'  -   19 BYTES

00000   C6C7C8C9  D16BC6C7  C8C96BC6  C7C86BC6    FGHIJ,FGHI,FGH,F
00004   C76BC6                                    G,F

KEY =X'000BB8'  -   39 BYTES

00000   7FD2D3D4  7F6B7FD2  D3D4D57F  6B7FD2D3    "KLM","KLMN","KL
00004   D4D5D67F  6B7FD2D3  D4D5D6D7  7F6B7FD2    MNO","KLMNOP","K
00008   D3D4D5D6  D7D87F                          LMNOPQ"

KEY =X'000FA0'  -   39 BYTES

00000   7FE7E8D9  7F6B7FE7  E8D9E27F  6B7FE7E8    "XYR","XYRS","XY
00004   D9E2E37F  6B7FE7E8  D9E2E3E4  7F6B7FE7    RST","XYRSTU","X
00008   E8D9E2E3  E4E57F                          YRSTUV"

KEY =X'001388'  -   39 BYTES

00000   F0F9F8F7  F66BF0F9  F8F7F6F7  6BF0F9F8    09876,098767,098
00004   F7F6F7F8  6BF0F9F8  F7F6F7F8  F96BF0F9    7678,09876789,09
00008   F8F7F6F7  F8F9F0                          8767890

KEY =X'001770'  -   19 BYTES

00000   F1F2F3F4  F56BF1F2  F3F46BF1  F2F36BF1    12345,1234,123,1
00004   F26BF1                                    2,1
```

The output of COPY ALPHA TO ME is familiar. It consists of the six alphanumeric records, each containing five strings. It is the second printout that is of interest. First, the letter X flags us that the data are printed in hexadecimal notation. A hexadecimal number follows each X. The six numbers are 0003E8, 0007D0, 000BB8, 000FA0, 001388, and 001770; their decimal equivalents are:

$3E8_x = 1000_{dec}$	$FA0_x = 4000_{dec}$
$7D0_x = 2000_{dec}$	$1388_x = 5000_{dec}$
$BB8_x = 3000_{dec}$	$1770_x = 6000_{dec}$

Dividing each of these numbers by 1000_{dec} yields the six key numbers 1, 2, 3, 4, 5, and 6. On the same line, following the key number, we find the decimal number of bytes in the record.

The hexadecimal numbers in the first column in each of the six records are for record keeping—they keep track of the location of bytes in the record.

Reading across the first record, the first byte is C1, the second 6B, the third C1, und the fourth C2. The decimal equivalent of C1($C1_x = C \cdot 16 + 1 = 12 \cdot 16 + 1 = 192 + 1 = 193_{dec}$) is the EBCDIC value of the letter A. The decimal equivalent of 6B ($6B_x = 6 \cdot 16$

+ B = 96 + 11 = 107_{dec}) is the EBCDIC value of "comma." The decimal equivalent of C2 ($C2_x = C1_x + 1 = 193 + 1_{dec} = 194_{dec}$) is the EBCDIC value of B. Similarly, C3 translates to the character C, and C4 to D.

To simplify reading these hexadecimal records, their keyboard equivalents are given in the last column on the right. The hexadecimal record itself is contained in columns 2 through 5. That the record for which the key number is 1 consists of 19 characters may be verified by counting. The remaining records are treated similarly.

What we have seen thus far is that the computer can print a BCD file at our terminal in two formats. It can return the data to us either in the form we entered it or in binary. Having these two representations of the same file helps us to understand how a BCD file is stored in binary.

Reading a Binary Record

We can now interpret the binary file ALPHA1. If we have the computer read ALPHA1 as if it were a BCD file all that we can tell is that the file contains three records. COPY ALPHA1 TO ME (X) produces the following printout.

```
!COPY ALPHA1 TO ME

Z
#
>

!COPY ALPHA1 TO ME (X)

KEY =X'0003E8'  -  120 BYTES

00000   3CE90078  0101C140  40404040  0201C1C2      .Z....A     ..AB
00004   40404040  0301C1C2  C3404040  0401C1C2         ..ABC    ..AB
00008   C3C44040  0501C1C2  C3C4C540  0501C6C7      CD ..ABCDE ..FG
0000C   C8C9D140  0401C6C7  C8C94040  0301C6C7      HIJ ..FGHI  ..FG
00010   C8404040  0201C6C7  40404040  0101C640      H   ..FG    ..F
00014   40404040  0301D2D3  D4404040  0401D2D3         ..KLM    ..KL
00018   D4D54040  0501D2D3  D4D5D640  0601D2D3      MN  ..KLMNO ..KL
0001C   D4D5D6D7  3CBD0000                          MNOP....

KEY =X'0007D0'  -  120 BYTES

00000   3C710078  0701D2D3  D4D5D6D7  D8404040      ......KLMNOPQ
00004   40404040  0301E7E8  D9404040  0401E7E8         ..XYR    ..XY
00008   D9E24040  0501E7E8  D9E2E340  0601E7E8      RS  ..XYRST ..XY
0000C   D9E2E3E4  0701E7E8  D9E2E3E4  E5404040      RSTU..XYRSTUV
00010   40404040  0501F0F9  F8F7F640  0601F0F9         ..09876 ..09
00014   F8F7F6F7  0701F0F9  F8F7F6F7  F8404040      8767..0987678
00018   40404040  0801F0F9  F8F7F6F7  F8F94040         ..09876789
0001C   40404040  3CBD0001                             ....

KEY =X'000BB8'  -  120 BYTES

00000   3C6E0040  0901F0F9  F8F7F6F7  F8F9F040      .>. ..098767890
00004   40404040  0501F1F2  F3F4F540  0401F1F2         ..12345 ..12
00008   F3F44040  0301F1F2  F3404040  0201F1F2      34  ..123   ..12
0000C   40404040  0101F140  40404040  3CBD0002         ..1      ....
00010   00000000  0501F0F9  F8F7F640  0601F0F9      ......09876 ..09
00014   F8F7F6F7  0701F0F9  F8F7F6F7  F8404040      8767..0987678
00018   40404040  0801F0F9  F8F7F6F7  F8F94040         ..09876789
0001C   40404040  3CBD0002                             ....
```

The key numbers are as before, but now the length of each record is 120 bytes. This is characteristic of all binary files on this computer. For the first record, the first four bytes are 3CE90078. The first byte, 3C, denotes the beginning of a physical record; it is used also to denote the end of a physical or logical record. The next byte in this first record, E9, is for internal bookkeeping and need not concern us. The next two bytes, 00 and 78, indicate the number of informational bytes used in this record; since $78_x = 120_{dec}$, all 120 bytes in record 1 are used. Similarly, all 120 bytes in record 2 are used, but in record 3, only $40_x = 64_{dec}$ bytes are used.

In record 1, the next eight bytes, 0101C140 40404040, are reserved for the first string. The first byte, 01, indicates the number of characters in the string; the second, 01, is more internal bookkeeping; the third, C1, is the hexadecimal representation of the EBCDIC value of the first character of the first string, which is A. In all, six bytes are reserved initially for each string, and if fewer than six characters are present, unused places are filled with spaces. The EBCDIC value of "space" is $64_{dec} = 40_x$. The letter A is followed by five spaces.

The next eight bytes 0201C1C2 40404040 are read as follows: 02 means this is a string of two characters, 01 is bookkeeping, C1 = A, C2 = B, and four spaces are added at the end.

We continue in this fashion until we come to the eight bytes 0601D2D3 D4D5D6D7, which are interpreted as a string of six characters consisting of the letters KLMNOP.

The first time a string of more than six characters appears is at the beginning of the second record. If a string contains between seven and 12 characters, two sets of eight bytes are used. Thus, the string KLMNOPQ is written 0701D2D3 D4D5D6D7 D8404040 40404040.

The end of a record is signaled by the hexadecimal number 3C. This is followed by BD, which need not concern us, and then by a four-digit hexadecimal number. These last four digits indicate the physical record number, beginning with the number zero. Thus, scanning down the page, the last four hexadecimal digits for the three records are 0000, 0001, and 0002.

The first and second records are similar, but the third is slightly different. The third and fourth bytes are 0040, indicating that this record has only $40_x = 64_{dec}$ meaningful characters. Therefore, 3CBD0002 appears before the end of the record; it is in row 4, column 5. Since each record in a binary file must contain 120 bytes, those that follow 3CBD0002 are merely filler.

As in the preceding printout, the keyboard equivalents of the legitimate graphic symbols are given at the right.

Comparing a BCD File and a Binary File

Another Look at a BCD File in Binary

Earlier, the original file ALPHA, consisting of 30 strings arranged in six records, was rewritten as 15 records of two fields each. That new version of the BCD file ALPHA was displayed under EDIT (see page 374). We display it again using COPY ALPHA TO ME, and then display its binary version using COPY ALPHA TO ME (X).

```
!COPY ALPHA TO ME

A    AB
ABC     ABCD
ABCDE     FGHIJ
FGHI   FGH
FG   F
KLM     KLMN
KLMNO     KLMNOP
KLMNOPQ     XYR
XYRS   XYRST
XYRSTU    XYRSTUV
Ø9876    Ø98767
Ø987678    Ø9876789
Ø98767890     12345
1234   123
12  1
```

```
!COPY ALPHA TO ME (X)
KEY =X'0003E8'  -  6 BYTES
00000   C1404040  C1C2                                A   AB
KEY =X'0007D0'  -  10 BYTES
00000   C1C2C340  4040C1C2  C3C4                      ABC   ABCD
KEY =X'000BB8'  -  13 BYTES
00000   C1C2C3C4  C5404040  C6C7C8C9  D1              ABCDE   FGHIJ
KEY =X'000FA0'  -  9 BYTES
00000   C6C7C8C9  4040C6C7  C8                        FGHI  FGH
KEY =X'001388'  -  5 BYTES
00000   C6C74040  C6                                  FG  F
KEY =X'001770'  -  10 BYTES
00000   D2D3D440  4040D2D3  D4D5                      KLM   KLMN
KEY =X'001B58'  -  14 BYTES
00000   D2D3D4D5  D6404040  D2D3D4D5  D6D7            KLMNO   KLMNOP
KEY =X'001F40'  -  13 BYTES
00000   D2D3D4D5  D6D7D840  4040E7E8  D9              KLMNOPQ   XYR
KEY =X'002328'  -  11 BYTES
00000   E7E8D9E2  4040E7E8  D9E2E3                    XYRS  XYRST
KEY =X'002710'  -  15 BYTES
00000   E7E8D9E2  E3E44040  E7E8D9E2  E3E4E5          XYRSTU  XYRSTUV
KEY =X'002AF8'  -  14 BYTES
00000   F0F9F8F7  F6404040  F0F9F8F7  F6F7            09876   098767
KEY =X'002EE0'  -  18 BYTES
00000   F0F9F8F7  F6F7F840  4040F0F9  F8F7F6F7        0987678   098767
00004   F8F9                                          89
KEY =X'0032C8'  -  17 BYTES
00000   F0F9F8F7  F6F7F8F9  F0404040  F1F2F3F4        098767890   1234
00004   F5                                            5
KEY =X'0036B0'  -  9 BYTES
00000   F1F2F3F4  4040F1F2  F3                        1234  123
KEY =X'003A98'  -  5 BYTES
00000   F1F24040  F1                                  12  1
```

Another Look at a Binary File

The program on page 375 was used to write ALPHA1 as a file containing 15 records with two fields each. A portion of the hexadecimal printout of that file follows:

```
!COPY ALPHA1 TO ME (X)


KEY =X'0003E8'  -  120 BYTES

00000   3CD60018  0101C140  40404040  0201C1C2    .O....A       ..AB
00004   40404040  3CBD0000  00000000  0401F1F2           ..........12
00008   F3F44040  0301F1F2  F3404040  0201F1F2    34  ..123    ..12
0000C   40404040  0101F140  40404040  3CBD0002        ..1       ....
00010   00000000  0501F0F9  F8F7F640  0601F0F9    ......09876 ..09
00014   F8F7F6F7  0701F0F9  F8F7F6F7  F8404040    8767..0987678
00018   40404040  0801F0F9  F8F7F6F7  F8F94040        ..09876789
0001C   40404040  3CBD0000                            ....


KEY =X'001F40'  -  120 BYTES

00000   3C630020  0701D2D3  D4D5D6D7  D8404040    ......KLMNOPQ
00004   40404040  0301E7E8  D9404040  3CBD0007        ..XYR     ....
00008   00000000  0301F1F2  F3404040  0201F1F2    ......123    ..12
0000C   40404040  0101F140  40404040  3CBD0002        ..1       ....
00010   00000000  0501F0F9  F8F7F640  0601F0F9    ......09876 ..09
00014   F8F7F6F7  0701F0F9  F8F7F6F7  F8404040    8767..0987678
00018   40404040  0801F0F9  F8F7F6F7  F8F94040        ..09876789
0001C   40404040  3CBD0007                            ....


KEY =X'002EE0'  -  120 BYTES

00000   3C2C0028  0701F0F9  F8F7F6F7  F8404040    ......0987678
00004   40404040  0801F0F9  F8F7F6F7  F8F94040        ..09876789
00008   40404040  3CBD000B  00000000  0201F1F2        ..........12
0000C   40404040  0101F140  40404040  3CBD0002        ..1       ....
00010   00000000  0501F0F9  F8F7F640  0601F0F9    ......09876 ..09
00014   F8F7F6F7  0701F0F9  F8F7F6F7  F8404040    8767..0987678
00018   40404040  0801F0F9  F8F7F6F7  F8F94040        ..09876789
0001C   40404040  3CBD000B                            ....


KEY =X'003A98'  -  120 BYTES

00000   3C740018  0201F1F2  40404040  0101F140    ......12      ..1
00004   40404040  3CBD000E  00000000  3CBD000C        ............
00008   00000000  3CBD000B  00000000  0201F1F2    ..............12
0000C   40404040  0101F140  40404040  3CBD0002        ..1       ....
00010   00000000  0501F0F9  F8F7F640  0601F0F9    ......09876 ..09
00014   F8F7F6F7  0701F0F9  F8F7F6F7  F8404040    8767..0987678
00018   40404040  0801F0F9  F8F7F6F7  F8F94040        ..09876789
0001C   40404040  3CBD000E                            ....
```

When we read the printout of the file, we must remember where the end of each record occurs. Because the length of the records used in this illustration are short, the 3CBD will occur early. In most of the records it occurs in the second row; in record 12,KEY=X′002EE0′,3CBD008 occurs in the third row. Characters appearing after the first end-of-record character are filler to complete the needed 120 bytes.

The essential difference between the two hexadecimal printouts is that the first is the binary version of a BCD file, ALPHA, where the second printout is that of a binary file, ALPHA1.

The PUT Statement

We can now describe the operation of the PUT statement. Although data strings of variable length are entered into the binary file, the PUT instruction attempts to wait until there are sufficient data to fill all 120 bytes before creating the record. This did not happen under two different circumstances. The first case, when it might be expected, occurs in the last record of the file when there are insufficient data to fill all 120 bytes. When the file is closed under a CLOSE statement, a short record is created. In general, when a CLOSE statement is executed, the PUT statement does not fill the current record; rather, the short (incomplete) record is put out into the file.

The other case occurred when line 160 of the program on page 375 was executed. The line is repeated for reference.

```
160 PUT :2; INT(I/2) + 1, N$(I), N$(I+1)
```

When this line is executed the first time, only a partial record is obtained. This partial record is not entered into the file; the computer waits for additional data to complete the 120 bytes. At that time, the whole 120-byte record would be transferred to the file. When line 160 was executed a second time, however, since it referred to a keyed record, the previous record was transferred to the file as a short record. In general, when a PUT statement does not fill the current output record being assembled in the computer, that record is not transferred to the file unless a keyed PUT statement is subsequently executed.

There is a third way to produce short records. Whenever a double asterisk appears in a PUT statement, the record currently being formed is closed and put into the file. The following illustrates how this may be done.

```
>100 PUT :2, N$(1), N$(2), **
```

If, before the execution of line 100, a partially filled record exists, then the result of executing line 100 would be to add to that partially filled record the data in addresses N$(1) and N$(2), close that record, and put it into the file. The next PUT statement would start a new record.

Another illustration follows.

```
>200 PUT :3, **, A$(1), A$(2), A$(3), **, B$(1), B$(2), **
```

If, before the execution of line 200, a partially filled record exists, that record is closed and put into the file. A new record is then started, and the contents of addresses A$(1), A$(2), and A$(3) are put into it. The record is closed and put in the file. A new record is opened, the contents of B$(1) and B$(2) are entered, the record is closed and put into the file.

Keyed Files

As with BCD files, binary files are also keyed. This permits us to reference a specific record by its key number. Thus, if we want to write to a specific record, the form of the instruction is:

```
PUT :channel ; key , variables
```

If we wish to retrieve a specific record, the instruction takes the form:

```
GET :channel ; key, variables
```

One word of caution. When working with a binary file, you must update the fields in a record carefully. If the number of characters in the new information exceeds the number in the data being replaced, and that record is full, the additional characters will overwrite information you may want to retain.

Summary

The concepts developed in this chapter are based on the following idea. We have at most 256 "letters" available in the EBCDIC "alphabet." These include the upper-case letters of the English alphabet, lower-case letters, digits, and some punctuation symbols (such as the comma, semicolon, or number sign). Other characters, called control characters, help us get the computer to respond to special needs. Examples include end-of-file, ESC F, and delete line input, ESC X. The RUBOUT function, which is considered neither a graphic character nor a control character, is another character in the set. As of this writing, not all 256 "letters" have been defined.

As we know, the computer does not know what the printed symbol A means. We tell the computer what the symbol A means: It means $193_{dec} = C1_X = 11000001_{bin}$. The computer's electric circuitry can handle 11000001_{bin}. Thus, each time we type one of the "letters" of our "alphabet," the computer gets an 8-bit binary number.

When the computer talks back to us, it could use several forms, including its native tongue, the binary language. It might say

```
1100100011000101110100111101001111010110
```

Or, it might group this greeting as follows:

```
11001000 11000101 11010011 11010011 11010110
```

It could also write

```
C8 C5 D3 D3 D6
```

If we recognize the hexadecimal equivalents of the computer's binary language, we can convert the pairs into their equivalent decimal forms: C8 → 200, C5 → 197, D3 → 211, and D6 → 214—and the message becomes:

```
200 195 211 211 214
```

If we still cannot understand what the computer is trying to tell us, we might refer to our EBCDIC-to-English dictionary and translate 200 in H, 197 into E, 211 into L, and 214 into O. The computer is saying HELLO.

In most situations, the computer gives us its messages in our language. If we do not understand what it is trying to tell us, we may have to examine the message in the computer's language. In this chapter, we used files in order to practice the computer's language. Two difficulties should be apparent: If the computer were to write all its messages in binary, the amount of paper generated would be enormous, and we would have difficulty recognizing the 256 different 8-bit patterns. For these reasons, and because translation between binary and hexadecimal is easy, the computer writes to us in hexadecimal. Thus, we have an exact description of what is being said; nothing is lost in the translation.

With that as preamble, let us review what we did with files. Using EDIT, we entered string data initially into six records of the BCD file ALPHA, which then was read (INPUT) by a BASIC program, by EDIT, and under the operating system. The file actually exists in the computer in binary form; each character in the file is stored as its 8-bit EBCDIC equivalent. Under the operating system, we read the file in this form and the printout was in hexadecimal. Remember, there are the same number of records in the two printed versions of the file, and there are the same number of EBCDIC characters in the two printed versions of each record.

Using a BASIC program, we then rewrote the BCD file ALPHA as the binary file ALPHA1. ALPHA1 can be read (GET) by a BASIC program; it cannot be read under EDIT. ALPHA1 exists in the computer in binary form, but the record lengths are uniform—120 bytes long. When read under the operating system, it was printed in hexadecimal form.

The internal structure of files created using PRINT and PUT were compared. When PRINT is used, the file exists in the "print" form. Each record in the file looks exactly as if it were printed as a single line on a page. When PUT is used, the data are stored in records of fixed length, 120 bytes.

This discussion was presented for an EBCDIC machine. The general methods and procedures will be comparable on an ASCII machine; some of the details will be different. Do not expect machines produced by different manufacturers to function identically. In fact, do not expect machines produced by the same manufacturer but in different series to function identically. (Most Cadillac and Chevrolet parts, for example, are not interchangeable.) To use this information effectively on your computer, repeat the several steps taken, noting and reconciling the differences as they occur.

Exercises

20.1 (a) Using a BASIC program, read the alphabet, as a single string, into a BCD file. The file will consist of a single record. Print the contents of the file in hexadecimal and visually verify that the printout gives the EBCDIC values of the letters A through Z.

(b) Using a BASIC program, convert the file constructed in part (a) into a binary file. Print the contents of this file (the printout will have to be in hexadecimal). Visually verify that the printout gives the EBCDIC values of the letters A through Z. How many records are in the file? Why?

20.2 (a) Using a BASIC program, read the alphabet, two letters at a time, into a BCD file. The file should consist of 13 records. Print the contents of this file in hexadecimal and verify that there are 13 records. Also, verify that the contents of each record are the EBCDIC values of the corresponding letters of the alphabet.

(b) Using a BASIC program, convert the file constructed in part (a) into a binary file. Print the contents of this file (the printout will have to be in hexadecimal). Verify that the printout gives the EBCDIC values of the letters A through Z. Does this file differ from the one in exercise 20.1(b)? Why?

20.3 Using either of the binary files constructed in Exercise 20.1(b) or 20.2(b), write a BASIC program that will produce another binary file consisting of 13 records. Each record is to contain exactly two letters of the alphabet. Print the contents of this file (the printout will have to be in hexadecimal). Verify that the printout consists of 13 records. Identify the meaningful EBCDIC values and translate them into their English equivalents.

Binary Numeric Files 21

Binary files are significant because they are the most compact way to store numeric data. In the familiar decimal notation, the square root of 2 to 15 decimal places is: $\sqrt{2}$ = 1.414213562373095. When stored in a BCD file, 36 characters are needed: $\sqrt{2}$ = 40F14BF4 F1F4F2F1 F3F5F6F2 F3F7F3F0 F9F5. The 40_x is the "space" and the $4B_x$ is the decimal point. When stored in a binary file, however, only 16 BCD characters are needed for the same accuracy: $\sqrt{2}$ = 4116A09E 667F3BCC. The obvious savings in storage space is important.

Although devices capable of storing hundreds of millions of bits are commonplace, and ones with capacities in the billions and trillions are feasible, even these can become saturated. For example, consider the amount of data transmitted from the many satellites orbiting the earth and probing the solar system and beyond. If there were only 1000 of these, and each transmitted only one megabit (one million bits) of data per second for one year, the total number of bits transmitted would exceed 3×10^{16}. One trillion is only 10^{12}, so we would need 30,000 trillion-bit storage devices if we wished to retain all that data. Therefore, any scheme—like binary file storage—that cuts requirements such as these down to manageable size is a boon.

In this chapter, we shall describe how numeric data are stored in binary files. Two concepts, previously presented, are needed: (1) the technique for storing decimal numbers as double-word floating-point binary numbers and (2) the organization of these double words into files.

After this description is completed, BASIC matrix instructions are used to construct numeric binary files.

The Structure of a Numeric Binary Record

A binary record, whether for strings or numeric data, contains 120 bytes, or 30 words. As discussed in the last chapter, two words, the first and last, are reserved for internal record keeping. The remaining 28 words are used to store 14 double-word binary numbers. As an illustration, consider the following digital numbers for which the internal computer representation (previously described in Chapter 13, "On Representing Numbers") may be readily verified. As an exercise, we can easily see that the sum of any number and its negative is zero.

1	41100000	00000000
2	41200000	00000000
3	41300000	00000000
16	42100000	00000000
17 = 16 + 1	42110000	00000000
$256 = 16^2$	43100000	00000000
$272 = 16^2 + 16$	43110000	00000000
$273 = 16^2 + 16 + 1$	43111000	00000000
$4956 = 16^3 + 3\times16^2 + 5\times16 + 12$	44135C000	00000000
−1	BEF00000	00000000
−2	BEE00000	00000000
−3	BED00000	00000000
−16	BDF00000	00000000
−17	BDEF0000	00000000
−256	BCF00000	00000000
−272	BCEF0000	00000000
−273	BCEEF000	00000000
−4956	BBECA400	00000000

We could have determined the hexadecimal entries for these numbers by following the rules described previously, but it is easier to let the computer do the work. The decimal representations of these 18 numbers are entered into a BCD file called BETA. They are then read from BETA and put into a binary file called BETA1. Printing the contents of BETA1 in hexadecimal and comparing them with the corresponding entries in BETA displays the equivalence of the two files. The BCD file, BETA, the program, and the hexadecimal file, BETA1, follow.

```
*EDIT BETA
*TY
   1.000 1,2,3,16,17,256,272,273,4956
   2.000 -1,-2,-3,-16,-17,-256,-272,-273,-4956

 10 OPEN 'BETA' TO :1,INPUT
 20 OPEN 'BETA1' TO :2, PUT,ON
 30 ENDFILE :1,80
 40 FOR I=1 TO 18
 50 INPUT :1,A
 60 PUT :2,A
 70 NEXT I
 80 CLOSE :1 \ CLOSE :2
 90 END

 RUN

!COPY BETA1 TO ME (X)

KEY =X'0003E8'  -   120 BYTES

00000    3C660078  41100000  00000000  41200000
00004    00000000  41300000  00000000  42100000
00008    00000000  42110000  00000000  43100000
0000C    00000000  43110000  00000000  43111000
00010    00000000  44135C00  00000000  BEF00000
00014    00000000  BEE00000  00000000  BED00000
00018    00000000  BDF00000  00000000  BDEF0000
0001C    00000000  3CBD0000

KEY =X'0007D0'  -   120 BYTES

00000    3C9A0028  BCF00000  00000000  BCEF0000
00004    00000000  BCEEF000  00000000  BBECA400
00008    00000000  3CBD0001  00000000  43100000
0000C    00000000  43110000  00000000  43111000
00010    00000000  44135C00  00000000  BEF00000
00014    00000000  BEE00000  00000000  BED00000
00018    00000000  BDF00000  00000000  BDEF0000
0001C    00000000  3CBD0001
```

In BETA1, the first 14 numbers are written in the first record, the remaining four in the second record. The computer representation of 1 is 41100000 00000000, printed in row 1, columns 3 and 4. The computer representation of 2 is 41200000 00000000, which is printed in row 1, column 5 and row 2, column 2. The last data entry in the first record, BDEF0000 00000000, appears in row 7, column 5 and continues in row 8, column 2. In decimal notation, it is -17_{dec}.

The first data entry in the second record is BCF00000 00000000, row 1, columns 3 and 4; its decimal equivalent is -256_{dec}. The last meaningful data entry in the second record is BBECA400 00000000, which appears in row 2, column 5 and row 3, column 2; -4956 is its decimal equivalent. The second record terminates at the first occurrence of 3CBD, in row 3, column 3.

Nonterminating Binary Fractions

Recall that the binary representation for 0.1_{dec} requires an infinite number of places. The computer, however, can allocate only a finite number of places, and the representation must therefore be approximate. The computer binary representation of 0.1_{dec} can be seen from the output of the following program.

```
10 OPEN 'BETA1' TO :2, PUT,ON
20 FOR I=1 TO 11
30 READ A
40 PUT :2,A
50 NEXT I
60 DATA .1,.2,.3,.4,.5,.6,.7,.8,.9
70 DATA .0625,.00390625
80 CLOSE :2
90 END

RUN
```

```
!COPY BETA1 TO ME (X)

KEY =X'0003E8'   -    120 BYTES

00000   3CDC0060  40199999  9999999A  40333333
00004   33333333  404CCCCC  CCCCCCCD  40666666
00008   66666666  40800000  00000000  40999999
0000C   9999999A  40B33333  33333333  40CCCCCC
00010   CCCCCCCD  40E66666  66666666  40100000
00014   00000000  3F100000  00000000  3CBD0000
00018   00000000  00000000  00000000  00000000
0001C   00000000  3CBD0000
```

The first data entry in the record is 40199999 9999999A. We will show how this translates to 0.1_{dec}. First, the two leading hexadecimal digits, 40_x, tell us that the greatest power of 16 in this number is -1 and $1/16 = 1/2^4$. Since the binary representation of $1_x = 0001$, of $9_x = 1001$, and of $A_x = 1010$, we may use this to set up the following correspondence.

$$\begin{array}{cccccc} 1 & 9 & 9 & 9 & 9 & 9 \\ \updownarrow & \updownarrow & \updownarrow & \updownarrow & \updownarrow & \updownarrow \\ 0001 & 1001 & 1001 & 1001 & 1001 & 1001 \end{array}$$

$$\begin{array}{cccccccc} 9 & 9 & 9 & 9 & 9 & 9 & 9 & A \\ \updownarrow & \updownarrow & \updownarrow & \updownarrow & \updownarrow & \updownarrow & \updownarrow & \updownarrow \\ 1001 & 1001 & 1001 & 1001 & 1001 & 1001 & 1001 & 1010 \end{array}$$

To get the decimal equivalent, we proceed as follows.

$$1_x = 0001_{bin} = \left(\frac{0}{2^1} + \frac{0}{2^2} + \frac{0}{2^3} + \frac{1}{2^4}\right)_{dec} = \left(\frac{1}{2^4}\right)_{dec}$$

For the first 9_x, we get

$$9_x = 1001_{bin} = \left(\frac{1}{2^5} + \frac{0}{2^6} + \frac{0}{2^7} + \frac{0}{2^8}\right)_{dec} = \left(\frac{1}{2^5} + \frac{1}{2^8}\right)_{dec}$$

For the second 9_x, we get

$$9_x = 1001_{bin} = \left(\frac{1}{2^9} + \frac{0}{2^{10}} + \frac{0}{2^{11}} + \frac{1}{2^{12}}\right)_{dec} = \left(\frac{1}{2^9} + \frac{1}{2^{12}}\right)_{dec}$$

Continuing this way, for the last 9_x we get

$$9_x = 1001_{bin} = \left(\frac{1}{2^{49}} + \frac{0}{2^{50}} + \frac{0}{2^{51}} + \frac{1}{2^{52}}\right)_{dec} = \left(\frac{1}{2^{49}} + \frac{1}{2^{52}}\right)_{dec}$$

Finally, we get

$$A_x = 1010_{bin} = \left(\frac{1}{2^{53}} + \frac{0}{2^{54}} + \frac{1}{2^{55}} + \frac{0}{2^{56}}\right)_{dec} = \left(\frac{1}{2^{53}} + \frac{1}{2^{55}}\right)_{dec}$$

The hexadecimal number 40199999 9999999A therefore translates to

$$\left(\frac{1}{2^4} + \frac{1}{2^5} + \frac{1}{2^8} + \frac{1}{2^9} + \frac{1}{2^{12}} + \ldots + \frac{1}{2^{49}} + \frac{1}{2^{52}} + \frac{1}{2^{53}} + \frac{1}{2^{55}}\right)_{dec}$$

This sum may be written $(0.1 + 3/(5 \times 2^{55}))_{dec}$. The difference between this number, which is the way the computer writes the decimal number one-tenth, and the exact value, 0.1, is $3/5 \times 2^{55} \approx 1.66533 \times 10^{-17}$.

The last data entry in the record is 3F100000 00000000. The 3F indicates that the greatest power of 16 is -2. Thus, $3F100000\ 00000000_x = 1/16^2{}_{dec} = 0.0039065_{dec}$, an exact correspondence. The computer hexadecimal (or if you prefer, binary) representations of the other decimals may also be verified from the printout.

Application to Matrices

We shall conclude our discussion of binary files by illustrating their applicability to matrices.

The MAT PUT Statement

The following program illustrates the MAT PUT statement. In lines 30–70, a test matrix A is created, and in line 80 it is printed at the terminal. Whatever the file MU1 was before, it is overwritten; this is done at line 90. Line 100 puts matrix A into MU1 in binary form, and line 110 closes the file MU1.

```
10 DIM A(10,10)
20 MAT SIZE A(7,5)
30 FOR J=1 TO 7
40 FOR I=1 TO 5
50 A(J,I)=I*(J+11)
60 NEXT I
70 NEXT J
80 MAT PRINT A;
```

```
90 OPEN 'MU1' TO :1,PUT,OVER
100 MAT PUT :1,A
110 CLOSE :1

RUN

12      24      36      48      60

13      26      39      52      65

14      28      42      56      70

15      30      45      60      75

16      32      48      64      80

17      34      51      68      85

18      36      54      72      90
```

After the binary file of matrix A was created, we had the computer print the file in binary. See below. The file MU1, which consists of three records, contains only the numerical values as data entries. There is no indication in the printout that the numbers came from a matrix. If, at some later time, these numbers are read back into a computer program, it will be necessary to specify in that program how they are to be assigned to variables. They need not be assigned to another 7 × 5 matrix; they could just as easily be assigned to a 5 × 7 matrix or to a list of 35 elements.

From the data in the file, we can recover the decimal values by using the transformation rules we have been describing. For example, if we drop the trailing zeros, the 14 hexadecimal entries in the first record are: $41C_x \rightarrow 12_{dec}$, $4218_x \rightarrow 1 \cdot 16 + 8 = 24_{dec}$, $4224_x = 2 \cdot 16 + 4 = 36_{dec}$, $423_x = 3 \cdot 16 = 48_{dec}$, $423C_x = 3 \cdot 16 + 12 = 60_{dec}$, $41D_x = 13_{dec}$, $421A_x = 1 \cdot 16 + 10 = 26_{dec}$, $4227_x = 2 \cdot 16 + 7 = 39_{dec}$, $4234_x = 3 \cdot 16 + 4 = 52_{dec}$, $4241_x = 4 \cdot 16 + 1 = 65_{dec}$, $41E_x = 14_{dec}$, $421C_x = 1 \cdot 16 + 12 = 28_{dec}$, $422A_x = 2 \cdot 16 + 10 = 42_{dec}$, and $4238_x = 3 \cdot 16 + 8 = 56_{dec}$. The 14 entries in the second record may be read using this same procedure. The last seven entries of the matrix appear as the first seven data entries of the third record. The end-of-record 3CBD appears in row 4, column 5. (Note that the elements of the first row are entered into MU1 first, then those of the second row, and so on.)

```
!COPY MU1 TO ME (X)

KEY =X'0003E8'   -   120 BYTES

00000    3C920078  41C00000  00000000  42180000
00004    00000000  42240000  00000000  42300000
00008    00000000  423C0000  00000000  41D00000
0000C    00000000  421A0000  00000000  42270000
00010    00000000  42340000  00000000  42410000
00014    00000000  41E00000  00000000  421C0000
00018    00000000  422A0000  00000000  42380000
0001C    00000000  3CBD0000

KEY =X'0007D0'   -   120 BYTES

00000    3CA70078  42460000  00000000  41F00000
00004    00000000  421E0000  00000000  422D0000
00008    00000000  423C0000  00000000  424B0000
0000C    00000000  42100000  00000000  42200000
00010    00000000  42300000  00000000  42400000
00014    00000000  42500000  00000000  42110000
00018    00000000  42220000  00000000  42330000
0001C    00000000  3CBD0001
```

```
KEY =X'000BB8'   -   120 BYTES

00000    3CEC0040  42440000  00000000  42550000
00004    00000000  42120000  00000000  42240000
00008    00000000  42360000  00000000  42480000
0000C    00000000  425A0000  00000000  3CBD0002
00010    00000000  42300000  00000000  42400000
00014    00000000  42500000  00000000  42110000
00018    00000000  42220000  00000000  42330000
0001C    00000000  3CBD0002
```

The MAT GET Statement

The next program illustrates how a MAT statement is combined with GET to read the contents of a numeric binary file. Still using file MU1, a matrix A, now a 5 × 7 matrix, is initialized to zero (line 30) and then used to store the contents of the file MU1, line 40. Line 50 prints the contents of the matrix A; they agree with the entries of the file MU1.

```
10 DIM A(5,7)
20 OPEN 'MU1' TO :1, GET
30 MAT A=ZER
40 MAT GET :1,A
50 MAT PRINT A;
60 CLOSE :1

RUN

12     24     36     48     60     13     26

39     52     65     14     28     42     56

70     15     30     45     60     75     16

32     48     64     80     17     34     51

68     85     18     36     54     72     90
```

Suppose we change the dimension statement in line 10 from A(5,7) to A(35). Upon reading the 35 entires from the file MU1, the computer will assign them to the subscripted variables A(1), A(2), . . . , A(35). In the program, line 50 MAT PRINT A; would print these 35 values as a row vector. This change to the program and the resulting printout follow.

```
LIST 10

10 DIM A(5,7)
10 DIM A(35)

RUN

12    24    36    48    60    13    26    39    52    65    14    28
42    56    70    15    30    45    60    75    16    32    48    64
80    17    34    51    68    85    18    36    54    72    90
```

For the final illustration, we again begin with the file MU1 and UPDATE it. To understand UPDATE clearly, consider the following. A file literally exists on a disk. In the computer's main memory is a buffer area where a copy of one record of that file is temporarily stored. When we modify the record or print it at our terminal, we are working with the copy of the record in the buffer, not the record on the disk.

All transfers between the file on disk and the buffer in the main memory are done in units of records, one at a time. Thus, when the computer needs data from the file, a record is read into the buffer, overwriting what was there before, and these new data are then used by the program. If more data are needed, a second record is brought in from the file on disk.

When data are to be stored in the file, they can be entered only as elements of a record, and only a complete record can be transferred from the buffer to the file. In other words, only after all 14 data elements have accumulated in the buffer is the record sent to the file. If fewer than 14 data elements accrete in the buffer, they remain there waiting for the rest—unless we take positive action in either of two ways. Using a special instruction—here, a double asterisk—we may tell the computer to send a partial record to the file. The second way to send a partial record is to close the channel between the buffer and the disk. Under this condition, a partial record, presumably the last record in the file, is sent. Also, see page 381.

```
10 DIM A(7,5),B(7,5),C(7,5)
20 OPEN 'MU1' TO :1,GET,UPDATE
30 MAT A = ZER
40 MAT GET :1,A
50 MAT C=(.01)*A
60 MAT PUT :1;1,C
70 PUT :1,**
80 MAT GET :1;1,B
90 MAT PRINT B;
100 CLOSE :1

RUN


.120000    .240000    .360000    .480000    .600000

.130000    .260000    .390000    .520000    .650000

.140000    .280000    .420000    .560000    .700000

.150000    .300000    .450000    .600000    .750000

.160000    .320000    .480000    .640000    .800000

.170000    .340000    .510000    .680000    .850000

.180000    .360000    .540000    .720000    .900000

    100 HALT
```

Line 30 initializes matrix A to zero. In line 40, the contents of the file MU1 are read from the disk into the computer and assigned to matrix A. At this point, the key pointer is no longer at 1 but at the last record taken from file MU1. Matrix A may be manipulated according to the needs of the programer; in this illustration, we have divided each element of A by 100 to produce a new matrix, called C, line 50. The elements of matrix C will replace the contents of the file MU1 on the disk. To do this, the key pointer must first be moved back to the first record; the ;1 following :1 in line 60 does this. The MAT PUT in line 60 starts putting the contents of matrix C into the file MU1.

As we have said above, as a record for a file is being assembled in the buffer, that record does not get into the file on the disk until all 14 data words are filled. Since there are 35 elements in C, 28 of them will fill 2 full records, and these elements will go to update the first two records in the file MU1. The remaining 7 elements, however, are still in the computer. We want them to be sent to MU1. Line 70 does this; the double asterisks closes the record in the buffer and it is then sent from the computer to the file MU1 on disk.

Again, the pointer is at key number 3. If the contents of the file MU1 are to be assigned to B, the pointer must be directed to key number 1. The ;1 in line 80 does this.

A word of caution on two points. When using GET,UPDATE, you should know the location of the key pointer at all times, and you should remember that incomplete records require a special instruction to incorporate them into the file.

Summary

The last five chapters were only an introduction to the extensive subject of files. We limited our presentation to keyed BCD and binary files and the several BASIC instructions needed to create and manipulate them. Although a BCD file is more easily created and modified under EDIT, we still need a BASIC program to manipulate its contents for whatever purpose we have in mind. Binary files were created and modified only through the use of BASIC programs.

The precise format for opening and closing a file and the exact verbs used, for example, PRINT, PUT, and GET, should be expected to vary from one computer to the next. Such details can be found in the manuals supplied by the manufacturer of your computer. The concepts introduced—keyed files, BCD and binary files—are universal. The transition from the specifics we have offered here to those of your computer should be smooth.

Exercises

21.1 The following table lists the prime numbers between 2 and 100 and their square roots to 19 decimal places.

n(prime)	$\sqrt{n}$			
2	1.4142	13562	37309	50488
3	1.7320	50807	56887	72935
5	2. 2360	67977	49978	96964
7	2. 6457	51311	06459	05905
11	3. 3166	24790	35539	98491
13	3. 6055	51275	46398	92931
17	4. 1231	05625	61766	05498
19	4. 3588	98943	54067	35522
23	4. 7958	31523	31271	95416
29	5. 3851	64807	13450	40313
31	5. 5677	64362	83002	19221
37	6. 0827	62530	29821	96890
41	6. 4031	24237	43284	86865
43	6. 5574	38524	30200	06523
47	6. 8556	54600	40104	41249
53	7. 2801	09889	28051	82711
59	7. 6811	45747	86860	81758
61	7. 8102	49675	90665	43941
67	8. 1853	52771	87244	99700
71	8. 4261	49773	17635	86306
73	8. 5440	03745	31753	11679
79	8. 8881	94417	31558	88501
83	9. 1104	33579	14429	88819
89	9. 4339	81132	05660	38113
97	9. 8488	57801	79610	47217

SOURCE: Milton Abramawitz and Irene A. Stegun, eds., *Handbook of Mathematical Functions* (Washington, D.C.: National Bureau of Standards, Applied Mathematics Series, No. 55, June 1964).

Using a BASIC program, enter the prime numbers into a list P(I), I = 1, 2, . . . , 20. Next, store the square roots of these numbers in two separate files, one a BCD file and the other a binary file. Enter the data into the BCD file in packed format, as elements of a matrix, or in any other arrangement that appeals to you. Using the binary (hexadecmial) representation of this file, count the number of characters needed to store these 20 numbers. Compare that number with the number of binary (hexadecimal) characters needed to store the same information in the binary file. Which is the smaller? Why?

21.2 Given the two matrices:

$$A = \begin{pmatrix} 1\,2\,3 \\ 4\,5\,6 \\ 7\,8\,9 \end{pmatrix} \text{ and } B = \begin{pmatrix} 11\,12\,13 \\ 14\,15\,16 \\ 17\,18\,19 \end{pmatrix}$$

write a computer program that stores matrices A, A^2, and A^3 in a binary file MATRIX. Print the file MATRIX. How many records does it contain? Without recomputing A^2 and A^3, update the file MATRIX so that the entires in it are the contents of A, B, A^2, B^2, A^3, and B^3 in that order. Without recomputing B^2 and B^3, update MATRIX a second time so that the *only* entries in it are the matrices B, B^2, and B^3.

21.3 Refer to the table in Exercise 21.1. Using the maximum number of decimal places available on your computer, raise each of the first 10 prime numbers to the 25th power and each of second 10 prime numbers to the -25th power. Store these 20 numbers both in a BCD file and a binary file. What is the hexadecimal representation of each number in the BCD file? What is the hexadecimal representation of each number in the binary file?

21.4 The equation of an ellipse whose semi-major axis is 3 and whose semi-minor axis is 2 is

$$\frac{X^2}{9} + \frac{Y^2}{4} = 1$$

To each value of X between -3 and $+3$, there are two values of Y, equal in magnitude but opposite in sign. Construct a binary file that lists these three numbers, X, Y, and $-Y$, for $X = -3, -2.9, -2.8, \ldots, -0.1, 0, 0.1, \ldots, 2.8, 2.8\ ,3$. How many data entires are there? What is the minimum number of records needed to store these data?

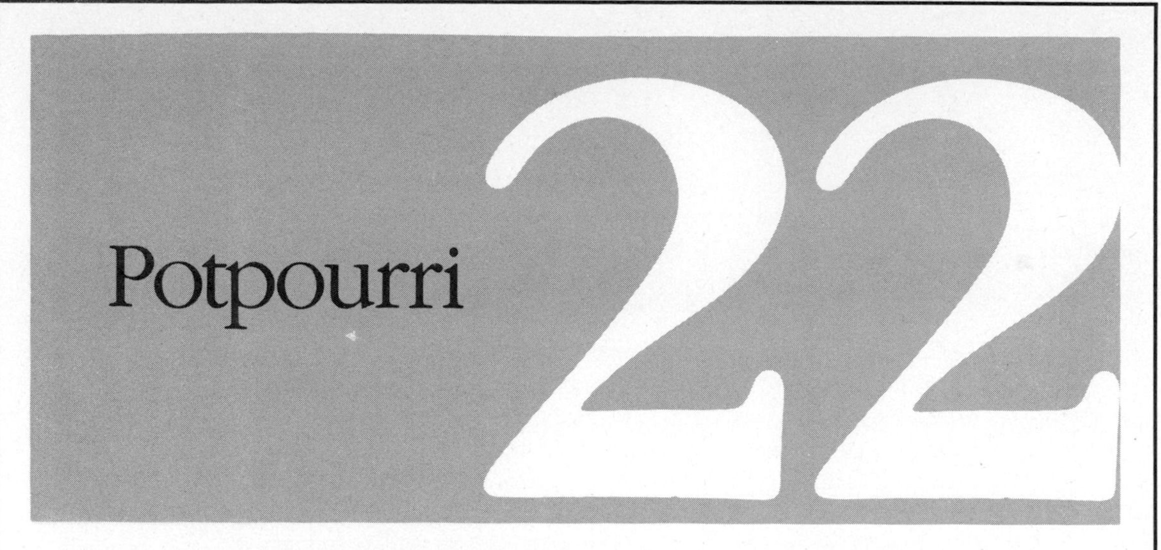

Potpourri

Scattered throughout the earlier chapters are descriptions of certain ancillary features provided by our computer systm to facilitate the writing of programs. In this chapter, we shall assemble and present a few more of these features as a collection of unrelated concepts. Their utility will depend, of course, on the specific problem we are attempting to solve.

Immediate Mode/Desk Calculator

When we introduced the Immediate Mode/Desk Calculator capabilities of BASIC in Chapter 2, the purpose was to use the similarities between a desk calculator and the computer to present the format for writing various arithmetic operations. The Immediate Mode can be used more extensively, however, to solve a limited class of arithmetic problems without resorting to writing a program. In other words, the computer can be used as a desk calculator. In this mode of operation, line numbers are not used. As we have seen, typical straightforward arithmetic operations are possible.

```
>PRINT 2*(3+4)^5
 33614

>PRINT 35/7-2
 3
```

In this mode, we have access to the several intrinsic functions, which we may then use in computation.

```
>PRINT 2*SIN(3.1415926/4)
 1.41421

>PRINT MAX(3,1,5,4,2)
 5

>PRINT MIN(3,1,5,4,2)
 1
```

A limited amount of storage is provided.

```
>X=4
>Y=5
>Z=6
>PRINT X*Y+Y*Z-Z/X
 48.5000

>X=3+4
>X=X^2+5
>PRINT X
 54
```

The Immediate Mode as a Debugging Aid

The frustrations of writing a program and getting it to work as intended should be painfully apparent to you by this time. Those errors the computer catches and reports provide some clues as to the source of the trouble. More dangerous and insidious errors come from programs that run but give incorrect answers. The immediate mode can be helpful as a debugging aid in this situation. To "debug" means to eliminate errors.

To illustrate, suppose we want to produce a multiplication table for the numbers 10 through 20. We wrote and started to run the following program:

```
 10 FOR I=10 TO 20
 20 FOR J=1 TO 20
 30 PRINT USING 60,I,J,I+J
 40 NEXT J
 50 NEXT I
 60 :      THE PRODUCT OF ## AND ## = ###

>RUN

     THE PRODUCT OF 10 AND  1 =  11
     THE PRODUCT OF 10 AND  2 =  12
     THE PROD_
     THE PRODUCT OF 10 AND  5 =  15

      40 RUN INTERRUPTED

>PRINT I
 10

>PRINT J
 5

>PRINT I*J
 50
```

As we saw the answers being printed at our terminal, we recognized that they were wrong; we were certainly not getting 10 times 10. We hit the BREAK key and the program stopped. Knowing the current values of I, J, and I*J would be helpful, so we ask for them in the immediate mode. The answers come back: 10, 5, 50. Thus, we have a clue that we have written an addition instruction instead of a multiplication instruction and that the J loop started at 1 instead of 10. Referring to the program, we detect these errors in lines 20 and 30.

If at any time we believe a program is not giving us the expected answers, we can stop it and, in the immediate mode, get the value currently assigned to any variable to see if it agrees with our expectation. In this way, we logically segment the program into parts and discover in which section the error occurs.

The previous printout may be interpreted as follows. The computer internally set up a print buffer to receive the values for I, J, and I+J. As these arrive, they are temporarily stored and then combined with the PRINTUSING instruction. The formatted combination is then sent to the terminal where one line is printed. During the time the line is being printed, a second line is received at the terminal. In this illustration, the second line was received and printed. During the printing of the second line, the third line was received, but before all of it could be printed, the BREAK key was struck and the printing stopped. However, the computer, obviously much faster than the terminal, was already transmitting the fourth and fifth lines for printing. The fourth line was lost because the terminal was jut not ready to receive it. The terminal, however, recovered in time to receive the fifth line and did print it. By the time the fifth line was printed, the computer was long aware that we wanted to stop further execution of the program. Accordingly, no more lines were sent. It also named the last line of the program it had executed—in this case, line 40—when it detected our BREAK signal.

On this computer, the symbol that the computer uses to indicate BREAK is the underscore, _ .

The Length of a File

Suppose we need to know the exact number of records in a file. If the name of the BCD file is 'VB', we would enter:

```
>OPEN 'VB' TO :3, INPUT                    <CR>
>INPUT :3;9999,A                           <CR>
```

We know that the key number 9999 far exceeds the number of records in the file. The computer responds:

```
        KEY NOT FOUND
```

We then type:

```
>PRINT KEY(3)                              <CR>
```

and the computer responds:

```
120
```

indicating that there are 120 records in that file.

If the file is binary, the sequence is as follows:

```
>OPEN 'MU1' TO :4, GET                     <CR>
>GET :4;9999,A                             <CR>

        KEY NOT FOUND

>PRINT KEY(4)                              <CR>
 3
```

There are three records in the binary file MU1.

RENUMBER (RESEQUENCE)

Generally, after writing a lengthy program in which there have been numerous deletions and insertions, it is desirable to renumber all lines in the program, if for no other than aesthetic reasons. As you know, the following command does this.

>REN <CR>

The first instruction is numbered 100 and subsequent instructions are increased by 10, that is, the instruction sequence is 100, 110, 120, ... The more general form of the renumbering command is

>REN l_1, l_2, n

where l_1 is the first of the new line numbers, l_2 is the line number in the old program that will become l_1, and n is the increment to be used from l_1 onward.

The following seven-line program was written starting with line number 10 and using increments of 10. The first listing exhibits the program. This is followed by the REN command, and the result is also listed. Finally REN 200, 130, 50 was used. The net result of this command is to leave all lines whose numbers are less than 130 untouched, to change line number 130 to 200, and to increase subsquent lines by 50. The third listing illustrates this.

```
>LIST

 10 FOR I=1 TO 10
 20 FOR J=1 TO 10
 30 PRINT I;J;I*J,
 40 NEXT J
 50 PRINT
 60 NEXT I
 70 END

>REN

>LIST

 100 FOR I=1 TO 10
 110 FOR J=1 TO 10
 120 PRINT I;J;I*J,
 130 NEXT J
 140 PRINT
 150 NEXT I
 160 END

>REN 200,130,50

>LIST

 100 FOR I=1 TO 10
 110 FOR J=1 TO 10
 120 PRINT I;J;I*J,
 200 NEXT J
 250 PRINT
 300 NEXT I
 350 END
```

Care should be taken when using this generalized form of the REN command. If improperly used, it can cause a considerable mix-up of line numbers and produce nonsense, as the following printout shows.

```
>LIST

 100 FOR I=1 TO 10
 110 FOR J=1 TO 10
 120 PRINT I;J;I*J,
 130 NEXT J
 140 PRINT
 150 NEXT I
 160 END

>REN 105,140,10

>LIST

 100 FOR I=1 TO 10
 105 PRINT
 110 FOR J=1 TO 10
 115 NEXT I
 120 PRINT I;J;I*J,
 125 END
 130 NEXT J
```

```
>RUN

 115 FOR-NEXT ERR
 130 FOR-NEXT ERR
```

We start again with the same program using the seven line numbers 100, 110, . . . , 160. We then issue the command REN 105,140,10. The first line number to be changed is 140; lines 100, 110, 120, and 130 remain as they are. Line 140 is renumbered 105, line 150 becomes line 115, and line 160 becomes line 125. This produces the jumbled mess seen in the second listing. Fortunately, the errors in this last version of the program are caught by the computer at execution time.

Different manufacturers implement the renumbering command differently. On some computers, when REN alone is used, the first line is numbered 10 instead of 100; the increment of 10 is fairly universal. On some, only the line number of the first line may be assigned although the choice of the increment remains an option. This is illustrated in the following printout. The renumbering command—the verb used here is RESEQ—renumbered the program with the first line starting at 10, and each subsequent line number increased by 10.

The command with specified options was then given and the result listed. The first of the two numbers specifies the starting number for the first statement, the second the increment between statements.

```
*LIST

100 FOR I=1 TO 10
110 FOR J=1 TO 10
120 PRINT I;J;I*J,
130 NEXT J
140 PRINT
150 NEXT I
160 END

*RESEQ

*LIST

10 FOR I=1 TO 10
20 FOR J=1 TO 10
30 PRINT I;J;I*J,
40 NEXT J
50 PRINT
60 NEXT I
70 END

*RESEQ 25,50

*LIST

25 FOR I=1 TO 10
75 FOR J=1 TO 10
125 PRINT I;J;I*J,
175 NEXT J
225 PRINT
275 NEXT I
325 END
```

The SET Command

SET Applied to the DIM Statement

In the past, when working with vectors, lists, arrays, and matrices, we always had to specify the maximum dimensions that might be encountered during the execution of the program. For the sake of generality, it would seem desirable to have these maximum dimensions themselves be variables to be set at some future time when the general program is applied to a specific problem. For example, the problem to determine the minimal polynomial of a matrix suggests the need for only 6 × 6 matrices to test the program. A general program to find the minimal polynomial should apply to an $n \times n$ matrix, where n is a number to be specified only when the specific matrix is given. While it is not difficult to change the dimension statements for each new problem, it is better not to have to modify a program once it is written and debugged. On some systems, a BASIC command permits this. Consider the following program:

```
10 DIM A(M,N)
20 FOR I=1 TO 7
30 FOR J=1 TO 5
40 A(I,J)=10+I*J
50 NEXT J
60 NEXT I
70 MAT PRINT A;
```

When an attempt was made to run it, an error message appeared.

```
>LIST

 10 DIM A(M,N)
 20 FOR I=1 TO 7
 30 FOR J=1 TO 5
 40 A(I,J)=10+I*J
 50 NEXT J
 60 NEXT I
 70 MAT PRINT A;

>RUN

 10 DIM ERR
 NO DIMSTMT ARRAY A
```

At this point, we use the SET command. Outside the program and as a direct instruction to the BASIC interpreter, the command takes the form:

SET M=9, N=7

With this done, the program ran as shown.

```
>SET M=9,N=7

>RUN

 11     12     13     14     15     0    0

 12     14     16     18     20     0    0

 13     16     19     22     25     0    0

 14     18     22     26     30     0    0

 15     20     25     30     35     0    0

 16     22     28     34     40     0    0

 17     24     31     38     45     0    0

 0    0    0    0    0    0    0

 0    0    0    0    0    0    0
```

There is a major difference between the SET command and the LET command. When LET M=9, N=7 is written, either in immediate mode or as an assignment inside a program, the computer interprets this as assignments to variables and as such are modifiable under program control. SET M=9, N=7 is a command to the BASIC interpreter to allocate space for the matrix, and this allocation remains in effect until explicitly changed by the programer or until the BASIC interpreter is replaced by another processor, for example, EDIT.

SET Applied to String Length

The SET command, again as a direct command to the BASIC interpreter, may be used to modify the maximum length of a string. If, on those systems that automatically set the length of a string at 72 characters when we sign on, a string of more than 72 characters is encountered, it is truncated to 72. The option to increase the string length up to 132 characters may exist, in which case the command is:

```
SET $=(number)
```

where "number" is the maximum length of any string. In some circumstances, it may be desirable to have this maximum length be less than 72. Thus, "number" may be any integer from 0 to 132 inclusive.

```
10 A$=""
20 FOR I=1 TO 14
30 A$=A$+"1234567890"
40 NEXT I
50 L=LEN(A$)
60 PRINT
70 PRINT "LENGTH OF STRING ="L
80 PRINT A$

>RUN

LENGTH OF STRING = 72
123456789012345678901234567890123456789012345678901234567890123456789012


>SET $=90
>RUN

LENGTH OF STRING = 90
123456789012345678901234567890123456789012345678901234567890123456789012
345678901234567890


>SET $=132
>RUN

LENGTH OF STRING = 132
123456789012345678901234567890123456789012345678901234567890123456789012
345678901234567890123456789012345678901234567890123456789012


>SET $=133
ILLEGAL

>SET $=5
>RUN

LENGTH OF STRING = 5
12345
```

The illustration should be read as follows. At lines 20–40, an attempt is made to construct a string A$ containing 140 characters The BASIC interpreter, however, truncates the string to 72 characters. The command SET $=90 is then given to BASIC and the program rerun; this time the length of A$ is 90. The exercise is repeated with SET $=132, and the length of A$ is stretched to 132 characters. If we attempt to increase the length of the string beyond 132, we are reminded that it is illegal. In the last example, SET $=5 is issued to the interpreter and the length of A$ is limited to 5 characters.

CHAIN LINK

At times, the inherent difficulties of writing a long program may be circumvented by writing it as a series of short programs. When they are run, however, we want them to run sequentially without our intervention. BASIC provides this capability with the CHAIN LINK instruction. We shall illustrate the use of this instruction with the following programs. First, there is a short program to produce a multiplication table for the numbers 5 through 10; second, a program to produce an addition table for the same set of integers. A third program prints the results of both the additions and the multiplications.

In the illustration, the first of these three programs is called MULTIPLY, the second ADD, and the third SHOW. Each program is listed below. In MULTIPLY, only matrix B is constructed and, therefore, only B needs a DIM statement. Once B is constructed, it must be carried along, through the ADD program, to the SHOW program. To do this, a DIM statement for B in ADD is required, although the matrix B is not acted upon by ADD. Failure to provide the DIM B(6,6) results in the loss of the data in B, and this will show up in the SHOW program when line 40 is executed; that is, 40 MAT PRINT B; will print the ZER matrix.

The other requirement for the use of the CHAIN LINK command is that the name of the program to be called be written within quotation marks.

The sequence of events is as follows. Write the program MULTIPLY, store it on disk, and clear the main memory. Next, write ADD, store it on disk, and clear the main memory. Then, write SHOW, store it, and clear the main memory. Finally, bring MULTIPLY in from disk and run it. The program constructs the matrix B and then automatically clears itself from main memory and brings in ADD. ADD constructs the matrix A and then automatically clears itself from main memory and brings in SHOW. SHOW prints A and B.

```
      MULTIPLY

>LIST

 10 DIM B(6,6)
 20 FOR I=1 TO 6
 30 FOR J=1 TO 6
 40 B(I,J)= (I+4)*(J+4)
 50 NEXT J
 60 NEXT I
 70 CHAIN LINK 'ADD'

      ADD

>LIST

 10 DIM A(6,6),B(6,6)
 20 FOR I=1 TO 6
 30 FOR J=1 TO 6
 40 A(I,J)=(I+4)+(J+4)
 50 NEXT J
 60 NEXT I
 70 CHAIN LINK 'SHOW'

      SHOW

>LIST

 10 DIM A(6,6),B(6,6)
 20 MAT PRINT A;
 30 PRINT & PRINT
 40 MAT PRINT B;
```

```
        MULTIPLY

>RUN


 10      11      12      13      14      15

 11      12      13      14      15      16

 12      13      14      15      16      17

 13      14      15      16      17      18

 14      15      16      17      18      19

 15      16      17      18      19      20


 25      30      35      40      45      50

 30      36      42      48      54      60

 35      42      49      56      63      70

 40      48      56      64      72      80

 45      54      63      72      81      90

 50      60      70      80      90      100
```

Suppression of the Header Message

On some BASIC systems, each program run is preceded by a header message, which prints such information as the time of day, the date, and the name of the program. At times, we may wish to suppress this. On one system, the command to suppress it is A=QFG(1), and it can be given either as a system command in BASIC or as a statement within a program.

To return to the normal mode, that is, to have the header printed, we use A=QFG(0), again either as a BASIC system command or within a program.

If your system does print a header message, you will have to consult the manual for the precise command needed to suppress it.

The Prompt Character for INPUT

The normal prompt character for INPUT is the question mark. The command A=PCH('string'), where 'string' is an arbitrary string, will change the prompt character to the first character of the string. Note that the quotation marks are necessary. For example, if the string is '#A$', then the prompt character will become #; if the first character after the leading quotation mark is a space, there will be no prompt character. This is illustrated in the following printout.

```
 10 PRINT "X="; & INPUT X
 20 PRINT "Y="; & INPUT Y
 30 PRINT "X+Y="X+Y

>RUN

X=  ?5
Y=  ?7
X+Y= 12


>A=PCH('#$%')
```

```
>RUN

X=  #5
Y=  #7
X+Y= 12


>B=PCH("  +*&@")

>RUN

X=   5
Y=   7
X+Y= 12


>C=PCH('?')

>RUN

X=  ?5
Y=  ?7
X+Y= 12
```

PROCEED/GO

On some BASIC systems, it is possible to interrupt the running of a program and then have it continue its execution. Imagine a program is running and you stop it by striking the BREAK key. If you now want the program to continue from that point forward, type PROCEED, or PRO for short, and press <CR>. In the following printout, after the run was interrupted the first time, we typed PROCEED <CR>; after the second interruption, we used PRO <CR>. In both cases the program continued.

We interrupted the execution a third time. This time, we used the direct statement GOTO10 <CR>; the program returned to line 10 and continued forward from that point.

```
 10 FOR I=234 TO 567
 20 PRINT "I=" I
 30 NEXT I

>RUN

I= 234
I= 235
I= 236
I= 237
I= 238
I=_
I= 248

      30 RUN INTERRUPTED

>PROCEED
I= 249
I= 250
I= 251
I= 252
I= 253
I= 254
I_
I= 263

      30 RUN INTERRUPTED

>PRO
I= 264
I= 265
```

```
I= 266
I=_
I=¯278

      30 RUN INTERRUPTED

>GOTO 10
I= 234
I= 235
I= 236
I= 237
I= 238
I= 23_
I= 248

      30 RUN INTERRUPTED
```

Suppose, being in BASIC, we need to go to the operating system level and we use control Y to get there. The advantage of using Y^c is that the current status of our BASIC program is suspended but not lost. When we are ready to return to BASIC, we can return to the suspended program and continue from the point at which it was interrupted. We have a choice of commands: GO, CONTINUE, or PROCEED. As the following program illustrates, however, output data may be lost.

```
 10 FOR I=234 TO 567
 20 PRINT "I=" I
 30 NEXT I

>RUN

I= 234
I= 235
I= 236
I= 237
I= 238
_
!PROCEED
I= 248
I= 249
I= 250
I= 251
I= 252
I= 253

_

!CONTINUE
I= 262
I= 263
I= 264
I= 265
I= 266
I= 267
I= 268
I= 269
_
!GO
I= 283
I= 284
I= 285
I= 286
I= 287
I= 288_
```

Note the different positions in which the BREAK and Y^c symbol, the underscore, __, appears. This simply reflects what the printer was doing when the interrupt was activated.

EXECUTE

When the RUN command is used, execution of the program starts at the first line of the program and continues to each succeeding line. At times, however, particularly when we are debugging a program, we want only a select subset of lines within the program to be executed. The EXECUTE command, available on many BASIC systems, provides this capability.

There are two forms for the EXECUTE command. The first is

>EXE (line number)

The second is

>EXE (line number)$_1$ – (line number)$_2$

When only one line number is specified, that specific instruction is executed. When two line numbers are specified, the program segment beginning at the first line number and ending at the line number immediately preceding the second line number is executed. The following printout illustrates the use of both.

```
 10 DIM A(3,3),B(3,3),C(3,3)
 20 FOR I=1 TO 3
 30 FOR J=1 TO 3
 40 A(I,J)= I^2-I+J
 50 NEXT J
 60 NEXT I
 70 MAT PRINT A
 80 MAT B=(2)*A
 90 MAT PRINT B
 100 MAT C=(.1)*B
 110 MAT PRINT C

>EXE 70
 NO DIMSTMT ARRAY A

>EXE 10
>EXE 70

 0             0             0

 0             0             0

 0             0             0

>EXE 20-70

      70 -EXEC- HALT

>EXE 70

 1             2             3

 3             4             5

 7             8             9

>EXE 90

 0             0             0

 0             0             0

 0             0             0

>EXE 80
>EXE 90
```

```
 2              4              6

 6              8              10

 14             16             18

>EXE 100-110

    110 -EXEC- HALT

>EXE 110

 .200000        .400000        .600000

 .600000        .800000        1

 1.40000        1.60000        1.80000
```

Lines 20–60 are to create matrix A for test purposes. Before the program is run, however, the command EXE 70 is issued. The computer is being asked to print matrix A without having been told the dimensions of A. It responds with an error message that we may interpret as a request for this information. Accordingly, we execute line 10, which assigns dimensions not only to A but also to B and C, and reissue the command to execute line 70. The matrix A = ZER and is printed as such. When EXE 20–70 is issued, the program executes lines 20 through 60 inclusive and assigns numerical values to the elements of the matrix A. Because line 70 is not executed, there is no printout. When EXE 70 is issued the third time, these values are printed.

The command EXE 90 is given before the program executes line 80 and therefore, the matrix B = ZER. Line 80 is executed and values are assigned to the elements of B. These values are printed when line 90 is executed a second time. The command EXE 100–110 causes only line 100 to be executed; finally, EXE 110 is given, and the matrix C is printed.

The PLATEN and PAGE Commands

On most printing terminals, the paper comes in a continuous roll or a sequence of connected sheets. Suppose, however, that we want to prepare information to appear as pages in a printed book, with margins on the top and bottom of the page as well as on the sides. To provide this flexibility, a command, PLATEN, may exist either in BASIC or at the operating system level that permits us to prescribe the width of the page (actually the desired number of characters per line) and the number of printed lines per page.

Generally, the format for the command is

```
PLATEN w,l
```

where w is the maximum number of characters that can be printed on one line and l is the number of lines to be printed per page. There may be a software constraint that l not exceed 255.

If only the width is to be changed, the command is abbreviated to:

```
PLATEN w
```

If only the number of lines per page is to be changed, the command is:

```
PLATEN ,l
```

It is clear that the comma is needed for the computer to distinguish between the two commands.

Controlling the Line Width

If a given string A$ has fewer than w characters, the string is printed on one line; if LEN(A$) exceeds w, the string is printed on two or more lines. The following printout illustrates the case in which the length of the string is 132 and the number of characters per line is 15.

```
>SET $=132

 10 A$=""
 20 FOR I=1 TO 14
 30 A$=A$+"1234567890"
 40 NEXT I
 50 L=LEN(A$)
 60 PRINT
 70 PRINT "LENGTH OF STRING="L
 80 PRINT A$

>RUN

LENGTH OF STRING= 132
123456789012345678901234567890123456789012345678901234567890123456789012
345678901234567890123456789012345678901234567890123456789012


!PLATEN 15

!GO

>LIST

 10 A$=""
 20 FOR I=1 TO
14
 30 A$=A$+"1234
567890"
 40 NEXT I
 50 L=LEN(A$)
 60 PRINT
 70 PRINT "LENG
TH OF STRING="L
 80 PRINT A$

>RUN

LENGTH OF STRIN
G= 132
123456789012345
678901234567890
123456789012345
678901234567890
123456789012345
678901234567890
123456789012345
678901234567890
123456789012
```

The command SET $ = 132 was issued to allow strings of that length. The program attempts to create a string A$ of length 140; however, the length is truncated to 132. When first run, the first 72 characters of the string are printed on one line and the remaining 60 on the next.

The key stroke Y^c (control Y) invokes the operating system, where the line width is changed to 15 with the command PLATEN 15. The GO command returns control to BASIC; none of the program is lost. A new list is called for. When printed, program lines 20, 30, and 70 appear on two lines because the number of characters in each exceeds 15. When the program is run, the string A$ is printed on 9 lines, the first 8 containing 15 characters each, the last containing the remaining 12.

If the platen width is inadvertently set to a number greater than the physical platen width of the terminal, the resulting printout depends on the specific terminal.

Standard-sized typing paper is 8 1/2 by 11 inches. In preparing a typed page, a margin of 1 inch generally appears on the left and right sides, leaving 6 1/2 inches for the characters. Most terminals print either 10 or 12 characters per inch. Thus, the normal line width would be either 65 or 78 characters.

Controlling the Number of Lines Per Page

Generally, there are six lines of printout material per inch. If a top margin of 1 inch and a bottom margin of 1 1/2 inches are used, the number of lines available for printing on standard-sized paper is 51. By specifying the number l in PLATEN w,l, we can control the number of lines to be printed per page. The default condition is l=0, which allows an unlimited number of lines per page. In general, there is an upper limit for specifying l; l>255 will cause an error message. For a value of l between 12 and 255, the computer considers the sheet to consist of l+11 lines. It first prints a header (think of this as line 0), skips five lines, and then prints the output on the next l lines. Five more lines are then skipped and the next header follows. There may be slight variations; for example, six lines may be skipped at the top or bottom of the page. In our first illustration, the page length is set at 15. The command PLATEN,15 had been issued before the next printout was prepared and remained in effect during its preparation. Since w is not explicitly set, the previous value, in this example, the default value 72, is in effect. In the illustration, which was done in the immediate mode, the variable A is assigned successive integer values so that you can readily see the number of lines used per page.

```
13:36 Ø1/31/81   2E-21              [1]




>A=1
>A=2
>A=3
>A=4
>A=5
>A=6
>A=7
>A=8
>A=9
>A=1Ø
>A=11
>A=12
>A=13
>A=14
>A=15





13:38 Ø1/31/81   2E-21              [2]




>A=16
>A=17
>A=18
>A=19
>A=2Ø
>A=21
>A=22
>A=23
```

```
>A=24
>A=25
>A=26
>A=27
>A=28
>A=29
>A=30



13:39 01/31/81   2E-21                [3]
```

The printout was generated in the following way. The computer printed the header message, then skipped five lines and printed the prompt character >. We then typed the next 15 lines: A=1 through A=15. After we entered A=15 <CR>, the computer took over, skipped five lines, printed the next header, skipped five lines, and waited for us to continue entering our information. The process continued.[1]

PAGE in a BASIC Program

The BASIC instruction PAGE uses these platen controls. To illustrate, suppose we want to print three 5 × 2 matrices, which are to be determined using a BASIC program. The printout is to be prepared so that it can be cut apart and used as pages in a small book. The number of lines of print per page is to be 15.

In the following program, only the instruction PAGE is unfamiliar. There is nothing significant about the matrices; their role is to provide an easily viewed printout. It should be remembered that each row of a matrix requires two print lines—the first is blank, the second contains the data—so that the printout of the matrix accounts for 10 lines of print.

```
10 DIM A(5,2),B(5,2)
20 FOR J=1 TO 3
30 FOR I=1 TO 5
40 FOR K=1 TO 2
50 A(I,K)=I^4+K^4
60 NEXT K
70 NEXT I
80 MAT B=(J)*A
90 PAGE
100 MAT PRINT B
110 NEXT J
120 PAGE
130 END
```

The matrix B is constructed in lines 30–80. At line 90, the instruction PAGE causes the print mechanism to advance to the next page. A header is printed, the margin at the top of the page is set, and the matrix is printed. After the matrix is printed, as it is on one page, the second matrix is constructed, again in lines 30–80. The PAGE instruction at line 90 again causes the print mechanism to advance to the next page, where after the margin at the top of the page is set, the second matrix B is printed, and the process repeats.

The instruction PAGE at line 120 does the following. On this computer, the termination of every program run is announced by the statement: (line number) HALT. To avoid having this printed on the last page of the printout, line 120 advances the paper to the next page, where the message appears. On computers that do not print a termination of run message, this line would be superfluous.

---

[1] If you take a ruler and measure the blank distance between 13:36 and >A = 1, it is not 5/6 of an inch. The reason is that the printout that came off the computer was reduced to 3/4 of size before being printed on this page. The reduced distance is therefore 3/4 × 5/6 = 5/8 inches and this may be measured. Similarly, the distance between >A = 15 and 13:30 is 5/8 of an inch, as are the distances between 13:38 and >A = 16 and between >A = 30 and 13:39.

```
14:16 11/Ø5/81  66-8                [1]


 2             17
 17            32
 82            97
 257           272
 626           641


14:16 11/Ø5/81  66-8                [2]


 4             34
 34            64
 164           194
 514           544
 1252          1282


14:16 11/Ø5/81  66-8                [3]


 6             51
 51            96
 246           291
 771           816
 1878          1923


14:17 11/Ø5/81  66-8                [4]


     13Ø HALT
```

Careful examination of the number of blank lines between the header and the first line of the matrix as well as between the last line of the matrix and the next header might lead you to believe that there is a discrepancy between what you see and the rules given above. Indeed there is. In order to fit the material onto one page of this text, not only were the printed characters reduced to 3/4 size but some of the blank lines were deleted. To demonstrate that the printout is actually as described, the first page is reproduced below in full scale. The distance between 14:16 and 2 is 1 inch; this corresponds to 5 blank lines after the header and the first blank line that occurs whenever a matrix is printed. The distance between 626 and the 14:16 and 2 is 1 inch; this corresponds to 5 blank lines after the header and the first blank line that occurs whenever a matrix is printed. The distance between 626 and the 14:16 on the second header is 1-2/3 inches. The matrix occupies 10 print lines, but the page length was set at 15. Therefore, there are 5 blank lines after the number 626. These 5 blank lines are followed by the 5 blank lines that precede each heading. Thus, there are 10 blank lines between 626 and the second header. At 6 lines per inch, 10 lines account for 1-2/3 inches.

```
14:16 11/Ø5/81  66-8                [1]





 2             17

 17            32

 82            97

 257           272

 626           641










14:16 11/Ø5/81  66-8                [2]
```

Security and Passwords

In Chapter 1, the series of steps required to enable you to log on were given. You had to give your ID number (the one used for the illustration was ST123456), the ID code word (HUMBLE), the intended use (SOC101), and the password (FANCY). The computer on which the log on procedure was illustrated operates in full duplex, and the password is not echoed back to you; the intent is to provide a means of securing your account and files from unauthorized persons.[2]

Changing Passwords on Accounts and Programs

A password may become compromised and need to be changed. Techniques for making this change vary from one machine to the next; the following illustrates how it is done on one. At the operating system level, the format is:

```
PASSWORD, OLD PASSWORD, NEW PASSWORD
```

Your old password is FANCY; you want to change it to ANGEL. Therefore, you would type:

```
PASSWORD, FANCY. ANGEL     <CR>
```

The computer will respond with a message, of which the following is typical:

```
PASSWORD CHANGE SUCCESSFUL.
```

There are two other situations that can arise. In the first, we start without a password and we want to introduce one; in the second, we have a password and want to remove it. In the first case, we type:

```
PASSWORD,,ANGEL     <CR>
```

In the second, we type

```
PASSWORD,FANCY,     <CR>
```

In both cases, the computer will respond

```
PASSWORD CHANGE SUCCESSFUL.
```

When we log on again, we will have to use our new password.

Passwords are usually limited to at most eight characters, although again this will be a function of the specific machine. It is advisable to use printable characters in your password because, if you should forget it, the manager of your computer installation can, with effort, retrieve it for you. If some or all of the characters in the password are nonprinting, retrieval can become a formidable task.

Passwords on Programs

In addition to using a password to prevent unauthorized access to our account, some of our programs may be so sensitive that we would like to provide additional security for them.

Assume we have written a program that we call ABC. What the program does is not important; to have something to work with, we use a program to add two numbers.

```
10 INPUT X
20 INPUT Y
30 Z=X+Y
40 PRINT Z
```

[2]On computers operating in half-duplex, multiple overprinting occurs in the space in which you are to type your password; this is in alternative procedure for securing your account.

We save it on disk for future use. We now want to assign a password of our choice to ABC to further secure it from prying eyes. The password we pick is HAY. With the program in main memory, we type:

```
PASSWORD HAY      <CR>
SAVE OVER ABC     <CR>
```

The password is now added to the program name.

If we attempt to load the program ABC using the familiar procedures, we should expect to fail. A typical sequence might be:

```
>LOAD ABC
 ABC
 UNABLE TO OPEN
```

Using the password, the new procedure is:

```
>PASSWORD HAY
>LOAD ABC
```

The program is brought from disk to the main memory. With the program in memory, we can run or modify it. Suppose we modified it by changing the numeric variables to string variables and, using SAVE OVER ABC, put the new version back on disk. If this new version is to be loaded from disk, the new load procedure using the password hay is still required.

If we save it under another name, say CBA, the password HAY is still attached to it.

Removing a Password from a Program When the program ABC is brought from disk to main memory, its password is brought along with it; the program and password exist simultaneously on disk and in main memory. Suppose, we now want to remove the password. We can do this only in main memory, never on the disk. Therefore, to delete a password from a program on disk, both must be deleted simultaneously from the disk. The following sequence illustrates how this is done. We start with the main memory clear and the program and its password on disk. Using the password HAY, we bring the program ABC into main memory. The password and program exist now on disk and in memory.

```
PASSWORD HAY      <CR>
LOAD ABC     <CR>
```

The disk copy of ABC, along with its password HAY, is deleted from the disk:

```
DELETE ABC     <CR>
```

To remove the password from main memory, we type

```
PASSWORD     <CR>
```

At this point, the unprotected program ABC exists in main memory and can be saved on disk as follows:

```
SAVE ON ABC     <CR>
```

Changing a Program's Password If we want to change from HAY to STRAW, the following sequence is required. The program and password are brought from disk to main memory; the copy on disk is deleted; the password in main memory is changed, and the program and its new password are saved on disk. The typing sequence is:

```
>PASSWORD HAY
>LOAD ABC
>DELETE ABC
>PASSWORD STRAW
>SAVE ON ABC
```

Passwords on Files

We have seen that we can create a file using a BASIC program. Suppose a file of names and salaries is to be created and protected by a password. The file name is to be PEOPLE and the password HAY. The program for creating PEOPLE, to be called NAME, is not to have a password.

```
     NAME

 10 OPEN 'PEOPLE';'HAY' TO :1, PRINT ON
 20 ENDFILE :0,70
 30 INPUT = $
 40 INPUT A$
 50 PRINT :1,A$
 60 GOTO 40
 70 CLOSE :1

>RUN

?SMITH, MARY : 28530
?WHALEN, HENRY : 18450
?BAKER, ANA : 19600
?KESSY, GEORGE : 16990
?F\
```

Line 10 is the only one that contains new information. To specify that the file PEOPLE is to have the password HAY associated with it, a semicolon separates PEOPLE and HAY, both of which are enclosed within quotation marks.

To read a file that has a password attached to it, we use the same format.

```
 10 OPEN 'PEOPLE';'HAY' TO :1, INPUT
 20 ENDFILE :1,70
 30 INPUT = $
 40 INPUT :1,A$
 50 PRINT A$
 60 GOTO 40
 70 CLOSE :1

>RUN

SMITH, MARY : 28530
WHALEN, HENRY : 18450
BAKER, ANA : 19600
KESSY, GEORGE : 16990
```

Passworded Files in EDIT As we have in the past, we may want to examine the file PEOPLE in EDIT. The format for doing this is

```
*EDIT PEOPLE .. HAY <CR>
```

The general rule is *EDIT (file name) .. (password) <CR>.

```
*EDIT PEOPLE..HAY
*TY
   1.000 SMITH, MARY : 28530
   2.000 WHALEN, HENRY : 18450
   3.000 BAKER, ANA : 19600
   4.000 KESSY, GEORGE : 16990
```

Copying a Passworded File and Removing a Password Because a file with a password cannot be copied over itself, this approach cannot be used to remove the password. If we try, it does not work:

```
*COPY PEOPLE. .HAY OVER PEOPLE
-SORRY. . .NO PASSWORD ALLOWED HERE
*
```

A file with a password, however, can be copied over a file not containing a password

```
*COPY PEOPLE..HAY OVER PERSON
..EDIT STOPPED
..COPYING
..COPY DONE
*EDIT PERSON
*TY
   1.000 SMITH, MARY : 28530
   2.000 WHALEN, HENRY : 18450
   3.000 BAKER, ANA : 19600
   4.000 KESSY, GEORGE : 16990
```

The file PEOPLE . . HAY can now be deleted and PERSON copied over PEOPLE. This effectively deletes the password from the original PEOPLE file.

Passwording an Unprotected File Suppose we have an unprotected file and we want to introduce a password. First, we cannot copy a file without a password over itself with a password. A file without a password, however, can be copied over a new file to which a password has been attached. In the following, the file PEOPLE is initially unprotected, the file PERSON does not exist. An unsuccessful attempt is made to copy PEOPLE over PEOPLE . . HAY.

```
*COPY PEOPLE OVER PEOPLE..HAY
-SORRY... NO PASSWORD ALLOWED HERE.
```

The file PEOPLE can be copied over PERSON . . HAY.

```
*COPY PEOPLE OVER PERSON..HAY
..COPYING
..COPY DONE
```

Now, PERSON . . HAY can be copied over PEOPLE . . HAY and PERSON . . HAY deleted.

```
*COPY PERSON..HAY OVER PEOPLE..HAY
..EDIT STOPPED
..COPYING
..COPY DONE

*DELETE PERSON..HAY
..EDIT STOPPED
..DELETED
```

Changing a File's Password To change the password on a given file, say from PEOPLE . . HAY to PEOPLE . . STRAW, the same procedure must be followed. First, PEOPLE . . HAY is copied over a new file PERSON . . STRAW; second, PEOPLE . . HAY is deleted; third, PERSON . . STRAW is copied over PEOPLE . . STRAW; fourth PERSON . . STRAW is deleted.

```
*COPY PEOPLE..HAY OVER PERSON..STRAW
..COPYING
..COPY DONE
*DELETE PEOPLE..HAY
..EDIT STOPPED
..DELETED
*COPY PERSON..STRAW OVER PEOPLE..STRAW
..COPYING
..COPY DONE
*DELETE PERSON..STRAW
..EDIT STOPPED
..DELETED
*EDIT PEOPLE..STRAW
*TY

   1.000 SMITH, MARY : 28530
   2.000 WHALEN, HENRY : 18450
   3.000 BAKER, ANA : 19600
   4.000 KESSY, GEORGE : 16990
```

In summary, using EDIT we can:

1. Start with a file with no password and add one.
2. Start with a file with a password and delete the password.
3. Change the password of a file.

Finally, if we want to BUILD a file directly in EDIT and use a password with it, we use the format:

```
*BUILD (file name) . . (password).
```

Extended Precision in Printing

On some computers, calculations are carried out internally to greater precision—that is, to more decimal places—than are printed at the terminal. Normally, for example, the result of dividing 1 by 3 is reported at the terminal as .333333, whereas we know that the internal representation, at least for the machine used as a model, utilized two machine words, or 64 bits. There may be times, and you have encountered such situations, when it is desirable to have the full decimal equivalent of the internally stored number printed at the terminal or in a file. Some BASIC interpreters provide this capability. On the BASIC interpreter used to illustrate most problems in this book, the command takes the form PRINT PRC(1). When issued either as a direct command to the interpreter or as an instruction within a program, the effect is to produce a sixteen-digit output. To return to the normal six-digit output, the command is PRINT PRC(0). The following illustrates the effect of the extended precision command.

```
>PRINT 1/3
 .333333

>PRINT PRC(1)

>PRINT 1/3
 .3333333333333333
```

```
>PRINT PRC(Ø)

>PRINT 1/3
 .333333
```

The manual for your computer should indicate how this extended precision in printing, if the capability exists, can be realized.

Conclusion

As promised in the introduction to this chapter, the computer commands we were to illustrate would not help us formulate an algorithm to solve any of our specific problems. That we must do using our prior knowledge, ingenuity, and the BASIC language instructions available to us. As we learn to solve more complex problems using these instructions and commands, we should also benefit from an increased mastery over the computer. It was the intent of this chapter to point us in that direction.

Glossary

A

Absolute Address. The specific physical location within a computer's memory at which data (a number, a set of characters, or other information) are stored. The format for specifying the absolute address is a hardware feature specified by the manufacturer.

Access Time. The time required to reach a given storage location and retrieve its contents.

Accumulator. A special memory location used to store the results of an instruction. Also referred to as a register.

Address. A location in memory where data are stored. There are diffrent ways to refer to a specific address, either directly, using absolute addresses, or symbolically, by means of a user-oriented language.

Algorithm. A specific procedure, generally step-by-step instructions, for solving a problem.

Alphanumeric. The set of characters consisting of the digits 0 through 9 and the letters A through Z. Sometimes extended to include the remaining printable characters, for example $ and &.

American Standard Code for Information Interchange (ASCII). An electronic code used to represent information internally within a computer. *See also* Extended Binary Coded Decimal Interchange Code.

ALU. The Arithmetic and Logic Unit. A fundamental element of the central processing unit (CPU) where both the arithmetic and logical operations are performed.

Analog Computer. An electronic computer in which numbers are represented by continuously varying physical quantities such as voltage or resistance. A familiar nonelectronic example is the slide rule.

Analog-Digital Conversion. The process of converting a continuous measurement to digital form. Often accomplished by sampling a continuous signal at discrete intervals of time and specifying the value of the signal in digital form.

ANSI. American National Standards Institute, an organization that coordinates the voluntary standards in the United States. It serves also as a clearing house for this information.

Argument. An independent variable used in the definition of a function. For example, in BASIC, X is the argument of the function ABS(X) (the absolute value of the number that X represents).

Arithmetic and Logic Unit (ALU). The unit in the CPU that performs the arithmetic and logical operations.

Arithmetic Constant. Any numerical value. It can be expressed in decimal, integer, or exponential form.

Arithmetic Expression. Any meaningful collection of variables, constants, and arithmetic operators. Thus, if X and Y are arithmetic expressions, so are, −X, X+Y, X−Y, X*Y, X/Y, X^Y.

Arithmetic Operators. The operations of addition (+), subtraction (−), multiplication (*), division (/), and exponentiation (^).

Arithmetic Variable Name. In BASIC, a variable name consists of a single letter A through Z or a letter followed by a digit, 0 through 9. Thus, Q and D7 are variable names.

Array. An arrangement of data, in one or more dimensions, under a single variable name. A one-dimensional array is known also as a list or vector; a two-dimensional array is known as a matrix. *See also* Matrix and Vector.

ASCII. *See* American Standard Code for Information Interchange.

Assembler. A computer program that converts a program written in a user-oriented language into machine language, the form that the computer understands.

Assignment Statement. A computer language statement that assigns an arithmetic (or string) expression to an arithmetic (or string) variable name.

B

Base. In a number system using positional notation, the value raised to successive powers moving from right to left. Synonym for Radix. *See also* Binary, Octal, Decimal, Hexadecimal.

BASIC. An acronym for *B*eginner's *A*ll-purpose *S*ymbolic *I*nstruction *C*ode, initially developed by John G. Kemeny and Thomas E. Kurtz of Dartmouth College. BASIC is a high-level user-oriented language specifically designed for time-sharing applications.

Binary Coded Decimal (BCD). A method for coding a character set, the digits 0 through 9, the alphabet A through Z, and the other printable characters, as well as the nonprinting characters such as "space." BCD is generally used when alphanumeric data are processed.

Binary Number System. A positional notation system employing only the two digits 0 and 1. A number system using the base 2. Most computers are constructed to operate in binary.

Bistable Device. A device, such as a switch, that assumes only one of two possible states, such as on or off. The use of bistable devices suggests the use of a binary number system, which also requires only two values, 0 and 1, for arithmetic and data-processing operations.

Bit. An abbreviation for *B*inary dig*it*.

Block Diagram. A chart indicating the logical flow of a program; a pictorial description of an algorithm. *See also* Flow Chart.

Branch. *See* Conditional Branch and Unconditional Branch.

Branch Point. A location within a computer program at which the order of the computation, the next step to be taken, depends on the value of a previously determined quantity.

Branch Statement. A statement that alters the sequential execution of instructions in a program by directing that the next step in the calculation be determined by and dependent upon a previously calculated quantity.

Brute Force Approach. Any technique that depends on raw power, the great speed with which a computer can perform the various arithmetic and logical operations needed to arrive at a solution to a problem.

Bubble Sort. A technique for ordering (alphabetizing) a list according to a specified rule. The sort is achieved by interchanging successive pairs of records until the desired ordering is achieved.

Bug. A programing term for an error, either in hardware or software.

Byte. A group of bits. Typically, a byte is defined as eight bits, although some authors prefer to k-bit bytes when k is a natural number different from eight.

C

Calling Statement. Any statement in BASIC that accesses a library function, a user-defined function, or a subroutine.

Carriage Return Abbreviated CR or <CR>. In a printing mechanism, the signal that the next character is to be printed at the left margin. Generally, <CR> implies a line feed also, so that the next character is printed at the left margin of the next line.

Cathode Ray Tube (CRT). A specialized version of the familiar home television tube used to display characters. In some systems, graphs, charts, drawings, and other art forms, in either black and white or color, can be displayed. A CRT is a major component of an input/output terminal.

Central Processing Unit (CPU). The unit of a computing system that controls and executes a program. It includes the control and arithmetic and logic units.

CHAIN (file name) and CHAIN LINK (file name). A BASIC instruction that automatically terminates the running of the current program and initiates the execution of the program named in the statement.

CHANGE (numeric list) **TO** (string variable) and **CHANGE** (string variable) **TO** (numeric list). The functioning of this statement depends on whether the computer operates in ASCII or EBCDIC. (For a complete description with illustrations, see Chapter 14.) In general, the first format assumes that the numbers in the list are the ASCII or EBCDIC values of characters and constructs the string corresponding to these values. In the second format, the first entry in the list is the ASCII or EBCDIC value of the first character in the string, the second entry in the list is the ASCII or EBCDIC value of the second character in the string, and so on.

For ASCII systems there is the additional specification: the zeroth entry in the list must contain the number of characters in the string.

Character. One of a set of symbols that include the digits 0 through 9, the alphabet, punctuation, the arithmetic and logical signs +, −, *, /, ^, <, >, =, and such special symbols as &, $, and #. These symbols and certain combinations of them can be "understood" and manipulated by a computing system in a meaningful way.

Characteristic. For a floating-point number, the part that represents the size of the exponent; for example, for 0.725861E+17, the characteristic is +17.

Character Set. The totality of characters acceptable to a given computer. Also, the totality of characters meaningful in a particular programing language.

Collate. Same as merge. To start with two or more ordered lists and produce a single ordered list.

Column Matrix. A matrix of 1 column and *n* rows. Also, a column vector.

Compiler. A specialized program that converts a program written in a user-oriented computer language through one or more steps into machine language. A different compiler is required for each computer language that may be used on a given machine. The purpose of each compiler is to match the user language to that machine language required by the given hardware, as well as to provide the user greater ease in program creation. FORTRAN and COBOL are compiler language acceptable on many computers.

Compiler Error. *See* Syntax Error.

Compiling. The process whereby a digital computer translates the instructions of a program written in a high-level language into their machine language equivalents.

Computed GO TO Statement. A multibranch conditional transfer statement used when a decision has more than two possible outcomes.

Computer. Any device that accepts coded information and transforms it into a more usable form in accordance with a program of instructions.

Computer Language. One of several methods of communicating with the computer. Each computer language, such as BASIC, FORTRAN, and COBOL, has its own rules of grammar, conventions, commands, and detailed restrictions.

Computer Word. See *Word.*

Concatenate. To join together two or more character strings into a single string.

Conditional Branch, or Transfer, Statement. A program statement that alters the normal sequence of execution of instructions in a program only when a stated condition is true. The IF—THEN— statement is an example of a conditional branch statement.

Connector Symbol. A flow charting symbol used to relate various parts of a flow chart. The symbol is a small circle containing an identifier.

Control Unit. The part of the CPU controlling all the tasks of the computer system.

Counter. A variable used to record the number of times a program segment has been executed.

CPU. *See* Central Processing Unit.

CRT. *See* Cathode Ray Tube.

Cycle Time. The time required to access a given memory location, read its contents, and, should the reading process be destructive, restore the contents.

Data. Any information introduced into a computer that is to be used during the execution of the program instructions.

Data base. A collection of many interrelated files from which specified categories of data may be extracted for further processing.

Data Element. One or more characters of data to be taken as a unit. Sometimes called a field. Several data elements make up a record; several records make up a file.

Data Processing. The collection, processing, and distribution of facts and figures to achieve desired results. Any procedure for the collection, processing, and distribution of data to achieve a more useful format.

Debug or Debugging. The process of finding and correcting errors in a computer program.

Decimal System. The conventional base 10 positional notation system.

Decision Instruction. A conditional branch instruction. An instruction used to alter the sequential execution of instructions when a given condition is true.

Decision Symbol. A flow charting symbol used to indicate where in a program alternatives are to be considered. A diamond-shaped figure is used for the decision symbol.

Decision Tree. A pictorial description of available alternatives in a process.

Declarative Statement. A statement that informs the computer's compilation programs of certain facts necessary for the compilation and translation to machine language process. Such facts may include data input and output formats, the dimensions of lists and arrays, and similar details.

DEF Statement. The BASIC statement form that allows the user to define her or his own functions. The function itself may be single or multiline.

Delimiter. A special character, often a comma or space, used to separate variable names or other items in a list or to separate one string of characters from another, as in the separation of data elements. In some cases, the quotation mark and semicolon are also used.

DET Function. A matrix function that yields the value of the determinant of the last matrix inverted by the INV function.

Diagnostic Messages. A computer-generated message to the programer informing the programer of one or more grammatical errors in the program. Also called "error messages."

Digital. In general, digital refers to computations that are based on the use of discrete symbols, particularly the digits 0 through 9.

Digital-Analog Conversion. The opposite of Analog-Digital Conversion. The process by which a series of numbers is converted into a continuous signal or measurement.

Digital Computer. A device employing an internally stored program to perform a sequence of computational steps. These steps are based on counting rather than measurement (as in an analog computer). If different internally stored programs can be used to solve different problems, the computer is called "general purpose."

DIM Statement. A statement used to alert the computer that a list or array is to be assigned to a variable name.

Document. As a verb, a detailed description of the problem to be solved and the logic and method by which a computer program is written to achieve that end. Documentation is necessary to convey the intent of the programer to others as well as to serve as a historical record. As a noun, all papers and data needed to provide a basis for understanding a program.

Double Precision. A programing technique in which each numerical value is allocated twice as many storage locations as would normally be used. The results of the computation are twice as accurate as would normally be given.

E

Editor. An intractive computer program designed to ease the writing and modification of another program. See Chapter 18.

END Statement. The last statement in any BASIC program.

Executable Statement. A statement that demands action on the part of the computer when the program is run, for example, PRINT.

Executive Program. The master program that controls the execution of all other programs (such as compilers, subroutines, user programs) in the computer. Synonyms: Monitor, Supervisor, Operating System.

Exponential Growth. A mathematical concept that states that the increase in a variable is directly proportional to the variable.

Extended Binary Coded Decimal Interchange Code (EBCDIC). An electronic code for representing information internally within a computer. *See also* American Standard Code for Information Interchange.

Extrinsic Function. A function, not internal to the system, defined by a programer in a program. *See* Intrinsic Function.

F

Field. A subdivision of a record consisting of one or more characters. A data element.

File. A collection of records, usually referring to a common subject; for example, an inventory file.

Fixed Record Length. When each record in a file has the same number of available spaces, although all need not be used for a specific record, the file is said to be a fixed record length. Social security numbers have a fixed record length of nine characters; a name file that allows for up to 30 characters has a fixed record length of 30 characters.

Fixed Word Length Machine. A computer designed so that a specified number of bits is treated as a unit, a word, during the course of a computation. Typically, the number of bits per word is a power of 2, for example, 16 or 32, or is divisible by 2, for example, 36 or 48.

Floating-Point Number. The representation of a number in scientific notation. For example, 1.234×10^5 means 123,400, that is, move the decimal point five places to the right; 1.234×10^{-2} means .01234, that is, move the decimal point two places to the left. The equivalent computer notation is 1.234E+5 and 1.234E−2.

Flow Chart. A diagram describing the logical structure and the processing sequence of a computer program. The degree of detail will depend on the information to be transferred. Thus, a summary flow chart should convey only the general flow of ideas from beginning to end; a detailed flow chart would indicate each step in the procedure for solving the problem. Standardized symbols (rectangles, parallelograms, diamonds) are used to indicate the various operations. A flow chart should be part of the documentation.

Format Statement. In BASIC, the PRINTUSING statement is a format statement used to control the graphic quality, the exact location of the printed characters, in the output.

FOR—NEXT— Statements. A pair of statements in a BASIC program that automatically executes a specified sequence of instructions a specific number of times. Used to perform looping.

Function. A rule whereby the specifications of the values of one or more variables yields a unique result.

G

Glitch. An unexpected and often unexplained electronic malfunction.

GOSUB Statement. The statement initiating a call to a subroutine.

GO TO Instruction. A BASIC instruction that directs that the next step in the computation be at a specified location.

Grammatical Error. Although each statement in the program may be correct, the combination of statements may be logically inconsistent, incomplete, or violate the grammatical rules of the computer language. Such errors are detected by the compiler as it converts the program into machine language. Diagnostic messages help direct the user to the source of error. *See also* Logical Error.

H

Hard Copy. The output as printed on paper or in similar permanent form, as opposed to the output as it might appear on the face of a cathode ray tube terminal.

Hardware. Physical components of a computing system.

Heuristic (From the Greek *heuriskein,* to discover.) In the context of computers, a heuristic method for the solution of a problem leads to an answer that is not far from the correct or true answer that, because of the complexity of the problem, cannot be found exactly.

Hexadecimal. A number system to the base 16. The symbols generally used to represent the digits in a hexadecimal system are 0, 1, 2, 3, 4, 5, 6, 7, 8, 9, A, B, C, D, E, F. One hexadecimal digit is equivalent to four binary bits, since $2^4 = 16$. For example: $C3F5_x$ means $12 \cdot 16^3 + 3 \cdot 16^2 + 15 \cdot 16^1 + 5 \cdot 16^0$.

High-Level Language. A computer language that is constructed to reflect the vocabulary, syntax, and logic used in the solution of a class of problems, such as scientific problems or business problems. The statements in this language must susequently be translated into the computer's machine language before processing can take place.

I

IF—THEN—ELSE Statement. An elaboration on the IF—THEN— statement to permit a more clearly defined description of the two alternatives. Not universally available in BASIC.

IF—THEN— Statement. A conditional instruction used when a decision between two alternatives is to be made. By permitting reference to the alternatives, departure from the normal sequence of execution of instructions in the program is possible.

Input Device. A unit that receives data and program steps from the programer and converts them to the appropriate signals for transmission, storage, and processing.

Input/Output. Any of the devices or techniques used for man-machine communication.

Input/Output (I/O) Symbol. A flow charting symbol used to indicate when data are to be entered into the computer or when information is expected from a program. The parallelogram is used to represent I/O.

INPUT Statement. A statement whereby the user of a program assigns data values to variables during the execution of the program. Generally, the computer prints a question mark at the terminal as a signal for the user to type in the value to be assigned to the variable.

Instruction. The combination of an operation and one or more operands. In BASIC, there are five fundamental categories of instructions: (1) Assignment; (2) Input/Output; (3) Transfer; (4) Matrix; and (5) Directives.

Instruction Repertoire. With reference to a given language, the set of instructions and commands, for example, LIST, PRINT, GOTO, DIM. With respect to a given computer, the set of instructions the hardware is capable of executing, for example, STORE, CLEAR, SHIFT, ADD.

Integer. A number without a fractional part; a whole number. One of the numbers 0, ±1, ±2, ...

Interface. A point in a computer system at which two different components connect to one another, usually for the transfer of information. By extension, used also to refer to the methods by which the human communicates with the machine, the man-machine interface.

Internally Stored Program. A computer program whose instructions are stored in the same locations as the data values so that the instructions themselves can be altered as the computation progresses.

Interpreter. A software program that translates each line of a program, as soon as it is written, from the high-level language syntax into machine language. A compiler, by contrast, waits until all lines of a program are written before translating them into machine language.

Intrinsic Function. A function defined by the system. Also called a *library function*. Examples are SIN, RND, and ABS.

I/O Device. An Input/Output Device. I/O is the accepted acronym for input/output.

J

Jump. *See* Conditional Branch and Unconditional Branch.

Justify. *See* Right Justify and Left Justify.

K

Key. With reference to the process of extracting certain information from a file, the word *key* is used to specify the desired characteristics that a record in the file should exhibit. In a personnel file, for example, each record can be searched for the individual's age and those records selected for which the age lies between 20 und 25. With respect to the sequence of records in a file, the *key* would be a number specifying the location of the record in the file.

L

Left Justify. To cause a string of characters to be printed at the extreme left of a given field with any blanks appearing to the right.

LET Statement. The fundamental assigning statement in BASIC. A valid BASIC expression consisting of constants and variables whose numerical values are known together with such operators as +, −, *, / and ^ is evaluated and the value so determined is assigned to a specified variable. The BASIC expression appears to the right of an equal sign; the variable assigned to the value that has been determined appears to the left.

Library Function. A function in BASIC that is permanently stored within the computer. *See* Intrinsic Function.

Light Pen. A device associated with a cathode ray tube I/O device that permits graphical input to the computer by "drawing" on the face of the tube.

Line Number. An integer that precedes each statement in a BASIC program. The line number is used to indicate the order in which instructions in the program are to be executed and for reference to nonserial program operations resulting from branching. *See also* Statement Number.

Logical Error. The meaning is not standardized. For some authors, logical errors and grammatical errors are synonymous, meaning that the totality of statements in a program is incomplete or inconsistent. For others, logical errors and pragmatic errors are synonymous, meaning that although the program as written is correct within the language, the problem that is being solved is either incorrectly or incompletely specified.

Logical Operators. Operators that combine two or more relations to form a more complex one. The logical operators are AND, OR, and NOT. In the case of NOT, the operator modifies only one relation.

Loop. A sequence of instructions that is executed repetitively, with modified addresses or data values.

Low-Level Language. A computer language that requires few, if any, translation steps before a program written in it is ready for direct machine processing. Being close to machine language, it is usually not user oriented nor machine independent.

M

Machine Error. Those possible, although relatively infrequent, mistakes in the results of a computer program that may be attributed to hardware difficulties originating within the computer, its memory devices, its peripheral devices, or its associated communication and remote terminal links. One source of machine error may be cosmic rays.

Machine Independence. A program is said to be machine independent if it will run on computers made by different manufacturers. In general, the manufacturer provides a compiler or interpreter that translates the program instructions, written in some standardized user language, into the machine language of the specific computer.

Machine Language. That form of symbolism that the machine can process without further translation. Machine languages are generally specific to a particular type of computer and frequently are written in binary.

Macro-Instruction. A term indicating a program instruction written in a high-level language that generates several program steps in a lower-level (machine level) language. Most user-oriented languages deal almost exclusively with macro-instructions.

Magnetic Disk Drive. A secondary storage device that stores magnetically recorded data. A disk resembles a phonograph record; a disk pack resembles several phonograph records stacked one above the other; one or more fixed or movable reading and recording heads can both record and read data. The entire mechanism, the disk pack, the reading and writing heads, the motor to spin the disk pack, and the associated circuitry are collectively referred to as the disk drive.

Magnetic Drum. A secondary storage device that stores magnetically recorded information on a rotating cylinder. While its storage capacity is generally less than that of a magnetic disk drive, its access time is much faster and consequently its cost is greater. The access time for a magnetic drum is much slower than that of internal high-speed memory, for example, magnetic core memory, and consequently, its cost is lower.

Magnetic Tape Drive. A secondary storage device that stores magnetically recorded data on tape similar to recording tape. The least expensive and also the slowest, of the memory storage devices.

Main Memory. The part of the computing system where programs currently being executed are stored.

Mantissa. That part of a floating-point number that indicates the significant digits. For example, in 0.642531E + 12, the mantissa is 0.642531.

MAT INPUT Statement. An input statement that permits the user to assign the elements of a matrix.

MAT PRINT Statement. An output statement that prints a matrix.

MAT READ Statement. An input statement used in conjuntion with DATA statements to assign data to the elements of a matrix.

Matrix. A rectangular, two-dimensional array. Implicit is the use of two subscripted indexes, the first specifying the row of a given element, and the second, its column position. Thus, the element $A(2,3)$ of the matrix A is located in the second row and third column. The data value to be assigned to $A(2,3)$ is dictated by the problem being solved.

Memory Device. One of many devices, usually constructed to exploit the recording properties of magnetic materials, that stores information for computer processing. Typical are Magnetic Core, Magnetic Disk, Magnetic Card, Magnetic Drum, and Magnetic Tape.

Merge. *See* Collate.

Microcomputer. A small self-contained general purpose desk-top computer.

Microsecond. One millionth of a second.

Millisecond. One thousandth of a second.

Monte Carlo Technique. Although a mathematical problem may be deterministic, that is, have a unique answer, the time and effort required to determine it may be prohibitive. Accordingly, simulations of the phenomenon underlying the mathematical formulation of the problem are done; the outcome of these simulations approximates the true answer to the problem. In general, such simulations use random number inputs.

Multiprograming. A term that indicates that a computer may process several jobs concurrently. The technique is to overlap or interleave the execution of the several programs.

N

Nanosecond. One billionth of a second.

Number System. A specific method of counting. For example, the decimal system uses the base 10 and represents numbers as powers of that base, or radix. Thus, the decimal number 123 means $1{*}10^2 + 2{*}10^1 + 3{*}10^0$. The binary system uses the base 2 and represents numbers as powers of that base. Thus, the binary number 11001 means $1{*}2^4 + 1{*}2^3 + 0{*}2^2 + 0{*}2^1 + 1{*}2^0$.

O

Object Program. The machine language program that results from the translation of a source (high-level) program.

Octal. A number system to the base, or radix, eight. The available digits are 0 through 7. One octal number is exactly equal to three binary bits, since $2^3 = 8$. For example, 6724_{octal} means $6{\cdot}8^3 + 7{\cdot}8^2 + 2{\cdot}8^1 + 4{\cdot}8^0$.

Operation. Specifically, one of the arithmetic operations permitted in a given computer language, for example, add, subtract, multiple, divide, and exponentiate. By extension, the term applies to other data-handling manipulations available in a given computer language, for example, concatenation of two strings.

Optimization Procedure. Any mathematical technique for finding the smallest or the largest value of a bounded mathematical function.

Output. The answers obtained from a computer program. In BASIC, the results are made visual when the PRINT statement is executed.

Output Device. A unit that displays or otherwise makes available for human understanding (for example, audio) the results of a computation.

Overflow. A technical term indicating that a number or result, usually as a consequence of a computation, is larger than the computer can handle. When overflow occurs, the computation usually stops and an error message is given.

P

Picosecond. One-thousandth of a nanosecond, that is, 10^{-12} seconds.

Precanned Programs. Programs that are coded by the manufacturer and supplied to the user in a machine-readable form.

Prescanner. A system program that checks for syntax errors as each line of the program is entered into the system.

Printer. A computer output device capable of printing alphanumeric characters on paper.

PRINTUSING. A BASIC PRINT statement that utilizes format statements to control the graphic arts quality of the output.

Program. A set of instructions produced by a programer to be used by a computer to process data.

Programer. An individual who converts the details of a problem's solution into a computer program.

Prompt Character. A character displayed by the computer to solicit a response from the user. Generally used as a request for input.

Pseudo-Random Numbers. A set of numbers that, although generated in a deterministic way, behaves as though it had been generated in a random fashion. For most computer programs, pseudo-random numbers can be used as random numbers.

R

Radix. *See* Base.

Random Access. The ability of a computer to go directly to a specific memory location independent of the physical location of the last memory location accessed. Contrast with Serial Access.

Random Numbers. A statistical term referring to a set of numbers. No one member of the set of random numbers can be predicted from any known sample of members of the set. In particular, BASIC provides a function that generates a uniform distribution of such numbers lying in the range 0–1. (Since, in fact, the computer generates these numbers by a known method, the numbers of the set are not truly random; they are called pseudo-random numbers. For most practical applications, however, they may be considered truly random.)

Range. (a) The block of statements contained between the DEF and FNEND statements in the multiline user-defined function; (b) The block of statements contained between the FOR—NEXT— statements.

READ DATA Statements. A pair of statements used to assign values to variable names. READ DATA statements are used primarily when large sets of data are needed and the interactive capabilities of the computer are not needed.

Read-Only Memory. A memory device containing permanently stored information that cannot be altered during processing. Memory of this type may be wired into the hardware, may be provided by optical media, or may consist of a segment of core or other magnetic memory that cannot be modified.

READ Statement. A statement for assigning data values to variables in a BASIC program.

Real Number. A number of the form $a_1 \cdot d_1 d_2 d_3 \ldots$ where the a_1 is an integer and $.d_1 d_2 d_3 \ldots$ represents an infinite decimal.

Real-Time Processing. Data processing operations in which computed results are obtained so quickly that they can be used to influence the operation of the process being studied.

Record. A group of information details consisting of one or more fields, usually descriptive of a given item, for example, an employer, a product, a customer. One or more characters create a field; one or more fields create a record; one or more records create a file; and one or more files create a data base.

Register. A high speed device used for temporary storage by the central processing unit of a digital computer.

Relation. In a computer language such as BASIC, there are six relations: equal to, not equal to, greater than or equal to, less than or equal to, greater than, and less than. Symbolically, they are written: =, <> or ><, >=, <=, >, and <, respectively. They are used primarily in IF—THEN— statements to establish test conditions, for branching purposes, for example, if A>B THEN—.

Remote Terminal. An input–output device used to communicate with a distant computer by means of telephone lines, hard wired circuits, or microwave relay links. A remote terminal may itself have limited computational capabilities and may both preprocess the information being sent to the computer and postprocess the data received.

REM Statement. REM stands for REMARK. A REM statement is nonexecutable. REMs are inserted at appropriate places in a program along with comments that should enable future users to understand the intent of the various sections of the program.

RESTORE Statement. A statement that returns the data pointer to the first data item in the first DATA statement in the program.

RESTORE (Line Number) Statement. A statement that returns the data pointer to the first data item in the DATA line specified.

Return Statement. A statement in a BASIC subroutine that transfers control from a subroutine back to the calling statement in the main program.

Right Justify. To cause a string of characters to be printed to the extreme right of a given field, with any blanks appearing to the left. See Left Justify.

RND Function. A special function that generates a pseudo-random number between 0.0 AND 1.0.

Round-Off Error. The error introduced in a calculation when a number requires more than the available number of positions in the machine to represent it, for example, the decimal number .1 requires an infinite number of bit positions to represent it in binary. Also, a round-off error occurs if an integer is too large to be stored as such in a computer and is converted and stored as a floating-point number, with the attendant loss of accuracy.

Routine. In general, a synonym for a program, but more precisely, a working program.

Row Matrix. A matrix of 1 row and n columns. A row vector.

S

Scalar Multiplication. The product of a real number and a matrix.

Semirandom Access. The method for locating information in memory that combines in the search for the desired item some form of direct access, usually followed by a limited sequential search.

Serial (Sequential) Access. A method of searching a file (or a memory) that starts at a fixed place and examines successive records (or memory locations) until the desired information is discovered. Equivalent to looking in a telephone directory for Smith by starting at the first name on page 1 and examining each successive name until Smith is reached. Contrast with Random Access.

Simulation. A mathematical model of a process or activity is created. A computer program is then written to obtain information from this model. The information thus obtained is assumed to be representative of the process or activity being modeled. The whole process is called a simulation. It is hoped that the information so gained can be used for predictive purposes.

Software. A collective term designating the programs used in a computer system. Generally applies to the executive or supervisory programs that manage a computer installation.

Sort. For a given set of objects, to arrange them according to some specified order. To alphabetize a list of names is to sort them lexicographically; a set of people may be sorted by height, from smallest to largest.

Source Program. A program written in a user-oriented language.

Square Matrix. A matrix having the same number of rows and columns.

Statement. A program line containing one logical step in a computer program.

Statement Number. A string of integers that specifies the location of a particular instruction within a BASIC program. *See also* Line Number.

STOP Statement. The BASIC statement that halts the execution of the program.

Stored Function. Synonymous with Library Function and Intrinsic Function. A function provided for the user; one that the user need not create.

Stored Program. A user-written program that, before execution, is stored in one or several of a computer's memory devices.

String. A contiguous sequence of characters.

String Variable. A variable that assumes strings as values. In BASIC, a string variable is identified by the presence of a dollar sign ($) to distinguish it from the numerical variables in the program. A string variable name is identified by a letter followed by the dollar sign, as in P$, or by a letter and a digit followed by a dollar sign, as in F7$ or N2$(5,10).

Structured Programing. A technique for writing programs that increases their reliability and makes them easy to read. As a by-product, it should increase the productivity of a programer. *See* Top-Down Programing.

Subroutine. A subprogram, essentially complete in itself, that is accessed by the main program (or another subroutine) one or more times in the process of computation.

Subscript. An integer, enclosed within parentheses, used to identify an element of a matrix or vector.

Subscripted Variable. A variable of the form A(K) or A(I,J) where the subscripts identify the particular element of the array A.

Substitution Statement. A program instruction that evaluates the numeric value of a valid BASIC expression appearing to the right of the equal sign and assigns that value to the single variable named to the left of the equal sign. Example: LET Z=X+Y; the numeric values assigned to X and Y are added and the result assigned to Z. See Assignment Statement.

Supervisory Software. The specialized programs that usually reside permanently in the computer's main memory and control the flow and processing of users' application programs. Synonymous with executive program and systems software.

Symbolic Address. A symbolic reference to a memory location: During the translation phase (compiling) from the user's program to machine language, the symbolic memory location is translated into an absolute address in the computer's memory.

Symbolic Language. The translation from a user's high level language to machine language generally is done in steps; an intermediate step is to the symbolic language that provides mnemonic clues to the actual machine languages. Generally, there is a one-to-one correspondence between the symbolic language statement and the machine language instruction and thus symbolic languages are usually machine dependent.

Syntax. The rules of grammar, such as sentence structure, spelling, and so on, that govern a language.

Syntax Error. An error caused by typing an invalid BASIC language instruction. Frequently the result of typos.

System Command. A user's instruction, not part of the program, that calls for action by the computer's executive program. Generally, in BASIC, a system command is distinguished from a program statement by the absence of a line number.

System Error. An instruction that is either not recognized by the operating system or is in violation of the procedural rules.

T

TAB Function. An intrinsic BASIC function used to position output in a desired format.

Teleprocessing. The use of telephone lines to transmit data and instructions between remote locations and a data-processing center or between two computers.

Test Cases. A series of computer runs for which the answers are known in advance. These are used to test and verify that the program is functioning as expected.

Time-Sharing System. The mutual and simultaneous use of a single computer facility by many persons. Time sharing enhances a programer's productivity by affording a psychological advantage: Each user feels that he or she has sole use of the computer and does not have to queue up with other programers and wait to see the results.

Top-Down Programing. The writing of a program in blocks so that the logical flow can be easily recognized as proceeding from top to bottom. The program uses structural techniques and permits only one entry point and one exit point. *See* Structured Programing.

Trace. To follow the changing numeric values of one or more variables in a computer program so that the program's progress may be followed in detail. *See* Debug.

Transfer Statement. *See* Conditional Branch.

U

Unconditional Branch. An instruction that alters the serial execution of program statements by jumping to a specified location. GOTO (line number) exemplifies an unconditional transfer statement. Same as unconditional transfer.

User-Defined Function. A function defined by a user in the program. After it has been specified, the function may be used by reference to its name, often following the same rules as for a stored function.

User-Oriented Language. A programing language whose vocabulary and grammar rules mimic those of a discipline. Programs written in such a language employ the jargon of the discipline and parallel the solution processes common to it.

V

Variable. A quantity represented by a symbol. The symbol is assigned various numerical values during the execution of the program.

Variable Record Length. A file consisting of records not necessarily of the same length, for example, a name and address file.

Variable Word Length Machine. A computer whose main memory is arranged so that words of varying length can be stored without wasting memory modules.

Vector. A row or column matrix. An ordered list or one-dimensional array. A singly subscripted variable.

Voice Output. An audio computer output, usually consisting of a limited number of phrases. Voice output has been used for credit checks and spelling and arithmetic games.

W

Word. A term used to refer to the information stored and manipulated as a unit.

INDEX

F

G

H

I

K

L

S

T

V

W

Z